Weill's Musical Theater

The publisher gratefully acknowledges the generous support of the Ben and A. Jess Shenson Endowment Fund in Visual and Performing Arts of the University of California Press Foundation, made possible by Fred M. Levin and Nancy Livingston, The Shenson Foundation.

The publisher also gratefully acknowledges the generous contributions to this book provided by Stanford University's School of Humanities & Sciences, by the Kurt Weill Foundation for Music, Inc., and by the Hibberd Endowment of the American Musicological Society.

Weill's Musical Theater

Stages of Reform

Stephen Hinton

UNIVERSITY OF CALIFORNIA PRESS

Berkeley Los Angeles London

University of California Press, one of the most distinguished university presses in the United States, enriches lives around the world by advancing scholarship in the humanities, social sciences, and natural sciences. Its activities are supported by the UC Press Foundation and by philanthropic contributions from individuals and institutions. For more information, visit www.ucpress.edu.

University of California Press
Berkeley and Los Angeles, California

University of California Press, Ltd.
London, England

Library of Congress Cataloging-in-Publication Data

Hinton, Stephen.
Weill's musical theater : stages of reform / Stephen Hinton.
p. cm.
Includes bibliographical references and index.
ISBN 978-0-520-27177-7 (cloth : alk. paper)
ISBN 978-0-520-95183-9 (ebook)
1. Weill, Kurt, 1900–1950—Criticism and interpretation.
2. Musical theater—History—20th century. I. Title.
ML410.W395H56 2012
782.1092—dc23 2011046514

Manufactured in the United States of America

21 20 19 18 17 16 15 14 13 12
10 9 8 7 6 5 4 3 2 1

In keeping with a commitment to support environmentally responsible and sustainable printing practices, UC Press has printed this book on Rolland Enviro100, a 100% post-consumer fiber paper that is FSC certified, deinked, processed chlorine-free, and manufactured with renewable biogas energy. It is acid-free and EcoLogo certified.

CONTENTS

ILLUSTRATIONS

FIGURES

MUSIC EXAMPLES

TABLES

PREFACE AND ACKNOWLEDGMENTS

In 1947, less than three years before his death at the age of fifty, Kurt Weill summed up his career in a single, matter-of-fact sentence: "Ever since I made up my mind, at the age of 19, that my special field of activity would be the theatre, I have tried continuously, in my own way, to solve the form-problems of the musical theatre, and through the years I have approached these problems from all different angles."[1] If the purpose of this book can be summarized in a similarly succinct fashion, it is to explore in detail the implications of Weill's terse autobiographical statement. What are the "form-problems"? What are the "different angles"? What is his "own way"? What happened in 1919, when he was nineteen?

"Activity," although it embraces composition, is not synonymous with it. Weill did not compose his first work for the musical theater, the ballet-pantomime *Zaubernacht,* until 1922. In the latter part of 1919, after interrupting his studies in Berlin, where he had been receiving instruction in composition with Engelbert Humperdinck and attending classes in musicology and philosophy at the university, he took a job first as *répétiteur* in his hometown of Dessau and then, on Humperdinck's recommendation, as second kapellmeister and soon thereafter as chief conductor in the South Westphalian town of Lüdenscheid, thereby gaining hands-on experience in the worlds of opera and operetta. Participation in Ferruccio Busoni's master class in Berlin, beginning in 1921 and lasting until the meister's death in 1924, only strengthened his already firm sense of vocation.

The "commitment to opera," as Weill called it in an early manifesto, and more broadly to the theater, remained with him throughout his professional life.[2] Trying "continuously to solve . . . form-problems" nicely captures the mix of pragmatism and idealism that informs his work. His protean gifts went hand in hand with an abiding urge toward significant innovation. Behind all the diversity of his work, he seems to be suggesting, lay a common artistic purpose—"my own way." In this book, I explore both the variety of Weill's solutions to the problems he continuously set himself and the common aesthetic underlying his approach.

The book's allusively ambiguous subtitle, "Stages of Reform," refers both to the forms of theater that were Weill's principal artistic territory and to his career as a whole, which can be divided into a number of distinct phases of development. (The ambiguity calls to mind, for example, John Gielgud's *Early Stages,* published in 1953, an autobiography covering the boards the celebrated actor trod at the beginning of his professional life as well as the figurative steps of his evolution during that early period. Another, perhaps more obvious, instance is the title of Richard Rodgers's autobiography, *Musical Stages,* published in 1975.)

"Reform" has a double meaning, too. On one level, it is meant to invoke a few of Weill's illustrious predecessors, chief among them Gluck and Wagner, who saw their creative work in terms of the reform of musical theater, an aim corroborated by their posthumous reputations. Weill harbored analogous ambitions. Whenever he made statements about his many projects—something he did almost habitually, both in public and in private—he focused not only on his vocation as a man of the theater but specifically on his aspirations as a renewer and innovator. The adjective *new* was as indispensable to his artistic vocabulary as it was to Busoni, with his "New Aesthetic." Despite the various stages (in both senses) of his career, covering all manner of institutions and genres, traversing two continents, and lasting some three decades, it is Weill's self-appointed role as theatrical reformer that arguably supplies the key to his relatively short but intense creative life.

Weill may have felt a greater affinity for Gluck's eighteenth century than for Wagner's nineteenth, but it was Wagner's lingering presence that haunted those musicians whose careers began, like Weill's, after the First World War. "Why," he asked referring to Beethoven in 1927, "are Mozart and Bach closer to the younger generation, in spite of our admiration for the master?" He laid the blame on transmission *[Überlieferung],* in particular Wagner's reception of Beethoven. Wagner had fostered a "prejudice from which we have to free ourselves."[3] "Our generation," Weill further declared in 1929, "could not listen to Wagner any more, even as children."[4] The relationship to Wagner was complicated. Although anti-Wagnerism became de rigueur in the 1920s, it should be borne in mind that the same generation that defined contemporary music and theater as a specific and emphatic negation of Wagner's art had formerly been utterly in thrall to it. Weill's backdating his aversion toward Wagner is not only misleading; it is also symptomatic of the intensity of the earlier devotion.

In his last year of high school, for example, Weill delivered a lecture on *Die Meistersinger* (as we know from a surviving manuscript), describing it with seemingly boundless admiration as the "most splendid work" and extolling its "healthy humor." In conclusion he states that this very quality allowed Wagner's work "to blaze a trail into the hearts of the Germans, who had treated one of their greatest geniuses so ignominiously." Shortly thereafter, as a seventeen-year-old, he took part in a recital that included the *Liebestod* from *Tristan und Isolde,* which he played on the piano from memory. He reported to his brother, Hans, that the concert received "thundering applause, especially for *Tristan.*" He further confessed to Hans that "a decent *Tristan* performance will always be something special for me. No other opera score contains so much. One cannot sink more deeply into any other kind of music when listening, or become more involved when learning or performing." Because Wagner exerted such a profound and defining influence on Weill and his contemporaries, the effort to displace him played itself out as a quasi-Oedipal struggle on a generational scale. Wagner had to be overcome through conscious, even self-conscious negation, though he was never fully exorcised.[5]

Weill preferred to cite other European men of the theater as models: initially Mozart, of course, but later also Verdi, Offenbach, and Puccini. A bit of each of them can be found in him, along with all the residual Wagner. He also invited comparison with Stravinsky and, during the 1940s, with American colleagues such as Gershwin and Rodgers. Perennially, though, the main point of positive reference was Busoni. Busoni's teachings on opera, in particular, had a lasting influence on Weill's own theoretical pronouncements, even when the source was not acknowledged, though it usually was. By honoring this particular mentor by name, Weill also established his own creative pedigree, as discussed in chapter 2.

Like the otherwise radically different Wagnerian kind, Weillian "reform" is not merely a technical or formal matter; it is a moral one as well. Despite the claims of numerous critics, Weill used the stage neither to engage in purely formalistic experiments nor merely to entertain, but above all to communicate with his fellow human beings: from his first to his last compositions for the stage, he felt bound to explore, on a range of levels, the very nature of humanity itself. Musical theater, which for him meant drama through music, was a help rather than a hindrance in this endeavor. As he stated in 1936, "The stage has a reason for existence today only if it aspires to a rarer level of truth."[6] Music, by enabling the exploration of characters in extreme situations where speaking yields to singing, offered a means of access to that "rarer level."

In keeping with political and aesthetic experiments conducted during the Weimar Republic, Weill's reforms also entailed seeking out new audiences for his art. Creating musical theater accessible not just to a new but also to a broader public obliged him continually to adapt as a composer. This is another sense of "reform." Emigration only strengthened that obligation rather than obviating it. It is this aspect of his reform, both personal and artistic, that has been the most contentious and pervasive issue in Weill reception and scholarship. Which aspects of his art remained consistent in his career? Which ones changed? These have been abiding questions, perhaps *the* abiding questions. And so they are here, too. Aesthetically, Weill's work would appear to have been based on the necessity, even the inevitability, of change, as he often insisted in his programmatic statements. Nor can the change that occurred when he moved from Europe to the United States—a radical and regrettable transformation, according to many of his detractors—simply be ignored or dismissed. On closer analysis, however, and despite the variety of idioms, genres, and styles that he pressed into service, Weill's approach to matters of musical dramaturgy remained remarkably consistent from beginning to end, as I conclude in the final two chapters. In this quite fundamental sense, at least, he could justifiably claim to have established "my own way."

Aesthetic issues combine with biographical ones. The persistent notion of "two Weills," inescapable in any reception history of the composer, posits two putatively distinct images of the man, each underpinned by its own aesthetic, one of them European, the other American. Yet the "two Weills" theory, based on the idea of an unbridgeable schism in his development as a composer, draws on traditional notions of integrity that have as much to do with biographical method as they do with compositional aesthetics. Addressing this last sense of "reform," the present study begins with a discussion of biographical issues before turning to the central facets of Weill's program as presented in his own writings and interviews. The remainder of the book, which deals with his career in more or less chronological sequence—concluding, in the coda, with a brief overview of posthumous reception history—does not pretend to cover everything. This is neither a new biographical study nor a comprehensive account of all the works. Rather, it is an investigation of Weill's musical theater from a number of different angles that include the biographical, the philosophical, the historical, and the music-analytical.

The idea for this book grew out of a commission. When I was invited to contribute the entries on Weill and his stage works to *The New Grove Dictionary of Opera,* the matter of which works to include proved anything but trivial. How many of them are "real" operas? Although Weill's case is by no means unique, especially in the twentieth century, it is certainly extreme. As extended discussions with the opera dictionary's editor confirmed, nearly all of his pieces for the musical theater are hybrids, presenting at once a case for and a case against their inclusion. The criteria I applied were of two basic and closely related kinds: institutional and structural. Although Weill's stage works rarely started life in an opera house, that does not necessarily preclude their being performed in operatic institutions. Nor does it prevent their being considered as sub-genres of opera. Throughout Weill's oeuvre, however, there is a tension, both institutionally and structurally, between the work itself and its generic traditions. Moreover, that very tension often seems to be, at least in part, what the piece is about. Weill trades in productive ambiguity.

An obvious case in point is his and Brecht's most famous piece, *Die Dreigroschenoper,* which did manage to be included in *The New Grove Dictionary of Opera,* edging out some perhaps equally deserving candidates. It was first performed (and often still is) in a medium-sized theater, not an opera house. The word *opera* in its title is partly ironic—but only partly. If it is opera, it is a kind of lowbrow opera, as compared with its highbrow antecedents. Or rather: it brashly and self-consciously mixes high and low in the manner of a burlesque. It is opera about opera. As Weill said, "It gave us the opportunity to make opera the subject matter for an evening in the theater." Opera as subject matter? Not only does Weill write about reforming the genre, but the work itself is conceived as a contribution to the debate. At the same time, he describes the work as a "prototype" *(Urform)* of opera that combines the traditional elements of the genre, its rudimentary forms and conventions, in a novel and provocative way.

When he came to compose *Street Scene* some two decades later, Weill produced another unconventional, if less crudely provocative, combination of elements, as illustrated by the trouble he took finding a suitable label. Before settling on "American opera," in contradistinction to the traditional "European" kind, he called the piece first a "dramatic musical" and then a "Broadway opera," all of these designations reflecting an attempt to capture the unusual mix of elements from traditional opera and Broadway musical. "Broadway" connotes both the work's first home, where *Street Scene* was performed, and the apparatus of the institution for which it was conceived, its scale. In a letter to his former European publisher, Universal Edition, Weill remarked that *Street Scene* "was written for a relatively small orchestra (33 players) for the special requirements of the Broadway theater and I wonder whether that would be sufficient for large opera houses." He would, however, "consider the possibility of doing a new orchestration as well as undertaking some musical alterations (less dialogue, more music)."[7] Sadly, the revised version never materialized.

As I considered each work on its own merits, Weill seemed to be saying, "I challenge you to include me in the history of opera," and no less emphatically, "I challenge you *not* to include me." His own commentaries tend to reinforce this sense of deliberate equivocation. From the beginning to the end of his career he talked about being in between, about creating musical theater that stood between opera and other genres. He was a composer who knowingly defied simple classification, despite pervasive attempts by others to squeeze him into established categories, as in the "two Weills" theory.

What goes for his works individually also goes for his career as a whole. The stages are complementary. The second half of Weill's career does not entirely revoke the aspirations of the first half, as conventional wisdom would have it, by turning a "German" composer into an "American" one, a serious purveyor of European art music into a Broadway entertainer.[8] Nor are the differences between the early and late works immaterial. The shifts are gradual, from one piece to the next, from stage to stage. There are continuities and discontinuities in his work, and the present study is an attempt to come to grips with them, neither making the composer homogeneously whole nor dividing him neatly into two. By way of conclusion, the final chapter explores these contrasts in Weill's career not just as expressions of the "divided world" he lived in (to use Ronald Taylor's phrase) but also as inherent, productive contradictions in the composer's own artistic make-up.

As is often the case, the study could have taken a form somewhat different from the one it did. It could have followed Weill's life and works in strict chronological sequence, describing each career step in turn. Or it could have presented aspects of his work for the musical theater more systematically than it does, taking key theoretical concepts and applying them to the entire corpus of works. Although both approaches have their merits, I have preferred to strike a compromise between the two. The chapters therefore focus, one by one, on the principal forms of theater both adopted and reformed by Weill, while adhering to a more or less chronological sequence in the discussion of individual works. Included, too, in a separate chapter is a discussion of Weill's involvement with the medium of film ("Stage vs. Screen"), in particular his aspirations to create a new genre of musical theater, "film opera." My aim has been to do justice as far as possible both to the historical and to the systematic aspects of Weill's work—"stages" in the twofold sense. Doing so involved going beyond immanent description and analysis of the works.

The notion of a work itself requires qualification here. For a theater composer such as Weill, a work is not synonymous with a text. His projects for the musical theater were always, to varying degrees, collaborative ventures; more often than not, their genesis did not precede but was rather inextricably bound up with the process of realization for specific events. Insofar as written materials were involved—principally, librettos and scores—they were subject to revision and adaptation as a part of the production process. Changes of cast or venue, revivals and new stagings—all these aspects of the work's realization called for further revisions and adaptations. It follows that each work's identity is dynamic, its status as written text not permanently fixed but mutable. As I propose in the final chapter, a work-concept based on the precepts of classical rhetoric offers a viable alternative to the conventional *Urtext* model. Rather than being excluded from consideration, production and reception history play an important role, both philologically and critically; they are essential to establishing an authoritative performing text, as well as to understanding the nature of Weill's various theatrical projects. The context contributes to the text, even becomes part of it. Documents of reception history, in particular reviews, convey the complexion and impact of the event. To that extent they are indispensable facets of the work.

While the discussions of individual works, in keeping with the rest of the book, are mainly historical and interpretive in their focus, I would not have bothered to write them without being convinced that many, if not all, of Weill's works for the musical theater are still viable today, as recent performance history of most of them has demonstrated. It is my hope, then, that the present volume, beyond appealing to music historians, may also be useful to a wide constituency of people interested in Weill's music. Prominent among my envisaged ideal readers are theatrical practitioners, especially those considering future productions.

The idea for this book grew out of research done for the entries on Weill and his works in *The New Grove Dictionary of Opera,* as described above. In addition, several of the chapters grew out of material initially presented in other publications (and vice versa); these are listed in the credits at the back of the book. I am grateful to the publishers for permission to use portions of these articles in revised form. I also extend my thanks to the music publishers listed in the credits for permission to reproduce the musical examples from Weill's works and to quote the lyrics from Rodgers and Hammerstein's *Allegro* and Sondheim's "Saga of Lenny," and to the organizations credited in the figure captions for permission to use the photographs.

Having enjoyed the privilege of combining research and teaching at three separate institutions over the last two and a half decades—at the Technische Universität Berlin, at Yale University, and at Stanford University—I should like to acknowledge the contribution of the many students and colleagues, too numerous to name individually, who have discussed with me the ideas that have found their way into this book. A large part of the research was conducted at the Weill-Lenya Research Center (in the Kurt Weill Foundation for Music, New York, N.Y.), the official home of Weill studies, with the friendly and expert support of its staff. The book's production was funded in part by the Kurt Weill Foundation for Music, Inc., which awarded a stipend to cover the cost of engraving the music examples and creating the index; by the Hibberd Endowment of the American Musicological Society; and by the School of Humanities & Sciences at Stanford. I am grateful to Don Anthony at Stanford's Center for Computer-Assisted Research in the Humanities (CCARH) for his beautiful engraving of the examples. I should also like to thank the Geheimes Staatsarchiv Preussischer Kulturbesitz (Berlin) for supplying photocopies of reviews from the archive's invaluable Steininger Collection. Joseph Auner, who alerted me to the collection's existence, also read the complete manuscript and provided invaluable feedback.

Above all, I am greatly indebted to all those Weillians whose published work and private counsel made this study possible: to Tim Carter, who provided invaluable input on chapter 9, in particular on *Johnny Johnson;* to Tamara Levitz, who read the chapter on Busoni; to Jürgen Schebera, coeditor of Weill's *Gesammelte Schriften;* to the editorial board members of the Kurt Weill Edition—the late David Drew, Joel Galand, Edward Harsh (coeditor of *Die Dreigroschenoper* and former managing editor of the Edition), Kim Kowalke (also president of the Kurt Weill Foundation), and Giselher Schubert, all of whom I have spent countless hours with discussing Weill and his works; to former director of the Weill-Lenya Research Center, David Farneth, and to his associates, Dave Stein (now the Foundation's archivist) and Elmar Juchem (the current managing editor of the Edition). Dave has delivered outstanding assistance during all stages of the project, from providing photocopies and digital images to responding rapidly to last-minute queries about sources. I have especially benefited from the matchless expertise of Elmar and Kim, whose extensive feedback and advice improved the final manuscript in innumerable ways. And I feel fortunate indeed to have enjoyed the support and expert guidance of my three editors: Anne Canright (copy editor), Rose Vekony (project manager), and Mary Francis (acquisitions editor). My wife, Grace, knows better than anyone how long this book has been in the works. It is dedicated to her and to our son, Harry, with love.

1

Biographical Notes

Lately he has been asked to write in the vein of Gilbert and Sullivan, or of Gershwin, and now of seicento madrigals. And this for a man who was notable for the curious individuality of his own style, for a man almost inflexibly remote from any other style but his own.

S. L. M. BARLOW, "IN THE THEATRE"[1]

I think of Weill as a composer who was able to put on any clothes—ranging from Protestant chorale to Jewish melisma to Euro-tango to Schoenbergian atonality to Richard Rodgers' popcorn—precisely because he was so confident that he had centered his art on the fundamentals of expression: on legible music-figures. He was not a fake, but a serious composer adept at wearing any sort of frivolous musical drag. . . . To learn what is the common property of all music theater, listen to Weill.

DANIEL ALBRIGHT, "KURT WEILL AS MODERNIST"[2]

How should Kurt Weill be remembered? The fact that posterity has been inclined to recognize him as the composer who didn't give a damn about posterity is an irony he would have acknowledged, if not entirely appreciated. Nor was he wholly blameless for this state of affairs. "As for myself, I write for today," he said in a much-cited and often paraphrased statement. "I don't give a damn about writing for posterity." It is hard to believe he was not protesting too much. Why else would he have brought up the issue in the first place? Those who really don't give a damn, frankly do not talk about it. Or perhaps he was not protesting enough. Posterity, after all—which *has* given a damn about Weill's statement—has been left to work out what he meant, and has done so in a variety of ways. The irony demands qualification, if not resolution.

The notion of his not having written for posterity contributes to the prevalent image of Weill as a composer without a stable identity, someone who "seemed to change styles more often than countries," to quote one of his biographers.[3] Part of this image no doubt stems from his lifelong commitment to musical theater as opposed to concert or "absolute" music. As the situation required, he sought to adapt to the needs and demands of those involved in the creation of musical theater: co-authors, directors, singers, conductors, et al. The patchy transmission of the works is another factor. Despite the value that Weill attached to the "sonic image" of his compositions, as he referred to his own instrumentation, and hence to preparing his own orchestrations—including on Broadway, where composers customarily assign the task to someone else—not a single full score of any of his works for the musical theater was published in his lifetime. In fact, some of his best-known music has circulated in the form of popular arrangements, as hit tunes lifted from the theater works—a practice to which he himself was not averse, and on occasion actively promoted.[4] Yet he always made a distinction between, on the one hand, the control exercised by the composer over the integrity of the work as a whole, including its "sonic image," and, on the other hand, the mutability of individual songs. And in a few notable instances, such as "Mack the Knife" and "September Song," he achieved that rare thing among classically trained twentieth-century musicians: having his identity as a composer eclipsed by his own music's popularity. The more people there are who whistle his tunes, the less likely it is they will know who wrote them—a way, perhaps, of *posterity* not giving a damn?

The image of a chameleonic artistic identity has above all to do with Weill's having worked with conspicuous success on two continents, changing countries as well as styles. Many of his critics and not a few of his admirers have had a problem with that success, reluctant to embrace the move he made with apparent ease from 1920s and 1930s European to 1940s American culture. Because the crossover was both literal and figurative, Weill was charged with having abandoned the values of his earlier, European work and reinventing himself. No one captured this labile aspect of his profile more colorfully than the director Elia Kazan, with whom Weill worked on two of his American shows: "I did admire his ability to make good in a new country, this one, and to adapt himself to the requirements of our musical theatre. If, when he left Germany, he'd landed in Java instead of the United States, within a year he'd have been writing Javanese temple music and receiving praise from their high priests. If he'd been dumped on an African savannah, he'd quickly have mastered the tribal drum!"[5]

Some have even claimed that after leaving Germany Weill "[attempted] to evolve a consistent secondary persona," as David Drew put it in 1975, adding that such an attempt "is unique in the history of significant composition"; it "requires a corresponding and difficult adjustment on the part of everyone who is accustomed to evaluate an artist's late works in the light of earlier ones."[6] Along these lines, while also raising the question "concerning the calibre of Weill's American work when compared with the European," the composer Robin Holloway has expressed the view that Weill "decisively relinquished" the European.[7] The "two

Weills" that emerge from this view are deemed mutually incompatible. Without my either wanting or needing to play down the tensions and apparent contradictions in Weill's life and work, one of the critical tasks of this study is to explore the reasoning behind such judgments.

To be sure, Weill's artistic positions were never entirely free of contradictions. Why should they be? The contradictions were challenges he set for himself as much as for his critics. Not surprisingly, his correspondence with his family tends to be much franker about such matters than the public statements. Of the early letters, which contain a wealth of detail about his career, none sets the stage better than one he wrote to his brother Hans on 27 June 1919. Here the nineteen-year-old writes about his sense of vocation as a composer and describes with revealing imagery his approach to composition. He compares himself to Beethoven, quite clearly the paradigmatic composer of instrumental music, but hardly one to be emulated: "I need words to set my imagination in motion," he declares; "my imagination is not a bird but an airplane."[8] For someone who would spend almost his entire career writing for the musical theater, this statement is remarkably providential. Words would indeed continue to set his imagination in motion; purely instrumental music would be the exception rather than the rule.

His description of the compositional process in terms of modern technology adds a sense of historical context that is never far from the surface of Weill's art. A decade later, for example, he would celebrate Charles Lindbergh's epoch-making transatlantic flight with a cantata, originally conceived as a piece for radio written in collaboration with Paul Hindemith and Bertolt Brecht. *Der Lindberghflug,* as the 1929 cantata is called, is one obvious case. Another is *Railroads on Parade* (a "Pageant-Drama of Transport," as it was billed), written for the New York World's Fair and performed there in 1939–40 as a celebration of the Transcontinental Railroad from its beginnings in the mid–nineteenth century through the present. And these are hardly exceptions. Very few of Weill's works conceal their connection to contemporaneous culture; indeed, most make a point of emphasizing it. Weill composed music that was both *for* and *of* its time.

Measuring himself against Beethoven was not just a question of instrumental or "absolute" versus vocal music or of establishing a vital link to the historical present, however. It was also a matter of racial identity. Wondering aloud in the letter to his brother whether he should abandon composition and turn instead to conducting, Weill mentions studying with Arnold Schoenberg as a solution. The following passage from the 1919 letter is nothing if not provocative, its layers of irony presenting a significant challenge, particularly where Weill invokes the anti-Semitic stereotype of the Jewish artist. Hardly expecting posterity to eavesdrop, he is no doubt appealing to a sense of sardonic humor he knew his sibling would appreciate:

> We Jews are just not productive, and if we are, then we have a subversive, not a constructive impact; if the musical youth declares the Mahler-Schoenberg direction to be constructive, that's because they consist of Jews or Christians with a Jewish accent. Never will a Jew write a work like the Moonlight Sonata. And the pursuit of this line of thinking wrests the pen from one's hand. I want to get to the point—and I could only do this through Schoenberg—where I write when I must, when it comes to me from the bottom of my heart; otherwise it is music of the mind, and I hate that.

If Weill accepts the stereotype—a stereotype notoriously promulgated by Wagner—it is less as a verdict on his own ability or productivity than as a fact of cultural life, as something he has to confront, not least politically. With youthful ardor he suggests that another solution would be to forget about everything else, including moving to Vienna, by "falling frantically in love." The latter course is the one he would end up taking. The plan to study with Schoenberg came to naught, a "what-if" scenario as tantalizing as it proved to be unlikely. But fall in love he did. The marriage to Lotte Lenya, for all its frantic and turbulent aspects, would provide the foothold he was looking for. As he writes to his brother in the 1919 letter, five years before he and Lenya first met: "People like us who are caught between two worlds need such a foothold." At which point in the letter, his musical paradigm reappears: "There is only one thing that has a similar effect on me to imagining what love must be like: Beethoven." Hearing the *Kreutzer* Sonata, he reports, moved him to tears; "that alone, if I were bad, could make me good." The characteristically self-deprecatory humor continues right up until he signs off: "My bed is waiting longingly for me in order to rock me soothingly to sleep, to face a new day, a new hope—a new disappointment. Good night!"

The inspiration provided by texts; the engagement with contemporary life, including technology; the biographical issues connected to his Jewish identity coupled with a sense of being caught between two worlds; the vexed relationship to the German musical models (whether Beethoven, Wagner, Mahler, or Schoenberg); the existential importance of marital ties; the pervasive sense of irony, in art as well as life; the painful proximity of hope and disappointment; the appeal to human goodness through love and through music; the ultimate belief in music's power to heal—all are evident in the letter and would remain so in one form or another throughout his career. The extent to which these aspects of Weill's life and work have informed posterity's image of him, however, is of course another matter.

Weill's attitude toward posterity and posterity's attitude toward him are sides of the same coin. At his own prompting, he is remembered as someone who wrote expressly for his own time, without regard for the future. That is part of the legacy, neatly summarized by one of his less charitable obituarists, Theodor W. Adorno, who remarked on Weill's singular ability not only to serve the present but to capture it in sound: "This most ephemeral aspect of him may endure."[9] Endured it has. Again, the challenge is to describe how. How did Weill serve his time? How did he capture it in sound; how—to use a favorite verb of his from the late 1940s—did he "musicalize" it? How have his works—principally works for the musical theater—been transmitted for posterity to savor?

Placing those works in a biographical context, the present chapter has a twofold aim. As well as reviewing Weill's career in terms of its continuities and discontinuities, it subjects to scrutiny the models on which such terms are themselves based. Asking how Weill should be remembered is not just a matter of reviewing and reassessing his image. It is also about examining the methods of biography and criticism that helped generate the image in the first place.

WEILL AND POSTERITY

Weill's posterity-shunning statement, inviting skepticism on account of its self-conscious appeal to posterity, first appeared in a newspaper interview in 1940.[10] He had been in the United States for five years, after having escaped Nazi Germany in March 1933 and spent the initial exile years in Paris and London. His experiments in musical theater, on which his reputation in Germany was based, continued. In Paris he revived his soured collaboration with Bertolt Brecht to produce a theatrical mix of vocal numbers and dance, the "ballet chanté" *Die sieben Todsünden* (The Seven Deadly Sins). He also wrote songs and instrumental music for the theatrical adaptation of Jacques Deval's novel *Marie Galante*. In London he completed for the Savoy Theater his satirical operetta *A Kingdom for a Cow*, initially conceived in German as *Der Kuhhandel* and intended for performance in Zurich and Prague. His next project, the vast biblical pageant *The Eternal Road*, had likewise begun as a German-language work, *Der Weg der Verheissung*, again with performance in Europe in mind. But plans for the pageant's realization in New York in 1936 (the postponed premiere eventually took place on 7 January 1937) brought the composer to the United States in September 1935, where he would end up living for the remaining fourteen years of his life.

The time of the interview was a turning point in his career. Apart from *The Eternal Road*, which had enjoyed 153 performances but was a financial disaster because of the huge costs, his two main American stage works up to this point had been relatively successful. The musical play *Johnny Johnson* (1936), with 68 performances, was something of a *succès d'estime;* and its successor, the musical comedy *Knickerbocker Holiday* (1938), which received 168 performances, achieved genuinely popular acclaim, even by Broadway's demanding standards. But in 1939 Weill had produced no new major works for the musical theater—not for want of trying. After the Federal Theater Project (FTP) productions of *Johnny Johnson* in Los Angeles and elsewhere, Weill and book author Paul Green received an FTP commission for a theater piece to celebrate the U.S. Constitution. Their "symphonic drama," entitled *The Common Glory,* remained unfinished, however, as did the plan to produce a work on the theme of Davy Crockett. Weill began work with Maxwell Anderson, book author of *Knickerbocker Holiday,* on a theater piece called *Ulysses Africanus;* although it was eventually abandoned, parts would be salvaged for Weill's last work for the stage, the "musical tragedy" *Lost in the Stars.* He worked on several films in an attempt to establish himself in Hollywood, but only one of them was produced with his music: Fritz Lang's socially critical gangster movie *You and Me,* starring George Raft and Sylvia Sidney, which was released on 3 June 1938. He also supplied music for the historical pageant *Railroads on Parade,* performed at the New York World's Fair in the Railroad Pavilion in 1939 and 1940, and allegedly described by the composer himself as a "circus opera."[11] In addition, he contributed stage music to two plays, *Madam, Will You Walk?* (by Sidney Howard) and *Two on an Island* (by Elmer Rice) and composed the songs "Stopping by Woods on a Snowy Evening" (Robert Frost) and "Nannas Lied" (Brecht).

The immediate occasion for the interview's publication was the first broadcast, scheduled for the following day, of the radio cantata *The Ballad of Magna Carta,* also written with Anderson. Weill was also just beginning work, this time with Moss Hart, on a musical play that would become one of his biggest theatrical successes and establish him as a major force on Broadway, *Lady in the Dark.* This, then, and the other works just mentioned are the practical purposes of which he speaks. And Schoenberg is still on his mind:

> I want to use whatever gifts I have for practical purposes . . . not waste them on things which have no life, or which have to be kept alive by artificial means. That's why I'm in the theater—the commercial theater. . . . I'm convinced that many modern composers have a feeling of superiority toward their audiences. Schoenberg, for example, has said he is writing for a time fifty years after his death. But the great "classic" composers wrote for their contemporary audiences. They wanted those who heard their music to understand it, and they did. As for myself, I write for today. I don't give a damn about writing for posterity. And I do not feel that I compromise my integrity as a musician by working for the theater, the radio, the motion pictures, or any other medium which can reach the public which wants to listen to music. I have never acknowledged the difference between "serious" music and "light" music. There is only good music and bad music.

Although the statement appeared in a newspaper interview, unlikely to transmit exactly what Weill said, it is still plausible that the words are essentially his. The gist, if not the precise wording, is arguably authentic. As reported, he is not discussing the issue of posterity in general so much as that of *writing* for posterity in particular. He is comparing himself with two constituencies of composers:

the "great 'classic' composers," on the one hand (for the Busoni pupil this meant, first and foremost, Mozart, but also included figures such as Verdi and Bizet), and Schoenberg on the other hand, his great "might-have-been" teacher whose obsession with posterity serves as his point of departure.[12] The metaphor he uses to characterize these two factions—having life versus being kept alive by artificial means—demands interpretation, if not deconstruction. He is distancing himself from subsidized art but also from the tradition of "artificial," "non-vernacular" music with which he was so familiar as a young man.

What rings especially true, and also requires amplification, is the rarely quoted remark that follows about not compromising his integrity. What does that mean, "integrity as a musician"? Weill raises the issue in a number of writings, both letters, private and public, and occasional pieces, usually written for newspapers in conjunction with premiere productions of his work. Movies presented an even greater challenge in this regard than the theater. Writing in 1946, having experienced mixed success as a film composer, Weill was still ready to declare that "the motion picture is a perfect medium for an original musico-dramatic creation on the same level as the different forms of the musical theatre: musical comedy, operetta, musical play and opera." He wanted his contribution as musical collaborator to be not only "original" but also "integral": "If we want to develop an art form (or a form of entertainment) in which music has an integral part, we have to allow the composer to collaborate with the writer and director to the same extent as he collaborates in the musical theatre." He wanted to "leave room for music to express emotions, to set the tempo, to 'speak,'" to "allow the composer to use his own musical language, to employ different orchestra combinations, to write with the same originality and integrity as if he were writing for the concert or the theatre."[13]

Working in the movies as opposed to the theater presented a more acute challenge to Weill's sense of artistic integrity owing to the divisions of labor required by the industry, even though his aspiration to compose for the general public remained the same for both media. Pondering the future of opera in 1929, for example, he had insisted on the need to write music that was useful to that public, which he referred to as an "Allgemeinheit"; the quality of the work would decide whether the music produced could be called art. He was therefore careful to distinguish between music that would be consumed and then disappear *(Verbrauchsmusik)* and genuinely useful music *(Gebrauchsmusik),* even though he hoped that the difference between these two categories, and even between them and art music *(Kunstmusik),* might eventually be erased, a historical process for which he uses the Hegelian expression *aufheben* (indicating the synthesis or "sublation" of opposites). He saw himself committed, and would remain committed throughout his career, to attempting something that many twentieth-century composers dismissed as futile, if not impossible: "conducting an experiment to create music that can satisfy the artistic needs of broad social strata, without sacrificing its artistic substance."[14] In this Weill stands in utter contrast to the Schoenbergian position against which he was now openly polemicizing.

The call to erase the distinction between *Gebrauchsmusik* and *Kunstmusik* echoes the aesthetic discourse of the time, particularly in debates about operatic reform. For Weill, such programmatic statements manifested themselves most fully in the Lehrstück, the genre of musical theater created expressly for didactic purposes. The programmatic statements are precisely that, however; they articulate artistic aims and ambitions, utopias of reform as much as, if not more than, realities. As an artist, as opposed to a propagandist, Weill may have succeeded less in completely erasing categories than in exploiting the creative tension between them. He was a composer whose work thrived on dualisms on a number of levels. Whether his embracing such creative tensions ultimately amounted to his overcoming them, thereby creating a new synthesis (the Hegelian *Aufhebung* or "sublation" that his language implies), or whether the posited antagonism perhaps even became moot in his work, is an open question. Weill reception has been characterized by deep, enduring divisions on this very issue. The nature of Weill's challenge—to himself, to his audience, and to posterity—is generally acknowledged, but the terms on which he attempted to meet it and his ultimate success in doing so are nothing if not disputed. Although his aims present themselves in terms of a binarism that he aims to overcome, the terms themselves vary somewhat.[15] In 1929, it was a matter of reaching "broad social strata" versus "not sacrificing artistic substance." The question of accessibility would remain, but it would later be expressed in terms of confronting the opposition between entertainment and education.

Audience appeal and artistic merit remained separate issues for him, at least in theory. The former, he thought, need not compromise the latter. By the time of the 1940 interview, although the importance of the earlier distinctions may have faded, he was certainly exaggerating when he claimed that he had "never acknowledged the difference between 'serious' and 'light' music." He had, after all, been engaged in the culture wars of the Weimar Republic that required composers to provide elaborate justification for writing "functional" as opposed to "autonomous" music. Translated, albeit roughly, into American terms, this could be taken as "light" versus "serious." And in the 1920s the differences were precisely the ones Weill was struggling to overcome, or at least to exploit. The slippery issue of quality remained: the difference between good and bad music.

Nor did Weill entirely relinquish the adjective *serious* in connection with his own art. In the 1947 article "Broadway and the Musical Theatre," for example, he asserted: "I never could see any reason why the 'educated' (not to say 'serious') composer should not be able to reach all available markets with his music, and I have always believed that opera should be part of the living theatre of our time.

Broadway is today one of the great theatre centers of the world. It has all the technical and intellectual equipment for a serious musical theatre."[16] A decade earlier, in "The Alchemy of Music," he had written: "I consider it one of the most important realizations of recent years that the distinction between good and bad music has replaced the distinction of light and serious, and that good light music is appreciated as being more valuable than bad serious music."[17] These are issues that never went away. Yet addressing them is not the same as resolving them—that remained a task for posterity.

Weill himself would touch on the transition from his earlier to his later work in connection with *Down in the Valley,* a folk opera for amateurs, including high schools and colleges, for which he was charged, shortly after the 1948 premiere, with writing "corny" music. His defense, which is quoted here at length, provides an eloquent expression of the aims of his art and the rationale behind his artistic choices. "Corn," he wrote on 24 July 1948, responding to Irving Sablosky, music critic of the *Chicago Daily News,*

> is really a part of life in our time, and life is what I am interested in as a basis of musical expression. My teacher Busoni, at the end of his life, hammered into me one basic truth which he had arrived at after 50 years of pure aestheticism: the fear of triviality is the greatest handicap for the modern artist, it is the main reason why "modern music" got more and more removed from reality, from life, from the real emotions of people in our time. I lost this fear through years of working in the theatre, and in doing so, my whole aspect *[sic]* towards musical composition changed. Instead of worrying about the material of music, the theory behind it, the opinion of other musicians, my concern is to find the purest expression in music for what I want to say, with enough trust in my instinct, my taste and my talent to write always "good" music, regardless of the style I am writing in.[18]

What did he mean by "good" while invoking his teacher, Busoni? His explanation of a chord with an "added" sixth provides a clue. Craftsmanship mattered, defined here in terms of "good" voice-leading, a concept for which he did not have the correct English term, only the German one.

> I am sorry I offended your ears with the sixth in the last chord. But you can see in the piano score that I arrived at the sixth entirely out of "Stimmführung" (development of voices), so it is not used as an "effect." But here again, it offends your ear because it is being used a great deal in popular music today. If you had lived in the 18th century, your ear would have been offended a thousand times listening to Mozart using over and over again the same cadenza [he means the German word *Kadenz,* i.e., "cadence"] which every other composer of his time used.

Musical training and a trust in "instinct, taste, and talent" aside, integrity is above all a biographical category; its study belongs in the realm of biographical method. It is the job of composer biographers to explore the elements of a life, to form them into an undivided or unbroken state—or not; to seek out wholeness and completeness, if they see fit; to synthesize the entirety, if they can. Integrity could also imply soundness of moral principle, uncorrupted virtue, and sincerity. Again, biographers may be ready and able to provide guidance. But what methods and criteria should they apply?

BIOGRAPHICAL METHOD

Biographical method is really two distinct, yet related, things. It signifies approaches to reading a life, something that in German would be called *Biographik,* a term that tends to be used in a collective sense referring to the whole business of biography but also to trends and tendencies of its various genres, either with respect to a particular figure or to biographies in general. "Weill-Biographik" would be the sum of knowledge to be gleaned from available studies, from the obituaries in 1950, and from David Drew's seminal overviews, including the entries in *The New Grove Dictionary of Music and Musicians* and the revised edition, through the monographs by Ronald Taylor, Jürgen Schebera, and most recently Foster Hirsch.[19] But in the field of musicology, biographical method means something else as well, referring to a particular way of reading musical works in terms of a life (or vice versa). In German this would not be *Biographik,* but rather *die biographische Methode,* a type of music analysis, a way of reading meaning in musical works, hermeneutics. There is some kind of narrative to present, which may entail gleaning information from the works themselves. Composer biographies may or may not offer such analysis beyond putting things in correct chronological order. In his 1980 biography, for example, Ronald Sanders offers almost no such analysis or interpretation.[20] Putting together the narrative may even entail having the works provide a story of their own, typically in terms of the evolution of a style. This is something David Drew has attempted in various ways, as have Ronald Taylor, despite the "divided world" of his monograph's title, and Douglas Jarman.[21] In turn, the narrative of the works may or may not tell us something about the composer's life. There are many options, often depending on the subject, of course, but also on the information available. The *biographische Methode* is *a* form, not necessarily *the* form, of *Biographik.*[22]

Biography, as a genre, tends to be implicated in establishing, confirming, or occasionally reducing the reputation of a figure deemed historically or culturally significant. Composer biographies are no exception, often presented as hagiographies, as tales of artistic integrity at the highest level. In this they serve various cultural purposes, as both criticism and history. There is no reason, then, why biography should be bracketed off from other forms of reception. Biographers are bound to make critical judgments based on certain expectations: on aesthetic criteria as well as on conceptions of personal identity and individuality. The significance accorded individuals and their creations will determine the narrative form of any biography but also vice versa: the narrative form comes laden with preconceptions that will influence the content and outcome of any story. From their various options, biographers have to be careful to choose the right approach to their subject. Hero worship does not work for everyone.

Wolfgang Hildesheimer, with his 1977 anti-biography of Mozart, offered a novel and strikingly provocative alternative.[23] This biography is cited as exemplary of a shift in *Biographik*—a shift, to quote from the seminal work of Helmut Scheuer, that involved "attempt[ing] to navigate around the cliffs of hero worship and myth creation."[24] Hildesheimer's work became a landmark, not because it offered lots of new information, or a huge amount of old information for that matter, but because it sought to debunk a number of prevalent myths about Mozart. And it did so through its studied avoidance of a traditional narrative, or rather, through a self-conscious variation thereof. We still get a *Lebenslauf,* albeit one constantly interrupted by lengthy excursuses into *Biographik* in general and a critique of the *biographische Methode* in particular. Yet Hildesheimer asks more questions than he provides answers to, somewhat like the envy-ridden composer Salieri in *Amadeus* (initially a play by Peter Shaffer, later a popular, award-winning movie directed by Milos Forman), which Hildesheimer seems to have influenced in substantial ways. Like Salieri, he is puzzled by the connection between the man and the music. And he is unhappy about earlier discussions that claim to have that connection sorted out. Not that he does not replace the old myths with a newer one—he does, as does the movie, with a vengeance. The movie brings together the two disparate and discrete parts preserved by the anti-biography: Mozart's debauched, scurrilous, scatological, and puerile character on the one hand, and his sublime, divinely absolute music on the other. This is surely a myth for the late twentieth century: the geek who transforms the world.

To the extent that Weill has not received the Great Composer treatment à la Mozart, he has not needed a demythologizer like Hildesheimer. Yet if biographies of Weill have tended toward the opposite of hagiography, that is partly because they still applied the old paradigms of nineteenth-century hagiography and consequently found their subject wanting, quite sorely so in some cases. Every biographer applies his own notion of integrity to Weill. Taylor's guiding notion appears to be "style"—a category that plays a critical role in the work of two enormously influential figures in Weill reception, Theodor W. Adorno and David Drew. Adorno's impact on postwar Weill reception has been as incalculable as it is widespread, and Drew's view of Weill likewise finds frequent echoes in the literature of music criticism.[25]

Taylor's monograph on Weill, which openly acknowledges Drew's influence, presents itself as a popular biography, "not addressed to specialists," as the author puts it in the preface. The readers he has in mind are "those who have whistled

'Mack the Knife,' 'Surabaya-Johnny' and the 'Alabama Song' for years and would like to know more about the man who composed them, his life, the people he knew, the things that mattered to him, the works he wrote." As a matter of principle, the author is "not . . . concerned with analysis of technique, or with the investigation of musico-historical issues" (viii). His choice of songs here is hardly casual, for it becomes clear as one progresses through the book that Taylor himself is especially partial to the Weill-Brecht works from which these titles originate.

No doubt Taylor's initial involvement with Weill's music parallels that of his intended readers. No doubt he, too, has whistled the Weill-Brecht evergreens. At any rate, his exposure to Weill's entire oeuvre, although it may have enlarged his knowledge, seems to have done little to alter his opinion or perspective. By way of emphasizing this point he temporarily forsakes his popular platform and resorts instead to the professorial language of Kantian essentialism in a brief discussion of "the phenomenon of Weill's music *an sich.*" He insists on an "unmistakable Weill musical accent, a Weill 'sound,' identified in most people's minds with the *Dreigroschenoper* and the works surrounding it, down to *The Seven Deadly Sins*" (212–13). (The mix of original and translated titles in Taylor's monograph seems, incidentally, to follow no system.) This "characteristic sound," he maintains, becomes "less characteristic, blander, almost more commonplace" beginning around the time of emigration. Yet the diminution is hardly a "purely musical" matter. The key to Taylor's analysis can be found in the following four sentences, which deserve therefore scrutiny: "The tensions and conflicts of the old Berlin environment had been the goad that drove him forwards. Take away these conflicts, remove the forces of opposition, and the raison d'être of the work evaporates. Paris was not Berlin. For reasons as much of survival as anything else Weill turned from confrontation to accommodation, to serving a market for which in Germany he had spent much of his time showing scorn" (213).

Beneath the scarcely concealed tautologies (the "characteristic sound" becoming "less characteristic"), knowing platitudes ("Paris was not Berlin"), and contradictions (*Die sieben Todsünden* was composed in Paris) lurks the bifurcation thesis. The Berlin Weill is the composer of confrontation, an active agent of stirring historical forces; the subsequent, postemigration composer is a willing victim of pernicious market forces. Taylor is quick to credit Weill with some autonomy in the matter, voicing the sentiment that he "was far too intelligent a musician not to know what he was doing." But he returns equally quickly to the familiar clichés of Weill criticism, presented as rhetorical questions: "A lapse of taste?" "A lowering of sights?" Of *The Eternal Road,* he concludes that it was "perhaps an early expression of that urge to accommodation and adaptability which was to become so strong in America" (213). In a judgment unfathomable to anyone acquainted with the innovations of Weill's American works, Taylor concludes that Weill "accepted . . . the Broadway musical . . . as he found it and placed his talent at its disposal." Whereas "in Europe, he had been a master of his forms. In America he became their servant" (306). It is a serious (if unoriginal) charge, which the author leaves largely unsubstantiated.

His biography's subtitle might suggest that Taylor had attempted to relocate the bifurcation thesis from the composer to the worlds in which he lived. Yet he ends up applying it in the customary way: to the composer himself. He begins with the question "Will the real Weill please stand up?" (vii) and concludes by asserting that "we do not mind how many Kurt Weills stand up" (334). In view of Taylor's view of the American Weill, his questions could imply that all but one of the Weills he describes are frauds—or worse, that none of them at all is real.

Theodor W. Adorno addressed the issue of identity at a more abstract, conceptual level than Taylor. As one might expect from this professional philosopher, he launched into his much-cited Weill obituary by signaling a possible category mistake: "The figure of the composer who died in America," he began, "was hardly commensurate with the concept of composer."[26] The obituary goes on to explain that Weill had in fact ceased to be a "composer" long before his actual death in 1950, at least according to Adorno's understanding of the term.[27] Instead, Adorno proposed, it would be more appropriate to label him a *Musikregisseur*, a "music director." Appearing here for the first time and recurring in several of Adorno's subsequent writings that either are about Weill or mention him explicitly, the term refers to how in dedicating his career to the musical theater he "subordinated" his music to theatrical function. At the same time, Adorno connects this creative approach to inherent artistic shortcomings, claiming in the obituary that Weill "made a virtue of subordination to function—artistic and, to a degree, also political—out of the necessity of limited powers of composition." In this normative sense, with its inescapably pejorative connotations, Adorno's "new type," as he calls it, echoes the backhanded compliment Hanslick paid Wagner when he dubbed him "the world's first *Regisseur*."[28]

Like Hanslick, Adorno believed that attention to the whole business of theater detracted from strictly musical considerations. The epithet *Musikregisseur* reduced the composer to his role as a cog in the larger machinery of theatrical life. And however much he may have wished with his new coinage to do justice to Weill's vocation as a man of the theater, there is no denying that the terms in which Adorno presented his assessment of Weill's career as a whole were comprehensively negative. Submission to theatrical function and lack of large-scale forms are just two of his charges. Others mentioned in the obituary include "avoidance of psychological affect, to the point of self-sacrifice"; "a certain monotony of style"; "paucity of musical means"; "a shifting of the compositional process into rehearsal"; "yielding to the constraints and temptations of exile"; and "obedience" as well as "conformism *par excellence*." By way of offering a paradoxical conclusion, he ascribes to Weill's music an enduring quality of ephemerality, as mentioned above.[29]

From this list of negative traits associated with Weill's development as a *Musikregisseur,* it is not difficult to infer how Adorno *positively* defines his concept of the composer. His paradigm is freedom from the kind of constraints that Weill was subjected to—in short, the paradigm of artistic autonomy. Although he is willing to concede aesthetic value in Weill's collaborations with Brecht, he construes the American period as one of utter subservience to popular culture, which for him is inextricably bound up with the capitalist "culture industry." In a later article, "Questions of Modern Opera Theater," Adorno thus distinguished between two phases in Weill's career: one in which he made a virtue of the perceived necessity, another in which he did not. "His extraordinary achievement as a *Musikregisseur,* his instinct for combining snatches of music in a montage on the 'threepenny' stage, lasted only as long as he rigorously foreswore actual composition. As soon as he allowed himself to be guided by larger musical forms, he failed; and precisely by harboring the higher aspirations he formerly ridiculed, he fell under the spell of a mere amusement-theater, the American musical."[30]

Around the time of Hildesheimer's *Mozart,* David Drew produced his seminal essay "Kurt Weill and His Critics," which, along with the slightly later (1980) *New Grove* entry, was the most informed and critically engaged overview of the composer's career up to that point in Weill scholarship. Both pieces, moreover, revealed Drew as one of Weill's staunchest critics in terms of his putative failure to develop along the lines adumbrated by the early, German compositions. Drew therefore left Weill at the end of the 1980 *New Grove* entry as "one of music's great 'might-have-beens,'" a composer "whose gifts were partly unfulfilled or partly squandered." What happened? Was it Weill? Was it history? Or were Drew's frustrated expectations based on unrealistic, inappropriate criteria? Or all three of these factors? "Weill," Drew wrote in *New Grove,* "is perhaps the only [notable artist] to have done away with his old creative self in order to make way for a new one." *Lady in the Dark* represented the principal stumbling block. Drew called it "outwardly the least personal score," yet salvaged the idea of a continuing biographical narrative by suggesting that "inwardly it is the nearest to being a subconscious form of autobiography" in which Weill almost succeeds in "banishing every trace of his musical background and upbringing."[31] The American Weill, he claimed, suppressed the European one. The development, if there was one, was negative, born of denial. Personal traces were significant only to the extent that they seemed to have been erased.

In "Kurt Weill and His Critics," meanwhile, Drew expanded on why *Lady in the Dark* was such a problem for him: "It is only with some sense of the whole that we can hope to understand, and be fair to, the individual works, be they weak or strong. That sense of Weill's art as a living and developing organism informs everything of value that was written about it by his contemporaries in Germany."[32] The organicist model, then.

Continuing the search for a "unified style" attempted by the musicologist Herbert Fleischer in 1932,[33] Drew found unity in Weill's European "manners," as he referred to the variety of Weill's music, in a "central style . . . defined not by superficial aspects that tended to attract attention at the time, but by the very bone structure," by which he meant "voice-leading and the interrelation of timbre and tempo, and so on."[34] (Weill's later talk of good voice-leading suggested that he felt he had in fact retained his good European manners.) Echoing Adorno's talk of *Selbstpreisgabe,* Drew spoke in *New Grove* of "a degree of self-sacrifice greater than any that would have been demanded by a totalitarian ministry of culture."[35]

Weill, needless to say, saw his development quite differently, in positive terms. Apropos *Street Scene* in 1947 as we saw in the introduction, he wrote: "Ever since I made up my mind, at the age of 19, that my special field of activity would be the theatre, I have tried continuously to solve, in my own way, the form-problems of the musical theatre, and through the years I have approached these problems from all different angles."[36] Solving form-problems, the Busonian legacy, provides a thread of continuity, even integrity, that belies the notion of a radically different American Weill. Different, yes, because of the "different angles," but nothing that need give biographers too much pause, Weill seems to be saying. He wants us to acknowledge the diversity of his oeuvre, certainly, to appreciate how theater makes its demands, yet ones that can be met in various ways, depending on the circumstances, whether dramatic or social. The statement nicely captures the provisional, ongoing nature of his solutions, while also creating an image for posterity. Avoid looking backward too much, he seems to be saying, "worrying about the material of music, the theory behind it," trying to identify how these developed consistently from one work to the next. Rather, appreciate the "different angles." Each solution, he emphasizes, is "in my own way."

Weill's "way" was a variant of the Busonian way, as he liked to stress. On numerous occasions, whether expressly or only implicitly, he invited us to identify continuity in his identity as a Busoni pupil, just as he pointed out that it was Busoni who taught him not to fear something that even his most sympathetic critics would charge him with: banality.[37] His European, "classical" roots remained an inalienable part of his artistic identity, even though his career unfolded in a way quite different from those of his European contemporaries. The other composers for the musical theater with whom he closely identified at various times were all European: Mozart, Offenbach, Verdi, Bizet, Puccini.

When it is described and accounted for using the models applied by Taylor, Adorno, and Drew, Weill's career inevitably comes up short. Even the "new type" proposed by Adorno, the *Musikregisseur,* is essentially a negative concept, reflecting an inability on Weill's part to qualify as a "real composer" (the "real Weill" whom Taylor wanted to "stand up"). Similarly, Drew's psychological model, which adopts Jung's notion of a "secondary persona," posits a biographical schism—Taylor's "divided world"—that manifests itself in stylistic pluralism and an attendant lack of musical authenticity. All of the conceptual models and their opposites, whether implied or explicit, seem a priori value-laden, prejudicing the outcome of the investigation before it even begins. Is there a more neutral, less obviously normative model that might serve as a conceptual guide to describing the totality of Weill's career and so allow for coherence and integrity? Or alternatively, how can traditional concepts be modified or reconceived to do justice to the peculiarities of Weill's case?

COMPETING CHARACTERS: WEILL AND HINDEMITH

Typecasting of any kind could appear to preclude change and development, and Weill clearly did change and develop. What is required is a model that somehow captures the very mechanisms that govern development and questions of conformity and nonconformity, or in Freudian terms, superego controls. What was it that changed and developed in Weill? And how did he cope with the upheavals of exile? However extreme the upheaval may have been in cultural and artistic terms, is there a way in which his response to it can be described as characteristic?

By way of exploring these questions I would like to continue a line of investigation initiated by Drew in his pioneering article "Musical Theatre in the Weimar Republic," published in 1961.[38] There Drew proposed a fruitful and telling point of comparison by considering Weill's early career in relation to that of his near-contemporary Hindemith—"an unusual but friendly game of artistic rivalry" (95–96), as Drew called it. Although other candidates suggest themselves, such as Weill's archrival in the United States, Richard Rodgers, the pairing with Hindemith makes particular sense not only because of the obvious points of convergence in their artistic biographies but also because of considerable divergences in their character types as artists.

The story begins in the early Weimar Republic, continuing into an American period, where each then goes his quite separate way. They were born within five years of each other, Hindemith in 1895 and Weill in 1900. Hindemith came from Hanau near Frankfurt. His father was a painter and decorator who wanted his children to become musicians. Starting in 1912, Hindemith studied composition in Frankfurt (at first with Arnold Mendelssohn and then with Bernhard Sekles), and by the time he was twenty-two he had become the concert master of the Frankfurt Opera Orchestra, which he had joined three years earlier. In 1927 he took up a professorship at the Berlin Hochschule für Musik, where he taught composition and theory. Weill's musical education followed a path that was similar in some respects, different in others. He grew up in Dessau, where his father was chief cantor in the synagogue. After composition lessons in Berlin with Humperdinck in 1918, he took a job in the opera house in Lüdenscheid in 1919, before resuming his training two years later as a composer in Berlin, this time with Busoni.

Their early successes in Germany swiftly established them as that country's foremost young composers, leaders of the New Music's second generation. For this reason, they were also in competition with each other. At one point the rivalry was such—that is, sufficiently strong but also sufficiently kept in check—that they collaborated on a radio cantata, *Der Lindberghflug*, which was performed with considerable success in 1929.[39] Both were forced out of Germany by Hitler's regime—Weill in 1933, Hindemith in 1938—with their work officially denounced as "degenerate." Both settled on the East Coast of the United States and acquired American citizenship, each becoming in his own quite distinctive way a respected figure of 1940s American cultural life.

For all the parallels in their careers—particularly evident in their Berlin years and underscored by their enforced exile—their music and personalities could scarcely be more different, as their respective contributions to *Der Lindberghflug* had already demonstrated. Each made his separate way to America: Weill in September 1935, Hindemith in February 1940 (after a stay in Switzerland and discounting the handful of short U.S. tours he made prior to emigration). But in a sense they and their generation had already made a spiritual journey to what they took for the New World a decade or so earlier. They had already "envisioned" America in the 1920s, influenced as they were by that era's *Neue Sachlichkeit* or New Objectivity, a salient ingredient of which was "Amerikanismus."[40] American values—or what was taken for American values—provided the younger generation of Germans with an alternative to the discredited nationalistic ones of their parents. Germany's dependence on America became not only economic, thanks to the Dawes Plan, but also cultural and spiritual. In music, the influence began most obviously with an infusion of dance music (or "jazz," as the musical idiom of fox-trots, shimmies, and ragtime was then called) into so-called serious music.[41] The resulting mix was frequently intended to shock, as illustrated by Hindemith's Suite "1922," composed in the year of its title. That the enterprise is impertinent and antimetaphysical in the extreme is reflected in the notorious note in the score described in French and English as "Mode d'emploi—Direction for Use!"; it appears on the first page of the suite's final movement, the Ragtime, instructing the performer to ignore what they learned in their piano lessons, "[not to] think very long about whether to play D♯ with the 4th or 6th finger," to "play this piece very wildly, but always rhythmically strict, like a machine," and to "regard the piano as an interesting kind of percussion instrument and act accordingly." Other such works include his first *Kammermusik*, with its notorious fox-trot finale, and the triptych of one-act operas, with which Hindemith temporarily acquired a reputation as an iconoclastic *enfant terrible.*

As for Weill, the extent of his musico-dramatic "Americanisms" has, if anything, been exaggerated. In his "Preface to the production book of the opera *Aufstieg und Fall der Stadt Mahagonny,*" for example, he warned against looking "for psychological or contemporary relevance." The name Mahagonny, he stated, "was chosen for timbral (phonetic) reasons. The city's geographical location does not play any role."[42] Nonetheless, Americanisms in his European works, from *Royal Palace* (1925–26) through *Die sieben Todsünden* (1933), are pervasive, their symbolism rich and contradictory.

The rivalry concerns the type of works Hindemith and Weill composed. On the surface this is unremarkable. Hindemith matched Weill's ballet-pantomime for children, *Zaubernacht,* composed in 1922, with his own "Christmas fairy tale" *Tuttifäntchen,* also from 1922. Both made settings of Rilke: Weill in *Das Stundenbuch* for baritone and orchestra; Hindemith in his song cycle *Das Marienleben,* completed in 1923. The parallels become more substantial, and the contrasts more obviously striking, in their works for the stage. Hindemith followed Weill's opera about artistic vocation, *Der Protagonist* (composed in 1924–25, first performed in 1926), with his own, *Cardillac* (1926). Riding the prevailing wave of anti-expressionism, both operas deal with the artist's fatal identification with his work, an identification so intense that he ends up committing murder. Both composers were indeed concerned as a matter of principle with the artist's responsibility to society, replacing what they saw as the isolationism of the Schoenberg school with social usefulness. In the spirit of radical artistic experimentation, but with a view to creating new platforms for art, they both wrote short operas for the Baden-Baden festival of 1927: Weill his "Songspiel" *Mahagonny;* Hindemith his "Sketch" *Hin und zurück.* It is also worth noting that Hindemith passed up the opportunity to write music for John Gay's *Beggar's Opera* after his publishers suggested it to him in 1925.[43] It was left to Weill to make his immortal setting, *Die Dreigroschenoper,* in 1928. And, as mentioned, 1929 brought their collective effort, *Der Lindberghflug,* also for Baden-Baden.

By this time, however, Hindemith had all but abandoned the use of popular dance music, whereas Weill had assimilated it as an idiom that people readily associate with his Berlin years, as easily recognizable as it is inimitable. Whenever Hindemith employs such popular idioms, they feel like quotations from a foreign language. Weill's approach was more, if not wholly, integrative. Some of the best examples are to be found in the otherwise ill-fated show *Happy End,* which attempted to repeat the stir *Die Dreigroschenoper* had caused a year earlier. Idiom is not personal style, however. Jazz was the idiom of the city, one that suited Weill's dramatic purposes at the time. If Weill's music is about its time, it is above all about city life. Nor does it embrace that life unequivocally, any more than the jazz-influenced song style should be mistaken for Weill's personal style. Writing about his *Berliner Requiem,* also to texts by Brecht, in the radio journal *Der deutsche Rundfunk,* for which he worked between 1925 and 1929 as a regular correspondent, Weill stated that the Requiem's content "undoubtedly corresponds with the feelings and views of the broadest strata of the population. An attempt has been made to express what the contemporary city dweller has to say about the phenomenon of death."[44]

By this time in their careers, around 1930, one basic difference had become evident. Weill was a man of the theater; Hindemith was not. Hindemith was a versatile and prolific all-rounder: an established soloist (on viola and violin), someone who had turned his hand to all kinds of music-making, including amateur music. This latter pursuit had revealed his affinity for the aims of the "youth movement" *(Jugendbewegung),* as the cultural movement was called.[45] Whereas Weill sought to capture the sentiments of the city dweller, Hindemith's *Musikantentum,* his instinctive musicality, which was lauded as much as it was criticized, made him a community (as opposed to a society) person. True, his early operas had earned him renown as a rowdy upstart. Yet his opera *Cardillac* had established him as a composer seriously to be reckoned with.[46] However, his approach to composition was not innately theatrical, as Weill's patently was. An analogous distinction can be drawn between Bach and Handel. The difference is not absolute but one of tendency, of general type. Much of Bach's music tends toward the cerebral, much of Handel's toward public effect, particularly in his operas and oratorios, of course. Similarly, Hindemith's guiding interests as they developed in his career lie with music as a craft, both compositional and performative, Weill's with music's expressive and theatrical potential.

Hindemith's appointment as a professor of composition and theory in 1927 thus brought to light a quite substantial discrepancy between the two composers. The former prankster of the *épatant* one-act operas and Suite "1922" now became a member of the academic establishment. Weill, on the other hand, was no pedagogue. He had previously taught music theory and composition only for money. Nor, moreover, would he try his hand at writing music-theoretical texts, as Hindemith was about to do.

One of Weill's few written statements on the subject is preserved in a letter from 1949 in which he was responding to the question "What are the most essential factors in composition?" His response begins with a general observation: "It is one of the hardest things for a composer to talk about his own work and even harder to develop a theory about the process of composition, since, in my opinion, it is one of the main factors of creative art to keep a certain innocence about this process of creation, to follow that stream of imagination (or, to use a much abused word, of inspiration) without looking around for the source of the stream." He then offers an analogy: "It is a bit like the process of falling asleep. If you try to watch how you fall asleep you'll have a hard time to pass into Morpheus' arms. By the same token, you cannot write music if you are watching yourself how you do it. That is, of course, the only comparison between falling asleep and writing music." The remarks that follow provide a potted summary of Weill's approach to musical composition, stressing in particular his vocation as a composer for the theater: "I have learned to make my music speak directly to the audience, to find the most immediate, the most direct way to say what I want to say, and to say it as simply as possible. That's why I think that, in the theater at least, melody is such an important element because it speaks directly to the heart—and what good is music if it cannot move people."[47] That was in 1949, a year before Weill's death, but the sentiments surely hold good for many of his European works as well.

The relationship between Hindemith's theory and practice is a considerably more complex one. Unlike Weill, he produced a number of theoretical tracts that earned him a reputation as a composer-theorist. While the theory, which he began writing in the 1930s, largely served to rationalize his own creative practice, the practice was also affected by the theory.[48] The development of the theory, in particular the invocation of Nature and universal harmony as a legitimizing authority, guided the composer through the turbulence of Nazi Germany. In general, then, Hindemith's *Unterweisung im Tonsatz* (Craft of Musical Composition), first published in 1937, both reflected the composer's pedagogical methods and defined the parameters of his own musical language.[49] In its specific appeals to universal values, however, it also documented a craving for continuity and identity at a time of increasing alienation from active musical life. That alienation was a direct result of National Socialism. Yet Hindemith's sense of it also continued after his return to Europe in the 1950s, despite widespread recognition and celebrity.[50]

Weill's departure from Germany was short and swift. He made his way first to Paris and then England, but two critical flops—a BBC broadcast of *The Threepenny Opera* and the premiere of *A Kingdom for a Cow* in London—were enough to suggest that that country was not the place for him.[51] And so he moved to the United States, under contract to oversee rehearsals and the production of *The Eternal Road,* which ended up being postponed for a substantial period. There he stayed, never permanently to return to Europe.

Hindemith's extrication from his native country was more protracted and full of more obvious pain, involving what has come to be known as the Hindemith Case *(Der Fall Hindemith),* the political tug-of-war between various parties over Hindemith's acceptability as a composer living in Nazi Germany. It was not just a matter of interpreting his oeuvre but of deciding what the criteria for that assessment should be in the first place.[52] Just how wide of the mark some of the assessments were is illustrated by the "Degenerate Music" exhibition staged in Düsseldorf in May 1938, where Hindemith and Schoenberg were lumped together as "theorists of atonality." The charge is absurd in both cases and indicative of the ideological opprobrium practiced by the Nazis. In Schoenberg's case the tribute referred to his harmony textbook of 1911, which deals only briefly, in an appendix, with the dissolution of tonality. And Hindemith's *Unterweisung im Tonsatz* is anything but a treatise on atonality. In the war of racist and ideological slander, musical details evidently mattered little.

Despite his professional successes in America, Hindemith eventually returned to pursue his academic vocation at the University of Zurich and also his career as a conductor. His ties to Germany and to Europe were patently stronger than Weill's. If he reveled in Americanisms in Germany, in America he seemed to crave attachments to Europe and its traditions.

Hindemith's invocation of universal laws of nature can be read as a response to his growing sense of isolation, an attempt to absolve himself from the pressures of history. His theoretical thought impinged on his practice as a composer such that he began to question the validity of earlier compositions in the light of his new ideas. The theory was not value-free, in other words, but had far-reaching aesthetic implications. In the first edition of the *Unterweisung* he even appended a list of his own works that he considered consistent with his theory, compositions in which "the realization of the views put forward in this book concerning compositional technique can best be followed."[53] Those he omitted were, by implication, aesthetically inferior.

In a handful of instances he undertook revisions in order to justify their inclusion in the newly defined canon of his oeuvre. One such, and the best known, is the song cycle *Das Marienleben,* originally composed in 1922–23.[54] Though not published until 1948 (with an elucidating foreword, completed in New Haven in June of that year), the revised version was apparently contemplated shortly after completion of the first. His diaries and work catalogues show that Hindemith did the bulk of the work on it a decade later and in two stages: in 1936–37, before his departure from Berlin while drafting the *Unterweisung;* and in the first half of 1941, shortly after joining the Yale School of Music full time.[55]

The foreword, in which Hindemith describes the motives, aims, and achievements of his revision, is a remarkable document of his artistic credo in matters general and particular. He sees *Das Marienleben* as having met an "interest in Western music."[56] The historical context in which he places himself is wide, stretching back to the Middle Ages. The contemporaries from which he distances himself are all those modernists who in their "new art" overstress "new" and forget "art."[57] For his part, he stresses the "ethical necessities of music and the moral duties of the musician"—qualities, he says, of which he had been aware since the performance of the first version of *Das Marienleben.* His revisions are undertaken in the spirit of approaching an ideal. He calls them "attempts at a solution which run parallel to the great issues of the general compositional development of our age."[58] He goes on to criticize the vocal lines of his first version as unamenable to the voice, as having been conceived in abstract musical terms, and says that the principles laid down in his own theory guided the revision. He concerned himself in the new version, he explains, with the coherence of the cycle as a whole. Its unity should be guaranteed not only by the text but also by musical means, by the repetition of motives, by piano postludes, and by tonal relations. The purpose behind the revision can be summed up in his concept of "the total vision of the work," to which all its elements are subordinate.[59] Of the original fifteen songs, Hindemith retained only one unaltered. Two were completely recomposed, and the remainder revised, most of them thoroughly.

The idea of returning to an earlier work with a view to revising it, particularly one from 1923, was generally anathema to Weill, except in the event of an actual production. Such productions were few and far between, however. Thus he revised *Aufstieg und Fall der Stadt Mahagonny* for the 1931 production in Berlin. And although he continued to entertain a revival of *Die Dreigroschenoper* during his American years, he insisted it would have to be "a completely new adaptation."[60] But there are numerous examples of his reusing earlier material, in a way comparable to Handel's self-borrowings.[61] He was more pragmatic than Hindemith, less concerned about matters of stylistic continuity and consistency within his oeuvre as a whole. In that sense, he really did not give a damn about composing for posterity. Hindemith's revising his own work may initially suggest discontinuity. But the consistency of his style, the similarity between his earlier and later works, was sufficient for him to consider the revision in the first place.[62] And the effort expended, including the self-justifying apology of the revision's foreword, speaks for itself.

When Weill died in 1950, a book came onto the market that was soon to capture the imagination of the thinking American public. It eventually sold over half a million copies in paperback, and a picture of its author, David Riesman, appeared on the cover of *Time* magazine as a result of its popularity. Called *The Lonely Crowd,* the book became famous for its character typologies, which were intended as ideal types to describe shifts in socioeconomic attitudes in the modern age.[63] The two principal types of modern character structure that Riesman constructs—again, with the broader aim of illuminating overall social and historical tendencies rather than individuals—are "inner-direction" and "other-direction." These are some of the ways in which he defines them in *The Lonely Crowd:*

> The source of direction for the individual is "inner" in the sense that it is implanted early in life by the elders and directed toward generalized but nonetheless inescapably destined goals. . . . The problem of personal choice . . . is solved by channeling choice through a rigid, highly individualized character. (15)

> Aims are ideologically interrelated, and the selection made by any one individual remains relatively unalterable throughout his life. . . . The inner-directed character . . . is very considerably bound by traditions: they limit his ends and inhibit his choice of means. . . . He cannot help becoming aware of competing traditions—hence of tradition as such. . . . The inner-directed person becomes capable of maintaining a delicate balance between the demands upon him of his life goal and the buffetings of his external environment. (16)
>
> The diary keeping that is so significant a symptom . . . may be viewed as a kind of inner time-and-motion study by which the individual records and judges his output day by day. It is evidence of the separation between the behaving and the scrutinizing self. (16)
>
> The inner-directed man becomes vulnerable to himself when he fails to achieve his internalized goals. Able to forget the invisible hand as long as he is successful, he seeks in his baffled failure to make it visible so that he can smite it. (196)
>
> He becomes a "moralizer-in-retreat." (195)

As for the other-directed type:

> What is common to all other-directeds is that their contemporaries are the source of direction for the individual—either those known to him or those with whom he is directly acquainted. The source is of course "internalized" in the sense that dependence on it for guidance in life is implanted early. The goals toward which the other-directed person strives shift with that guidance: it is only the process of striving itself and the process of paying close attention to the signals from others that remain unaltered throughout life. (22)
>
> I am inclined to think that the other-directed type does find itself most at home in America.
>
> The other-directed person wants to be loved rather than esteemed; he wants not to gull or impress, let alone oppress, others but, in the current phrase, to relate to them; he seeks less a snobbish status in the eyes of others than assurance of being emotionally in tune with them.[64]

It should be evident by now which type best describes which composer, in particular their quite different reactions to emigration. Weill's success in adapting to other musical cultures and generally feeling "at home in America" aligns with the "other-directed" type, whereas Hindemith, in accordance with Riesman's concept of "inner-direction," became something of a "moralizer-in-retreat" and increasingly "bound by tradition." In some ways, however, such typologies may seem no more and no less relevant than astrology charts or I-Ching readings. Not only can they be applied in a statically essentialist way, despite their having been intended to capture a historical process, but the positing of just two types can also be too limited, like any binary opposition.[65] These and other objections have already been voiced in the substantial secondary literature on *The Lonely Crowd.*[66]

To some extent, Riesman's categories function as historical variables rather than as fixed types that apply in all epochs and cultures. For example, Quentin Bell has appropriated them to describe artistic types as they change throughout history.[67] Thus Bell's analysis refers to "the social situation of the artist in the state of inner-direction," that is, to the nineteenth- and early-twentieth-century, principally European conception of the artist as autonomous, nonconformist creator.[68] Such an application seems appropriate here insofar as one is dealing less with Weill's individual character traits than with how he plotted his career. The model of "other-direction" may suggest unity and continuity where in previous accounts of his artistic evolution disruption and discontinuity obtained.

In inner-directed terms, the purported differences between early and late Hindemith may seem less marked than is often suggested. Adorno perhaps sensed that inner continuity when he remarked apropos the Suite "1922" and the fox-trot finale of the first *Kammermusik,* "'It can't go on like this' is, as it were, part of the composition."[69] Hindemith's gyroscopic sense of European tradition is pronounced, whether he is apparently opposing or affirming it.[70]

As for Weill, diagnosing his American works in terms of "doing away with his old creative self," to paraphrase Drew's remark quoted above, or describing his development as abnormal seems informed by expectations that closely resemble Riesman's inner-directed type. In other-directed terms, the transition from Weill's European to his American career seems utterly "normal."

However limiting typologies as such may initially seem, their possibility alone can be used to challenge preconceptions about composers, whether Taylor's, Adorno's or Drew's. An alternative model may invite us to consider differently how creative energies can be channeled, in spite or because of adversities. In that sense, the type holds a possible key to the individual, a framework for interpretation, or, as Elisabeth Young-Bruehl describes it, "a map for further inquiry."[71] Descriptions of émigré artists and intellectuals based on the inner-directed model seem to be the norm: Adorno's own writings, informed as they are by German musical expressionism, supply an especially drastic example.[72] This is understandable. In many ways, as the stereotype of the European artist, it is a model that has defined the very image of the exile experience.[73] The other-directed type, however, suggests another, quite different experience, one that ultimately subverts the very notion of "exile."[74]

In his book *Culture and Imperialism,* Edward Said offered a definition of exile that is as true for Hindemith as for Weill, but relevant for each in differing degrees. "Exile," he says, "is predicated on the existence of, love for, and a real bond with one's native place."[75] Said precedes this truism with what he calls a "hauntingly beautiful passage" by the twelfth-century monk Hugo of Saint Victor.

> It is a . . . source of great virtue for the practiced mind to learn, bit by bit, first to change about in visible and transitory things, so that afterwards it may be possible to leave them behind altogether. The person who finds his homeland sweet is still a tender beginner; he to whom every soil is as his native one is already strong; but he is perfect to whom the entire world is as a foreign place. The tender soul has fixed his love on one spot in the world; the strong person has extended his love to all places; the perfect man has extinguished his.[76]

Seymour Martin Lipset has argued that "other-directedness may permit, or even demand, inner autonomy."[77] That would appear to accord with Hugo's "strong person." Studies of musical émigrés thrive on the fact that nobody is perfect.

It is arguably a variant of the "inner-directed" type that brings together life and work while tracing an organic development of an entire oeuvre and its underlying personal style. Weill, by way of comparison with Hindemith, could be seen to be resisting the type by claiming not to give a damn about writing for posterity and by making a point of not "worrying about the material of music, the theory behind it, the opinion of other musicians." There is also a strong sense, evident quite early on, of his moving from one theatrical collaboration—one "practical purpose"—to the next without stopping to look back. Although earlier works might matter again as the possibility of revival presented itself, "[keeping them] alive by artificial means" held little interest for him. Otherwise, he would return to works not destined for revival as sources of useful material. He did not preserve them "intact," as it were, but neither did he let them go to waste. Self-borrowings from earlier works in fact abound, especially from works written during his years of European exile.

Those reconsidering biographical method with a view to capturing Weill's "way" (his "other-directed" way, specifically) could do worse, then, than begin by reassessing one of the central concepts that underpins traditional notions of "inner-directed" identity and that has proved something of a stumbling block in discussions of Weill's oeuvre: namely, style. In what way and to what degree is it still useful for Weill? In what way does it need to be qualified, and with what, if anything, does it need to be supplemented or even replaced?

STYLE: PROBLEMS OF DEFINITION

Consider the following statements on style. The first, already quoted above, comes from Ronald Taylor's biography of Weill, published in 1991. Weill was a composer, Taylor writes, who "seemed to change styles more often than countries." The implication, something made explicit elsewhere in the book, is that Weill not only adapted to changed circumstances to a degree that undermined his identity and development as a composer, but that he changed even when the circumstances didn't. As quoted earlier, Taylor had begun by asking "the real Weill" to "stand up," and concluded: "We do not mind how many Kurt Weills stand up." He seems to be implying that there is one Weill for each of the styles in evidence, even though he really recognizes the legitimacy of only one of them. "In Berlin," he asserts, "[Weill] had created his own idiom, taken out a patent personal musical language," adding that "here one approaches the heart of the matter."[78] Compare this with the contrasting view, recently voiced in connection with a recording of excerpts from the 1937 biblical pageant *The Eternal Road.* "It amazes me," the reviewer remarks, "how quickly and how often Weill's style changes throughout his career, to remain throughout recognizably himself."[79] The question begged here is, if not through his style, how does the composer remain "recognizably himself"? If a diversity of styles can both undermine identity and not undermine it, how can Taylor and the reviewer be talking about the same thing? What, in other words, is style in Weill, and how does it relate to other notions, such as the identity of the composer?

One of the first people to discuss this issue, some sixty years before Taylor, was Herbert Fleischer, who in 1932 published an essay entitled "Kurt Weill: Versuch einer einheitlichen Stilbetrachtung"—an attempt at a unified view of style. Fleischer had studied in Berlin with philosopher Max Dessoir, professor of psychology and of the theory of art, and written under his supervision a dissertation in which, in a mere one hundred pages, he provides a remarkable summary of recent trends in music aesthetics, with attention paid not just to schools of composition but to key individuals, such as Schoenberg and Stravinsky.[80] In his study Fleischer is concerned above all with the tendency displayed by both of these composers toward "certain sonic abstractions." Yet he identifies a key difference, namely Stravinsky's exclusion of human sentiment.

That was in 1928. Stravinsky continued to abide his question, and his next major publication was a monograph on the composer, which appeared in 1931.[81] Somewhat amending the earlier view and thereby humanizing his subject, he attempts in this new study to balance Stravinsky's architectural and constructivist tendencies with his role as a "tone poet."

After the Stravinsky monograph, Fleischer turned his attention to Weill. The composer evidently approved. When Fleischer submitted the article to *Anbruch,* the house journal of Weill's publisher, Universal Edition, it was forwarded to the composer, who returned it with the comment that he thought it "adequate to the purpose" *(zweckentsprechend);* he "welcomed" the publication, he said, because it "viewed his work from a somewhat larger perspective."[82] He also lent Fleischer materials for his research, though the materials were eventually lost and Fleischer never finished the book. Even so, after moving to Italy Fleischer did publish a more general book on contemporary music in which, in a short section on Weill, sandwiched between Křenek and Hindemith, he essentially recycled the 1932 style essay.[83]

Fleischer's style article, appearing just a year before Weill made the first of several changes of country, served as a double prolegomenon: to the unfinished book on Weill and to the part of the book that he did eventually finish. Equating style with "physiognomy," he identifies "traits" of the Busoni School, but argues that "Weill's physiognomy shines through" in those early German works nonetheless. As characteristically Weillian, he identifies a "gesticulating" quality: "gesture, mime . . . direct expression." Weill's art becomes "language, representation." According to Fleischer, "In its penetrating quality, its imposing thrust, it becomes the distinct opposite of the reserved spirituality of Busoni's music." Thus he begins by stating that Weill is one of the "few contemporary musicians who have developed a well-defined, vital style, recognized by us all."[84]

In the course of his essay Fleischer introduces no fewer than eight separate style concepts to characterize different facets of Weill's music. These are "revue style," "song style," "aggression style," "stage style," "didactic style," "oratorio-dramatic style," "lapidary style," and "representational and descriptive style." Their function is both diachronic and synchronic. On the one hand, he uses these concepts to trace a development from Weill's earliest stage works through 1932; on the other, he suggests the simultaneous presence of several of these styles in the then-latest work, the opera *Die Bürgschaft*. The terms are at once discrete and, as facets of Weill's development, complementary. Some are mutually exclusive, while others overlap. A closer look, however, reveals that the style concepts do not possess the same logical status: those that overlap describe different aspects of the same thing. The "revue style," used pejoratively to describe superficial Americanisms, refers in particular to works such as *Der neue Orpheus* and *Royal Palace,* both collaborations with the surrealist poet Iwan Goll. It is hard to tell whether Fleischer is referring more to the subject matter than to the musical style, but he is relieved that Weill does not continue to compete with Křenek and works such as *Jonny spielt auf* and glad that he moves instead to the opera buffa *Der Zar lässt sich photographieren,* whose gramophone tango, like the very end of *Royal Palace,* anticipates what Fleischer calls the "song style."

He sees the transition to the song style fully achieved in several of the collaborations with Bertolt Brecht, some of Weill's best-known works. These include *Mahagonny-Songspiel, Die Dreigroschenoper, Das Berliner Requiem,* and *Happy End.* In this style, Fleischer asserts, "Weill found himself, that which is very much his own: the ability to let music become language." This is not a matter of personal expression. The "essential characteristic of the song style," Fleischer observes, is that "it is the expression of a world." He identifies "the melody line's slight dynamic motoric nuances" as responsible for the "lapidary simplicity of the musical language," a language that reveals the "essential face," the *Urgesicht,* of Weill's music.[85] The rhetoric of physiognomy could scarcely get more essentialist than that!

The song style relies on a combination of two basic elements: the motor rhythms of the accompaniment, derived from contemporaneous dance idioms; and the lyrical melodic line. It's not just a hit tune, Fleischer asserts; it's a ballad: "People of the lower class, creatures of the street, sing their bit of life, bit of romanticism, lust for adventure, their love."[86] That is the world of which the song style is an expression: the modern world. Hence Weill's definition of the dance music on which he based his style as "the expression of the masses." It is at once free and strict—agogically supple lyricism held in check by the discipline of the dance.

It is hard to say whether, for Fleischer, the "aggression style" is synonymous with the "song style" or whether it is a contrasting, discrete style. In fact, he talks of two "aggression styles," one from the period of the song style that may or may not be synonymous with it, and one that postdates the next style in Weill's development, the "didactic style." Some of the songs are certainly more aggressive than others, and it is tempting to see Weill cultivating a distinct idiom akin to the marching songs of Hanns Eisler, beginning with his quotation of "Die Internationale" in the *Mahagonny-Songspiel* and acquiring particular prominence in *Happy End.*

There is another overlap here with the so-called didactic style of works such as *Der Jasager,* in which Weill cultivates a sparse, bare-bones contrapuntal style for the Lehrstück, the genre of didactic theater that flourished around 1930 and of which Weill was one of the chief practitioners along with composers such as Eisler and Hindemith. The referent in the term *didactic style* is as much the genre of the work and its content as it is the musical language employed. Perhaps the language itself is better described as "lapidary," as in Fleischer's concept of "lapidary style." Derived from the Latin word for stone, the adjective generally applies to something either literally engraved or figuratively done in the manner of an inscription, especially monumental stones. A lapidary style is therefore one characteristic of, or suitable for, inscriptions. That figurative meaning would certainly apply quite readily to the opening of *Der Jasager,* with its terse pronouncement of the theme of collective consent, and to substantial stretches of *Der Lindberghflug* and *Die Bürgschaft.*

If "lapidary style" and "didactic style" overlap in capturing both the form and content of *Der Jasager,* then the terms *stage style* and *oratorio-dramatic style* do not describe any one stylistic idiom so much as accommodate a diversity of idioms within a range of theatrical works. In fact, "stage style," when applied to works such as *Happy End* and *Mahagonny,* circumscribes an approach to composition predicated precisely on stylistic diversity. Such diversity, motivated by dramaturgical concerns, could also be said to be the essence of the "representational and descriptive style" that Fleischer applies to *Die Bürgschaft,* with its basic division into dramatic action and epic commentary. "Representation" refers to the action itself and "description" to the commentary and interpretation by a chorus, done in the manner of an oratorio. Such is the synthesis that Fleischer sees in that latest work: the gathering together of previous theatrical experiments in a multifaceted musical language, a plurality of stylistic idioms cultivated at the service of a dramatic concept—in short, a style of the stage.

So what does Fleischer mean by "style"? His approach reflects a fundamental tension between competing concepts—between, on the one hand, the systematic delineation of contrasting and complementary styles within an overriding commitment to musical theater and, on the other, the identification of a singular "physiognomy" in the context of the composer's evolution. One concept leads to the plurality reflected in Fleischer's seven style compounds, the other to the singular concept of a "stage style."

A similar tension exists in Weill's own accounts of his development. An often-cited instance of self-commentary relating to matters of style is a letter to his publisher from 14 October 1929 in which he spoke of the abandonment of the "song style" in the Mahagonny opera: "Almost everything added to the Baden-Baden version," he wrote, referring to the difference between the "Songspiel" and the opera, "is written in a perfectly strict, thoroughly responsible style," adding that "I presume that it will endure longer than most of what is being produced nowadays."[87] He was referring above all to the neo-baroque turn taken by a number of his compositions, but also to certain numbers in *Happy End*. He shared his publisher's perception of a "style change" *(Stilwandlung)*, a "great development" *(grosse Entwicklung)*, which "hasn't stood still *for one moment*" (Weill's emphasis) and was making "a new advance *[Vorstoss]*."[88]

Exactly where the neo-baroque fits into Fleischer's taxonomy is hard to say, except as a facet of the broad category of "representation and descriptive style." This raises a question about Weill's remark concerning the style's longevity: the music written in this style is not something that necessarily endures; rather, it is something that *represents* an enduring, timeless quality. Its counterpoint partakes of the putatively timeless, stylistically unassailable substance of music. When Weill referred to the "Songspiel" version of *Mahagonny* as a "style study," which he did on a number of occasions, he seemed to be opposing the notion of an unceasing development, still less positing an enduring physiognomy. The "song style" was something that had to be worked on, experimented with, as one element among many. Its abandonment was above all dramaturgically motivated.

Going beyond the period of Fleischer's purview, there are many further such instances of Weill discussing the style or "styles" of his work after he left Germany, and they do so in contradictory ways. It was not until he had, as he said, "worked his way" into the style of the biblical pageant *The Eternal Road*, begun in 1934 in German as *Der Weg der Verheissung*, that he could make good progress on the piece.[89] Just a year earlier, he had described his satirical operetta *Der Kuhhandel* as being written "in a very beautiful, new style," presumably not the same "responsible style" of *Mahagonny.*[90] The epithet *beautiful* attaching to the new style should not necessarily be taken as an automatic guarantee of aesthetic value or quality, as can be seen from a Busoni-inspired statement Weill made some years later, in 1940, with several changes of style behind him and more to come. Style and quality are invoked here as discrete matters: "Instead of worrying about the material of music, the theory behind it, the opinion of other musicians, my concern is to find the purest expression in music for what I want to say, with enough trust in my instinct, my taste and my talent to write always 'good' music, *regardless of the style I am writing in*" (my emphasis).[91] Even if the style changes, the quality need not.

Weill reiterates the idea of his changing style for each new work—or even the idea of the style of each work creating itself—in the mid-1940s. He develops his argument in two steps, first by defining "standard formulas" and then by describing his approach to them.

> Our theatre has developed a number of standard formulas for musical entertainment—revue, musical comedy, musical play, operetta, light opera and grand opera, each of which follows a time-tried recipe. At the same time there has always been a special fascination for the composer in trying out different mixtures of the same ingredients. The special brand of musical entertainment in which I have been interested from the start is a sort of "dramatic musical," a simple, strong story told in musical terms, interweaving the spoken word and the sung word so that the singing takes over naturally whenever the emotion of the spoken word reaches a point where music can "speak" with greater effect.

The singularity derives from blurring generic boundaries and mixing conventions. "This form of theatre has its special attraction for the composer," he continues, "because it allows him to use a great variety of musical idioms, to write music that is both serious and light, operatic and popular, emotional and sophisticated, orchestral and vocal. Each show of this type has to create its own style, its own texture, its own relationship between words and music, because music becomes a truly integral part of the play—it helps to deepen the emotions and clarify the structure." The result is a unique "work style" that arises from studied diversity.[92]

Two preliminary conclusions follow from these quoted remarks about style. The first is that shifts in the meaning and significance of the term are considerable, in both Weill's and Fleischer's uses. The second is that when people talk about style they may well be talking at cross purposes, even with themselves—more about different than the same things. Style in music functions in the manner of an "essentially contested concept," to use the notion put in circulation by W. B. Gallie. There is, to cite Gallie, who was writing about the concept of "freedom" in political science, "no one clearly definable general use" that could be "set up as the correct or standard usage." Style serves a variety of purposes, whether complementary or mutually exclusive. Even though disputes about its meaning ought to be considered genuine, they are unlikely to be resolved by argument, even though (as Gallie said about freedom) it is "perfectly respectable arguments and evidence" that sustain them.[93] The task is rather to recognize the plurality of meanings. Style, however defined, is coherence—or at least, in view of its labile nature, it is the *rhetoric* of coherence. As such, it is one of the indispensable keys but also one of the potential hindrances to our appreciation of music, including Weill's.

For this reason, there is an additional matter to pursue. For all its lability, the terminology is not entirely arbitrary; it is historically and culturally informed. Looked at in a broader context, the various connotations of "style" invoked so far reflect the broader historical evolution of the term. In his outstanding entry on style in the encyclopedia *Musik in Geschichte und Gegenwart,* Wilhelm Seidel plots several shifts.[94] The key shift with respect to the current discussion is that in the nineteenth century toward the notion of a "personal style." As Seidel demonstrates, in addition to this connection to individuals, style as a concept of classification has been called upon over the centuries to describe (1) functions (as in "church," "chamber," and "theater style"); (2) epochs (as in "baroque," "classical," "romantic"); and (3) nations (as in "German," "French," "Italian"). Historically, Seidel writes, beginning in the mid-sixteenth century, "the first systems compare styles of musical motion, movements, function and genre; the eighteenth century includes styles of nationality, expression and sentiment; the nineteenth century above all personal style." He also notes an increasing connection between "style theory and the idea of unity," which explains the fact "that the nineteenth century, including Adler, saw the organic constitution of works of art as the innermost condition of stylistically perfected creations."[95] Although style was originally a function of genre, its career followed a path from outer to inner, from social function to personal expression, and eventually to individual identity. All of these connotations play a role in the discussion of Weill's music.

Studies such as Richard Crocker's *History of Musical Style* (1966), Charles Rosen's *The Classical Style* (1971), and Leonard Meyer's *Style and Music* (1989) testify to the centrality of the concept of style in musical discourse. But where do they fit into Seidel's broader framework? And what is their relevance to critics and biographers such as Ronald Taylor who apply the category of style to Weill's oeuvre, albeit with negative conclusions? Crocker, Rosen, and Meyer are all concerned with epoch style, or "style periods," as they used to be known. In this they build on the legacy of Guido Adler and the ideas contained in his book *Der Stil in der Musik* (1911) and his *Handbuch der Musikgeschichte* (1924), both of which had a profound influence on the historiography of succeeding generations. Adler's theory was shot through with biological metaphors: a style was something that developed in "an organic process."[96] More specifically, "Each main style, appearing in numerous offshoots and other branchings-off, each has its growth, its full bloom, and its decline, and each of these phases has its symptoms, its criteria."[97]

Thus Crocker's history of music presents itself as a study that "stresses the continuity of basic musical principles . . . seeking the reasons for stylistic change within the history of style itself." It is an account that, as the preface states, "tries to show how music, growing out of its past, has shaped its own development"—in other words, it is a narrative of style's autonomous evolution.[98]

Rosen's "classical style" takes a different course, between a generally valid notion of style and the individuality of the exceptional work. The latter, he says, "seems to deny even the possibility of the history of art," at least history seen as a history of style, even of personal style. "Even with the work of one artist, it is not his usual procedure that characterizes his personal 'style,' but his greatest and most individual success." Rosen's compromise solution is the idea of the style of a group, a style that "avoids this impossible fragmentation without falling into the difficulties of the 'anonymous' period style."[99] Rosen's narrative is also organicist, a matter of life and death, with Mahler's ironic appropriation of the classical style occurring within "a shadowy life-in-death."[100]

Meyer's style concept is different again. Although he divides his book into period styles, along traditional historiographic lines (classical to romantic etc.), his approach is more systematic than historical, drawing as it does on linguistic theory, and it is certainly less organicist. His notion of stylistic analysis pursues the goal of establishing a unifying principle conceived in terms of a "hierarchy of constraints."[101] It tends to be based, therefore, more in a particular repertory than in a personal style.

Rosen and Meyer reflect an increasing shift away from epochs and individuals to contextually situated works, a shift that typifies the structuralist paradigms of the postwar period. They have little room for Fleischer's subject-oriented physiognomies. But as Ernst Gombrich stated in a somewhat resigned way in his brilliant, and brilliantly entertaining, entry on style in the *International Encyclopedia of the Social Sciences* (1968), in which he dismisses "stylistic physiognomics" as fallacious: "The intuitive grasp of underlying *Gestalten* that makes the connoisseur is still far ahead of the morphological analysis of styles in terms of enumerable features."[102] In other words, any underlying principle of stylistic unity is a critical rather than a scientific matter. The unity resides in the eye or ear of the beholder and in his or her critical competence and authority rather than in any features that can be readily generalizable. Meyer would most certainly agree, referring to his conclusions as "hypotheses," which "do not pretend to be definitive."[103] Seen another way, they are like Kant's "aesthetic idea," an idea that cannot become a scientific insight or cognition "because it is an *intuition* (of the imagination) for which an adequate concept can never be found."[104] More is at stake, in short, than musical style. Style is coherence, however defined. And coherence is hard enough to define, still more to prove. If the concept itself is contested, then so should the criteria be whereby coherence—or lack thereof—is attested, whether it is the organic evolution of a genre, a historical epoch, an artist's life, or even a single work.

Weill, Taylor said, was a composer who "seemed to change styles more often than countries." This is no doubt true if by "style" he meant idiom in the seventeenth- and eighteenth-century sense, with the kind of topical changes we associate with the operatic music of Handel and Mozart, whether that idiom is a "song style" or something more "lapidary" or even "neo-baroque." Style, in that sense, refers to forms of musical rhetoric analogous to the eighteenth-century kind, the means deemed suitable to the artistic end. If "the real Weill" is to "stand up" as a composer of stylistic coherence and, unlike Taylor, we do mind how many Kurt Weills stand up, then we need to adjust our notions of identity with regard both to the artist and to his individual works. One place to do this would be in the aesthetics of "stage style." Another would be in the area of orchestration or "sound image," as Weill called it. Yet another is in the habitually reappearing figures and patterns that occur across his oeuvre. These things are not so much to do with what we usually call style, however, but rather with what one might call "signature"; they are also what makes Weill Weill. After all, a defining feature of the "stage style" that Weill cultivated is irony, a category predicated less on stylistic unity than on incongruity. Cultivating a musical style in the idiomatic sense did not amount to the adoption of Drew's "secondary persona," a mask or façade presented to satisfy the demands of the situation or the environment and not representing the inner personality of the individual—in short, a public personality as opposed to the "anima." Style in Weill, if it is to be used as a positive term of coherence, is rather the cultivation of opportunities, within a theatrical context, among other things for a richness of topical allusion—a well-nigh inexhaustible richness, as study of his scores continues to reveal.[105]

STYLE AND *GESTUS*

The notion of "stage style" overlaps but is not entirely synonymous with *Gestus,* a concept initially employed by Weill in 1929 and later adopted and developed by Brecht beyond that initial usage. The concept itself was not new, however, having been used in the eighteenth century, as Marc Silberman has shown, "to describe the rhetoric of passions as a language of gestures."[106] Moreover, in his *Hamburgische Dramaturgie,* Lessing discussed how *Gestūs* (used here in the Latin plural) serve as a means for the actor "to return the symbolic aspect of morals to immediate [i.e., intuitive] apprehension," connecting the general with the specific.[107] Such gestures contained in a work for the stage turn a story into a parable—a dimension of Lessing's concept preserved in Brecht's later theories, which seek to prevent the equation of gesture merely with personal expression.

In the voluminous Brecht-Weill literature, *Gestus* is nothing if not a contested concept.[108] The first documented source is Weill's essay "Über den gestischen Charakter der Musik" (1928–29). Following the lead of his teacher Busoni, Weill posed in that essay two fundamental questions: "What occasions are there for music on stage?" And "How is music in the theater constituted . . . are there certain characteristics that brand music as theater music?" These characteristics, he claims, can be summarized as "the gestic character of music." That doesn't take us very far, of course, so Weill provides examples. Generally speaking, he says, he is referring to music's ability to "establish the basic tone, the basic gesture of an event or process" and to do so in such a way "that a false interpretation can at least be avoided." Mozart, he claims, "never relinquishes the gestic character." He specifically cites Tamino's aria "Dies Bildnis ist bezaubernd schön" from *Die Zauberflöte*. Thus he writes: "The music determines by itself the attitude of a man who is looking at a picture. He can hold the picture in his right or left hand, pointing up or down, he can be illuminated by a spotlight or standing in the dark—his basic gesture is correct because it is correctly dictated by the music" (85).[109] What, Weill inquires further, are the gestic means? One is the "rhythmic fixation of the text" in terms of accents, syllable length, etc. (86). But he also includes, using his "Alabama Song" as an example, a "basic gesture" that is "rhythmically established in the most primitive form" as an accompaniment, composed here of anapests. But the potential for this approach depends, he stresses, on the dramatic content of the text, which may or may not allow such a relationship between melody and accompaniment. "The problem touched on here," he concludes, "is no less a problem of modern drama" (88). In other words, *Gestus* has to do with the congruence—or rather, with the *possibility* of congruence—of form and content. And that is a problem he would seek to resolve, throughout his career, both with and without Brecht, and with all manner of musical styles.

Style in Weill is the theatrical means. *Gestus* is the dramatic end or result, itself a function of reception and hence susceptible to interpretation. In his theory of epic theater, in which *Gestus* forms a central tenet, Brecht would define that end as sociological rather than psychological. Thus, for example, the opera *Aufstieg und Fall der Stadt Mahagonny* is the story of a city, not of a particular hero or antihero.

Style in Weill's music should be considered a poietic rather than a biographical category—the clothes, not the man, to refer back to Daniel Albright's observation quoted at the beginning of this chapter: something inseparable from dramaturgical function. So too is instrumentation. Yet instrumentation not only functions to cast intentional stylistic banality, even corniness, in an unusual light; it also serves as a complementary category to personal style: as signature. As Weill put it in 1932, formulating one of his basic maxims: "the sonic image . . . is always especially important with me."[110] Like "good" voice-leading, it was another essential facet of his craftsmanship. Weill's "own way" had much to do with his personal sonic images. His emphasis on this parameter of music, as the transfiguration of the commonplace and as personal signature, is critically bound up with the importance of scores in the transmission of his works. He may, as Adorno observed, have "shifted the composition process into rehearsal."[111] That came with the territory of the collaborative venture that is musical theater. Yet the sonic image remained fully under his personal control for posterity to savor. Each work has a more or less recognizable identity as a text, even if the performance materials sometimes seem like nothing more than multiple sets of scripts for diverse, even unique occasions.[112]

Where does all this leave the biographer? The tools of the trade have to be reconceived for Weill. And it is surely no coincidence that the rise in his critical stock began when writers such as Hildesheimer and critics such as Scheuer were questioning traditional narratives of the life and works of artists. Describing the life of a man of the musical theater such as Weill will entail, in terms of biographical method, steering a judicious course between a biography of the man, who remained elusive even to Lenya,[113] and a biography of the works, which tend to take on a life of their own. Traditional notions of autonomy will in either case be of little help.

Weill's work as a composer invites us to understand his life forward, not just backward, as Kierkegaard's much-quoted and -paraphrased principles seem to demand: "It is quite true what philosophy says: that life must be understood backwards," Kierkegaard wrote in 1843. "But then," he added, "one forgets the other principle: that it must be lived forwards."[114] Put in their anti-Hegelian context, Kierkegaard's words can be taken as a critique of teleological historical thinking and hence as a corrective to the first principle, that of understanding life backward. In their theological context, however, the same words refer to the Christian ideal that embraces the totality of an individual's existence as the artifact on the basis of which he or she is judged (in this case, by God) for his or her eternal validity. Referring in the first instance to philosophers and theologians, Kierkegaard insisted we should focus on the whole life, not just on one part of it, such as the art.[115] Biography may be implicated in both of these endeavors: reading lives backward and passing judgment on their totality, as if for eternal validity. Artistic biography, however, needs to acknowledge where such a holistic view is appropriate and where it is not. It needs to decide, on the one hand, where backward-reading (because ultimately teleological) narrative is called for and, on the other, where the connections between the life, however construed, and the work can convincingly be established. Just as Weill, the man and the artist, needs to be understood in all his "other-directedness," and not least because of the fact of emigration, so the realization of the musical-theater works and their meaning in performance (Weill's sonic control notwithstanding) invite an approach in which questions of material progress and personal style (the questions, that is, of conventional teleology) yield to those of music's dramaturgical and sociological significance. These, then, are the matters with which the remainder of this study is principally concerned. After focusing in the next chapter on Weill's self-proclaimed identity as a Busoni pupil, I explore the various stages of Weill's career as a composer for the musical theater, a career defined in terms of the conventions that he both adopted and, through committed experimentation with hybrid genres, reformed.

2

The Busoni Connection

Brecht, Busoni, Mozart, and Wagner. To judge from how often they appear in his published writings and interviews, these were the names that were uppermost in Kurt Weill's artistic consciousness. (Other, not quite so prominent figures included Bach, Beethoven, Georg Kaiser, Puccini, Schoenberg, Strauss, Stravinsky, and Verdi.) The frequency is hardly surprising, given the significance that Weill attached to these four composers, above all to Busoni, whose master class he attended in Berlin from 1921 through 1924. The connection to his teacher is something Weill was not only pleased but evidently quite proud to acknowledge in numerous public statements. Even when he extolled Mozart and disparaged Wagner—which he did throughout his career—he was also testifying to Busoni's profound influence on his own thought.

The Brecht connection was of a somewhat different order, at once professionally beneficial and productive but also personally fraught. Here, too, Busoni's teachings made themselves felt, even if Brecht preferred not to see it that way. Writing in his journal in 1941, Brecht described his collaborator as a "Busoni-pupil," no doubt intending to invoke a gulf between himself and Weill's teacher. "When I met Weill," he recalled, "he was a Busoni- and Schreker-pupil, a creator of atonal, psychological operas, and I whistled to him measure by measure and, above all, performed for him."[1] The description "Schreker-pupil" is a telling slip. Like Busoni, Schreker taught in Berlin. But Weill did not study with him, as he did with Busoni, despite his early admiration for Schreker. In 1919, as he told his brother, Schreker was "supposed to be the most significant *Musikdramatiker* of our times," his music belonging together with that of Reger and Schoenberg as "the most modern."[2] Weill would soon change his mind. By 1926 he saw Schreker as a composer continuing in the Wagnerian mold, something that he himself claimed to have broken away from, thanks in part to Busoni's example. Schreker's version of Wagner's "total work of art" *(Gesamtkunstwerk),* he contended, still "has as its theme the problematic nature of the erotically overcharged man from the prewar period."[3] Though hardly atonal, Schreker's operas can indeed be described as "psychological." Weill's early operas, on the other hand, may contain some elements of atonality, but "psychological" is hardly an apt description; "anti-psychological" would be a better choice.

By linking Weill to a teacher with whom he never studied and to an aesthetic he actively rejected, Brecht managed to convey his own prejudice and at the same time imply that it was he who was largely responsible for transforming Weill. He was implying far too much. Whether or not he whistled them to Weill, the influence of Brecht's settings of his own texts on Weill's later versions is negligible, as the composer made clear in his 1929 essay "On the Gestic Character of Music." Brecht, he said, had "transcribed the speech rhythm" and captured a "thoroughly personal" and "inimitable way of singing." But although Weill's settings follow the same basic *Gestus* of the speech rhythm, the text (Weill cites "Alabama Song" as his example) is "really composed" with the "much freer means of the musician."[4] Nor do Weill's versions mark a radical departure from his earlier practice, in the way Brecht suggests. Granted, they signal another step in the simplification of Weill's musical language and means, but this too is something for which Weill preferred to give Busoni credit, albeit perhaps more credit than the teacher ultimately deserved. As far as the artistically fruitful Brecht-Weill partnership is concerned, the obverse of Brecht's account applies: in a number of critical areas the Busoni pupil transformed Brecht.[5]

Busoni's influence was as profound as it was enduring. More than anything, it served as a stable point of reference throughout the various stages of Weill's career, from the fulsome panegyric published on the first anniversary of Busoni's death in 1925 to the anecdotes of indebtedness and affection that appear in various essays and interviews in the 1940s. In 1941, for example, Busoni was not only his "old friend and teacher"; he was also his authority on language acquisition: "My old friend and teacher Ferruccio Busoni used to say: you don't feel at home in a language unless you dream and count in this language." The occasion for the remark was the broadcast "I'm an American!," an NBC radio program aired "in cooperation with the United States Department of Justice" to celebrate Weill's American citizenship (though some two years before he actually received his naturalization papers).[6] Apart from testifying to Weill's artistic pedigree, Busoni is invoked here as a model, presumably because of the way he himself had adapted to living in a foreign culture. "Home of choice" *(Wahlheimat)* was how Weill once described Busoni's Berlin; by analogy, New York had now become his.[7]

One of the more fascinating, even tantalizing pieces of testimony is the 1936 interview in which Weill made the following terse statement: "And I would say that what Liszt did for Wagner, Busoni did for me."[8] What elicited the statement was a suggestion made by interviewer Ralph Winnett of the *Brooklyn Daily Eagle* that Busoni might be compared to Liszt. Whereas Liszt could be seen as someone who was primarily "a springboard for others," composers such as Wagner, Winnett proposed, echoing a suggestion of the critic Olin Downes, "took comparatively undeveloped Lisztian material and transformed it into something valuable. . . . Without this undeveloped material," he went on, "Wagner might have done little." That Weill should agree with this as "all very true" is intriguing on more than one level. Busoni, musical polymath, certainly had an important predecessor in composer-pianist Liszt. And Weill was always happy to acknowledge Busoni as a springboard for his own work. But putting himself in Wagner's role, a composer whose music he specifically and consciously negated after a period of youthful infatuation with it, adds a nice nuance to the negation. As he did with Busoni, he continued to relate in various ways to several of his European forebears.

Busoni the man, then, was as much a model as Busoni the musician. In 1925 Weill eulogized him as nothing less than the "last renaissance man," comparing him to Leonardo. "Such figures are immortal," Weill wrote,

> not only because of their oeuvre but also because of the aura of their personality, because of the gradual influence of their humanity. . . . Just as the man's oeuvre evolved from the significant musical production of the past into a new art with a promise for the future, so every utterance of his life was apt to forge a link between the great personalities of earlier times and the ideal of humanity that we are endeavoring to attain. He combined for the first time all the characteristics of the European intellectual of the future; all those not infected by general Western pessimism must recognize the mission of a man who in the heyday of imperialism could place himself above nations, who despite the nationalism of his environment established a life of beauty, who knew no weapon other than ridicule, no privilege other than personal achievement, who could despise bourgeois morality because he was good, and who could be free in an age of slavery because he saw no one as being above himself. Let one thing be said which may be characteristic enough: it is impossible for anyone who knew him to imagine a situation in which Busoni would have lied. The unconditional truth, which formed the supreme law of his art, also governed his life.[9]

Weill made the same point a few months later, perhaps even more fulsomely, in a piece titled "Busoni and New Music":

> Among the great creative artists there are those whose name lives on only in their works, whose own life and influence completely disappear behind their creations; and others who, through the aura of their personality, exert such an influence in their own lifetime that the memory of the purity of their being remains as alive as

their artistic legacy. The spheres of Ferruccio Busoni's life manifested themselves in the light of an intellect that strove to embrace all possible fields, a cast of mind whose very integrity already placed him above his contemporaries. Not only did the enchanting harmony of this artist cause people within his immediate orbit to feel happier, but those at a distance also sensed the invisible influence of a figure whose serene goodness would disperse any malice or badness. Few were conscious of it, but everyone felt it: that Busoni had become the invisible leader in European musical life; everyone intuited that here was someone in the face of whose righteousness only a true and great art could exist. The powerful influence exerted by such a life is not terminated by death; it so strongly impinges upon the events of its age that its traces remain well into succeeding generations. And if Busoni had not left us his compositions and writings, his Bach edition and the memory of his unforgettable piano playing, then at least the influence of his personality would be handed down for ages to come.[10]

Not that he downplayed Busoni's artistic achievements. He saw him as a trailblazer, almost a prophet. Yet in doing so he concentrated less on the compositions than on the ideas and teachings: "All the stylistic innovations of recent times were either prompted or proclaimed by him. He was the first to see that Wagner had so perfectly realized his own intentions that there was nothing more to add. He was the first to bring the French Impressionists to Germany, the first to champion Schoenberg, the first to coin the word 'new classicality' *[junge Klassizität]* to which the creative musicians of all countries now subscribe."[11]

Busoni is depicted as a kind of cultural luminary, even an oracle, someone recognized as embodying the *Zeitgeist* and whose calling it is to impart that spirit to his contemporaries. Weill was hardly alone in his views. In 1923, for example, the critic Paul Bekker dedicated to Busoni the foreword written to accompany a new edition of Bekker's 1919 book *Neue Musik,* honoring him as "the finding searcher and searching finder . . . the epitome of the good, true artist of our time."[12] Hugo Leichtentritt, émigré musicologist and composer and Busoni's first biographer, was no less adulatory in the description he gave of Busoni's achievements in his 1939 book *Music, History, and Ideas:*

In Berlin, Ferruccio Busoni was for twenty years the advocate of all ideas that aimed seriously at creating something vitally new. As an incomparable master of the piano, as a composer, conductor, teacher, essayist, and philosopher of art, Busoni was an outstanding personality of the highest artistic and intellectual type. In Busoni all the various tendencies of the modern movement met; all were familiar to him, and all were searchingly investigated and approved or rejected. Debussy and Ravel, Mahler and Strauss, Delius and Sibelius, Stravinsky and Schönberg, Casella, Malipiero, Pizzetti, Bartok—they were all known to him minutely. Almost every night there was a gathering of young artists from many countries at his hospitable residence, Victoria [*recte:* Viktoria] Luise Platz 11 in Berlin. There were

> heated controversies on the artistic problems of the day in which everyone spoke freely and which were given great distinction by Busoni's own *esprit* and wit, superior understanding, mature judgment, and illuminating criticism. It is probable that in our confused, nationalistic, impoverished age such social intercourse no longer exists at all. Indeed, those gatherings were a sort of modern parallel to the Socratic symposiums of which Plato gives us so vivid a picture.[13]

When he celebrated Busoni's sixtieth birthday in 1926, two years after his teacher's death, Weill mourned the loss of a multifaceted artist: "'the greatest pianist of all time,' the creative musician of genius, the great theoretician and author, the inspiring educator, the wonderful human being." In his rousing conclusion he went even further, apostrophizing the composer of *Doktor Faust* as "the Faustian man of the 20th century." "His life was a struggle," Weill wrote. "And his victory is the work that endures, the love of the thousands he enchanted."[14]

Never would Weill write more expansively or gushingly about his teacher. How could he? But he would continue to acknowledge a huge debt, publicly and privately, as his 1941 naturalization broadcast indicates. He would continue to feel that Busoni was responsible for fundamental changes in his own attitudes. In a letter to his parents, dated 1 January 1926, he traced the source of his "flight from the bourgeois world *[Bürgerlichkeit]*" back to Busoni.[15] And toward the end of his life, in 1948, he was still crediting his teacher with having "hammered" into him "one basic truth" central to his own development:

> My teacher Busoni, at the end of his life, hammered into me one basic truth which he had arrived at after 50 years of pure aestheticism: the fear of triviality is the greatest handicap for the modern artist, it is the main reason why "modern music" got more and more removed from reality, from life, from the real emotions of people in our time. I lost this fear through years of working in the theatre, and in doing so, my whole aspect *[sic]* towards musical composition changed. Instead of worrying about the material of music, the theory behind it, the opinion of other musicians, my concern is to find the purest expression in music for what I want to say, with enough trust in my instinct, my taste and my talent to write always "good" music, regardless of the style I am writing in.[16]

He even recognized Busoni's importance in the realm of film music: "He had a vision of the changing social order. He foresaw the enormous musical possibilities of the film as the vehicle of a new form of tone-drama."[17] And it was Busoni, he joked privately to Lenya in 1947, who taught him the "Anglosaxon rule of law: everyone is innocent until proven guilty."[18]

The admiration between Weill and Busoni was mutual. In a letter dated 7 October 1923 to Philipp Jarnach, for example, Busoni included an enthusiastic, quite poetic appraisal of his pupil.

> He has any amount of "ideas" . . . but they are concealed or inferred, so that only "the likes of us" can discover and admire them. He—Weill—does not seem to be conscious of when he has arrived at the right place; instead, he passes over it as if over sand and rocks between which beautiful, individual flowers grow, which he neither tramples on nor plucks, and over which he does not linger. His wealth is great, and his selectivity at present inactive. One envies him and would like to help.—But he will come to the right thing of his own accord!—The eternal question: is he still developing, or has he already reached his peak?

The teacher then turned the question on himself, couching his answer in terms redolent of his own idol Goethe, but also with an element of self-doubt: "The greatest are 'in the making' until their death and leave behind unfulfilled expectations. The *'arrivés'* are to be pitied, and one asks oneself despairingly if one numbers amongst them."[19]

What is to be made of Weill's own account of the connection? With its unrestrained declarations of indebtedness it suggests the very opposite of Harold Bloom's "anxiety of influence." The model is in danger of being acknowledged too much, not too little. Rather than downplaying Busoni's influence, Weill tends to play it up. The rationale invites analysis in terms of a rhetoric of exaggeration, even hyperbole. Nor is it hard to find reasons for the rhetoric. Busoni inspired such unqualified devotion from most of his other pupils, too, as it evidently did from the two biographers who knew him personally, Leichtentritt and Edward Dent. But in Weill's case it is also tempting to see Busoni as supplying continuity in the face of unsettling change. It can seem like overcompensation when Weill invokes him: Busoni represents the artistic roots from which the pupil did not want to be seen to be straying too far. The teacher is the European imprimatur, the guarantor of artistic credentials. He is also the authority called upon to sanction change. It is Busoni, as Weill claims, who set him on his path toward simpler means, for example. The teacher was a catalyst—*the* catalyst. None of this should serve to diminish the connection, only to complicate it, make it richer.

Comparing Weill with fellow students such as Wladimir Vogel and Philipp Jarnach, or with would-be student Stefan Wolpe, one can see that Busoni was an important catalyst for them as well.[20] Yet he hardly created an identifiable school of composition, even had he wanted to.[21] Unlike Schoenberg with his twelve-tone method, a method subsequently adopted by his pupils Berg, Webern, and even Eisler in their compositions, Busoni did not develop, still less propagate, a method of composing. Whereas Schoenberg's Second Viennese School owes a large part of its coherence as a school to dodecaphony and its philosophical underpinnings, there is no correlate for a Busoni school. The master's influence was less technical or stylistic than it was aesthetic and intellectual, based on ideas and teachings. And these changed over time. Nonetheless, as discussed below, Weill's early works do reveal the direct impact of his teacher's music, especially

FIGURE 1. Ferruccio Busoni (center) with pupils from his Berlin master class, c. 1923; left to right: Kurt Weill, Walther Geiser, Luc Balmer, Wladimir Vogel. Courtesy of the Staatsbibliothek zu Berlin—Preussischer Kulturbesitz, Musikabteilung mit Mendelssohn-Archiv (Busoni Nachlass P I, 235).

the opera *Arlecchino,* whose influence extends to matters of musical language and texture, not just operatic philosophy.[22]

Above all, however, Busoni's tutelage allowed his students to develop in all manner of directions, and they did. Weill made this point in the 1925 anniversary essay. Reminiscing about his attendance at the Berlin master class, he even rejected the notion of having been "a pupil."

> At this stage there were no longer any "pupils." He called us "disciples," he gave no lessons, but he let us breathe his being, which, though manifesting itself in all realms, always culminated in music. The hours spent in these daily meetings are too recent for me to be able to talk about them. It was an exchange of ideas in the highest sense, without any pressure to voice opinions, without any self-satisfaction, without any trace of envy or malice; and the recognition of any creativity that betrayed talent and ability was unqualified and enthusiastic.[23]

Another Busoni pupil, Egon Petri, nicely captured the nature, if not extent, of Busoni's pedagogy in a piece called "How Ferruccio Busoni Taught": "To say that

Busoni was a teacher is both an understatement and an overstatement, depending upon one's point of view. In the sense of guiding a pupil's technical and artistic problems in a steadily progressive manner, he was not a teacher at all. But in the higher sense of imparting to a pupil a consummate understanding of art, and the need for cultural and spiritual completion, he was the most inspiring teacher of our time." Petri's words serve as an epigraph at the beginning of Tamara Levitz's ground-breaking book on Busoni's master class, a study that allows us to gain a fairly good idea of what actually occurred in those "daily meetings."[24] Busoni's classes comprised far more than the kind of technical exercises and analysis taught, for example, by Schoenberg and Hindemith, to mention just two other prominent teachers working in Berlin during the Weimar Republic. By the time Weill came to study with Busoni, the core of his pedagogy was an entire aesthetic or philosophy of art which the master disclosed to his disciples in a multifaceted program of instruction, or what Germans more adequately describe as *Bildung.*

Adopting an almost priestlike stance, Busoni strove to form the whole person and character of his pupils. Technical facility was but one—by no means the central—focus. As Weill put it in a letter dated 13 February 1922, "Indeed, your influence went much deeper than mere compositional matters. For me it culminated in the realization that we can create a true work of art only if we reduce the complexity of our human natures to their simplest and most concise form."[25] In fact, Weill took instruction in counterpoint not from Busoni, but from another of his students, Philipp Jarnach.[26]

NEW CLASSICALITY

The philosophy of art espoused by Busoni in his master class was *Junge Klassizität* or "New Classicality," as Weill mentioned in his obituary—an aesthetic adopted by "creative musicians of all countries." It is a concept at once elusive and potentially far-reaching in its implications, as Busoni's classes themselves were. After all, a composer as different from Weill as, say, Jarnach would claim to be continuing the legacy. The most succinct, if somewhat curtailed formulation can be found in Busoni's famous letter to the music critic Paul Bekker, itself a response to a polemic Bekker had published against the composer Hans Pfitzner.[27] Nor is it hard to see these ideas echoed in Weill's writings, especially the early ones.

By New Classicality Busoni meant, according to the letter to Bekker, "the mastery, the sifting and the turning to account of all the gains of previous experiments and their inclusion in strong and beautiful forms." This art, he said, "will be old and new at the same time." Along with this synthesizing notion, Busoni espoused what he called "the idea of the Oneness in music": "There is no music which is Church music in itself, but only absolute music to which sacred words are put or which is performed in church. . . . Join words to a movement from a string quartet and an operatic scena grows out of it." To this definition he added "the definite departure from what is thematic and the return to melody again as the ruler of all voices and emotions (not in the sense of a pleasing motive) and as the bearer of the idea and the begetter of harmony, in short, the most highly developed (not the most complicated) polyphony." Finally, he called for a "casting off of what is 'sensuous' and the renunciation of subjectivity (the road to objectivity, which means the author standing back from his work, a purifying road, a hard way, a trial by fire and water) and the reconquest of serenity *(serenitas)*." He rejected not only "profundity" but also "personal feeling and metaphysics."

In responding to Bekker's response to Pfitzner, who in turn was reacting to Busoni, Busoni was not only justifying his own aesthetic; in formulating it under the banner of a New Classicality he was also reflecting the shift in his ideas that had occurred since the first edition of his *Entwurf einer neuen Ästhetik der Tonkunst* (1907). True, he was setting forth the tenets of a philosophy of music put into practice in the master class; but he was also signaling something of a retreat from certain "progressive" trends of the postwar era that his earlier philosophy could be seen to embody. In wishing to clear up "misunderstandings between [Pfitzner] and what he opposes," Busoni was probably edging closer toward Pfitzner than Bekker wanted him to.

Busoni's program of New Classicality went far beyond the oft-quoted definition of the letter to Bekker, however, as Levitz has shown: "In contrast to the popular image, Busoni's New Classicality was a multi-faceted theory which included not only lessons in objectivity, Bach's counterpoint and Mozart's orchestration, but also explorations of the supernatural, an aesthetic of opera, historical studies, musical parody, the dramaturgy of Italian puppet theater and writing about music."[28] Most pertinently for Weill, it emerges from Levitz's comprehensive account of the master class that "every aspect of compositional teaching . . . led towards the ultimate goal of composing opera."[29] Here it could be argued that Weill was even more effective in realizing his teacher's precepts than the teacher himself. To the extent that his magnum opus *Doktor Faust* remained unfinished, Busoni did not fully realize the precepts of his late teachings. This magnificent fragment represents, in the words of Levitz, "an unrealizable ideal of perfection, a philosophical project, a pedagogical tool, a vision, the expression of his entire life and person."[30] The description highlights both the strengths and weaknesses of the teachings.

At best, *Junge Klassizität* was the source of boundless inspiration to those who came under the master's spell. At worst, it may appear like a veil, woven from an eclectic intellectual fabric—deriving especially from Goethe and a number of nineteenth-century, mostly German idealist sources—with which to cloak any number of failed aspirations and pretensions. And it is to his credit that, of all Busoni's pupils, Weill not only profited enormously from the teachings of the New Classicality, but he also—no doubt thanks to his unqualified respect—remained largely silent about the more unpalatable and pretentious facets from which his career can be seen as a successful liberation. Busoni's synthesis was left for his students to achieve.

URFORM

Immediately suggestive of Busoni's influence because of its German-idealist flavor is the concept of *Urform* that Weill employs in the latter years of the Weimar Republic as a key concept in his thinking about music. Although the conceptual ground it covers is adumbrated in earlier writings, *Urform* first appears in connection with the composer's thoughts on *Die Dreigroschenoper.* "What we were aiming to create," Weill declared, "was the *Urform* of opera."[31] In 1929 it served as the unifying concept underpinning the diversity of his works for the musical theater: "I have been working for years consistently and without concession, as the only creative musician and against the opposition of the snobs and aesthetes," he wrote in a gesture of defiant self-justification to Hans Heinsheimer, his principal correspondent at the music publishing house Universal Edition, "on the creation of *Urformen* of a new, popular *[volkstümlich]* musical theater."[32] In 1930 he uses the term in connection with his cinematic aspirations, predicting the emergence of "sound movies whose overall design is so extensively determined from the musical side that one could see them as prototypes *[Urformen]* of a future film opera."[33] The concept evokes *Urmusik,* a term that Busoni used just once in his *Entwurf einer neuen Ästhetik der Tonkunst* but that serves to encapsulate his thinking about music. Yet although both concepts refer to an ideal, as signaled by the *Ur-* prefix, the ideals are hardly identical, despite much common ground.

Busoni's *Urmusik* refers to some kind of "original music," a primordial state from which all subsequent music derives. At the same time, the "original essence" *(Urwesen)* constitutes an evolutionary goal. In his conclusion to the first edition of the *Entwurf* (1907) the author wonders "how music may be restored to its primitive, natural essence." His declared aim is to "free it from architectonic, acoustic and esthetic dogmas."[34] The musical art-work, he claims, "exists, before its tones resound and after they die away, *complete and intact.* It exists both within and outside of time, and through its nature we can obtain a definite conception of the otherwise intangible notion of the Ideality of Time."[35]

Although it is tempting to trace *Urmusik* as far back as Plato, to the idea of a universal harmony implicit in the proportional relations of the harmonic series, it differs markedly from such a music-theoretical conception. One key difference is the unqualified freedom and immateriality of Busoni's conception, symbolized by his recurring metaphor of a "floating child"; another is its connection to a work-concept, however cryptically defined. Nor does Busoni subscribe to the kind of ethos typical of Neoplatonic thought. His *Urmusik* is fundamentally "absolute" in character, save perhaps where he discusses theatrical music in the second edition of his *Entwurf*: "The public does not know and does not wish to know that in order to receive a work of art, half the work must be done by the receiver himself."[36]

For Busoni, the transcendental ideal of a musical *Urwesen* is most closely embodied by the music of Bach and Beethoven. "Of all 'modern' tone poets," he writes in the second edition of the *Entwurf*, "Beethoven is the one who made the fewest concessions to the demands of instruments."[37] Both of these composers are "to be conceived as a beginning," though "not as unsurpassable finalities." "In spirit and emotion," he maintains, "they will probably remain unexcelled . . . What still remains to be surpassed is their form of expression and their freedom."[38] At once music's original essence and its goal, *Urmusik* must also hold the promise of a state of unfettered freedom of means and expression.

Yet the conception outlined in 1907 undergoes a small but significant shift in the postwar years, when the earlier goal of complete freedom of means and expression is held in check by the artifice of "completion as perfection." It is precisely the idea of such completion that becomes an important aspect of *Junge Klassizität*. Busoni refines his conception of an *Urmusik*, no doubt as a response to what he felt to be the extremes of modernist experimentation, something in part perpetrated by the reception of his own aesthetic writings. *Junge Klassizität* is thus both the culmination of the earlier work and a reaction against implications and consequences that the author was reluctant to accept, especially the music of Schoenberg.

Busoni's *Urmusik* c. 1920 was no less idealistic and, at least in certain respects, scarcely less reactionary than, say, Heinrich Schenker's contemporaneous *Ursatz*. Both theorists entertained timeless essences in reaction to the times. The later position is reflected above all in the essentializing essay "The Essence of Music" (Vom Wesen der Musik), published in his last year, 1924. There he writes, emphatically endorsing an aristocratic stance comparable to Schenker's, that "our conception of the essence of music is still fragmentary and dim; . . . only very few are able to perceive it and fewer still to grasp it, and they are quite unable to define it."[39] Unlike Schenker, however, he eschews nationalistic distinctions. "What is the essence of music?" he asks rhetorically, supplying a characteristically quixotic answer, defined more negatively than positively:

> Not the virtuoso's performance, not the overture to *Rienzi*, not the theory of harmony, not the locally embellished folk-song of the various nations, developing behind brightly-painted boundary posts (in this case the separation into countries

> is already a denial of the essence of music). Even though every single one of these examples contains a tiny seed of the supreme whole, in so far as music includes all the elements, it is just because they do fall into sections that they will again be subdivided, as if the vault of heaven were to be torn into little strips. What can the individual do in the face of such an abundance of material? From the depths of our hearts, therefore, let us be thankful to the select few who are privileged, at least on a small scale, through taste and form, inspiration and mastery, to set up a miniature model of that sphere from which all beauty and power flow to them. Mankind will never know the essence of music in its reality and entirety; would that they could at least arrive at distinguishing what does *not* belong to it! . . . At times, and in rare cases, a mortal is by listening made aware of something immortal in the essence of music that melts in the hands as one tries to grasp it, is frozen as soon as one wishes to transplant it to the earth, is extinguished as soon as it is drawn through the darkness of our mentality. Yet enough still remains recognisable of its heavenly origin, and of all that is high, noble and translucent in what surrounds us and we are able to discern; it appears to us as the highest, noblest, and most translucent. Music is not, as the poet says, an "ambassador" of heaven, but the ambassadors of heaven are those chosen ones on whom the high charge is laid to bring us single rays of the original light through immeasurable space. Hail to the prophets![40]

Weill's *Urform*—needless to say—does not aspire to such a universal theory of absolute music, here expounded in perhaps the most absolute sense conceivable. The differences are telling and critical. Weill was never as poetically or aristocratically lofty as his teacher; he also restricts himself to the sphere of musical theater. *Urform* is nonetheless informed, quite extensively, by Busoni's thought. Like *Urmusik,* the notion of *Urform* is both backward- and forward-looking. "The success of our piece," Weill said in connection with *Die Dreigroschenoper,* "does indeed prove not only that the creation and realization of this new genre came at the right moment for the situation of art but that the audience seemed actually to be waiting for the renewal of a favorite type of theater."[41]

In the way it is articulated in his writings, Weill's *Urform* reflects many of Busoni's own aspirations with regard to musical theater. His reference to *Die Dreigroschenoper* as an *Urtyp* provides a terminological variation, but it is conceptually consistent with *Urform.*[42] And although *Urform* disappears entirely as a term in Weill's English-language writings, it remains conceptually—albeit necessarily transformed, for example as "form-problems." Thus Weill stated, apropos the premiere of *Street Scene,* that he had "tried continuously to solve, in my own way, the form-problems of the musical theatre, and through the years I have approached these problems from all different angles."[43] A similar notion linking earlier and future efforts is also in force in the claim, made in 1936, that "a reestablishment of the true musical theater is scheduled to take place inside of the enormous territory between the two genres [of opera and musical comedy]."[44]

REFORM

Whenever Weill invokes the idea of an *Urform* of opera, whether or not he actually uses the term, he does so as a committed reformer. This is perhaps hardly surprising: schemes to reform musical theater have always been Janus-faced. The hopeful gaze toward a brighter future goes hand in hand with a nostalgic look back to putative origins. By way of adopting adequate distance from immediate tradition—a tradition viewed as a regrettable aberration—reformers have sought justification for renewal in the values embodied by a remote, fondly remembered past. *Urform* is similarly equivocal. The *Ur-* refers to past achievements, now corrupted or totally obscured. At the same time, it points to renewed attempts—for example, under the banner of "epic theater," the "Lehrstück," or "American opera"—at the ideal's eventual realization.

The way back is also the way forward: this is a mode of thinking that characterized the very birth of opera. When the genre came into existence around 1600, it did so under retrospective auspices—as an attempt to revive a form of musical theater from antiquity. Ancient Greek tragedies, according to the humanists of the Florentine Camerata, had been sung throughout. Composers such as Peri and Monteverdi, standing on the threshold of the Baroque era, took part in a renaissance in the literal sense, the "re-birth" of antiquity. From its very beginnings opera was conceived of and also justified as an *Urform* of theater, as Weill himself observed in 1936: "In the great theater cultures of the past, music was an inevitable and intrinsic feature of the drama. . . . In the beginning opera was musical theater in the best and purest sense of the phrase; it sought a new blending of song and speech on the basis of great theater tradition. In fact, the music of Monteverdi's *Orfeo,* which was really the first opera, bears a strong resemblance to ancient drama."[45]

Reform has always focused on the relationship between music and text, Weill's included. In Monteverdi's so-called *seconda prattica,* music placed itself at the service of drama by giving priority to declamation and the representation of textual content over the prescriptions of compositional theory—the *prima prattica.* Expressiveness arose from rule-breaking. Theoretically sanctioned order gave way in affective song to textually inspired mannerism. Although, in that sense, opera was manneristic from the start, the spur to Gluck's and Wagner's programs of reform was a dissatisfaction with an operatic practice that, it was felt, had drifted too far from the earlier ideal. Musical mannerisms had lost their purpose by detaching themselves from the text they were originally designed to express. Vocal melisma in particular and virtuosic display in general—so the reformers thought—had become ends in themselves.

Thus Gluck and his librettist Calzabigi were concerned, in principle, with "true declamation." In this they echoed the views of Francesco Algarotti, who complained in his influential "Essay on the Opera" that Italian opera had degenerated in the mid–eighteenth century into a series of "affectations and languishing airs."[46] Wagner's critique was more radical still, and more emphatic. The development of opera, according to him, was nothing but a story of decline, a steadily compounded confusion of ends and means. As he wrote in *Oper und Drama:* "the error in the genre of opera consisted in the fact that the means of expression (music) was made an end, while the end of expression (drama) was made a means."[47] Thus he rejected Rossini's melodies as "absolute music"—music, that is, with little or no connection to either text or drama. And he found a chief propagandist for his reforms in Nietzsche (prior to their falling-out), who incorporated Wagnerian ideas into *The Birth of Tragedy out of the Spirit of Music.*

A reformer in the Gluckian or Wagnerian mold Weill was not. Quite to the contrary: he departed from the models and aims of his historical forebears fundamentally, and from Wagner quite explicitly. Nor, as already suggested, should his aims be equated with Brecht's, despite the success of their partnership and their common opposition to Wagnerian aesthetics. For all their shared interests, their goals were ultimately quite different. If they both pursued an ideal circumscribed by the concept of "epic theater," each understood something quite different thereby. Weill came from musical theater, Brecht from spoken theater (albeit one with a heavy reliance on music). Whereas Weill was interested in spoken theater insofar as it served his envisaged reform of opera and musical theater, Brecht viewed music as just one of several indispensable elements in the "epicization" of traditional drama—indispensable, yet also dangerous. Brecht tended to harbor a deep mistrust of music, not least of its irrational power. Whereas Weill maintained his "commitment to opera" (to cite the title of his 1925 essay "Bekenntnis zur Oper"), for Brecht the genre eventually became the embodiment of all that was "culinary," which for him meant that it was something to be opposed and overcome.

That Weill's reform writings are Busonian at core can be seen by studying them in relation to the principal printed source of his mentor's thinking about opera: the second edition of the *Entwurf einer neuen Ästhetik der Tonkunst* (1916). Much of the new material added to that edition appears in the sections on opera and reflects better than anything else in the tract Busoni's thinking immediately prior to the time that Weill joined the master class.[48] As he had already stated in the first edition of the *Entwurf* in 1907, the type of musical theater on which Busoni based his thinking was the "mode of old opera," by which he meant eighteenth-century Italian opera, precisely the "mode" against which Gluck and Wagner had directed their polemics. "I consider justified, albeit with qualification, the mode of old opera, which captured in a closed number (aria) the mood attained by a dramatically propelled scene, allowing it to resonate. Words and gestures conveyed the dramatic course of the plot, more or less inadequately followed by music in the form of recitative; having arrived at a point of rest the music again assumed the dominant position *[Hauptsitz]*."[49]

"Justified," but "with qualification": Busoni was quite aware that much had been written in this "mode" that Wagner rightly criticized as undramatic. The gap between Busoni's position and that of Gluck and Wagner is nonetheless quite apparent. While the latter primarily sought a reform of singing declamation, Busoni focused on the specific genre of the number opera, in which dialogue alternates with formally closed arias. The premise for reform efforts that proceed from the number opera as *Urform* is no longer the assumption that dramas should be sung throughout but rather a more fundamental question, namely, the extent to which drama admits music at all. Replacing, or at least displacing, the issue of the nature of sung declamation is the more basic consideration of which kinds of theater allow music—and where.

In his 1929 essay "Über den gestischen Charakter der Musik," Weill summarized his idea of opera, echoing Busoni, in the form of two questions, to which his works attempted to offer answers: "With my attempts to arrive at the *Urform* of the musical stage work I have made a number of observations which initially seemed like wholly new insights but which on closer inspection could be placed in historical contexts. During my own work I have repeatedly forced myself to answer the question, 'What occasions are there for music on the stage?' Yet retrospective observation of my own or other operas produced another question: 'How is music in the theater constituted, and are there certain characteristics that mark music as theater music?'"[50]

In the second edition of his *Entwurf*, Busoni had already expressed the dilemma facing the opera composer as follows: "The sung word on stage will always remain a convention and an obstacle to any genuine impact: in order to emerge from this conflict with any degree of propriety, a plot in which people act while singing has to be based on the unbelievable, the untrue, the improbable, so that one impossibility may support the other and both become possible and acceptable."[51] In the same sense Weill wrote in "Korrespondenz über *Dreigroschenoper*" that "with every musical work for the stage the question arises: how is music, particularly song, at all possible in the theater? I had a realistic plot, so I had to set the music against it, since I do not consider music capable of realistic effects. Hence the action was either interrupted, in order to introduce music, or it was deliberately driven to a point where there was no alternative but to sing."[52]

Considering the future of opera, Busoni had also posed the question "At what moments is music on the stage indispensable?" His answer: "During dances, marches and songs—and when the supernatural enters the plot." The opera composer should be guided by the "idea of supernatural subject-matter." The stage should be viewed as a "clear and unabashed distortion." Its essence resides "in the idea of the joke and unreality as opposed to the seriousness and verity of life. . . . Hence it is fitting that people assert their love and unleash their loathing while singing, and that they fall in a duel to a melody, that they linger on high notes during emotional eruptions; hence it is fitting that they behave differently from how they would in real life instead of unintentionally doing it the other way round (as in our theaters and especially opera houses)." For this reason, he saw "so-called Italian 'verismo' on the musical stage as untenable."[53]

Within the context of German letters, Busoni's and Weill's ideas represent the greatest conceivable contrast to Wagner. In almost all details, and definitely in principle, their respective opera aesthetics can be interpreted as a specific negation of Wagner's, even if one allows for the qualifications that teacher and student did not espouse identical positions and that Wagner's own position shifted quite radically during the conception of the *Ring* cycle. Writing about "new opera" in 1926, Weill stated: "The musical development of recent decades led to the insight that one had to withdraw as far as possible from Richard Wagner's sphere of influence."[54] Along with the concept of number opera ("the mode of old opera"), in conscious opposition to music drama, the other key term is *absolute music*. In espousing the unity of music—a unity that transcends genre differences, among other things—Busoni accused Wagner of having caused a decline: "The name of Wagner leads back to program music."[55] Number opera, in contrast, made possible a return to closed, "absolute" forms of music-making, with Mozart as the paradigm. Nonetheless, as with Mozart, music should contain "the animation of scenic events," to quote Weill from his early manifesto "Commitment to Opera" (Bekenntnis zur Oper). The debt to Mozart is as much a debt to Busoni, formulated here with a paraphrase of Busoni's definition of the unity of music from his letter to Bekker:

> Central to all this is the realization that we cannot set about the creation of a work for the stage by changing our musical thinking, that we must make music in opera with the same abandon and unfolding of our imagination as in chamber music. It is not a matter, however, of transferring the elements of absolute music to opera; that would be the path to cantatas, to oratorio. On the contrary: the dramatic impetus which opera demands can be an essential component of all musical creation. Mozart taught me this. He is no different in opera than he is in the symphony and string quartet. He always possesses the rhythm of the stage, which is why he can remain an absolute musician, even when he has the infernal din intervene in *Don Giovanni*. If, then, our music possesses the typically operatic elements—strict accentuation, concise dynamics, eloquent melodic lines—opera can once again become the most precious vessel for currents of our inner song. . . . It was only when I sensed that my music contains the animation of scenic events that I turned to the stage.[56]

"Inner song" could be seen to function here as a synonym for *Urmusik*, to be evoked by the opera composer in his pursuit of a theatrical *Urform*.

MODERN CLASSICAL ART

Equally suggestive of the Busoni connection as the ideal of an *Urform* of musical theater is Weill's promulgation of "modern classical art," an unmistakable variant of Busoni's "New Classicality." As with Busoni's term, the pairing of the adjectives *modern* and *classical* is not without its oxymoronic side. One could argue that the "modern" part serves to cancel out the "classical" part, or vice versa, even though subscribing to such an interpretation would be to take a rather one-sided view of modernism, if not classicism. It is a view that has enjoyed considerable currency, especially in the early 1950s. Its (so to speak) classic formulation came from Adorno in *Philosophie der neuen Musik,* with his injunctions against "concert museums" in general and the reception of his teacher Alban Berg's music in particular. Complicit in the classicizing process are both the composer and the audience, as Adorno infers with mention of *Wozzeck:* "Those who extol *Wozzeck* as one of the first enduring products of New Music do not realize how much their praise compromises a piece that already suffers from serenity."[57] At the other extreme, one could argue, as Ernst Robert Curtius did, that classicism is part of a timeless dualism, the other half of which is mannerism. All ages have their classical elements, some more than others, and "modern classicism" is simply any form of classicism in the modern age. Curtius, it should be remembered, had reservations about the modern age; emblematic of that age's sensibility, he suggested, was the work of James Joyce, which he characterized as a "gigantic manneristic experiment."[58]

This brief digression into terminology raises a linguistic problem that is only compounded in English, especially when terms switch grammatical identity from noun to adjective: German distinguishes quite clearly between *Klassizismus* and *Klassik;* English does not do this so readily, at least not as far as the substantive form is concerned. While *Klassizismus* translates into "classicism," there is no precise equivalent of *Klassik*. It is not that German speakers are necessarily more precise in distinguishing between the two, but rather that English either uses the word *classicism,* and hence makes neither a linguistic nor semantic distinction, or else it uses a phrase such as "the classical age" or "classical music." Turning the noun into an adjective is a good idea, then, for it precisely mirrors the German distinction: *klassizistisch* becomes "classicist," and *klassisch* becomes "classical." But again, usage is sloppy; someone inclined toward the classical can be described as having "classicist" leanings.

What useful semantic distinction between these adjectives does the lexical one, if observed, connote? *Klassizismus* is at one remove from that which is classical—from classical epochs and models (neoclassicism may even be at two removes). *Klassik* either is that epoch or model, or it is being used by someone laying claim to such a status or achievement. To make public such aspirations is also to risk hubris. "Classicality"—the state of being classical—is not for creative artists to determine or expect for themselves. In that sense it is an aesthetic rather than a poietic category, a matter of reception rather than production. In practical terms we might say that *Klassizismus* readily applies to Stravinsky, who used classical models in a manneristic way, at one or more removes, while *Klassik* applies to Schoenberg, who not only subscribed to a classical aesthetic (albeit while eating his "expressionist" cake at the same time), but also demanded a place for himself in the pantheon of Austro-German classics.[59] Moreover, he fondly declared those classics, among which he desired inclusion, as universally predominant. Historians and critics have still not decided on the degree of hubris he committed here.

One need only consider Schoenberg's and Stravinsky's respective uses of earlier music for the chief differences to become apparent: Stravinsky defamiliarized surface gestures of the models he used, more often preclassical compositions than classical ones. Rudolf Stephan has fittingly invoked the tenets of Russian formalism in this connection.[60] As an aesthetic trend, Stravinsky's neoclassicism tended toward mannerism. Schoenberg, in contrast, relied on formal and structural devices, which, except for their names, were often hidden beneath the musical surface. If such devices were also part of a poietics, then it was only to the extent that they remained largely subcutaneous, as classical aesthetics required. Seeing the two composers in this way prompts a review of a much-discussed issue: are Stravinsky and Schoenberg two sides of a common trend in the 1920s, or are they antipodes? The answer lies partly but also critically in their respective relationship to the classical tradition, and in the implications of the distinction being drawn here between "classicist" and "classical." Transferring that distinction to nouns, Stravinsky and Schoenberg represent "classicism" and "classicality," respectively. Busoni's own *Junge Klassizität* translates as "classicality," not "classicism." Nor was his position without its hubristic aspects. Like Schoenberg, he also aspired toward a classical status among his peers.

To talk of "modern classical art" in connection with the composer of *Die Dreigroschenoper* and *Lady in the Dark* may seem odd, if not entirely inappropriate. Weill's art was, if anything, of the mannerist, Stravinskian kind rather than the Schoenbergian. Didn't he, after all, proclaim in 1940 that he didn't "give a damn about composing for posterity"? Rather than aspire to "klassische Vollendung," he openly shunned it, even satirized it. Recall the ironic invocation of "die ewige Kunst" in *Aufstieg und Fall der Stadt Mahagonny.*[61] And if his music utilized established models, wasn't it to defamiliarize them and by doing so to derive from them richly layered dramatic meaning? One might not rush in so readily or confidently if Weill himself had not used the phrase "modern classical art" in the first place.

The source of his concept is a survey, published in Polish in 1929, on the topic "romanticism in music."

> I am sending you a few words as a contribution to the survey concerning "Romanticism in Music." I am of the opinion that the announcement of a new romantic epoch in music, being proclaimed at present in Germany by the defenders of an obsolete artistic taste, is a highly reactionary phenomenon. That which the proclaimers of that theory call romanticism is nothing other than the form of expression of the 19th century, which has now already been completely overcome by musicians of today. It would amount to a complete lack of understanding of the musical development of our epoch if we were to take pains to smooth the path toward a direction that we have already quite consciously given up.
>
> That which characterizes recent music [*mloda muzyka*—literally, "young music"], namely, the simplification of the means of expression, the avoidance of affective overload, the forging of a clear musical language—all this is unromantic in a certain measure; it is only necessary to attach the great human idea to those artistic achievements, and there will arise a modern *classical* art, which will be in the most complete opposition to romantic art. Modern times abound in great, all-embracing ideas, which are able to find artistic expression solely in classical form. There is no place in them for romantic art.
>
> After all, the public for whom we are writing these words do not require of music that it should drug them like opium. They ask of it the same as of all other great art: the reflection of their life and of their experiences on a sublime level of artistry.
>
> We protest against those who would gladly deny our epoch the manifestation of great artistic revelations only for the reason that it is unromantic. On the contrary, we believe that precisely this unromantic character of our epoch favors the creation of art that would be an expression of the great events being played out in our days.[62]

Weill defines his notion of "classical art" in contradistinction neither to modernism nor to mannerism but rather, as he says, as "the most complete opposition to romantic art." He may well be polemicizing against Adolf Weissmann and his 1928 book *Die Entgötterung der Musik* (The Secularization of Music; the title of the English translation published in 1930 was *Music Come to Earth*), one of whose chapters is titled "Die unweigerliche Romantik und der neueste Musiker" (Inexorable Romanticism and the Contemporary Musician). By way of illustrating the semantic context, one might add that Goebbels spoke of "romantischer Realismus," as indeed in a deplorably opportunistic or at best miscalculated moment did Theodor Adorno in 1934 when he approvingly quoted Goebbels's phrase in praise of a "new romanticism."[63]

Technically, Weill's classical art involves simplicity, clarity, and the avoidance of what he calls "affective overload." Obvious parallels can be found in Busoni's letter to Bekker. In this case Weill seems to be echoing Busoni's call for a "casting off of what is 'sensuous' and the renunciation of subjectivity," both aspects of his championing of absolute music heedless of genre.[64]

Another aspect, related to the last one and no less familiar from his teacher's writings, is the matter Weill raises regarding reception. Music should not "drug [the audience] like opium." The idea recalls Nietzsche's critique of Wagnerism, which Busoni reiterates with his criticism of "strong human experiences." Such experiences, he thought, were demanded from the stage as compensation for the audience's dull daily lives. Placing greater responsibility on the listener, Busoni required that "half the work" in the reception of a work of art "must be done by the receiver himself."[65] Brecht was to give this sentiment a more obviously Freudian-cum-Marxist twist in his notes on *Aufstieg und Fall der Stadt Mahagonny,* in particular in the following verbatim quotation from Freud's 1930 publication *Civilization and Its Discontents:* "The life imposed on us is too hard; it brings us too many agonies, disappointments, impossible tasks. In order to stand it we have to have some kind of palliative. . . . The pseudo-satisfactions offered by art are illusions if compared with reality, but are none the less psychologically effective for that, thanks to the part played by the imagination in our inner life. . . . Such drugs are sometimes responsible for the wastage of great stores of energy which might have been applied to bettering the human lot."[66]

An analogous passage, with a similarly Nietzschean twist, can be found in Weill's article "Über den gestischen Charakter" from the same year as the Polish survey: "The theater of earlier eras was written for pleasure seekers. It wanted to tickle, arouse, stir up, overpower the audience. . . . The other form of theater that is beginning to establish itself assumes an audience that follows the action on stage with the calm attitude of the thinking person and which, because it wants to think, must perceive any demands made on its pleasure nerves as an intrusion. . . . This theater is unromantic to the highest degree. 'Romanticism' as art extinguishes thought; it uses narcotic means."[67]

SOCIOLOGICAL AESTHETIC

The difference between Busoni on the one hand and Weill and Brecht on the other reflects the shift from the former's ideal of *Junge Klassizität,* as manifested in his opera aesthetic in the *Entwurf,* to a more manifestly sociological variant characteristic of the younger generation in the 1920s. The difference—gradual rather than absolute—can be seen in the reformist zeal with which Brecht and Weill voiced their opinions. Their reform not only affected the substance and constitution of their work; it also addressed the nature and behavior of their audience. Like Busoni, they were critical of traditional opera audiences. But they were also keen to act on that criticism by attracting new audiences, even to the point of moving outside the traditional institutions.

This aspect of Weill's work is captured in the term *gesellschaftsbildend*, which he employs on a number of occasions. The first occasion, at least in print, seems to have been his essay about the impact of radio on musical life ("Der Rundfunk und die Umschichtung des Musiklebens"), which appeared in *Der deutsche Rundfunk* in June 1926. In recognizing the contribution to be made by the medium of radio, Weill registered the decline of the "type of concert that serves only as a figurehead for a social event." The "socially regenerative power of music" *(gesellschaftsbildende Kraft)*, in contrast, "is beginning to have an impact on the masses." Radio music, he thought, could directly oppose "superficially oriented concerts that are full of pomp and circumstance, and which have become superfluous."[68]

In the same spirit, the program for the *Mahagonny* "Songspiel," from one year later, contained the following programmatic statement, also including the term's antonym, *gesellschaftlich*: "In his more recent works Weill is moving in the direction of those artists of all forms who predict the liquidation of arts engendered by established society *[gesellschaftliche Künste]*. The small epic piece *Mahagonny* merely takes the logical step from the inexorable decline of existing social structures. It already addresses an audience that naively demands its fun in the theater."[69] And in the reform-oriented notes to *Dreigroschenoper* he took the next constructive step, in which he saw radio as colluding: "Today . . . there is no other artistic form in the entire world whose bearing is so unabashedly engendered by established society *[gesellschaftliche Haltung]*. The theater in particular has moved quite decisively in a direction that can rather be described as socially regenerative *[gesellschaftsbildend]*."[70]

The term *gesellschaftsbildend*—literally, "socially formative"—has its origins in the writings of Paul Bekker, the critic and musicologist whom Weill extolled in 1919, before his own association with Busoni, as "the most significant writer on music alongside [Romain] Rolland."[71] The term plays a significant role both in Bekker's 1918 book on the symphony, which Weill expressly recommended to his brother for information about Beethoven, and in his book *Das deutsche Musikleben* of 1916.[72] The similarities between Weill's and Bekker's thought are not merely terminological but also substantive. Weill's borrowing of the term makes utter sense in the context of his and Bekker's common rejection of Romanticism and their promulgation of what Bekker calls a "sociological aesthetic."[73]

A quotation from the foreword to Bekker's *Deutsches Musikleben* should speak for itself, especially in light of the earlier quotation from Weill's essay on music's *gestischer Charakter*: "The one essential thing is this: we must learn to replace our approach to art as one of enjoyment with one of activity. . . . The doctrine of our times is to move beyond enjoyment to activity, even in art. . . . That is the fundamental idea behind the sociological aesthetic." For Bekker, such an aesthetic took up where Beethoven had left off. Between the death of Beethoven and 1916 stood a Romantic retreat into what he calls the "sphere of sensuality" *(Gebiet des Sinnenlebens).* Music, in his view, had lost touch with the socially active and activating power of Beethoven's compositions.[74]

In the symphony book, Bekker cherishes music's ability, especially in Beethoven symphonies, to "form a unified, specifically individualized essence from the chaotic mass of the audience," to create what he calls "communities of feeling" *(Gefühlsgemeinschaften).* The music of which he approves possesses a "community-forming capacity" *(gesellschaftsbildende Fähigkeit).*[75] Bekker, of course, had in mind Mahler of the Eighth Symphony, not the composer of *Die Dreigroschenoper.*[76] Even so, Weill's appropriation of Bekker's values for the promulgation of a democratically inspired musical theater, as opposed to the bourgeois symphony, leaves those values basically intact.

Weill justifies his modernity through a contemporaneous opposition to and "specific negation" of romanticism, in the sense in which the turn-of-the century and later postwar generation understood that term. His classicality is more Busonian than Schoenbergian. With respect to musical theater, the opposition involves the use of number rather than through-composed forms. It also requires a "classical" mode of listening, which can be distinguished from the "romantic" approach defined according to the typologies drawn up by Heinrich Besseler in his "Grundfragen des musikalischen Hörens" and later writings.[77] Bekker's notion of "activity" is also relevant here.

Weill's classicality also affects the choice of topics—perhaps the most contentious aspect of his article espousing "modern classical art." This aspect needs to be understood in light of his association with the phenomenon of *Zeitoper,* against whose more ephemeral aspects he polemicized quite extensively in other articles.[78] Especially relevant here are the works he composed around this time, such as the contentiously didactic "Lehrstück" *Der Jasager* and the parabolic epic opera *Die Bürgschaft.* The concern with audience attitudes also has institutional implications: Weill's is a classicality bent on reform rather than preservation of the status quo.

If the notions of *Urform* and "modern classical art" most immediately define his relation to his teacher and his own musical production around 1930, they also draw attention to the salient differences between him and the romantically "classical" Schoenberg, on the one hand, and the manneristically classicist Stravinsky, on the other. They are differences that identify an important strand—a "third strand"—in 1920s German music. The appropriation of Busonian "classicality" obviously has much in common with the aspirations of other composers of his generation, such as Paul Hindemith, Hanns Eisler, Ernst Toch, and fellow Busoni pupil Philipp Jarnach. Comparing them reveals differences of compositional technique, to be sure. No less critical are criteria derived from Bekker's sociological aesthetic. Applying such criteria reveals a gap between Weill and Jarnach (despite the latter's championing of his version of Busoni's "Junge Klassizität") greater than that between Weill and many of his other contemporaries.

Of all of his generation, Weill remained perhaps truest to Bekker's principles, while the others, Eisler and Jarnach included, increasingly closed the gap between themselves and Schoenberg. Compare, for example, Jarnach's 1924 essay "Das Romanische in der Musik," in which he espoused the post-Nietzschean enthusiasm of the Busoni school for Mediterranean (literally, "Romanic") musical culture, with his panegyrics to Schoenberg from the early 1950s.[79] After Schoenberg's death in 1951, Jarnach wrote: "His work is at an end and with it the quarrel about his oeuvre as a whole, an oeuvre that stands above the times because, as the only one of its time, it takes to its conclusion while perfecting at the highest level the classical synthesis of a personal style."[80] Nothing could be further from Weill's own position, as Jarnach himself indirectly demonstrated seven years later when, in a letter to Heinz Tiessen, he trashed Weill's American works as lacking "stylistic significance." Weill turned "to a type of creative activity," he suggested, "in which the artistic ambition [of *Dreigroschenoper, Mahagonny,* and *Jasager*] is no longer recognizable."[81] Weill, in contrast, never had occasion after he left Germany to pass official judgment on his former fellow student and counterpoint teacher.

WORK-CONCEPT

Busoni's notion of *Urmusik* is closely tied to his conception of the musical work, and it is here that it is not only tempting but also legitimate to see yet a further link with his pupil Weill. Like *Urmusik,* Busoni's work-concept is hard to pin down. Its elusiveness, however, is part of its essence. For Busoni, composition—like editing, arranging, and performing—was an ultimately imperfect attempt to realize a musical *Urform.* Notation, according to this view, is a form of transcription, an attempt to transcribe an abstract, universal idea: "Notation, the writing out of compositions, is primarily an ingenious expedient for catching an inspiration, with the purpose of exploiting it later. But notation is to improvisation as the portrait is to the living model. It is for the interpreter to *resolve the rigidity of the signs* into the primitive emotion. But the lawgivers require the interpreter to reproduce the rigidity of the signs; they consider his reproduction the nearer to perfection, the more closely it clings to the signs."[82]

In admitting imperfection, Busoni leaves room for the interpreter, whether in the guise of editor, transcriber, arranger, or performer. The distinction between these roles is blurred—"confused," as John Williamson has put it—in Busoni's case.[83] Confusion obtains in a neutral, even positive sense. It is a function of "transformation" or "metamorphosis" *(Verwandlung),* which Albrecht Riethmüller has identified as something quite fundamental to Busoni's poietics.[84] Examples from his oeuvre would include numerous transcriptions, literal and free; the *Nachdichtungen* after Bach (*Fantasia nach Johann Sebastian Bach,* 1909;

Fantasia Contrappuntistica, 1910; *Sonatina brevis,* 1918); parody of genre characteristics (nineteenth-century Italian opera in *Arlecchino,* 1917; Mass and choral fugue in the Easter Vespers and tavern scenes of *Doktor Faust*); "transliteration" of style elements (Mozart in the *Divertimento* for flute and small orchestra, 1921; Johann Strauss in *Tanzwalzer,* 1922); and the revision of old works into new (*An die Jugend,* 1909, and Sonatina, 1910; and the numerous so-called "satellite works" related to *Doktor Faust*).

"Every notation," Busoni wrote, "is, in itself, the transcription of an abstract idea."[85] The original idea is thereby not only captured; to an extent, it is also lost. Composition, insofar as it is transmitted as notation, is no exception; it, too, amounts to a kind of transcription, a transformation of the idea into the realm of musical material. Conversely, a new edition or arrangement could be seen to recover some of what was lost in the compositional transcription. "The performance of a work is also a transcription," Busoni stated, "and still, whatever liberties it may take, it can never annihilate the original."[86] What does he mean by "original"? Williamson has rightly questioned its ontology, suggesting that several senses of the term *original* might fit the bill here.[87] One thing is certain: it is not synonymous with the idea of a fixed, definitive text, an *Urtext.* It may be closer to the realm of *Urmusik,* where the idealistic Busonian work-concept also resides. As a performer-composer-transcriber-arranger-editor, Busoni was following in the footsteps of Franz Liszt. For both of these multifaceted musicians, transcription mediated between the predilections of the composer and those of the performer. Notions such as authenticity and fidelity are applicable only insofar as they can refer to the apprehended, intuited spirit of the work, not the notated text.

It is in this context that Busoni's central statement (quoted above) belongs: "The musical art-work exists, before its tones resound and after they die away, *complete and intact.* It exists both within and outside of time, and through its nature we can obtain a definite conception of the otherwise intangible notion of the Ideality of Time." As something located outside of time, the work is replete with all forms, motives, and combinations of past and future music, "through an unremitting effort to accumulate all previous achievements and those yet to be achieved."[88] This is a later formulation of the central tenet of the New Classicality as espoused to Bekker.

Although Busoni's aesthetic sensibilities were self-consciously historical, as were Liszt's, they contain more than a tinge of Nietzsche, increasingly so in the late writings. Though concerned about the future of music, Busoni increasingly espied an "eternal recurrence." This ancient cosmological idea, seized upon by Nietzsche, posits that everything happens as part of an endlessly repeating cycle or sequence of events. As Busoni puts it, "Everything that is to happen has already and for all time happened."[89] Although Nietzsche entertained the idea as a kind of cosmological hypothesis, he employed it hypothetically as a test—for those, that is, seeking to affirm life in the aftermath of all disillusionment. Without fully exploring the philosophical implications of this idea, Busoni provides an important link, both explicit and implicit, between Nietzsche's late work and the neoclassical turn in music.

A consequence of this turn is Busoni's pronounced eclecticism in matters of musical style, his "rhapsody of styles," to use Céléstin Deliège's apt characterization.[90] In the realm of opera, toward which his late work leaned heavily with his unfinished magnum opus, the mix of styles serves to furnish a vocabulary of dramatic signifiers. The role of convention is key. Style generates meaning through a network of historical and functional associations. Understanding the idea of absolute music in this light—an idea that shifts in significance throughout his career, as mentioned above—entails coming to terms with the potential for such meaning, not precluding it. If anything, freedom from the immediate constraints of traditional genres and forms—a freedom that engages with convention rather than rejecting it—only enhances that potential.

Here, too, is the most obvious link to Weill: to his cultivation of style as "stylus theatralis," not *Personalstil*. Another is Busoni's idea of "absolute orchestration." By this he was referring to instrumentation "demanded and directed by musical thought," as opposed to "the instrumentalisation of what was originally only an abstract musical composition or one conceived for another instrument." He believed that "absolute" orchestration is the only genuine one." The second kind "belongs to 'arrangements'." "Orchestration," he stated, "is composition, not 'instrumentation.' The choice of means: formulating the thought, the clothing of the form, the form itself."[91] Considering the state of music, he bemoaned the fact that "there are more composers who transcribe for the orchestra than those who invent and feel purely orchestrally." Among the "genuine composers" for orchestra he counted Mozart, Weber, and Wagner, although "even Wagner lapses into orchestration [i.e. instrumentation]." Beethoven, he felt, "almost always 'orchestrates'." Judged according to Busoni's criteria, Weill aspired to be a "genuine composer" for orchestra. "When I write music there's no piano around," Weill said in 1936.[92] And in 1932 he emphasized the importance of the "sonic image" (the *Klangbild*) of his music, something conceived as part of the compositional process, not merely added as part of an "arrangement."[93] For this reason, he rarely relinquished the job of instrumentation to another hand, even on Broadway, where that practice generally obtained. (This was also among the reasons why in Hollywood, where such a division of labor was enshrined in the structure of the institution, Weill felt his art to be severely compromised.)

Even arrangements, however, can transcend the status of mere "instrumentation." Busoni extolled, for example, Liszt's version of Schubert's *Wandererfantasie,* which he described as "symphonically transcribed." He was "obliged," he wrote, "to recognise how helpfully Liszt shows the way over certain 'stretches' in the original."[94] The "original" version is not necessarily the ideal one. Transcription may bring the work closer to that ideal, closer to the *Urmusik.*

Underpinned by the notion of *Urmusik,* Busoni's concept of the musical-work is subversive in several respects. Traditional notions of textual fidelity and authenticity in performance don't apply. They are subverted. The ideal of "absolute orchestration" posits an adequacy between musical thought and the means of presentation, which may or may not obtain. The idea is echoed in the "sonic image" that accompanies Weill's musical thought. At the same time, conceived as it is from the perspective of a performer in thrall to idealist thinking, Busoni's work-concept is predisposed to accommodate and thereby transcend the contingencies and compromises of time, place, and space. Even the greatest geniuses, he insisted, had to battle with the limitations imposed by the musical culture of their time.

Although Weill never ventured into this cosmically heady realm, there are undeniable Busonian traces to his work-concept, too. It is as if he had stood his teacher's *Urmusik* on its feet. Although not a performer, like his teacher, he was a practical musician. Performance, however compromised, was the attempt to realize an idea imperfectly transmitted in notation. While seeking to protect his own "absolute orchestration" by insisting on close control over the performance of his theatrical collaborations, he composed music that never ceased to aspire toward universality in matters of the human predicaments portrayed. That is the thread that runs through all his work. Having just arrived in the United States, he put it this way:

> Music can only express human sentiments. Often, it is true, these sentiments arise out of the political tendencies of an epoch. For this reason Beethoven's music is different from Mozart's, since by Beethoven's time a new idea of democracy, not known in Mozart's era, had arisen. But this is all merely historical. No music of any value can be written on a purely political basis, as some of the moderns in Russia and Germany would have us believe. Nor would I ever compose a single bar for esthetic reasons in order to try to create a new style. I write to express human emotions, solely. If music is really human, it doesn't matter to me how it is conveyed.[95]

Deep down he believed music to be something universal, beyond the contingencies of history and society. It had an essence for Weill, a human essence, just as it did for his teacher. Music can express the "inner voice," as Weill said in 1946 apropos the movie *You and Me.*[96] It can become "the most precious vessel for capturing streams of our inner song," as he wrote in 1925.[97] A quintessentially romantic belief, all "classicality" notwithstanding, it constituted the central dramatic idea behind *Lady in the Dark.* Finally, realization through performance depended on conventions in the way outlined in Busoni's notes on the future of opera. But the use of convention was hardly conventional. The aim was to transcend it. It is an aim that brought Busoni into the realm of Nietzsche's "eternal recurrence." From a similar premise, Weill took a distinctly different path. With his feet more firmly planted on the ground (or rather, on the stage), transcending convention meant a commitment to permanent reform: "Our theatre has developed a number of standard formulas for musical entertainment—revue, musical comedy, musical play, operetta, light opera and grand opera, each of which follows a time-tried recipe. At the same time there has always been a special fascination for the composer in trying out different mixtures of the same ingredients."[98]

Unlike Busoni, Weill never saw himself as someone with a calling to be a teacher. Nor did he have significant ambitions as an aesthetician. He never contemplated anything comparable to Busoni's *Entwurf.* When he voiced his opinions, in short articles or interviews, also in letters, it was invariably in conjunction with the project he was currently working on (or was about to work on). His rationalizations tended to be pragmatic. Busoni, by contrast, could even be seen to be compensating with his aesthetic positions for the fragmentary nature of his oeuvre. Where Busoni tended toward the aristocratic and the cosmic, Weill embraced the democratic and humanistic.

Expressed in terms of the ancients, Busoni was enormously attracted to the concept of a *musica mundana.*[99] Like Boethius, he apprehended music as an all-pervading force in the universe. His writings are frequently an invitation, as he writes at the beginning of his 1910 essay "Das Reich der Musik," to follow him into that realm beyond "the barrier separating the earthly from the eternal."[100] Weill's thinking, although far less theoretically inclined, tends more toward a *musica humana.* However disinclined he was to speak metaphysically, in radical contrast to his teacher, music certainly held a fascination for him as something that mediated between the rational and the irrational. He never relinquished the view he expressed in 1925 that "music is, after all, a language of the soul, it speaks to us with its own words."[101] Music was essential to his commitment to musical theater, to the belief, as he put it in 1936, that "the stage has a reason for existence today only if it aspires to a rarer level of truth," insofar as he believed that music alone was capable of access to that "rarer level."[102] In order to account for the differences between himself and his teacher, he would no doubt have put them down to different times and different customs. Yet there is also something more at stake, a fundamental difference of personal disposition, of character.

ARLECCHINO

Apart from invoking the general precepts of his teacher's writings, sometimes almost verbatim, Weill repeatedly acknowledged Busoni's *Arlecchino* as the work that he particularly admired and as one that had left an indelible mark on his output (as well as that of his contemporaries). One of the reasons is the attention Busoni paid to *Arlecchino* in his master class. His students, as Levitz reports, "not only became intimately familiar with *Arlecchino* in class, but also attended performances in Berlin, Hamburg, Dresden, and Weimar."[103] Of all his works for the musical theater, *Arlecchino* illustrates, even better than his unfinished Faust opera, the theoretical precepts he promulgated to his pupils, precepts that Weill subsequently adopted and adapted as the basis of his own work.[104] With *Arlecchino,* Weill wrote in 1927, Busoni had "created anew *[neu geschaffen]* the number opera."[105] And writing about his own school opera *Der Jasager* in 1930, he listed *Arlecchino* along with his own *Dreigroschenoper,* Hindemith's *Hin und zurück,* and Milhaud's *Le pauvre matelot* as an *Urform* of opera, all of them works that met the task of "placing the genre 'opera' on a new footing and redefining the boundaries of this genre."[106] "Without his 'Arlequino' *[sic],*" he would later say, "an opera in which the principal character was not a singer, but an actor, there might possibly have been no music for 'Johnny Johnson,' 'Mahogany' *[sic],* or the rest."[107] (In the same interview he went so far as to ascribe Busoni's influence to a contemporary more often associated with the Second Viennese School: "Whether or not Hanns Eisler realizes it, he is undoubtedly in the Busoni tradition. He studied with Schoenberg, you know, but you couldn't tell it from his music, which is, on the other hand, pleasant and simple.") The following year, in 1937, he noted in an article titled "The Future of Opera in America" that "already, during the war, Busoni had written an opera *(Arlecchino)* which used an actress in the principal role. In Stravinsky's *L'histoire du soldat* a speaker carried the action; the *Dreigroschenoper* was written for an actress who could sing."[108] As elsewhere, Weill was generous in acknowledging the debt to his teacher, also on behalf of others.

Designated on its title page "ein theatralisches Capriccio *[a theatrical caprice],*" *Arlecchino,* composed in 1913–16, is an early example of the kind of neoclassical playfulness and self-consciousness that clearly appealed to Weill and directly influenced the ballet *Zaubernacht* and his first opera *Der Protagonist.* Above all, the element of operatic parody in *Arlecchino,* which "gives rise to all manner of quotations and allusions, from Gluck to Wagner, and bel canto to ragtime," as Antony Beaumont has observed, legitimized an approach that Weill would very much make his own, tending to prefer allusion to direct quotation.[109] His indebtedness to classical models rarely amounts to mere pastiche, as it so memorably does in Busoni's opera. The connection to Busoni's work nonetheless makes itself felt in a number of places, particularly in *Der Protagonist,* where one can hear Weill adopting expressive gestures, while not exactly reproducing them. The similarities are more those of texture, tone, and overall melodic contour, especially in the kinetic writing for winds, than of specific turns of phrase. Compare,

EXAMPLE 1. *Der Protagonist,* First Pantomime

EXAMPLE 2. Ferruccio Busoni, *Arlecchino,* Matteo's Monologue

for example, the end of Weill's First Pantomime in *Der Protagonist* with Matteo's Monologue in *Arlecchino* (examples 1 and 2).

The "objectivist" march styles both look and sound similar, especially in their use of repeated chords with oscillating chromatic alterations (or "semitonal instability," to use John Waterhouse's term), without it being possible to say that the Weill passage is derived directly from the Busoni.[110] To paraphrase Herbert

Fleischer, one can identify "traits" of the Busoni School, but Weill's "physiognomy" nonetheless "shines through."[111]

Weill's thinking, like that of his teacher, changed over time, reflecting the evolving character of his work. For this reason, his approach to musical theater can no more be systematized than can Busoni's. If there is one central and persistent idea, however, it lies in the permanent challenge of ongoing reform suggested by notions such as *Urform* and "form-problems." For all their cultural and generational differences, there remain numerous points of contact between teacher and pupil, points that are readily identifiable and remain remarkably consistent throughout Weill's career. Through the Busoni connection, above all, Weill gives the lie to the popular, if somewhat dated, notion of multiple artistic identities. That he succumbed on occasion to the temptation to exaggerate the strength and continuity of the connection is perhaps not surprising, given a tendency on the part of his critics to do just the opposite.

3

One-Act Operas

DER PROTAGONIST

When, in the last year of his life, Weill said that "I'm always in right at the beginning. I'm never lucky enough to find a libretto and set it to music," he had forgotten how lucky he had been with *Der Protagonist.*[1] His first surviving opera began as the exception to what would become the inviolable rule: it is his only musical theater piece to use a preexisting dramatic work almost wholesale, with little adjustment. Otherwise he was indeed "always in right at the beginning," always involved in shaping the musico-dramatic product, often quite extensively, from inception until opening night and beyond. (This is even true of *The Eternal Road,* despite its troubled genesis, and even though Franz Werfel, who was largely uninvolved in the work's production, produced the book in effect as a self-sufficient text.)

With Georg Kaiser's one-act play *Der Protagonist,* Weill described his choice of libretto as the solution to a creative "block." The text was evidently just what he was looking for. And because of how he set it, adhering closely to the original source, the resulting piece could qualify as an early example of the genre known as *Literaturoper,* albeit with an important caveat.[2] "Literature operas" not only set their texts more or less word-for-word; they also tend to thrive on the reflected glory of the original, on its status as "literature" in the emphatic sense of the term. Written in 1920 and first performed two years later in Breslau, Kaiser's play would hardly have passed muster as an established literary work at the time. *Der Protagonist* is not comparable in this respect to *Pelléas et Mélisande* or *Lulu* or even to *Salome.* Weill was principally interested in the fame-cum-infamy of the author, as he would be with the other distinguished writers he sought out as collaborators throughout his career. Kaiser appealed to Weill as an actively creative man of the theater, not as an icon. Granted, Weill would later draw on finished and established literature as the thematic or dramatic basis of a number of stage works, notably in *Die Dreigroschenoper, Der Jasager, Street Scene,* and *Lost in the Stars* (as well as the unfinished adaptation of Twain's *Huckleberry Finn*); yet he always worked together with his chosen librettist on the actual text that would be set to music. The final version of these pieces departed from the original, often quite significantly, even when the librettist himself was the author of that source, as with Elmer Rice's *Street Scene.*

Der Protagonist is different: it is the closest Weill came to setting a preexisting dramatic text without adaptation. Kaiser's participation as librettist was thus both nugatory and absolute. Although his contribution essentially ended before the collaboration began, the composer for his part scarcely tampered with the playwright's work. The changes to the original—for the most part cuts, ranging from individual words and lines to whole speeches—were made largely for musical reasons, most likely by the composer.[3]

Kaiser, who had written his one-act play before getting to know Weill, reverted to it as the basis for a musical stage work when the two of them failed to complete a ballet they were writing at Kaiser's invitation.[4] This is how Weill himself described his situation in 1924 in a program note written for the Dresden premiere of *Der Protagonist:*

> I felt happy and honored when Georg Kaiser offered to write me the scenario for a full-scale ballet. We began working together. In ten weeks nearly three-quarters of the piece was written. The score of the prelude and the first two acts was complete. Then came a block. We had grown out of the subject matter, the muteness of the characters bothered us, we had to burst the chains of the pantomime: it had to become opera. Georg Kaiser reverted to an earlier piece that he had at one point conceived in his mind in terms of opera, the one-act play *Der Protagonist.* Here we had what we were looking for: an unforced, unintentional dovetailing of opera and pantomime.[5]

Despite (and perhaps because of) Weill's note, the work's genesis remains somewhat vague. David Drew has described the explanation of the shift from ballet to opera as "remarkably unconvincing," finding it more likely that a commission for a dance piece "suddenly evaporated."[6] The creative moment described by Weill is critical, however, given the title he attached to the note—"Commitment to Opera"—and the significance that the first opera came to assume in his career, in both the short and the long term. The explanation may be "unconvincing" in terms of what actually transpired (Weill may be suppressing mundane contingencies), yet the "official" account accurately reflects the composer's sense of his artistic development, even before the opera's favorable reception. He had to burst the chains of ballet and pantomime and find a way to compose vocal music for the stage.

By way of emphasizing the career trajectory of "bursting the chains," Weill also mentions in the essay his first work for the stage, *Zaubernacht,* a "Ballett-Pantomime," as it was called at its premiere in Berlin in 1922. Referred to by the composer himself as a "children's pantomime," the work remains something of a curiosity in his oeuvre. All that survived of the performance materials until quite recently was the piano rehearsal score, which includes occasional details of instrumentation and staging, but two of whose sixty-eight pages are missing. In 2005, however, the parts used for the work's two productions, the second of which took place in New York in December 1925, resurfaced in a vault at Yale University. The discovery has allowed for most of the full score to be reconstructed and added to the Kurt Weill Edition, except for the second of the two framing songs, both of which were cut in the New York production.[7]

With its theme of magically animated toys and intended as entertainment for children, *Zaubernacht* belongs to a venerable tradition of dramatic artifacts, looking back to works such as Tchaikovsky's ballet *Nutcracker* and forward to the movie *Toy Story.* Although the ballet scenario by Wladimir Boritsch has not survived, David Drew constructed the following synopsis based on the various notes in the surviving piano score and a handful of press reports:

> As "the Girl" and "the Boy" fall asleep, the Fairy enters and sings her magic spell. One by one the children's toys, and the characters from their story books, are brought to life. Presently, the children themselves become involved in a phantasmagoria where, for instance, Andersen's Tin Soldier helps rescue Hansel and Gretel. At the end, the Witch is hunted by the assembled company, and at last disposed of. The Fairy then vanishes, the children sink back into a dreamless sleep, and their mother tiptoes into the room to close the curtains.[8]

According to a review of the premiere published in the *Berliner Börsen-Zeitung,* the "delicate pair of children" and "the wicked witch" literally emerged from "the pages of the book . . . a thick volume of Grimm's fairy tale *Hänsel und Gretel.*" All the characters, including the animated toys, "performed dances that were both beautiful and funny, and it was hilarious to see the Kitchen Stove dancing with the Doll or the Ball bouncing around the clumsy Bear."[9]

Before the discovery of the 1920s parts in 2005, previous recent performances of the work relied on the arrangement by Meirion Bowen, which was first performed for the Cologne Triennale in 2000 and recorded with the same performers in 2001. Bowen's version drew on a variety of sources: Weill's annotations in the surviving piano rehearsal score; the original version of some of the music in his string quartet op. 8; and *Quodlibet,* the suite subtitled "four orchestral pieces from a children's pantomime" and scored for double-wind symphony orchestra that Weill assembled in the wake of the ballet's handful of performances and modest success.

Falling into the period of tutelage under Busoni, *Zaubernacht*'s composition can be seen as an almost programmatic realization of Busonian precepts and, as such, an important precursor of the first one-act opera. To the fundamental question posed by Busoni's aesthetics of opera—when and how should music be implemented on the stage?—Weill's ballet responds with functional forms such as dances (gavotte, waltz, can-can) and marches (à la Mahler). The requisite transition to the sphere of fantasy occurs right at the outset with the "Lied der Fee" ("Song of the Fairy"). The central conceit of the song, to use its own descriptions, contrasts the "rigid and mute" daytime with the nighttime of "joyful play and jest." The singer, the toy fairy, who "breathes life into all," invites the toys "into the wide magical realm." "Under the canopy of stars," she sings in lilting tones redolent of the later Weill's *Frauentanz,* "mine is the beautiful world." It is into this realm that Weill's music is conceived to transport us—a world that incorporates his first stage use of popular dance music (the fox-trot, also known in a slightly earlier version as the "Algi-Song"), but that also borrows from his two string quartets, the earlier B minor Quartet and the contemporaneous Opus 8. In that sense the ballet score also subscribes to Busoni's idea of the "unity of music"—music whose essence and purpose transcend the boundaries of genre. *Zaubernacht* is at once a worthy conclusion to Weill's apprenticeship and a springboard to his first full-blown opera.

As early as 16 February 1924, in his first letter to Universal Edition, Weill had stated that he was "working on a full-length stage-work for which *Georg Kaiser* is writing the text."[10] Presumably he meant the "Kaiser pantomime," as he himself described it, and on which he reported resuming work in early summer. In an undated postcard to his sister sent either in late June or early July he wrote that he had befriended the Kaisers, "who have become dear friends and will perhaps become the only people who can replace a part of what I lost with Busoni"; completed a "new large piece, a violin concerto"; and returned "now finally to the Kaiser pantomime."[11] In the earlier letter to Universal, he had listed among his next plans a "new (comic) opera," without identifying the librettist. *Der Protagonist* hardly fits this description—despite comic elements, especially in the first pantomime. It better describes the next collaboration with Kaiser, *Der Zar lässt sich photographieren,* which calls itself an opera buffa; but Weill cannot have been thinking of this just yet.

Concerning *Der Protagonist,* a tragedy with comic interludes, he could write about an "unforced, unintentional dovetailing of opera and pantomime" because the original already contained the structural contrast between play and pantomime. Perhaps not coincidentally, it is a contrast that recalls Shakespeare's

Hamlet and perhaps also *A Midsummer Night's Dream. Der Protagonist* is set, after all, in "Shakespeare's England," as the libretto tells us. An obvious parallel to *Hamlet* is the device of a play-within-a-play, which in both cases provides an ironic counterpoint to the action of the plot proper.

The opera amounts to a cautionary tale about an actor who suffers from a fatal surfeit of talent, a *déformation professionnelle.* So completely does he identify with his role that he can no longer distinguish between art and life. The crime of passion he commits—a confusion of *Dichtung* and *Wahrheit*—results from the way he practices his craft, that is, from *method acting.* At once expressionistically intense and estranged from its own intensity, chiefly thanks to the pantomimes, the work can also be seen as a variant of the genre known in German as *Künstleroper,* opera that treats as its theme "The Artist." Other examples of "artist operas" are Hindemith's *Cardillac* (composed shortly after *Der Protagonist*) and *Mathis der Maler.* Both have a message to convey about the production and reproduction of art; both invite speculation about the artistic views of their creator. Like E. T. A. Hoffmann's figure Cardillac, the nameless Protagonist is absolutely and, moreover, lethally obsessive about his art. How, then, does Weill's first opera reflect his own artistic views? What is the message? What, for better and for worse, is the musical equivalent of method acting?

Absorbed by the demands of the role with which he utterly identifies, the eponymous Protagonist ends up murdering his own sister during rehearsal. It is a *Liebestod* of sorts. He is the lead actor in a troupe of players that, at the outset of the opera, has been invited to present a comedy in the presence of the Duke. With their international audience in mind, they rehearse a wordless pantomime. The sister has a crucial role to play: it is her job to bring her brother back to reality after his high-voltage performances. She is normality; lightness after the creative darkness of his art.

Following the rehearsal it is announced that a bishop is to join the guests; the troupe must switch to something more serious—a tragedy. The horseplay of the comedy, after all, entails a man's adulterous assignations with his mistress while his wife is distracted by a monk—hardly the thing for a visiting bishop. "Turn the backcloth *[Kulissen]* around!" the Protagonist demands; "the rehearsal was in error." (At one point Weill told his publishers that the opera's title had been changed to *Kulissen.*) "It must end in horror," the Protagonist declares, not without dramatic irony.

In the tragedy, which the troupe begins to act out, the monk is replaced by a rich and somewhat dissipated gentleman. In the plot proper, as opposed to the rehearsed pantomime scenes, the Protagonist's sister, to whom he is incestuously close, has been trying all along to disclose to him her own amorous relationship with a young man. When, at the end of the comedy, she tries to break her news to him, he casually dismisses it in a rather incredulous way. But in the midst of the rehearsal of the tragedy, in which he now reacts to his stage wife's own unfaithful activities by drawing a dagger, he fails to snap out of his role as his sister interrupts the action. "Happiness reigns over me," she sings with wide intervals of ecstasy, explaining how she and the young man have been secret lovers until now. "Even you failed to discover anything. Now you will laugh at yourself." But the actor is still caught up in the tragedy. He is anything but amused: "Whoever laughs when he is bruised by a whore . . . The first lie breeds an obscene swarm of more lies." In measured rhythm he exclaims *(in a hoarse whisper):* "This must be nipped in the bud." Whereupon he plunges the dagger into her neck.

Life invades the stage; the stage invades life. For an absolute artist like the lead actor, these two spheres are virtually indistinguishable from each other—fatally so, as the tale tells us. At the very end, after committing the murder, the Protagonist has one final request: the Duke must delay his arrest. "He would otherwise deprive me of my best role, which no longer permits a distinction between genuine and feigned madness." He concludes: "It must be a pleasure for the Bishop and Duke to watch me."

How did Weill go about setting all this to music? This is what he wrote in his program note:

> The melodramatic acting of the protagonist could only be conveyed by an operatic character; the high points of the action could only be expressed by music: the dialogue between brother and sister, the clandestinely hasty love scene, the transition to dance, and the sudden shift from comedy into tragedy. The two pantomimes afforded an opportunity for lyrical expansion. In order to lend the proceedings a musical framework, I gave the eight musicians, as it were, the role of the chorus in Greek tragedy: they are supposed to open the drama, passively accompany it until they themselves intervene, and, at the end, create the impression that we are guests of the Duke and have witnessed the unique performance of the Protagonist.[12]

In terms of the means of presentation, the two spheres of play and play-within-a-play are initially quite separate. Apart from emphasizing the basic divisions of the piece, with its "musical framework," Weill establishes a necessary connection between opera and melodrama: the medium of opera befits melodramatic characters, with traditional operatic means serving the plot proper. The Protagonist's virtuosic vocal lines are those of a dramatic tenor, and the music of love and passion also partakes of this *espressivo* sphere. The rehearsals, by contrast, are presented as pantomimes in a wholly different musical style, a distinction that becomes increasingly blurred during the second pantomime, as art spills over into life. Weill's operatic career begins, then, with a demonstration of his celebrated and oftentimes decried stylistic diversity. Style in opera, however, is more a dramaturgical than a personal matter, as the distinguished critic Oskar Bie recognized in his fine review of the premiere.[13] Writing to his parents on 1 April

1926, Weill proudly noted: "The review by Bie, which I just sent, is according to him the best thing he has ever written about opera."

The review also acknowledged another aspect that would continue to characterize Weill's approach to composition: the critical, constitutive part played by orchestration. Apostrophizing the composer and his work as "the future of opera," Bie admired the "novel and effective way" in which Weill employed the two orchestras "as instrumental material." The traditional opera orchestra in the pit, he suggested, is the material "of life." The orchestra above—an octet comprising two flutes, two clarinets, two trumpets, two bassoons—represents "that of the stage." Yet Bie argues that it is no longer "the old division into principal and stage music. . . . It is a double soul," he writes, going on to report in detail how the stage musicians (in costume) descend during the opening music into the orchestra pit and "take part in the general symphony because the stage is still life to begin with." They climb up again to perform the comical pantomime, but not for the second, tragic one: "life reenters." (The actor's "profession," Bie had remarked earlier in the review, "kills life," at the same time as "life kills the profession".) Only at the end do the musicians remount the stage in order to "blow a fanfare at life with sardonic pomp."

This is archetypical stage music provided for classic dramas. Yet it is also more than that, not "merely" incidental music but an integral part of the work. The stage musicians, as Weill put it, "create the impression that we are guests of the Duke and have witnessed the unique performance of the Protagonist." In a piece whose theme is the confusion of art and reality, it is fitting that the traditional brass fanfares end up no less essential to the plot than the through-composed, fully orchestrated melodrama. The highly charged murder music similarly has a double identity: it is both extrinsic to the theatrical presentation on stage (the play-within-a-play) and part of the "unique performance."[14]

The "stage" musicians are principally responsible for the separation of plot proper and the pantomime within the opera (the musical framework Weill likened to the chorus in Greek tragedy), and it is the music's job first to make the distinction between the two spheres and then to blur it. Their music introduces taut rhythmic discipline generated by repeated figures such as ground basses and ostinati, all of which contrasts markedly with the preceding rhythmic or agogic flexibility that serves the representation of individual expressive intensity. (Relevant here is Henri Bergson's distinction between *temps-espace* and *temps-durée:* abstract, merely quantitative time versus experiential, felt time.) Weill thus pits music that stays in the same place, as it were, through repetition, against music that unfolds in time through development. He does so both in the large and in the small. The pantomimes provide a large-scale, structural contrast, but the interchange can be swifter, especially toward the end of the piece. "Never before in an opera," Bie enthused, "has the plurality of orchestral groups been grasped so spiritually, so symbolically. It is not orchestra here, chamber music there; it is expressive elements of different worlds, the struggle between which is the content of the piece. It is also a drama of the orchestra."

In all these things—pantomimic action, the visibility of instrumentalists, and mechanical, "objective" repetition—Weill exhibits a debt, which he readily acknowledged at the time, to Igor Stravinsky. Others, including Bie, sensed this as well. The critic Siegmund Pisling, for example, writing in the *8-Uhr Blatt der National-Zeitung* on 29 March 1926, thought that the "work betrayed the influence of Igor Stravinsky in the formulation of grotesque-parodistic moods." Bie described Weill's style as oscillating "between the psychological intellectuality of Busoni and the quasi-graphic quality of Stravinsky's writing for winds." Theodor W. Adorno also noted the specific influence of a Stravinsky piece that would remain his all-time favorite, *L'histoire du soldat,* both "on the musical surface and throughout in spirit." Weill himself, too, would cite the *Soldier's Tale* as a model of the mixed genre he was seeking to create.[15]

Where the critics tended to focus on dramatic effect through style, the composer acknowledged Stravinsky's influence in larger formal matters. Both style and form are tied to content, as Bie recognized in his review: "It is expressive elements of different worlds, the struggle between which is the content of the piece." *Der Protagonist* produces a mixed genre almost programmatically, with parodistic pantomime and conventional opera "dovetailed," to use Weill's expression, in the large and the small. It is the kind of mixture that can also be found in much later works of his, even full-length ones, such as *Street Scene,* where stylistic juxtapositions are similarly motivated by dramaturgical considerations to the point of informing the piece's overall form, which in turn conveys content. In a sense, the form *is* the content.

The first pantomime begins with a much-repeated mechanical ground bass in the bassoon, with metrical irregularities (characteristically Stravinskian hiccups) contradicting throughout the established pattern of the opening figure (ex. 3). The score includes the following description of the action and performance instructions:

> *The First Pantomime is performed entirely balletically and unrealistically, with exaggerated gestures, in contrast to the Second Pantomime later, which is to be played dramatically throughout, with vivid expression and passionate moments.* On the left the Wife turns back and entices her Husband to her with languishing gestures.

We also hear these gestures, which provide yet a further foil to the ostinato (ex. 4). Meanwhile, when the husband is eventually alone under his mistress's window, he vocalizes a wordless serenade with a line that inverts the original languishing gestures (ex. 5). And we know exactly when the monk enters the picture thanks to the quasi–Gregorian chant in parallel fourths.

EXAMPLE 3. *Der Protagonist,* First Pantomime

EXAMPLE 4. *Der Protagonist,* First Pantomime *(cont.)*

EXAMPLE 5. *Der Protagonist,* First Pantomime, wordless serenade

Although the *espressivo* music that contrasts radically with that of the pantomime-within-the-opera draws on the conventional language of operatic individuality, the purpose of the story (why else the parodistic parts?) seems to cast the evident excesses of that convention in a critical light. Weill embraces the movement known as expressionism and at the same time distances himself from it. The keyword here is "excesses." The convention as such remains central to Weill's musical language; and the radical split in *Der Protagonist* between objectivism and subjectivism is something the composer bridges in various ways. The wordless vocal parts are lyrical—"lyrically expansive," to invoke his own description—while the accompaniments are mechanically repetitive. And so it will continue: the combination of lyrical expressivity and ostinato-like accompaniments will form the basis of the much-vaunted song style, whose roots can be traced back to Weill's next one-act opera, *Royal Palace,* but whose essential aesthetic dualism is adumbrated already by *Der Protagonist.* With its contrast between melody and accompaniment, it is a style that suggests a parallel with another "song style"—that of Franz Schubert. There are differences, of course. In addition to Schubertian anapests, Weill will draw on modern dance rhythms, and his cantilenas are not exactly Romantic; they are post-Romantic. *Espressivo* in quotation marks, as it were.

Der Protagonist takes as its theme unconditional identification with art, but it does so at a remove, as indicated. This is something that commentators at the time readily appreciated. The opera uses the means of operatic psychology—the late-Romantic tradition—only to have the purpose of those means undermined. Maurice Abravanel, a pupil of Weill's who would become one of his foremost interpreters, put this point in a nutshell when, in his published review of the opera in *La revue musicale,* he praised the work as "the first successful attempt at an opera that moves the audience while leaving its feelings of sympathy completely untouched."[16] Adorno echoed Abravanel's point when, in 1928, he wrote that "the unity of the dramatic figure, hitherto invariably the focus of dramatic music, is dismantled. The pantomime music is rather a means to destroy that unity."[17] In other words, the reception of the piece seems to be making a Busonian point. Rather than inspiring sympathy with the Protagonist, still less identification, the opera is constructed to leave the audience with its critical faculties intact. An "artist opera," it is art about art.

As the setting of a contemporaneous one-act play in terms of both "literature opera" and "artist opera," the first of Weill's three one-act operas has a double-edged relationship to the literary traditions on which it draws. It is both symptom and antidote. By describing Kaiser's spoken play as a "camouflaged drama *à clef,*" meaning a key to the author's own preoccupations, Walther Huder has indicated that this was one of Kaiser's own "Künstlerdramen." Not only does Huder see the author "confessing to the necessity of lies in the business of art," but he also identifies a number of other "typical tendencies." He lists these as "his tribute to Shakespeare, the problem of play and reality, a taste for incest, the hankering after an experience of demonstrative intensity and the incorporation of pantomime into spoken theater."[18] All of the above serve well the central idea of the play: artistic absorption and its attendant dangers. Himself a recovering expressionist, Kaiser no doubt felt ambivalent about these dangers, as must have Weill at this stage.[19] Yet thanks to its setting, with the silent pantomime scenes acquiring a distinctly parodic musical voice, the operatic version only enhances any critical tendency of the original. Kaiser was as much an expressionist artist as he was not one, just as Weill spoke two musical languages: the emotionally charged, "subjective" one of late-Romanticism and its mechanically "objective," neoclassical antithesis.

Der Protagonist is a close relative of the expressionist one-act play, even though its eponymous lead role appears in a more obviously critical light than the typical protagonist of a full-blown exemplar of the genre. The designation of types for main characters (such as "Der Protagonist") is itself typical. The type essentializes, creating distance almost clinically, in a way suggestive of a case study. The "Schwester" is "humanized," of course, with the name Catherine, but otherwise only the three players get individual names (again an ironic inversion). Musical antecedents for expressionist one-act operas can be found in Arnold Schoenberg's prewar monodrama *Erwartung* and the "drama with music" *Die glückliche Hand,* with their archetypical men and women. More immediately, Weill would have been aware of Paul Hindemith's triptych of one-act operas composed between 1918 and 1920 (even though he never entertained performance of his own three one-acters as a group, at most only two of them at one sitting). The first of Hindemith's three, *Mörder Hoffnung der Frauen,* is a rather tame setting of Oskar Kokoschka's 1907 one-act play that set the shape and tone for the entire movement of theatrical expressionism.

Weill's first effort is at once more intense than Hindemith's Kokoschka opera and closer in overall character to the last of the Hindemith triptych, *Das Nusch-Nuschi,* which seems better suited to Hindemith's instrumental playfulness and, with its *Tristan* parody, a more characteristically post- or even anti-Romantic document. Weill's first effort at a one-act opera is, in itself, as ambivalent in its aesthetic purpose as Hindemith's triptych is as a whole. But there was no doubting its theatrical effectiveness at its premiere in Dresden (27 March 1926), thanks in large measure to the sureness, even authenticity, with which Weill embraces different expressive worlds.[20] The largely favorable reception, which overwhelmed the composer, only reinforced his "commitment to opera" and sense of artistic avocation, even if these would take him still further from his expressionist roots. That rapid artistic development, in part a symptom of the eclipse of expressionism in German culture, might account for the relatively small number of productions that took place following the premiere. In 1927 there were just two: in Erfurt and Nuremberg. In 1928 there were four: in Altenburg, Berlin, Frankfurt, and Erfurt. After that, the work had to wait until 1958 for another performance.

The congenial and fruitful collaboration with Kaiser would continue. As mentioned, Weill told his parents that he and the Kaisers had "become dear friends" and predicted that they "will perhaps become the only ones that can replace a part of what I am losing with Busoni," who was gravely ill and would die the following month (on 27 July 1924).[21] Weill and Kaiser even attended the premiere of Berg's *Wozzeck* together in December 1925, just three months before the premiere of their own opera.[22] Before the artistic partnership continued, however, Weill entered into a brief partnership with Iwan Goll. It was certainly an unusual meeting of artistic minds, a collaboration with weaker—or at any rate, less evident—chemistry than that between Kaiser and Weill. It was Kaiser who facilitated their first meeting. But the young composer joined up with the bilingual surrealist at a decisive point in his flourishing career; this brief intersection of their otherwise quite different paths would leave a lasting impression.

ROYAL PALACE

It is in Iwan Goll that Weill found the somewhat unlikely librettist for the opera he envisaged as a companion piece to *Der Protagonist.* On 26 September 1925, with his first one-act opera recently completed and in the middle of negotiations for its premiere in Dresden, he told his publisher that "very soon I will be receiving a new libretto (half opera, half ballet) that I hope to finish by early 1926 and include in the same evening."[23] Although he completed *Royal Palace* on schedule, the hoped-for double bill failed to materialize. Instead, the new work was first given in March 1927, preceded by another Weill composition to a text by Goll, the cantata *Der neue Orpheus,* op. 16. (*Der Protagonist* would eventually be paired, quite successfully, with the third one-act opera, *Der Zar lässt sich photographieren,* also to a libretto by Kaiser. As a double bill, the two received their premiere in Altenburg on 8 April 1928.)

Although not a stage work as such, *Der neue Orpheus* is connected on several levels with the one-act opera. For that reason alone it deserves mention here, but also and especially because it can be seen as seminal in Weill's development. The composer himself said as much, as others have since. In a letter to his parents sent during work on *Royal Palace* toward the end of October 1925, he wrote: "I am dug into this new opera, leaving the house only for the most important outside matters. I must master a form of expression that is still new to me. And I'm pleased to say—as I discovered with *Der neue Orpheus*—that I am gradually approaching 'my real self,' that my music is becoming much more secure, much freer, looser and—simpler."[24]

Weill ascribed the turn in his music to his increased independence, the fact that he felt "more secure, more cheerful and less inhibited." And he gave much of the credit to Lotte Lenya, whom he would marry three months later on 28 January 1926: "It is the only way I can tolerate another human next to me: a conjunction of two different artistic interests, without inner ties, each supported in their endeavor by the other. How long can it last? I hope: very long."[25]

And so it did, in the manner presciently described by Weill—not entirely without inner ties, but with loose, sporadic ones. The expression "without inner ties" *(ohne innere Bindung)* is nonetheless curious. Was Weill playing down his attachment to Lenya, given his parents' apparent disapproval and perhaps also drawing attention to the fact that she was not Jewish? Or was he responding to her lack of such ties, rather than his? To be sure, theirs was an unusual alliance, but over the years some kind of "inner tie" certainly bound Weill to his wife, whom he would end up marrying twice. At times they seemed tied to each other in the way that close siblings are. Weill follows the quoted remark with typical self-ironizing: "Puh, this is becoming a philosophical letter." There would be rifts. As he knew already, the couple's artistic interests were certainly different, enormously so, but they provided long-lasting mutual support.

Another factor in shaping the "new form of expression," in helping him to write music at once "surer, much freer, looser and—simpler," was the text of *Der neue Orpheus,* which could seem in retrospect to be just what Weill was looking for. Kaiser's one-act play had provided an opportunity to breathe the cooler air, if only intermittently, from the Stravinskian planet. Now Goll's poem, a contemporary take on the Orpheus myth, led him further along that path, requiring him to draw freely on traditional idioms as dictated by the bizarre, surreal imagery of the poem.

Goll's poem *Der neue Orpheus,* dating back to 1918, or even 1917, had undergone a significant transformation through several incarnations in two languages. Weill set the substantially revised German text from 1924, one quite different in tone from the almost Whitmanesque original published six years earlier. Between the two German versions there had also been a French one, published in 1923. It makes for a fascinating story of a poem's—and a poet's—development.[26] In the first version Orpheus had assumed the role of the god of art, an almost Christ-like outcast, whose second coming was supposed to bring about universal absolution. The version set by Weill recasts the classical figure of Orpheus as an everyman of the modern city. The "New Orpheus" of 1924 is just a regular guy, a democratic "Musikant," whose job it is to furnish music of various kinds: as piano pedagogue, as variety artist, at the circus, at veterans' gatherings, as emaciated organist, as Mahler conductor at subscription concerts, as "torture pianist" playing in suburban movie theaters.

The centerpiece of the cantata, whose solo violin stands in for the mythical lyre, is a set of seven variations, one for each of the seven incarnations of Everyman Orpheus, in which Weill provides appropriate musical "intonations." We hear the Alberti bass of the piano lesson, the waltz of the variety show, the defamiliarized circus band, the veterans' march, the organist's chromatic meanderings, a Mahlerian scherzo, even a snatch of Wagner's Pilgrims' Chorus. As for Eurydice, who appears at the end, she is the "beloved of longing," representative of "unredeemed humanity," with "too much make-up on her mouth." Is she ultimately unredeemable? And Orpheus, who shoots himself in the train station—is he simply not up to the job? The answer is left open.

If Weill claims to have come closer to his "real self" here, it is not so much to an identifiable style of composition as to an aesthetic stance. Goll's surrealist vision of a demythologized Orpheus trying to find a place in the modern city evidently appealed to a sympathetic musical sensibility. It allowed the young composer to draw on preexisting musical idioms and refunction them in a characteristic way. Busoni's "new classicality" acquires thereby a bluntly ironic twist: Weill tackles the predominant musical myth of antiquity, the myth that fueled the birth of opera and its subsequent reform by Gluck, but he does so with essentially surrealistic means. The classical, even pastoral allusions are there, but they are placed firmly in the urban "now" of the 1920s. That the composition is designed for the concert hall at a time of crisis for that institution only increases the tension between the work's form and its content. It is a concert-hall work, musically and textually, but one that transcends the four walls that contain it. It is a piece of aesthetic propaganda. Weill began an article published at the time he was working on *Der neue Orpheus,* and in which he for the most part rehearses Busonian ideas about musical performance, by bemoaning the "untenable situation of our music business." Concert life, he declared, was "useless, unusable and superannuated."[27]

Read as aesthetic tract, *Der neue Orpheus* can be—and indeed was—seen as a fitting prologue to the ensuing theater piece. Preceded by the cantata at its premiere under the musical direction of Erich Kleiber at Berlin's Staatsoper on 2 March 1927 (the composer's twenty-seventh birthday), *Royal Palace* was much less of a critical success than the piece it was originally supposed to be paired with, *Der Protagonist.* If anything, the critics tended to prefer the cantata. And they directed most of the blame at the librettist. Although the failure does not diminish the opera's general significance for Weill's development, it did mean that he would continue the search for another companion piece. It also meant that *Royal Palace* would soon be neglected, such that the full score was lost. What survives is the published piano-vocal score with its numerous, though not complete, instrumental cues.

This raises a question about the work's authenticity in its surviving form. In 1933, asked about recordings of his own music, Weill rejected most of the gramophone recordings of his music as arrangements. The "correct, the *original* piece of music," he said, "depends exclusively on . . . respecting the composer's own instrumentation"—a principle that guided him throughout his career.[28] One might therefore argue that the loss of the full score of *Royal Palace* and the orchestral parts used in the two productions during Weill's lifetime divests the work of its Weillian signature. In this case, however, there is enough of the recognizable combination of musical elements—in large part thanks to the surviving instrumental cues—to make the 1971 reconstruction seem sufficiently "original" in Weill's sense of the word.

Weill found in Goll's words, both in the cantata and in the opera, one of the sources of the artistic emancipation he claimed to have experienced at the time. By the same token, it is in Weill that Goll claimed to have found the solution to an artistic dilemma. Here is what the poet wrote in the program booklet to *Royal Palace:*

> Lyric poetry is an orphan nowadays, standing begging on the perimeter of the great avenues of the arts. Then princess music suddenly drives by in her high barouche, resounding with stars and flowers. Does she remember that they are blood-related? She lifts the lonely being up into her carriage.
>
> Opera is the most perfect and complete form of poetry.
>
> It doesn't belong to the genre of drama merely because it's played on the stage. Opera and drama are antipodes. The soul of drama is action, plot; that of opera is rhythm. In drama there is thinking, in opera feeling. The material of drama is logic, that of opera is dream. Drama is life, opera is fairy tale.[29]

The metaphorical language of the first paragraph is redolent of the libretto itself, which cries out for allegorical interpretation. The second and third paragraphs accurately define an opera aesthetic that Weill's subsequent career renders somewhat anomalous. Brecht would soon try to turn such ideas on their head (or on their feet, as the later Marxist might have said). Brecht wanted drama with music: not feeling, but thinking; not a fairy tale, but life. And although Brecht and Weill would never agree completely in theoretical matters, it is hard to imagine that Goll's theory of opera would have met with Weill's wholehearted approval. Nonetheless, he seems to have gone along with the spirit of Goll's ideas on "Escape into Opera," as these thoroughly un-Brechtian notes were entitled.

Goll goes on to assert that "the fundamental element for the opera composer is not the sentence, the verse, the dactyl, but the word, the syllable, the vowel. . . . From the word 'Dejanira' [the opera's female protagonist], what has Weill not created! This word plays the principal part in the opera."

The opera begins, not with the word *Dejanira,* or with any word for that matter, but with the single vowel *Ah,* intoned by a "wordless" female chorus against the background of an ideal Italian landscape. (Recall that the singing in the pantomimes of *Der Protagonist* is also wordless.) The three notes intoned correspond, in retrospect, to the first three syllables of Dejanira's name. All four notes of the name finally sound, albeit without their respective syllables, when Dejanira appears on the terrace of the hotel Royal Palace with three men, identified (again in quasi-expressionist manner) as nameless types: her husband, yesterday's lover, and tomorrow's lover. They are joined by a group of "red boys" who jump around Dejanira as they perform a short ballet—one containing lots of modern syncopations borrowed from contemporaneous popular music, for which Weill had already acquired such an absorbent and infallible ear. This change of tone marks a critical step in his development, not just because of the injection of popular music as *couleur locale,* but also because the stylistic contrast is absorbed from the outset into the overall texture of the music—the plot proper, as it were, even though the dramatic concept "plot" is hardly applicable here, as Goll's own commentary suggests.

Montagelike juxtapositions nonetheless remain a central device, as Weill's description "half ballet, half opera" neatly conveys. The next element inserted into the mix is no less "modern": a film. (It would be another ten years until Berg's *Lulu,* with its film sequence. In this connection it is worth nothing that the director of *Royal Palace,* Franz Ludwig Hörth, had previously staged Weill's *Zaubernacht* as well as Berg's *Wozzeck.*) This is the first of three balletlike sequences, set in motion by each of the three men respectively: the husband "[gives] you the rich continent"; yesterday's lover "[gives] you the heaven of our nights," a symbol of the past; the lover of tomorrow "[gives] you eternal nature," a vision of the future. But all is ultimately not enough for the insatiable Dejanira—a figure transplanted, like the new Orpheus, from classical literature (although none of the critics seemed to pick up on that at the time).

Dejanira's mythological origins are hardly auspicious. Wife of Hercules, she killed her husband by accident, in an act intended to secure his love. She gave him a robe steeped in the blood of Nessus, a rival suitor whom Hercules had slain. But the blood acted as a poison, contrary to the dying Nessus's promise, penetrating into Hercules' limbs and causing him intense agony. When Hercules tried to remove the garment, it stuck to his flesh, and with it he ripped away pieces of his body. Seeing what she had unwittingly done, Dejanira killed herself.

The relevance to Goll's libretto is obvious, especially with the implication of a time-honored conflict between the sexes, given here a modern twist. As a representative of womankind, Dejanira sticks to men like the mythological robe. Her attraction tears them to pieces. For their part, the men are incapable of understanding her. They merely project their own fond imaginings. "Poor suitors!" she mocks in chromatically inflected, appoggiatura-rich declamation. "You always cried: Me! Me! Me! I need, love, have you, you, you!" The more they try to possess her, the more she eludes them. "Like children from a playpen, you took pieces of a foreign world and put me in there like a wooden queen."

Dance plays a constitutive role in the piece on more than one level—because of the structural function of the extended choreographed sequences; because of the symbolic significance the types of dance music used in those sequences assume: fox-trot, fugue, and tango; and because of the implied aesthetic polemic attaching to dance in a self-consciously post-Wagnerian age.

Weill already nudges the proceedings into the present with the wordless motif accompanied by modish syncopations. The film sequence does the same thing, with a vengeance, for the husband's gift of the rich continent: three notes blasted out on a car horn (an instrument already introduced after the wordless prelude).

The notes are not any three notes, but the same pitches as the wordless motif, already familiar from the love music of the first pantomime in *Der Protagonist.* They also form, incidentally, the same set of notes that begin the "Moritat von Mackie Messer," the "Lied von der Unzulänglichkeit menschlichen Strebens," and "Surabaya-Johnny." They even provide pitch material for the main motif at the beginning of *Der Weg der Verheissung* and the song "This Is the Life" from *Love Life.* In these later examples, the motif has clear harmonic implications as the linear presentation of a tonal verticality with an added sixth. Here the motif is, for the most part, less obviously harmonic. It suggests a kind of dreamy pentatonicism, suffusing the entire opera with Dejanira's siren call, whether in the ethereal wordless chorus at the opening or here in the fox-trot of the film interlude with the rudest of all modern appurtenances, the car horn. Weill also plays with the motif in the symphonic manner of *motivische Arbeit*—a procedure somewhat ironized by the all-too-modern means of presentation. Even a car horn can do this! And so it does, both at the beginning and at the end of the film interlude. Unity within sonic diversity: the horn imported as ambient noise but made with rudimentary musical means to fit.

Although the film has unfortunately been lost, the piano-vocal score describes it as showing "all contemporary delectations: Dejanira in Nizza, in the sleeping car en route to Constantinople, a ball, Russian ballet, flight to the North Pole, etc." The two main parts of the dance prominently feature the piano to articulate its modish dotted rhythms and syncopations. Apart from supplying the opening and closing material, Dejanira's motif also introduces the second half of the dance, which looks forward to the song style of the *Mahagonny-Songspiel* (ex. 6). The style's key ingredients are already in place: a variably tonal, rhythmically disciplined dance accompaniment beneath a sweeping cantilena marked *espressivo* (here with saxophone and solo violin). The opening harmony is also familiar from many later works: minor tonic with added sixth.

The second interlude, in which Yesterday's Lover gives Dejanira "the heaven of our nights," presents a very different backdrop, with the twelve signs of the zodiac. Dejanira's motif has become a pervasive ornament, like an augmented turn, first in the twinkling celestial textures of the upper woodwinds and strings (as indicated in the piano-vocal score) and then in the melismatic duet of a soprano solo (behind the scenes) and a young fisherman. This sequence concludes with shadows and stars "frenziedly intertwining," again with the opening briefly returning at the end before the beginning of Lover of Tomorrow offers "eternal nature." Eternal nature finds her traditional representation—as fugue. In keeping with the Italian setting, however, the lilting fugue theme is a siciliano (in 6/8 time). Orpheus is supposed to appear as part of this aquatic pastoral setting, followed by "all living creatures, who eventually enact a prayer to the God." (Critics who had read the score in advance noted that they had failed to identify Orpheus

EXAMPLE 6. *Royal Palace,* film sequence (Dejanira's motif)

in the original production, even though his presence was no doubt intended to supply an obvious link to the New Orpheus of the preceding cantata.) Dejanira's complaint of being misunderstood by her "poor suitors" yields to the "Dance of the Waterwoman," here a tango. This, Dejanira's death dance, is an extended ensemble in which both the men and women indulge in the verbal equivalent of *motivische Arbeit,* mixing up the syllables of the word *Dejanira* in different combinations, like Dadaist *Lautgedichte.* The three abandoned men do this, too. The bells of the opening return and then die out as Dejanira's husband appears before the curtain "as if tearing himself away from a deep dream." He cries out in a hoarse whisper, "Help, someone has drowned!"—then jumps himself.

A piece of modish musical property, the tango not only functions appropriately enough as Dejanira's "dance of death," with the traditional erotic connotations, but it also brings about the dissolution of the opera itself into the realm of the purely musical, with only the chopped-up syllables of Dejanira's name left for the singers to intone. The whole amounts to a very rich, verbally "glutinous" piece of more or less obscure symbolism which the critics found for the most part fairly unpalatable. Even Oskar Bie, the most favorably disposed critic, had his problems with the text. "Flowery phrases, decorative images, imaginative perspectives," he wrote, "cannot overcome the somewhat bland odor and essentially very antiquated arrangement of the subject matter." He praised the music with its manifold contrasts demanded by the libretto and an intensiveness that he compared favorably with Křenek's *Jonny spielt auf,* whose "extensiveness," he suggested, was directed more toward superficial effects. But he felt that the composer and librettist had miscalculated the "balance of lyric poetry, drama, scenery, and pantomime." The "overflowing of the scenic apparatus" dominated all the other elements.[30]

Similarly well disposed toward the composer, Karl Holl also criticized the ensemble of elements as "late Romanticism in modern garb." He described "the newness of the dramaturgical design (with automobile, film, revolving stage, circular horizon etc.)" as "merely superimposed."[31] Rudolf Kastner, focusing on these elements, questioned whether the work was an opera at all, finding the label *revue* more appropriate. "Weill," he wrote, "has unreservedly subjected himself to Iwan Goll's 'tragic revue.' . . . How could he be inspired by this book? He wasn't. He leaves a large part of this weak plot to the realm of dance, pantomime, film, and the planet revue."[32]

Rather than let Kastner have the last word, one might spring to the piece's defense by pointing out that Weill and Goll's conception precisely aimed at a provocative hybrid of opera and dance, of classical myth and contemporary setting (as in the cantata). And Weill was no doubt grateful for a libretto that gave him an opportunity to compose such an "absolutely musical" finale in keeping with Busoni's classicism. Whatever its own intrinsic shortcomings, the negative criticism played an important role in that it sealed the fate of *Royal Palace* as a potential companion for *Der Protagonist.*[33] Weill's search would have to continue.

Three-quarters of a century later, in the year of Weill's centenary, *Royal Palace* witnessed a revival. In 2000, two productions occurred within weeks of each other, both using the orchestrated version prepared for a performance in 1971 by Gunther Schuller and Noam Sheriff, one fully staged, the other a concert performance. With the concert performance, part of the BBC Weill festival at London's Barbican Centre, the audience had an opportunity to relish the vast richness of the musical invention, with the inspired peroration, even though they could not relish Weill's actual instrumentation, which must have been lighter and more transparent than the reconstruction. Forced on them as supertitles in all-too-literal translation were the idiosyncrasies of Goll's lyrical invention. (The poet would surely have disapproved, valuing as he did the words' phonetic quality over their semantic content.)

The fully staged production, presented under the direction of Jonathan Eaton at the University of Cincinnati College–Conservatory of Music, interpreted the piece as a prewar political allegory with an elaborate staging, leaving little of the symbolism uninterpreted. Dejanira appeared to be in a sanatorium (a neat way of reconciling plot problems), while her three male suitors literally represented the past, present, and future. According to the director,

> It is logical to associate Yesterday's Lover with a past world, perhaps a threatened, cultivated Germany, perhaps the more liberal-humanist but ultimately ineffectual side of a defeated Prussian-German state. Today's wealthy Husband can be associated with the resurgent industrialists of the struggling Weimar Republic, the Thyssens and Krupps and Voeglers that Hitler so successfully courted. And Tomorrow's Lover, the impassioned, strutting, and incoherent posturer, perhaps with the mad seductions of the fascist world to come. . . . Why are the men, these representatives of past, present, and future, so keen to possess Dejanira? What does she offer them? She seems to be a desperately sought after, redemptive spirit, a female sensibility in a masculine German world, a yearning for Italianate light in a Teutonic consciousness. Perhaps, pursuing particularly German issues of identity, she can be considered a sort of *Germania,* a binding force for disparate factions and peoples. The men, however, no matter how hard they woo her and seek to understand her, are irredeemably obsessed with themselves, with materialism, possession, and an inflated notion of their own passions. They cannot comprehend Dejanira's true nature.[34]

The "perhaps" can be found in the score, in the "Italianate light" (siciliana) and the "Teutonic consciousness" (the fugue). But these are what tomorrow's lover has to offer, before the suicidal tango. Although the libretto posits a rift between the sexes, it does not offer such a neat division between dark and light, male and female. Its sexism—a variant of the Eternal Feminine—is surely more traditional than Eaton suggests. His production functions rather as a political corrective, and not just in terms of sexual politics. Why should tomorrow's lover, by implication, have to be the worst of an already bad bunch? The piece's symbolism invites and then resists consummation. Its message remains equivocal: Dejanira's behavior is both emancipatory and nihilistic, her "modern" tango at once erotic and destructive.

The theatrical potential of *Royal Palace* is no better served by allegorical "director's theater" *(Regietheater)* than it is by a mere concert performance: it cries out for elaborate realization on stage, by all means including the technology with which the short-lived premiere experimented, namely cinema. After all, the modern means can do a vastly more elaborate job than Weill and Goll could ever have imagined when the medium was in its infancy. By way of proving this point, the production at the Bregenz Festival in 2004 offered a high-tech extravaganza, making opulent use of back projection and computerized video. In a symbolic sense, the technology was an end in itself. As the director Nicolas

Brieger stated in his eloquent program notes to the well-received double bill: "The pieces *[Der Protagonist* and *Royal Palace]* reflect the illusion machine that is the theater, thereby bringing us into our own world, in which all information is subjected to permanent visual transformation and none of these pictures can be verified anymore—they point toward our own time of total visualization. The play of reflection and projection, a topic that both pieces deal with, finds itself on stage. It's not that videos are shown as part of the staging; rather, projection is the staging itself."[35]

Early critics were correct in seeing the piece as woven from disparate threads, generically and stylistically. Yet one need not share their negative assessment, especially with fine productions such as the one in Bregenz. Directors face the challenge of bringing all the threads together without committing interpretative violence. And they will find the solution somewhere in the large creative space between historical allegory, on the one hand, and a concert performance, on the other.

DER ZAR LÄSST SICH PHOTOGRAPHIEREN

As he implicitly stated in a short essay written in connection with the premiere, which took place in Leipzig on 18 February 1928, Weill saw his third one-act opera, *Der Zar lässt sich photographieren,* as superseding *Royal Palace,* if not totally suppressing it.

> The opera *Der Zar lässt sich photographieren* was written in the summer of 1927. The necessity arose to write a companion piece for *Der Protagonist,* albeit of a buffo kind, for a full evening in the theater. During a summer stay at the home of Georg Kaiser I reminded Kaiser of an idea about a photographer's camera with a built-in machine gun that he had once mentioned in jest. We invented the character of the typical postwar prince as frequently portrayed in the movies by Adolphe Menjou. Within a few days we drafted the outline together and soon thereafter I received the completed libretto from Kaiser. My collaboration on the draft of the libretto had been directed toward shaping the piece formally as an opera buffa. Having created new musical possibilities with *Der Protagonist* with the invention of a musical frame, the opposition of the eight wind players from the orchestra and the vocal expansion of the pantomimes, I similarly reworked the new text. By adding the male chorus to the orchestra, whose text I put together myself, I attempted to create a connection between stage and audience. In many places I expanded the dialogue to give myself room for small ensembles, arias, buffo duets etc. Finally I believed that an inner build-up, such as I imagined for the flight scene, was only to be achieved by a complete change of tone color. This is why I introduced the gramophone scene, in which I gave a mechanical instrument and dance music plot-advancing significance. For this *Tango Angèle* (as I called it) I could reserve saxophone and jazz sound. After careful gramophone studies I orchestrated this

> self-contained dance piece specifically for gramophone disc and recorded it at Lindström A.G.
>
> This opera concludes a number of one-act operas in the sequence of my works. Currently I am working on the three-act opera *Mahagonny,* whose libretto I have written in close collaboration with Bert Brecht.[36]

No mention here of *Royal Palace* or of the actual number of one-act operas. Weill may or may not have been including in his mental list the *Mahagonny-Songspiel* on which the full-length opera was based. Its composition for the Baden-Baden Festival the previous summer had briefly interrupted work on *Der Zar.* Having received the Baden-Baden commission for a short opera in March, Weill initially turned to Kaiser. He soon discovered, however, that the outline Kaiser and he had drawn up was inappropriate: "it bursts the bounds of Baden-Baden," as he wrote to his publisher on 23 March. He also admitted that it would "be wasted on the snobbism of a music festival. It will be something for the public at large and a wonderful complement to the 'Protagonist.'"[37]

Whether or not Weill included the *Songspiel* among his collection of one-act operas, he soon consigned it, like *Royal Palace,* to the margins of his oeuvre, eventually describing it as a mere "stylistic study." In any event, with the completion of *Der Zar* he was drawing a line in his output, and there are grounds to locate that line both before and after the *Songspiel.* Conventionally, the move from Kaiser to Brecht is seen as a radical shift, and on several levels it was. The *Songspiel* is hardly an opera; its home is not the opera house; nor was it ever seen as a companion piece. It is more provocatively and self-consciously a reform piece. Yet the preceding one-act operas were not without their provocative aspects and did much to prepare the ground. For listeners familiar with subsequent works, especially *Aufstieg und Fall der Stadt Mahagonny, Der Zar* contains many pre-echoes, especially in the dynamic orchestral writing.

Weill's commentary serves, among other things, to demonstrate how he was "in right at the beginning," as he would later say. Kaiser receives some credit, of course, but Weill's persistent use of the first person singular to lay claim to his own intellectual property is striking. According to him, the critical creative decisions were mainly his because they chiefly arose from musical considerations. Not only is the quantity of textual revisions and additions to which he alludes considerable; so is their quality.

Especially pertinent here is the concept of the "musical frame" that informs the conception of *Der Protagonist* and *Der Zar* and that can also be applied to *Royal Palace.* In *Der Protagonist* the frame created by the onstage musicians sets up the principal juxtapositions of the piece: between musical styles, between the two plot levels, between appearance and reality, thereby facilitating multilayered ironies. In *Royal Palace* the frame is delineated by the three sequences centered around the visions of the three men. By means of stylistic contrast the sequences also generate an ironic interplay between illusion and reality. However much they are grounded in reality, especially the husband's vision with realistic film footage and vernacular music, the men's interludes are fueled by their own misguided fantasies. The elusive Dejanira literally slips from their grasp as her name turns into a jumble of vocalized syllables. *Der Zar,* for its part, really has two musical frames. Weill claims authorship for both. The principal one, in evidence throughout, is the men's chorus located in the orchestra. It functions like the knowing camera in a movie, sometimes just humming away omnisciently, at other times pointing to things of which the antagonists are themselves unaware. A further musical dimension, however, is provided by the gramophone scene, again with the all-important tango. If the men's chorus functions centripetally, leading us with its commentary step by step toward the dramatic center of the piece, the gramophone scene, by contrast, is centrifugal. It is located, as it were, at the dramatic center of the piece, timbrally isolated from the surrounding scenes. And yet it spreads its stylistic waves as far back as the Czar's entrance. On a symbolic level his own fox-trot, sounded at his entrance, adumbrates the gramophone's tango.

The opera's title itself changed twice. An early version was the innocent-sounding *Photographie und Liebe,* a phrase that echoes one of the duets between the Czar and his would-be assassin. The love, of course, is anything but innocent. Spoofing the Wagnerian notion, it is likely death. Before the ultimate title was eventually adopted, Weill and Kaiser considered reducing it to *Der Zar lässt sich . . . .* with the nudging triple ellipsis. Their aim was presumably twofold: to have the opening chorus fill in the dots, and to leave the premiere audience guessing at the verb prior to hearing it on opening night. They might not have guessed correctly, especially if they happened to recall the famous censoring ellipsis from published editions of Goethe's *Götz von Berlichingen,* inserted to mask a colloquial idiom considered (at the time) taboo. Although the dots would have nicely reflected the ambiguity of the dramatic situation as well as the intended spirit of the piece, Weill and Kaiser were persuaded to abandon the idea, which Weill's squeamish publishers found unacceptable, as they would the "love" part of the full-length version of *Mahagonny.*

Entering to fox-trot accompaniment as "Monsieur," not as an old-fashioned tyrant, the up-to-date Czar gets both more and less than he bargains for. He wants to appear as a regular citizen by having his photograph taken in everyday dress. He also ends up wanting to have the photographer. But the photographer's appearance is as illusory as his is. In reality she is an impostor, a revolutionary whose aim is to assassinate him. He thinks she is shooting his picture while in reality she has a gun concealed in her camera. Much of the comic tension derives from their cross-purposes, expressed through verbal puns. For example, the leader sings to his accomplice with delicious ambiguity, "Hit the tyrant in the heart." And so she does, but not in the way intended, at least by her. The revolutionary leader is the opera's tenor, a passionate and essentially serious figure. The Czar, by contrast, is a baritone, a would-be Don Giovanni, both serious and comic. His vocal range connects him to the amatory as well as to the "buffa" aspects of his fabled predecessor.

Although Weill likened the musical frame of *Der Protagonist* to a Greek chorus, his description suits the men's chorus in *Der Zar* equally well, if not better. At the premiere production its members wore formal dress: top hats and tail-coats. They literally frame the work, singing the words of the title in unison both at the beginning and (transposed up a half tone) at the end (ex. 7). In between, they spend a fair amount of time, in a way redolent of a children's pantomime, pointing to the cloth covering the camera/gun ("Dort unter dem Tuch"); they affectedly repeat words sung by the cast members; and they hum. For the most part they stand outside the proceedings, creating distance, coming literally and figuratively in between the stage and the audience.

The Czar's quest for normality—at least, normality as he sees it: having his photograph taken in civilian clothing—is futile. As in *Royal Palace,* the tango mediates between desire and death. With the Czar in disguise having allowed himself to be taken in by the terrorist posing as photographer, the gramophone scene brings the cross-purposes of the unlikely couple to a head. The false Angèle winds up the gramophone, not to facilitate love-making, but to provide a foil for her escape. Her name, as Alexander Rehding has suggested, alludes to the image of "the plump naked angel writing with a quill" that appeared on early labels of Berliner's Gramophone Company. Accordingly, there is a sense in which all Angèles are false: "the writing angel becomes a visual euphemism of what is actually a demonic absence. . . . Can such spiritless sounds still be called music," Rehding asks, "or are they merely noise?"[38] Transferring the same argument to the visual realm, it could be claimed that even the "real" Angèle trades in such absences, using modern technology to create soulless two-dimensional images that can be serially reproduced. Normality, indeed!

The tango accompanies the disappearance of the vainly desired female, as it does in *Royal Palace.* Superficially, the gramophone stands as an emblem of the everyday world, like the telephone at the beginning of the opera, which rings when a representative of the Czar calls Angèle to make an appointment. Both pieces of stage property epitomize the clichéd notion of *Zeitoper.* But the tango is much more than that, implicated as it is in an ultimately sinister purpose. If the Czar is going to be modern, he has to expose himself to modern music, with all its seductive dangers. The tango functions on three levels: it gives the piece its contemporary flavor; it serves as an equivocal symbol; and it is an essential ingredient of the opera's dramaturgy.

Comedy in *Der Zar* is, above all, a function of timing. The gramophone scene,

EXAMPLE 7. *Der Zar lässt sich photographieren,* opening motto

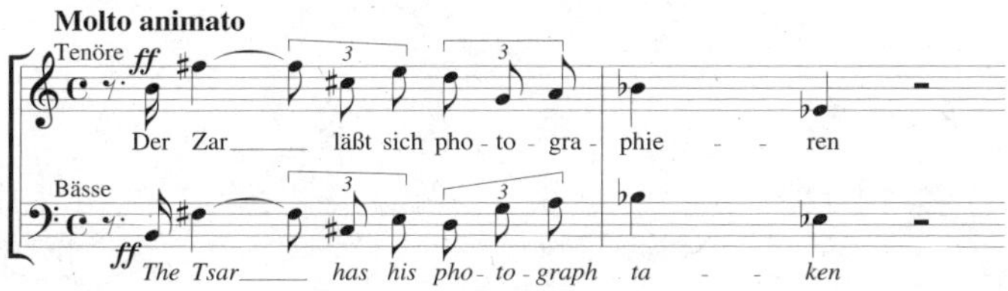

EXAMPLE 8. *Der Zar lässt sich photographieren,* ground bass

juxtaposing mechanically reproduced dance music and live singing, is the only closed musical number. Otherwise Weill generates dramatic tension through a series of more or less discrete poetic-musical periods defined by various musical gestures, which are repeated both in the large and in the small. Ostinato is a common device, often defining the expressive content of each period as well as prolonging suspense. Particularly prevalent is the ponderous, almost funeral march–like theme employed at several points as a ground bass, a kind of fate figure (ex. 8). The dotted-rhythm motif outlining a (usually) rising third can also be found in isolation as the object of developing variation. Its pitch contours seem for their part derived from the opera's opening choral exclamation. The opening itself functions as a complete semantic unit that undergoes its own motivic transformations. The winds occasionally accompany the action with a variant of the opening motif, as if to remind the audience of the ironic connection between the work's title and the action onstage. To similar effect, the motif also sounds at the point where the Czar sings, "How beautiful you are, Angèle!" (ex. 9). Earlier, after his show-off fox-trot, the Czar had begun his seduction of his

EXAMPLE 9. *Der Zar lässt sich photographieren,* motto in orchestra

would-be assassin to the strains of a waltz—a polite prelude to his more blatantly *espressivo* outpourings during the tango. In this way the musical continuity, breathing the rhythms of the comic stage, oscillates between the syntax of social dance, on the one hand, and brief motivically derived orchestral gestures apt for repetition, on the other. The flow of the composition is at once spontaneous and tightly controlled.

Der Zar proved to be a welcome companion to *Der Protagonist,* with which it was frequently paired. But the two works did not become utterly inseparable. Other combinations would occur. A brief anecdote, by way of conclusion, illustrates the limits of reception history in the early years, as well as telling us something about the opera that negatively critical reactions often do better than gushing panegyrics, particularly in the case of art designed to provoke. The month after the premiere in Leipzig, Hans Heinsheimer of Universal Edition wrote to Weill to report the reaction of a representative from the Moscow State Opera, who had written the following:

> Kurt Weill's opera is an excellent work. I should also like to become acquainted with his other works. It is very amusing, of course, but the ideology of this opera precludes any performance in Soviet Russia. The composer is only satirical. He does not take sides. He views the Czar just as satirically as the revolutionaries; the latter even supply the comical part of the opera and we absolutely do not like seeing comical revolutionaries on the stage. Nonetheless I will report on the opera in our journal and consider how one might adjust the content to fit our situation.[39]

The reaction echoes Abravanel's comment about *Der Protagonist:* Weill appears equivocal about his characters, inviting the listener neither to identify nor to sympathize with them. Yet the revolutionaries are not wholly comical. Perhaps if he had listened more closely to their leader, the Russian commentator would also have heard a passionate operatic tenor, not just a comic caricature. The leader sings a familiar musical language. In itself, however, it is hardly comic, but stirring and dramatic. For it is the juxtaposition of the starkly contrasting elements that creates the overall, lasting effect, something that is both satirical and comical—a modern opera buffa.

Weill's one-act operas document his successful attempt to establish himself as a composer for the theater. Both hoped for and, to a degree, realized with these works, his ultimate aim was to compose material for a full evening in the opera house. In this sense, the one-act operas form a self-contained group of works as well as stepping stones to the full-length works that followed. Although he would eventually turn his back on state-subsidized theater, all three operas belong, institutionally speaking, to that world, however much they also challenge its values and assumptions. Yet there are telling differences between them, partly because Weill conceived the operas to complement one another in various ways and partly because of his rapid development during this period.

All three treat the thematic opposition of appearance and reality, in each case brought to the fore by the metadramatic use of a musical frame. All three articulate the frame through blatant stylistic contrast. Although none of the operas is strictly speaking a number opera, they all include interpolated numbers as part of the frame, kept separate from the surrounding material by virtue of the radically different style invoked. The musical diction in each is, however, quite distinct. *Royal Palace,* a surrealist dream, is the least conversational of the three, while *Der Zar* is the most.[40] *Der Protagonist* radically juxtaposes conversation and wordless pantomime. Ultimately one can see why Weill continued the collaboration with Kaiser and not with Goll. He wanted his music for the theater to mediate between life and dreams—an endeavor germane to the two Kaiser operas and, above all, to the "play with music" *Der Silbersee.* But this last piece would come only toward the end of Weill's partnership with Bertolt Brecht, which had begun during the composition of *Der Zar* with the creation of a new genre, the "Songspiel." While both pieces—*Der Zar* and *Mahagonny*—contain the rhythms of the fox-trot, sharing common melodic material, the differences are as marked as the similarities. Whereas the Czar bursts into the opera with his fashionable dance, contaminating the spheres of high and low, both socially and artistically, the *Songspiel* raucously commences with it, following the cue of a gun shot. The symbolic significance attaching to the dance may remain the same, but the aesthetic context has shifted. The gentle provocations of the 1920s opera buffa have become decidedly ruder, coarser, more "in your face," with the traditional set of the opera house supplanted by a boxing ring. A new stage, indeed!

4

"Songspiel"

Which came first, the *Mahagonny* "Songspiel" or the *Mahagonny* opera? Regarding their performance history, the answer is quite straightforward. *Mahagonny: Ein Songspiel nach Texten von Bert Brecht* received its premiere at the festival Deutsche Kammermusik Baden-Baden on 17 July 1927.[1] After supplying the credit "by Kurt Weill," the program went on to characterize the work as "the small epic piece." The full-length epic opera *Aufstieg und Fall der Stadt Mahagonny,* whose text was credited solely to Brecht, followed nearly three years later, with a premiere in Leipzig on 9 March 1930. Both premieres sharply divided critical opinion. Both, but especially the opera, provoked a scandal.

With respect to their genesis, however, the sequence of the two works is harder to determine unequivocally. In a note written at the time of the opera's premiere, Weill stated that he had already begun the full-length work before undertaking the "Songspiel." Yet there are reasons to doubt him. The opera effectively suppressed the "Songspiel," which after the premiere received just one more production in Germany prior to its publication and revival in the 1960s. By asserting that the project for the opera came first, Weill appeared, with hindsight, to be emphasizing the provisional character of the Baden-Baden piece. Backdating the opera's inception as far as possible also helped him to counter an accusation of plagiarism.

Another, quite different account of the genesis came from Hans Curjel, dramaturg at the Berlin Kroll-Oper in the late 1920s. Writing in 1972, Curjel claimed to have been responsible for persuading the composer to undertake the opera project only after the *succès de scandale* of the "Songspiel" had occurred.[2] Which version of the story is correct? Answering this question is hardly a straightforward matter. To be taken into account is the admittedly self-serving nature of Curjel's story as well as the circumstances influencing the composer's own testimony. Yet another—indeed, perhaps the principal—complicating factor is how little we actually know about the beginning of the partnership with Bertolt Brecht.

THE BEGINNING OF THE PARTNERSHIP

Exactly when, where, and how Weill and Brecht came together remains something of a mystery. Chiefly because of the paucity of available primary sources, accounts in the numerous secondary sources, including the memoirs of friends and acquaintances, tend to be either vague or full of speculation and conjecture. The favorable conditions under which they worked make it correspondingly hard to reconstruct their movements. They were both living in Berlin: Brecht in Wilmersdorf, Weill in neighboring Charlottenburg (in the year 2000 the two boroughs were joined together with a hyphen as Charlottenburg-Wilmersdorf). Any correspondence between them from the period prior to enforced exile in 1933 is nonexistent, or at least has not survived. And unlike the inhabitants of the fictitious Mahagonny who plaintively enquire, "Is here no telephone?" they were able to call each other whenever they wished. Even Weill's frequent letters to his publisher, normally an indispensable guide to the genesis of his works during these years, leave some crucial gaps in the story.

Here is David Drew's version of their coming together from his classic essay "Kurt Weill and His Critics." Drew begins with an extended simile that nicely captures the unavoidable note of uncertainty surrounding the whole matter:

> It was as if two "highly gifted" men from different lands had chanced to meet in the twilight at the point where their paths crossed. Each, as it were, had liked the tone of the other's voice without understanding much of what the other was saying; and since neither was quite sure of finding his way in the gathering darkness, they had agreed to repair to a nearby inn. After a mug or two of ale their language difficulties had seemed to dissolve and their conversation about the deplorable weather conditions in those parts had turned to a discussion of the state of the world. This, they had agreed, was no less deplorable, but certainly more susceptible to human influence once it was seen for what it was. On that assumption they had commenced work on the opera *Mahagonny.*
>
> It was a collaboration that would hardly have survived long enough to produce a single work, let alone six in the space of three years, but for a high degree of self-deception and mutual incomprehension. It remained feasible so long as the characteristic tension was confined to the subconscious creative levels and was no stronger than the natural affinity between such dissimilar yet strikingly complementary minds. But once the tension had begun to manifest itself in terms of the age-old rivalry between words and music, it gained in strength what it lost in meaning.[3]

Drew's figure of speech does not translate back into a factual narrative; the invoked "darkness" corresponds to the state of our knowledge of the event. Of course, the figure of speech is not meant to describe the actual meeting between Brecht and Weill. Rather it conveys, however allusively, Drew's own interpretation of the partnership, with the full-length opera as its center. What does the "gathering darkness" stand for, the "nearby inn," the "deplorable weather conditions in those parts"? What is the connection between the so-called local weather and the state of the world? Why is the state of the world more susceptible to human influence than the local conditions described here in terms of the weather? How and when did Weill and Brecht actually begin work on the opera? The narrative derives not from the meeting itself, but from an interpretation of its consequences. The fictional origin has the job of representing the essence of the historical whole, and the historical whole has more to do with the opera than with the "Songspiel."

Drew thus introduces some of the key issues surrounding the partnership once it was established, at least as he sees them: mutual incomprehension, tension, dissimilar yet complementary minds, a rivalry between words and music. His point of retrospection is the rift over the opera, the work in which the tension and rivalry became manifest, quite obviously so in Brecht's theoretical notes on the piece and in the reported falling-out at the time of the Berlin production in 1931. According to impresario Ernst Josef Aufricht, Brecht went so far as to denounce Weill as "a phony Richard Strauss."[4] Later in Paris, while working on the sung ballet *Die sieben Todsünden,* a brief but also fraught resumption of the collaboration, Weill remembered his work on the *Mahagonny* opera from three years earlier as a "battle against B."; he and Brecht "had become enemies."[5]

About their dissimilar minds, even mutual incomprehension, Weill would make the following statement in a 1934 interview, a full year after their collaboration on *Die sieben Todsünden:* "I almost have the impression that Brecht was going through a period in which he actually despised music."[6] Brecht's comments about music tend to sound like those of a recovering music lover. He had his reasons both to love and to hate music. He was, above all, wary of its power. And he was loath to cede that power to a collaborator. Privately, Weill had admitted to Felix Jackson, librettist of the unfinished opera *Na und?:* "Music has more impact than words. Brecht knows it and he knows that I know. But we never talk about it. If it came out in the open, we couldn't work with each other any more."[7] Brecht's notorious business dealings, about which Weill complained on occasion, also took their toll. So much for the ending of their relationship—chronologically, personally, and aesthetically. The work in Paris, which involved other mutually estranged émigrés and occurred to all intents and purposes *after* the Weill-Brecht partnership had already been dissolved, must have been strained (to say the least) for personal as well as artistic reasons.

One of the earliest documents of possible relevance to the beginning of the partnership is the letter from Weill to Lenya dated 24 March 1927. Weill writes about "Baden-Baden . . . pressing me about the one-act opera," and then closes by saying enigmatically that he had to "go see B."[8] If "B." is Brecht, then Weill is already indicating acquaintance, if not familiarity. The previous day, in the middle of intensive work with Kaiser on *Der Zar lässt sich photographieren,* Weill had written to his publisher saying that this piece would be too large to fulfill the Baden-Baden commission for a short opera, adding that it would in any case "be wasted on the snobbism of a music festival." He was considering instead setting scenes from *Lear* and *Antigone.*

Weill's comment about the "snobbism of a music festival" is both remarkable and telling, especially in light of the piece he was soon to write for Baden-Baden. A similar sentiment would be voiced years later by his wife, Lotte Lenya, who sang in the first performance of the "Songspiel." Shortly after Weill's death, Lenya wrote to music critic Olin Downes: "I never forget the horror he created at the music festival in Baden-Baden in 1927, when he suddenly had stoped *[sic]* writing atonal music and wrote the first short version of 'Mahagonny.' I still can see his colleagues rushing up to him after the performance and almost shouting at him: 'Weill, do you know what you're doing? You are writing in G major.' And Kurt smiled and said very calmly: 'I know, what's wrong with it? It's not a new invention.'"[9] And in an interview she gave in 1971, Lenya recalled that Baden-Baden was "at that time what I would call now Tanglewood . . . very highbrow." She continued: "It was quite shocking for the people in the middle of that culture-carrying crowd. . . . *Mahagonny* was so new, it was so entirely new. Real avant-garde, you know, for a festival like that: to come into a highbrow festival with *tunes* again. At that time it was all atonal music, and here was somebody who wrote tunes people could sing. Like a Verdi or a Puccini. That was the great sensation."[10]

Like Weill before her, Lenya offers a clue to the "horizon of expectation" that informed the piece's purpose and impact. According to her, the shock of the new derived not so much from the piece's dissonances as from its lyrical tunes—from the all too familiar (the tunes parodying popular idioms) rather than the absolutely new. By introducing a kind of cultural property not usually expected at an avant-garde festival, Weill and Brecht had created, as it were, a piece of inverted snobbism.

Another relevant document from the time of the work's inception is the review of Brecht's play *Mann ist Mann* that Weill wrote as the regular musical correspondent for the radio journal *Der deutsche Rundfunk* on the occasion of the work's broadcast. The review, published on 27 March 1927, had an almost apologetic tone: "A poet, a real poet," Weill enthused, in the manner of one of his own manifestos from the time, as though the alliance between the two had already been formed. Perhaps it had. "In the unproblematic, vibrant plot," he noted, "in the infinite richness of the language, which runs the whole gamut of modern humor, and in the unusual terseness of the form, there can be seen a new kind of dramatic production, which acquires significance as the manifestation of a new type of person." In 1931 Weill would supply incidental music of his own for a production of *Mann ist Mann,* putting his musical money, so to speak, where his critical mouth was.

Weill's initial involvement with *Mann ist Mann,* previewing and then reviewing its broadcast, was undoubtedly an impetus for him to stake out his own territory as a new type of composer. After receiving a commission from the Festival of German Chamber Music in Baden-Baden to write a short opera, he had at first hesitated. As mentioned, he considered submitting *Der Zar* but soon dropped the idea, perhaps because things were already brewing with Brecht. Nor did scenes from *Lear* and *Antigone* seem to get him anywhere. Then, in early May, he wrote to his publisher of his "very nice idea" to write a "Song-Spiel." He had decided to set the "Mahagonny Songs" from Brecht's poetry collection *Hauspostille,* whose title can be translated as "Domestic Breviary," intended to invoke Lutheran allusions but with contents anything but pious, still less Protestant. Since the *Hauspostille* had been published only the previous month, in April, it is conceivable that his reading of that collection, along with his enthusiasm for *Mann ist Mann,* prompted the idea of a collaboration with Brecht.[11] Conversely, it is possible that he had had some direct contact with Brecht, the details of which remain unknown, which in turn prompted his enthusiasm for *Mann ist Mann* and his reading of the *Hauspostille.* Lenya, in any event, recalls that it was Weill who first approached Brecht, not the other way round.[12] Perhaps he did so even prior to the broadcast of *Mann ist Mann.* Brecht may even have given him an advance copy of the *Hauspostille* on 24 March, if "B." was indeed Brecht.

It is also possible that the two may have met as early as 1925 in connection with a meeting of the Novembergruppe, the group of left-leaning artists from various media, including painting, architecture, and music, that formed in December 1918 and took its name from the German revolution that had occurred the preceding month, at the end of World War I and prior to the establishment of the Weimar Republic in 1919.[13] At the end of a report for *Der deutsche Rundfunk,* which mainly deals with the occasion's musical offerings, Weill mentions Brecht's having read his own poetry that evening in 1925, "even though [his] significance lies more in drama."[14]

Be all that as it may, who approached whom, when and where and for what reason—these are questions that may never be definitively answered. How the partnership literally began will remain a mystery, at least until further documentation is unearthed. What we do know are the circumstances under which the partnership began to flourish. Whether those circumstances included work on the opera before any on the "Songspiel" is something for which there is some circumstantial but certainly no conclusive evidence. As early as 1924 Brecht had jotted down in his diary the words "Mahagonny-Oper" in connection with "Mar," the opera singer Marianne Zoff, his wife at the time.[15] And there has survived a brief outline entitled "Auf nach Mahagonny!!!" from the time of his coming together with Weill that describes a cabaret diva named Irma who parodies contemporary hit tunes.[16] It is to the title of this outline (coincidentally the opening words of the "Songspiel") that Weill would refer in his account of the genesis.

In any event, it was with the fulfillment of the Baden-Baden commission that the partnership with Brecht really took off. Between his receiving that commission and the work's premiere, Weill was approached to write music for *Das Ruhrepos,* a musico-dramatic documentary about the industrial region known as the *Ruhrgebiet,* and in June he and Brecht traveled together for preliminary discussions with city officials in Essen and to familiarize themselves with factory life, including a visit to the Krupp steelworks. (The project, however, was eventually canceled.) Was Weill misleading his biographers, then, when he published a version of the story that suggests a genesis of the *Mahagonny* "Songspiel" and opera somewhat different from the one sketched here on the basis of the scant evidence available? This is what he wrote in the month of the full-length opera's tumultuous and highly controversial Leipzig premiere in March 1930:

> It was already at my first meeting with Brecht early in 1927, in a conversation about the possibilities of opera, that the word "Mahagonny" cropped up and, along with it, the idea of a "paradise city." In order to develop this idea, which instantly took hold of me, and to try out the musical style that I envisaged, I first of all set the five Mahagonny songs from Brecht's *Hauspostille* and assembled them in a small dramatic form, a "Songspiel," which received its premiere in Baden-Baden in the summer of 1927. This Baden-Baden *Mahagonny* is nothing but a stylistic study for the opera, which, already begun, was continued after the style had been tried out. Brecht and I worked on the opera's libretto for almost a year. The score was completed in November 1929.[17]

The critical part is the "already begun." Exactly when—and to what extent? Weill seems to contradict himself, having previously said, "I first set. . . ." At any rate, he would have a very real need to repeat this story when, a few months later, following the Leipzig premiere, he and Brecht were accused of plagiarism by the author Walter Gilbricht, a resident of that city. In their defense, Weill again referred to the earlier incarnation of the *Mahagonny* material as merely a "study work *[Studienwerk]* for the opera." He also drew attention to Brecht's sketches and drafts for a piece to be called "Auf nach Mahagonny," drawn up in the course of his discussions with Brecht in March 1927.[18] The date is not necessarily accurate, however, since Weill goes on to state that the "Songspiel" was also written in March, two months earlier than it really was.

Having finished his play *Die Großstadt mit einem Einwohner* (The Metropolis with a Population of One) in 1927, Gilbricht had offered it to Erwin Piscator in the spring of 1928. Piscator, with whose theater Brecht was associated, rejected it, or at least ignored it. Correspondences between the texts of the two works are indeed "striking," as the press report by Fritz Voigt put it at the time: "In both cases, the city is founded by three not exactly honorable people in a desert; in both, an avaricious woman is the motivating element for the founding; in both, because of their greed, people become the objects of the big business of the metropolis. . . . Finally a higher power intervenes (a world war and a hurricane, respectively), destroying the business of the metropolis. Inflation ensues and the whole comes to a tragic end: Mahagonny goes up in flames, [Gilbricht's] metropolis freezes." Apart from these basic parallels between the two works' plots, moreover, there are some more specific ones, such as references to Alaska, leading Voigt to the conclusion that "one of these two authors must have been influenced by the other!"[19]

Gilbricht appears not to have pursued his plagiarism charge in any formal way, however. The question remains: did Weill and Brecht begin work on the opera *before* the "Songspiel" and hence conceive the latter from the start as a "stylistic study" with the intention of proceeding to the full-length opera? Hans Curjel thinks not:

> We do not know in detail what came to pass. However, it cannot have been anything other than Weill, with the Baden-Baden commission in hand, visiting Brecht and making the suggestion to write something from the poems, music, and some other ingredients that would pass as "scenic" for Baden-Baden. . . . It was Weill's hour. The spark came from him, he had brought in Brecht. . . . Weill and Brecht returned to Berlin, where the echo of the *Mahagonny* performance had reached. But no further performance of the short *Songspiel* was forthcoming. New plans were envisaged, among them, at my request, the expansion of *Mahagonny* into a full-length piece, which we considered giving at the newly opened Kroll-Oper under Klemperer. But things dragged on. Weill and Brecht were two great men with much to do.[20]

The matter may seem as inconsequential as Curjel's account is self-serving. On a purely factual level, the composition of the opera grew out of the "Songspiel," not the other way around. That Weill should wish to play down the significance of the earlier work is characteristic and also understandable in view of the central position the opera had meanwhile acquired for him, eclipsing in scale and importance all the other stage works written up to that point with Brecht, the two "plays with music" *Die Dreigroschenoper* and *Happy End*, the cantata *Der Lindberghflug*, and the radio commission *Das Berliner Requiem*. Yet the relationship between the two versions of *Mahagonny* is not simply one between *chef d'oeuvre* and *parergon*, between main work and occasional piece, as suggested by Weill's term "stylistic study" and by his official account of the opera's genesis.

The "Songspiel" served its purpose as a provocative contribution to the opera discussion of the 1920s, a discussion that questioned the traditions of the genre from both a formal and an institutional perspective. Besides, "stylistic study" is hardly an appropriate description insofar as the "Songspiel" marks a stage in a musical development already started before Weill's collaboration with Brecht, one that culminates in his cultivation of the austere classicism of the didactic piece *Der Jasager* (1930), a thoroughly different style. This new style (Weill called it "responsible") also leaves traces in the *Mahagonny* opera as well as in *Die sieben Todsünden*. The full-scale opera, in other words, is not stylistically congruent with the "Songspiel." Nor is the style of the "Songspiel" wholly new, even if in the context of Weill's theater works the "song" as such is.

If Weill had indeed begun by discussing the possibilities of opera, as opposed to creating the "Songspiel," the partnership with Brecht also came to grief with their attempt to give the "Songspiel" experiment a full-scale operatic treatment. As suggested by Drew's remarks, it might be more appropriate to ask how the partnership could have lasted so long.[21] On a personal level, their relationship was never close; remarkably, perhaps, they always retained the formal mode of address, *Sie* instead of *Du*. Concerning Brecht, Weill's letters to Lenya contain mainly negative bickering, especially during the American years. Brecht's devious, covetous way of doing business, in particular, was a constant source of frustration for Weill.

Artistically, their collaboration seems to have been predicated on a number of fruitful misunderstandings, as Drew has indicated. Politically they had a common sympathy for liberal causes (whether to do with local or global conditions), but Brecht developed a marked affinity for Marxist theory and practice; Weill did not. In fact, this affinity sharpened precisely during the fruitful years of the collaboration, such that Brecht sought retroactively to correct and sharpen the works' political messages. In this spirit he revised the texts of *Die Dreigroschenoper, Der Jasager, Der Lindberghflug*, and even the opera version of *Mahagonny* for publication in his collected works, the *Versuche*. In doing so he at once belied and confirmed the provisional concept of *Versuch* ("experiment"). Although both Weill and Brecht were interested in opera, the actual formulation and realization of their ideas eventually proved those ideas to be incompatible. As Drew remarks, and as Aufricht's anecdote about the *Mahagonny* rehearsals suggests, the differences boiled down to the age-old question of the primacy of music. Ultimately they seemed happier working together in mixed genres, such as the "Songspiel" and the "plays with music," where the question of music's primacy was not so acute, rather than in opera proper, which belatedly brought to light their artistic and personal differences.

Despite these differences, Brecht had much to learn from Weill's own ideas about opera reform, themselves adapted from those of his teacher Ferruccio Busoni. The influence was reciprocal. The new collaboration brought Weill, on the one hand, a broadening of his institutional horizons and, on the other, a willingness to experiment with different types of singers. Yet these were developments already under way. Brecht's first wife, as mentioned, was an opera singer for whom he had originally conceived the idea of a *Mahagonny* opera in 1924. Weill's wife was a singer, though hardly one whose natural habitat was the opera house. It had been Kaiser who had introduced Weill to Lenya; Weill and Lenya were already married the year before Weill began working with Brecht. And it was Lenya's last-minute addition to the "Songspiel" that inaugurated the experimentation with nonoperatic singers, one of the piece's evident novelties.

INSTITUTIONAL HORIZONS

A brief note at the bottom of the program for the Baden-Baden premiere of the "Songspiel" addressed the matter of institutional horizons head on. There it states: "In his more recent works Weill is moving in the direction of those artists of all forms who predict the liquidation of arts engendered by established society *[gesellschaftliche Künste]*. The small epic piece *Mahagonny* merely takes the logical step from the inexorable decline of existing social structures. It already addresses an audience that naively demands its fun in the theater."[22]

Again, the immediate addressees should be borne in mind. Weill and Brecht were making their programmatic statement at a music festival devoted to avant-garde experiments. The audience in attendance was hardly one that "naively demands its fun in the theater," as the program describes the people for whom *Mahagonny* was allegedly conceived. In view of this anomaly, the statement itself could be seen as nothing less (but also nothing more) than a nose-thumbing provocation directed at "established society." As artists proclaiming the overturn of existing social structures, Weill and Brecht were merely rehearsing the uprising, hardly enacting it. Weill himself recognized this when he wrote a year later, apropos *Die Dreigroschenoper*, that "nearly all worthwhile operatic experiments in recent years have been basically destructive in nature."[23]

As the work of a reformer, the "Songspiel" is the kind of reform that does more to rudely sweep away the old than create the new. Many of the pieces after it, on the other hand, can be said to subscribe to Weill's philosophy of social construction—that is, they are *gesellschaftsbildend*, as opposed to *gesellschaftlich*. If the "Songspiel" is a study, it is of the kind that ends up blowing the roof off the institution in which it is being conducted.

Yet there is also a sense in which the composers for the Baden-Baden festival were being actively encouraged to challenge conventions. In his essay on the history of the festival that he contributed to the Baden-Baden program in 1927, Heinrich Burkard, one of the codirectors (along with Joseph Haas and Paul Hindemith), described "the guiding thought" behind the commission of the one act-operas:

> a retreat from grand "opera," with its giant apparatus, and the creation of a stage work with only a small cast, with music that is pure chamber music in scale and treatment, and with minimal scenery. If Toch's "musical fairy tale" *[Die Prinzessin auf der Erbse]* can be seen as a reduced opera, then Milhaud's "Opéra-Minute" *[L'enlèvement d'Europe],* Weill's "Songspiel," and Hindemith's "Sketch" *[Hin und zurück]* also come close to realizing the envisaged new type: the comic stage-capriccio, bordering on the neighborhood of the revue, little concerned with truth, logic, and psychology, speaking the unaffected, realistic language of the present, and aspiring to be nothing more than an entertaining "piece of theater" *[Theater-Spiel].*[24]

Weill's settings of Brecht's poems met the terms of the commission inasmuch as they followed Burkard's recipe for an "entertaining *Theater-Spiel*" in a novel and provocative way. The label "Songspiel" (initially spelled "Song-Spiel" by Weill) conflates old and new with a pun that combines the German tradition of singspiel and the modern American song. Unlike the vernacular singspiel, comprising arias, duets, and ensembles interspersed with spoken dialogue, the "Songspiel" consists of a sequence of vocal numbers in "song" form interspersed with instrumental interludes. The interludes (Kleiner Marsch—Vivace—Vivace assai—Sostenuto [Choral]—Vivace assai) accompany the scene shifts, yet they have more than a merely incidental function. Weill extensively, though not exclusively or uniformly, employs his so-called *Songstil.* "Song" form and "song style" are not synonymous. The forms of the popular American song are new to his musical theater works, but the style itself is not (having been introduced in earlier works). Insofar as the composite noun *Songspiel* can also be understood as a "playing with songs," the distance implied from both the singspiel and the song is equally great.

The term would later have two connotations for Weill. One was the sense that fits *Mahagonny,* namely "a new form between concert and theater," as he wrote to his publisher in 1929. His idea was to publish in a single volume "Three Songspiele by Weill and Brecht—1. *Mahagonny* Songs [that is, the Baden-Baden version], 2. the *Berliner Requiem,* and 3. the *Lindberghflug,*" and to have them performed together.[25] The idea was never realized, nor did the label *Songspiel* ever stick to the other two works. (In a letter dated 16 December 1929 to Universal Edition, Weill referred to *Der Lindberghflug* as a "bona fide concert work.")[26] He also used the same term in 1932, when contemplating a concert version of *Happy End,* to connote a sequence of songs lifted from their original theatrical context but with connecting dialogue.[27] In 1927, however, the new coinage, applied to just one piece, was more than just a neutral designation to describe a sequence of pieces largely in song form. Rather, it must have come across as a willful corruption of the German tradition of opera represented by works such as Mozart's *Entführung aus dem Serail* and *Die Zauberflöte* or Albert Lortzing's *Zar und Zimmermann,* the latter perhaps the best-known example of the lighter genre called *Spieloper.* Weill himself had described the context for such an interpretation in 1925. "*Singspiele,*" he wrote, had begun as "small, harmless pieces," but in Mozart's hands they had become "the foundation stone of 'German' opera."[28]

But it is to another classic of German opera that Weill specifically alludes in the music: Weber's *Der Freischütz,* technically also a singspiel. (One other quite specific musical allusion, of a very different kind, occurs later in the piece, as discussed below.) In 1926, invoking the opinion of his teacher Busoni, Weill had put Weber at the top of the list of those composers whose "huge facility" connected them to Mozart.[29] Here, in the opening "Mahagonny-Song," Weill quotes Weber's "bridesmaids' chorus" at the words "schöner, grüner Mond von Alabama." How campily surreal! In the opera, the bridesmaids celebrate their chaste bride, Agathe. Here, in the "Songspiel," the men await their "Weiberfleisch" (female flesh), that is, the girls from Mahagonny. The American "song" part of the punning equation literally precedes the "Singspiel" part: at their first entrance, to fox-trot accompaniment, the male singers deliver their exhortation "Auf nach Mahagonny!" with a very different allusion.

This opening, as Jürgen Schebera has noted, can be heard as a reference to "Komm nach Mahagonne," the well-known song by hit-tune composer Leopold Krauss-Elka, recordings of which, as well as two sheet-music versions, had been in circulation since 1922.[30] Subtitled an "African shimmy" with an oxymoronic "slow shimmy tempo," the song is really a cakewalk. Musical parallels between Weill's sprightlier fox-trot and Krauss-Elka's mislabeled "shimmy" seem to be nonexistent. There are textual ones, however. Where "Komm nach Mahagonne" stutteringly repeats the *Zieh-* of *Ziehharmonika,* in a kind of poetic word-painting (the instrument is being pulled out, not pushed in), Brecht copies the device, to less innocent effect, by repeating the first syllable of *Zivilis,* a play on *Syphilis* and *Zivilisation.* Which of them is "cured there," as the words claim? (The words are poignant, given that Baden-Baden was then, as now, a famous spa town!) Brecht has transformed the utopian "Mahagonne" of Krauss-Elka's hit into the rather different "Mahagonny" of his poetry collection. All the more reason, then, especially in light of the context of the commission and its first performance, to hear the first number as a veritable clash of musical cultures—a mixed genre, indeed.

Weill did not set the poems from the *Hauspostille* as he found them. After Brecht had agreed to the plan, Weill divided the piece into three parts: Prologue, Life in Mahagonny, and Finale (the latter being a textual addition). Another departure from the original entailed moving the pidgin-English "Alabama-Song" and the "Benares-Song" from the end of the cycle to the first part and the second part, respectively. Among the music Brecht had included in the *Hauspostille* is a setting of the "Alabama-Song" done in collaboration with the composer Franz S. Bruinier. The similarities with Weill's own setting, such as they are, are purely rhythmic, however. The melodies are quite different, with Weill's having much wider intervallic contours. Weill also links the songs with four instrumental interludes for the ten-piece orchestra.

Names are used to distinguish the six members of the cast (sopranos, Jessie and Bessie; tenors, Charlie and Billie; basses, Bobby and Jimmy), but beyond that they do not acquire any individual identity. When they sing in the first person, it is the plural. Their job is largely narrative: to tell the story of Mahagonny. As the first "Mahagonny-Song" tells us, it is a city with four main attractions: whiskey, women, horses, and poker. All of these pastimes involve "the next little dollar" ("Alabama-Song")—five dollars a day, to be precise (second "Mahagonny-Song"). But the whiskey, money, and girls run out, and the longed-for alternative perishes in an earthquake ("Benares-Song"). God comes to Mahagonny and orders the inhabitants to hell. They revolt: "we have been in hell all along" (third "Mahagonny-Song"). The paradise city exits only because everything is so rotten, "there is nothing to hold on to." Set designer Caspar Neher, who would collaborate on subsequent Weill-Brecht productions and who also wrote the libretto for *Die Bürgschaft*, met Burkard's requirement of "minimal scenery" and contemporary relevance by staging the piece in a boxing ring.

Although Weill had not yet finished *Der Zar*, and had in fact interrupted work on it to produce the "Songspiel," the intertextual connection between these two works is similarly striking. Compare the Czar's self-introduction, "Ich bin Monsieur" (ex. 10), with the opening "Auf nach Mahagonny!" and the closely related passage at the end of the "Songspiel" (ex. 11). The vocal parts share the same simple motif, an upper-neighbor-note motion followed by a falling fourth. The parallel is even plainer following the concluding words "Mahagonny ist nur ein erfundendes Wort," where the dotted rhythm that had accommodated the text "Auf nach" disappears, while the fox-trot rhythm originally preceding it becomes part of the instrumental texture, as it is in *Der Zar*. Again, as he does in *Der Zar*, Weill complicates the opposition of illusion and reality. Mahagonny, symbolized musically by the popular dance idiom, is qualified as an illusion, it is "only a made-up word." Turning into an ostinato, the dotted rhythm (also a feature of Weber's bridesmaids' chorus) swells to forte and then dies away, into nothing. It is a throwaway gesture, both verbally and musically. By extension, *Mahagonny* the piece is made up. The end itself, then, illustrates the sense of a "playing with songs."

Only two of the numbers of the "Songspiel" are actually entitled "Song": the

EXAMPLE 10. *Der Zar lässt sich photographieren,* the Czar's entrance

EXAMPLE 11. *Mahagonny-Songspiel,* ending

"Alabama-Song" and the "Benares-Song," both of them to English texts. Both are cast in a binary "song form" with alternating verse-refrain pattern. But the "Benares-Song" is somewhat complicated by a central section, which breaks up the pattern, as well as by the end, which fades away to the words of the verse, "Where shall we go?," before segueing into a chorale. Nor is the beginning entirely self-contained; the central motif of the number, eventually joined to the words "Where shall we go?," is repeated over and over during the last third of the preceding instrumental interlude. As for its style, the "Benares-Song" also illustrates the fact that the so-called song style relies heavily on expressive cantilenas from bel canto opera, with characteristic Italian doubling of the swooping melody in thirds.

Echoes of Stravinsky's *L'histoire du soldat* can be heard both in the instrumental chorale and in the "Kleiner Marsch" of the first instrumental interlude that leads *attacca* into the "Alabama-Song." In fact, with its double- and triple-stopping technique, the violin part of the march almost sounds like a quotation from the earlier work, which had made such an impression on Weill. As a piece of refashioned functional music, the "Marsch" can be grouped together with the defamiliarized "Waltz" when God comes to Mahagonny. Both constitute a stylistic quotation that complements the "Songstil." The production notes describe *Mahagonny* as a "Totentanz" ("dance of death")—a description supported above all by the positioning of the waltz. Stylistic becomes literal quotation in the succeeding instrumental interlude after the men of Mahagonny say "no": the trumpets play snippets, in thirds, from the revolutionary song of the proletariat "Die Internationale." Continuing the idea of a dance of death, the ensuing finale intones a tarantella reminiscent of Verdi's *Il trovatore* (act 4). But at the words "weil es nichts gibt, woran man sich halten kann" ("for there is nothing that one can hold on to"), the dance—perhaps fittingly—breaks off. After all, as the epilogue then tells us, "Mahagonny" is only a made-up word.

CRITICAL RESPONSES

One of the more substantial critical responses to the premiere came from the American critic Olin Downes, who in the 1940s would become one of Weill's more prominent supporters in the United States. In his largely favorable review, published in the *New York Times,* Downes mentioned having seen "the original sketches of *Mahagonny* made in Berlin," adding that "they were not pleasant." The stage production at Baden-Baden was, according to Downes, "skeletonized." At the same time, he wrote: "Quite enough was done under the circumstances."[31] Downes may have been referring to plans not only for a fuller staging but also for less clothing. Brecht, who was credited as the premiere's director, had apparently wanted to have the two women (Jessie and Bessie) appear in the nude.[32] In the event, they appeared clothed. Although unrealized, the plan nonetheless confirms the general intention to provoke, even to shock. Expecting dissension, customarily expressed by German theatergoers through loud whistling, Brecht had issued the members of the cast with their own whistles with which they could respond in kind, which they did.

Downes concluded his review by asserting that "the question of the worthiness of the subject can go begging here." On the other hand, he saw in Weill a "composer who knows his business. . . . As a craftsman he can afford to stick his tongue in his cheek." The "Songspiel" thrives on its playing the invoked cultural worlds off one against the another. And it does so more tersely and more pointedly than any of the one-act operas. Herein lies a connotation of Weill's term *Zwischengattung,* usually (and somewhat misleadingly) translated as "mixed genre," the sense, that is, of the work not so much synthesizing its various ingredients as combining them through juxtaposition. Such ambiguity in the case of *Mahagonny* was nicely captured in the *Prager Tagblatt* (21 July 1927), in a brief, not wholly sympathetic report. The critic, [Dr.] Erich Steinhard, somewhat mystified, describes *Mahagonny* as a "dadaist operetta-oratorio." Overall Steinhard, sharing Downes's own critical distinctions between text and music, considers the piece a failure because of the text by the "radical communist Bert Brecht." He praises Weill, however, for being "exceptionally inventive, with a powerful gift for the theater." He also credits him with a "talent for parody, ostensibly not intended." There can be little doubt, however (and as Steinhard sensed), that the parody, which takes place on a number of levels, is utterly intended; little doubt as well that Weill not only skillfully parodies various idioms and styles, but that he does so with a heavy dose of irony, as humorous as it is critical. That is the point of the term *Songspiel,* a knowingly sardonic twist on the tradition of German opera with a surreal injection of Americanism.

Allusions to traditional opera, especially German opera, multiply in the full-length *Aufstieg und Fall der Stadt Mahagonny.* And the surreal Americanisms remain, as does the finale. But much will change. For the critic Paul Bekker, writing an open letter to Weill in 1932, the full-length version turned out to be a "coarsening of the basic idea" *(Vergröberung der Grundidee).*[33] By expressing his implied preference for the earlier work, Bekker states a truism: in order for the "Songspiel" to be transformed into an opera, Weill had to abandon some of its basic precepts. Principal among these are the circumstances of the original commission and the explosive brevity of the initial design. Writing for an opera house for a full evening's entertainment required quite different measures. In this sense, too, the "Songspiel" was anything but a "stylistic study," however much Weill might have felt obliged, even pressured, to see it as such. The basic idea was not so much coarsened as, of necessity, radically revised. Weill admitted as much when, in a letter to Hans Heinsheimer at Universal Edition dated 14 October 1929, he stated that "almost everything added to the Baden-Baden version is written in a perfectly strict, thoroughly responsible style," that is, not in the song style.[34] He was referring to the neo-baroque turn taken by his compositions.

Discussions about the opera version of *Mahagonny* followed soon after the premiere of the "Songspiel." A month later, on 25 August, Weill wrote to his publisher observing that "a completely new kind of stage work is evolving, one that is directed to a different and much larger audience and whose appeal will be unusually broad."[35] For the time being he could write "in long discussions with Brecht I have become convinced that his idea of an operatic text largely coincides with my own." They still had a long way to go, however. "The piece we are going to create won't exploit topical themes, which will be dated in a year, but rather will reflect the true tenor of our times. For that reason it will have an impact far beyond its own age. The task is to create the new genre that gives appropriate expression to the completely transformed manifestation of life in our time." Although planning to write an opera, then, Weill still anticipated creating a new genre. By December, the director of Universal Edition, Emil Herztka, had received an outline of the new work, which led him to voice the following reservation: "What emerges from your outline *[Exposé]* is a new style of opera, yet one that nonetheless signifies merely a sequence of scenes, admittedly sometimes quite gripping and original ones, that can form a new type of 'opera-revue' . . . boxing, murder, homicide, drunkenness and the like predominate, and that could be difficult to bear for a whole evening."[36]

Weill responded by saying that he was "already occupied with a change, moving the love plot between Jimmy and Jenny more into the foreground."[37] But the plan would have to wait. As Curjel reported, Weill would have "much to do." First came Brecht's invitation to supply music for an adaptation of John Gay's *Beggar's Opera*. This more pressing, if smaller project would force the opera to take a backseat, for quite a while as it turned out, as the new commission became both bigger and more significant than Weill initially imagined. Like the "Songspiel," the new "play with music" came to constitute yet another important stage of theatrical reform, and certainly his best known.

5

Plays with Music

Even more than the preceding one-act operas, Weill's *Mahagonny-Songspiel* reflects an abiding interest in creating mixed genres or "in-between genres" (*Zwischengattungen*, as the composer himself called them). The three works discussed below likewise draw on a variety of theatrical conventions and musical styles. Mixing dialogue and musical numbers, comedy and morals, they hark back to the precedent of the eighteenth-century singspiel, as *Mahagonny* had overtly done through its punning subtitle "Songspiel." Apart from describing the ingredients of spoken dialogue and musical numbers, and unlike "singspiel," the label "play with music" *(Stück mit Musik)* refers to the pieces' home outside the opera house as well as to the mainly nonoperatic performers for whom they were written. Anything but incidental, however, the music is as much "the thing" as the play itself. This will continue to be the case in Weill's "musical plays," the American counterpart to his "plays with music."

DIE DREIGROSCHENOPER

"I'm not exactly asking for an opera here," says Macheath, *Die Dreigroschenoper*'s antihero. The occasion for the comment is a wedding reception, held in an illegally entered stable. The wedding (by no means his first) is that of Macheath himself, a dashing and notorious criminal known as Mack the Knife. Given his dangerous lifestyle, several widows will presumably survive him, among them Polly, whom he has just married, and Lucy, daughter of his old friend Tiger Brown, London's chief of police. Along with his excessive fondness for the bourgeois institution of marriage, Macheath displays *nouveau riche* pretensions to taste: when his men supply stolen furnishings, he claims to know the difference between Chippendale and Louis Quatorze. Later, under arrest and awaiting an execution that is ultimately aborted, he requests his favorite food: asparagus.[1] Why does he receive a pardon? Why the happy end? "So at least in opera," as his father-in-law and archrival Peachum concludes, "you can see for once how mercy comes before justice." Neither Macheath nor his creators ask for an opera, but a connection to high culture is part of his (and the piece's) style, however ironic the effect. High culture, Macheath seems to be suggesting, is for anybody with sufficient pretensions and access—with or without cash.

If *Die Dreigroschenoper* is an opera, it is one with significant differences, materially and institutionally. The premiere took place on 31 August 1928 in a small theater (Berlin's Theater am Schiffbauerdamm), not an opera house. Playing to a broader audience than traditional opera, the first production drew on a wide spectrum of performers from various theatrical constituencies. None of the cast was a professional opera singer. The instrumentalists, drawn from the world of dance bands, remained in full view on the stage as visual property—opera turned inside out, as it were. Yet thanks to these differences, Weill and Brecht, each in his way, managed to say something about the genre. "It presented us with the opportunity," Weill remarked at the time, "to make 'opera' the subject matter for an evening in the theater."[2] Hence Peachum's conclusion; the audience is supposed to see how the genre works. *Die Dreigroschenoper* thus makes explicit a tendency of Weill's musical theater evident already in *Der Protagonist:* it is art about art.

The work begins like many an eighteenth-century piece for the operatic stage, with an overture. While recognizably related to baroque music (the form being loosely based on the three-part French model, including fugal writing in the middle section), the musical idiom is "defamiliarized" by linear counterpoint, by bold modern harmonies, and by an unusual instrumental lineup.[3] Both texture and timbre impart a 1920s flavor, with two saxophones, two trumpets, a trombone, a banjo, timpani, and a harmonium. This is parody, not pastiche. Underscoring the generic ambiguity, the playbill described *Die Dreigroschenoper* as a "play with music," but it also informed the audience that they had come to watch an adaptation of an early-eighteenth-century piece, *The Beggar's Opera,* presented "in a prologue and eight scenes after the English of John Gay." Brecht received credit, not as author, but for the adaptation; his assistant Elisabeth Hauptmann provided the translation.

The idea of updating a theatrical "classic" informed the work from the beginning. Alerted to the huge success of Sir Nigel Playfair's revival of Gay's *Beggar's Opera* at the Lyric Theatre in Hammersmith, London—a production that opened on 5 June 1920 and ran for a record-breaking 1,463 performances over a three-year period—Brecht had Hauptmann prepare a working translation of the piece in the winter of 1927–28. The project took off when Brecht met the young impresario Ernst Josef Aufricht, who was in search of a play for his new company at Schiffbauerdamm.[4]

Between its inception early in 1928 and its first performance on 31 August, eight or so months later, the hybrid opera–cum–play with music underwent numerous and substantial reworkings, especially during the chaotic final month of rehearsal under the direction of Erich Engel. Apart from Gay's text, Brecht also used "interpolated ballads by François Villon and Rudyard Kipling," as the playbill indicated. Given such open borrowing, it might seem ironic, if not downright perverse, that Brecht should later have become embroiled in a plagiarism suit. The theater critic Alfred Kerr charged Brecht with having failed to credit the German translator of the Villon poems, K. L. Ammer, whereupon Brecht responded with an immortal line about his "fundamental laxity in matters of intellectual property."[5] The upshot was that Brecht had to cede to Ammer a small portion of his royalties.[6] The 2.5 percent that Ammer received from German-language performances of *Die Dreigroschenoper* ended up being enough for him to be able to buy a small vineyard near Vienna and produce a wine labeled "Threepenny Drops" *(Dreigroschentropfen).*

When it came to contracts, however, Brecht was not at all lax about what he considered *his* intellectual property—the reason, perhaps, for failing to acknowledge the Villon translator. Even so, he was also making a statement of his own aesthetic, his way of doing creative, as opposed to financial, business. A key concept is that of "montage." *Die Dreigroschenoper* juxtaposes its separate and separated elements almost in the manner of a film: the musical numbers; the spoken dialogue; the actors that speak and sing, with separate lighting *(Songlicht)* for the latter; the stage property, including the visible instrumentalists and the prescribed placards narrating the plot. The elements themselves are drawn from diverse sources, some acknowledged, some not.

The principal, openly acknowledged source is Gay's play itself. Then there are the Villon ballads (wholesale borrowings from which appear in Macheath's "Ruf aus der Gruft" and "Grabschrift"; there are also free adaptations of Villon's translated verse in "Zuhälterballade," "Die Ballade vom angenehmen Leben," and the "Salomon-Song"). Kipling, the other declared source, is somewhat harder to identify. "Polly's Lied," based in part on Kipling's "Mary, Pity Women," was cut for the premiere (and also omitted from the published libretto). And the "Kanonen-Song," which Brecht had written in various versions before it found its way into *Die Dreigroschenoper,* was derived only loosely from a German translation of Kipling's ballad "Screw-Guns."[7]

Not that the extent of Kipling's influence really mattered. Throwing in a few more names would scarcely have detracted from the piece's originality. On the contrary, if anything it would probably have enhanced it. In a work of radical montage, one that subscribes to the theory of epic theater, the roll call of elements forms part of the work, as the playbill seemed to be indicating. This was an era of creative recycling of earlier, classical art, an era of neoclassicism. In music, the label principally applied to Stravinsky, which irked his rival Schoenberg no end. But Satie, Picasso, and Cocteau, brought together for the 1917 ballet *Parade,* had all been enormously influential, too. And Brecht and Weill's piece, itself heavily indebted to Stravinsky (as Weill readily conceded), fit right into this trend. Symptomatic of the revivalist tendency were the contemporaneous stagings of other classics—Shakespeare in particular in the spoken theater (in 1928, Berlin saw a modern-dress staging of *Macbeth,* for example) and Handel at the opera.

Although the work was not expected to succeed, mainly because of turmoil during rehearsals, the premiere proved to be the biggest theatrical success of the epoch, running for more than 350 performances over the next two years. The main roles were created by singing actors from the spoken theater (Lotte Lenya as Jenny, Erich Ponto as Mr. Peachum), from cabaret (Rosa Valetti as Mrs. Peachum, Roma Bahn as Polly, Kurt Gerron as Tiger Brown), and from operetta (Harald Paulsen as Macheath). The Lewis Ruth Band, a seven-man outfit of versatile studio musicians, named (*Amerikanismus*-style) after the band's flautist and saxophonist, Ludwig Rüth, provided the instrumental accompaniment. Pianist Theo Mackeben (later famous for his film music) directed from the keyboard. In its final form, which included revisions made by Weill immediately after the premiere, the full score deploys a total of twenty-three instruments.

Weill's score, his second collaboration with Brecht, retains just one of the airs arranged by Pepusch for *The Beggar's Opera:* "Morgenchoral des Peachum." Initially this number was to follow the overture, as it does in Gay's work, but the last-minute insertion of "Die Moritat von Mackie Messer" disturbed the "neoclassical" parallel. A high-low stylistic mix drawing on baroque idioms, traditional and popular song, opera and operetta, even (at the end) Lutheran chorale, and colored throughout by the sonorities and idioms of the modern dance band, the music made a decisive contribution to the work's multilayered effects. A classic it was, albeit a provocatively refashioned one.

A number of prominent observers saw the piece as an operetta, but again with a difference. Oskar Bie, writing in the *Berliner Börsen-Courier,* extolled *Die Dreigroschenoper* as "an exemplar of modern operetta such as it should be."[8] Theodor Wiesengrund-Adorno talked about an "exalted operetta form."[9] Elias Canetti suggested a "Berlin operetta."[10] Aufricht himself recalled: "We saw the piece, as written, in terms of a comical literary operetta with a few flashes of social criticism."[11] The desired effect was created not merely by the use of familiar and stylistically diverse means. Critical here is the way the elements are juxtaposed (as they had been in the "Songspiel" version of *Mahagonny*), surrealistically and ironically. Even where Weill comes close to reproducing the real thing, the text usually provides a jarring counterpoint. The "Zuhälterballade" (Pimp's

Ballad), a tango written in the wake of the 1926 craze for this dance form, was Weill's own favorite example: "The charm of the piece," he wrote, "rests precisely in the fact that a rather risqué text (not, by the way, as offensive as a lot of operetta texts) is set to music in a gentle, pleasant way."[12] This mode of juxtaposition is not dissimilar to Gay's own practice of setting new ribald texts to well-known ditties associated with familiar, more innocent words (for example, refunctioning the air "Oh London is a fine town" as "Our Polly is a sad slut!").

Weill's work is hard to pin down in terms of genre because genre is one of its topics, as Weill suggested.[13] Yet this facet of the piece has not uniformly endured. One reason is obvious: Brecht turned his work into a classic by publishing a revised version of the libretto in the 1931 collected edition of his works (the *Versuche*), thus changing the complexion and purpose of the piece. Although he now referred to it as "an experiment in epic theater," he removed all references to Gay and many musical cues, as well as much of the stage business—the very elements that convey the work's neoclassical playful subversiveness. He also rewrote much of the dialogue to sharpen the piece's political message, thereby becoming the work's first anachronistic interpreter or "re-reader." In addition, he published a set of notes to accompany this reprint, bridging the gap between the piece's initial form and reception, on the one hand, and his own changing conception of the function of theater, on the other. Drawing on Brecht's notes and his new, ideologically sharpened material, exegetes have often insisted on a political significance the work never possessed, even in its later version. Such readers have even claimed the initial reception to have been a misunderstanding on the part of the audience.[14]

The distance Brecht adopted from the work's original incarnation at its 1928 production is nowhere more succinctly or transparently expressed than in a self-interview from 1933, first published in 1994.

> *What in your opinion created the success of the "Dreigroschenoper?"*
>
> I'm afraid it was everything that didn't matter to me: the romantic plot, the love story, the musical elements. When the "Dreigroschenoper" was a success it was turned into a film. They put into the film everything I had satirized in the play: the romanticism, the sentimentality etc., and omitted the satire. The success was even greater.
>
> *And what did matter to you?*
>
> The critique of society. I had tried to show that the mind-set and emotional life of street robbers is immensely similar to the mind-set and emotional life of respectable citizens.[15]

Brecht presents a dichotomized view of the work: the sentimental, "romanticized" one he claims to have been the reason for its success versus the subversive, "critical" one he claims to have intended and had attempted to supply with his revision. The "critical" aspect of the original production, however, had emerged from the self-conscious manipulation of artistic practices: it was not primarily directed at the political system of the Weimar Republic.[16] Brecht's stark oppositions of "sentimentality" and "critique" are not so much mutually exclusive alternatives as they are two sides of the same "Threepenny" coin. The Third Threepenny Finale, with its chorus, recitative, and happy ending, is at once the formal reality of eighteenth-century opera seria and, in its dramatic artificiality, a surreal reworking of it. On yet another level, it is a true indication of social corruption and injustice.

Distributed as sheet music and on shellac discs, the evergreen songs detached themselves from the work as a whole in all manner of arrangements for domestic and public performance, whether for piano, piano and violin, or various sizes of dance band, with or without singer. Weill provided his own new arrangement, the *Kleine Dreigroschenmusik,* another "neoclassicist" throwback, in this case to the instrumental arrangements of operatic hits *(Harmoniemusik)* of Mozart's time. Weill and Brecht became involved—though not as involved as they would have liked—in the production of the movie version of the piece directed by G. W. Pabst and released in 1931. A celebrated lawsuit ensued, putting on trial the matter of intellectual property in the incipient age of the mechanical reproduction of art.

What had begun as a lighthearted, occasional adaptation of a theatrical classic, and had then turned into a vehicle for artistic experimentation and programmatic reform, eventually acquired a much wider significance. *Die Dreigroschenoper* became an enduringly resonant, multifaceted sign of the times—for better and for worse. The National Socialists, whose reading of the piece lacked any sense of irony, declared it the epitome of degenerate art, according it pride of place in their 1938 exhibition of "Degenerate Music." During the years of Nazi rule Weill's music, officially banned, became dangerous in not only an aesthetic but also a practical sense. Listening to it with confidants, huddled in front of a wind-up gramophone, was tantamount to an act of conspiracy. *Die Dreigroschenoper* remained his best-known and most frequently played composition in Germany, as the memoirs of German émigrés attest almost without exception. Erich Fried, for example, recalled the last screening of the Pabst film prior to the annexation of Austria as follows: "We actually managed to see the last performance. It had been banned in Austria, and had only been on for the last few days. Now we hummed the tunes. But we hummed them softly. We looked to left and right as we came out of the cinema. No brown uniforms yet."[17]

Apart from functioning as a symbol of resistance against suppression, Weill's music became—with the aid of hindsight—an unheeded warning against barbarism. In his Weill obituary, the director Karl Lustig-Prean wrote: "Weill had recognized these brown portents well in advance and alerted us to them. The hammering rhythms of his music to Brecht songs, to workers' agitational ballads, to whiplashes against a reactionary bourgeoisie arrogantly becoming stupefied while betraying its own kind, were signals, nay screams, of warning about the horror to come; but in a tragic chain of tragic circumstances, they were no more heard than their texts (to which they gave the vital spur) were turned into deeds."[18] The music also fostered feelings of nostalgia for the good old days, the glorious Golden Twenties. It still does. Yet the premiere audience at Schiffbauerdamm could not possibly have understood Weill's music in either of these senses, either the political or the transfiguring sense. Diagnosing the work's popular reception as a misunderstanding is largely anachronistic. Nonetheless, the subsequent understanding of his works in these terms has lastingly shaped Weill's postwar image in Germany on both sides of the wall.

After the war, partly because of its previously banned status, *Die Dreigroschenoper*'s cultural capital as emblem of the Golden Twenties only increased. For years, both before and after unification, it has maintained its top ranking as Germany's most frequently attended theater work.[19] In the United States, with the work having remained largely unknown in the English-speaking world in Weill's lifetime, it took the country by storm during the 1950s, and by decade's end *The Threepenny Opera*'s "Mack the Knife" had put Weill and Brecht on the hit parade.[20]

The label "play with music" is inclusively neutral. Covering a wide spectrum of possibilities, it leaves open both the extent of the music and the nature of its role within the play. *Die Dreigroschenoper* is located at the musically richer end of the spectrum. Amounting to so much more than the sum of their already considerable parts, the musical numbers are anything but incidental. The Third Finale is the most obvious case in point: the irony of the *lieto fine* is achieved through the quotation of convention. As Weill put it, "The concept of opera was used directly to resolve a conflict, as a plot-advancing device, and hence had to be presented in its purest, most primordial form."[21] Even the instrumental interludes, played during scene shifts, may have something substantive to contribute. Sketchily notated in the band parts and indicated by cues in the first published libretto, the interludes followed standard operetta practice. Yet the actual choice of the number to be repeated and where that repetition occurs seems hardly arbitrary. For example, having the "Kanonen-Song" follow Mac and Polly's "Liebeslied" bespeaks a satirical intention: Mars juxtaposed with Venus. If the insertion of interludes suggests the influence of operetta, the instruction that the "Moritat" be employed as a recurring leitmotif has a double significance, at once parodying the leitmotivic practices of Wagnerian music-drama and pointing to the emerging medium of film, where such "underscoring" was to become commonplace.[22] The overall musical organization is hardly "organic," however. Both the genesis and the documented performance practice emphasize the montage principle.

Weill's own evolving conception of *Die Dreigroschenoper* is nicely illustrated by the respective cover pages of his autograph piano-vocal score on the one hand and the published version on the other. The differences are telling in two respects. In the autograph, he described the contents as "Musik zu 'The Beggar's Opera,' op. 25," suggesting that, initially at least, he conceived of his contribution as nothing more than music for a preexisting play, but of sufficient substance and import to warrant an opus number. By the time the piano-vocal score was published shortly after the premiere, however, the opus number had disappeared. Nor would Weill ever use one again, for any of his compositions. And the title had changed to align with the playbill (minus the references to Villon and Kipling):

> *Die Dreigroschenoper (The Beggar's Opera): Ein Stück mit Musik in einem Vorspiel und acht Bildern nach dem Englischen des John Gay, übersetzt von Elisabeth Hauptmann, Deutsche Bearbeitung von Bert Brecht.*

The sensationally successful *Dreigroschenoper* proved transformative for Weill in a number of respects. More than just a change in the importance that the work assumed in his partnership with Brecht, the difference between the title pages symbolizes a shift that was occurring in his career as a composer for the musical theater. What began as an occasional project takes center stage in his artistic evolution. The musician schooled in the tradition of "opus music" leaves the exclusivity of that culture behind him to embrace more overtly popular forms of composition.

HAPPY END

Conceived among other things to capitalize on the earlier work's huge success, *Die Dreigroschenoper*'s successor not only includes an artificial happy end, but it is called *Happy End.* All is not well that ends well, the piece seems to be saying with the help of its pervasive Americanisms, freely throwing in other *Fremdwörter* as well, such as *Girl* and *sex appeal.* While the message is more blatant and aggressive than before, it is also more ironic. The irony begins with the title. And if this in itself does not make the piece's purpose clear, the Prologue soon does, cast in free verse with Americanizing neologisms. Here is the last stanza:

> Ach, Sie fragen nach dem Weltbild? Das ist hollywoodlich
> Wie vermutlich
> Und das Ganze endet happyendlich
> Selbstverständlich.
>
> (You inquire about the worldview? It is Hollywoodish
> As suspected
> And the whole ends happy-endingly
> Naturally.)[23]

Here, at least, Hollywood endings are as much a topic as they are a device. In this case, however, the ironically happy end may well have been principally responsible for the lack of success. The device-cum-topic did not work, despite the presence of several members from the original team. Elisabeth Hauptmann again played a pivotal role in the work's creation. Having supplied the German translation of *The Beggar's Opera,* this time she wrote the book herself under the pseudonym Dorothy Lane, claiming to have based it on a "magazine story" and thereby leaving people to speculate for years about the author's identity. She was listed as having done the adaptation this time, as Brecht was before. Brecht apparently encouraged Hauptmann to undertake the project. Apart from stressing the financial benefit that she might reap, the surviving fragment of a letter he sent Hauptmann supplied a succinct plot outline:

> Dear Bess: I was wondering today whether you wouldn't like to partake of the Massary business. I'd supply you with a story-line *[Fabel]* etc. and you would craft from it a little play *[Stück],* rough and ready, even fragmentary, if you like. A partly affecting, partly comical thing for c. 10,000 marks. You would have to sign for it, but that would be of enormous benefit to you. The whole thing could be quite decent through plain openness and a kind of affecting modesty!
>
> Story-line roughly as follows:
>
> Place: Salvation Army and gangster bar.
> Content: Struggle between good and evil.
> Conclusion: Good triumphs.[24]

The following three paragraphs of the letter provide a few more details of the story—but with different names from the ones eventually used—up to the point where the female lead (whom Brecht calls "Mimosenbess," echoing the appellation in his letter to Hauptmann) drinks whiskey. But there the letter, as it survives, stops. The only song Brecht mentions is the "Lied vom Branntweinhändler," which he reminds Hauptmann comes from his *Hauspostille* collection. But he obviously intended for there to be more. "Massary business" refers to Fritzi Massary, megastar of stage, cabaret, and shellac. Although Massary did not sing in *Happy End,* songs do play a crucial role, and Brecht seems to have expected that the 10,000 marks would come from engaging a star such as Massary, if not Massary herself.

Apart from the one poem he mentions, the plot outline, and his general encouragement, Brecht did eventually contribute texts for other musical numbers, although he probably did not write all of them, contrary to the playbill, which listed him as sole author of the lyrics.[25] He also functioned as codirector with Erich Engel. Caspar Neher again designed the sets, and the instrumentalists remained the same: Theo Mackeben and the Lewis Ruth Band, also collaborating as before with the composer during rehearsal. The collaborative, interactive rehearsal process was also similar to that of the previous year. In an interview given just days after the premiere, Weill remarked how "during the rehearsals for 'Surabaya-Johnny' . . . it occurred to me that the violin could be accompanied by the clarinet playing an octave lower. I had the band stop, amended the score, and the resulting sound was greatly enriched. This would have been impossible with a large orchestra. The conductor would momentarily say: 'Are you unable to write for orchestra, since you're making adjustments to the score during rehearsal?'"[26] The surviving band parts for *Die Dreigroschenoper* and *Happy End* contain amendments of various kinds evidently made during rehearsal. For example, in the original band parts for "Surabaya-Johnny," the alto saxophone doubles on clarinet (as well as flute), and the player of the tenor saxophone switches to violin. Moreover, the clarinet accompanies the violin an octave lower, just as Weill states in the interview. All additions are in pencil, apparently entered by the players, not by Weill.

Carola Neher, who would soon return to the *Dreigroschenoper* cast as Polly after dropping out before the premiere, took the lead role of Lilian Holiday, a Salvation Army officer committed to the "unceasing struggle with sin." Here Lilian's principal target for religious conversion is the hardened gangsters of Chicago, whom she tries by various means to bring into her fold. One of the main points of the piece, of course, is that they also bring her into theirs. Kurt Gerron, who had played Tiger Brown, took the part of Sam Worlitzer, one of the gang members; and Brecht's wife-to-be Helene Weigel (an original *Dreigroschen* cast member who had become indisposed at the last minute) played the gang's leader, the mysterious Lady in Grey. All came to nothing—or at least relatively little. With *Die Dreigroschenoper* still going strong, the production closed on 1 October 1929, just four weeks after its premiere on 2 September. Advertisements published in the *Berliner Tageblatt* confirm that the new play was performed at least six times per week for the entire month, thereby contradicting assertions in the secondary literature that the production folded after just a matter of days.[27] What did endure were Weill's songs, evergreens such as the "Bilbao-Song" and "Surabaya-Johnny." In 1932 Weill himself still considered them among "the best song instrumentations I have done," "the best thing I have done of this kind."[28]

Although the songs have led a rich life quite separate from the theater piece, as Weill intended, the obverse is neither true nor possible. The *Stück* is literally unperformable without the *Musik*. Like *Die Dreigroschenoper, Happy End* is not only a play with music, it is a play *about* music. If, as Weill said, the earlier piece makes opera its subject matter, *Happy End* casts its net even wider. A central theme is the effect of music in general. Whereas Peachum's beggars use all manner of props and playacting to reach the "hardest of hearts," Lilian and her fellow Salvation Army workers use music. Their chief means of religious conversion is their songs.

Most of the music in *Happy End* is integral to the plot in the way that, exceptionally, "Seeräuberjenny" had been in *Die Dreigroschenoper.* Polly's ballad performed at her wedding to Macheath elicits a reaction from him: he orders her to desist from such "playacting" in the future. He admits, however, that her performance is not just "nice" but rather "art," which is not "nice." By the same token, Lilian Holiday (the Salvation Army officer committed to the "unceasing struggle with sin") sings as much to the other cast members as to the audience. The reaction to her music is part of the story. Not just a mode of the narration, the music is an indispensable part of the narration itself. In that sense, it is "diegetic." The mode is the message. Or rather, the modes are, for Weill provides different types of songs, some more integral, in terms of the story, than others. The musical numbers are required to play themselves, as it were. There are short and simple, traditional-sounding anthems, such as "Bruder, gib dir einen Stoss" and "Fürchte dich nicht." This maudlin hymn style stands for the sphere of the Salvation Army at its most conventional (even though Weill's simple harmonies are deceptively so). Other numbers, notably "Geht hinein in die Schlacht," sound like music of political agitation and propaganda. Their tone is close to the *Kampfmusik* manner cultivated by Hanns Eisler for use at communist rallies. And in "Der kleine Leutnant des lieben Gottes" Weill makes a brief allusion (at the words "Denn die armen Leute") to the hymn of the international proletariat, "Die Internationale," something he had already done in the "Songspiel" version of *Mahagonny* (ex. 12). This militant agitprop style lends Lilian's actions a note of political, if not personal, liberation, even though the ending of the piece casts that liberation in a caustically ironic light. Good does not so much triumph over evil, as suggested in Brecht's outline. Rather, the two sides unite, the implication being that religion and big business are really a lucrative alliance made in heaven.

But even the most belligerent-sounding hymns do not always work as intended. Like Peachum, Lilian needs something new to be successful in her business. The play's turning point is at once alcoholic and musical. Emboldened by whiskey, Lilian enters the risqué sphere of the "Matrosen-Tango." Recall the earlier uses of tango in *Royal Palace, Der Zar lässt sich photographieren,* and even *Die Dreigroschenoper.* Here the dance topic is not just representative of the here and now; it also suggests an up-to-date "Liebestod," as it had in the earlier pieces. In any event, it does the trick in softening up the hard nut, gangster Bill Cracker. Lilian seems to know what she is doing, as Bill loses his head. He has already revealed himself as susceptible to music. "As long as you don't sing any Salvation Army songs," he proclaims, "you can kiss . . ." And when she visits him before the planned bank robbery on Christmas Eve, he repeatedly pleads with her not to sing. She resolutely ignores him with her rendition of "Surabaya-Johnny." It reduces him to tears, despite the warning explicit in a line from his "Lied von der harten Nuss": "Don't go soft" (*Nur nicht weich werden*). So much for his earlier

EXAMPLE 12. *Happy End*, "Der kleine Leutnant des lieben Gottes" (allusion to "Die Internationale")

complaint that his gang members have a "soft head." It turns out that he has one, too, at least whenever music enters the picture.

Hard and soft are pervasive metaphors in the piece, with music mostly located on the "soft" side, however hard its apparent exterior. Because of the song style's particular association with "softness," as conveyed through the "Bilbao-Song," the "Matrosen-Tango," and "Surabaya-Johnny," its role in the context of the piece, its "markedness," is nothing if not equivocal. The style of the moment, as introduced through the "Bilbao-Song," is also the song of long ago, a function of nostalgia. What is more, the style is morally ambiguous, sexually and politically. Ambiguity informs its very elements: it is at once free and disciplined, its agogically flexible, *espressivo* cantilenas coexisting in constant tension with the mechanically repeated dance rhythms. Personal freedom asserts itself, as far as possible, against unyielding ostinato. Weill tellingly referred to jazz as the "instinct of the masses."[29] How much more unyielding that libidinous dance ostinato is than the um-pahs of the Italian bel canto style!

And how rich the symbolism of the original musical ending! In its brief incarnation on the stage of the Theater am Schiffbauerdamm, *Happy End* concluded with the number "Hosiannah Rockefeller," a panegyric to three giants of American capitalism: Ford, Morgan, and Rockefeller. Highlighting the ironic relevance of the number to the play's plot were set designer Casper Neher's huge portraits, done in the manner of stained-glass windows. Organized crime and organized religion thus unite to pay homage to these establishment icons of big business: St. Ford, St. Morgan, and St. Rockefeller (fig. 2). A playful, amusing point, perhaps, but it is hardly just burlesque, especially in light of the Lady in Grey's introductory words delivered in a speech that would eventually find its way, only slightly altered, into the revised text of *Die Dreigroschenoper.*

THE FLY: The days when you minor artisans, working with a conventional jemmy in your callused palms, broke into metal safes containing nothing more than shares and credit notes—these days are gone. You are being swallowed up by big corporations with the banks behind them. What's a jemmy compared with a share certificate? What's breaking into a bank compared with founding a bank?

ALL: Nothing!

Nowhere is the Marxist turn in Brecht's writing more palpable. The speech, evidently a late revision to the play's text, after Brecht replaced Erich Engel as director, paraphrases a passage from the introduction to Karl Marx's *Contribution to the Critique of Political Economy*: "Is the view of nature and of social relations which underlies the Greek imagination and Greek [mythology] possible with self-acting mules, railways, locomotives and electric telegraphs? What is a Vulcan compared with Roberts and Co., Jupiter with the lightning conductor and Hermes with the Crédit mobilier?" Marx's text continues: "All mythology subdues, dominates and fashions the forces of nature in the imagination and through imagination, it disappears therefore with real mastery over them."[30] (A delicious irony here, in that Hermes is the Greek god chosen to adorn American Express credit cards!)

By the same token, the dialogue of *Happy End* has shifted from being a gentle spoof of gangster stories (plausibly lifted from an American magazine) to the rhetoric of the stump address; from light entertainment to political rally. According to Alfred Kerr, Helene Weigel read her speech from a scrap of paper. Was it an insertion not yet memorized, or was she adding an authentic political touch? For the punning Kerr, at any rate, the effect was "angepappt" (pasted on).[31]

FIGURE 2. The final scene of *Happy End* from the premiere production in Berlin, 1929. Caspar Neher's set design depicts three giants of American capitalism canonized on stained-glass windows: St. Ford, St. Morgan, and St. Rockefeller (swinging a golf club). Widely criticized in the press, the scene concluded with the song "Hosiannah Rockefeller," following a political speech delivered by Helene Weigel (Brecht's wife) that was based on a passage from Karl Marx's *Critique of Political Economy.* Courtesy of the Weill-Lenya Research Center, Kurt Weill Foundation for Music, New York.

The play had abruptly turned into a vehicle for a hard-hitting point of materialist social critique: the truly successful criminals are the big corporations, run by the so-called robber barons, three of whom the finale celebrates in person as "saints." Weill brings them closer to home by singing their praises to the melody of "Berlin im Licht–Song," a shimmy he had composed the previous year as part of Berlin's electric light exhibition. It makes for a rousing conclusion. The seductive strains of contemporary American dance music, albeit spoken with a German accent, not only soften up gangsters such as Bill; they also fill the air of Berlin, like electric light, as the glory of international big business shines all around. We are all being seduced!

The premiere audience did not like it, however. Nor did most of the critics. Even Weill and Brecht's supporters turned against them. Oskar Bie, usually a sympathetic advocate of Weill's work, thought the play "weak, poor, and thin, even boring." When its "political tendency was sharpened" at the end, he reported, "this ignited opposition. . . . Someone in the audience cursed the republic. A huge din ensued, drowning out the end of the play. The pointed applause that accompanied the early scenes and was directed at the actors' performances, notably the complicated criminal (Homolka) and the touchingly untouched Salvation Army girl (Carola Neher), became problematic."[32] Another reporter complained that the piece became "draped in morality and social ethics. . . . It was shatteringly strange," the anonymous critic continued, "after all that parody, suddenly to receive a lecture about noble communism and the great criminals Ford and Morgan and Rockefeller. The audience took exception and started to play along, and they were right."[33] While the performances for the most part received jubilant ovations, only one newspaper—the Communist *Die rote Fahne* (4 September 1929)—liked the ending, approving of the "political seriousness" that Helene Weigel's speech lent the proceedings. Otherwise the ending was uniformly rejected. "Activism intrudes with force," wrote Junghans of the *Kreuz-Zeitung* (4 September 1929); "the moral of the story is stuck on and dispensed in a violent manner." Writing for the *Neues Wiener Journal* (6 September 1929), Rudolph Lothar described the "political apotheosis" as bringing about a "murderous scandal." People, he said, "shouted, whistled, called stop; the whole performance came to a halt for a number of seconds." Hans W. Fischer of the *Welt am M.* (9 September 1929) described the effect in thoroughly sinister terms: "The piece," he wrote "which is all surface, suddenly turned into a black mass." Even Herbert Ihering, usually an avid Brechtian, had to admit that the ending "seemed like a tableau from a different piece." At three and a half hours, the work outstayed its welcome; it "broke its own bounds," Ihering wrote, "placing greater demands than planned." Like others among his colleagues, he thought it a mistake to have conceived of the piece as a repetition: "The style petrifies when it is overburdened. It does not permit stasis. Repetitions are wrong. Either you build a fortress or move on. Both are not possible."[34]

Musically, *Happy End* is a drama of jostling styles invested with complex layers of significance that not only relate to the plot but are actually part of it, musical theater in an emphatic sense. The description "Stück mit Musik" is an understatement. More accurate would be an inversion of the label: "Musik mit einem Stück"—and not a very good play at that. Rudolph Arnheim put it this way: "much good meat but no skeleton."[35] Several of the critics offered an explanation for the failure of the play by reporting dissonance among the members of the production team, especially between the codirectors. Erich Engel, who had apparently developed misgivings about the production, abandoned it before opening night, leaving Brecht to continue as director on his own. "When, Mr.

Engel, are you going to write the next play yourself?" was the conclusion to a scathing review in the *Berliner Tageblatt* (3 September 1929) by Alfred Kerr, who sustained his diatribe against Brecht's lack of originality with a pun on the work's title, "*Happy entlehnt*" (i.e., "happily borrowed").

Still standing up for his own contribution, Weill would soon refer to the piece as "bad." In a letter to his publishers dated 14 October 1929, he urged them to recognize that his music had been "badly integrated" into a "bad play." He also felt that it had been "misunderstood." "Pieces such as the 'Salvation Army March' and the 'Sailor Song,'" he wrote, "go well beyond the song style *[Songcharakter]*."[36] Yet it was not until three years later, in June 1932, that he took steps to rescue the piece. The initial plan was to work with Brecht on a revised version of the piece, despite their having fallen out over the Berlin production of *Aufstieg und Fall der Stadt Mahagonny. Happy End* was to be "depoliticized," Weill said.[37] "Hosiannah Rockefeller" would "go altogether."[38] Yet when he received the revised book, he was "amazed that Brecht and Frau Hauptmann have left the piece *completely unaltered*." He had been expecting "a thorough revision in the sense of tightening the plot and thereby providing the framework for the songs." If Brecht could not provide one, he concluded, then he would "drop the whole matter." An important motivation had been "that I would like to give Lenya this wonderful role and the fact that I am confident that the music can have an impact along with a great performance in the theater, despite the weak piece."[39] But Brecht and Hauptmann did not deliver. Besides, they had already recycled some of the *Happy End* material, including several of the songs, in the much more politicized *Die heilige Johanna der Schlachthöfe*. Weill seemed to know nothing about it.

A further resuscitation attempt by Weill followed six months later. In a letter dated 26 December 1932, he mentioned the need for a companion piece to the "small version" of *Mahagonny*. This time *Happy End* would be altered to match the form of the earlier work: "The obvious thing to do (an old plan of mine) would be to turn *Happy End* itself into a kind of *Songspiel* with short spoken scenes from the life of a Salvation Army girl. Brecht could do that, of course, but the thought of subjecting oneself to all the difficulties of working with Brecht just for such a small and simple matter is dreadful. I'll give it some thought nonetheless. . . . At any rate I'll pursue this plan, which could give us a nice evening for six performers and eleven-piece orchestra."[40]

The plan never materialized, and one is left to speculate on how Weill would have turned this "Stück mit Musik" into "a kind of 'Songspiel.'"[41] Although his intention to make the piece principally a vehicle for the female lead is clear, how much of *Happy End*'s comedy he would have retained is not. A comedy the original piece most certainly is—one with humor complicated (or rather, enhanced) by parody. If the parodic element is either suppressed or overlooked, then the book can seem particularly flat. What killed the first production was two things.

The piece was overlong. Weill was right to want to cut it. Brevity is the spice of wit. And responding to critics, he was also right to want to fix the ending, with its abrupt shift of genre from comedy to agitprop.[42] In *Die Dreigroschenoper* he and Brecht used the means of opera to provide a resolution while also making a satirical point. In *Happy End* the point was spelled out in an all-too-blunt, even patronizing way foreign to the rest of the piece. So the songs survived, in their own right and also recycled in later works. Several found their way into his French play with music, *Marie Galante,* and one, "Das Lied vom Branntweinhändler," served as part of the overture to *Johnny Johnson.* That it might be possible to produce a comedy with a more or less overtly political conclusion was an idea Weill did not abandon but attempted to realize with *Der Silbersee.*

DER SILBERSEE

It was not until three years after *Happy End*'s aborted run that Weill again considered the combination of play with music. (In the interim he had devoted a significant portion of his creative energies to three other works: the two full-length operas, *Aufstieg und Fall der Stadt Mahagonny* and *Die Bürgschaft,* and the school opera *Der Jasager.*) *Der Silbersee: Ein Wintermärchen* (The Silver Lake: A Winter's Fairy Tale), his third and final collaboration with Georg Kaiser, marks the end of an era for the composer. The triple premiere took place in Leipzig, Erfurt, and Magdeburg on 18 February 1933, less than a month after Hitler's accession to power as chancellor of Germany. It was just a few more weeks before Weill left Germany for the relative safety of Paris. And two years later, after a brief stay in London, he emigrated to the United States, where he would spend the rest of his career until his death in 1950.

Even today, it is hard to ignore the circumstances of that 1933 premiere. In transcending its time, the work seems to reflect it. How else to interpret the conclusion, where "the hours of the night give way to the dawning of the light"? The seemingly bizarre turns of plot delineate a conception as musical in its shifts of character and mood as it is dramatic, from the stark privations of a community stricken by poverty and hunger, via the unlikely, fantastic interventions of fate and fortune, to the promise of escape and redemption.

The full significance of the work's title and subtitle emerges only gradually. As the titular Silver Lake freezes over, the meaning of "A Winter's Fairy Tale" is revealed; the season of discontent is both literal and figurative, even transfigurative. Magically, the frozen water of the lake becomes for the two principal men, Olim and Severin, a means of escape from their oppressive world. Fate has brought them together, at first in their respective, antagonist roles of policeman and perpetrator of a hunger-induced theft, and then as friends, led by the serene Fennimore to their salvation.

The narrative's overall structure contains fairy-tale elements, with Olim's winning the lottery and the intervention of the wicked witch in the form of Frau von Luber. But it is the backdrop of hunger and class conflict and the insertion of a ballad about a dictator that makes the allegorical potential of the story especially rich. Nor would that potential have been lost on audiences at the time. The critic of the *Leipziger Volkszeitung* put it quite succinctly when he wrote, "There are a number of possibilities of allegorical interpretation that, if formulated too specifically, would drag the deeper significance of the whole down into banality and, moreover, into a sphere closely covered today by emergency measures."[43] He thereby offered two reasons why he and his colleagues stuck largely to literal plot summary—one essentially aesthetic, the other self-protectively political.

Der Silbersee is "of its time" in that it relates on various levels to conditions "at the time." Going where the critic of the *Leipziger Volkszeitung* feared to tread, Andreas Hauff has specified an allegory at the political level, suggesting that the work can be read in terms of the fate of the political parties in the late Weimar Republic and the early period of National Socialist rule.[44] According to such a reading, Olim and Severin stand for the Social Democrats and Communists respectively, fatally divided in their sociopolitical interests. Their future, Kaiser and Weill seem to be saying, is possible only as a common one. (And in reality it proved tragically impossible, as we know with historical hindsight.) For such a future to come about would require something of a miracle. Olim's repentance for having shot Severin when he caught him stealing a pineapple marks a first step. The literal steps he and Severin take together over the frozen lake in spring point the miraculous way forward. However, not only was the consummation of the symbols into an allegorical narrative dangerous for political reasons, as the Leipzig critic warned—the very danger being no doubt one of the reasons for the work's impact at the time—but such an interpretation may also seem inept now, for historical reasons. Allegorical potential is fueled by symbolic power: the piece struck a chord at the time, and retains the potential to do so today, precisely because it at once reflected and transcended the circumstances of its creation. The "purely human" appeal strengthened the immediately political one.

Most of the critics concentrated on the Leipzig premiere, even though it was the one in Magdeburg that had the greater—and thoroughly ominous—political impact.[45] And irrespective of whether they were sympathetic or hostile, most of them remarked on the piece's peculiar mix of fairy tale and social realism. The *Deutsche Zeitung* (20 February 1933), only slightly inclined in this case in the hostile direction, reported that Kaiser had "spun his fairy-tale image from the tough threads of reality." And like nearly all the reviews, this particular one devoted most of its space to summarizing the rich details of the plot, with all its bizarre developments. Reduced to the bare minimum of action by and interaction among the principal characters, the plot can be summarized as follows:

> It is winter. Severin and his unemployed, starving comrades are trying symbolically to extinguish their hunger by burying a life-size straw doll. Hunger, however, persists. After raiding a grocery store, they are fired upon by the country policeman Olim. Severin is wounded and arrested. On discovering that his victim has stolen only a pineapple, Olim feels such remorse that he alters his report to feign Severin's innocence, and retires from duty. He then learns that he has won the lottery and buys a castle, where he devotes himself to serving as Severin's generous but guilty benefactor. Confined to a wheelchair and seething with revenge, Severin is initially ignorant of his host's identity. Olim's housekeeper, Frau von Luber, is intrigued by the relationship between the two men, and in order to discover more about them she enlists her charming and guileless niece Fennimore. It is through Fennimore that Severin will discover Olim's secret. When Severin's doctor prescribes music as a palliative, Fennimore sings a ballad about "Caesar's Death," accompanying herself on the harp. But this only fuels his wrath, as does the sight of a pineapple, a reminder of the cause of his misery. A jaunty shimmy doesn't help either, even though the sight of bananas dancing on the ends of forks (an allusion to the bread rolls in Chaplin's *The Gold Rush*) entertains everyone else. To make matters worse, Frau von Luber discovers Olim's secret. Fennimore discovers it, too (at Severin's behest, she had visited his comrades at the Silver Lake). Hiding in the attic from the vengeful Severin, Olim is duped by Frau von Luber into signing away his property to her. She also enlists one of Olim's colleagues to reveal his identity. But Fennimore manages to bring about reconciliation between Olim and Severin, explaining that "whoever must continue will be carried by the Silver Lake." Instead of drowning, as intended, the two men escape across the lake, which has miraculously frozen over, even though it is spring.

Just as the work's narrative is richly allusive, so are the work's title and subtitle and also its artistic means. Possible associations include Shakespeare *(The Winter's Tale),* Karl May *(Der Schatz im Silbersee),* and, above all, Heine *(Deutschland: Ein Wintermärchen).*[46] By analogy with Heine's bitter poem, written from Parisian exile, *Der Silbersee* stands for contemporary Germany; to those familiar with the poem (however superficially), the connection is already obvious in the title. But they might also be tempted to draw more substantial parallels between Heine's focus on hunger on earth (railing against those who "secretly drink wine and preach water") and the miserable lot of the starving workers near the Silver Lake driven by their circumstances to petty theft. And they might note a further connection between the singing of "the little harp girl" in Heine's poem and Kaiser and Weill's figure of reconciliation and redemption, Fennimore, who accompanies herself on the harp. But Heine has "the little harp girl" sing the "Entsagungslied" (Song of Privation) on behalf of organized religion. It is a caustic irony that pursues a critical purpose somewhat different from that of *Der Silbersee.* True, Fennimore's "Ballad of Caesar's Death" is clearly meant as an allegory, not of organized religion, but of contemporaneous politics, which imposed its own forms of "privation." Her ultimate message will be one of hope and transcendence, however, a message almost completely absent from the conclusion of Heine's cynical poem.

The richly allusive quality is partly a function of the work's uncertain generic status. When he first described his conception of *Der Silbersee* to his publishers in 1932, Weill made it clear that he was not returning to the formula of *Die Dreigroschenoper,* as he had intended with *Happy End.* From the outset he made an important distinction between the earlier works and the new one he was contemplating: "Kaiser wants to write a musical folk play *[Volksstück]* with me. . . . By no means should it become an opera, but rather an intermediate genre *[Zwischengattungsstück].* It is up to me whether I turn it into a 'play with music' *[Stück mit Musik]*—that is, with quite simple songs that can be sung by straight actors—or whether I do something musically more ambitious and produce music on the scale and difficulty of, say, a musiquette by Offenbach. The latter would appeal to me because I would like to go here beyond the model created in *Die Dreigroschenoper.*"[47]

According to Weill's initial conception, then, *Der Silbersee* is not a *Stück mit Musik* for at least three reasons. One is the demands made by the vocal parts. Another is the scale of the music (something considerable in *Dreigroschenoper* nonetheless). A third is "difficulty" (beyond that of the vocal parts). And yet, a few days after his initial description, he not only explained further what he meant but also modified his earlier statement by qualifying what kind of play with music it was actually going to become: "In no way is it an opera but rather a play with well-integrated *[gut eingebauten]* musical numbers, somewhat along the lines of a singspiel. Since I have intended for a while to fit in a few smaller, less demanding works for practical theater use before my next big opera, here is an opportunity to realize this aim at the highest level and without any risk to my name."[48]

"Well integrated" is something one could say of the numbers in the earlier works, of course. Weill seems to have shied away from calling the new piece a mere *Stück mit Musik,* not only in order to accentuate the differences from other works of his, but also to stress the proximity to the earlier singspiel. Each piece, he appears to be saying, requires to be understood in two ways: on its own terms and in relation to generic precedents. He was at pains both to point up the unique character of the piece vis-à-vis his previous compositions for the spoken theater and to place his work within the classical traditions of German theater. Nor is the invocation of the eighteenth-century model tongue in cheek, as it had been with the Americanizing *Mahagonny-Songspiel. Der Silbersee* may be a comedy, but it is not brazenly ironic or satirical, as *Happy End* is, nor does it tend toward burlesque, still less farce, as *Die Dreigroschenoper* does. Its humor serves a solemn purpose.

The ending—something hopefully transcendent, not satirical—is key. In this respect the piece is closer to *Die Zauberflöte* than it is to its immediate predecessors. It is less art about art than it is art about the political situation in particular and human relations in general. Weill was perhaps also concerned that the contribution of his music to the whole would be downplayed or wholly misunderstood if the inclusive term *Stück mit Musik* were used. Even so, if the earlier pieces are more at home in the spoken theater, as Weill's reference to "straight actors" indicates, *Der Silbersee* is not exactly a singspiel in terms of its institutional underpinnings. As an in-between genre, it is between the opera house and the spoken theater, if anything closer to the latter. It is still very much a *Stück*, albeit one that makes remarkable musical demands on various levels. Not only do those demands need to be appreciated; so does Weill's expression "well integrated."

There is a third crucial aspect as well: the circumstances of the initial productions after Hitler's seizure of power need to be considered. Those circumstances lend the work's brief critical success a remarkable poignancy as well as a significance that is hard—and for that reason, perhaps, all the more necessary—to recapture.

Scored for an orchestra of at least twenty-five players, Weill's music to *Der Silbersee* comprises sixteen numbers, including solo songs, duets, choruses, melodramas, and instrumental interludes.[49] From the start there seemed to be a tension between Weill's thinking in terms of a singspiel and the length of Kaiser's text. Even before the work went into rehearsal it became clear that the extensive dialogue would need some pruning in order to let the music have its say and to keep the performance to a manageable length. After reading the book and inspecting some of the score, Hans Heinsheimer of Universal Edition expressed in a letter of 11 November 1932 the hope that "above all the matter of cuts will rapidly be resolved. The piece is baffling, I have convinced myself, because of its length and gives no sense of closure."[50] Weill responded: "Kaiser has declared himself wholly unprepared to make cuts for the time being and adopts the attitude that the piece is much shorter than any of Shakespeare's plays, and that it is a purely practical matter to remove the necessary few sentences."[51] But the composer agreed that "work still needed to be done on the book, especially cutting." The score, however, was a different matter: "I consider it out of the question to touch the music," he asserted, insisting on the integrity of his orchestration. "It is completely impossible with this work to use the piano-vocal reduction as the conductor's score. This is not an operetta in which the instrumentation does not matter, but a fully developed, carefully crafted score."[52] And so it is. The play is literally inconceivable without the music, of which instrumental timbres (the "sonic image," to use Weill's own expression) form an integral part.

But the basic problem remained, summarized by a critic of the Magdeburg premiere: "A play with too much music? Or an opera with too much dialogue?"[53]

The critical answer may be neither, despite the length of the dialogue. "Play with music" may be a catch-all for the intended "intermediate genre," but the role of the music needs to be understood on its own terms, not as diluted opera or overblown incidental music. It is a problem of classification similar to the one that surrounds Henry Purcell's so-called semi-operas, works that mix spoken plays with often quite discrete masque elements. History has been cruel to these works by viewing them, so to speak, through opera glasses. Purcell is seen as a frustrated, even failed opera composer, with his one small school opera *(Dido and Aeneas)* given far more importance for seventeenth-century England than it properly deserves, at the cost of more representative theater pieces such as the semi-operas (a label that already prejudices the issue). Despite Weill's own operatic aspirations, *Der Silbersee* deserves consideration as a type of theater in its own right, as something sui generis. Perhaps the most apt label was the one used for a recording of two songs from *Der Silbersee* ("Das Lied vom Schlaraffenland" and "Der Bäcker backt ums Morgenrot") recorded at the time of the premieres by Ernst Busch, who played Severin in the Magdeburg production. The disc describes the work as a *Schauspiel-Oper* ("play opera"), thereby accentuating the musical substance as much as the mixed genre.

In tackling the question of topicality it is worth recalling Weill's remarks on *Aufstieg und Fall der Stadt Mahagonny.* "It is," he said, "a parable of contemporary life," but he then went on to say: "Looking for psychological or contemporary relevance beyond this basic idea would be wrong."[54] He further clarified: "The idea of a theater of the times *[Zeittheater]*, something of enormous significance for the development of recent theater, can only be applied to musical theater when action of contemporary relevance *[aktuelle Vorgänge]* is cast in a grand form, in heightened language."[55] In his article "Zeitoper," written already in 1928, he had warned against "constructing themes of contemporary relevance valid only for the briefest period of the work's genesis."[56]

Fennimore's role is complicated by her pointing the way both to contemporary relevance and away from it. Her siren song about the Silver Lake, which returns at the end, may suggest a role for her as the "eternal feminine" along the lines of Gretchen in Goethe's *Faust.* But it is another Goethe allusion at the beginning of the piece that introduces the initial obstacle to be overcome. Whereas Goethe had written in his poem "Das Göttliche" that "people are noble, helpful, and good" ("Edel sei der Mensch, hülfreich und gut!"), the gravediggers omit any reference to nobility. One man digs another man's grave because people are like that: "helpful and good." It is an equivocally ironic twist induced by the desperate conditions. Are the men digging a grave or burying hunger? At this point, the latter activity is only symbolic. And the rhythms of the march music—quite distinct from those of the dance—will reappear throughout the piece to remind us of the source of Severin's anger. For hunger to be removed, people will have to become truly "helpful and good," if not "noble." Olim, who sees "people as changeable when their neighbor lends a hand," will play a role in this. So will Fennimore, who owes her awkward position to the fact that she is, by an unfortunate accident of birth, Frau von Luber's niece.

In her introductory song (her "Cavatina," as it were), "Ich bin eine arme Verwandte," Fennimore would all the more readily "offer her neighbor [her] hand" if she "didn't have to be related." The audience would no doubt have "related" to this sentiment given the racial policies of the National Socialists, instigating investigations into so-called racial purity and moving to bar "racially impure" citizens from state employment. Fennimore is not poor in a pecuniary sense; in this case, through family ties, she is expected to do the bidding of a vengeful, divisive aristocracy.

The "Ballade von Cäsars Tod" is unmistakable in its political implications. By way of emphasizing its importance, it already dominates the second, "contrasting" group of the overture. Although Fennimore's rendition of the ballad is supposed to help Severin overcome his rage, in fact it only exacerbates it, at least initially. (Like "Seeräuberjenny" in *Die Dreigroschenoper* and most of the songs in *Happy End,* it is a piece of diegetic or "source" music that disturbs the remaining characters on stage.) Severin is visibly provoked by the final verse ("Caesar wanted to rule by the sword and was felled by a knife"), which leaves him holding his food knife in his fist, as if about to stab someone. Frau von Luber, for her part, is left wishing that Fennimore would rather "stuff her mouth" with food than sing "murder ballads." To make amends, Fennimore performs her Chaplinesque "banana dance." With her back to the audience and her shoulders bobbing up and down, she entertains the company by attaching bananas to forks and making them dance, like puppets. (In *The Gold Rush,* Chaplin used bread rolls, but here the rolls are "too round.") Or rather, she entertains Olim and Frau von Luber, not Severin. One can even hear Olim's "unbuttoned laughter" with the orchestra's irregular phrase-lengths inserted between the four-square sentences of the shimmy.

The middle section of the song adopts a different tone, however. It is a belligerent march, presumably reflective not only of Severin's reaction to the dance but also of the psychological origin of that reaction. He is not amused. His face is "dangerously twitching" until, at the end of the dance, he lunges at the pineapple with his knife and shreds it to pieces in a blind rage. Although his guardians, the good and the bad, have been temporarily diverted by the shimmy, Severin is inadvertently forced to focus on the origin of his pain—the desire "overstimulated by phantasies brought on by hunger . . . to slurp juices . . . at the gates of paradise," as he later explains. Such is the symbolic import of the pineapple!

Again, Fennimore has not had the effect intended. That is part of her significance as musical siren with extraordinary powers. Olim had hoped to allow

EXAMPLE 13. *Der Silbersee,* Severin's revenge aria

"grass to grow over history" with the aid of food and music—the history, that is, of his crippling of Severin. Instead he has nurtured his victim's urge for revenge. After climbing onto his wheelchair seat and standing on it, Severin delivers his vengeance aria (No. 11). Over a driving accompaniment, with its triplet-dominated ostinato (such as can be found in the *Mahagonny* opera), Severin belts out his message of retribution in tones that recall the march of agitation and propaganda "Das Komintern-Lied" by Eisler (ex. 13).[57] The autobiographical narrative joins with music of collectivity; the personal sounds political, as if Severin were singing in solidarity with his fellow proletariat from the Silver Lake. At the end of each stanza, his refrain includes the words "There will be no forgiving, there will be no forgetting," followed in turn by "eye for an eye," "tooth for a tooth," "blood for blood," and in the last stanza, "life for a life," this time with "forgiving" and "forgetting" reversed.[58] Most of the syllables receive a whole measure to themselves as part of a drawn-out crescendoing incantation, first with just an oscillating minor third and then, at the end of the refrain, with a jarring tritone (ex. 14).

The reminiscence of Severin's aria (No. 12a) for chorus (a repetition of the final strophe) confirms the collective sentiment. Here, as elsewhere, the chorus articulates the two men's states of mind and, as the unity of multiple voices, transforms them into a kind of collective unconscious. In the first of the three melodramas

EXAMPLE 14. *Der Silbersee,* Severin's revenge aria, end of refrain

(No. 5), they goad a reflectively speaking Olim on, asking him, "Aren't you sorry?" and "Does this not concern you?" Like an epic Greek chorus, they also predict the turn of events (namely, his becoming rich) that will sustain his largesse toward Severin. Intertextual reference again enriches the dramatic and generic context: the prodding that leads to Olim's change of heart is introduced by a short but fairly explicit reference to the first-act finale of *Die Zauberflöte* (recall Weill's wish to create something approaching a singspiel).[59] The reference occurs via the dotted motif in the bass that accompanies the chorus's answers to Tamino's searching questions, such as "When will the cover be lifted?" The chorus replies: "Soon the hand of friendship will lead you to holiness and an eternal bond." Tamino continues: "O eternal night! When will you disappear? When will light find my eyes?" "Soon, soon, stranger," the chorus answers, "or no more," eventually confirming "Pamina is still alive!" (ex. 15). Weill's chorus, having asked the questions, also provides the answers: "Now you are on your way, keep thinking hard!" (ex. 16). One may not wish to pursue these parallels too far, however. Severin is hardly Pamina! But the metaphysical weight of Olim's quest is certainly increased, as Weill no doubt intended. The chorus plays a crucial role here.

Fennimore becomes Severin's messenger, volunteering to relay his fate to his friends at the Silver Lake and help discover the identity of the constable who shot him. But first of all he has to tell her how to find the place, in their duet "Auf jener Strasse." Like the "Kraniche-Duett" in *Aufstieg und Fall der Stadt Mahagonny,* with its rapid exchanges, "Auf jener Strasse" also has a text rich in nature imagery. Humanity is dissolved here into nature, as if into its primordial state. *Der Silbersee* is both the literal and metaphorical home. Fennimore says she will cross the lake as if on a wooden plank. Severin asks with obvious biblical allusion: "How can one walk on water?" Fennimore answers: "Whoever must continue will be carried by the Silver Lake." Just as these words have a multilayered resonance throughout the piece, so does their musical setting, with both music and words

EXAMPLE 15. Wolfgang Amadeus Mozart, *Die Zauberflöte,* act 1 finale

EXAMPLE 16. *Der Silbersee,* Melodrama

recurring at the open-ended conclusion of the piece. Although the duet begins in a fairly plodding duple meter, the final instrumental section switches to triple meter for the sparkling slow waltz. Dancing rather than walking may be required.

The Silver Lake owes its color, literally and metaphorically, to the light cast on it, as the duet makes clear at the words "Am Himmel sind doch Sterne aufgezogen und scheinen in die Finsternis hinein." Whoever continues also needs that light. The appropriate timbre and texture are provided at these words by two flutes, which create a static, "impressionistic" sonority built from a chain of superimposed thirds. In tonal terms, and depending on its deployment, the sonority might be seen as either a major or a minor triad with added seventh and ninth (again, either major or minor). The ambiguity is inherent in the construction: the common denominator is the aggregation of thirds, while the actual deployment in tonal contexts varies. The effect is a kind of coloristic stasis. The chains of thirds shine as detached motifs through the time-marking texture. They also become motivically derived harmony: the duet ends on a D♭ major chord with added major seventh (and in the pre-penultimate bar also a ninth) (ex. 17). The song's material, in other words, is at once generator of contextual harmony and musical emblem of the work's title. As such it makes itself felt in other parts of the score in significant ways, in terms of absolute musical coherence as well as dramatic salience.

The topic of musical metaphor in *Der Silbersee* has been discussed by Ian Kemp, who analyzed Weill's "tonal organism," identified "key symbolism," and explored "how Weill's harmony achieves its expressive effects." Kemp established, above all, a tendency on Weill's part "towards the flat side of a tonic," key areas traditionally "associated with introversion, darkening, pessimism, tragedy."[60] But there is, as suggested, another dimension of metaphor intimately linked on a motivic level to the work's dramatic content. To what degree and in what ways does the musical emblem of the Silver Lake, at once linear motif and harmonic collection, pervade the score? Answering such a question is hampered by the nature of motivic analysis in general and the rudimentary nature of Weill's motif in particular. Like many of Wagner's leitmotifs, Weill's "motif of illumination," as it might be called, can be reduced to extremely basic elements. Only with such elements can a composer create what Thomas Mann called the "sorcery of associations" *(Beziehungszauber)*, leaving the listener and analyst uncertain where connections do and do not exist. That which is most specific, as Adorno put it, is also most general. Ultimately almost any note—even a single note—can end up *seeming* motivic.[61]

As presented in "Auf jener Strasse," the motif of illumination is articulated rhythmically and timbrally (see ex. 17). With its staccato sixteenth notes, however, the rhythm has the effect of an arpeggiated chord—harmony more than melody. The instrumentation is more specific: upper-register flutes highlighting the motif's signification of luminescence. From a motivic perspective, the identi-

EXAMPLE 17. *Der Silbersee,* "Auf jener Strasse" ("motif of illumination")

cal presentation at the work's conclusion is unmistakable (if not unequivocal); the associations of this literal recapitulation are indeed magical.

There are degrees of specificity and generality. Measured in degrees of abstraction, the distance of the motif's presentation from the duet varies. Chains of thirds appear at various points in the score. They begin already in the Overture, whose bustling opening gesture could put the listener in mind of another overture, that to Mozart's *Figaro.* This is the *buffa* aspect of the piece by way of radical contrast to the central section, "Cäsars Tod," the work's extremely *seria* aspect. The piling up of thirds appears with a vengeance in the Overture's second subsection. The same approach to the generation of linear figures continues in the pseudo-baroque chorus following the Overture, and is echoed again frequently in subsequent numbers. In a number of cases, notably the song of the Lottery Agent, such variably diatonic lines, which result from tertiary elements being juxtaposed, generate the entire melodic material.

In its most general abstract form, stripped to its basic constituents as a collection of thirds, the motif can seem almost omnipresent. In the final measures it presents itself as a self-sufficient simultaneity, the sonority of the illuminated Silver Lake. With Olim and Severin having overcome their differences thanks to their faith in Fennimore, it is a magical moment of maximum integration. The entire play seems to be carried by the music, concluding on an unresolved leading note, itself thematic. But leading to where?

Political developments at the time unquestionably inspired Kaiser and Weill's utopian thinking. Events surrounding the Magdeburg production of the piece in particular, despite the largely favorable reception, demonstrated all too forcefully that the artists' vision would indeed remain utopian.[62] Germany was not ready to tolerate, let alone overcome, perceived difference. Yet the ending of the piece can also be read in baldly realistic terms: human sympathy, such as that developed against the odds between Olim and Severin, is a necessary but hardly a sufficient condition for the peace and well-being of the community. Faith must ally itself with action. That action must necessarily take place outside of the theater. And so it did, with tragic consequences: action allied to a barbaric faith.

6

Epic Opera

The epithet *epic* is laden with conceptual baggage. In the expression "epic theater" it conjures up theory rather than practice, tracts rather than plays. The literature on the subject is voluminous, most of it on theoretical aspects of works written by Brecht and his associates. Yet the relevance of the concept for Weill extends well beyond the plays and operas he wrote with Brecht or the theoretical texts that accompany them. Busoni's teachings, which foreshadowed some of Brecht's ideas about epic theater, exerted a vital influence, and not just on Weill's pre-Brecht operas. Another defining influence came from the music-theater works of Stravinsky, in particular *L'histoire du soldat,* but also *Oedipus rex.*[1]

Just as Busoni and Stravinsky were decisive in shaping Weill's commitment to forms of theater that can be described as "epic," that commitment endured long after the partnership with Brecht had foundered. While there is no denying that the *Mahagonny* project (both the "Songspiel" and the full-length opera) and other Brecht works furnish the classic examples against which the idea of epic musical theater can and has been tested, the opera Weill composed with stage designer Caspar Neher as co-librettist, *Die Bürgschaft,* is a no less deserving candidate. Heinrich Strobel voiced a hardly eccentric opinion when he stated in his Weill obituary that "epic music theater, the object of Weill's constant striving, achieved its most opportune formulation in *Die Bürgschaft.*"[2]

In an interview given in connection with the premiere of *The Eternal Road* in 1937, Weill demonstrated that he by no means abandoned the principles of epic theater, at least as he understood them, after moving to the United States. "The musical theatre is predominantly epic in character," he maintained, echoing earlier writings.

> The role played by music is not that of drawing out the inner action, knitting together transitional phases, bringing out events and causing passions to flare high; rather does it go its own way chiming in at static moments of the action. This is possible only with an epic-narrative form of action which makes the course of events on the stage perfectly clear to the audience, so that the music framed in this quiet development can retain its concertistic character and achieve its purely musical effect in undisturbed harmony. Not to interpret musically the objectively presented course of the action, but to let this action run parallel to an equally objective flow of music—that is the inner sense of the new musical theatre.[3]

The comment is as general in its relevance as it is problematic in its details. General, because "musical theater" and "epic theater" are almost synonymous, at least in Weill's mind. Problematic, because of the questions his explanation raises. What does he mean by "concertistic character," "purely musical effects in undisturbed harmony," and "objective flow of music?" How can these essentially musical matters be connected, first, to Brecht's theories and, second, to Weill's non-Brecht works?

A comparison of Brecht's and Weill's theoretical writings reveals anomalies in their conceptions of epic theater, alongside commonalities. At the same time, Brecht's writings have been particularly influential to the extent that they have determined interpretations of the works, including production decisions. The present chapter begins, then, with a comparison of the writings, before discussing how Weill's theoretical conceptions apply in particular to the operas *Aufstieg und Fall der Stadt Mahagonny* and *Die Bürgschaft*.

THEORETICAL ANOMALIES

Lotte Lenya was epic without knowing it—or at least without *thinking* that she knew it. When she visited Bertolt Brecht at his East Berlin home in 1955, he asked her to sing for him. Yet because they had not seen each other for a number of years, she at first demurred, feeling apprehensive about her grasp of the playwright's celebrated theories. Brecht, for his part, was quick to supply words of encouragement. "Lenya," he said, "whatever you do is epic enough for me."[4] The anecdote, however fanciful, serves as a reminder that Brecht's approach to theater was thoroughly pragmatic, notwithstanding his numerous and widely publicized theoretical statements. The proof of the pudding, as he is often quoted as saying, using an unabashedly culinary metaphor, is in the eating. By the same token, the test of epic theater is in the performing, requiring for its impact the likes of Lenya and Helene Weigel. "Epic," according to Lenya's story, belongs to the sphere of performance; it defines a particular artistic quality or distinction, a way of performing. She was (unwittingly) "epic enough" for Brecht. Yet Brecht's remark indirectly illustrates a point of more general significance. When dealing with his theories in terms of creation or performance, it is as well to consider the relation of those theories to actual practice: not just how the theories apply (if they actually do) to the works and their realization, but also the circumstances under which the theories themselves came about.

Of Brecht's tracts, none more warrants such circumspection than the best known of all: "Anmerkungen zur Oper *Aufstieg und Fall der Stadt Mahagonny,*" written jointly with Peter Suhrkamp and published in 1930 as part of volume two of the *Versuche.*[5] Not only do these "Notes" represent the most often quoted source of the theory of epic theater—remarkable enough for a text purportedly about opera; they also provide the frequently invoked Brechtian precepts of epic opera and, equally remarkable, what many have taken to be the theoretical foundation for the Brecht-Weill collaboration in general.[6] As a closed system, the words have been mistaken for the thing itself; or, as the seventeenth-century British empiricist philosopher John Locke put it in his celebrated *Essay Concerning Human Understanding,* the nominal essence has been substituted for the real essence.[7]

In a much-quoted definition, Brecht described the role of music in the shift from "dramatic" to "epic" opera as one whereby the music "mediates . . . setting forth the text *[den Text auslegend],* taking the text as known *[den Text voraussetzend],* taking up a position *[Stellung nehmend],* and indicating the attitude *[das Verhalten gebend].*" By adopting wholesale Brecht's definition, one influential commentator has drawn the conclusion that in Weill and Eisler Brecht had found composers who created "vermittelnde, den Text auslegende, Stellung nehmende, das Verhalten gebende, Partei ergreifende Musik."[8] Another has expressed the view that "in the *Mahagonny* opera both [Brecht and Weill] achieved the profoundest artistic realization of their theoretical postulates."[9] Closer examination of the "Notes"—considering, that is, the collaborators' divergent notions of what constitutes epic opera, and including the circumstances of the notes' genesis—reveals such assumptions about a harmonious correspondence between theory and practice to be illusory. Significant anomalies emerge.

The first and most obvious ground for questioning the adequacy of Brecht's "Notes" could be seen to rest in the fact that he formulated them only after the tumultuous first performance of the *Mahagonny* opera, which took place in Leipzig on 9 March 1930. *Postfestum* theory is not in itself a questionable undertaking. If anything, it is preferable; or in this case—given the opera's two-year genesis, during which time the authors' respective conceptions and styles changed considerably—it is the only kind of theoretical abstraction possible.

What invites circumspection is not simply the fact that Brecht wished to reflect on his work or on opera in general. It was, after all, a period when the genre's very existence and justification were permanently under discussion. Rather, it is that Brecht's views diverge in several fundamental respects from

Weill's own. And Weill's views may well have been partly responsible for prompting Brecht's proclamations in the first place. Before the "Notes" appeared in 1930, Weill had published the "Vorwort zum Regiebuch der Oper *Aufstieg und Fall der Stadt Mahagonny*" and two other articles that share common material: "Zur Aufführung der Mahagonny-Oper" and "Anmerkungen zu meiner Oper *Mahagonny*."[10] Brecht, in the words of David Drew, "retaliated."[11] It is possible, then, to read the "Notes" more as an aggrieved answer to Weill's contrary opinions—opinions also conveyed in reviews of the premiere—than as the expression of common aims.[12]

"What principally appealed to me about this subject matter," wrote Weill, "was the fact that it offered me the best possibilities for realizing my musical and formal intentions in the field of opera."[13] Or as he expressed it in the "Vorwort," "The subject matter of the opera *Aufstieg und Fall der Stadt Mahagonny* made possible a *structure based purely on musical laws*." The prefatory remarks to the "Vorwort"—remarks that Weill formulated in a letter, dated 11 December 1929, to his publishers, Universal Edition—refer to Weill's working "jointly with Caspar Neher and Bertolt Brecht on a production book *[Regiebuch]* for the opera Mahagonny." Originally intended for distribution to theaters together with Neher's projections, the *Regiebuch* was in fact solely the creation of Neher and Weill. Brecht had no hand in the matter.[14] From the start, it would seem, Weill had conceived of the work along "purely musical" lines. As he wrote to his publisher as early as 18 November 1927, "I am in the middle of working on 'Mahagonny.' I have been working daily with Brecht on the libretto, which is being formed completely in accordance with my directions. This type of collaboration, on the basis of which a libretto is actually structured from a purely musical point of view, opens up whole new possibilities. The composition [of the music] has already begun."[15] Weill would echo these ideals eight years later when he wrote that the music in epic theater could, as quoted above, "retain its concertistic character and achieve its purely musical effect in undisturbed harmony"—ideals that hardly define themselves, however.[16]

Weill was evidently instrumental in shaping the libretto. At all events, the espoused primacy of music in the overall conception must have incensed Brecht, whose central idea behind epic opera—an antithesis to the Wagnerian *Gesamtkunstwerk*, as he saw it—was the "separation of the elements." As Brecht wrote in the "Notes," "The penetration of opera by the methods of epic theater leads principally to a radical separation of the elements."[17] To Brecht's chagrin, Weill was expounding a theory of opera that gave music primacy over the word and hence upheld what Brecht wished "simply to abolish": "the music occasioning the events on stage," or vice versa.[18] Admittedly, Weill no longer saw the music as the "motivating *[handlungtreibendes]* element"; rather, "the music enters where certain situations or states *[Zustände]* are arrived at." Yet it was precisely the juxtaposition of such "states" or "situations" that, "in their musically fixed, dynamic sequence, yield a dramatic form."[19]

Where Brecht was seeking to overturn, Weill was being a traditionalist. For each collaborator, translating the principles of epic theater to the opera house meant something different. For the composer, it meant primarily the restitution of the number opera: "dividing the plot or action *[Handlung]* into closed numbers and the dramaturgic utilization of absolute musical form."[20] Weill's aim, as he expressed it in December 1929, was "a form of opera founded on musical principles."[21]

On several points the collaborators of course saw eye to eye. How else would their partnership have been possible? It could just as easily have been Brecht who wrote, "This theater is, to the highest degree, unromantic. 'Romanticism' as art switches off our capacity to think; it operates with narcotic means; it shows human beings only in exceptional states; and in its heyday (in Wagner) it avoids representing human beings at all." But the words are Weill's, from his 1929 essay "Über den gestischen Charakter der Musik."[22] In his "Notes," Brecht circumscribes Weill's first clause with "Together with their hat, they [grown men] also give up their normal behavior, their attitude 'in life.' . . . The old opera completely excludes any discussion of content."[23] Weill's clause about "narcotic means" finds expression in Brecht as "A state of intoxication is indispensable."[24] Weill's last two clauses are covered by Brecht's notion of the "culinary" or *geniesserisch:* "The degree of enjoyment is directly dependent on the degree of unreality."[25] "Those composers who are addicted to Wagner even persist in adopting a *Weltanschauung*—one that is otherwise quite useless and is dumped on the public purely as a means of sensual pleasure!"[26]

Where Weill and Brecht part company is, as mentioned, on the question of music's predominance. But they also differ on a more basic question—namely, the prospects for the genre as such. Brecht is pessimistic: "Today one has to ask whether opera is not already in a state in which innovations no longer lead to the rejuvenation of this genre but rather to its destruction." He summarizes the innovations of the *Mahagonny* opera as "those that make it possible for the theater to present moral tableaux (revealing the commodity status both of entertainment and of those being entertained) and those that put the spectator in a moralizing frame of mind." Yet he then applies the self-destruction metaphor of sawing off the same branch one is still sitting on: "but *Mahagonny* has at least started (absent-mindedly or out of bad conscience) to saw [the branch] through. . . . Real innovations," he argues, "attack the base"—the economic base which determines, as Brecht sets forth at the outset of his "Notes," the very nature of the operatic establishment. With a subtle shift of terminology Brecht then implies in his final paragraph, by introducing the superscription "Für Neuerungen—gegen Erneuerungen," that *Mahagonny* also falls under the second category: rejuvenation rather than real innovation. Consequently, Brecht devotes his closing remarks to promoting what came after his opera: "experiments [which] emphasize more and more the didactic at the expense of the culinary." In other words, his Lehrstücke (didactic theater pieces).[27]

Weill, too, wrote Lehrstücke after *Mahagonny.* Yet he never proffered a Marxist analysis of the operatic establishment. His didactically conceived pieces were part of his declared aim of reaching a new, wider audience, as had been his other hybrid forms such as *Die Dreigroschenoper.* But all along, large-scale opera remained a goal. For all his scathing criticism of the musical establishment, Weill never opposed opera, as Brecht appeared to, as an essentially reactionary, untenable, and ultimately dispensable institution. On the contrary, he viewed all the other collaborations with Brecht written between the inception of the *Mahagonny* opera in the summer of 1927 and its completion in the winter of 1929—*Die Dreigroschenoper, Happy End, Das Berliner Requiem,* and *Der Lindberghflug*—as "building blocks toward this opera." Even the *Mahagonny-Songspiel*—the "Baden-Baden *Mahagonny,*" as Weill described it—he considered a "stylistic study to prepare for the operatic work."[28] Weill's public articulation of these views no doubt prompted Brecht to exaggerate or polarize his own position. Yet the crucial theoretical difference remains: Brecht was expressing a negative, destructive intent; Weill a positive, constructive one.

The disparity between Brecht's and Weill's theoretical stances is not merely to be put down to a matter of temperament, nor explained away by invoking the age-long quarrel between librettist and composer over the primacy of their respective media, words and music. Brecht's negative attitude toward opera no doubt reflects his ambitions as a playwright, his professed anti-expressionist mistrust of music and, not least, his Marxian opposition to the institution of opera as such, to the genre's representative function, its embodiment of oppressive power relations. All these factors have a role to play. Yet there is also a sense in which the very notion of "epic" as applied to the theater functions as an essentially negative category—in Brecht's words, where "innovations no longer lead to the rejuvenation of this genre but rather to its destruction."

Within the strictly defined terms of classical poetics, the concept of epic theater can be seen to represent a paradox or, to use Emil Staiger's hyperbole, "babylonian confusion." True, the adjectives *epic, dramatic,* and *lyric* denote qualities whose application is not restricted to the genres that their cognate nouns signify: *epos, drama,* and *lyric.* As Staiger puts it, "nicht jeder Mensch ist menschlich."[29] Similarly, not every drama is dramatic, but can contain other qualities or elements, either lyric or—in Brecht's case—epic ones. Brecht's experiments in epic drama begin, as Peter Szondi observed in his *Theorie des modernen Dramas,* where the contradiction becomes evident between social subject matter and dramatic form.[30] Yet within the context of the theater, the injection of these epic elements is to be understood in terms of liberties taken with the dramatic unities. "In place of dramatic teleology there is the epic freedom to linger and reflect."[31] Indeed, Szondi's theory of modern drama, underpinned as it is by the seminal idea of the "epicization" of the dramatic (an idea borne out particularly in Brecht's work), propounds a fundamentally negative thesis or ideal model—namely, that "developments in modern writing for the theater lead away from drama."[32]

The rules of epic theater are not in themselves normative, as Szondi remarked in his "Nachtrag zur *Theorie des modernen Dramas*." Epic structure in plays tends to be interpreted in terms of the impossibility and therefore specific negation of the dramatic.[33] In purely formal terms, Brecht achieved his renunciation of traditional drama by means of epic "liberties," which, because of their intended impact on the audience, he labeled *Verfremdungseffekte*. In early Brecht, such "effects"—for example, the intervention of the auctorial voice in *Mann ist Mann*—are clearly intended as *épatant* (something also planned for the scene before Macheath's proposed hanging in *Die Dreigroschenoper*, but ultimately suppressed). Later, however, they serve a positive, pedagogical purpose, as the theory expounds: "The object of the effect is to allow the spectator to criticize constructively from a social point of view."[34] Willful disruption of the illusion of dramatic unity and socially critical didacticism are two faces of the same epic coin.

The crux of Brecht's "Notes" is the underlying assumption that his theory of drama neatly translates, with the additional element of music, into a theory of opera, that the shift of emphasis from dramatic to epic in the former also applies to the latter. Just as, by drawing up the ubiquitously cited parallel columns, he posits an ideal model of the "epic form of theater" as the conceptual opposite and specific negation of the "dramatic form of theater," so he similarly distinguishes an epic and dramatic form of opera. What goes for these theater pieces, Brecht seems to be saying, also goes for his opera, *Mahagonny*. The assumption, however, is flawed, as becomes apparent when one attempts to apply the Szondian model.[35] Opera is different. Furthermore, Brecht's basic understanding of opera derives from a facile and uncharitable concept of Wagnerian music-drama.

In its essentials, opera can be both more and less dramatic, more and less epic, than spoken drama. This is not to presume a fundamental generic structure, as Erik Fischer has done with systematic, and hence abstractly ahistorical, pretensions.[36] It is simply to draw attention to two salient differences between the two types of theater—differences that, for diametrically opposed reasons, serve to undermine Brecht's proposed "epicization" of opera. The first historically specific difference is that, formally or poietically speaking, opera has tended all along toward "epic" construction. Thus, Brecht's model of the epic form of theater—entailing, in contradistinction to the dramatic form, not "one scene for another" but "each scene for itself," not "growth" but "montage," not "linear action" but action "in curves," not "evolutionary inevitability" but "jumps"—applies quite readily to operas Brecht would no doubt have considered as belonging to the old, dramatic form. As Carl Dahlhaus observed (adopting Brecht's own terminology), "Non-aristotelian dramaturgy, a sign of modernity in plays, appears in opera as a piece of tradition."[37] This, at least, is why Weill could see *Mahagonny* as an opportunity to compose an opera with closed musical numbers, thereby reinstating the *Urform* of opera, as he called it in his notes on *Die Dreigroschenoper.*[38] As Weill remarks in his "Vorwort zum Regiebuch," "The epic theater form is a successive juxtaposition of situations. Hence it is the ideal form of musical theater; for it is only situations that can be performed as music in a closed form, and a juxtaposition of situations from a musical perspective produces the heightened form of music theater: opera."[39]

Symptomatic of this structural anomaly between opera and drama is the differing importance the two collaborators attach to the use of projection. What principally concerned Weill with the composition of *Mahagonny* was "to give the links between the musical numbers a form that obstructs as little as possible the musical design of the whole. . . . For this reason, we have replaced the dialogue with inscriptions."[40] Brecht, in contrast, saw the inscriptions as a significant innovation constituting one of the separated, discrete elements of epic theater that serve to disrupt dramatic illusion and unity and thereby create "Verfremdung" or "V-Effekt." He similarly draws attention to the importance of the independent images supplied by Caspar Neher's projections, a "Novum" intended to "adopt an attitude toward the events onstage."[41] That Weill openly declared the inscriptions an expedient measure, a solution to the opera composer's abiding problem of dealing with bothersome dramatic dialogue, must have only provoked Brecht further. (Given the extent of Chaplin's influence on Brecht, the latter's written titles may well have been inspired by silent films, irrespective of the fact that here, as for Weill, their use was largely a matter of expediency.)

Both collaborators were at one in consciously rejecting the principles of Wagnerian music-drama. "The penetration of opera by the methods of epic theater," as Brecht makes plain, is directed specifically at the *Gesamtkunstwerk.*[42] Where Brecht writes of the music in dramatic opera as "heightening the text," "asserting the text," and "illustrating," he had in mind not just "attempts to hypnotize" as well as "undignified states of intoxication," but in particular those perpetrated or unleashed by Wagner.

One side of Brecht's critique of traditional, "dramatic" opera refers to its effect on the audience—"the undignified states of intoxication," which on Brecht's own admission did not escape him either. The other side addresses the question of music's relation to the text, which Brecht defines as tautologous in dramatic opera. The view is based, among other things, on a misunderstanding of Wagner's leitmotif technique, on the assumption that the music merely doubles the action on stage or what the *dramatis personae* are declaiming. In the words of Carl Dahlhaus, "It is simply absurd to accuse a technique of being tautologous whose point and dramaturgic function consist, on the contrary, in constituting a 'second plot' alongside the events made manifest by verbal and scenic means—an imaginary drama, that is, compounded of references backward and forward and which outstretches the consciousness of the characters involved."[43] Where, in Wagner, Brecht described the music as "painting the psychic situation," it may well in fact be "indicating the attitude." Leitmotif technique often represents auctorial intervention and comment on the composer's part. To that extent it serves what Brecht would define as an epic purpose.[44]

Based on Weill's theoretical understanding, opera before *Mahagonny* contained a number of "epic" elements—elements that Brecht's "Notes" scarcely acknowledge. Moreover, such elements are prominent in Weill's own operas composed before his partnership with Brecht. In that sense they are Busonian rather than Brechtian. Insofar as Weill's debt to his teacher Busoni was more an aesthetic than a stylistic matter, that debt seems especially evident in his first opera, *Der Protagonist,* completed in 1925. When the critic Oskar Bie declared Weill's achievement in this work as pointing to "the future of opera," he may well have had in mind Busoni's essay of the same name, "Von der Zukunft der Oper," which appeared in *Von der Einheit der Musik* in 1922. And even if he did not, it is scarcely an exaggeration to regard *Der Protagonist* as a practical realization of Busoni's programmatic reflections. For this reason one could be forgiven for assuming that Weill had specially commissioned the libretto from Kaiser. (The text already existed as a play, written in 1920.)

Much like *Der Protagonist,* Weill's third one-act opera, the opera buffa *Der Zar lässt sich photographieren,* is concerned with the typically Kaiserian dialectic of illusion and reality. With all its "epic" elements—the stylistic dualism embracing chromatic espressivo and jaunty tango, the impassively commenting chorus, the confrontation of old and new, "false" and "real"—*Der Zar* can be seen, on a meta-level, as an opera about opera. By placing a lyrically amorous member of the old order (the Czar) in the altogether up-to-date setting of a photographer's studio, with the property of telephone and gramophone playing an integral role in the proceedings, Weill and Kaiser have a serious point to make, albeit with delightfully witty and undogmatic means. In the prefatory material to the *Mahagonny-Songspiel* (whose composition held up progress on *Der Zar*) there is talk of "the liquidation of aristocratic art forms"—an issue of cultural politics that the *Songspiel* formulates in a stridently question-begging fashion and that later finds its way into Brecht's "Notes." The creators of *Der Zar,* however, would appear no less aware of the agenda. Yet they employ a more equivocal approach, nudging rather than shaking their audience into drawing its own conclusions.

The other seminal difference between opera and drama that potentially undermines Brecht's theory of the "epicization" of opera has to do with nothing less than the distinction between modes of delivery: speech on the one hand and song on the other. It is not a purely formal matter, for it has to do as well with reception, belonging in the same category as Brecht's objection to music's intoxicating effect. Music, according to W. H. Auden, is "immediate actuality"; opera "an imitation of human willfulness . . . rooted in the fact that we not only have feelings but insist upon having them at whatever cost to ourselves."[45] If Auden's observation applies, according to which "every high C accurately struck demolishes the theory that we are the irresponsible puppets of fate or chance," then the very idea of opera is at loggerheads with the central notion behind epic *Verfremdung*, which, as Szondi perceived, emerged as an attempt to resolve the contradiction between social subject matter and dramatic form.[46] Opera, as described by Auden, stubbornly upholds that contradiction—a fact with potential ramifications for *Mahagonny.* Either Jimmy Mahoney sings himself out of the plot, or the plot demolishes the music.

Echoing Auden, Peter Conrad put his finger on this anomaly when reviewing a production of the opera at the New York Metropolitan Opera in 1979. "Though Brecht's *Mahagonny,*" he wrote, "is a study of economic villainy, Weill's musical commentary changes it to a work about the pursuit of pleasure. . . . Song in this work is a medium not of alienatory critique, as Brecht wished, but of wishful fantasy . . . and an assertion of appetitive freedom: during the hurricane Mahoney sings defiantly."[47] This is always assuming—something Conrad omitted to mention—that the protagonist's high C is accurately struck. The conviction and defiance lie as much in the performance as in the musical score, just as the *Verfremdungseffekte* vary in frequency and degree from production to production. Whether or not a work is perceived as epic is ultimately not decided by the librettist or by the composer; as a matter for realization in the theater it is subject to what William Empson termed "dramatic ambiguity."[48]

A distinction needs to be drawn, then, between epic structure and epic effect, between means and ends. Seen in this light, Lenya's anecdote about being "epic enough" is anything but flippant or trivial, emphasizing as it does the extent to which epic theater relies for its impact on certain qualities of production and performance, while at the same time serving as a reminder that Brecht's notion of "epic" is not only a theory of creation, a poietics, but also a philosophy of performance and reception, an aesthetics. The distinction is all the more crucial for opera, in view of the genre's inherent tendency toward epic structure but also toward both dramatic and lyrical effect. As a category in the poietics of music theater, "epic opera" can be seen as a tautology; in terms of a *Wirkungsästhetik*, in contrast, it functions as an oxymoron. Where, however, in the Brechtian sense, the epithet *epic* may appear most meaningful and appropriate is as a style of production. The influence of Brecht's theories on opera may have been greatest in the realm of production techniques. What, after all, is director's theater, *Regietheater,* if not an attempt, through the imposition of extraneous, often didactic concepts, to point beyond the work and potentially undermine music's immediate dramatic impact—in other words, to make opera epic? The result is often called music theater, as are later attempts to implement more emphatically at the compositional stage Brecht's "separation of the elements."

The differences are of course gradual rather than absolute. Weill himself was keen to cultivate what he called *Zwischengattungen,* mixed genres, alongside "pure opera." Yet as he remarked in an interview published in 1930, "Particularly dangerous are the sort of aspirations that can be described as modernistic. . . . Some people preach a dissolution [of opera] in a theatrical direction but do nothing other than those older opera directors who, out of an aversion toward music, destroy every musical form with a theatrical gimmick or surfeit of 'production ideas' *[Regieeinfälle].*"[49] Weill clearly stopped short of such "epic" invasions. That he did so is characteristic of his commitment to opera and, moreover, of the tensions and anomalies in the Brecht-Weill partnership.

AUFSTIEG UND FALL DER STADT MAHAGONNY

Concerning the many differences between the two incarnations of the *Mahagonny* material, Weill himself observed: "Almost everything added to the Baden-Baden version is written in a perfectly strict, thoroughly responsible style," adding that "I presume that it will endure longer than most of what is being produced nowadays."[50] The occasion for the comment was a letter from Weill's publishers, Universal Edition, in which Hans Heinsheimer conjectured that Weill had "abandoned the style of 1928."[51] The coexistence of the two styles in the opera—the "song style" and the "perfectly strict, thoroughly responsible style"—not only reflects Weill's development during the work's two-year genesis. As *Die Bürgschaft* also demonstrates, the coexistence contributes to the music's "concertistic character," its "purely musical effect," as Weill called it, the significance of which will emerge in the following discussion.

There ought to be little disagreement about the central theme of *Aufstieg und Fall der Stadt Mahagonny.* The title makes it clear enough, and in his own plot summary the composer goes so far as to state that "the main character of the piece is the city, which emerges from people's needs." The full description, quoted here from the "Vorwort zum Regiebuch," is written very much from the composer's perspective; all the events described have musical consequences.

> Two men and a woman, fleeing from the police, get stuck in a desolate area. They decide to found a city in which men coming from the Gold Coast will have their needs satisfied. In the "paradise city" that emerges people lead a tranquil, idyllic

> life. In the long run, however, such a life cannot satisfy the men from the Gold Coast. Dissatisfaction prevails. Prices go down. In the night of the typhoon that approaches the city Jim Mahoney invents the new law of the city. The law is: "You may do everything." The typhoon changes course. People continue to live according to the new laws. The city flourishes. Needs increase—and with them, prices. You may do everything—provided you can pay for it. Jim Mahoney himself is condemned to death when he runs out of money. His execution gives rise to a huge demonstration against the inflation that heralds the city's demise. That is the story of the city of Mahagonny. It is represented in a loose juxtaposition of "images of twentieth-century customs." It is a parable of contemporary life. The main character of the piece is the city, which emerges from people's needs. It is people's needs that bring about the city's rise and fall. We merely show the individual phases in the city's history and how they affect people. Just as people's needs influence the city's development, so in turn the city's development changes people's attitudes. All the opera's songs are an expression of the masses, even where they are performed by the individual as spokesman of the masses. The group of founders at the beginning confronts the group of new arrivals. At the end of the first act the supporters of the new law struggle against its opponents. The fate of the individual is portrayed only where it exemplifies the fate of the city. Looking for psychological or contemporary relevance beyond this basic idea would be wrong. The name "Mahagonny" connotes merely the name of a city. It was chosen for timbral (phonetic) reasons. The city's geographical location is immaterial.[52]

Not only does the word *city* appear in the work's title; it occurs in the plot description no less than fourteen times.

It is worth recalling here the interview Weill gave in 1936, just over a year after coming to the United States: "In Germany I'm known as a Kulturbolshevist: my music is un-German, un-Aryan. They call it asphalt-music, because it smacks of the city, which is to me a great compliment!"[53] In the preceding decade the city had become an irresistible fascination for many creative artists. For Weill, as for many of his contemporaries, among them Bertolt Brecht, it was a fascination that was double-edged. The city stood for many things, positive and negative, real and imaginary, utopian and dystopian.[54] The question, then, is not so much, what is the theme of the opera? (that much is evident), but rather, how does Weill's music "smack of the city"?; what does the music tell us? how is the urban theme treated musically? Again, the stylistic shift that Weill reported to Heinsheimer has an important role to play.

In view of Weill's generalization about his music "smacking" of the city, it is also worth recalling when and how he came to that theme. His musical urban studies began already in 1925 with the cantata *Der neue Orpheus,* a work that he saw as path-breaking in his evolution as a composer. The city serves here as the site for a surreal recasting of the Orpheus myth, located somewhere between heaven and hell. In the one-act opera *Der Zar lässt sich photographieren* of 1927, written with Georg Kaiser, the city is specified as Paris, the place where the eponymous Czar fails in his attempt to appear both normal and up-to-date—that is, urbane. Traditional absolute rule and modern democracy don't mix too well, despite any appearances to the contrary. The 1929 play by Brecht and Hauptmann with music by Weill, the ironically titled *Happy End,* brings a mix of another kind: gangsters and the Salvation Army. Set in Chicago, the piece ends with the canonization of the saints of capitalism, Morgan, Ford, and Rockefeller, as the local gangsters join forces with the street peddlers of religion. Another example is the collection of songs and choruses called the *Berliner Requiem* written in 1929 and about which Weill commented that its content "undoubtedly corresponds with the feelings and views of the broadest strata of the population. An attempt has been made to express what the contemporary city dweller has to say about the phenomenon of death."[55] The city has a crucial role to play in *Die Bürgschaft* as a symbol of modern, industrial society and the attendant alienation between family and friends. In *Die sieben Todsünden,* a secular parable of exile, various American cities represent the urban obstacles that threaten personal and artistic integrity.

The city continues to play a role in Weill's American works, above all in the "American opera," *Street Scene.* New York is Weill's "melting-pot" symbol of a cultural mix as well as the locus of passion and death. He called the house of "Lonely House," the theme song, "a prison for the human spirit"—a comment that recalls the earlier fascination with the Lamentations of Jeremiah, with their opening line "How doth the city sit solitary, that was full of people!" *Love Life* pursues the theme of interpersonal estrangement over a 150-year period of American history, echoing concerns about industrialization that similarly informed *Die Bürgschaft.*

All of Weill's city pieces amount to essays on the human condition, viewed from a variety of perspectives, a condition at once formed and threatened by modern urban life. The *Mahagonny* project with Brecht, then, is just one among several of his visions of urbanity.

The two and a half years between the conception of the *Songspiel* and the premiere of the opera critically defined the careers of the two collaborators, just as their project marked both the beginning and the end of their partnership, if not literally, then at least spiritually. If Weill's commentaries tell a quite different story from Brecht's, so does the music. It was during the realization of the opera version that the Weill-Brecht partnership came to grief, with Brecht proclaiming the death of opera and reportedly denouncing Weill as a "phony Richard Strauss" (whatever that might be in the Brechtian lexicon, as if Strauss weren't phony enough for him already).[56] To say that there were differences in their conceptions is to put it mildly, above all their respective takes on the reform of opera, as described above. Weill had more constructive uses for traditional opera, theoretically and practically, than Brecht did.

The allusions to traditional opera already present in the *Songspiel*, especially those to German opera, multiply in the full-length version. The more obvious allusions occur in the following places: No. 11 ("Haltet euch aufrecht") recalls the armed men of Mozart's *Zauberflöte;* the introduction to No. 7 recalls Beethoven's *Fidelio* ("Abscheulicher"); the middle of No. 1 (preceding "Sie soll sein wie ein Netz") alludes to the opening of Wagner's *Tristan und Isolde;* the ostinato in the middle of No. 20 ("Aber dieses ganze Mahagonny") is similar to the one in act 4 of Verdi's *Il trovatore.* Such allusions are common in Weill's work, creating a rich context of interpretation for the musically educated listener.

And the surreal Americanisms remain, as does the finale, with God coming to Mahagonny "mitten im Whisky." But much will change. The basic idea was not so much coarsened as, of necessity, radically revised. When he wrote to Heinsheimer about "a perfectly strict, thoroughly responsible style," he was referring, above all, to the neo-baroque turn taken by a number of his compositions. But it would be wrong to talk about this shift merely in terms of personal style. Serving a dramaturgical purpose in the full-length opera, the neo-baroque has a significant—or rather, a *signifying*—role to play in the musical parable of the rise and fall of the city, acting as a foil to the temporal *couleur locale* of contemporary dance music (as it does in *Die Bürgschaft,* too).

As the city emerges, so do the rhythms and sounds of dance music. These are radically contrasted with the timeless topics of academic counterpoint and the compound melodic style of J. S. Bach. The opening scene with the fugitives from justice and the founding of the city is accompanied in the opening orchestral prelude by music written in an austere style of linear counterpoint, a musical symbol of flight, perhaps, but also of unadulterated craftsmanship. Bit by bit the style is contaminated by the trappings of modern civilization, epitomized by the rhythms and textures of dance music (ex. 18). The hurricane—the threatening force of nature—comes and goes as pure polyphony (ex. 19). A relevant parallel here is the example of Mozart in his later works such as *Die Zauberflöte,* where the "learned style" *(stile antico)* is played off against the more modern and more obviously popular "gallant style." Weill's chorale melodies in the full-length opera may sound like Bach, but their dramaturgical function is Mozartian.[57]

The love duet between Jenny and Jimmy known as the "Cranes' Duet"—the parody of a text by Dante that was inserted late in the genesis of the opera—is one of Weill's finest neo-baroque compositions. It seems to owe its existence to Weill's intention to "shift the love plot between Jimmy and Jenny more into the foreground," an intention initially voiced as a response to the director of Universal Edition, who a few months after the premiere of the *Songspiel* had written to Weill with the following admonition: "What emerges from your outline is a new style of opera, yet one that nonetheless signifies merely a sequence of scenes, admittedly sometimes quite gripping and original ones, that can form a new type of 'opera-

EXAMPLE 18. *Aufstieg und Fall der Stadt Mahagonny,* act 1 (introduction of dance rhythms in opening)

EXAMPLE 19. *Aufstieg und Fall der Stadt Mahagonny,* "Typhoon" (fugato)

revue' . . . boxing, murder, homicide, drunkenness and the like predominate and that could be difficult to bear for a whole evening."[58]

In his discussion of the duet's relationship to the rest of the work, David Drew asserts that the "truthfulness of *Mahagonny* may well be greatest when the 'Kraniche-Duett' is omitted," mentioning that it was omitted in the Berlin production of 1931, "but not for that reason." He then discusses the difficulty of finding a suitable place for its insertion. "The very nature of the work," he concludes, reflecting on the enormous philological and interpretive challenges *Mahagonny* presents, "compels us to continue searching for ideal solutions long after we have recognized that there are none to be found."[59] The work continued to evolve as a function of its production history well beyond its initial publication as piano-vocal score and libretto in 1929; the question of the duet's placement is just one of the many questions facing editors and performers alike. Informed, unequivocal decisions are hard to come by.

In his exhaustive survey of the numerous surviving documents, Esbörn Nyström marshals a considerable array of sources, including Weill's correspondence with his publisher, to come to the conclusion that it would be "wholly justified" to have the original brothel scene (the "Mandelay" section) and the "Cranes' Duet" in sequence in scene 14, thereby "complementing, not mutually excluding each other."[60] In this, he argues against the 1969 edition of the piano-vocal score, in which Drew transferred the duet "to the only possible place in Act III," arguing that it had been "omitted from Act II" in Berlin—"and rightly so, for it is completely at odds with the style and structure of the other *'Sittenbilder.'*"[61]

Whether one sees the duet as an enhancement or as a detraction, as "complementary" or "at odds," its existence poses not only a philological but also an interpretive challenge. The poem's nature imagery of two birds in flight finds its musical equivalent in gorgeous cantilenas, a musical image of timeless order—an order disturbed elsewhere in the opera by the all-too human interventions of life in the city. Readings of the duet, which are various, depend on two crucial factors: where it is placed in the piece and whether the text is treated separately or in relation to the music. In the brothel scene, the duet is juxtaposed with the "Song of Mandelay." Two forms of "love" are contrasted, along with two musical styles. Sung before Jimmy's execution, the text may appear more existential. Either way, love and the question of transcendence are the principal themes invoked. Before its being set to music and included in the opera, the text was published separately, in 1928, as "Die Liebenden."[62] The love of which the text speaks offers the lovers something to hold onto ("ein Halt"), however transient. Yet that transience is also celebrated as unavoidable—that, at least, is what the text tells us. The music, for its part, created a lyrical enclave amid the surrounding squalor of love-for-sale and rough justice. Its contrapuntal texture, with compound melody à la Bach, constitutes a musical emblem of natural order that will find significant echoes in the musical imagery of *Die Bürgschaft* (as discussed below). As such, it represents a critical link, developmentally and in terms of musical meaning, between Weill's two epic operas.

Based on the musical symbolism, one might even be tempted to make a case for an interpretation of the opera as more ecological than Marxist in import. Cities in Weill's artistic imagination are expressions of the human spirit, at once vital and debasing, necessary but in many ways ephemeral, the focal point of hope but also of life-threatening corruption, as the opening plot description describes.

At the 1930 premiere in Leipzig, the principal couple did not perform the duet. Rather, in an intriguing departure from the various published versions of the libretto and score, it was sung by "a pair of lovers" *(ein Liebespaar),* as the playbill described cast members Hans Lissmann and Ilse Koegel. (Both Lissmann and Koegel were residents of Leipzig, and Koegel had in fact sung the part of Angèle in the Leipzig premiere of *Der Zar lässt sich photographieren.*) According to the review published in the *Leipziger Neueste Nachrichten* (11 March 1930), they performed the duet "very beautifully," even though the critic, Alfred Baresel, was critical of the fact that the number had been "taken out of the mouths of Jenny and Jim and sung instead at the front of the stage, as a kind of interlude, by a gentleman and a lady in formal dress." This might also explain a similar departure in the unauthorized adaptation of the *Mahagonny* materials known as the "Paris version," or "Das kleine *Mahagonny,*" the surviving text of which describes the duet as an "Intermezzo" with the inscription ERINNERUNG AN DIE WAHRE LIEBE ("Reminder of True Love"), prescribing that it be sung by the characters Jessie and Charly as a "konzertantes Duett."[63] In keeping with Brecht and Weill's theoretical precepts of epic opera, the duet was thus formally set apart from the rest of the scene as a "separated" and "concertistic" element.

The "musical principles" on which Weill founded *Mahagonny* are not only a return to the structure of the number opera as a reaction against the uninterrupted flow of the Wagnerian *Gesamtkunstwerk,* but also a juxtaposition of musical styles whose symbolic import tells its own story about the human condition, about the individual and the masses, about love in the city, about the corruption of nature by so-called civilization, about human values in general—a story more universal in its lyrical way than the didactic parable that Brecht wanted the piece to be. The fate of the individual exemplifying the fate of the city, as the composer defines his piece, is expressed in terms of purely musical laws, as he understands them; in both cases, in sociological and in musical terms, that fate has to do with the clash of laws, the new with the old. Weill's vision of urbanity is complicated, then, by his neoclassical aesthetic—an attempt to balance the new with the old, tradition and modernity, responsibility and freedom, order and anarchy, etc. However much it echoed Busoni's aesthetics of absolute music, Weill's theory of epic opera should hardly be read as a piece of dry formalism. ("Purely musical" is not synonymous with "formalist.") It is utterly in keeping with an approach to idiom in which style functions as a form of musical semiosis—not as something readily resolvable into the specificity of allegory so much as an essentially nonverbal symbolic language.

DIE BÜRGSCHAFT

Lecturing about his works for the musical theater to members of the Group Theatre in Connecticut in 1936, Weill referred to *Die Bürgschaft* (which had received its premiere at the Städtische Oper in Berlin on 10 March 1932) as an "epic opera with social idea, sentence of Marx, proved by 3 stories of the life of two men."[64]

EXAMPLE 20. *Die Bürgschaft*, chorale ("People do not change by themselves")

It was the only work in the lecture to which he applied the label "epic opera." *Mahagonny,* whose premiere predated that of *Die Bürgschaft* by exactly two years, was just *Mahagonny,* with no distinction made between "Songspiel" and opera, presumably because in Weill's mind the former had effectively been superseded by the latter, and with no genre label. The description of *Die Bürgschaft* leaps from the pages of Weill's lecture notes for two reasons: it is the longest for any of his works and the only one with a summary of its content. As such, it provides a convenient entry point for a discussion of the work in the context of the composer's ideas about theatrical reform.

Convenient, perhaps, but hardly self-explanatory. In using the word *sentence* (and perhaps also *proved,* as I discuss below), Weill was still thinking in his native language. He likely had in mind the word *Sentenz,* the German expression meaning "maxim" or "principle," referring here to the choralelike intonation, sung by the small chorus, that functions as a kind of motto for the whole work: "Es ändert sich nicht der Mensch, es sind die Verhältnisse, die seine Haltung verändern" (People do not change by themselves; it is [social] relations that alter their attitude) (ex. 20). Apart from its being intoned at the beginning and end of the first act, the maxim appears again in act 3—this time, however, with a dialectical twist that expands on the "social idea": "Auch das System, das die Verhältnisse schafft, verändert sich bis zu dem Tage, da es an seiner Veränderung untergeht" (Even the system that creates the relations continues to change up to the point at which, because of change, it suffers its demise).

If there is a single well-known passage in Marx that corresponds to the motto, at least to its first and second appearances, it is the following one from his 1859 text *Zur Kritik der politischen Ökonomie:* "Es ist nicht das Bewußtsein der Menschen, das ihr Sein, sondern umgekehrt ihr gesellschaftliches Sein, das ihr Bewußtsein bestimmt" (It is not people's consciousness that determines their being but, conversely, their social being that determines their consciousness).[65] The motto's expansion in act 3 would similarly parallel the continuation in Marx's text: "Auf einer gewissen Stufe ihrer Entwicklung geraten die materiellen Produktivkräfte der Gesellschaft in Widerspruch mit den vorhandenen Produktionsverhältnissen oder, was nur ein juristischer Ausdruck dafür ist, mit den Eigentumsverhältnissen, innerhalb deren sie sich bisher bewegt hatten. Aus Entwicklungsformen der Produktivkräfte schlagen diese Verhältnisse in Fesseln derselben um. Es tritt dann eine Epoche sozialer Revolution ein" (At a certain stage of their development, the social forces of production come into contradiction with the existing relations of production or, to use what is merely a legal expression for the same thing, property relations, within which those forces hitherto operated. These relations turn from being developmental forms of the forces of production into shackles of the same. An era of social revolution ensues).

The opera's motto and its elaboration are not, however, a literal quotation of Marx's "social idea." Nor are they even a faithful summary, containing nothing about "consciousness" or "relations of production," let alone "social revolution." Weill's *Sentenz* is at once more concise and more abstract: relations are not qualified explicitly as those of "society" or of "the forces of production"; they are merely *Verhältnisse.* What creates those "relations," we learn in *Die Bürgschaft,* is "the system." Insofar as it is subjected to change, the system will, as the chorus tells us—and indeed the system does—"decline." Marx's "era of revolution" finds no mention. The opera's ending (to be precise, the ending of the libretto) is unremittingly bleak, not hopeful: the Great Power, which seizes control in act 2, is still in force at the conclusion of act 3, ruling not according to the principles of late capitalism, as diagnosed by Marx, but merely according to the "law of money and power."

However they might be supported by the legal system, "money and power" do not in themselves constitute a socioeconomic law defined in Marxist terms. Missing from *Die Bürgschaft* are the class-specific "relations of production" (the legal "property relations") that form Marx's economic base. It is this base, according to Marx, that underpins the laws of commodity production and distribution and hence monetary circulation. Power, enshrined as it is in the legal system and in political ideology, is also part of what Marx calls the superstructure that both supports and is supported by the base. "The law of power and money" is not something to which Marx would have referred as such. Nor is it valid as a distillation of his political economic theory, something historically specific. Rather, it is a poetic abstraction devised parabolically for the purposes of an "epic opera."

The libretto of *Die Bürgschaft* is Marxist, then, only in a qualified sense. Because of the omissions and abstractions, it does not actually *present* a "sentence of Marx"; nor therefore can it serve to "prove" it either, even if it does demonstrate "the law of power and money" to be a corrupting one, in itself hardly a specifically Marxist idea. What's omitted is not only the crucial historical context but, along with it, a representation of the "relations of production" with their revolutionary potential. Insofar as the piece contains historical significance, it does so allegorically, not literally. As in *Der Jasager*, the action functions as a parable, not a historical analysis. Its unspecified time divides itself into two distinct epochs, occurring either side of a brutal imperialist-cum-dictatorial takeover by the "Great Power." Insofar as there is any revolutionary potential (and there may be none), it has to be inferred, not deduced. Marxist ideas about social relations, if not full-blown Marxist ideology, were nonetheless an important source for the opera, as Weill readily identified. More than that, as discussed below, they were also the touchstone for many of the critical responses, including extensive reviews from some of the best-known critics of the time, such as Paul Bekker, Oskar Bie, Ernst Bloch, Karl Holl, and Hans-Heinz Stuckenschmidt.

Several critics—those writing at the time of the premiere and also since—have noted parallels to Wagner's *Ring* cycle, an operatic work that similarly has as its central focus the "law of money and power."[66] In creating his mythological world, Wagner, too, drew on nineteenth-century socialist theory without necessarily espousing it, ultimately preferring an apocalyptic over an affirmative ending, a message of resignation over one of social liberation.

Weill and Neher's own recasting of Marx's dialectic is both cause and effect of the parabolic quality of the opera. Chiefly responsible for this quality, no doubt, is another source: Herder's story "Der afrikanische Rechtsspruch" (The African Judgment), which supplies the idea and some of the content for the central act.[67] The playbill for the premiere, in the neoclassical manner of *Die Dreigroschenoper* with its various named sources, described the opera's text as being by "Caspar Neher (using a parable by Herder)."

In seven terse paragraphs, quoted *in extenso* in the piano-vocal score and the original program booklet, the "parable," as the authors refer to it, tells the story of a visit by Alexander the Great to a "remote, auriferous province of Africa," where he witnessed the King issuing the eponymous legal judgment. A man had bought a sack of chaff and found "a sizable treasure" therein. Claiming ownership only of the chaff, the buyer tried in vain to return the gold to the seller, who refused to accept it. The King's verdict: "Have your children marry each other and give them the found treasure as a dowry." Alexander was astonished: "In our country," he said, "the disputing parties would lose their heads and the treasure would become the property of the King." Whereupon the King asked Alexander whether the sun still shone and rain still fell in his land. Alexander said, "Yes."

"Then that must be," the King continued," because of the innocent animals: on such people no sun should shine, no rain should fall!"

Herder's parable juxtaposes two radically different systems of social relations as reflected by their respective legal systems: the one essentially feudal, defined by social status; the other more enlightened, characterized by social harmony and civil, even natural law. In his legal analysis, which explores the historical roots of Herder's parable, Ulrich Fischer describes and contrasts the various historical precedents of Herder's fictional model and, by extension, Weill's and Neher's.[68] Not that Herder's parable or its operatic adaptation in *Die Bürgschaft* suggests any sense of historical progress or enlightenment. On the contrary, both works, the opera more than the parable, highlight the corruption of natural and civil law by tyranny. The decline of the opera is one from the legal order of enlightened civility (not without an element of prelapsarian innocence inherited from Herder) to the modern condition of anarchy, greed, and terror. But the break isn't absolute. Even under the old, more humane system, it is still possible for the protagonist to accrue gambling debts; and unlike in the parable, the seller of the chaff is deceived by the person he apostrophizes as his "best customer." After the Great Power's takeover, with its attendant trappings of modern industrialization, perhaps the most dramatic change that occurs is the character transformation undergone by the seller of the chaff, offered as concluding "proof" of the maxim that social relations change people. But is that really the message of the opera? The underlying parable, after all, entertains its ahistorical, nonrevolutionary alternative.

Die Bürgschaft takes place, not in any historically or geographically distant place like Herder's story, but in an entirely mythical land called "Urb." The title's "pledge" concerns the relationship between "two men" (as Weill referred to them in his lecture notes): the cattle dealer Johann Mattes and the grain dealer David Orth. The "3 stories of the life of two men," narrating the fortunes of their relationship within two contrasting systems of social relations, serve as the exemplary case of people who change as society changes. Rather than illustrating the basic motto, the Prologue creates the premise for its later demonstration. Having lost all his money through gambling (emblematic perhaps of the anarchy of market relations), Mattes is being pursued by creditors. Echoing Tamino's opening lines in Mozart's *Die Zauberflöte,* Mattes declares in the first person plural (rather than Tamino's singular): "We are lost" ("wir sind verloren"). His wife, Anna, persuades him to seek help from Orth, who lives across the lake. "He [her husband] has always been like that since I've known him," she muses, "and will never change." Orth, however, is prepared to make a pledge on behalf of his friend and "best customer." The creditors, about to dispossess Mattes, accept. Mattes repays his debts.

Act 1, occurring six years later, puts the relationship to a much sterner test.

Mattes buys two sacks of chaff from Orth. Jakob, Orth's son, points out that the sacks were in fact a hiding place for his father's savings. Unlike his counterpart in the Herder parable, Orth knows about the money but remains nonetheless sanguine: Mattes will return it. Mattes is mugged by three highwaymen (the Gang of Three) on his way home, but they take only his purse. Mattes assumes that Orth does not know about the contents of the sacks either. Three blackmailers (again the Gang of Three, in a different guise) discover the secret and threaten to reveal it to Orth. Mattes races them across the lake and confesses to Orth, whose reaction is remarkably tempered. Although he considers Mattes's confession "too late," he also questions his own right to the money: the judge in the city shall decide.

Continuing with the gist of Herder's parable, act 2 presents "the judgment." The Judge decrees that the money belongs neither to Mattes nor to Orth but shall be set aside for the former's son and the latter's daughter (Herder's condition of marriage between the two is not retained). Meanwhile, an announcement is made that the Great Power, which has seized control of Urb, is to send its Commissar. Henceforth the new law will prevail, the law of money and power. The Commissar, eager to assert his authority as a "warning and a sign of discipline," forces the Blackmailers, under threat of execution, into assisting him; he then retries Mattes and Orth. Declaring both parties criminals, he will release them only if they, like all civil servants, actively support the regime. Meanwhile, Anna bemoans the temporary loss of her husband and of her daughter, Luise, who has left for the big city.

A further six years elapse. As the chorus reports, times have changed; man has not. Under the new rule, the rich have become richer, the poor poorer. As if in a pageant, the inhabitants of Urb have to pass through four gates: War, Inflation, Hunger, and Disease. But thanks to the war, Mattes and Orth have come into money. Although Anna wishes to leave, Mattes, seized by greed, wishes to stay. The aftermath of the war brings inflation, followed by hunger. Mattes and Orth exploit these for their own gain, but Anna falls victim to disease. As she lies dying, Luise can be seen in a dancehall in the city, pursued by suitors. The people of Urb rise up in anger against Mattes, who, contrary to his expectation, fails to receive support from the Commissar, or from Orth, who is no longer willing to help his friend. Instead they fight, and Orth leaves Mattes, blinded by blood, to be finished off by the crowd. Orth delivers the conclusion: "Everything happens according to a law, the law of money, the law of power."

Weill described *Die Bürgschaft* to his publisher as "the first substantial outcome of a new form of expression that began with *Der Lindberghflug* and, above all, with *Der Jasager*,"[69] thereby drawing a distinction on stylistic grounds between his new epic opera and its predecessor, *Aufstieg und Fall der Stadt Mahagonny*. That was toward the end of November 1931, as UE was putting together performance materials for the new opera. The following month, which saw the two works jostling for attention because of preparations under way for the first Berlin production of *Aufstieg,* Weill went even further in distinguishing the one from the other while prompting his publisher to do the same: "Perhaps you can write a few lines commenting on the curious coincidence of circumstances with *Mahagonny,* already three years old, not being produced in Berlin until now, just as a new, quite different work of mine has been completed, one that again represents pure opera as opposed to the experiments *[Versuche]* to create a mixed genre between play and opera *(3 Groschen Oper, Mahagonny).*"[70] Weill was no doubt overstating the case by drawing attention to the differences rather than to the similarities between the two works, mentioning the origins of the earlier work in the "song style" of 1927 rather than the evidence of the neo-baroque turn that separates the opera from the *Songspiel,* as discussed above. Even so, the opposition of "mixed" or "intermediate" versus "pure" is telling, given the high esteem in which Weill continued to hold *Die Bürgschaft* throughout his career. Stylistic and structural considerations no doubt informed this view. Yet in that *Mahagonny* was about to be transferred to a theater that included members of the cast of *Die Dreigroschenoper,* he may also have been bearing in mind institutional aspects, including questions of casting.

If *Die Bürgschaft* counts as "pure opera," in comparison with the more mixed-genre, "in between" traits of *Mahagonny,* then the role of the double chorus, which is extensive, creates a mixture of a different kind, pushing the work in the direction of "opera-oratorio" (no doubt influenced, as several commentators have remarked, by Stravinsky's *Oedipus rex*).[71] Drawing heavily on the neo-baroque style, the chorus functions as one of the main ingredients that justify the epithet *epic.* After Mattes has dramatically burst onto the stage and recounted his woes (supported by the almost *molto perpetuo* energetic eighth notes in the orchestra), the small chorus calmly delivers the motto, as cited above, in unison, beginning in even quarter notes (see ex. 20). But the chorale sounds less austere than it otherwise might, thanks to the lilting, siciliano-like dotted accompaniment, a rhythmic figure that anticipates the setting of "die Verhältnisse" (the relations) that change people's attitude. It is the same dotted rhythm—traditionally evocative of the pastoral sphere—that will convey Anna's heartfelt expression of fear and resignation before she herself returns to the regimented, unchanging quarters with which the chorus had commented on her unchanging husband, just as she now comments, "and he will never change." So the music makes a difference: Weill's combining of the lapidary chorale and the melancholy expressive gesture common in baroque arias complicates the epic moment of verbal commentary. Social relations cause both motion and emotion, as Anna soon demonstrates; these belong to her (and our) being a "Mensch."

No wonder, then, that Weill had reservations about distributing the words on their own, without the music: "Reading the libretto can at best allow a given theater director to decide whether there are any political or other kinds of objections to the piece," he wrote to UE. Political objections were, as discussed below, very much part of the opera's reception. "Only studying the score," Weill emphasized, "will permit an appreciation of the artistic merit."[72] The chorale passage, and much else in the opera, prompts yet a further point about the composer's contribution. Studying the score allows us to appreciate the music's potential to subvert the epic design and along with it the epic theory of the piece. Weill's music rarely has a tautological relationship to the words that he sets; more likely than not it will, in some way, be at variance with them, altering their sense and even their putative political purpose. The motto is no exception. "Der Mensch" in *Die Bürgschaft,* whether or not he is construed as unchangeable, is no mere sociological abstraction, but a vital and sensuous musical presence.

The chorus, with its homophonic style and epic-narrative role, serves as a neoclassical foil to the drama of individuals that plays itself out with tragic inevitability, culminating in the demise of the protagonists' friendship and Mattes's death. Not only does the choral writing tend to recall the oratorios of Handel, the passions of Bach, and also Stravinsky's *Oedipus,* but the role of the small chorus harks back to the chorus of ancient tragedy. In this latter regard the functions of the small chorus are various. They include framing the narration, with descriptions of the passing of the years between the acts, setting the scene, either forecasting or describing the action (such as the chase across the lake), posing rhetorical questions about the unfolding events, even directly addressing the protagonists. Compared with the small chorus, which is extensively involved musically, the large chorus is more limited, and more traditional, in scope. It has but few appearances, representing the crowd as an integral part of the action onstage.

Occasionally individual members of the small chorus have solos, such as the alto at the beginning of the "Fog Scene" (No. 9), the spoken melodrama between Mattes and Orth. Integrated into a quasi–trio sonata texture, the words sung by the alto and the rest of the chorus, as well as the measured orchestral accompaniment, paint the scene: "Now it is evening," the alto reports. "We're on the banks of the river. The wind gently drives the clouds and the coolness of the evening makes itself felt" (ex. 21). This is Weill at his most Bachian, continuing in the "thoroughly responsible style" of the "Cranes' Duet" of *Mahagonny.* As there, and in several places in the cantata *Der Lindberghflug,* the style betokens some kind of natural order. A direct precedent can be found in the corresponding fog scene in the latter work, where Lindbergh is described as having had "to struggle with fog almost throughout his entire flight." The personified fog, sung by the tenors in the chorus ("Ich bin der Nebel . . ."), comprises one line of a three-part invention that invokes the C minor fugue from the first volume of Bach's *Well-Tempered Clavier* (ex. 22). Here, in *Die Bürgschaft,* the alto soloist describes the accumulat-

EXAMPLE 21. *Die Bürgschaft,* "Fog Scene"

ing fog, after which the basses exclaim: "That's how the law of nature would have it . . . the colder streams of the night breach the zones that have warmed up . . . that's how fog forms."

The scene is nothing if not allegorical: the fog is both literal and figurative. The protagonists literally and figuratively lose sight of each other, as Mattes evades Orth's questions about his money. Instead of singing, they speak their lines, avoiding any musical communication between them as well as resisting the accompanying counterpoint—a poignant symbol of the weakening of their pledge. The alto soloist concludes: "The eye of the one seeks in vain the eye of the other; the words they speak are impenetrable, like the fog." Yet the scene also suggests that their friendship, now shrouded in fog, is itself subject to timeless laws and forces beyond their control. Unlike the cyclical laws of nature, however, the law of money brings no relief. The friendship will be irreparably damaged. That is the ultimate price.

EXAMPLE 22. *Der Lindberghflug,* "Fünftens: Fast während seines ganzen Fluges hatte der Flieger mit Nebel zu kämpfen" (Fifth: During almost all of his flight the pilot had to battle against fog)

Just as the *Mahagonny-Songspiel* could be seen, according to Weill, as a "stylistic study" for the full-length opera, so the Lehrstücke served as stylistic studies for *Die Bürgschaft,* however much Weill saw them as "fully fledged works of art." If the later work seems stylistically more homogeneous, that is because the balance between the styles has shifted significantly and because individual numbers are integrated into larger musico-dramatic units. Stylistic heterogeneity remains nonetheless. Even though the neo-baroque may predominate as a musical signifier, elements of the song style still have an important role to play.

As in *Mahagonny,* the song style invokes modernity, characterized by transience, human susceptibility, and corruption. Or rather, those particular traits are signified by reference to contemporary music, even in the preindustrial world of Urb. The style is chiefly, though not exclusively, associated with the Gang of Three, who variously play the roles of creditors, highwaymen, blackmailers, henchmen, and agents. As highwaymen, for example, they perform an insinuating waltz (No. 5). As blackmailers, they have a fox-trot (beginning of No. 10: at first slow, then more animated) and a tango (second part of No. 13), this last, following the takeover by the Great Power, to the lines "Those are conditions such as we need, those are conditions that appeal to us . . . now things will get better in a bad world."

The associations between music and libretto are usually thick with irony. The hunger scene (No. 22), for example, is underpinned by the dotted fox-trot rhythm, redolent in a bizarre way of the *Mahagonny-Songspiel.* Mattes and Orth are figuratively dancing with the agents while the populace starves. There follows the opera's *coup de théâtre* (No. 23): a split stage, to the left Mattes's daughter, Luise, in the city dancing with a strange man on a raised floor, to the right Mattes's wife, Anna, lying sick in the hospital. Binding together this double scene of Anna's abandonment, by her daughter and by her husband, is a muted tango. "Relations" could scarcely be bleaker.

At the head of the finale to act 3 (No. 24) are two indications presented in the score in parentheses and both germane to the work's musico-dramatic design. The first is "2nd Finale," in contradistinction to the "1st Finale" (No. 10). Emphasizing the parabolic structure of the opera, the first finale illustrates the enduring bond of friendship, the second its corruption by the law of money and power. The second parenthetical indication is "Ritornell," placed before the tempo marking "Breit (♩=58)." This refers to the opening figure, whose profusion of dotted rhythms evokes French baroque in a gesture of solemn grandeur. Framing the scene at the beginning and the end, with intermittent recurrences throughout, the ritornello not only provides the main musical gesture of the opera's conclusion; it also creates a sense of structural balance and unity. That instances of such ritornelli pervade the opera, from the very beginning to the very end, no doubt contributes further to its neoclassical character. It is also a key factor contributing what Weill called the "concertistic character" of the music in his epic opera. Yet the ritornello's double function—as an element of formal articulation and as topical gesture—should serve to qualify what Weill meant by the music retaining "its purely musical effect in undisturbed harmony." The congruence embodied by the ritornello between dramatic context and topical gesture is also part of that effect.

To talk of motives, however, as Diana Diskin has done, and to provide those motives with labels in the tradition of Wagner reception, is to push the matter too far in a semantic, hermeneutic direction. Diskin describes the energetic opening of the opera in terms of the "first rhythmic-thematic motive," which she labels "the crisis motive," and claims that the motive recurs "throughout the opera," without making it entirely clear what the constituent rhythmic and diastematic components are or how they are motivically transformed or, indeed, what the dramatic or epic significance of the motive's recurrence might be.[73] The nineteenth-century concept of semantically charged motives seems foreign to Weill's neoclassical conception. Insofar as the elements of the ritornelli resemble one another reflects more their derivation from Weill's rich stock of musical gestures than it implies any leitmotivic transformation. (Telling in this regard is the fact that Weill "borrows" several of the ritornelli, almost intact, in subsequent works, notably *Der Silbersee* and *Die sieben Todsünden.*)

Commonalities of melody and harmony, beyond being matters of mere stylistic consistency, are rare. A case in point might be made for the introduction to the "Fog Scene" (No. 9) and the beginning of act 3, both featuring the alto solo from the small chorus. Yet the transformation of expressive character is the principal expressive point here, as the alto sings to accompaniment marked "very energetic" (not elegiac, as before): "And a further six years have elapsed, and the times have changed." Tellingly transformed here, too, is the accompaniment to the reiterated motto, now expanded to include not just the changing relationships but, with them, the demise of the entire "system" that creates them (as discussed above). The original siciliano-like accompaniment has been replaced by even quarter notes that become gradually louder and more emphatic.

Diskin is surely right, however, to observe that the form of the first number, and by the same token the form of other scenes, "is not constructed in any stereotypical form, but rather as a succession of musical phrases that occasionally (but not regularly or predictably) repeat according to the dramatic impulse."[74] Each scene is articulated and punctuated by its respective ritornelli, whose recurrences are dictated not only by formal but also by textual considerations. As Weill and Neher worked on the libretto and its revisions, the exact character of those ritornelli and their occurrences was not yet fixed. And textual revisions to the completed score, including the insertion of the new scene and various excisions, no doubt called for musical adjustments. Formally speaking, each scene is not so much a "purely musical" form, in the sense of a concertolike aria, still less a song, than it is an extended musico-dramatic unit unified in terms of its overall musical form and its expressive affects by ritornelli structures. In this regard, *Die Bürgschaft* is not that different from certain large sections of *Mahagonny*. Rather, it represents an expansive and integrative refinement of procedures already in place in the earlier opera.

The bleak, tragic ending of *Die Bürgschaft* presented a problem, not only to critics but to the creators themselves. To what extent do the "3 stories of the life of two men" presented as epic opera "prove" Marx's axiom, as Weill claimed? How much does the opera at the same time convey Herder's humanistic message? The relationship to these textual sources is no doubt complicated, as Weill himself suggested, by the particular relationship between text and music that his epic opera represents. That he and Neher might nonetheless have tipped the balance too much in the negative direction is reflected both in their own efforts to redress it and in various responses to the score and early performances.

One of the first to express reservations about the ending was conductor Otto Klemperer. Having been initially enthusiastic about the libretto and a likely candidate, as Weill hoped, to conduct the premiere at the Staatsoper, Klemperer rewrote the final scene and sent his new version to the composer. As Weill reported to UE, "this scene was unusable for us, of course, since this opera hardly permits a religious perspective at the end," and he told Klemperer as much "in a roundabout way." "Under no circumstances," he continued, "can I get involved with him in philosophical debates *[weltanschauliche Debatten]* about the text of *Die Bürgschaft*. If the score sufficiently appeals to him, such that he can support it with his whole person (and only then), then he can perform it. Otherwise not."[75] It was hardly to be avoided that an opera such as this, composed at this turbulent time in history, would provoke "weltanschauliche Debatten," as it has done since the time of its premiere. Even so, Weill's insistence on making a distinction between libretto and score is critical.

Given the way that Weill and Neher derived the opera's parabolic structure from Herder, the ending was not only inevitable but perhaps also unalterable. Two radically different systems obtain, as reflected in the respective "Verhältnisse." That is the point of the two finales: the first is optimistically humane, the second bleak and pessimistic. The conclusion no more admits of a religious perspective, as Weill insisted, than it does of a Marxist, revolutionary one (and this despite the underlying motto, adapted from Marx).

No doubt intended to counterbalance the character and mood of the latter half of the opera, the most substantial revision made during the opera's production process was the insertion of a new scene in the second act that replaced the original ending of No. 13 with the Commissar and the three blackmailers. Instead, following the blackmailers' extolling the favorable conditions of the "bad world," there is a stark exchange between the Judge and the Commissar. While the Commissar declares his commitment to the new authoritarian and industrialized system, the Judge advocates a form of passive resistance ("Don't take from the bread they give you . . . Don't believe the promises of the Great Power") with the repeated refrain, eventually adopted by the large chorus, "Be wise and don't defend yourselves." Before the new scene, the Judge was notable for his Solomonic decision under the old system, a decision made in silence, or rather, during a cerebral piano interlude that lends itself to interpretation as a concealed homage to the composer's teacher, Busoni. Now, with his express opposition to the new system, the Judge's role becomes significantly enhanced and a specific connection is forged between the two halves of the opera. In addition, as documented in the revised piano-vocal score published in 2000, Weill also proposed an extensive cut to the second act following the interpolated new scene, no doubt partly a response to complaints about the work's length, which approached almost four hours at the premiere on 10 March 1932.

Critical reaction to the premiere at the Städtische Oper Berlin and the almost simultaneous productions in Wiesbaden (16 March) and Düsseldorf (12 April) was decidedly—and not unexpectedly—mixed. Even the most favorable reviews voiced reservations; even the more negatively disposed critics conceded artistic virtue. Frequent among the topics of discussion was the length of the work—"almost Wagnerian," as the critic ("H.J.") of the *Thüringer Allgemeine Zeitung* described it (13 March 1932). More frequent still, however, were the opera's politics. How did they affect the work's character and form? What was their relevance to broader ideological matters?

Among the work's detractors, the *Deutsche Zeitung*'s music critic, Paul Zschorlich, devoted considerable space to discussing not only the work itself but, more generally, the cultural politics of opera in Berlin (12 March 1932) and, in a separate piece, to reviewing the actual production (13 March 1932). Given Zschorlich's record, it is hardly surprising that in his preview, characteristically entitled "Musical Proletarian Culture in the Red Opera," he would dismiss Weill's music as "utterly un-German." Or that in his review he would declare the music "superficial," though conceding "melodic invention" and "consistently competent work." He saved the most damning and most overtly political condemnation for his conclusion, telegraphed by the review's attention-grabbing title, "Hindenburg and Weill in the Städtische Oper."

Zschorlich seems to have been the only critic to have reported on the event that immediately preceded the Berlin premiere—namely, the radio broadcast in the opera house auditorium of a political speech by Reichspräsident Paul von Hindenburg, who was standing for reelection three days later, on 13 March. Zschorlich's comments put the election in the broadest possible cultural context. Hindenburg, he implied, was responsible for allowing works such as *Die Bürgschaft* to be performed at the publicly funded Städtische Oper. For Zschorlich, unabashed Nazi sympathizer and purveyor of the rebarbative Nazi rhetoric of denunciation, Weill's opera, if successful, would reflect "the cultural decline of the German people," thereby generating a "wave of filth" that would "sooner or later sink and silt up the masterpieces of German opera." This "weighty question," as Zschorlich saw it, was to be decided by the election.

Such was the cultural-political context surrounding the opera's premiere. And although Hindenburg would defeat Adolf Hitler with the requisite absolute majority in a runoff election the following month, on 10 April, it wasn't long before Zschorlich's perspective became part of official cultural policy. By the time Hindenburg died in 1934, allowing Hitler to consolidate his power further, Weill was no longer living in Germany or expecting his work to be performed there.

None of the other reviewers makes such a wide-ranging, undifferentiated connection between the opera and the political scene. But many do stress its contemporary relevance, for better and for worse. Two issues predominate: the nature of the political message and the opera's didactic purpose. Both, of course, are linked to the question discussed above concerning the work's connection to Marxism. Otherwise sympathetically disposed, the drama critic Bernhard Diebold (*Frankfurter Zeitung*, 15 March 1932) objected to the unswerving, rather naive didacticism of the reiterated motto, which presents man as the puppet of epic forces rather than as an active agent in the drama of life. Yet in his 1936 Connecticut lecture, Weill would still state that the opera "proved" this maxim.

Also generally supportive of Weill, Hans-Heinz Stuckenschmidt (*BZ am Mittag*, 11 March 1932) nevertheless found fault with "the so-called political conclusion drawn from the material, or rather not drawn from it. . . . Missing here," he opined, "is the antithetical extension [to the motto]: 'collective action changes the circumstances.'" In a similar vein, but more expansively critical of this aspect, was the review of *Die Bürgschaft* by the conductor and pianist Herbert Trantow.[76] The title—"Questions for Kurt Weill Concerning his *Bürgschaft*"—makes clear the largely interrogative nature of Trantow's critique, quoted here at length.

> Why the line "People do not change; it is social relations that change their attitude"?
>
> Why not "People change decisively on the basis of gradual development through intellectual insights and spiritual experience; whoever changes his attitude because of external conditions does not deserve, with such elastic beliefs, to be called a human being"?
>
> Do "social relations" exist in the Weill-Neher sense? Would Weill-Neher allow themselves to be changed at a critical moment by such "relations"? Wouldn't they assert themselves in spite of such "relations"?
>
> If so, why the proclamation of this dogma by all three acts of *Die Bürgschaft?* Does one want to provide the audience with a comfortable excuse for its spiritual corruption ("It's not your fault; social relations have made you bad"), or does one want to teach them by example not to resist the "Great Power" because human beings are victims of "social relations" (50 years ago: products of the "milieu")?
>
> Since, after all, *Die Bürgschaft* presents itself as a didactic opera *[Opernlehrstück]*, why isn't it used to demonstrate that there are people who preserve their humanity by resisting the temptations of capitalism? Why is it tragic or instructive that Matthes is killed at the end as punishment for his unsocial behavior? Orth, after all, remains alive, having become just as much of a shady dealer under the influence of the "Great Power," and having shamelessly betrayed his friend to the mob, although he once made a pledge to him.
>
> How are war, inflation, hunger, and sickness exclusively the result of capitalism? Assuming they are, why aren't we shown how this bad capitalist system is overcome? On the contrary, Weill-Neher teach us that capitalism remains the victor and that outwardly one can do just fine under this system if one becomes involved in "shady dealing" (the case of Orth); that one is only badly off if one resists (the case of the wise judge). Why aren't we given the victory of idealism and enduring human rights and honor over the "Great Power"?
>
> Will Weill create his next Lehrstück around a theme that shows how human beings are happier under a better system, so that listeners can go home wanting to contribute to the construction of this new, better, and pedagogically presented world? Shouldn't he also be aware that there are more people than he thinks who don't attach the slightest value to money and outward well-being—the kind of value, according to Weill, that determines human values, as he has been telling us since *Die Dreigroschenoper* (with the exception of *Der Jasager*)?

> Couldn't he write a Lehrstück in which he demonstrates that money fails miserably as compared with spiritual power, and that it is more necessary to ponder pure humanity in our time than to struggle against a superficially superior power? Doesn't the history of all spiritual activity prove that in the long run outward power comes up short?

Trantow's questions, which were published in the journal *Melos,* prompted Weill to respond in an open letter to the editor,[77] quoted here *in extenso:*

> Dear Professor Mersmann,
>
> In the latest issue of *Melos* you published a series of questions directed at me concerning *Die Bürgschaft*. I have attempted to answer these questions. That is hardly possible, however, because these questions represent only another form of subjective criticism. Whenever the basis and self-evident assumptions of a work of art are either doubted or disputed, then it is one opinion against another.
>
> I maintain that our line about social relations changing human behavior is right and that Trantow's is wrong; we did not want to show heroes or supermen but rather human types whose "intellectual insights and spiritual experiences" are less important than how they behave. Of course there are "social relations" in our sense that determine our behavior. Perhaps it will help the questioner if he can conceive of the "economic relations" we are talking about as a concretization of what the Ancients called "fate."
>
> I maintain that the conclusion of *Die Bürgschaft* is both tragic and "instructive." Yet the tragedy lies less in the death of Matthes than in the explanation given by Orth in his closing words; and in the wretchedness of this perception rests the "moral" that members of the audience can take home with them.
>
> This brings us to the "main point of the prosecution": the accusation of negativity. The questioner forgets that socially representative art of all ages was at pains, often excessively so, to show things as they are, and only through the manner of representation to suggest to the audience a critique of what was being presented. Such art limits itself to leaving the audience with the sense that existing conditions must be changed, and it seeks to achieve this by revealing the conditions in their most blatant, unvarnished form. This was the approach taken by *Die Bürgschaft,* especially because it was intended all along to be a tragic opera. It would have been nice, of course, against the same ideological background to come up with something positive and affirmative, and I would be the first to seize such an opportunity with both hands were it to present itself. I consider looking for such an opportunity in the realm of the "purely human," however, to be particularly dangerous in opera because I believe that the task of opera today is to move beyond the fate of private individuals toward universality.
>
> In conclusion, a point that I consider important: *Die Bürgschaft* is not a Lehrstück but an opera. It is written for the theater. It does not want to demonstrate dogmas but rather, in accord with the tasks of the theater, to present human activity against the background of a universal idea.

> One more thing: in an age in which some engage in artistic frivolities while others prefer to be entirely unproductive in order to avoid rubbing anybody the wrong way, *Die Bürgschaft* undertakes an attempt to adopt a position on matters that concern us all. Such an attempt must elicit discussions as a matter of course. That is part of its job. Yet for a discussion to occur, it is necessary that the opposite point of view is precisely and carefully analyzed. The questions that you publish are very well suited to add yet further misconceptions to the ones that already exist.
>
> *With best wishes,*
> *Kurt Weill*

Weill's reply touches on several critical points. Trantow, who later worked as a film composer in the German Democratic Republic, appears to subscribe to a variant of "socialist realism"; he expects a vision of a better society rather than a "blatant and unvarnished" portrayal of "things as they are." Weill and Neher's realism, in contrast, might be called "critical" in that it focuses on the bleaker, negative aspects of society as they knew and saw it. They leave the audience to draw their own conclusions about any contemporary relevance.[78]

In his obituary of Weill, quoted at the beginning of this chapter, Heinrich Strobel defined epic theater as "the object of Weill's constant striving" and *Die Bürgschaft* as the work in which that concept had "achieved its most opportune formulation." At the time of the opera's premiere, however, Strobel performed the dual role of apologist and critic. On 8 March, two days before its premiere, German radio broadcast highlights from the opera with Strobel providing commentary. The commentary, in Diskin's words, "did not bother to hide Strobel's enthusiastic support for Weill's career; it was a very good piece of marketing for Weill's music and the opera."[79]

The notice Strobel published in the *Danziger Neueste Nachrichten* on 14 March 1932, however, took a more critical view. While echoing some of UE's pre-performance publicity, which in Weill's own words described him as "returning to pure opera," Strobel qualified this description both generically and in relation to the opera's sources. Calling the work "half Lehrstück, half music opera," he saw it as an "interaction of the oratorical and didactic with the pure form of opera." Specifically, he identified the "operatic element" as being "derived from the parable" and the "didactic element determined by the maxim that it is not people who change but relations that change." It is this arrangement that created, for Strobel, the "problem of the opera, combining human emotive action and epic didacticism." He laid the blame chiefly with "the text of Caspar Neher, which in the didactic parts of the second and third acts . . . drifts too far into theory." (Although Neher was billed as the librettist, the text was in fact the product of a close collaboration between him and Weill; they were originally going to receive joint credit.) Strobel's verdict: "The balance between music and ideology has not yet been achieved." "It will take a few more experiments," he concluded, "before this order [of new elements], this synthesis, fully succeeds."

Another major critic of the time, Paul Bekker, was even more actively involved in the work's dissemination, as director of the production in Wiesbaden. Bekker's view, formed through practical contact with the work and in extensive exchanges with the composer, was more conciliatory than Strobel's. It found its most enduring expression in an open letter to Weill that he included in his 1932 collection *Briefe an zeitgenössische Musiker* (Letters to Contemporary Composers).[80]

Like Weill before him, Bekker warned against judging the work solely on the basis of the book, not the score. It was "important for me . . . to confront the danger of overestimating and misconceiving the significance of the opera's subject matter." Weill, he claimed, had succeeded in achieving "something higher: solving the problem of forming and constructing opera, an opera that emerges from a traditional foundation and becomes, in an unforced way, a new, by all means special phenomenon." The danger, Bekker thought, "was equally real for friend and foe, and both parties succumbed to it." To that extent, he was describing not merely the potential but also the reality of the opera's reception, a reality to which Trantow's and other reviews bear testimony.

Bekker questioned whether *Die Bürgschaft* is really a political opera at all. "I can only imagine a political opera being one where the political attitude as such determines the way in which the whole is developed and constructed, such that the music is at best incidental and provides accentuation here and there." In *Die Bürgschaft*, on the other hand, "the underlying political character of the text as such has not given you the omnipotence of relations vis-à-vis people's will. It is the way of dividing and writing for the chorus, the treatment of the vocal crowd. . . . It also places human beings so emphatically at the center that the individual voice had to dominate from the stage over the orchestra. . . . The fundamental political meaning, properly understood [as a form-creating element], remains, not as a naturalistic fact but insofar as it has created for itself a sonic equivalent."

David Drew has characterized Bekker's defense of the opera as involving an "ostensibly unpolitical and unblushingly formalistic approach to the topic of political actuality."[81] This is certainly the tendency of Bekker's approach. His focus on the way in which the political idea of the piece manifests itself on a formal level nonetheless brings into play important issues of interpretation. Does the opera really "prove" the maxim, as Weill seemed to be claiming, and if so, what does that mean politically? Moreover, what is the significance of Bekker's notion of political meaning, not as "naturalistic fact," but as "form-creating element" and "sonic equivalent"? To be borne in mind here is that the idea of didactic theater as it was realized in the Lehrstücke informs stylistic matters as much as it does the character of the libretto. The choralelike setting of the motto is one such matter, an ingredient (and a central one at that) contributing to epic opera's generic mix.

But a mix it is, as Strobel observed, a combination of operatic and didactic elements, "human emotive action and epic didacticism." As such, the mix derives not merely from a musically eclectic approach on Weill's part, but also from the musico-dramatic design. Weill's "borrowed" choral and instrumental styles are thus both absolute and emblematic—or rather, emblematically absolute. The affinity to sacred models is a case in point. In presenting the motto as chorale in an operatic context, Weill produced a piece of staged didacticism, secular opera about sacred oratorio.

"*Die Bürgschaft* is not a Lehrstück," Weill asserted, "but an opera." He thus sought to distinguish it from the *Der Jasager* and *Der Lindberghflug,* his Lehrstücke proper. In saying, "It is written for the theater," he was defining the obvious institutional difference between operas and Lehrstücke. But his assertion also suggests something else. In his reply to Trantow, and in flagrant contradiction of his Connecticut notes, he stated: "*Die Bürgschaft* does not want to demonstrate dogmas but rather, in accord with the tasks of the theater, to present human activity against the background of a universal idea." That is to say, the motto freely derived from Marx is *not* the "moral" *(Lehre);* it is not even the didactic part, however epically, even didactically, it happens to be presented. Rather, it is the basis of the enacted drama, just as much as the parable is. The enacted drama *shows* how people and hence personal relations change because of social and economic relations. (Perhaps in his Group Theatre notes, if he was still thinking in German, Weill had in mind the word *zeigen,* which can mean either "show" or "prove.")

Strobel's comment that the "operatic element" is "derived from the parable" and the "didactic element determined by the maxim" is simply wrong. Or rather: the distinction between the operatically dramatic and the epically didactic is not that simple. Insofar as the piece has anything to teach, it is a moral to be derived from the juxtaposition of the two systems. As Weill states, "The tragedy lies less in the death of Matthes than in the explanation given by Orth in his closing words; and in the wretchedness of this perception rests the moral that members of the audience can take home with them." The tragedy, in other words, is not an individual but rather a universal one, and one that was certainly topical at the time.

Lending a tragedy didactic traits—or conversely, a Lehrstück tragic ones—is also part of the peculiar mix that is *Die Bürgschaft.* The mix occasions Weill, in his reply to Trantow, to shift the discourse about the work from the rational theory of "Verhältnisse" to terms more amenable to drama theory: "Perhaps it will help the questioner if he can conceive of the 'economic relations' we are talking about as a concretization of what the Ancients called 'fate.'" Mattes and Orth are not just lifeless puppets of social relations; they are, in all their operatic irrationality, human beings, as evidenced by the music. And if their personal fate is universal, then it is indeed wretched.

That it might not be so, that the "moral" of the opera and hence the "universal idea" might be different from the repeated motto, is the political spark that the work ignites at various junctures. Systems change as well as people, the chorus tells us. The parable itself posits an alternative state of affairs, personified in Orth's humane behavior and especially in the Judge. Predicated on Herderian ideals of humanity, the posited alternative embodies not fate but character.

"Such art," Weill said, "limits itself to leaving the audience with the sense that existing conditions must be changed." The critical realism of the drama's outcome obscures any positive message that the audience "can take home with them." What the ideological import of that intended message might be has become therefore, perhaps necessarily, a matter of considerable exegesis and speculation. Herder and Marx as sources have had to share the stage with others. Prominent among them is Gandhi, first proposed by the unidentified critic of the *Magdeburgische Zeitung*, whose review of the premiere production (12 March 1932) noted the "Gandhi-traits" of "the wise judge who is deposed"; it also mentioned the "khaki uniforms . . . bayonets, rifles, railways" by way of suggesting a British colonial context. Such a perspective might explain the effort expended on highlighting the message of passive resistance in the revisions to the second act. Other ideological perspectives invoked—in particular by Drew and Diskin—are those of Tolstoy, Lenin, and Ruskin. But again, discerning such perspectives has more to do with a literary reading of the text than with an analysis of the score. Diskin's extensive survey is surely right to offer a final note of circumspection. "Whether or not Weill and Neher worked consciously under the influence of Lenin, Tolstoy, Gandhi and Ruskin," she concludes, "the particular philosophical tenets that each writer held dear may easily be discerned in all the versions of the libretto of *Die Bürgschaft*."[82]

Reactions to the music tend to be at odds with such purely literary analysis, as Weill predicted. Trantow's second response to the opera, published in the *Sozialistische Monatshefte* in October 1932, made this point quite explicitly. Reinforcing his critique of the libretto's "acquiescent pessimism," he conceded that "the composer allows the listener at least a presentiment . . . of a new world to come, of the true realm of freedom, as Marx would say."[83] Ernst Bloch, in what Drew has called "the finest of the major contemporary contributions to the *Bürgschaft* debate," echoes Trantow's sentiment with his characteristically utopian reading of the work: "Behind the opera *Bürgschaft* there is a fourth act at work, or rather a new opera; one of 'melancholy' rising up against the 'great power.' . . . The increasingly intolerable state of affairs that the music reveals at the same time anneals revolution."[84] For Bloch, the difference that music makes is one between resignation and hope. As it does, too, for Drew, who concluded his first essay on the opera with an observation that captures something essential about Weill's music generally, not just in *Die Bürgschaft*:

> Whilst Orth commits an act of consummate perfidiousness, the music indicates, with almost unbearable serenity, those positive and purely humane values against which all perfidy must be judged if the totality of human experience is to be understood. And again, at the very end of the tragedy, when Orth apostrophizes his dead "friend" and proclaims the law of money and the law of force, the music continues to say (though in terms quite different from those of the preceding duet) that this need not be, that man is capable of far finer things. Here, then, is the second and, to my mind and ear, the unquestionably humane conclusion of the opera. It is Weill who says the last word, the all-important word.[85]

In its universality, the music tells us that the tragedy is as much Anna's and Luise's as it is Mattes's or even Orth's. But in doing so, it also emphasizes the ambiguity of the "Verhältnisse." As Weill specified, they are economic relations, certainly. But they are also human ones. (To mention one small but telling sonic detail: the ubiquitous, exquisite solo woodwind writing, particularly for the oboe and flute, suggests a wordless parallel with Beethoven's *Fidelio,* a work "whose political background is a humanizing one," as Weill put it.)[86] The premise of the *Die Bürgschaft*'s intractable title is at once social and personal.

The dichotomy of the social versus the personal or individual has proved to be, on a number of levels, one of the central tensions in Weill's two full-length German-language operas, *Aufstieg und Fall der Stadt Mahagonny* and *Die Bürgschaft.* Defining each of them as "epic operas"—as operatic variants of "epic theater"—only enhances that tension. In part, this has to do with the theoretical anomalies in the Brecht-Weill partnership, as reflected in the critical discourse. The epithet *epic* carries a lot of theoretical baggage insofar as it is pressed into service in various ways: as a category that covers both production (poietics) and reception (aesthetics), but also performance or "reproduction." Not only does Brechtian theory not adequately apply to actual practice; some of it is also at odds with Weill's own ideas.

Weill focuses his theoretical statements largely, albeit not exclusively, on matters to do with musical form and style. Writing about the form problem in modern opera in 1931, for example, he described his approach in terms of "new style elements, which in part date back to the pure opera forms of earlier times."[87] For Brecht, the theory of "epic opera" not only addressed matters of form and content in ways that do scant justice to Weill's scores; it emphasized above all issues of reception and questions of institutional politics. He foresaw a more adequate realization of his theoretical postulates not in opera performed in traditional venues but rather in the genre of the Lehrstück (the topic of the next chapter).

"Epic opera" remains a challenging, controversial concept. Even "the most opportune formulation," to use Strobel's description of *Die Bürgschaft,* necessarily reflects the subgenre's inherent contradictions. After a closer look at the work itself, one could even say that it positively thrives on those contradictions. In the much-cited chart that Brecht included in his theoretical notes on *Mahagonny*, intended to capture "some shifts of emphasis from the dramatic to the epic form of theater," he defined the dramatic form as "thinking determining being" and the epic form as "social being determining thinking"—the latter inversion recalling Marx's materialist critique of Hegelian idealism.[88] *Die Bürgschaft*, whose reiterated motto paraphrases Brecht's postulate, does not demonstrate the theory of epic opera so much as provide a spirited engagement with it.

7

Didactic Theater ("Lehrstück")

In an interview published in April 1930, two months before the premiere of his "school opera" *Der Jasager,* Weill stated that "this 'Lehrstück' [literally, "teaching piece"] should become a fully fledged work of art, not a by-work." In the same interview he described himself as a "simple musician," for whom "the simple style is no problem, the simple works . . . no mere *parerga [Nebenwerke],* but *chefs-d'oeuvre [Hauptwerke]*."[1] And in 1935, newly arrived in America, he was to call *Der Jasager* his most important work to date.[2] Yet there is no denying an element of special pleading, expressed in the pre-premiere interview with characteristically feigned modesty. Declaring a "school opera" a *Hauptwerk* rather than a *Nebenwerk* meant nothing less than inverting traditional priorities—priorities that might account for the style and scale of the piece in terms of some aesthetic concession or sacrifice on the composer's part.

Weill was not alone in his views, despite the apparent need to plead his case. The first performance of *Der Jasager* was originally planned for a festival of New Music at which it and similar compositions took center stage. (The reasons for its withdrawal will be discussed below.) The plan of the festival was symptomatic: for a brief period, which coincides with the zenith of cultural activity in the Weimar Republic before the abrupt and tragic demise of that era, the genre of music theater known as "Lehrstück" became the focus of interest for a number of Germany's leading musicians and writers, Weill and Brecht included.

The field of Brecht studies has had much to say on the Lehrstück. Yet most accounts say little, if anything, about the term's origins or about the relevance of those origins to theatrical developments during the Weimar Republic.[3] The present chapter attempts to fill that lacuna by dealing with five related issues: (1) the etymology of the term; (2) the inception of the Brecht-Hindemith piece itself entitled *Lehrstück;* (3) the aesthetic trends that characterize the second half of the Weimar Republic; (4) the emergence of the Lehrstück as experimental music theater; and (5) the musical implications of the genre for the composers involved, Weill in particular.

ETYMOLOGY

Lehrstück can denote anything of didactic import. The Grimms' *Wörterbuch* defines the compound tautologically by dismantling it: "Stück einer Lehre"—that is, "a piece of a teaching or doctrine."[4] More recent dictionaries restrict their definitions to a type of theater; some mention Bertolt Brecht; and they all ignore the earlier history of the concept, which predates Brecht by several centuries.[5] For the development of Brechtian theater, the first part of the compound, *Lehr-,* is crucial. For understanding the etymology of *Lehrstück,* however, it is the second part, *-stück,* that requires special attention.

Applied to theater pieces, the term *Lehrstück* is best translated as "learning play." Brecht generally preferred to call all his stage works *Stücke* (literally, pieces), eschewing the traditional term *Schauspiel* and its various subcategories—*Lustspiel* (or *Komödie*), *Trauerspiel* (or *Tragödie*), etc.—and he styled himself a *Stückeschreiber* rather than *Dramatiker* (the latter label hardly apt for a practitioner and theorist of "epic theater"). Since many of his Stücke have a strong didactic (or "Lehr-") component, however, the subcategory *Lehrstück* might seem to border on the tautological.[6] Aren't the majority of his Stücke in one way or another intended as Lehrstücke?

This latter question has given rise to a considerable amount of critical commentary in the secondary literature on Brecht. How do the Lehrstücke proper relate to the remainder of his stage works?[7] Yet it is that literature's almost exclusive focus on Brecht that has perpetuated a somewhat myopic understanding of the Lehrstück, thereby precluding a more comprehensive account of its history. In most studies the term first appears in 1929, as if out of thin air, with the Hindemith-Brecht piece entitled *Lehrstück,* which subsequently serves as a generic designation for a number of didactic pieces, including some by writers and composers not directly associated with the Brecht camp. The most recent and at the same time exhaustive treatment of Brecht's Lehrstücke, that by Klaus-Dieter Krabiel, declares that "the origin of the concept 'Lehrstück' remains unexplained. . . . Even though it may not be a coinage of Brecht's," Krabiel writes, "the term became common through him."[8]

The Grimms' dictionary traces the compound *Lehrstück* back to the seventeenth century. In both religious and secular contexts, it meant "lesson" in the sense of an illustration of a general truth.[9] That meaning is still preserved today, usually in the sense of a lesson or moral to be derived from specific historical situations. When it is applied to a piece of fiction, "cautionary tale" might be the best English equivalent.[10] *Lehrstück* is also encountered as a synonym for *Lehrsatz,* in the sense of "theorem" or "dogma," as in "das . . . aristotelische Lehrstück von der Seele als Form des Körpers" (the Aristotelian dogma of the soul as the form of the body).[11] But there is a precise technical meaning, which is documented neither by the Grimms (the relevant volume of whose dictionary was compiled in 1885) nor by any other German-language dictionary, but which is familiar in theology, both Protestant and Catholic. Here the word *Lehrstück* has less to do with theater than with catechistic instruction.[12]

Although the word *Lehrstück* did not become part of established catechistic terminology until the early twentieth century, with the introduction of the so-called *Lehrstück-Katechismus,* it originated in the teachings of Luther, whose own *Small Catechism* (*Kleiner Katechismus*) of 1529 represents one of the earliest attempts to codify oral religious instruction, particularly for children. Luther's work also provided the prototype for all future catechisms. According to the general meaning of the term detailed above, the entire catechism may count as a Lehrstück: it is "a piece of a teaching or doctrine" in that it sets forth the tenets of the Christian faith.[13] But to apply the term in this colloquial way is to deny, first, the special sense of *-stück* and, second, the form of the catechism known as *Lehrstück-Katechismus,* whose involved history has a special relevance to the emergence of secular theatrical Lehrstücke in the late 1920s.

Luther divided his *Kleiner Katechismus* into five parts (later six), which he called *Hauptstücke* or "main elements." They are (1) the Decalogue, (2) the Apostles' Creed, (3) the Lord's Prayer, (4) Baptism, and (5) Holy Communion. *Hauptstück* used in this sense commonly signifies a central premise or argument, as in the Hauptstücke or "principal sections" of a philosophical or instructional tract; or it can merely describe the sections themselves.[14] But *Hauptstücke* in this theological context can also have the more specific meaning of the *capita religionis christianae:* the principles of Christian faith. Each section of the catechism constitutes a principal dogma, especially the first three Hauptstücke. (The term *article* is reserved for the elements of the tripartite Creed.) As Luther wrote in his *German Mass* of 1526, "What we need first of all is a plain, good Catechism . . . For such instruction I know no better form than those three parts which have been preserved in the Christian Church from the beginning—the Ten Commandments, the Creed, and the Lord's Prayer—which contain, in a brief summary, nearly all that a Christian ought to know."[15]

The educational nature of Luther's Catechism—his mission to inculcate the Hauptstücke of Christian faith in the face of ignorance and incompetence—is quite obvious in its construction in terms of questions and answers.[16] This expressly didactic part, known as the *Fragestück*, was further expanded by subsequent authors, especially for the purposes of instructing confirmands.[17]

So much for *Hauptstück* and *Fragestück*. What about *Lehrstück?* The spirit, if not the letter, of the concept comes from Luther himself. When the German Union of the Evangelical Church (*Evangelische Kirche der Union*, or EKU) proposed a revision of the Protestant Catechism in 1953, they removed what they called the "Lehrstück vom Amt der Schlüssel und von der Beichte."[18] This section, originally absent from the 1529 text, was interpolated by Luther in his 1531 revised edition between the fourth and fifth Hauptstücke, though not initially under the heading "Amt der Schlüssel," as in later inauthentic editions, but simply as "Wie man die Einfältigen soll lehren beichten" ("How plain people are to be taught to confess"). Here, then, is the specific theological sense of *Lehrstück:* a didactically motivated supplement to the Hauptstücke of the Catechism.

But Luther did not use the term as such. In fact, it was not coined in a catechistic context until the middle of the nineteenth century, when it was used to challenge the methods of instruction enshrined in the Fragestücke. In general, the history of catechistic teachings reflects an involved discourse on questions of form and content—that is, it reflects attempts to find adequate means for imparting central truths, and an acceptable balance between upholding Christian belief, in its integrity, and subjecting that belief to rational pedagogic processes informed by the Enlightenment.[19] The envisaged audience was also an important factor, and it was to play a crucial role in the emergence of the *Lehrstück-Katechismus.* Whereas Luther's *Small Catechism* was compiled expressly for the instruction of children, its Roman Catholic counterpart, the *Catechismus Romanus,* published in 1566, was commissioned by the Council of Trent expressly for adults.

The mid-nineteenth century brought a critical development with John H. Newman's work, which sought to consolidate the disciplines of theology and science. Both of these, Newman thought, could be founded on the same epistemological premises. "If religion," he wrote, "is consequent upon *reason* and for *all* men, there must be reasons producible for the rational conviction of every individual."[20] For Newman, that meant inductive, as opposed to deductive, method. The general should be derived from the particular, not vice versa.[21]

Newman's ideas soon found advocates on the Continent, for example Gustav Mey, who similarly sought to combine scholastic methods derived from Aristotle with biblical catechetics. It was Mey, according to the theologian Franz Michel Willam, who first introduced the term *Lehrstück* in connection with these reforms.[22] Mey's Lehrstücke, for example in his *Vollständige Katechesen für die unterste Klasse der katholischen Volksschule,* are designed as organically constructed lessons for use in schools.[23] As such, they represent a Catholic attempt to formulate catechistic teachings expressly for children, from the Lutheran perspective once scorned by the Catholic Church.

But it was not until the early twentieth century that Mey's innovations bore fruit in catechisms proper. The first so-called *Lehrstück-Katechismus* was Heinrich Stieglitz's *Grösseres Religionsbüchlein*, published in Kempten in 1916. Stieglitz, a Catholic teacher (and also a reviser of Mey's work), replaced the traditional Fragestücke with a continuous narrative text in a lively and uncomplicated language, including illustrations from biblical legends. Stieglitz applied what was termed the "Munich Method" (also referred to as the "psychological method"), an approach to catechistic teaching developed by reformists in Munich, Stieglitz among them, that stressed the didactic importance of interaction between teacher and pupil. This, then, is the precise theological sense of *Lehrstück:* an instructional unit related to the catechism, presented in a language accessible to children, and based on inductive rather than deductive principles. Writing in 1905, E. Christian Achelis stated "the principle of providing a religious grounding for all Christian morality and the goal of enabling students to become morally autonomous are inalienable."[24] It is to the spirit of such autonomy that the religious Lehrstück owed its emergence, and to which the later secular one also aspired.

LEHRSTÜCK (BRECHT-HINDEMITH)

At its premiere at the Baden-Baden Festival on 28 July 1929, the Brecht-Hindemith piece entitled *Lehrstück* caused a scandal.[25] The critic of the *Badische Volkszeitung,* Elsa Bauer, called it "a subjugation that made a mockery of all the laws of aesthetics and morality."[26] Sensationally offensive to the sensibilities of the audience, according to reports, was the second of two "investigations" into the question of "whether one man will help another." The scene involves three giant clowns. The first and second clowns answer this question by attending in a gruesome way to the bodily ailments of the third, called Herr Schmidt: they amputate his limbs, one by one, and then unscrew his head. Conclusion: Man *does* "help" man! According to reports, one member of the premiere audience fainted. The rest of the piece concerns a crashed pilot, as it were a refugee from the Brecht-Weill-Hindemith collaboration *Der Lindberghflug,* also given its premiere at the Baden-Baden festival.[27]

Lehrstück is divided into seven parts: (1) "Report of the flight"; (2) "Investigation: Whether man helps man"; (3) "The chorus addresses the crashed one"; (4) "Looking at death" (film); (5) "Teaching"; (6) "Second investigation: Whether man helps man" (scene for clowns); (7) "Examination." The story of the crashed pilot is of course a parable, especially in view of the existentialist exhortation from the speaker in the chorus after the first "Investigation": "If you want to overcome death, then you will overcome it when you actively acquiesce to *[einverstanden seid mit]* death." When Brecht revised the text of *Lehrstück,* he gave it the new title *Das Badener Lehrstück vom Einverständnis.* As will be seen, the word *Einverständnis* ("active consent") becomes a key term in Brecht's Lehrstücke on several levels.

In *Lehrstück,* the crashed pilot is reduced, as the chorus declaims at the end, to "his smallest denominator": "now he knows that no one dies when he dies." That is the sober conclusion, from which performers and audience alike are left to draw their own moral. What does *Lehrstück* mean? One of the most comprehensive discussions of the piece to date, that by Reiner Steinweg, considers the possibilities of "mysticism, substitute religion, or parody."[28] By rejecting all three of these possibilities, Steinweg seeks to defend Brecht against the attacks of his Marxist critics such as Ernst Schumacher, who criticized the piece's "ideological nebulosity" *(ideologische Unklarheit).*[29] Instead, Steinweg interprets the piece as "philosophy," posited for discussion in the sense of Brecht's later theory of the genre "Lehrstück." He also asserts that "Brecht apparently coined the term *Lehrstück* while writing [the first version of] the text."[30] Yet there are several reasons to believe not only that Brecht was aware of the theological associations of his title, but also that those associations inform the significance of the work. For all its connections with the philosophy of the later Lehrstücke, *Lehrstück* relates to the theological tradition of *Lehrstück-Katechismus* in an openly provocative way. In his detailed survey of 1993, *Brechts Lehrstücke,* Krabiel traces Brecht's first use of the term *Lehrstück* to one of the so-called Augsburg Sonnets from 1926, a poem entitled *Lehrstück Nr. 2,* in which, to quote Krabiel's description "a prostitute instructs a younger colleague in the art of commercial love."[31]

Brecht's pervasive use of theological motives in his work is well known. Several studies have already documented his use of the Bible. "You will laugh," he himself said in an interview in *Die Dame* in 1928 when he named the "strongest influence" on his work: "the Bible."[32] His religious background was mixed: his mother was a Protestant, his father a Catholic. At the Augsburg *Realgymnasium* he received religious education as a Protestant, although the school also offered classes for Catholics and Jews. During his nine years there, the first four included intensive study of the Catechism.[33] Consequently, his knowledge of the formulations of Lutheran doctrine must have been exhaustive. It is fairly safe to assume, therefore, that the title *Lehrstück* was intended to have religious echoes similar to those of his poetry collection *Hauspostille* (House Breviary; derived from the Latin *post illa verba texta*), named after books of biblical exegesis, of which Luther's collection of that name also serves as a model.

The ultimate test is the works themselves, and in this the Brecht-Hindemith *Lehrstück* remains consistent: both its diction and structure are redolent of catechistic teachings, not just in the interrogative style but in the inductive method of investigation as well. Only after concrete demonstration are any generalities formulated. Against such a background, of course, the content of the piece is ultimately blasphemous. Sacred means (underscored by Hindemith's sparse polyphonic choral style) serve highly profane ends. The "Stück" of *Lehrstück* professes an article of antifaith.

Whereas the relationship between *Lehrstück* and its religious source is quite apparent—substantially intended as provocative negation—any overall didactic aim behind the piece seems at best unclear. The confusion is reflected in the collaborators' published theoretical statements. Hindemith said one thing; Brecht said several things, some agreeing with Hindemith's aims, others in flat contradiction of them. Open dissension ensued, specifically over Hindemith's preface to the piano-vocal score of *Lehrstück*, published by Schott in October 1929, three months after the Baden-Baden premiere. Hindemith concentrated on musical matters, such as in his description of the work's adaptability: "Since the Lehrstück has the sole purpose of engaging all those present in the work's execution and does not, in the first instance, aim to create particular impressions as a musical and poetic utterance, the form of the piece is, if possible, to be adapted as required. The order given in the score is therefore more a suggestion than a set of instructions. Cuts, additions, and reorderings are possible."

Brecht took exception to Hindemith's preface, describing his instructions as based on "a misunderstanding": "Even if one expected . . . that certain formal congruencies of an intellectual nature came about on a musical basis, it would never be possible for such an artificial and shallow harmony, even for a few minutes, to create on a broad and vital basis a counterbalance to the collective formations which pull apart the people of our times with a completely different force." Brecht wrote these words for the preface to his revised *Badener Lehrstück vom Einverständnis.* He was prepared nonetheless to shoulder the burden of responsibility: "Mainly to blame for this misunderstanding is my own willingness to subject to purely experimental purposes as unfinished and misleading a text as the version of *Lehrstück* performed in Baden-Baden. Consequently, the only didactic purpose that could be served was a musical one of a purely formal nature."[34]

Had Hindemith really misunderstood Brecht's text? The evidence suggests not. Brecht's mea culpa for the "misunderstanding" in the preface to his revised version serves, as it were, as a smoke screen. In 1928–29, for example, he could still maintain that "it is not necessary that action *[Handeln],*" by which he meant making music, "be directed toward useful ends. . . . Music [as] *feeling aloud* (whereby it does not matter whether there is singing or whether the 'animal that makes tools' uses instruments) lends the feeling of the individual, insofar as it wishes to become general, a general form and is thus the organization of people on the basis of the organization of tones."[35]

Moreover, accompanying the performance at Baden-Baden was a huge placard that bore the motto of the proceedings: "Besser als Musik hören, ist Musik machen" ("Making music is better than listening to it"). And projected on the wall during the previous day's performance of *Der Lindberghflug* (with music by Hindemith and Weill) was a text, purportedly by Brecht, which corroborated that motto:

> Following the principle "the state should be rich, man should be poor," the state should be duty bound to be capable of much, man allowed to be capable of the little he can—the state should, concerning music, produce everything that demands special study, special apparatus, and special skills, but the individual should learn everything that is necessary for pleasure. For pleasure in music, it is necessary that no distraction is possible. Freely associating feelings occasioned by music, certain thoughts without consequence such as those thought while listening to music, exhaustion which easily sets in while just listening to music, are distractions from music and reduce the pleasure in music. In order to avoid these distractions, the thinking person takes part in music, thus following the principle "action is better than feeling," by following a score of the music and humming the missing parts or following the music with his eyes or singing loudly in unison with others. In this way the state delivers incomplete music, but the individual makes it complete.[36]

Like the textual backdrop to *Der Lindberghflug,* the motto on display during *Lehrstück* the following day proclaimed that its original purpose, apart from its shocking "alienation" of religious pedagogy, was largely of a musical nature (it was after all given its premiere at a music festival) and that Hindemith's preface accurately reflects that purpose. The *Frankfurter Zeitung* (21 May 30) specified the piece's objective, praising *Lehrstück* as an example of a new "community music . . . in ideal rapprochement with the youth singing movement." Brecht's 1930 version changed all that: rather than resolving any "misunderstanding," Brecht sought completely to radicalize the content of the original, calling for political action and change, augmenting its structure, and substantially reducing its musical portion. His chief motivation behind the revision, as with his 1931 reworking of *Die Dreigroschenoper,* appears to have been one of "de-musicalization," effectively suppressing the work's musical origins and revising its ideological function in line with his more recent ideas about didactic theater.[37]

GEBRAUCHSMUSIK

The fact remains that *Lehrstück,* despite its later "de-musicalization" by Brecht, owed much to trends in music pedagogy and that those trends, while epitomized by the work of Germany's youth music movement *(musikalische Jugendbewegung),* had also taken hold of that country's cultural avant garde. The positive notices of *Lehrstück* readily acknowledged this fact. Heinrich Strobel, Hindemith's first biographer, called *Lehrstück* "nothing but the creative realization of the music-pedagogical idea," by which he was referring to the totality of pedagogical reforms that characterized the epoch.[38] Casting a yet wider net was the report on the Baden-Baden festival written for the *Zeitschrift für Musik* by Karl Laux. Laux's article is worth quoting extensively, not because it is exceptional, but because it offers a succinct rehearsal of ideas that many musicians and critics were airing at the time. Laux begins by describing "the situation":

> We are living in a new age. Our image of music has also changed. What comprised a city's musical life twenty years ago? Symphony concerts, choral concerts, recitals. People attended because they wished to delight in the performances of others, but also because it was the thing to do to have been there. People attended, at least physically. How far they participated spiritually could not be ascertained. They could indifferently allow a symphony to wash over them or they could experience it inwardly, as a storm over one's soul, a struggle with intellectual forces. This was a matter for the individual. Concerts were more or less an affair of great passivity.
>
> That has now changed. Just as the audience's sociological mix has changed—the working masses rising upward, wishing to participate in cultural activities—so the internal structure has also changed. People no longer sit in subscription seats. They sit together in rows, wishing to form a community. Moreover, this community is no longer content with just listening. They want to make music themselves. Inner involvement is thus guaranteed. *Activity of the community* replaces passivity of the individual.
>
> It is something new, but it also existed before.
>
> *Heinrich Besseler,* in his essay "Basic Issues of Musical Listening," juxtaposed *practical Gebrauchsmusik* with *autonomous concert music.*[39] The latter contrasts with Being as "in some way self-contained"; with the former the emphasis is "wholly on the active execution of the music." Such execution is "essentially bound up with practical behavior, with prayer, avowal of beliefs, work, recreation in dance and community, entering into a mythical or magical constellation: it always comes about as ornament or intensification, as a specifically 'musical' manifestation of such behaviour."
>
> Such *Gebrauchsmusik*—that is the word that everyone is using—has (according to Besseler) always existed: in dancing, work songs, communal singing, anthems, liturgical music, in the mythic and the magic, in vocal intensification during the narration of fairy tales, lullabies, and incantations.
>
> The youth-music movement as well as the younger generation of composers wishes to rejuvenate such *Gebrauchsmusik.* They no longer want concerts that release listeners *from* life but music-making that redeems the listener *in* life. In the summer of 1927 people decided to act collectively. The yearly *Deutsche Kammermusik Baden-Baden* was to coincide with the annual meeting of the youth movement. They wanted "to support amateur music in every form."
>
> In 1929 three such *utility forms* of contemporary music were to be discussed in Baden-Baden.[40]

Laux goes on to report on the "sensation" of *Lehrstück* under the rubric "music for amateurs"; the other categories are "music for radio," including the Hindemith-Weill-Brecht collaboration *Der Lindberghflug,* and "music for film." By invoking Besseler, Laux places *Lehrstück* in a context that had been a controversial talking point ever since Besseler's lecture was published in 1926.[41] Although Besseler's theory of *Gebrauchsmusik* had begun as methodological reflections on the study of early music, it soon expanded into a critique of contemporary music, culminating in emphatic support for the youth movement.[42] And his theory's relevance was stressed again when, in 1930, the left-liberal journal *Musik und Gesellschaft* presented an abridged version of Besseler's essay in its first issue as a kind of aesthetic manifesto.

Following Besseler's essay in the next issue of *Musik und Gesellschaft* were two articles, the first entitled "Lehrstück" by Hilmar Trede and Hans Boettcher, the second "Lehrstück und Theater" by Gerhart Scherler, a dramaturg in Oldenburg. The authors dealt not merely with one piece but with a whole collection of pieces, several of which had been written for (though not necessarily performed at) "Neue Musik Berlin 1930," the successor to the 1929 Baden-Baden festival. Within the space of a year, "Lehrstück" had become the designation for a thriving genre of musical theater. "I see therein," Scherler wrote, "a new and great movement, capable of radically changing the whole condition and nature of our contemporary theater." The pieces specifically referred to in the articles are *Lehrstück, Der Jasager, Das Wasser* (Ernst Toch and Alfred Döblin), *Der neue Hiob* (Hermann Reutter and Robert Seitz), and *Wir bauen eine Stadt* (Hindemith and Seitz). Stravinsky's *Oedipus rex* is also discussed as an "anticipation of what the 'Lehrstück' . . . can achieve."[43]

The journal *Melos* followed developments with comparable interest. By 1931 it could offer a brief "history of the 'Lehrstück'" in an article entitled "Lehrstück und Schuloper" by Siegfried Günther. Further pieces mentioned by Günther are: *Das Eisenbahnspiel* (Paul Dessau), *Das schwarze Schaf* (Paul Höffer), *Cress ertrinkt* (Wolfgang Fortner), *Jobsiade* (Theodor Jacobi and Robert Seitz), and *Der Reisekamerad* (Hans Joachim Moser).[44]

"LEHRSTÜCK" AS EXPERIMENTAL MUSIC THEATER
Der Lindberghflug

The most frequently performed and extensively discussed Lehrstück of the era was, without doubt, Weill's "school opera" *Der Jasager.* It followed by a year—and in a sense superseded—his first piece that arguably belongs to the genre of Lehrstück, namely *Der Lindberghflug,* written and produced in collaboration with Hindemith and Brecht for the Baden-Baden festival and performed at that festival, as mentioned above, the day before Hindemith-Brecht's *Lehrstück.* Ostensibly a cantata celebrating Charles Lindbergh's 1927 solo flight across the Atlantic, *Der Lindberghflug* began—and was given its premiere—as a multimedia experiment for radio. Ernst Schoen, artistic director of Southwest German Radio, introduced it, prior to its premiere, as an "epic poem full of pathos" *(pathetische Epopöe)* about Lindbergh's flight.[45] The nature of the celebration, however full of pathos, would prove problematic, not least because of Lindbergh's later support of National Socialism. Brecht's various revisions of the text, the last of which makes an express point of expunging Lindbergh's name, document shifts in his conception of the Lehrstück, as is the case with *Der Jasager.* Initially conceived as a piece of *Gebrauchsmusik* for the "listener," who is invited to contribute to a performance broadcast on radio, *Der Lindberghflug* was an ephemeral experiment for Weill, too, who likewise produced his own revised version that also modifies the work's original purpose. In other words, the considerable philological muddle that surrounds the piece reflects a number of aesthetic and ideological issues, nicely captured in the fact that one of Brecht's additions to the text, not set by Weill, is entitled "Ideology."[46]

The first complete version of *Der Lindberghflug* was a pasticcio, mixing numbers set by Hindemith and Weill. For his revision, Weill set the whole thing, replacing Hindemith's settings with his own. The division of labor between the composers in the pasticcio version was about equal, as table 1 illustrates. Yet the collaboration was not without conflict. Rumors about differences between the two artists, which Weill attempted to quell by refuting them in a public statement published shortly after the premiere, contained more than a grain of truth.

Weill's strenuous denial of tensions between Hindemith and himself, which may well have been largely of his own creation, was no more accurate than the description included in his statement concerning how the two of them had divided up their respective tasks. Weill was certainly correct in stating that the project had begun with a commission to compose *Der Lindberghflug,* like his *Berliner Requiem,* for Frankfurt Radio. Before "the idea emerged to create an interesting experiment for Baden-Baden by doing it together," as he explained, he had intended to set the whole thing himself. Accordingly, only Weill is mentioned in the first publication of the text, which appeared in the journal *Uhu* in April 1929. Hindemith had already completed his portions of the collaborative version of the composition by the middle of April—that much is known. Yet who was responsible for bringing about the collaboration in the fist place remains unclear. Weill's account is silent on the matter; it even contradicts what was actually written and performed: "Hindemith took over the composition of the words of America, I the part where Germany speaks."[47] As table 1 shows, Weill in fact composed the numbers associated with America and with the eponymous hero as well as the opening chorus; Hindemith contributed the numbers linked to Europe and to "nature" (i.e., fog, snow, sleep) as well as the concluding chorus.

A month before the premiere, Weill wrote to Hans Curjel, dramaturg at Ber-

TABLE 1 The two versions of *Der Lindberghflug:* A list of musical numbers

Numbers in revised version (all set by Weill)	Numbers in first version (Hindemith/Weill)
1. American pilots are being challenged to cross the Atlantic	1. American pilots are being challenged to cross the Atlantic (Weill)
2. Introduction of the pilot Charles Lindbergh	2. Introduction of the pilot Charles Lindbergh (Weill)
3. The pilot Charles Lindbergh leaves New York on his flight to Europe	3. The pilot Charles Lindbergh leaves New York on his flight to Europe (Weill)
4. The city of New York addresses the ships	4. The city of New York addresses the ships (Weill)
5. During almost the entire flight the pilot had to battle fog	5. During almost the entire flight the pilot had to battle fog (Hindemith)
6. A snow storm came during the night	6a. A snow storm came during the night (Hindemith)
	6b. Lindbergh (Weill)
7. Sleep	7. Water (no music)
	8. Sleep (Hindemith)
8. During the entire flight, all American newspapers spoke incessantly about Lindbergh's luck	9. During the entire flight, all American newspapers spoke incessantly about Lindbergh's luck (Weill)
9. The thoughts of the lucky one	10. The thoughts of the lucky one (no music)
10. The French newspapers wrote: And so he flies, above him the storms, around him the ocean, beneath him the shadow of Nungesser	11. The French newspapers wrote: And so he flies, above him the storms, around him the ocean, beneath him the shadow of Nungesser (Hindemith)
11. Lindbergh talks to his motor	12. Lindbergh talks to his motor (Weill)
12. Finally, not far from Scotland, Lindbergh sees fishermen	13. Finally, not far from Scotland, Lindbergh sees fishermen (Weill)
13. At 10 o'clock on the night of May 21, 1927, at Le Bourget airfield near Paris, a huge crowd awaits the American pilot	14. At 10 o'clock on the night of May 21, 1927, at Le Bourget airfield near Paris, a huge crowd awaits the American pilot (Hindemith)
14. Arrival of the American pilot Charles Lindbergh at Le Bourget airfield near Paris	15. Arrival of the pilot Charles Lindbergh at Le Bourget airfield near Paris (no music)
15. Report concerning the unattainable	16. Report concerning the unattainable (Hindemith)

lin's Kroll-Oper, complaining that "Hindemith has really messed things up for Baden-Baden. . . . I'm resolved," he continued, "to go on the offensive, since he [i.e., Hindemith] has already abandoned any pretense of objectivity." He also insisted to his publisher that "things have happened (in my absence) while the Baden-Baden program was being put together that have only confirmed my earlier unpleasant impressions of this whole event." He therefore requested that the following announcement be issued: "The latest composition by Kurt Weill is a cantata *Lindberghflug* to a text by Bert Brecht. The work will receive its premiere in the autumn. A few movements from this composition will be performed at this year's music festival in Baden-Baden."[48] The publisher duly complied with Weill's wishes, thereby creating the impression that the composer had already completed his version of the movements set by Hindemith, which in fact he had not. Weill did not stop there, however, in distancing himself from the joint venture. In a further letter to Curjel, he made a point of unconditionally rejecting Hindemith's music: "Hindemith's work on *Lindberghflug* and *Lehrstück* was unsurpassable in its superficiality. It has become quite evident that his music for Brecht's texts is too innocuous. It's amazing that even the press has noticed this and cited me as a glowing example of how to set Brecht."[49]

In the absence of statements from Hindemith or, indeed, of any press reviews corroborating Weill's assertions, Giselher Schubert has aptly concluded that "in a grotesque fashion this collaboration with Hindemith must have seemed to Weill an imaginary competition from which, applying sly tactics, he could then feel he had emerged triumphant."[50] (As such, Weill's machinations serve to corroborate the perceived rivalry between the two composers, at least on Weill's part.)

When his revised version of *Der Lindberghflug* received its premiere at a concert given by the Berlin Staatskappelle on 5 December 1929, Weill continued to stress the work's pedagogically motivated conception over the use in the concert hall. As he observed in his program note, the concert hall prepared for pedagogical application, not the other way round. The initial motivation of composing "radio-specific" music is mentioned, but only as one of several possibilities (following a theory of Brecht's):

> With vocal music I consider it obligatory to indicate, beyond its use in the concert hall, the practical purpose for which it was written. Brecht's text *Der Lindberghflug,* set to music in an earlier version as a radio play, is presented here in a musical version intended for performances in schools. The role of Lindbergh should be sung simultaneously by several boys in order to preclude the private attitude of a single Lindbergh performer. The musical apparatus could be supplied by radio (following a theory of Brecht's, which was demonstrated in Baden-Baden). The musical design of the piece, as presented here, is kept intentionally simple, such that it can, with sufficient study time, be learned by school children. For this reason, the instrumentation has also been arranged to fit the available forces of a school orchestra.
>
> The concert hall faces new tasks nowadays. It is relinquishing its exclusively solemn nature and its exclusively pleasure-dispensing function. It is becoming a laboratory in which music's new attitude and the new connections between audience and author have to be proved. It can also become a kind of exhibition room. Thus, for example, *Der Lindberghflug* is meant to be "exhibited," as it were, through concert performance—that is, the performance is meant to prepare the other means of utilization, whereby the piece is no longer presented to an audience but fulfills its practical pedagogical purpose.[51]

Der Jasager

Der Jasager, a "school opera *[Schuloper]* in two acts after the Japanese Noh play *Taniko,*" received its premiere in Berlin at the Zentralinstitut für Erziehung und Unterricht on 23 June 1930. Although the festival "Neue Musik 1930" had commissioned the work, Brecht and Weill withdrew it. The text of another Lehrstück, *Die Maßnahme,* which Brecht had submitted for scrutiny to the festival's committee (Eisler not yet having composed the music), was rejected on "purely artistic grounds." Not only Eisler and Brecht, but also Weill, sensed that there were other reasons for the rejection of the work, namely its political content.[52] *Der Jasager*'s withdrawal was intended as a protest against the inferred politics of the committee's decision.

Weill himself associated three aims with his school opera, all of them basically musical: "a schooling for composers or a generation of composers, in order to place the genre of 'opera' on new foundations"; "a schooling in operatic presentation" requiring "simplicity and naturalness"; and the placing of music "at the service of institutions" such as schools, "rather than its being created as an end in itself."[53] Yet there is no denying that the didactic content justifying the designation *Lehrstück* is also highly political, as the intense debates surrounding *Der Jasager* testify.

The piece's genesis began with Elisabeth Hauptmann's translation of the fifteenth-century Noh play *Taniko.* (Her source, Arthur Waley's English version, is itself a free rendering of the Japanese original.) Although Brecht uses about 90 percent of Hauptmann's translation, he departs from it in one significant respect by introducing the concept of *Einverständnis. Der Jasager* is divided into two acts, each of which begins with the chorus standing on either side of the stage (as it does throughout) and singing the exordium, both a musical and a moral canon: "Above all, it is important to learn consent." When the teacher visits one of his pupils to bid farewell before a school trip across the mountains, he learns that the boy's mother is ill, even though the mother reassures the teacher about her condition. The teacher says the journey will take them to a town in which the great doctors live, but the route is too dangerous for the boy to accompany him. The boy urges the teacher to allow him to join the group so that he can obtain medicine for his mother. Although the mother is reluctant to let her son go, the boy is adamant. All finally agree that he may go. The chorus concludes the first act by confirming the boy's resolve, after which the mother and teacher sing, "Such profound consent! Many accept what is wrong; yet he does not accept the illness but rather that it should be cured."

After repeating its exordium at the beginning of the second act, the chorus comments on the journey: the boy is not equal to the task. When the boy tells the teacher and three other pupils that he is feeling unwell, the teacher suggests a short rest. The other pupils ask whether they should follow the old custom and hurl the sick boy into the valley. The boys repeat their question. The teacher reminds them that the custom also requires that he who has fallen ill must be asked whether the others should turn back on his account. If the boy agrees to that, the students will still want to hurl him into the valley. The teacher explains the custom, adding that it also requires that the answer to the question should be not to turn back. The boy complies, explaining that he had been aware of the possible consequences, and asks that the others should fill his jug with medicine for his mother. The chorus concludes: "Thereupon the friends took the jug and bemoaned the sad ways of the world and its harsh law and hurled him down. Foot to foot they stood at the edge of the abyss and hurled him down with closed eyes, none more guilty than his neighbor, and flung down clods of earth and flat stones as well!"

The central character of the boy thus demonstrates *Einverständnis* in his willingness to act in the interests of the community, even to the point of sacrificing his own life because of his illness. Therein lies the critical difference from the Noh play: whereas his suicide in the Japanese original represents unquestioning obedience to tradition, the new version attempts a demythologization, with the boy being allowed to make his own rational and autonomous decision. (An obvious parallel can be drawn with the innovations of the "Lehrstück-Katechismus": tradition and custom are subjected to inductive scrutiny.)

Having been rejected by the New Music festival, *Der Jasager* was first performed by pupils of the Akademie für Kirchen- und Schulmusik (under the auspices of the Berlin Zentralinstitut für Erziehung und Unterricht) and broadcast simultaneously on radio. The piece, as planned, encountered a further obstacle with its critical reception. A number of critics with differing political views appeared to misconstrue the intended message. Some greeted favorably what they saw as confirmation of their conservative Christian principles, while others interpreted the piece as lending support to authoritarian and reactionary tendencies. It also provoked discussion among the performers themselves. As a result, Brecht made two separate revisions. In the first, the changes mainly served to stress the autonomy of the boy's decision. In the second revision, *Der Jasager* ("the affirmer") becomes *Der Neinsager* ("the refuser"). In this alternative version the boy contravenes convention by refusing to commit suicide. The additional music supplied by Weill for the first revision has never been published, no doubt because it disrupts his original design. Weill declined to set *Der Neinsager*. Brecht's assumption that it could be performed to Weill's music for *Der Jasager* reflects how out of tune he was with Weill's musical aesthetics.

The literary scholar Peter Szondi has rightly drawn attention to the most pressing reason for Brecht to offer *Der Neinsager* as an alternative to the original libretto: in a political climate in which *Der Jasager* could be misconstrued as underwriting sacrifice to the wrong cause, it was just a matter of months before naysayers would not be tolerated.[54] Yet focusing exclusively on the text when either justifying or at least accounting for the revisions, as Brecht and Szondi did, is to ignore the contribution of the music and the ambiguous light it casts on those potentially misconstrued messages.

With its austere contrapuntal style, *Der Jasager* consolidates changes in Weill's musical language already evident in *Aufstieg und Fall der Stadt Mahagonny.* In the same interview in which he described himself as a "simple musician," Weill said that "the rhythms are no longer expressly dance rhythms, but have been transformed, 'digested' *[verdaut].*"[55] The simplicity and restraint, a function of the Lehrstück, go hand in hand with the urge toward a "new classicality" (to use Busoni's term). The boy's sacrifice has nothing to do with the legacy of Bismarckian "blood and iron," however. It occasions, rather, immense human grief, as expressed by the sparse orchestral commentary in the D minor conclusion. Particularly notable in this connection is the major-seventh clash on an accented upper auxiliary note in the orchestra's final iterations of the march tune, moments of heightened melodic expressivity—no less poignant for all their brevity—that qualify the music's underlying rhythmic gesture of uniformity (ex. 23).

In his detailed musical analysis of the piece, which focuses largely on voice-leading structure, Paul Humphreys posits a musical "shock of recognition" at the conclusion "that enables a feeling member of the audience to experience the powerful emotional conflict to which the act of agreement has given rise." The composer, he writes, "has chosen not to sit in judgment of the text or of the characters that it portrays; he takes rather a more compassionate stance that has allowed him (and his audience) to perceive both the tragedy and the inevitability of its outcome." By way of conclusion, Humphreys describes *Der Jasager* as "an expression, rather than an espousal or a rejection, of the act of agreement and its accompanying consequences." It is an ambiguity that the music admits, but which the text on its own does not. For those who care to listen, the qualifications presented by the two revised versions are already embedded in the musical setting of the original.[56]

In Danish exile, Brecht was asked to comment on an interviewer's opinion that "there are many instances in *Der Jasager* where the music creates a lot of feeling and is highly enjoyed by the audience." He responded, effectively ducking the issue, by stating quite correctly that "the music does not exist for the benefit of the audience, but for the performers. *Der Jasager* and *Der Lindberghflug* are truly *Gebrauchsmusik* and are to be performed by children for the benefit of their own enrichment."[57]

In its original form, *Der Jasager* proved to be one of Weill's most successful compositions in Germany, receiving more than three hundred performances before the Nazis came to power in 1933. Celebrating its success, *Melos* reported in

EXAMPLE 23. *Der Jasager,* conclusion

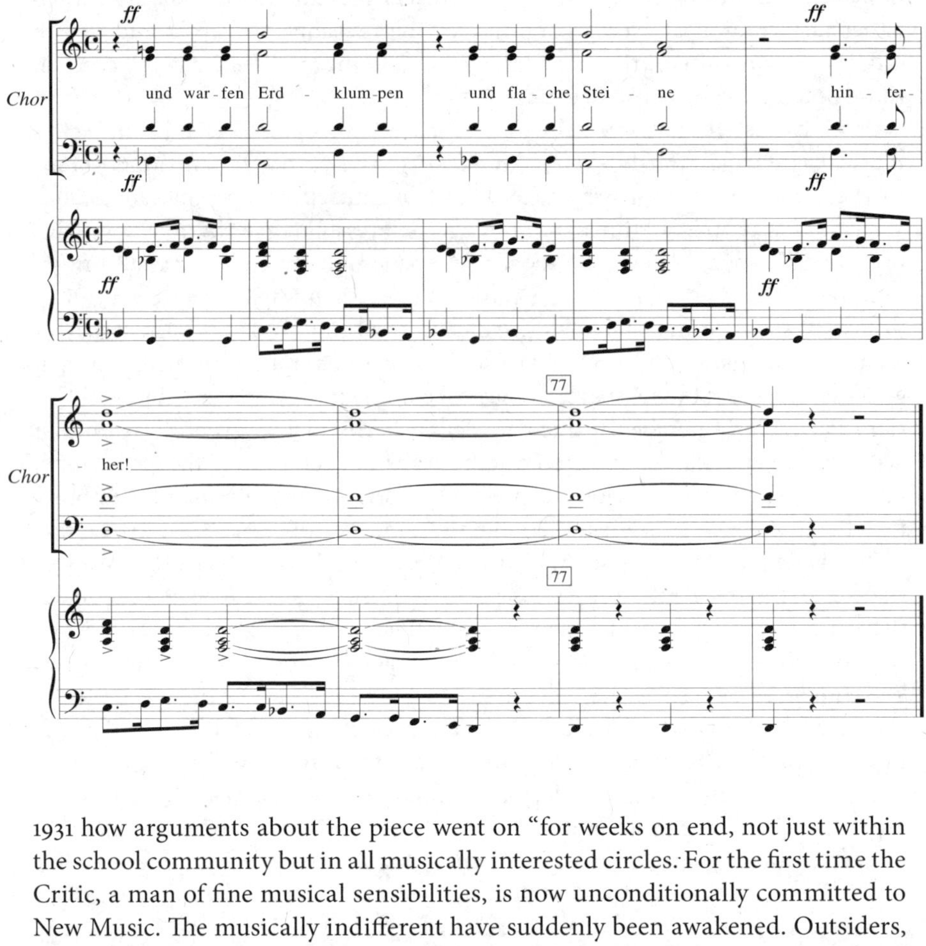

1931 how arguments about the piece went on "for weeks on end, not just within the school community but in all musically interested circles. For the first time the Critic, a man of fine musical sensibilities, is now unconditionally committed to New Music. The musically indifferent have suddenly been awakened. Outsiders, not just the parents of performers, enter the battle over New Music. Centers of resistance include the Nationalists, the Wagner Youth (led at our institute by a philologist), and the orthodox wing of the church (because of the un-Christian thought)."[58]

Frank Warschauer, for example, writing for *Die Weltbühne* (8 July 1930), castigated the work for its reactionary tendencies: "In this school opera young people are inculcated with a philosophy that finely mixes in, while still effectively containing, all the evil ingredients of reactionary thought based on senseless authority."[59] (It was precisely such criticisms that prompted Brecht to prepare his revisions.)

Der Jasager even provoked a direct creative response, albeit a negative one.

Hans Joachim Moser conceived his "Schuloper" *Der Reisekamerad,* mentioned above, expressly as a corrective ("per oppositionem") to the Weill-Brecht work.[60] Freely based on Hans Christian Andersen's fairy tale, Moser's academically eclectic piece stresses the "good deed" of the individual over the notion of his or her subjugation to the collective moral preached by Brecht. Apart from his response to the success of *Der Jasager,* Moser no doubt had in mind Brecht's more recent Lehrstücke as well, such as *Die Maßnahme* and *Die Ausnahme und die Regel,* both of which placed the issue of *Einverständnis* in a party-political context. As Eisler reportedly described *Die Maßnahme,* "It is a political seminar of a special kind on questions of the party's strategy and tactics. . . . The Lehrstück is not intended for concert use. It is only a means of pedagogical work with students of Marxist schools and proletarian collectives."[61]

Brecht was just one of many artists who were finding overtly political outlets for their art. To that extent, the furor over *Die Maßnahme* was wholly symptomatic. Criticism of the traditional social apparatus of music-making, both concert and opera, was widespread, expressed in terms of a preference for the organic community *(Gemeinschaft)* over the inorganic, anonymous society *(Gesellschaft).* Such opposition could be heard on both sides of the political spectrum. The call for "Gebrauchskunst" was similarly widespread and similarly unrestricted to any one political stripe. In dispute was the nature of the "use" being proposed and the type of community that the new "utility" art should serve. By way of making its voice distinct, the left replaced the neutral notion of *Gebrauchswert* (use value) with the ideologically more colored criterion of *Kampfwert* (the value of didactic art in the service of a specific political struggle). Traditional aesthetic values had to yield to the requirements of agitprop.[62]

The development of the Lehrstück can be seen to reflect the general course of Weimar culture whereby the simple opposition to cultural institutions characteristic of the early and middle years of the republic (often involving parodistic iconoclasm) gives way to the grounding of countercultures. Thus the parodic "alienation" of the Christian catechism in *Lehrstück* was transformed into the serious "secular" catechetics of *Der Jasager.* But like the republic itself, the movement that produced Lehrstücke was only short-lived. Although strongly influenced by the *Schulmusikbewegung,* those Lehrstücke were principally produced by an experimental avant-garde; they owed their inception directly to the music festivals for which they were written, and, as exemplified by *Der Jasager,* they relied for their further dissemination on the willingness of pedagogical institutions to collude in the experiment. When the National Socialists came to power, the musicians associated with the New Music festivals largely fell out of favor. With their works being branded as "degenerate," most of them left Germany.[63] But if Lehrstücke necessarily ceased, their influence did not. Ingredients of the Lehrstücke—the involvement of the audience, the cast of "types" rather than individuals, the use of a chorus, judicial scenes in which the chorus acts as intermediary, the central theme of the relationship of the individual to the community, a theme played out by the performers, who themselves form a microcosmic community—all of these aspects have been identified in the so-called *Thingspiele* of the Nazi period prior to 1937, in particular the ritualistic stage spectacles of Eberhard Wolfgang Möller.[64]

MUSICAL IMPLICATIONS

Although the Lehrstück owed much to the burgeoning amateur music movement of the 1920s, one might readily assume that its implications for the composers of New Music were aesthetic rather than stylistic, especially in view of the apparent concessions that amateur music necessitated—not just technical simplicity but also adaptability in matters such as instrumentation. Yet the cases of two of the most prominent composers who contributed to the Lehrstück movement, Hindemith and Weill, illustrate that such an assumption is far from the truth. As Weill said in the interview cited above, *Der Jasager* should be considered central to his output: a *chef-d'oeuvre,* not a mere *parergon.* For him, as for Hindemith, amateur music not only corresponded with his personal philosophy of music but also influenced how he would compose. And for Hindemith, the experience was to affect his music theory as well.

In his stage works prior to *Der Jasager,* Weill utilized modern dance music to powerful dramatic effect. *Der Jasager* seems to consolidate this development. As he said, "the rhythms are no longer expressly dance rhythms, but have been transformed, 'digested.'" Moreover, in a work that debates the question of individual responsibility (absent the self-abandonment and recklessness of *Mahagonny*), Weill cultivates his own musical embodiment of such responsibility, a kind of musico-dramatic *prima prattica.*[65] The influence of *Der Jasager* is perhaps most strongly felt in Weill's next full-scale opera, *Die Bürgschaft* (1931–32), with its terse parabolic plot, neoclassical musical textures, and moralizing chorus. Yet while such stylistic and dramaturgical traits imbue *Die Bürgschaft,* it cannot really be called a Lehrstück in the strict sense. The generic tradition certainly persists, however, in Weill's "folk opera" *Down in the Valley* (1945–48) and, to a certain extent, in the various pageants produced for the American war effort.[66]

With Hindemith, the connection between pedagogy and composition is still more far-reaching. For him, too, the new simplicity prompted by writing for amateurs affected what traditional musicology terms his "personal style."[67] Writing about the musical language of *Lehrstück,* Heinrich Strobel identified a "strength and monumentality," as opposed to the earlier "broad playing-away" *(breites Ausmusizieren),* which he felt "often endangers Hindemith's operas."[68] In other words, *Lehrstück* signals a shift in Hindemith's approach to composition, and it is a shift that continues to make itself felt in the immediately succeeding instrumental works. It is these works—for example, the symphony *Mathis der Maler* (1934)—through which Hindemith established his later reputation. The connection between pedagogy and composition is intensified in Hindemith's case inasmuch as he based the music theory published as *Unterweisung im Tonsatz* (Craft of Musical Composition) on his own musical language. The very mobility and flexibility required by *Lehrstück* and other amateur pieces generate, as I have demonstrated elsewhere, the type of harmonies and part-writing that become the cornerstones of Hindemith's theory.[69]

In an attempt systematically to distinguish between Brecht's Lehrstücke and his other Stücke, Reiner Steinweg has posited a much-discussed axiom, or "Basisregel."[70] He suggests that Lehrstücke are different from other theatrical pieces insofar as they are conceived primarily for the players themselves. Steinweg drew his axiom from Brecht's last written observation on the genre: "This designation *[Lehrstück]* is valid only for pieces that are instructive for the *performers*. They do not require an audience."[71] The rule emphasizes less the didactic content of the works than the mere fact of active participation. In defining our involvement in an aesthetic act, the rule is phenomenological. As such, in circumscribing an aesthetics of performance, it reflects a pervasive trend in Weimar culture.

The present investigation has also identified a connection between the innovations of the theatrical Lehrstück and those of its religious predecessor that goes beyond mere etymology. Just as the early-twentieth-century Catholic Catechism sought to further an active comprehension and interpretation of Christian creed, so the creators of the secular Lehrstück hoped to break down traditional barriers between composers, performers, and audience in the dissemination of music. The inductive-deductive dichotomy addressed by theologians such as Heinrich Stieglitz thus has a precise analogy in the active-passive debates that characterize 1920s musical aesthetics. To that extent, the Lehrstück represents a remarkable example of the secularization of religious thought. The connection is encapsulated in an *aperçu* made by a reviewer of *Die Maßnahme,* albeit with a significance beyond the intended one, which was to draw a parallel between Brecht's work and the religious dramas of the Baroque. "It is remarkable and it is important," wrote Julius Bab, "that after Catholicism Communism is now developing a 'Lehrstück.'"[72] That the development of this type of didactic theater came to grief on the platform of ideological disputes is utterly in keeping with the political republic whose spirit the Lehrstück embodies perhaps more than any other artistic genre.

8

Stages of Exile

Weill's life and work after his departure from Germany suggest a pattern that resists the concept of exile, at least as that term is normally applied to German émigré artists. More appropriate in his case, as suggested earlier, is the notion of "other-directedness," a character typology that runs counter to conventional conceptions of artistic identity and development. Eschewing the concept of exile is no trivial matter, however. Terminology is critical for historical as well as cultural reasons. The editors of the 1993 book *Musik im Exil,* for example, warned against replacing the term *exile* with *emigration.*[1] "Emigration," they contended, represents a "neutralization *[Entschärfung]* . . . a dispossession of the history and identity of those who fled abroad from the Nazis." Their objection is wholly justified in one sense, yet it necessarily invites difficulties in another. "Exile" is an equivocal concept. It can signify both the process of enforced emigration and a feeling of alienation and loss in the foreign culture to which the emigrant has fled. While the historical process is an inescapable, appalling fact, the matter of cultural identity is hard to determine on an individual basis. In the field of German exile studies, especially where the nature of an artist's departure from Germany is concerned, distinguishing between "exile" and "emigration" has been a matter of heated, sometimes even acrimonious contention.[2]

Weill and Brecht were both exiled from Germany, but only Brecht continued to insist on his status as an exile in America. As he wrote in his poem "Über die Bezeichnung Emigranten" (On the Designation Emigrants) from the *Svendborger Gedichte,* "Und kein Heim, ein Exil soll das Land sein . . . Aber keiner von uns / Wird hier bleiben" (Not a home, the country should be an exile . . . but none of us will remain here). Not so Weill. He would willingly adapt to the new culture;

proudly proclaim in a radio broadcast in 1941, "I am an American," even before receiving citizenship; and then happily spend the remaining years of his life in the United States.[3] Even *he* thought this was unusual. On 21 August 1944, after an evening spent with other émigrés, he wrote to Lenya that he was "[beginning to think] that we are almost the only ones of all these people who have found American friends and who really live in this country. They all are still living in Europe."[4] And in 1947, after being described in *Life* magazine as a "German composer," he responded with his often-quoted "gentle beef": "Although I was born in Germany, I do not consider myself a 'German composer.' The Nazis obviously did not consider me such either and I left their country (an arrangement that suited both me and my rulers admirably) in 1933. I am an American citizen and during my dozen years in this country have composed exclusively for the American stage."[5]

In light of such personal testimony, talking of "Weill's enforced exile in America," as Arnold Whittall has done, seems odd.[6] Doing so almost always involves more than the "mere" fact that the composer fled Germany in 1933 and continued to work in the United States even after the end of the war. Matters of artistic identity and/or the quality of his music, before and after emigration, are never far away. Not only does the use of the term *exile* with respect to cultural identity require interpretation; the implications are also both political and aesthetic, as urged on the inside cover of *Musik im Exil:* "As a whole, the volume accomplishes a further act of coming to terms with a past whose consequences are still with us and, at the same time, an act of spiritual atonement, coupled with the attempt to uncover progressive traditions."

Yet the question remains concerning the extent to which national history, collective guilt, political significance, and aesthetic judgment are separate and separable. Weill reception, it could be argued, has been the story of this very question being answered in disparate, even mutually exclusive, ways. According to Hanns-Werner Heister, for example, the above factors are all of a piece. Heister seeks to "rescue" Weill as a "progressive" by claiming his alienation from the "ideologically dominant 'mainstream'" and thereby appropriate him for German history, in particular by positing a link with "left oppositional Germany before 1933." Weill, he claims "was in exile, in an emphatic sense in foreign parts *[in der Fremde]*."[7]

Heister even speculates that Broadway works such as *Street Scene* compensated for a sense of failure on Weill's part to realize the ideal of a political aesthetic. Construing such personal, artistic, and political alienation by setting Weill in opposition to a putative mainstream is motivated above all by the desire to turn him into a worthy subject for German exile studies (Heister is writing, after all, for a volume called *Musik im Exil*). As an interpretive strategy, this approach stands in stark opposition to the two-Weills theory, which typically requires excluding the American works from serious consideration or at least bracketing them off from Weill's German works. Heister, by contrast, is quite willing to entertain continuity in Weill's thinking and even offers evidence of it. He nonetheless finds a perhaps inevitable gap between ideal and reality, theory and practice. It is this gap that provides him with his main reason for invoking the exile concept. Yet to do so, with respect both to life and works, seems a stretch.

Distinctions can and indeed should be drawn, following Weill's lead, between his European period of exile and his life in the United States. In the "I am an American" broadcast he talks of finding in America "everything I needed to continue where I had left off." By this he is referring to a sense of continuity between his German and American years, with a hiatus during the years in France and England after "all that we had done was wiped out by an iron hand." When he invokes "a theatre full of creative impulse, freedom, technical possibilities," he is no doubt thinking about his institutional affiliations rather than matters of generic convention, form, or style, insofar as these things can be kept separate. Those affiliations were lacking more than ever during the period 1933 through 1937.

Each of the stage works conceived after the departure from Germany and prior to the move to the United States deserves to be treated as a "stage of exile," in the twofold sense of having been written both in and for foreign institutions. It could seem platitudinous to say that each of these projects for the musical theater reflects the specific historical and cultural circumstances of its conception, for that is equally true of the American and German works. However, the theme of "exile" in particular does offer a useful, even necessary, key toward an understanding and appreciation of these interim works. Applying the concept of exile is not just a matter of biography. Each work requires that the constellation of politics and aesthetics (national history, collective guilt, political significance, and aesthetic judgment) be assessed anew. Each also possesses potential, up to a point, to transcend those circumstances. The interpretive task is to determine that point. In what sense do the works remain bound to their stages of exile, in what sense not?

A biographical starting point is the interview that Weill gave in 1934 to the Danish newspaper *Berlingske Politiske og Avertissements-Tidende* and that was published in the paper's evening edition *(Aften-Avisen)* on 21 June under the heading "Kurt Weill i Exil." The composer had been in France for over a year, and after a brief introduction setting the scene of the interview, which was conducted in Louveciennes near Paris (his "new home"), the author of the article, Ole Winding, quotes verbatim Weill's own remarkable view of his situation.

> Even in Berlin last year I felt the need for a change of air; everything was gradually becoming too easy for me; and there was reason to suppose that this would affect my music. I'm only human, and it's human to be conquered by one's vanity. So

> before Hitler and the Nazis thought about renewing me, I had already hit upon the idea myself! I traveled abroad without the slightest bitterness and of course hopeful of returning at some point; at least certain that my right to love the fatherland was as great as that of the current German patriots! My family has served the country to the best of its capabilities and in accord with its position for eight hundred years; I also hoped to serve it, and perhaps I will now have even more chance to do so through the renewal that exile has meant for my music. . . . Naturally Paris had to become my new home! I knew that fresh battles awaited me here, that battles long ago endured at home had to be waged all over again, and I felt that would do me good. It is hard but nice to start life from the beginning.

The passage nicely captures resilience in the face of what could only have been the most wrenching personal and artistic upheaval. In a fairly short time, Weill had chosen to put the negative aspects of his circumstances behind him. He viewed the disruption in a positive light, as a creative opportunity for self-reform or "renewal," as he says. Necessity became a virtue. This public view needs to be supplemented, of course, by a more private one, and indeed, the correspondence with Lenya supplies several poignant counterexamples.

In the interview he goes on to talk about his new plans, which included a projected "singspiel" version of *Marie Galante* (in the end a play with music), his "opéra comique" (*Der Kuhhandel,* really a satirical operetta), and his symphony for the princess de Polignac, which, perhaps tellingly, he refers to as his first (it was actually his second). No less fascinating than his personal, idiosyncratic definition of exile is the account of his work with Brecht. Having fallen out with Brecht over *Aufstieg und Fall der Stadt Mahagonny,* he offers insight into how he was still able to renew the collaboration on *Die sieben Todsünden,* his first "exile" work:

> Brecht is one of the most talented writers of modern Germany; yet being a great writer does not mean you are also a good composer. Brecht is an artist; of course we talked with each other during our collaboration; but the fact that, for example, music possesses the same value and enduring validity as the words in the text is not a specially Brechtian idea, as some believe. It is an old musical idea! Every sung text should match the music, so that the senseless stretching of words and breathless blather are both avoided equally. Brecht is a genius; yet the responsibility for the music in our joint works is mine alone. Our collaboration was not my debut, as some have believed.

DIE SIEBEN TODSÜNDEN

The extent of Brecht's contribution to *Die sieben Todsünden* remains a matter of conjecture. Whereas Brecht himself preferred to play down his involvement, Esbjörn Nyström has uncovered textual evidence to support the notion that "the idea of Brecht's pronounced lack of interest in the work should be revised."[8] This is hardly a unique case, however: the extent of Brecht's contribution to many of his collaborative theater works has given rise to lively scholarly dispute.[9] Here, as elsewhere, the authorship of his poetry is less in question than that of other parts of the work. Here, as elsewhere, too, biographical questions spill over into exegetical ones. What influence did Brecht exert over the work's final form and over its reception? How "Brechtian" is it?

One of the most extensive studies of the work to date, a master's thesis by Barbara Münch, presents *Die sieben Todsünden* as "philosophically the end of an artistic partnership." Using Brecht's writings as her point of reference, Münch concludes that the work is "not wholly successful" in implementing the demands of Brecht's opera theory; rather, it "represents a regression."[10] Scholarship in the German Democratic Republic, as Jan Knopf reported in his *Brecht-Handbuch,* displayed a similar tendency by placing the "ballet" with the "operas" and describing the renewed collaboration as "anachronistic."[11] In accord with Brecht's materialist theories, Münch maintains, Brecht aimed to use the female protagonist of the work "merely as an object to demonstrate an opprobrious social situation."[12] Yet given the situation at the time, historically and in terms of Brecht's biography, Anna with her split personality was more than just a representative of her class or even her gender. She also stands as "the prototype of an artist whose means of articulation are trapped in inner and outer exile."[13] Seeing the work in this way raises a question concerning the significance of Brecht's revised title, *Die sieben Todsünden der Kleinbürger:* What motivated the change? How much did it serve, for example, as a corrective to Brecht's impression of opening night, communicated in a letter to his wife, as "nice enough *[ganz hübsch]* but not all that significant"?[14]

Although this premiere performance, which took place in Paris on 7 June 1933, was in German, the title was announced in French: *Les Sept Péchés capitaux: Spectacle sur des poèmes de Bert Brecht.* Brecht did indeed write the sung texts, into which he injected his customary "genius," but he may have had little to do with the final version of the scenario, and seems to have had nothing whatsoever to do with the actual production. He was present at the most for only two weeks during the work's inception (his precise movements at the time have proved difficult to reconstruct) and did not return to Paris again until the time of the premiere.[15]

Responsible for the initial idea for the piece was the wealthy impresario and British eccentric Edward James, who had agreed to fund the first season of Kochno and Balanchine's Parisian company "Les Ballets 1933" on the condition that the company commission a work from Weill. James wanted a piece for his estranged wife, the German dancer Tilly Losch, and for Lenya, whom he had admired when she performed in Paris before, in December 1932. Weill first approached

Jean Cocteau to work with him. Only when Cocteau declined did Weill instruct Kochno, on 5 April 1933, to send a telegram to Brecht inviting him to come to Paris and start work as soon as possible ("baldigst"), which he apparently did.

In a letter dated 18 April to Erika Neher, wife of set designer Caspar Neher, Weill could report that he had been "working with B. [Brecht] for a week." He also writes that Caspar Neher was "reluctant to work with B. and myself" for reasons "completely plausible and understandable to anybody of a reasonable disposition." Weill was in the middle of an intense, ardent affair with Erika. Moreover, the week working with Brecht had made Weill "more than ever of the opinion that he [i.e., Brecht] is one of the most repulsive, unpleasant characters on the face of the earth." No love lost there! Yet he immediately states that he is "able to separate this completely from his [i.e., Brecht's] work."[16]

The private thoughts Weill shared with Erika concerning this particular text are revealing, not just about *Die sieben Todsünden* but about the collaboration in general: "I don't believe it is immortal poetry; but it contains several elements that really suit my music (and that is decisive for me and really should be for you as well); it displays an intellectual attitude completely in control (all Frenchmen who read it—and they really aren't all idiots—compare it to *Candide* by Voltaire); it contains—as always—formulations of great individual beauty and phrases of a simple human expressiveness, which you recognize only when you hear the music I have come up with for it." Elsewhere in the letter he confirms that "every text I've set looks entirely different once it has been swept through my music." It is a sentiment that would have been as irritating to the playwright as it should be indispensable to interpretations of the piece.

The French label *spectacle*, connoting a theatrical "show," does nothing to convey the particular mix of song and dance presented by the work's two principal performers: a dancer and a singer. Rather, it functions as a kind of umbrella term broad enough to accommodate the work's provocatively hybrid nature. More precise is Weill's own description in his autograph score: *ballet chanté* (sung ballet). Three years later he would talk about it as his "ballet-opera."[17] Other descriptions used at the time ran the gamut of genres from "more of a cantata than a ballet" to "short opera" to "immorality play."[18]

It is customary for critics to puzzle over how to categorize Weill's work—hardly surprising when the composer himself often wavered over how best to label his hybrid genres. In this instance all the descriptions manage to tell us something about the piece: about its main ingredients (song and dance), about its silent dancing protagonist ("ballet"), about its length (about forty minutes) and its ties to the 1927 "Songspiel" *Mahagonny* (also conceived as a "short opera"), and about its purposely ironic subversion of Christian theology. All of these elements, coupled with the generic uncertainty, are familiar and significant. In that sense, Weill's work was not cut short by his departure from Germany, an impression echoed in Walter Mehring's much-quoted description of opening night: "Two 'undesirables' from Germany, namely composer Kurt Weill and the poet Bert Brecht, continued their successes in Paris. . . . It was a glorious evening. An elite group of celebrated artists and interpreters, just as one was accustomed to during the days of the great German theater, was there."[19]

Radically separating song from action is an idea that can be traced back in Weill's case to two principal sources. The first is his teacher Busoni, who espoused an ideal of opera as "a kind of sung pantomime."[20] The other is Stravinsky, whose works from the teens and early twenties experiment with alienation devices and were likely influenced by the work of theater director Vsevolod Meyerhold. Both *Les Noces* and *Renard,* in which singers are not identified with particular roles, separate voices from action. (Not coincidentally, perhaps, it was Kochno, Diaghilev's secretary in the early 1920s, who was responsible for adapting Pushkin's narrative poem *The Little House in Kolomna* for the libretto of Stravinsky's *opéra bouffe Mavra* [1922].) Weill, as he openly acknowledged on a number of occasions, drew inspiration from Stravinsky's *L'histoire du soldat,* also a pantomime, albeit with a spoken rather than sung narration. The "separation of the elements" would of course become an indispensable, critical ingredient of epic theater as defined in Brecht's later theories. *Der Protagonist,* Weill's pre-Brecht "debut," with its interpolated, essentially mute pantomimes, marks a decisive step in this direction. The same principle manifests itself—albeit as an aspect of production—in the "Songbeleuchtung" that Brecht and Weill prescribed to illuminate the discrete numbers of their *Dreigroschenoper.* And separating song from action is something Weill would return to with the pageant *Railroads on Parade.*

There is no work of Weill's more thoroughly or consistently informed by the idea of separating its constituent elements, however, than *Die sieben Todsünden.* This is presumably what Weill was referring to as "an intellectual attitude completely in control." The protagonist herself is split in two: Anna I and Anna II. One is a singer; two is a dancer. But as Anna I sings in the opening Prologue, they are "really only one person." Her alter-ego sister is "beautiful" and "somewhat crazy"; she is "practical" and "sane." But they are, as she sings, "one heart and one savings book"—the latter substituting for the expected "soul," as in the common, even clichéd expression "ein Herz und eine Seele." The sacrifice of Anna II's soul to satisfy the family's greed is the common thread linking the seven cardinal sins of the work's title. Committing any one of them jeopardizes that overriding objective, for which Anna's coerced thrift functions as a corollary.

The split of the protagonist is hardly just a formalist matter, then. At stake is nothing less than the human soul and its relation to the social mores enshrined in the moral code of Christianity. Each of the separate musical numbers represents one of the sins, danced by Anna II, sung about by Anna I, and commented on by their family, traditionally performed by an all-male quartet, with "Mother" sung by the bass.[21] By seeking their fortune in large American cities (Memphis, Los Angeles, Philadelphia, Boston, Baltimore, and San Francisco), the sisters aim to earn enough to return to Louisiana and "build a little home," supposedly an ideal of domestic harmony. The authors appear to have believed that Louisiana was a city, not a state. Summarizing the plot in unpublished biographical notes from 1949, Weill described how, on arriving in Paris in 1933, "I got a commission from 'Les Ballets 1933' to write a ballet for Tilly Losch, and from a scenario by Bertholt *[sic]* Brecht I wrote a sort of Ballet-Singspiel called *Les Sept Peches Capitaux,* or *Anna-Anna* [the title used for the London production], the story of two young girls who were sent out by their family to earn money for a little house, and how they went through seven cities and seven sins. It was produced that same summer in Paris and London."[22]

Whether or not the domestic harmony is petit bourgeois is left open in the original title but made explicit in Brecht's revised one, *Die sieben Todsünden der Kleinbürger.* The ideal thereby becomes one that is entertained by a specific class (the petty bourgeoisie) and underpinned by questionable, theologically informed values. When *Kleinbürger* was added is uncertain. The latest Brecht edition indicates that the revised title was not used for any of the early European performances—Paris, London, Copenhagen—but that it did appear as early as 1937 in Brecht's correspondence.[23] The intention is nonetheless clear: to underline the sociological dimension of the work's didacticism.

According to the description in Brecht's typescript, Anna I represents the sales person and Anna II the commodity.[24] Their precarious union personifies a social unit, one that upholds the prevailing system morally and economically. By specifying their class allegiance, Brecht could be seen to be invoking a Marxist-influenced analysis of the system and hence of fascism. Yet such an analysis, which Brecht's revision invites, also limits interpretive possibilities of the work as a whole. (*Die Dreigroschenoper* offers a similar example of Brecht's retroactively enhancing, even augmenting, the sociopolitical dimensions of his work.) The context for interpreting Anna II's sins is certainly social, though not necessarily "petit bourgeois." The American setting—particularly in the context of 1933—suggests other avenues of interpretation.

The secularization of traditional religious motifs is hardly new in Brecht and Weill's work. *Mahagonny* (both "Songspiel" and opera), *Die Dreigroschenoper,* and *Happy End* are all replete with such motifs. The genre of the Lehrstück, as discussed in the previous chapter, stood a whole tradition of religious teaching on its head—or as Marxists might say, on its feet. On one level—the one that Brecht was keen to stress by changing the title—*Die sieben Todsünden* can be read as a kind of parodistic Lehrstück, too, about the complacent hypocrisy of middle-class values. The theologically classified "deadly sins" are seen here in terms of their material, secular worth; they appear less in terms of our personal lapses and ultimate guilt before God, as conventional theology would have it, than as an oppressive means directed toward the creation of wealth. Anna's proscribed behavior might be seen in a different world as purely human needs, not as "sins," in some cases even as virtues. In this world, they are luxuries only the wealthy can afford.

The scenario is straightforward enough. Still in their home state of Louisiana, the two sisters have devised an exploit whereby Anna II causes a scene in the park by accosting men and Anna I offers to have her removed for a fee. But the plan fails when Anna II falls asleep. In Memphis, the audience demand to see something for their money, coercing Anna II to do a striptease as part of her dance show. "Pride is something for the rich," her sister admonishes her. In Los Angeles, the sisters work as film extras, but Anna II is sacked when she protests at the ill treatment of a horse. Her sister has to teach her to curb her anger, including "open disapproval of injustice." In Philadelphia, where Anna II works as a solo dancer, she is obliged to watch her weight or lose her job, with two servants with revolvers assisting her in this endeavor. In Boston, she is forced to remain faithful to Edward (no doubt an in-joke about Edward James, the dancer's husband). Edward has money, but Anna really loves Fernando (originally called Adolphe). Financially ruined, Edward shoots himself; others follow suit. Through her naked displays of greed Anna achieves temporary fame that soon turns into notoriety. Moving from Baltimore to San Francisco, Anna II envies all those who commit "sins" with impunity. She is rebuked by her sister and repents. With enough money saved, they can now return to Louisiana to live in their little house.

Sloth (sleeping instead of working); pride (about one's occupation); anger (about injustice); gluttony (especially on the part of dancers); lust (for an impecunious lover); avarice (in the public eye); envy (for those who sin with impunity)—all get in the way of the life Anna is forced to lead, involving menial and demeaning work, in order to achieve the goal prescribed by her family and reinforced by her alter ego.

Furnishing a synopsis of the *Die sieben Todsünden* such as this involves conflating two of the work's elements: the texts of Brecht's songs and the scenario. A collective product, with markings in several hands in one of the surviving manuscripts, the scenario must have undergone several incarnations before the first production. Brecht no doubt had some say in its creation as he worked with Weill in mid-April, though it is likely that some of it was already conceived before he arrived in Paris.[25] And some of it, as David Drew has speculated, may have been written *after* the composition of the musical numbers.[26]

In an interview he gave to a Danish radio journal in Copenhagen a month after the premiere, Brecht flatly denied authorship, stating that "Weill wrote [the text] based on a poem, which I had made, but he is himself responsible for the making of the dialogue."[27] He was asked in the same interview whether Weill "share[s] your views upon art." He replied, "Unfortunately, not totally."

Weill "is on his way to move away from the ideas, and is too much concerned with the audience and with what pays," Brecht continued. "He insists on writing grand opera, and in this I cannot join him. Therefore I must definitely dissociate myself from his ballet *Die sieben Todsünden*." Whether Brecht chose to dissociate himself from the work because of his relative lack of involvement in its creation or because of his disapproval of the premiere production remains unclear; it was likely a bit of both.

Caspar Neher, despite his own initial misgivings about being involved at all, provided the set designs for the premiere production in Paris. In a painterly style familiar from his earlier collaborations with Brecht and Weill, he created sets that are described in the published text as follows:

> On the stage there is a small board showing the route of the tour through the seven *[sic]* cities, in front of which Anna I stands with a small pointing stick. On the stage there is the constantly changing market to which Anna II is sent by her sister. At the end of each of the scenes, which show how the seven deadly sins can be avoided, Anna II returns to Anna I, and on the stage there is the family of both—father, mother, and two sons—in Louisiana, and behind them the little house grows that is earned by avoiding the seven deadly sins.[28]

Reconstructable from surviving sketches and photographs of the premiere production, Neher's designs include seven arches whose openings are covered with paper. Each sheet of paper has a title on it, in the manner of the earlier experiments in epic theater, specifying in Latin the sin in question. Every time Anna II commits a sin, she passes through one of the arches, thereby ripping the paper. Seven lamps hang above the set. The two Annas' personal unity is symbolized by their wearing a dark cape that covers them both at the beginning and end of the piece.

At the end of each scene, the "Family," a male-voice quartet, receives the fruits of the "practical" daughter's efforts. The quartet sings in all but the outer movements. Its linking commentaries and admonishments between each "sin" range in style from the German *Singverein* to barbershop quartet and quasi-cantorial intonation, at all times in parodistic vein. They, as much as anything else, inject a note of comedy into the proceedings.

There is much to be made of the basic dualism introduced in the *Todsünden* as practicality and sanity versus beauty and craziness. Interpretations have differed markedly, however, covering a lot of ground, lending differing weight to the significance of the American milieu, and drawing on an array of theoretical support, from Rousseau and Marx to Freud. For those given to such interpretation, the work also resonates with autobiographical significance. The collaborators on the premiere production were themselves trying to make their way in new surroundings. In addition to a common estrangement from Germany, many of them were also estranged from one another. Weill and Brecht had fallen out in 1931 over the Berlin production of their opera *Aufstieg und Fall der Stadt Mahagonny.*[29] Weill wrote the part of Anna I for his wife, Lotte Lenya, with whom he was going through divorce proceedings (they later remarried). Lenya's then current lover, Otto Passetti, sang in the Family. The British impresario Edward James saw the ballet as a way of appeasing his wife, Tilly Losch, who danced the part of Anna II and from whom he was soon to be divorced. Weill himself, as mentioned, was romantically involved with the set designer's wife. Pride, anger, lust, and envy were no doubt evident off as well as on the stage.

As one of the discrete elements, the score is both separate and separable from the scenario, a fact demonstrated by countless concert performances and recordings of the piece. While this self-consistency of the score has no doubt been an important factor in the work's reception, it may also lead to an impression at odds with the music's dramatic purpose, especially if not only the scenario but also the sung texts are ignored. One may indeed marvel at the remarkable coherence of the musical material, a satisfying sense of unity that the music creates in the small and in the large, but a further question that such unity should provoke concerns its dramaturgical function. This is no Wagnerian web of leitmotifs employed to articulate a complex epic narration and lend support to a mythical worldview. Yet the music's thematic homogeneity and its sense of symmetrical closure demand interpretation, not merely formalist approbation. The motivic material makes its affective impact; the ending has its dramaturgical motivation.

Weill ensures continuity through the pervasive employment and transformation of motivic material introduced at the outset. The first component of that material is a sequentially descending figure traditionally symbolic of lament, articulated here with a dotted rhythm. This is immediately followed by a second component composed of rising and falling scale steps that outline the interval of a third (ex. 24). The latter, especially, is so pervasive as to raise the suspicion of being a stylistic mannerism. But like the first component, it appears in striking expressive contexts. Beyond creating a kind of symphonic coherence to the musical fabric, then, the leitmotif serves both the text and the drama. Some of the ways it does this are described below.

In the Prologue the expressive affect of the semitonal shift downward is set in relief against the foursquare rhythm of the accompaniment. For its part, the accompaniment alternates between quarter-note vamping and more agitated anapests. Both of these variants support the Andante sostenuto, a tempo too slow to be a purposeful march, even when the dotted rhythms of the melody signal the sisters' having "gotten under way a month ago." The oscillating third dominates the melodic motion, with a particularly striking moment when Anna I reports on their mission: "Von dem Gelde soll gebaut werden ein kleines Haus" (A little home shall be built from the proceeds). The minor third blossoms into a major third

EXAMPLE 24. *Die sieben Todsünden,* Prologue

EXAMPLE 25. *Die sieben Todsünden,* Prologue

on the word *Haus* over a sustained, full-measure C♭ major chord, unstably based on a second-inversion foundation. Anna delivers the following qualification: "ein kleines Haus am Mississippi in Louisiana," with both the bass and melody sinking chromatically (ex. 25). The expressive ambiguity of the moment is both poignant and telling: the theme briefly conveys optimistic longing for a "kleines Haus" amid a pervasive sense of lament, itself held in check by uniform motion. It is a moment nicely captured by the description Weill sent to Erika Neher in summarizing the quality of Brecht's text: one of the "formulations of great individual beauty and phrases of a simple human expressiveness, which you recognize only when you hear the music I have come up with for it." Talk of "ein kleines Haus," especially in April 1933, was something to tug at the musical heart strings.

EXAMPLE 26. *Der Silbersee,* fox-trot (for two bananas)

EXAMPLE 27. *Die sieben Todsünden,* "Anger"

The incongruity of Sloth's furious tarantella is intentionally ironic: a "dance of death." Both parts of the principal motif appear as breathless effusions from the woodwinds: the first "descending" element before the Family enters with its admonishment (the proverbial "Müssiggang ist aller Laster Anfang"), the second during the jittery dance sequence. Concluding the cantorial coda, the first element appears in the winds in a basic form, like a motto (single pitches in a slow, even rhythm), over tremolos in the bass.

In Pride, the first element is incorporated into a harmonic sequence, no doubt denotative (as elsewhere) of the sisters' journey. In the second half of the number, however, the same falling motif is absorbed in a quick waltz, the social dance that accompanies Anna's reluctant striptease.

Anger includes a fox-trot adapted from the play with music *Der Silbersee.* This is no straight borrowing, however. The pitch content of the Chaplinesque "Banana Dance" is adjusted to foreground the work's second motivic component (exx. 26 and 27).

Gluttony is for the Family only, with no obvious motivic signposts, save the motion by thirds, so pervasive as to be a stylistic fingerprint.

Lust works in both an ornamental version of the rising third as an accompaniment figure and the descending motif with pronounced dotted rhythm, announced fortissimo by the trumpet in the orchestral introduction. After stating that Anna II loved not the man who paid her and that she paid the one she

EXAMPLE 28. *Die sieben Todsünden,* "Lust"

loved, Weill inserts a brief reference to the opening measures of Wagner's *Tristan und Isolde,* followed immediately by an allusion to his own "Wie man sich bettet" from *Aufstieg und Fall der Stadt Mahagonny.*[30] The number concludes with another "phrase of a simple human expressiveness" as Anna I tells of hearing her sister crying (with a wrenching minor ninth between bass and melody) and saying, "It's right like this, Anna, but so hard!" Anna II does indeed speak these lines, accompanied by the winds playing the motivic motto over tremolos in the strings. The chromatically moving harmonies find tonal resolution on E♭, albeit without a major or minor third, only at the beginning of the next movement, which follows *attacca* (ex. 28).

Like Sloth, Covetousness is a number solely for the Family. It includes the same descending woodwind effusions with ascending slide. Much of the movement is presented in the stark, modally ambiguous linear-counterpoint style that emerged in *Der Jasager* and informed large portions of *Die Bürgschaft* as well as *Der Silbersee,* again leaving open the question whether the prominence of motion by thirds is motivically derived or merely an idiomatic fingerprint, especially when the rhythmic profile of the material is also fairly generic or part of a *molto perpetuo* texture, as here. This is not an open-and-shut case for the analyst. Maybe it was this aspect of the piece that caused Henry Prunières to remark that

EXAMPLE 29. *Die sieben Todsünden,* "Envy"

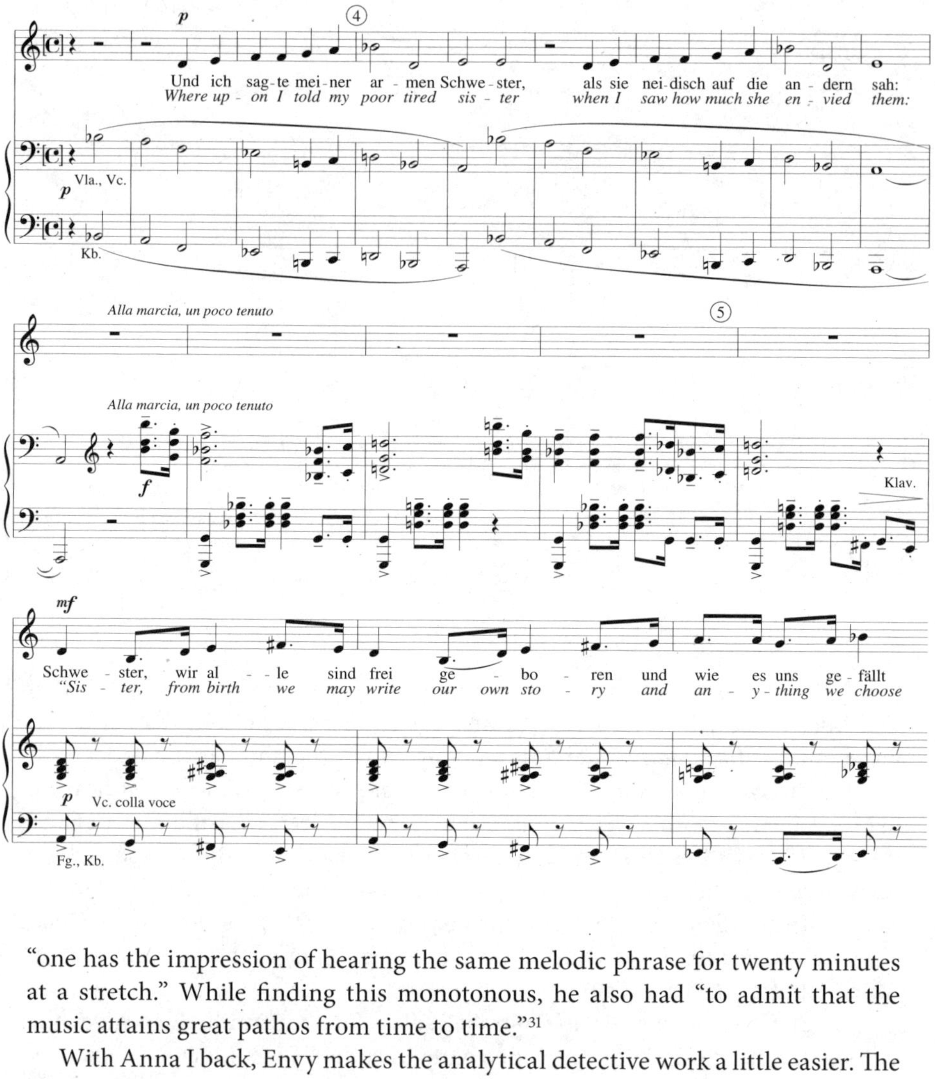

"one has the impression of hearing the same melodic phrase for twenty minutes at a stretch." While finding this monotonous, he also had "to admit that the music attains great pathos from time to time."[31]

With Anna I back, Envy makes the analytical detective work a little easier. The lower strings play a quasi–ground bass figure clearly derived from element one, with the solo voice utilizing element two as a melodic variation on the opening Prologue. But this yields to a neo-baroque gesture of woodwind interjections that seem lifted from the conclusion of *Aufstieg und Fall der Stadt Mahagonny,* as Anna I explains that "everything went well"—well, that is, except for the sins that Anna was forced to avoid. The ground bass returns as introduction to an *alla marcia* section that begins as a livelier variant of the Prologue (ex. 29). But the

EXAMPLE 30. *Die sieben Todsünden,* Epilogue

upbeat, almost belligerent tone (this is *Kampfmusik* of the Salvation Army kind found in *Happy End*) belies the song's negative message: the sisters don't know where their going through the triumphal gates will lead. Simply resist temptation! Conquer yourself and you'll get the prize!

The Epilogue has the sisters returning to Louisiana to the same music with which they left. Seven years—roughly the length of the artistic collaboration with Brecht!—seven years, she sings, "we spent in the cities, trying our luck, and now we've done it, we return, return to our little house . . . Right *[Nicht wahr],* Anna?" Anna II concedes, again with a spoken interjection. The descending motto sounds for the last time, resolving via the sonority of the *Tristan* chord into a radiant, albeit *piano,* C major (ex. 30).

If it is the sacrifice of Anna's soul that links the sins thematically, it is not hard to see how the main musical motto does something similar on a motivic level, especially when her own spoken lines have her reluctantly acceding to her family's wishes. The literal monotony of the repetition is justifiable in dramatic terms. Anna II has conquered herself, as the motif of lament reminds us.

Among his works for the musical theater, *Die sieben Todsünden* is undoubtedly one of Weill's most self-contained scores, this despite its drawing on earlier material. Does the Epilogue represent some kind of domestic harmony, mere mechanical repetition, or the hankering after an unrealized dream? For Weill and Brecht personally as much as for anyone in their position at this point in history, nothing could have seemed more poignant—or ironic. They could no more have returned to the roots of their artistic partnership than they could have returned to their respective homes in Germany. For Weill at least, the further irony was to be that before too long he would find a home in the country of the sins, the United States. The return to the little home in Louisiana is nothing if not equivocal, especially in the context of exile.

For the creators and for the audience at the time, Anna's plight was not just that of the petty bourgeoisie. Brecht's addendum of *Kleinbürger* to the title may reflect an attempt to highlight Anna's behavior as symptomatic of her social class—the theoretical aim being to point to that class's self-sacrificing complicity in wealth creation. In the context of Brecht's mid-1930s political theory, such complicity served not just capitalism but ultimately also fascism. Weill's music, however, highlights rather Anna's plight in terms of her suppressed humanity. It conveys her experience less as a type than as an individual, despite and because of the bifurcation. And although her "human expressiveness" might be fairly simple, sung by Anna I about Anna II, the personal predicament portrayed is not.

By stressing Anna's class allegiance, Brecht might have been hoping that his piece could transcend its original incarnation as the collaboration of estranged exiles, to give it the significance he found missing at the premiere. Weill's musical contribution transcended those circumstances, too, though in a different direction: through the creation of a wonderfully self-consistent score, of course, but also by giving expression to estrangement of exile in a way that extends relevance to *Die sieben Todsünden* beyond the confines of the petty bourgeoisie. Anna II is also an artist trying to find a home. She finds one, of sorts, but at an unacceptable price. Writing in French to Boris Kochno two weeks after the premiere, Weill declared himself "pleased with the success." He, too, thought of the piece in terms of "philosophical ideas": "My musical theater is meant to incite discussion rather than amusement. I believe that it was not only important, but absolutely essential to introduce my philosophical ideas—a human attitude—into the ballet. That for me was a task well worth the effort."[32]

Not only does Anna belong to a social class; she is (hardly a trivial fact, this) a woman. Whereas Brecht analyzed her plight as a function of capitalism, the fate of her sex goes well beyond any strictly class-based analysis. A feminist perspective would shift the emphasis from Anna's being reduced, in art and life, to the status of a commodity, to her general subjugation by men, including her all-male family. In other words, as an allegory of the female self, divided by male design into two incompatible halves, *Die sieben Todsünden* is not just about the petty bourgeoisie. A gender studies approach might well be inclined to question Brecht's theoretical aims while also broadening the scope of possible interpretations.[33] Weill's evident sympathy for Anna's suppressed humanity—his own "human attitude"—certainly leaves room for an interpretation along the lines of sexual politics, not just political economy. At the same time, in terms both more specific and more general than gender, the tragedy that the work portrays was also that of its creators. *Die sieben Todsünden* is an allegory of the artist in exile, the artist who sacrifices her art in order to work and survive in a hostile environment, the artist whose identity is threatened or even suppressed, the artist who loses her soul.

However interpreted, whether on Brecht's theoretical terms or Weill's musico-dramatic ones, whether in terms of Marxist materialism, gender studies, or artistic biography, the C major resolution at the end of the symmetry-creating Epilogue ought to be quite unsettling. Somewhat unexpected in the minor-mode harmonic context, and coming as part of a Tristan-inflected plagal cadence, the Picardy third is no less equivocal in its significance than the major-key march that precedes it. Whose march is it anyway? Echoing Rousseau, Anna I had exclaimed in those optimistically martial tones: "Sister, we are all born free." How, then, is the final resolution to be understood? Which of the several options suggested already are at work? Perhaps all of them. The equivocating effect of the ending is inherent in the music's symbolism. In its immediate context, major-key resolution may seem ironic, an invoked device with all the hackneyed associations that contradict the tragedy of Anna's decline. The resolution may nonetheless prefigure a context that, while ironic, may still admit the hope for true wholeness. It is an ambiguity that made Brecht wary of music but that Weill's musical humanism was increasingly inclined to embrace. Again, the distinction made earlier must apply: epic structure does not guarantee epic effect. In the last analysis, the idea of epic theater that so thoroughly informs *Die sieben Todsünden* has to find its realization in a style of actual performance. Through its words and music, the piece questions the conditions under which the freedom posited by Anna I might continue. Yet it is possible, as Constant Lambert remarked in his review of the London production of *Die sieben Todsünden* (under the title *Anna-Anna*), "that the music would lose much of its savor without the ironic counterpoint of the stage action."[34] Scenic realization—a relative rarity with this frequently performed piece—adds a variable to the mix, even more than vocal style does, whereby the conditions of Anna's freedom may or may not become more explicit.

MARIE GALANTE

Like Anna II in *Die sieben Todsünden,* Weill had to move to other cities to make his living, leaving Paris for London in January 1935 and continuing on to New York nine months later. Of the remaining musical-theater projects begun during his time in the French capital, only *Marie Galante* was completed and performed there. The other two works served their existential purpose as artistic passports to other exile locations—*A Kingdom for a Cow* to London, *The Eternal Road* to the United States—where they received their respective premieres.

Based on the novel of the same name by Jacques Deval, *Marie Galante* has enjoyed virtually no afterlife as a work for the musical theater following its premiere production at the Théâtre de Paris, which opened on 22 December 1934 and closed after a run of less than three weeks. The recent revivals—by Rome Opera in 2007 and Opéra Français de New York in 2008—are rare exceptions to the rule of obscurity and neglect.[35] What has endured, however, is the music, the songs and some of the incidental pieces that Weill composed, which have made their way in the world independent of Deval's theatrical adaptation of his novel. This reception beyond the confines of the theater has taken a number of forms and gone through various phases, starting with the publication of selections from *Marie Galante* in conjunction with the premiere production. Issued by the French publisher Heugel in December 1934, the album comprised the following seven numbers in piano-vocal format, also available singly as sheet music:

1. Les filles de Bordeaux
2. Marche de l'armée panaméenne
3. Scène au dancing
4. J'attends un navire
5. Le Roi d'Aquitaine
6. Le train du Ciel
7. Le grand Lustucru

On its first page the album memorializes the Paris premiere by reproducing the playbill with the full cast-list. The titular Marie was played by Odette Florelle, listed on the playbill simply as "Florelle," the name also used for the singer's subsequent recordings of Marie's four solo songs (1, 4, 5, and 7). The star *chanteuse* was already well known to Weill because of her role as Polly in the French version of Pabst's film *Die 3-Groschen-Oper,* which was released simultaneously with the German version as *L'Opéra de quat' sous* in 1931. Lys Gauty, another *chanteuse* who worked with Weill at the time, also recorded "J'attends un navire," which would become the work's most popular number by far thanks to its adoption by the French Resistance during the Second World War.

Even later still, in the 1980s, two concert arrangements of some of the music emerged, both of them released on CD. One is the *Marie Galante Suite* (devised by Kim Kowalke and Lys Symonette), which incorporates the numbers included in the piano-vocal score and adds to the other instrumental pieces (2 and 3) the Introduction and the rediscovered instrumental version of the song "Youkali," a tango-habañera. The other is the purely instrumental *Suite panaméenne (*devised by David Drew), which places the "Youkali" tango between numbers 2 and 3 and inserts a tango based on a few surviving parts in an arrangement by H. K. Gruber at the beginning, following a brief introduction.

The play with music nonetheless deserves its rightful place in the current narrative, not only because of its well-known songs, but because the work itself marked a critical stage of exile for the composer. *Marie Galante* was Weill's first work for the musical theater conceived in a vernacular language other than his native German, a switch that goes hand in hand with the deft transfer of his song style to the new cultural milieu.[36] The transfer is Janus-faced, however: not only does Weill reuse some of the music in later English-language works, but some of that same music derives from earlier, German-language compositions. The melody of the instrumental Introduction and "Les filles de Bordeaux," for example, is borrowed from "In der Jugend gold'nem Schimmer" from *Happy End*. The instrumental interlude "Scène au dancing" is a reworking of "Das Lied von der harten Nuss," also from *Happy End*. Yet another number from *Happy End*, "Das Lied vom Branntweinhändler," does double duty, as the orchestral "Complainte" and the duet "L'arreglo religioso." Later, partly as a consequence of the work's lack of impact in the theater and partly on account of Weill's departure from France, the composer saw fit to recycle portions of the score of *Marie Galante* in works performed in London and New York. The English waltz "Le Roi d'Aquitaine" became "Two Hearts" in *A Kingdom for a Cow;* and the melody of "Les filles de Bordeaux," already borrowed from *Happy End*, underwent yet another transformation as "The Trouble with Women" in *One Touch of Venus*.

Although exile forced Weill to adapt to setting the language of his new home countries, the copious musical self-borrowings that he used in the process represent a thread of stylistic continuity—a form of common currency, as it were—from one stage of his career to the next. According to an interpretation proposed by David Drew, however, the lingering presence of material from *Happy End* may still support the notion of a fundamental break in his career when he left Germany. Neither simply a matter of artistic expediency nor merely a reflection of consistency in his approach to musical theater, Weill's returning to the earlier German work in the new French work served, Drew suggests, "to cover the break with his past which it represented."[37] The questions that arise from this suggestion are common enough in the secondary literature on Weill: To what extent do stylistic choices in exile reflect aesthetic continuity or a lack thereof?

Do the self-borrowings, insofar as they are susceptible to biographical exegesis, compensate aesthetically and psychologically for an otherwise unbridgeable rift in Weill's output? And, accordingly, how should the more or less direct transfer of his song style to a new context be interpreted? As a pragmatic artist's expedient response to a commission? In intertextual terms? Or at some deeper level of creative psychology?

There can be little question that the circumstances under which *Marie Galante* came into being were far from ideal. Moreover, the fact that the collaboration with Deval would end up falling far short of Weill's initial expectations provides all the more reason to invoke compensatory mechanisms. Initially, however, when he was invited to provide music for the new play, the composer thought well enough of the French author and his work that he could describe him to Lenya as "the season's most in-demand and most frequently performed French playwright, whose play *Tovarich* is the biggest international theatrical hit of the year. . . . We want to dramatize his most successful novel, *Marie Galante,*" Weill continued, declaring it "an excellent, *serious* subject." In the same letter he also provided his own highly condensed summary of the plot: "A French peasant girl runs off with a man and ends up somewhere in Panama, but once there she wishes only to go home again; she earns money in a whorehouse, and when she has saved up enough and has already bought her steamship ticket, she dies."[38]

At the time of writing, in late January, he expected the play to open "as soon as May at the most beautiful theater in Paris, the Théâtre Marigny, and then in the fall in London and New York." Yet the collaboration would prove frustrating in the extreme. It had already gotten off to a slow start because of distractions on both sides, including overtures to Weill from Josef von Sternberg (which ultimately come to naught) to write music for a film starring Marlene Dietrich. By the end of March, Weill was referring to Deval as a "skunk" and wishing to "tell him I'm no longer interested in this thing."[39] A week later, the opprobrium only intensified: Deval had become "the worst yet of all the literary swine I've met, and that's a bunch." The collaboration contained an especially bitter twist because of the role played by Hollywood:

> [Deval] came back from his trip and assured me he'd start to work immediately, that he didn't have anything else in mind and could concentrate completely on *Marie Galante.* If I go to Hollywood [for the von Sternberg film], he said he'd go with me, because he could work there very well. But he would oblige me in all respects. Today I phoned him, and now he tells me he's leaving in two weeks—for Hollywood! Which means, in other words, he'll never write the play; he's cashed in on the advance and that's the end of it. You can imagine how embarrassing this is for me with Bertrand [the music publisher]; the first theatrical venture I wanted to undertake with him is a total failure, because the 25,000 francs he's given to Deval are as good as lost.[40]

It was not the first nor would it be the last time that the film industry would interfere with Weill's creative plans. The novel on which Deval planned to base the play had been published to considerable acclaim in 1931, appearing the following year in English as *That Girl,* and thanks to that success, Deval was invited to sign a contract for a movie version, also called *Marie Galante,* which starred Spencer Tracy and was released in October 1934, two months before the premiere of the musical play. As the composer was trying to collaborate on the stage work, the author was focusing on the screen version. Small wonder that Weill ended his complaint to Lenya with the observation: "Even Brecht could still learn something from Deval!"

Weill would continue with his disparagement of Deval after the show had closed in mid-January 1935. In a letter to his former pupil, the conductor Maurice Abravanel, who would become one of his staunchest supporters on Broadway, he felt impelled to denounce Deval as "the nastiest pig I have ever met in my entire life." However much he might have been venting in reaction to the "disgraceful flop" of the production, as he described it to Abravanel, he was nonetheless accurate in summarizing the view of the press, which was that this was a "horrid performance, but the music made a tremendous hit."[41]

The "excellent, *serious* subject" of Deval's novel captured by Weill's summary bears a striking resemblance to that of *Die sieben Todsünden:* the story of a woman's enforced exile and her attempts to return home that necessitate her subjecting herself to male exploitation. Unlike Anna's quest, however, which concludes with her return to Louisiana, Marie's efforts to return to Bordeaux are in vain. Responsible for her tragic demise is not so much prostitution as her unwitting involvement in international espionage, a facet of the story missing in Weill's summary.

The *galante* of the title is an adjective, ambiguously embracing the connotation "elegant" or even "blessed" and the euphemistic *fille galante,* meaning a "loose woman." Pascal Huynh in his French-language biography of Weill, which offers the most detailed treatment of *Marie Galante* to date, describes the titular character as "une prostituée chaste."[42] When the good-hearted Marie is abducted from her native France and taken on a cargo ship to South America, she resists the advances of the captain who has abducted her and, as a consequence, is placed ashore at the port of Carúpano in Venezuela—the city where Christopher Columbus set foot on the American continent for the only time and where, in 1814, Simón Bolívar issued a decree ending slavery. Eventually, after arriving in Panama, she works in a brothel, hoping to earn enough money to pay for passage home. Two things subvert her plan. First of all, she spends her savings caring for an old, dying black man called Josiah. Second, she finds herself an accomplice in espionage, simultaneously working for the German and the Japanese sides. The plot calls to mind the political intrigue and nightclub milieu of the movie

Casablanca. As a result of Marie's unwitting involvement, she is murdered before being able to board the ship bound for France.

Divided into ten scenes, seven of which feature musical numbers with lyrics by Deval and Roger Fernay, the play adheres closely and somewhat mechanically to the structure of the novel. Lacking both time and interest, the playwright did little to adapt *Marie Galante* to the requirements of the stage. He resorted instead to the insertion of whole sections of his novel, "as though he cut the book up with scissors and repasted them for actors to speak," to quote John Mucci and Richard Felnagle's apposite description.[43]

Deval's lack of engagement left Weill little opportunity for musico-dramatic innovations of the kind he achieved with his earlier experiments with the genre. As a "play with music," *Marie Galante* pales in comparison with its predecessors in Weill's oeuvre. Neither does it signal the reform of musical theater he successfully attempted with *Die Dreigroschenoper,* nor does it approach the condition of a full-blown singspiel, as *Der Silbersee* had done. (By referring to *Marie Galante* as a "singspiel," as he did in the Danish interview from June 1934, cited above, Weill seems to have signaled ambitions for the piece that remained sadly unfulfilled.) Nor, although it draws on *Happy End* for two of its musical numbers, does it display that work's self-reflexive questioning of music's power. Yet the music does possess considerable power, a power that allows the rather blandly drawn characters, especially Marie, to come to life.

Although Foster Hirsch is doubtless right to observe that there are "no audacious music-theatre concepts" in *Marie Galante,* it seems unfair to assert categorically that "there is no revelatory dialogue between book and score."[44] For the most part, as in *Happy End,* the vocal numbers are interpolated ballads that tell a story at something of a remove from the narrative of the play, separate but nonetheless relevant. The text of "Les filles de Bordeaux," for example, exhorts the girls of Bordeaux to "drown themselves first before they leave Béhague"—before, that is, they "go away to perish in the four corners of the earth to serve as booty for all the skunks." Appearing not only in the instrumental Introduction but also as a musical reminiscence in the final scene, the song's melody in turn foreshadows and reflects upon Marie's fate, which is presaged by the text. "Le grand Lustcru," a macabre and belligerent anti-lullaby that warns of a bogeyman who "eats everything alive uncooked," has its origins in an old Breton air collected by the French singer-songwriter Théodore Botrel. Since both the text and the melody depart quite substantially from the original, however, paraphrase would be a better description than adaptation. But the original gist of the song—"It is I whom he is looking for . . . this night I can sleep no more"—is preserved, delivering in the ninth scene of the play a grim premonition of Marie's impending assassination.

In Weill's oeuvre, the source and origin of such inserted ballads is "Seeräuberjenny" from *Die Dreigroschenoper.* Of the earlier songs in opera that perform a similar dramaturgical function, one might cite the example of Azucena's "Stride la vampa" from Verdi's *Il trovatore* or Desdemona's "Willow Song" in the same composer's *Otello.* The most pertinent precedent, however, is surely "Senta's Ballad" from Wagner's *Der fliegende Holländer.* Senta, like Polly's Pirate Jenny and Marie herself, is waiting for her ship to come in.

In addition to the songs that tell tales at a provocative tangent to the story of the play, and belie in the process the naïveté of the singer's dramatic character, *Marie Galante* contains several pieces of instrumental music performed by an onstage band. These are the "Scène au dancing" and the two tangos, all played in the third scene, which is set in a Panamanian dance hall. If this were a film, the aforementioned songs and the dance music would count as so-called source music, sonic events integral to the visible action. (The catchy "March of the Panamanian Army," essentially a piece of incidental music, similarly adds musical local color while providing a transition to the succeeding dance-hall scene.) The exception among the vocal numbers is "J'attends un navire," which comes closer than any of them to the style of a French cabaret chanson. A torch song of sorts, it lends powerful and stirring expression to Marie's immediate predicament—the longing of a woman in exile. The predominant tone is not maudlin or self-pitying, but almost operatically defiant. It is the kind of longing that generates resistance in the face of adversity, as reflected by the song's history during World War II.

A KINGDOM FOR A COW

Six months after the "disgraceful flop" of *Marie Galante,* Weill wrote to Lenya: "Whenever I think of London at night, I'm robbed of my sleep."[45] These bitter-sounding words were Weill's way of conveying a feeling of deep despondency after recent performances of two of his works in the British capital. Both were signal failures. The first blow came in February with a live performance of *Die Dreigroschenoper* broadcast by the BBC. The second, to which the letter alludes, occurred just a few months later in June with the premiere of the satirical operetta *A Kingdom for a Cow,* a work started but left unfinished in German as *Der Kuhhandel.* After receiving its premiere at the Savoy Theater London on 28 June 1935, *A Kingdom for a Cow* stayed in the repertory for barely two weeks. In both cases, the press was largely negative.[46]

Writing for the *Daily Telegraph* (June 29), Jack Westrup thought the satire of *A Kingdom for a Cow* little more than a "riotous burlesque" and praised the music only faintly as "a hotch-potch, no less." The reviewer ("E.L.") for the *Sunday Times* (June 30) adopted a similar critical stance to Westrup, remarking that the "grim topicality runs in uneasy double harness with the lighter moods of musical comedy," though he did credit Weill with "some wistful little tunes and several good choruses." The least negatively critical thing written about the music, by "H.H." in the *Observer* (June 30), was that it was "confident and resourceful, and seemed to me to range among the masters in various genres with academic versatility." Dyneley Hussey was outright dismissive, particularly of the composer, claiming in his report for the *Spectator* (July 5) that "Herr Weill has sacrificed integrity to popular appeal. . . . His music," Hussey continued, "drones its way though the mire with a despondency that surpasses the bluest of Blues. It acts like a wet blanket on what promised to be an amusing satire." But perhaps the most dismissive notice of all was the unsigned review that appeared in the *Times* (June 29), especially the obnoxious sting in its tail, presumably intended in humorous vein: "Weill writes a particularly nauseous form of jazz with every beat of a bar of common time regularly made into a strong beat, and his waltzes are more sympy than the old-fashioned kind. It is not stated whether his recent departure from Germany was occasioned by his partiality for politically tendentious satirical texts like this one or for the kind of music he writes, but the music would be the German authorities' most valid justification."

No laughing matter. A reaction to this critical reception as well as to the production's swift demise, Weill's words were not exactly his own, however, even if the feelings they captured more or less were. The phrase "When I think of London at night, I'm robbed of my sleep" parodies a line from Heinrich Heine's famous poem "Nachtgedanken" (Night Thoughts): "When I think of Germany at night, I'm robbed of my sleep."[47] The allusion to Heine both distances Weill from his own experience and suggests a fascinating parallel to his own situation. Like Heine, he was a German-Jewish artist forced into exile. Like Heine, he had initially chosen Paris as his new home. Save for a few brief absences, he had resided there from March 1933 until December 1934. But unlike Heine, he moved on. Nor is the departure from Paris the only important difference. Whereas Heine's poem "Night Thoughts" is about his place of birth, Weill's parody refers to a foreign city that he had hoped, for a while at least, could become his new domicile.

What follows the Heine allusion is no less remarkable, adding yet a further twist. "This London flop was a severe blow for me," he remarks, whereupon he introduces another modified quotation, this time from his own work: "Aber nur nicht weich werden!" (Just don't get soft!). Weill has lifted the line from "Das Lied von der harten Nuss" in *Happy End,* the source also for the "Scène au dancing" melody in *Marie Galante.* The parallel to his method of composing is striking. In order to express an emotion or affect, he draws on preexisting phrases or figures, sometimes well known, sometimes quite hackneyed, whose message he then contrives to retract, undermine, or relativize in some way. The ironic effect can be dizzyingly rich and multilayered, as with the quotation from Heine, an author also given to biting irony. The principle, if not its purpose, will continue in the American works: the convention of affective expression is not to be taken literally or at face value. Convention is a means, not an end; what is conveyed is itself seldom simple. And Weill's reaction to the reception of *A Kingdom for a Cow* was undoubtedly complex. His quoting a line from *Happy End* suggests that the possible interpretations of self-borrowings mentioned above—a pragmatic artist's response to the situation, an intertextual allusion, and even a glimpse into creative psychology—need not be mutually exclusive.

The choice of a new home depended exclusively on opportunities to compose for the musical theater.[48] Unlike Křenek, Hindemith, Toch, Eisler, and Schoenberg, all of whom emigrated to the United States, he would not have been disposed to consider a teaching appointment. True, he had taught private music lessons to a few students in Berlin, but only to make ends meet. His journalistic contributions for *Der deutsche Rundfunk* were similarly motivated by a need to supplement his income as a composer. Nor was he given to music-theoretic explanations of his own or other people's music, as can be seen from his writings, in which technical matters are largely absent. Often serving as propaganda for his own works, the writings are for the most part addressed to the nonspecialist. His theatrical art was always directed toward its imminent realization; composing for the bottom-draw was not an option for him. Paris had initially proved favorable, not only because of immediate projects, but also because a number of his works had already met with some success in that city. The move to London in January 1935 occurred chiefly because of the expectation that an English version of the operetta *Der Kuhhandel* would be performed there.

Back in Paris after his first trip to England in May 1934, Weill had written to Lenya that "London was glorious . . . for me personally there is definitely more to do there than here."[49] Apart from *Der Kuhhandel,* he had discussed a number of other projects, including a theatrical revue with the director Charles Cochran as well as the work that would eventually become *The Eternal Road.* He would refer to the latter in further letters to Lenya as his "Bible piece" or "the Bible thing," perhaps intentionally avoiding not only the title, which changed, but also the generic designation. For now, London—the Royal Albert Hall, to be precise—had become a likely venue for that vast project.

But that was not to be. Instead the Old Testament pageant, a work that reacquainted Weill with the religion of his upbringing, would occasion the next stage of his career, with the departure from London to New York in September 1935, as discussed below. Like *Der Kuhhandel,* however, the work was conceived and largely written in Paris, even though that city could not provide the performance venue. And like the operetta, much of the pageant was written in German before the realities of exile forced it to become an English-language work.

Shortly before his trip to London, Weill described the operetta project to his friend Hans Curjel, principal dramaturg at the Corso-Theater in Zurich.

> It is an excellent book, drawing on the best operetta tradition, yet far from the Viennese operetta trash. Its structure is complete; 12 of the musical numbers, which I have composed and which have turned out brilliantly, already have words; the book will be completely done in May. I am in negotiation with a big local theater and with Cochran in London. We would like to have a German production before ones in French and English. I would have discussions about this in Vienna, if, as is possible, I visit Reinhardt there next week. But I would almost prefer Zurich.[50]

He was keeping his options open with regard both to the location and to the language of the premiere. In case Curjel was interested, he offered to send him an outline. Curjel's response seems not to have survived, but it must have been encouraging. Just four days later, on 23 April 1934, Weill wrote to Curjel again to thank him for his reply and send along the promised outline as well as provide some additional remarks about the music and the overall conception of the new piece. The thirteen-page "Exposé," as the typewritten document is called on its title page, describes an "operetta in two parts" (it would later become three acts), with a "book by Robert Vambery."[51] (Weill knew fellow émigré Vambery from the Theater am Schiffbauerdamm, where he had been a dramaturg and a member of the production team for *Die Dreigroschenoper* before moving to the Kroll-Oper.) At this point the work was to be called *Die Verlobung von Santa Maria* (The Betrothal of Santa Maria), qualified here as the "provisional title." The title page also contains a full cast-list and specifies the "location of the action" as "the Republic of Santa Maria," which Weill further specifies in parentheses and in his own hand as "South America." The parallel to the setting of *Marie Galante* is striking: both works address topical issues at a geographical remove from the European mainland.

In the accompanying letter to Curjel, Weill pinpoints "the great advantages of the piece" in that it "finally reconnects with the best tradition of operetta, which had been buried for decades." He characterizes that tradition as "representing a very skillful application of serious and serene, of lyric and dramatic, showing the most topical things (things that are much more topical than the Third Reich) in an ingratiating, comical manner." Among the musical numbers already composed, he lists "a very popular march song of the general, a barcarole, a downright hit-tune 'Auf Wiedersehen' (English Waltz), the Song of the Great Pharaoh, and the Song of the Cow." By way of illustration, he quotes the "very nice text" of this last-mentioned number:

> Ich habe eine Kuh gehabt,
> Ich habe die Kuh nicht mehr,
> Ich hab dafür,
> Gott helfe mir,
> Jetzt ein Maschinengewehr.

The translation of the song done for the London production by Desmond Carter rendered the verse thus:

> A year ago I had a cow
> But I have one no more
> I have this fine machine-gun now,
> But I don't know what it's for.

Lyrics and music of this excerpt nicely reflect Weill's approach to creating a satirical operetta through the "skillful application" of contrasting, counterpointed elements. Pitched at the lyrical-comic end of his defined spectrum (the simple strophic setting is lyrical, the words comical) and sung by the male lead, Juan (lyric tenor), the third-act song nonetheless alludes to the reason for Juan's loss of his cow: the deadly serious matter of the arms trade, a topic treated here in burlesque fashion.

How and why does Juan lose his cow? Leslie Jones (baritone), an international arms dealer, has instructions to start an arms race between the two halves of an imaginary Caribbean island, the republics of Santa Maria and Ucqua. Despite being a pacifist, President Mendez of Santa Maria (tenor buffo) allows himself to be bribed, and orders an assignment of arms that he has no intention of using. Warned by Jones, Ucqua responds by planning to invade its neighbor. President Mendez in turn responds by calling a peace conference. Jones then organizes a coup d'état by General Conchas (high baritone), Santa Maria's war minister. War, which threatens the pastoral idyll, seems inevitable.

The work's original title, *Die Verlobung von Santa Maria* (with Kleistian overtones), refers to the engagement of two villagers—Juan and his bride-to-be, Juanita (lyric soprano)—whose wedding has to be deferred after their cow, hence their livelihood, is confiscated in lieu of extra taxes for the war effort. The work's eventual German title is an untranslatable pun: the metaphorical "Kuhhandel" ("shady dealing" or "horse trading") becomes literal ("cow trading"). Juan is conscripted and earns money for a second cow by unloading armaments; Juanita is forced to work in a brothel. After refusing to swear allegiance to the General and instead heroically clipping him round the ear, Juan is sent before a firing squad. The contrived happy end makes a satirically pacifist point: none of the weapons works, whereupon the General extols the virtues of peaceful coexistence, pardons Juan, and, amid rejoicing, blesses the couple.

If it seems uncontroversial to assert that no other work of Weill's, including the later *Firebrand of Florence*, approaches the condition of operetta to the degree that this one does, the debt to generic precedents nonetheless remains a matter of conjecture. There are a number of complicating factors, not the least of which is a perceived gap between the incomplete German version and its completion and production as an English-language "musical play" for the London stage. Two related questions are thus in play. How much of a departure was *Der Kuhhandel* from Weill's previous works for the musical theater? And how did the work change in becoming *A Kingdom for a Cow?*

Weill knew the operetta repertory intimately, a hands-on familiarity with the genre dating back to the beginning of his career in the musical theater. After being engaged as second kapellmeister in the South Westphalian town of Lüdenscheid for a six-month tenure, beginning in January 1920, he was soon invited to assume the duties of chief conductor, in which capacity he conducted performances of more than a dozen operettas over the next six months. Correspondence with his family during that period mentions works such as *Die tolle Komtess* by Walter Kollo, *Die schöne Galathee* by Franz von Suppé, and *Der Zigeunerbaron* by Johann Strauss. Others, not mentioned in the correspondence, included *Ein Walzertraum* by Oscar Straus, *Der Graf von Luxemburg* by Franz Léhar, and *Das Dreimäderlhaus* by Heinrich Berté. All did not go smoothly. Already in the middle of his first month at the Lüdenscheid municipal theater, Weill was complaining bitterly about the "endless operetta nonsense," which was "getting on my nerves."[52] And by the end of April, he was inviting his brother to imagine how "sick and tired I am of endless operetta and how much this unproductive life is tormenting me."[53] Even with the full-blown operas that he conducted and of which he evidently did approve, such as *Cavalleria rusticana* by Mascagni, he still bemoaned the lack of rehearsal time and the "unbelievable . . . difficulties with the orchestra."[54] It was an arduous apprenticeship, but ultimately rewarding. "I have learned a huge amount," he declared in the same letter to Hans.

Total immersion into the world of a provincial opera house was double-edged: although it afforded Weill the opportunity to absorb the language and routines of light operatic entertainment, the experience left him hankering for something else. After moving back to Berlin later the same year, and before deciding to continue with training in composition under Busoni, he initially contemplated a quite different calling as a musical scholar, mentioning the possibility of a doctoral dissertation on synagogal music, a repertory already familiar to him from his father's profession as cantor. Such was the disparate nature of the musical cultures that contributed to the young composer's formation: from Jewish liturgical music to Beethoven and Wagner (both of whom he revered above all others), from Viennese operetta to Busoni's anti-Wagnerian, pro-Mozartian "young classicality." All would remain enduring influences on his creative output in various ways, including operetta.

The disparaging remarks about his activities in Lüdenscheid notwithstanding, the close encounter with Léhar, O. Straus, J. Strauss et al. left a lasting impression. More than that, as Weill himself sought to reach a wider audience with his own compositions, he increasingly embraced operetta as a positive model. In 1936, for example, in making a quintessentially Busonian point about "the distinction between good and bad music" as replacing "the distinction of light and serious," he extolled operetta as "the light muse [that] has produced such geniuses as Offenbach, Sullivan, and Johann Strauss."[55]

Already in 1925, in his capacity as critic for *Der deutsche Rundfunk,* while still making a clear distinction between "the spirits of light and sentimental music" on the one hand and "serious artistic work" on the other, he bemoaned the general lack of operetta performances on radio. In making his plea on behalf of operetta composers, he divided them into two distinct groups: the "classic masters of operetta (that is, Joh. Strauss, Millöcker, Suppé, Offenbach, Lecoq, Sullivan)" and "the world-famous representatives of so-called Viennese operetta." Among this last group he counted Leo Fall, Franz Léhar, Oscar Straus, and Emmerich Kálmán.[56]

The following year there was one work he welcomed in particular: Offenbach's *Grande Duchesse de Gérolstein.* Devoting an entire column to reviewing the broadcast, he extolled the operetta in terms quite similar to those used to describe his own work in the above-quoted letter to Curjel. (It should be recalled here that Offenbach was himself a German-born Jew and that he had his greatest successes in Paris.) Even though Weill dismissed the plot of "a nymphomaniac petty princess who promotes a simple soldier because she finds him attractive" as "not in keeping with the times," he still considered the work to display "the authentic, essential elements of operetta: humor, pacing, gaiety in their purest and most beautiful form." The following passage seems especially relevant to his artistic purposes: "One is simply overwhelmed by the wealth of parodistic ideas. With Offenbach, as with all masters of this genre, from Cervantes to Chaplin, satire is another form of expression for serious, philosophically motivated content, which, in topsy-turvy fashion, appears with utmost concision. Music is able to translate this type of serious parody into exhilarating dance, and never has a musician availed himself of these brilliant means like Offenbach."[57]

Elements of operetta employed to parodistic effect already find their way into *Die Dreigroschenoper,* such that several critics referred to that work as a "Berlin operetta," in contradistinction to the Viennese kind. Macheath and Polly's "Melodram," with its parody of the saccharine romanticism of conventional operetta plots, is a case in point. Another is the allusion in Polly's "Barbarasong," musically and textually, to "Ich bin ein armer Wanderergesell" from Künneke's *Der Vetter aus Dingsda.*[58]

Die Dreigroschenoper also provided the pretext for Weill to establish a specific connection that others would also make between himself and Offenbach. After Weill suggested to his editor at Universal Edition, Hans Heinsheimer, that a planned journal article on his new work appear as an epistolary exchange between the two of them, with Heinsheimer supplying a preface in the form of a letter to the composer, Heinsheimer wanted to include the lines "People's opera

[Volksoper]. Weill as Humperdinck." Weill vehemently objected, saying that he harbored a "quite personal antipathy" toward his former teacher. Instead, as a more appropriate lineage, he proposed "From Offenbach to Weill." (In the end, neither Humperdinck nor Offenbach appeared in the published letter.)

It should also be recalled that Weill had described his full-length stage work *Na und?* as "a kind of operetta." Other descriptions of the lost work, which he composed in 1925–27 prior to the *Mahagonny-Songspiel,* included "musiquette," "a type of light-hearted opera," and "a work of a lighter genre."[59]

Last but not least, while working with Georg Kaiser on *Der Silbersee,* he had wondered whether he should turn it into a "play with music," by which he meant a piece "with quite simple songs that can be sung by straight actors," or whether he should do "something musically more ambitious and produce music on the scale and difficulty of, say, a musiquette by Offenbach. . . . The latter would appeal to me," he commented, "because I would like to go here beyond the model created in *Die Dreigroschenoper.*"[60]

An additional, arguably quite decisive factor to consider in connection with Weill's turn toward composing a full-blown operetta is his acquaintance with the Viennese satirical writer Karl Kraus, well known for his vigorous advocacy of the genre in general and Offenbach in particular. A friend and admirer of Brecht's, Kraus had been present during rehearsals for *Die Dreigroschenoper,* and Weill no doubt interacted with him then. This encounter led, in turn, to a brief collaboration at the time of the first Berlin production of *Aufstieg und Fall der Stadt Mahagonny.* On 11 and 12 January 1932, three weeks into the production's run, Kraus gave a presentation that formed part of his ongoing project "Literary Theater" *(Theater der Dichtung),* on this occasion with incorporated readings from the Weill-Brecht opera along with songs by Wedekind and also by himself. Weill provided the piano accompaniment. Reporting back to his publisher, with whom he had been having discussions about a possible collaboration with Kraus on a new work, Weill remarked that "Karl Kraus's reading from *Mahagonny* was very interesting, but—just between us—corresponded so little with my own conception, and was musically so deficient, that I really didn't know what to make of it. This attempt at a collaboration has led me to believe that Kraus belongs to an earlier generation from which I have little to gain, creatively speaking."[61] Even though the experience made it seem less likely that Kraus would succeed Brecht as Weill's librettist, Weill did report approvingly on another possible project, this time involving his wife and the music of Offenbach. "He [Kraus] is blown away by Lenja and continually mentions his fervent wish that she do *Perichole* [of which Kraus had prepared his own adaptation]. He has now hit upon the idea of producing *Perichole* with Lenja in Vienna."[62] According to Hans Heinsheimer, who replied from Vienna two weeks later, Kraus wanted to rent a theater and direct the work himself, which meant that the idea came to naught.[63]

In addition to the *Mahagonny* readings, Kraus presented two "Offenbach evenings" in Berlin around the same time, again performing all the roles himself, accompanied only by a piano, as was his custom. On other such occasions, for which he attained both fame and notoriety, Kraus offered one-man performances of theater works by writers that included Shakespeare, Goethe, Gogol, and Nestroy. Starting in 1910 for a period spanning a quarter of a century he presented some seven hundred such readings; the Offenbach readings began in 1926.[64] It so happened that at the second of the aforementioned Offenbach evenings in Berlin (that is, after *Mahagonny*), he presented *Die Herzogin von Gerolstein,* in his own translation and adaptation.

Reservations about Kraus's performance style notwithstanding, the satirist's perspective on the genre no doubt left its mark on Weill's own views. Nor was Weill alone. Thanks to his frequent and earnest discussion of operetta in his journal, *Die Fackel,* as well as the well-publicized theater performances and broadcasts of his adaptations, Kraus played a pivotal role in the Offenbach renaissance that took hold toward the end of the Weimar Republic, whether in the antiromantic production of *Hoffmanns Erzählungen* at the Kroll-Oper, for example, or in the engagement with Offenbach by a number of prominent critics and intellectuals.[65]

It was Kraus who, above all, defined the terms on which "the best operetta tradition," as Weill referred to it, would be resurrected against a perceived decline of the genre into Viennese "trash." Already in 1909, in a column entitled "Grimaces at Culture and Stage," Kraus emphatically rejected "the devotional exercises of a Wagner opera" as "theatrical nonsense" in favor of "the twofold perfection of theatrical effect that lends the works of Offenbach their magic."[66] Echoing Nietzsche's critique of Wagner, Kraus's strategy relied on interpreting the world of operetta as one "in which causality has been suspended, cheerfully existing according to the laws of chaos from which the other world was created, and where song has been authenticated as a means of understanding," a world where "nonsense goes without saying and never invites the reaction of reason. . . . The sum of serene impossibility," Kraus suggests, "signifies for us that attractive occasion to recover from the disconsolate possibilities of life."

Understood in this way, the perceived satire of operetta, rather than being directly confrontational, is gently indirect. Kraus's spirited apology places Offenbach's operettas above all other forms of theater. "If the dissolving effect of music unites with an irresponsible serenity that allows us, amid all this turmoil, to espy an image of what is amiss in the real world, then operetta proves to be the only dramatic form wholly suited to the possibilities of theater." According to him, the form's perfection is "twofold" insofar as "the singing of operetta conspirators parodies the deeds of opera conspirators." Nor, for this very reason, does Kraus spare operetta from critique if, as he maintains is the case with Viennese operetta, it ends up taking itself too seriously by "availing itself of the gesture of opera." He thus derides a recent tendency toward psychology as "the *ultima ratio* of inability. . . . Opera conspirators are serious in their intention and spoil the seriousness of their enterprise because their singing is unmotivated. . . . The idea of operetta is the intoxication *[Rausch]* from which ideas are born; sobriety comes away empty-handed." Privileging the intoxicating nonsense of operetta harbors a utopian element, he concludes: "the liquidation of all social differences for the purpose of musical concord *[Eintracht]*."

Music in Kraus's own performative "readings" remained the most utopian element of all, more implied than realized. Yet for philosopher-critic Walter Benjamin it was those readings as much as the writings that captured his imagination and inspired the report "Karl Kraus Reads Offenbach *(Pariser Leben)*," one of five pieces on Kraus that he produced between 1926 and 1931.[67] These commentaries, as Theodor W. Adorno suggested, reveal an "elective affinity" between Kraus and Benjamin based on a shared propensity to "view profane texts as if they were sacred ones."[68] Offenbach's operettas, interpreted with the benefit of Kraus's readings, represent the extreme case, where Benjamin deems the absence of music a decisive plus. The "true music" of these operettas, he writes, is "anarchy as the only moral, only humane worldview. Kraus's voice speaks this inner music more than it sings it." The anarchic impulse of Kraus's performance, in Benjamin's interpretation, conveys both the origin and the goal of the genre with critical force, gesturing toward music's "cry of sheer desire," as the expression of both pain and longing. Thus when Benjamin celebrates "Offenbach's secret," it seems unlikely, if not impossible, that he would have done so without Kraus's intervention: "That is Offenbach's secret: when in the midst of the deep nonsense of public discipline and order *[Zucht]*—be it that of the upper ten thousand, a dance floor, or a military state—the deep sense of private licentiousness *[Unzucht]* opens a dreamy eye." Ultimately, however, it is precisely on account of this inherent tension between public and private that in his essays on Kraus Benjamin considers Offenbach's music indispensable: "Operetta transfigures stupidity through music."[69]

"No doubt," Siegfried Kracauer asserted in *Jacques Offenbach und das Paris seiner Zeit*, "operetta grows out of a democratic spirit."[70] Making this assertion in the chapter entitled "Democratic Intoxication" (Demokratischer Rausch), Kracauer effectively acknowledges the profound impact that Kraus had on the conception of his book—a "social biography," as the author writes in the foreword, not a traditional "private biography" (11). He specifically credits Kraus with having "fought fanatically for the revival of Offenbach" and with having "corrected" the view that "operetta is a dream because of its improbability." Concerning Offenbach's *La vie parisienne*, Kracauer observes that Kraus "formulated the most apposite sentences" and quotes with approval his statement that in this operetta "life is almost as improbable as it actually is. . . . If they [the

Parisian audiences at the time] had been awake," he concludes, "they would have recognized the improbable reality of their own existence" (276f.). Written in Paris at the same time as Weill's *Der Kuhhandel* and published in Amsterdam three years later, in 1937, Kracauer's study aimed to disclose, as the author himself put it, "information about the revolutionary function of frivolity, parody, etc."[71] Echoing both Kraus and Benjamin, he heard Offenbach's music as "including a utopian element, something not yet realized," as "foreshadowing a condition of society in which all dark forces are dispelled" (94). He also drew explicit parallels to his own situation: "The conspicuous fact that both Offenbach and Ludovic Halévy had German ancestors stamps operetta as a phenomenon of emigration" (139).

To state that Kracauer's study of Offenbach was itself "a phenomenon of exile" is, in terms of its genesis, to state the obvious. Yet it is emphatically so in terms of its content as well. This is not just a matter of Kracauer's identification with Offenbach as a German-Jewish émigré. As Kracauer writes in his foreword, "In view of what is happening nowadays, no one can overlook the actuality that the phantasmagoria of the Second Empire possesses" (12). *Jacques Offenbach und das Paris seiner Zeit,* as Harald Reil has demonstrated in detail, can be read as an extended reflection on social and political relations in Hitler's Germany, with the Second Empire of Napoleon III serving as a "precursor" *(Vorläufermodell)* of National Socialism.[72] It was against this sociopolitical background that Kracauer, taking his cue from Kraus, interpreted the subversive nature of Offenbach's satirical operettas.

The comparative nature of the Offenbach study lends it a self-reflexive quality. Writing in enforced exile, Kracauer presents his work as scholarship about a fellow émigré from an earlier epoch whose political conditions the author construes as comparable to those of his own time. In this regard, the choice of subject matter and its treatment share traits with the literary production of other émigrés driven from Germany, in particular the shift exhibited in their work toward historical topics. Notable examples include Heinrich Mann's *Die Jugend des Königs Henri Quatre,* Lion Feuchtwanger's *Der falsche Nero,* and Brecht's unfinished novel *Die Geschäfte des Herrn Julius Caesar.* The predilection for such themes from the past constituted less an escape from the historical present, as some critics have maintained, than an engagement with it from a remove. True, authors such as Kracauer were keen to identify subjects that would carry sufficient appeal to provide themselves with the material means of subsistence in straitened circumstances. Yet this did not prevent them from making history relevant. On the contrary, history offered the *literary* means for the writer in exile—who, as Alfred Döblin put it in the 1936 essay "The Historical Novel and Us," had been "displaced from the forcefield of the society in which we lived"—to continue to engage with that culture from which he had become estranged. In the same essay, which discusses the titular genre generally but also reflects on his own contributions, Döblin contends that when a writer is "inserted into a new forcefield . . . there arises here a certain compulsion to create historical novels." His explanation is at once psychological and social: "Apart from the lack of the present, the desire exists to find historical parallels, to locate and justify oneself historically, the need to reflect, the inclination to console and, at least on an imaginary level, to avenge oneself."[73]

Analogous factors to the ones identified by Döblin can be said to have informed Kracauer's attraction to Offenbach and, by extension, the genesis of Weill's *Der Kuhhandel.* Satirical operetta presented the philosopher–cum–social critic as well as the composer with the opportunity to produce a work in their adopted culture—specifically, a musical culture with roots dating back to the previous century—that offered the prospect of commercial success while also satisfying a need to relate, albeit obliquely, to contemporaneous circumstances in their own country. Kracauer's understanding of the genre is therefore doubly significant: it circumscribes the phenomenon of exile literature and culture that influenced Weill's decision to revivify the Offenbach tradition according to the terms of the renaissance defined by Kraus and his followers, while at the same time furnishing a framework for an interpretation of the work itself.

In his searching essay "Reflections on the Last Years: *Der Kuhhandel* as a Key Work"—the most sustained discussion of Weill's operetta to date—David Drew recognizes Kraus's influence by calling him "the spiritual father" of the work.[74] Yet he is also at pains to qualify direct comparisons with Offenbach for a number of critical reasons, reasons that, in turn, reflect qualities that make *Der Kuhhandel* "a key work" in Drew's view. Not only is he responding to Weill's self-fashioning comparisons with Offenbach mentioned above; he is also taking into account Adorno's obituary of Weill, which he uses to frame his interpretation. The decisive point is not simply that Weill, in the words of the obituary, "believed himself to be a kind of Offenbach of his century"; it is that Adorno himself believed "the model wasn't repeatable": "The grimness of reality," he maintained, had become "too overwhelming for a parody to measure up to it."[75]

Such reasoning may well have informed the decision of Vambery, the librettist, after witnessing the atrocities of National Socialist dictatorship, to resist revivals of the work on account of its pacifist message. That is not Drew's concern, however. Instead he draws attention to the work's ability to "[survive] even such an enormity" precisely because of "its authors' prescient recourse to the absurd" (254). In so doing, he appears to be rejecting Adorno's blanket dismissal of Weill's orientation toward Offenbach and, up to a point, defending the creative decision to respond to the historical situation by turning toward satirical operetta as an appropriate model. A key difference from Offenbach himself is Weill's use of the model from a position of political awareness and engagement—less as a latter-day

Offenbach per se, as Adorno would have us believe, than as a creative appropriator of Offenbach's *example* in the spirit of his critical reception. Drew can thus write of the concluding cadence of *Der Kuhhandel* that its "latent energies . . . and the perceptions that helped generate them are surely a truer measure of Weill's achievement in the coming years than any that Offenbach could provide" (255).

What Drew is not prepared to defend in the slightest, however, is the work's transformation from *Der Kuhhandel* into *A Kingdom for a Cow*—a putative shift in approach of which he is unsparingly critical. His defense of the former is inextricably bound up with his rejection of the latter, which he refers to as "the London travesty" (220). *A Kingdom for a Cow* marks a watershed in Weill's career, according to Drew: the beginning of an artistic decline from serious composer to servant of the entertainment industry. That, too, makes it a key work: "*Der Kuhhandel* was the unquiet resting place between the old way and the new" (243). More nuanced with his detailed analysis than Adorno, Drew is nonetheless indebted to him ideologically.

Drew bolsters his critique in the large and in the small. "*A Kingdom for a Cow,*" he suggests, "was the unhappy result of an attempt to superpose the conventions of modern musical comedy on an incomplete formal structure that had been designed according to the quite distinct if related conventions of operetta." But he goes further by precluding the possibility of a successful hybrid: "For the very reasons that had ensured the decline of operetta and the rise of the musical, the two sets of conventions were incompatible" (242). He apportions blame more or less equally, among the composer (because of creative compromises), the production (for being too conventional and for downplaying the element of political parody), and the audience (on whose behalf the creative compromises had been made). Josef Heinzelmann, who worked with Drew in the 1970s on an ultimately unsuccessful attempt to produce a performable version of *Der Kuhhandel* in the original German, agrees that the London version "comes across as inferior to the idea of a finished *Kuhhandel*"; still, he is willing to concede that "even *A Kingdom for a Cow* is a successful, rich, compelling piece of musical theater."[76]

The differences between *Der Kuhhandel* and *A Kingdom for a Cow* that influence Drew's assessment of Weill's composition, and which he catalogues in detail, are of two basic kinds: cuts and additions. The principal cuts are "Die Ballade von Pharao," which was replaced by "San Salvatore," and two numbers toward the end of the second act (still act 1 in the two-act design of *Der Kuhhandel*). These last are "O trüber Tag" and "Es zog zu Salomon"; they are replaced by a new song for Juanita, "As Long as I Love." A further addition is Juan and Juanita's duet "Two Hearts," sung in the first scene and reprised before the finale. It is hard to disagree with Drew that the excision of the ballad, in particular, robs the piece of an element of political agitation and bite, which amounts to "a call for strike action" by Juan and his fellow workers in the first half and, in the second half, "effects the transition from class politics to national and (in Biblical guise) racist politics" (225). In a variant strikingly similar to the Negro spiritual "Go Down Moses," the text of the song derives from Exodus 7:26, where Moses exhorts Pharaoh to "let the people go." By contrast, notes Drew, "the railway workers in *A Kingdom for a Cow* seem altogether content as they blithely whistle the refrain that links the verses of 'San Salvatore'" (226). Moreover, the added duet "Two Hearts" (a musical self-borrowing taken from "Le Roi d'Aquitaine" composed for *Marie Galante*) and Juanita's "As Long as I Love," in expanding the principals' romantic music, tip the balance away from the social and toward the personal dimension of the piece. (Each of the added songs was published separately as sheet music in conjunction with the London premiere.) The final line-up of numbers as printed in the program booklet for the premiere of *A Kingdom for a Cow* is as follows:

PROLOGUE (MALE CHORUS)

ACT 1

Fishing Scene (Juanita and Juan)
Two Hearts (Juanita and Juan)
Trio: Hush, Not a Word (President, Ximenez, and Leslie Jones)
A Military Man (The General)
Wedding Scene (Juan, Juanita, and Ensemble
Goodbye My Love (Juanita and Juan)

ACT 2

San Salvatore (Juan and Male Chorus)
Song: Since First I left my Home (Juan)
Sleep on Santa Maria (General, President, and Ximenez)
If You Should Meet Me (Bailiff)
Reprise: Goodbye My Love (Juan and Juanita)
Song: As Long as I Love (Juanita)
Finale and National Anthem of Santa Maria (Full Company)

ACT 3

Ballad of Robber Esteban (Juanita)
A Jones Is a Jones (Leslie Jones)
Life Is Too Sad (General)
Song of the Cow (Juan)
Reprise: Two Hearts (Juan and Juanita)
Finale (Full Company)

EXAMPLE 31. *A Kingdom for a Cow,* Prologue (national anthem)

The various cuts and additions can no doubt be accounted for in terms of exigencies of the London production. Weill himself mentioned to Lenya after visiting prospective producer Charles Cochran that the latter was "afraid it's not popular enough for the broad masses and that the subject might be too 'satirical.'"[77] For their part, the added numbers for Juan and Juanita not only served to meet generic conventions of traditional musical comedy, but Weill himself conceded that the part of Juanita "is not a big role" and was prepared to augment it musically, as the principal female singer required.[78] The dramaturgical consequences of these changes are both nugatory and significant. They are nugatory insofar as the cuts that make the political and satirical import of the piece less overt do not affect the overall conception of the work as operetta. The tension between public and private that lies at the core of Benjamin's analysis of "Offenbach's secret" remains intact. One could even argue that this very tension constitutes, musically and in terms of plot, the underlying dramaturgical idea of the work as a whole. Emblematic of the former is the national anthem, more pastiche than parody, which could easily be mistaken for the real thing (and which Weill found suitable enough to reuse in *The Firebrand of Florence*) (ex. 31).

A patriotic march, the national anthem initially serves as the first part of the overture, succeeded by the contrasting, more lyrical concluding section. The latter music is derived from the "Youkali" tango and recapitulated as a framing device during the pastoral Prologue. Juan and Juanita's musical spheres are doubly marked, being both pastoral and subjectively romantic. Each of these spheres is threatened by the industrial-military complex (Benjamin's "military state"), here an essentially urban milieu. Juan's aria, "When First I Left My Home," a catalogue of personal sacrifice mixed with hope, whose melody became the basis of "September Song" from *Knickerbocker Holiday,* begins in the original German version with the line "Seit ich in diese Stadt gekommen bin" (Since I arrived in this city).

The juxtaposition of oppositions reaches its apogee in the second finale. Framed by operetta-style waltzes, the extended dramatic unit evolves into a remarkable scene of simultaneous action, with counterpoint that is at once dramatic and musical. Following the finale's opening (a waltz later recycled in *Lady in the Dark*), in which the chorus sings an encomium to state officials, the President enters (to repeated oom-pahs) in order to give one of his public addresses, whose content is always as vacuous as the melody and its cello and harp accompaniment are piously saccharine. Meanwhile Jones and the General surreptitiously plan their putsch as the chorus intones the national anthem to the words "Heaven, smile upon our Motherland, while the old flag floats above." To heighten the irony still more, the chorus then celebrates the peace accord with the neighboring state, while Juan and Juanita lament their respective fates in an epistolary duet. The envisaged blocking, which is made explicit in the German libretto, emphasizes the couple's separation, with Juan to the right of the stage among his fellow soldiers, Juanita to the left sitting at a table in a shabby room. (Juanita sings/writes: "My darling Juan, I've come to town, I've left the village behind me, living on dreams that tumbled down, until you can come back and find me.") As Juan and Juanita continue their impassioned entreaties, the General enters to place the President under arrest, while the chorus celebrates the delights of champagne to the strains of a waltz, thereby "[translating] . . . serious parody into exhilarating dance," to invoke Weill's characterization of Offenbach.

Not only is the bucolic, prelapsarian idyll of Juan and Juanita's romantic attachment disturbed by the machinations of the industrial-military complex, but those machinations are directly responsible for their ritualized nuptials being deferred twice before the topsy-turvy denouement of unwitting disarmament finally makes them possible. "The amorous element," notes Andreas Hauff, who otherwise recognizes numerous parallels between *Der Kuhhandel* and earlier operettas, especially by Offenbach, "is forced to take a backseat."[79] Repeatedly celebrating Juan and Juanita's romance through the newly inserted and reprised songs arguably undermines the large-scale logic of deferral. Whereas the original *Kuhhandel* reinforces the element of satire by withholding the elements that Weill had identified as "Viennese trash" and that Kraus had rejected for similar reasons, *A Kingdom for a Cow* allows those very elements to reassert themselves. Whether or not the revisions justify the verdict "London travesty," their presence does significantly alter the work's dramaturgical design.

Couched as it is throughout in dichotomizing terms, Drew's comparison of the German and English versions implies the existence of two discrete pieces with distinguishable identities. Yet in positing a "fundamental difference" between them, he draws a critical distinction between "work" and "production," thereby privileging the incomplete German version over the completed English one. "The production process that gave *[A Kingdom for a Cow]* an appearance of completeness," he observes, "left it without some of the structural supports that ensure the survival, against all odds, of the unfinished *Kuhhandel.*" The latter should be considered a "work-in-progress," he believes, "but a work for all that" (243). The work thus exists only as an idealistic, essentialized construct—"the idea of a finished *Kuhhandel,*" to use Heinzelmann's expression. The drama's conclusion, Drew writes, "confirms that *Der Kuhhandel* was—in essence—an expression of artistic and intellectual convictions. . . . The same could hardly be said of the *Kingdom for a Cow* numbers (except for the choral prologue, whose origins are in any case rather obscure)" (242).

The fact that the choral Prologue was composed only in connection with the London production is one of several factors that weaken Drew's argument about an underlying "fundamental difference." Another is the fact that, as Drew states in *Kurt Weill: A Handbook,* "Weill did not start orchestrating until *Der Kuhhandel* had been transformed into *A Kingdom for a Cow.*" As he further remarks, "There is no reason to suppose that the demands of the London theatre significantly influenced the orchestration of those *Kuhhandel* numbers that were transferred to *A Kingdom for a Cow.*"[80]

It should also be stressed that the principal shift in Weill's compositional style occurred, not as a response to the exigencies of the London production, but with the commitment to write a satirical operetta in the first place. In his correspondence with Lenya, Weill remarked how the first seven numbers he composed "turned out extraordinarily well, in a very beautiful, new style."[81] Earlier he had referred specifically to having "done a very beautiful barcarole, sung by the President, the General, and the Secretary while gazing on the sleeping Santa Maria."[82] The lilting accompaniment with its harp-colored sonorities is certainly the most obvious allusion to Offenbach in the entire piece, specifically to the "Barcarole" from *Les contes d'Hoffmann.* More important than this moment of homage, however, the musico-dramatic style that Weill employs relies throughout the operetta on a more or less wholesale appropriation of the various rhythms traditionally associated with the genre (march, waltz, can-can, etc.), along with others appropriate to the South America setting (tango, fandango, and rumba). And as with the march discussed above, the overall effect, for all the unmistakable Weillian fingerprints, is one of masterful pastiche rather than defamiliarizing parody, a fidelity to the generic style implicit in the composer's characterization "very beautiful." The operetta, to paraphrase Benjamin's remark about Offenbach, transfigures the satirized "dizzying stupidity" of the plot through music.

That Weill conceived of *Der Kuhhandel* from the outset as a "work-in-progress," uncertain in which country and in what kind of theatrical institution it would first be produced and without precluding productions in other countries and other kinds of institutions, represents the extreme case of the rule that applies to the majority of his works for the musical theater. The production process necessitated revision. (As discussed in the concluding chapter, the distinction between composition and realization is blurred; creation and production go hand in hand.) According the unfinished German version in effect greater authenticity than the "complete" English-language realization, as Drew does in his essay, is to base an aesthetic judgment not only on a comparison of two ultimately incommensurable versions but also on a wistful appreciation of unrealized potential. Had the circumstances of Weill's exile not dictated the move to London but instead to, say, Zurich, *Der Kuhhandel* would doubtless have turned out differently—though just how different must remain pure speculation. And for a while, it seems, the composer did contemplate a further revision. That openness and fluidity of the work's identity is surely the fullest but also the most controversial sense in which *Der Kuhhandel* can be construed as a "key work." Of all the musical theater pieces written by Weill, a composer whom Drew famously celebrated as "one of music's great 'might have beens,'" this is his "might-have-been" work par excellence.[83] There is, however, another sense in which it can be viewed as a key work—that is, in the way it continued to leave its mark on the rest of his oeuvre. In part because of its rapid slide into obscurity after the brief run at London's Savoy Theatre, but also because of its popular, operetta style, the completed *A Kingdom for a Cow* became the composition on which Weill would draw for self-borrowings more than any other single work.[84]

THE ETERNAL ROAD

Of Weill's "stages of exile," *The Eternal Road* is the paradigmatic case. It is a work informed by "exile" at every level—in terms of its conception, its genesis, its content, its performance history, and its reception. At the same time, and for all these reasons, it is also Weill's most problematic work, one that raises a whole host of questions likely to affect any assessment of its place and significance in his oeuvre. The questions touch on a range of interconnected matters, from the aesthetic and theological to the biographical. How does Weill tackle the task of writing an overtly religious work? How is his approach here different from the preceding secular compositions? How not? How, if at all, does that approach reflect his own sense of identity as a German composer whose background is also Jewish? What criteria should be applied to a piece such as this in order to judge its success or failure, conceived as it was (among other things) with political motives? In what sense were Weill's theatrical aims realized, in what sense not? Does *The Eternal Road* deserve a firmer place in the repertory alongside Weill's other works for the musical theater, or is it destined to remain something of a historical curiosity, more document than work?

Both symptom and cause of its singular status is the fact that *The Eternal*

Road has been transmitted in various forms, none of which can or should be considered definitive. While this is more or less true of all Weill's theater works, *The Eternal Road* is arguably an extreme instance. The text-script dichotomy is especially acute: there is nothing approaching a text that coordinates the parameters of words, music, and stage action, nor is there one that could be construed, or even reconstructed, as such. Neither is there a script that reliably reflects a performance event. Conceived in the German language, like *Der Kuhhandel,* it was eventually realized in an English-language premiere in January 1937. Dogged by delays, mainly because of mounting costs, the premiere production was not only a financial disaster, despite a run of 153 performances; it also demanded uncommonly severe creative compromises from the artists and tested the patience of everyone involved, all of which threatened the venture at every turn. At one point, for example, some four months before the premiere finally took place, Weill was driven to complain bitterly about aspects of the production process. "Never in my life I had to go through such a degradation," he wrote in his still imperfect English. He had "made every sacrifice to bring about this show."[85]

The story of the genesis is remarkable in itself, and has been described in considerable detail in a number of publications.[86] Over time, the context has become much better documented than the actual piece. That is probably as it must and even should be with a work of this kind, whose transformations seem to belong to its essence. In hindsight, the process rather than the result becomes key: it is an "exile" piece, after all, not least because of the conditions, and preconditions, of its creation. How else would the famed theater director Max Reinhardt, the poet, playwright, and novelist Franz Werfel, and the composer Kurt Weill have come together as a creative team, except through their common fate as assimilated German-speaking Jews forced by historical circumstances to leave their homeland and apply their considerable but ultimately incompatible talents to a project intended, among other things, as an act of politico-cultural consciousness raising?

More than just recognition of their common fate, of course, it was more specifically the initiative of impresario Meyer Weisgal that brought them together. Weisgal's role was crucial: he was responsible for conceiving of the project in the first place and for seeing it through to realization, despite numerous practical setbacks. During its conception, as mentioned above, Weill referred to the project privately as his "Bible thing" *(Bibelsache).* But what kind of "thing" was it? Any uncertainty reflects not merely Weill's fondness for mixed genres, which this work undoubtedly is; partly, too, it reflects divergent expectations as well as shifting conceptions as the piece evolved from idea to budget-busting reality. Precisely because Weisgal's original conception for the project would prove to be at odds with the aims of the artistic team he assembled, it remains indispensable to an understanding of the piece's fluid identity.

When he approached Reinhardt in 1934, Weisgal was still basking in the success of *The Romance of a People,* a biblical pageant seen by several hundred thousand people at the "Century of Progress" exposition at Chicago's World's Fair in 1933 and later that year in New York and Philadelphia, and for which Weisgal had served as executive director. The pageant's purpose is well described by German-born Democratic senator Robert Wagner, who accepted an honorary vice-chairmanship of the New York committee of sponsors: "No one whose heart beats in sympathy with the hopes and simple ideals of humanity can fail to be profoundly stirred by the desperate plight of innocent men, women and children of Germany who have become the targets of the unspeakable wrath of a small group of uncivilized bigots. . . . Christians and Jews alike will make the pageant in New York a demonstration of good-will that will resound throughout the world and shame the forces of intolerance, wherever they may be at work."[87]

The Romance of a People, Weisgal's model for *The Eternal Road,* served the dual purpose of fund-raising and consciousness raising, with proceeds going mainly to support Jewish refugees leaving Germany for Palestine. It was a truly monumental event, as can be seen from a description of one of the Chicago performances: "On a stage that rose tier by tier at the north end of the field, the cast, under the direction of Isaac Van Grove, conductor of opera and the symphony, portrayed in the mediums of music, light and mass, the trials of Israel from the day of creation. It was a striking spectacle; the benedictions sung by the white-robed priests whose bejewelled breast plates glittered; the roar of rams horn trumpets, the tolling of bells, the waving of palms, and the movement before the eye of the shifting lights and masses of the drama."[88]

Grove's engagement as the conductor of *The Eternal Road* was not the only thing Weisgal's two projects had in common. It began with the title: Werfel's first draft bears the title *Das Volk der Verheissung* ("The People of Promise," i.e. God's promise), with *Volk* crossed out and replaced by *Weg.* The German title—*Der Weg der Verheissung*—remained and, for a while, the English version was referred to as "The Road of Promise." ("The Road," in a temporal sense, is synonymous with "The Romance," although the question of God's promise is one of the thornier questions surrounding the piece's message, as discussed below.) Alexander Ringer has called Ludwig Lewisohn's translation of the title as *The Eternal Road* "a most regrettable, albeit no doubt unintentional faux pas. . . . It invited," Ringer argues, "if anything, painful associations with the notorious myth of the 'eternal Jew' condemned to roam the earth forever for denying the Christian savior—paradoxically a Jew who is said to have died for all mankind's sins." Moreover, "national socialism was making the most of that age-old vilification for its own nefarious reasons."[89]

As indicated in Werfel's script, and as existing photos of the set illustrate, *The Eternal Road,* like *The Romance of a People,* was conceived as spectacle; it too had a multilevel stage; it too was intended as a pageant and succeeded as such in various senses of that term. Both pieces can be linked back to the tradition of medieval mystery plays; both rely on fairly elaborate stage machinery, although only *The Romance of a People* remained in the open air, something considered only an initial possibility for *Eternal Road;* both risked favoring show and spectacular effect over substance; both presented scenes and events central to the identity and history of the Jewish people—though in the case of *Eternal Road,* the sometimes tension-creating differences between the key members of the creative team and Weisgal were significant and telling matters of emphasis.

Lasting some ninety minutes, *The Romance of a People* presented the history of mankind from Genesis to the present. Props included a giant Torah and a huge six-pointed star that towered over the entire stage. As something of a public relations coup, Weisgal persuaded Chaim Weizmann, who had been president of the World Zionist Organization and would become the first president of the state of Israel, to be the principal speaker before the pageant—undoubtedly an added attraction for the national Jewish organizations to participate in Jewish Day in Chicago. The cast, comprising actors, dancers, and singers, including professional cantors, numbered some 3,500 in all.[90] The production was such a success, not least financially, that it was repeated the following week, before moving to New York and Philadelphia. The press was uniformly favorable and enthusiastic. A reporter for the *Daily Jewish Courier* described the event as "a fitting answer to Hitler and Hitlerism . . . it told the doubters and the skeptics that the Jewish people are an undying people."[91]

In his initial pitch to Reinhardt about the sequel, Weisgal echoed that reaction to *The Romance of the People,* stating that "this spectacle must be our answer to Hitler." Yet despite the similar aspirations with which it was conceived, *The Eternal Road* would end up taking a very different route, partly because the project was to bring together "some of the greatest artists of our time," partly, as already suggested, because each of those artists approached it with his own artistic and political purpose, and partly because of the challenges of staging such an ambitious work in a large New York theater with over three thousand seats.[92]

From the outset, Weisgal felt that Werfel, as an assimilated Jew with leanings toward Roman Catholicism (partly due no doubt to the influence of his wife, Alma Mahler), had ideas about the project not wholly in accord with Weisgal's own. As he explains in his autobiography,

> The mystic strain which might have identified with Chassidism he transferred to the Catholic Church, but the advent of Hitler kept him from formalizing his conversion. I spent the whole night walking with Werfel in the garden and explaining to him, as well as I could, that this was a *Jewish* play—that and nothing else. It was our history, the history of his and my people, that had to be portrayed—not some alien or abstract concept. Remote as he was from Judaism, there was enough of the poet in Werfel to grasp at the idea even through my barbarous German.[93]

For his part, Werfel resisted the incorporation of music, which he accommodated in his libretto only in an incidental capacity. He conceived of the piece essentially in terms of a spoken drama—an impression promoted by the publication of the text, which appeared in the original German as *Der Weg der Verheissung: Ein Bibelspiel in vier Teilen* in 1935 (Vienna: Paul Zsolnay Verlag). Weill is not mentioned, nor are any of the other collaborators. Nor, indeed, is there any distinction made between lines spoken and lines sung. Musical indications are limited to calling for offstage trumpets, "Tafelmusik," "solemn march," and the like.

Ludwig Lewisohn's translation appeared the following year, in January 1936, as a more or less literal rendering of the Viennese text. The full title is given as *The Eternal Road: A Drama in Four Parts* (New York: Viking Press). Preceding the translator's note, there is a short note informing readers of the New York production: "The English version of *The Eternal Road* is the first to be performed. With Max Reinhardt as director, Kurt Weill as composer of the music, Norman Bel Geddes as stage designer, and under the management of Meyer W. Weisgal, Franz Werfel's drama was first given at the Manhattan Opera House in New York, in January 1936."

That, at least, had been the hope when the translation went to press. It should be noted that the published text, one of the principal sources, did not represent faithfully the version ultimately performed at the premiere, which took place exactly one year later than envisaged. Cuts would be made, principally the excision of the entire fourth part save for the very end. And a certain amount of editorial intervention would be necessary in an attempt, not entirely successful, to fit Lewisohn's translation to Weill's music. It should come as no surprise, then, that the composer adopted a perspective quite different from Werfel's. On receiving the finished text, Weill exclaimed to Reinhardt that it "cries out" for music.[94]

In addition to Weisgal's autobiography, the surviving Weill-Lenya correspondence provides colorful documentation of a collaboration that on occasion left the composer on the brink of utter exasperation. Reporting from a working session with Reinhardt and Werfel in Salzburg on 11 August 1935, for example, Weill writes to Lenya that "[Werfel] is scared of every note of music." He continues, however, that "he's easy game because he's a coward and immediately gives in, as long as one remains firm. Max behaves nobly, is very outspoken and unequivocally on my side, deciding all discussions in favor of the music. He understands completely what I want, and he's crazy about the music as he is about me . . . there's always a sort of quiet understanding between him and me. I hope that this Werfel beast will leave on Tuesday; then I still want to work alone with Max for one or two days."[95]

As this brief excerpt vividly illustrates, there was a clash not only of competing conceptions, but also of personalities. Unlike Werfel, with his tendency to deemphasize the music, Reinhardt and Weill, in talking about the piece, both invoke oratorio as the generic model. In his layout, Reinhardt states that *The Eternal Road* "is not a play with musical interludes and with melodramatic accompaniment. . . . It is rather an oratorio like the Matthew Passion by Bach, albeit in a new half-spoken, half-sung form, yet fixed (notated) and determined musically throughout."[96] Early on, in February 1934, Weill could report that "the big biblical thing seems to be progressing. . . . It would be a giant task for me, since it's a real oratorio." At that stage he also reported that the premiere was "supposed to be at London's Albert Hall."[97]

Some eighteen months later, in October 1935, with rehearsals under way and the hope that the New York premiere would take place in December, Weill described the piece in an interview with N.S. [Nicolas Slonimsky?] as follows: "On the whole I have conceived of the music in the spirit of popular oratorio. . . . About 70 per cent of the play will have a musical setting. I resort not only to arias, ensembles and choruses, embedded in the continuous music between the spoken parts, but use as well 'Sprechstimme' or half-song, 'parlando' and recitative." In the same interview, Weill addressed the relationship between the work's style and its content. "It is Mr. Weill's conviction," N.S. summarizes, "that the Old Testament, of which the play is a résumé, is primarily a great human document belonging in its appeal, not to any particular era, but to all time. For this reason he considers 'local color' of small importance and feels justified in employing a contemporary style."[98]

The relationship between old and new, with regard to both the content and the style of the piece, is complicated, much more so than the interview suggests. The play—and this is one of the bones of contention between the collaborators—is more than merely a "résumé" of the Old Testament, because of the relevance to contemporaneous political events. Similarly, what is meant by "local color" and "contemporary style" both require qualification. The latter, certainly, is already suggested by Reinhardt's reference to the *Matthew Passion.*

Although Werfel's published text ostensibly presents a "literary" version of the piece, analogous in this respect to Brecht's *Versuche* versions of his own plays with music, it doesn't entirely suppress reference to its theatrical realization. Stage action is an integral part of the text, with frequent mention of the five stages described in "The Plan of the Stage" that follows the *dramatis personae.*[99] "The total set," it states there, "is constructed in such a manner that it consists of five stages which rise in ascending order like the steps of a stairway." Here are the salient details, with the emphasis (from Werfel's text) highlighting the significance attached to each level: The first, lowest stage "represents a **house of prayer** or synagogue. . . . The background wall is low; in it, between two small square barred windows right and left, is the sacred niche (Aaron Hakodesh) which contains the scrolls of the Torah, the Law." The second stage "represents a gently ascending **road,** and the construction is such that the synagogue wall serves as the foundation of the road." The third road "broadens into a square of such dimensions that it consists of three spaces for action, a large middle space flanked by two others in the form of raised platforms. These will be referred to as the **Middle Space,** the **Right Space,** and the **Left Space.**" With the fourth stage "we enter the realm of mystery, for this stage symbolizes in the course of the action the top of the mountain Moriah, the ascent of Sinai, and the altar-place of the Temple. Hence, this stage is called the **Altar Stage.**" Finally, the fifth stage is "**the stair to heaven.**" This is "the sphere of the Angels and of the divine Voice." Werfel further specifies that the fifth stage is "framed within a gigantic door of rock and removed from the traffic of mortality by mystic veils."

The scene itself is also specified, immediately before the list of the *dramatis personae,* as "the timeless community of Israel"; the time as "the equally timeless night of Israel's persecution."[100] The Prologue establishes the context for that timeless night, with the Rabbi and the community gathered in the synagogue in the midst of a pogrom, thus establishing the epic frame for the entire piece: the Rabbi's recitation of various passages from the Torah at the lower level and their dramatic enactment on the other levels of the stage. The four parts bear the following titles:

1. The Patriarchs
2. Moses
3. The Kings (Saul, David, Solomon)
4. The Prophets (Isaiah, Jeremiah, The Angel of the End of Days)

Although the content summarized at length in the souvenir program issued in connection with the premiere[101] corresponds to this four-part outline, the program booklet had to be revised to accommodate the removal of the fourth act, as follows:

Prologue
1. Abraham, Jacob and Rachel, Joseph and His Brothers, Joseph in Egypt
2. Moses in Egypt, In the Wilderness
3. The Synagogue, Ruth, David, Solomon, The Synagogue

In addition to act 4, Saul in act 3 was cut, again for reasons of time.

Over time, memory of opening night made the premiere performance even longer than it was, with several authors remembering a show that still included the fourth act and did not finish until well after midnight. Gottfried Reinhardt's account, a frequently cited source in the secondary literature, seems to have conflated the rehearsals with the public performance:

> The curtain did go up that night, an hour and a half late. In retrospect, I am glad I only learned subsequently of yet another technical difficulty delaying it . . . the Fire Commissioner popped in and condemned the building out of hand. . . . After a heated argument, during which the opening, with a full, unsuspecting house, teetered in the balance, the Mayor gave the green light, provided forty firemen were present [because of lighted candles]—and would attend all future performances. . . . And then a miracle happened. It continued throughout two whole acts. They were of extraordinary power and beauty, and immensely moving. The high point was the second-act curtain: the exodus. The audience was so engrossed that it forgot about time. It was past midnight. But as the night interminably progressed, the audience remembered the hour. It was utterly drained. On the stage the flow of the last two acts became increasingly vicious. Play and performance seemed to dissolve in some kind of haze. What specifically concluded the agony, I do not recall; or when.[102]

Evidence from the time tells a different story. The drama critic for *Variety* (13 January) reported that the premiere curtain came down just before midnight, a fact confirmed by the very precise-sounding information in the *New York Times* (8 January): "The curtain rose at 8:43 and came down at 11:50, though the producers last evening said they will cut the running time until it is of standard length, two hours and a quarter." As reported by *Variety:* "Some 20 minutes had been cut after several dress rehearsals, but the German refugees who had a large part of the presentation were against further deletions." The magazine's synopsis lists three (not four) acts, as does the program and a number of other reviews. Substantial cuts had evidently already been made, with more to come.

The "Revised Script" presents a radically truncated version of the text, no doubt quite close to the version performed at the time.[103] Acts 3 and 4 are spliced together, with all but the latter's final pages gone: as in Werfel's published version, the seven-year construction of Solomon's Temple is followed by the Watchman's announcement of the imminent threat posed to the synagogue, whereupon the Congregation sings "Kol Nidre." At this point, the text cuts all the way to the choir exclaiming, "Messiah—Messiah—Messiah" (three pages before the end of act 4 in the Lewisohn translation). In the manuscript that initially bore the title *Das Volk der Verheissung,* Werfel included the "Messiah" *(Messias)* as the third and final prophet (after Isaiah and Jeremiah). In subsequent versions the designation disappears and the text is assigned to "The Angel of the End of Days." The lines are now spoken by "Voice of God." With minor cuts, the text continues as before, with the expulsion of the members of the synagogue from "this Royal Territory by nightfall on pain of death" and the closing scene bringing together the entire cast of biblical figures followed by "the [timeless] Congregation of Israel."

The ending of the piece had been an issue since the beginning, and not just for reasons of length. In an early progress report to Reinhardt (6 October 1934), written after he had received all four parts of the text, Weill expressed his particular enthusiasm for the work's conclusion: "I find what he [Werfel] has done splendid *[grossartig]*. . . . I am pleasantly surprised, in particular, by the conclusion of the work. This vision of the Messiah, in its genuine naïveté and simplicity, has a real greatness about it, and all questions concerning the 'intention' *[Tendenz]* behind the piece are thereby resolved, because the meaning of the work is entirely revealed." What that *Tendenz* was (the "intention," "meaning"; literally: "tendency" or "slant")[104] Weill does not say, and it would anyway potentially change, including the nature of the Messianic message, thanks to subsequent revisions and the removal of the fourth act. The implications of any such changes are potentially significant—aesthetically, theologically, and politically. At the same time, like the language switch, itself no trivial matter, the disappearance of the fourth act can be seen as emblematic of deeper tensions in the whole enterprise.

In the same letter to Reinhardt, Weill summarizes his approach to setting Werfel's text to music as follows: "I believe that I have succeeded in solving the formal question by creating large musical forms, interrupted by spoken scenes, without changing the text in the slightest. . . . It is a music that for the most part, vis-à-vis the other elements of the music, places melody in the foreground, whereby I have used original Jewish melodies only very sparingly, i.e. only where there is a connection to the liturgy." Weill's interest in collecting (or recollecting) Jewish melodies for *Der Weg der Verheissung* marks a departure in his approach to composition. Not only did he conduct research in the Bibliothèque Nationale in Paris, but he also contacted the original source of his own knowledge, his father (Cantor Albert Weill). Using such musical material in a predominantly melodic style had its limits, nonetheless. "Jewish liturgy," Weill explains to Reinhardt, "is lacking in real 'melodies'; it consists mainly of melodic formulae and short motifs, which I have occasionally given in particular to the Rabbi's readings. Often, however, whenever the Rabbi's song is part of the whole musical form, it is integrated into this form and he sings like the characters of the biblical stage."

In this way, Weill creates ensembles that contribute to the crossing and blurring of boundaries between the different stage levels, musically connecting the biblical action and the action in the synagogue, for example.[105] He also identifies where his work is at once most Jewish and most Christian: in the Rabbi's readings, which of all the oratorical features most resemble Bach's *Matthew Passion,* in accordance with Reinhardt's observation, while incorporating the cantorial intonations ("melodic formulae and short motifs") derived from the Jewish liturgy. But these are not Weill's only musical sources, of course. Apart from overtly religious music, both Jewish and Lutheran, Weill draws on a range of idioms, deriving notably from Mahler and Wagner, but also from baroque counterpoint, Mozartian opera, Viennese operetta, and popular dance music. Above all, he "borrows" from himself. This is nothing new, of course. Yet the stylistic mix is

TABLE 2 An excerpt from act 1 of *The Eternal Road:* Translation and adaptation compared

Ludwig Lewisohn's translation	William A. Drake's adaptation
FIRST ANGEL: Rise, Father Jacob, thy Joseph calls thee.	FIRST ANGEL: Arise, Father Jacob, 'tis Joseph who calls thee.
JACOB: 'Tis night and 'tis death that call me.	JACOB: 'Tis Night that is calling and death.
SECOND ANGEL: It is day, it is life and the crown of life that are calling.	SECOND ANGEL: It is life, it is life that is calling to Jacob.
JACOB: Inscrutable God, give time that I grasp this . . .	JACOB: Inscrutable God, give time that I grasp this . . .
FIRST ANGEL: The time is ripe and thy journey begins.	FIRST ANGEL: The moment has come and thy journey begins.
JACOB: My old heart fainteth . . .	JACOB: My senses are fainting . . .
BOTH ANGELS: Behold, we shall guide thee.	BOTH ANGELS: Behold we shall guide thee to thy beloved son.
JOSEPH: Rise ye up and suffer remorse no more! God rules us and though ye were planning evil, yet was He planning a good thing through you. Not ye—'twas He sent me into Egypt that I might prepare a stead and a fate for Jacob's house. Come close, come unto me! My heart hears my father, we go forth to meet him.	JOSEPH: Rise up, and suffer remorse no more. The Lord is my shield. For your purpose was evil. But good was the purpose He made you serve. Not you, He brought me a slave into Egypt that I might prepare a home and a faith for Jacob's house, come closer to me, my heart hears my father. Now let us go and meet him.

perhaps richer than in any of his other works. Not only that, but the aesthetic purpose of his characteristically allusive approach to musical idiom, here in a work with an ostensibly religious message, calls for reconsideration. Is it ironic, as in other contexts?

If this last question is directed to the listener, then the answer can only be a qualifying "it depends." Borrowings may not be perceived as such, still less as deliberate allusions to incongruous contexts. Although only a few of the audience members in New York would have been familiar with Weill's earlier work, or even with the other works alluded to, the catalogue of potential ironies, deriving from provocative juxtapositions, is nonetheless considerable. A description of the end of act 2 and the beginning of act 3 may serve as a representative sample.

Act 1—the story of Abraham and the other Patriarchs—concludes with the death of Jacob and the reconciliation of Joseph with his father. Werfel wrote the scene as "double action," with Joseph in the palace and Jacob lying at the mouth of a cavern by a road, accompanied by the First and Second Angels. Weill has them sing consecutively, Jacob and the Angels first. William A. Drake's adaptation (right-hand column of table 2) of Lewisohn's translation (left-hand column) served two purposes: to simplify Lewisohn's intentionally antiquated language and, more important, to fit the words to the music. In doing so, however, Drake distanced the text even further from Werfel's original.

Weill turns the double action into an expanded dramatic unit, setting the texts as successive musical utterances. The initial effect is akin to a varied strophic design, first with Jacob and the Angels and then with Joseph. But the overall musical form is more complex than that, with melodic material repeated at different functional points, derived from within the unit and from without. The principal melody of the section, as Christian Kuhnt has shown, draws on part of a traditional synagogal melody from the Rhineland, pressed here into a new tonal context, suitable for sectional repetition at the beginning and end of phrases and for transformation, in the course of the scene, into an instrumental march (ex. 32).[106] The purely instrumental central section, with the same melody serving as the "solemn march" prescribed in Werfel's text, accompanies the stage action, as the Angels lead Jacob along the road to meet with his son. Before reverting to the principal melody as part of the march, however, Weill introduces a new melody as a linking section. It is familiar from its association with the words "Schnalle deinen Gürtel enger um ein Loch" that Severin sings as a refrain in his song "Der Bäcker backt ums Morgenrot" in *Der Silbersee.* Coming as it does from Weill's considerable repertory of marches, the borrowing makes sense in purely generic terms, of course; yet one is left to speculate whether he had any further connection in mind.

If the instrumental interlude functioned formally as a further variation of the opening, the following section signals closure. With voices from the synagogue crying, "May it be for good!" Jacob sings his lament to a falling figure that is doubled in the orchestra, the traditional baroque topos for such an occasion, followed by a broken-chord figure that appears as if from nowhere (ex. 33). Or rather, from somewhere else. Mozart aficionados may recognize it as deriving from the end of the opera *Le nozze di Figaro,* in a similar dramatic context of resolution and closure accompanying the words "Ah, tutti contenti / saremo così. / Questo giorno di tormenti, / di capricci, e di follia, / in contenti e in allegria solo amor può terminar" (ex. 34).

That is not all: Weill's dramaturgy requires yet more concluding music for the extended scene. The draft piano-vocal score transmits two versions of the closing measures. Both recall material from earlier in the act, thereby serving the dual purpose of dramatic reminiscence and large-scale closure. The second ending, presumably intended to supersede the first one, recalls the more urgently passionate version of the Jacob-Rachel duet in the rehearsal score. The first, somewhat longer ending quotes the first version of the same duet contained in Weill's initial draft, itself another not quite literal borrowing, this time from *A Kingdom for a Cow*—namely, the brief duet between Juan and Juanita in the second-act finale of that work. Insofar as the passage constitutes an allusion, it likely suggested to Weill Juanita's (rather than Juan's) words, with which she affirms her constancy:

EXAMPLE 32. *The Eternal Road,* act 1 (double-action scene)

"Ich wusste mir nicht anders Rat, mein Herz bleibt dir immer verbunden" (in Desmond Carter's free translation: "Living on dreams that tumbled down, until you come back and find me"). Its replacement suggests that the melody was initially adopted mainly for reasons of time, until Weill composed the more suitable affect of the new version.

Either way, apart from recalling the Rachel duet (and in the initial incarnation echoing a duet from an earlier work), this closing music literally underscores the ongoing discourse that characterizes the synagogue scenes throughout. Its principal participants, including the Rabbi, are nameless types, somewhat in the manner of expressionist drama: The Estranged One, The Estranged One's Son (a thirteen-year-old boy), The Pious Man, and The Adversary (in other scenes they are joined

EXAMPLE 33. *The Eternal Road,* act 1 ("Figaro allusion")

EXAMPLE 34. Wolfgang Amadeus Mozart, *Le nozze di Figaro,* act 4 finale

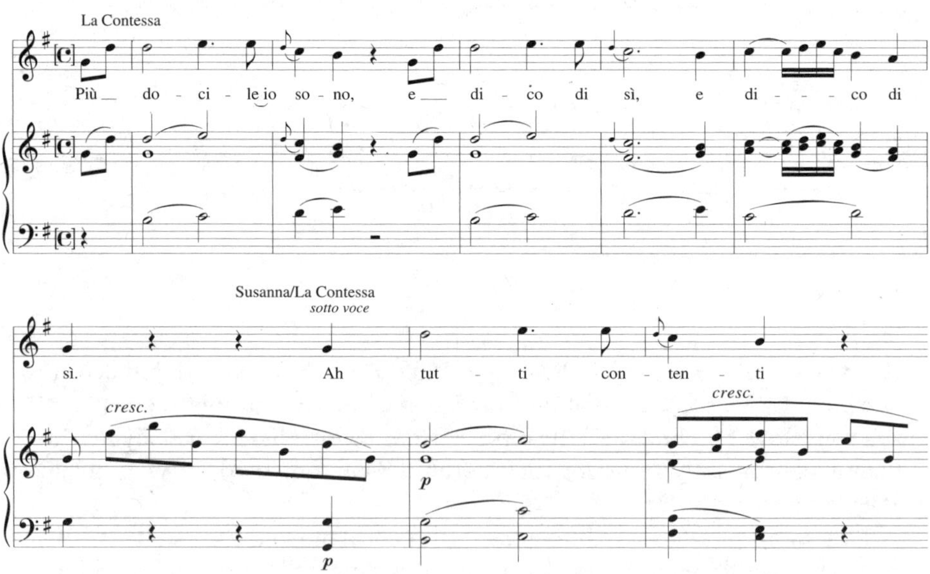

EXAMPLE 35. *The Eternal Road,* act 2 (march theme)

by The President of the Congregation, The Timid Soul, The Rich Man, et al.). At the end of the scene just described, for example, The Estranged One's Son, inspired by the biblical story, ecstatically exclaims: "I am myself Joseph." The Pious Man generalizes the relevance: "All Israel is Joseph. After long bitter parting he will embrace his father once again." The Rabbi conflates the general with the specific: "Fill your souls with the thought of Jacob and Joseph. It will give you strength to bear the long separation." The boy wishes to apply the lesson to his father, The Estranged One, who is not yet convinced. "Go alone, my child," he exhorts his son. "I have forgotten too much. It may be that you will bring it back to me." The Pious Man is skeptical: "What does this boy want? . . . He is the renegade's son." The Rabbi questions the question: "How are you to know *who* this boy is?" The Adversary counters: "Who is he? Why, another dreamer." Wrapping the boy "in a praying-shawl," the Rabbi has the last word of the act: "Come to us and listen and watch!"

In the same vein, act 2 turns its (as well as the community members' and, of course, the audience's) attention to two episodes, beginning with the Liberation from Egypt, "played out among the Israelites on the upper stages," as the program describes it, again emphasizing the interaction: "Its echoes reverberate continuously through the Synagogue below and through the audience."[107] And the stylistic mix continues as before. The main recurring elements include the Mahlerian "quiet march" heard at the beginning of act 1 to accompany Abraham's entrance. Notes printed in the souvenir program and entitled "Kurt Weill's Music," drawing on an interview with the composer that was published during the week of the premiere in the *American Hebrew,* state that the march "is to be taken as the musical symbol of eternal wandering from place to place," adding that it also "brings the entire drama to an exalted close" (ex. 35). At each of its appearances

FIGURE 3. The scene from act 2 of the premiere production of *The Eternal Road* (1937) in which Moses smites the Egyptian with his golden rod. "The total set," as prescribed by Franz Werfel's published text, "consists of five stages which rise in ascending order like the steps of a stairway." These progress upward from "a house of prayer or synagogue" at the bottom to "the stair to heaven" at the top. Photo: Lucas-Pritchard Studio. Courtesy of the Museum of The City of New York (Theater Collection).

the march acquires a different character and color, thanks mainly to the orchestration, even though its rhythmic and diastematic content are repeated basically intact, ranging at the beginning of act 2 from hushed woodwinds to raucous brass with glissandos in the trombones. The march binds the whole act together, in fact, with its reappearance at the end as well.

After his introductory recitative at the beginning of act 2, the Rabbi briefly joins the unison central section of the march to introduce the ensuing story: "Pharaoh commanded all his servants / All first born sons of Israel shall ye throw into the Nile." The Chorus of Israelite Women intone their lament ("Woe") over a new accompaniment figure—new in this context, that is. Before Moses' sister, Miriam, begins her ballad (sung in the premiere production by Lenya), Weill has the violins accompany the voices with a figure "borrowed" from "Lust" of *Die sieben Todsünden.* Why Lust? Was Weill recalling another stage of exile? Moses'

EXAMPLE 36. *The Eternal Road,* act 2, *Ring* allusion ("sleep motif")

refrain delivers the often-quoted line that underscores this work's exile theme: "A stranger am I in strangers' land."

In protest at the subjugation of the Hebrew men, Moses "smites" the Egyptian with his golden rod to strains of an especially brutal variant of the principal march theme, with Wagnerian associations (fig. 3 and ex. 36). More precisely, the combination of the bass and the melodic rhythm generates a motif from *Der Ring des Nibelungen,* first heard in its minor variant in *Die Walküre* when Brünnhilde expresses dread at being "easy prey for a coward" (ex. 37). The better-known major variant is generally referred to as the "motif of slumber." Again, one can only speculate as to what Weill might have had in mind with these allusions, if intended as such. That the richly eclectic music evinces a Wagnerian flavor at this crucial moment is nonetheless indisputable, allusion or no. In *Die Walküre,* Brünnhilde is reluctantly put to sleep by her father, Wotan. Here the Egyptian is buried in sand by Moses. Be that as it may, Weill's motif never turns into slumber in either mode: it reappears at the very end of the work in the triumphant C major of the final procession.

In 1937, a matter of months after the premiere of *The Eternal Road,* just as the run was coming to an end after 153 performances, Weill reflected on the question of "so-called artistic freedom." His thoughts acquire special poignancy in view of his recent experiences:

> So-called artistic freedom is something special. The creative artist seeks independence, he wants to conceive his work freely, unaffected by outer compulsion. On the other hand, he needs some restraining influence to prevent his wandering in

EXAMPLE 37. Richard Wagner, *Die Walküre,* act 3, scene 3

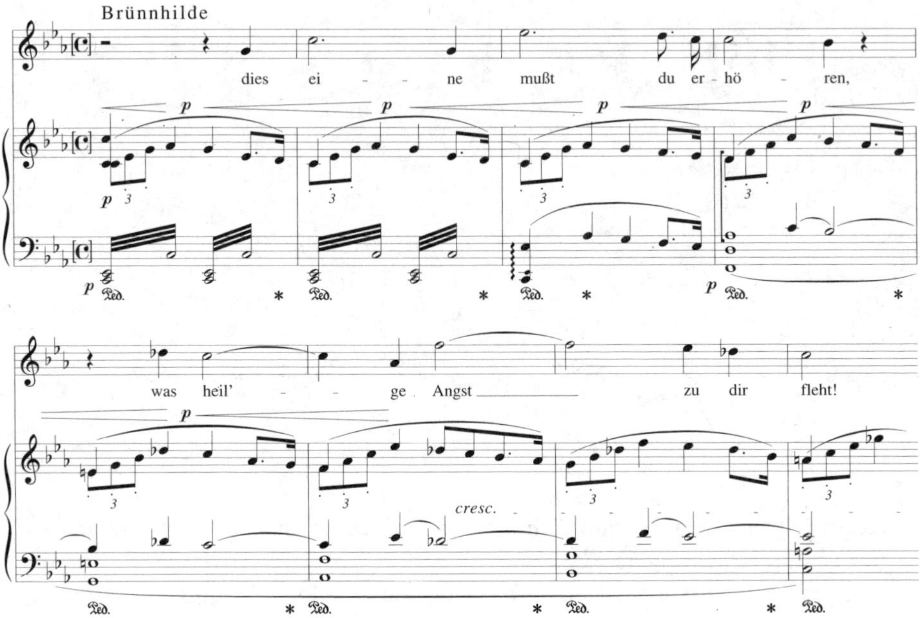

> abstract spheres. He must know for whom he is creating. Only by considering his objective will he find the necessary spiritual background that prohibits an empty play with forms. Most great works of art were produced as commissions, for a definite purpose and audience, that is, between the millstones of outer compulsion and inner freedom, between "must" and "will."[108]

Weill makes it quite clear that "inner freedom" is something to be balanced by "outer compulsion." Even allowing for any characteristic irony in his diction, it is perhaps surprising that he should refer to both in the same terms, as "millstones." Does he mean "milestone"? Be that as it may, he is keen to focus on the critical importance of knowing for whom he is composing—namely, not for posterity, but for a contemporaneous audience. *Der Weg der Verheissung* is unusual also in this respect: whereas Weisgal's initiative identified the work's "definite purpose" (even if this would necessarily change over time), the audience was, from the beginning, something of an unknown. Reinhardt, Werfel, and Weill started work without knowing exactly where the work would be performed and hence for whom they were writing.

The mounting costs of the production were due in no small measure to the profligacy of Norman Bel Geddes, whose extravagant set designs threatened the viability of the show even as they contributed greatly to its critical success. Weill could thus express both concern and admiration. Just five months before the premiere, he confided in a letter to Werfel (3 August 1936) that Geddes "will spend a fortune, without bringing the performance to realization and . . . no-one will be there to stop him." Two months into the run, however, before the extent of the budget deficit had been established, he reported in a letter to Werfel's wife, Alma Maria Mahler (1 March 1937), that "through his lighting artistry Geddes gave the piece a unique visual beauty."

Geddes's extravagancies notoriously entailed the removal of the orchestra pit to accommodate the five stages, with the synagogue eventually replacing the orchestra and thereby incurring two additional budget items: an extremely costly repair to a water main damaged by the dynamite used to remove the pit; and the replacement of the live music by recorded sound, save for the sixteen musicians required by union rules. The solution involved cutting-edge technology, on the viability and benefits of which Weill sought counsel from none other than Leopold Stokowski, who later that year would discuss with Walt Disney plans for the movie *Fantasia* (1940), in which he used the latest recording techniques.[109] Initially an expedient measure for Weill, recorded sound also offered potential benefits. On the one hand, he thought it would "achieve a better sound quality" than "with an ad hoc orchestra and all the acoustic difficulties of live theater." On the other hand, he wondered how a singer could "shape the music on the spur of the moment with full intensity and devotion, if he is bound with rigid necessity to the tempo prescribed to him by a machine."[110] It was a problem that particularly concerned him with *The Eternal Road* because of the half-sung, half-spoken portions not created until the rehearsal period and because of the need for "a flexible, adaptable orchestra." With assurances from Stokowski that both the technical and musical problems could be resolved, Weill acceded to the "compromise solution," with partial recorded music and partial live performance.[111]

Sound recording was something Weill had used before, as he reminded Stokowski, notably in *Der Zar lässt sich photographieren*. Its employment in *The Eternal Road* was of such greater magnitude, however, as to adumbrate a potential reform of the musical theater—something he considered in his letter to the maestro in favorable terms but which he would never entertain again. (Some of the issues surrounding the experiment have acquired renewed relevance for Broadway theaters with recent discussions about the merits and demerits of piping orchestral music, either live or recorded, through loudspeakers.)

Such was the theatrical novelty at the time of utilizing the new technology that the experiment received extensive documentation in specialist journals such as *Electronics* and *Radio-Craft*. According to the author of one *Electronics* article, who supplied every conceivable detail of the machinery used, the "RCA ultra-violet push-pull method was chosen because of its large volume range and freedom from distortion."[112] Readers are also told that "after the orchestra recordings had been completed, preliminary prints were made for the purpose of synchronizing the subsequent chorus recordings."[113] (Unfortunately, the tapes appear not to have survived, despite numerous efforts to track them down.) How much money was saved, if any, by replacing live musicians with recorded sound is impossible to calculate. For a run of 153 performances there may indeed have been savings, except that the reason the recordings were used in the first place (the removal of the orchestra pit) no doubt wiped out any economies in a production that ended up losing more than $500,000, a substantial deficit by any theatrical measure of the time.

Money problems notwithstanding, and with the nickname "The Eternal Postponement" because of the premiere's having been delayed some ten times, the production met with wide critical acclaim when it finally opened. Brooks Atkinson's review in the *New York Times* (8 January 1937), praising both the spectacular staging and Weill's music, is indicative of the favorable tone adopted by most of the critics, beginning here with reference to the show's uncertain generic status:

> Call it a pageant, if you will, or call it opera, spectacle, fantasy or profound religious teaching, for it is all of these things in equal measure. . . . Dr. Reinhardt has before now demonstrated his genius for handling mobs in stupendous productions. But as far as this reviewer knows he has never before had Kurt Weill at his elbow to give his mobs the lift of song, and that is a privilege devoutly to be cherished. For Mr. Weill's music, instrumental as well as vocal, invests the spectacle with vitality and exultation. It is the principal life-giving force along "The Eternal Road." When the portals to heaven open, disclosing a sacred choir of angels, the glory that floods the theatre is the voice of an inspired composer. Mr. Weill is said to have fashioned his score out of tribal motives, which is the sort of thing a musicologist might appreciate. But whatever the derivation of the music may be, it is enormously stirring and enormously alive and it spares "The Eternal Road" the heaviness that lurks in most religious spectacles.

Atkinson's equivocation over what to call *The Eternal Road* nicely captures not only the work's various ingredients but also the different directions in which the piece was being tugged from its conception to initial realization on the Broadway stage and beyond. In the end the tensions between the various parties involved were more creative than destructive, thanks to the critical success of the production. But it was a close thing. No doubt an important aspect of the Weill-Werfel rift, beyond the question of music's relative importance for the enterprise, is the composer's interest in emphasizing the dramatic frame. On the surface this may seem surprising, since it is in the biblical portions where the composer enjoyed relative freedom to create extended musical forms, despite the obvious restrictions placed on his creativity by the interests of the other collaborators and the exigencies of the production process. But Weill was quite explicit in his suggestion to Werfel, in a letter dated 3 September 1936, that, based on his having "carefully studied the American theater and public . . . we should do everything to expand the action in the synagogue into a unified, suspenseful drama that begins in the first scene and continues through the entire piece and holds the Bible scenes together more cohesively than at present." Werfel disagreed. On 8 September he responded that "since it was and is our task to bring the whole Bible to life, the balance and pathos of the giant tableau would be disturbed in favor of a realistic piece, as one has seen a hundred times before (Eastern pogrom drama)." This would not, he believed, "provide any substantial increase in interest. . . . Believe me, dear Weill," he urged, employing the vocabulary of religious ceremony, "the essence of our work is the musical-poetic-optical lustration that it must invoke." He did not want to "sprinkle any more realistic pepper into our strong broth."

Suspenseful realistic drama or lustration? As performed, *The Eternal Road* was evidently both—or rather, somewhere between the two. Whereas Werfel preferred to let "the whole Bible" speak for itself, Weill leaned more toward emphasizing the context of the "timeless night" of persecution. The reasons for his wanting to do so were surely several—aesthetic, theological, and, increasingly, political. Werfel, as other aspects of his oeuvre attest, was evidently more invested in the theology of the work's "Messianic" message—or at least, differently invested—than Weill. Whether God's promise would lead to the coming of the Messiah (the "Anointed One") as savior (specifically as "Yeshua," or Jesus); or whether he served as the prophet of a new, more peaceful age ("the End of Days"); or whether he was to bring the Jewish people back to Israel and restore Jerusalem—this is the crux on which the more salient differences between Weisgal and his collaborators doubtless hinged.[114]

In the context not only of Weill's own exile but also of the fate of his fellow compatriots and other Europeans being persecuted by the Nazis, Jews as well as Gentiles, both the Bible portions and the dramatic frame of *The Eternal Road* function best as parables, even Lehrstücke, that may or may not apply to the historical situation. They raise rather than answer theological questions. It follows, therefore—and there may be a certain artistic justice here—that Weill felt he could raid *The Eternal Road* for the pageants that followed with a more obviously direct relation to contemporary history: *Fun to Be Free, We Will Never Die,* and *A Flag Is Born.* These are all functional, agitprop pieces, more overtly so than *The Eternal Road.*

While the published texts of *Der Weg der Verheissung* and *The Eternal Road* could be read as some kind of cipher for Werfel's religious beliefs and sense of personal identity at the time (if not later), it is harder to say the same for Weill and

Reinhardt. Not least because of its shifting identity, it seems more appropriate to read the work as a reflection of the struggles of émigrés trying to make their way as artists at a precarious historical moment, a moment soon to be succeeded by a worse one. It is a "stage of exile" in every sense, not a theological tract. As such, it will remain a work whose various achievements and failures are hard to disentangle from one another. Anyone who concerns him- or herself with the complex of materials that the project left in its wake will have to tackle the rather bizarre juxtaposition they engender of recondite existential theological puzzles and the more mundane matter of getting a show on the boards without bankrupting the entire city of New York.

Art, religion, propaganda, and entertainment—all contribute in some way to the unique mix. For Reinhardt, as he stated in undated lecture notes, the Bible was "a sacred work of art of inconceivable mysterious greatness, an incomparable contribution to the history of mankind and, at the same time, a mirror of the reality that stirs the world." The task, as he saw it, was not to create propaganda. To quote his paradoxical formulation, "Propaganda has never produced a work of art and there is no better propaganda than a pure work of art." *The Eternal Road,* he stressed, "glorifies only God, not the people, which like all mankind is shown full of weaknesses and shortcomings."[115]

The question remains: a mirror of what reality? As the piece progressed from conception to realization, not only was contemporary relevance of the "realistic" synagogue scenes heightened, but ultimately it was overtaken by historical developments. How timeless was the "timeless night," how eternal the "eternal road"? In the version performed, the road is a road of exile, of diaspora, the road to be traveled by "the community of Israel" that has been expelled "on pain of death." By 1937, however, it was becoming all too clear that for many Jews, and not only for them, not even exile was an option. The pogrom was a fact; death was the reality. In this dire context, as several commentators have argued, the dramatic frame becomes at best problematic. Werfel biographer Norbert Abels has attempted to capture the problem in the form of a set of trenchant questions, which likely posed themselves to the creators of *The Eternal Road,* if not during the work's genesis then at some later point, and whose relevance has only increased with hindsight:

> How timeless can a night be that one senses might be the last? What use is the comfort of eschatological certainty about being as a whole when it is quite certain that one will not be allowed to see the dawn of Messianic light with one's own eyes? How is it possible that even the objection to the monolithic block of a community whose fate was originally established in theological terms is itself asserted as an integral part of this community's historical teleology? The question surrounding

> the dramatic frame of *The Eternal Road* could be: what binds us, apart from the fact of our collectively suffered persecution? From where do we derive the certainty that this fact can be a heuristic function of our future? What does such certainty mean for the ethical principles of hope and responsibility? Doesn't the certainty of being part of a divine plan paralyze any sense of responsibility?[116]

As with *Die Bürgschaft* and *Der Silbersee,* both works written in the midst of a gathering political crisis, it is hard not to read the dramatic frame of *The Eternal Road* as a scarcely concealed allegory. Hence one of the overwhelming problems for reviving the piece today. There is no question that Weisgal's principal aims—the operative aims of fund-raising and consciousness raising—both failed. And it is this failure that necessarily informs the assessment of recent commentators. Atay Citron has couched his discussion of *The Eternal Road* in the bluntest of terms, more with reference to Weisgal's initial goals than to the production itself: "The idea of employing theatre as a weapon in the struggle against Nazism seems naive and pathetic after the Holocaust."[117] Stephen Whitfield strikes a more conciliatory tone. Starting from the premise that "pageants are hybrids of art and propaganda" (in opposition to Reinhardt's aspiration toward "pure art"), he questions our ability to evaluate the power of a work such as this. "Even if the precise effect of *The Eternal Road* cannot be measured, the historian cannot accuse its progenitors of cramped ambitions or of parochial values."[118] Grouping it with Weill's other pageants, he is forced to conclude that "the grandiose hopes that their organizers nourished were unfulfilled. . . . It asks too much of art to expect it to halt tyranny."[119] Most recently, in a monograph that addresses the work's "literary, cultural, and historical significance," Jonathan Friedman locates the problem chiefly with the public at large. The efforts of Weisgal's artists were, he concludes, "doomed to fail," because "the cultural majority" lacked the "desire . . . to change dispositions and confront prejudice." *The Eternal Road* was a "moment in the history of European and American Jewry," he suggests, stressing the piece's political function, "that should have been repeated as often as possible."[120]

These views are all pertinent to the postpremiere history of the work, a history that includes, perhaps not surprisingly, only a handful of attempts at revival. Performing the work has had to confront a number of daunting challenges, chief among them the fact that it is neither possible nor wholly desirable to disengage it from the circumstances that prompted its creation and original purpose. In that sense, it constitutes a far different "stage of exile" from *Die sieben Todsünden,* one of Weill's most frequently revived works (albeit usually unstaged). The challenges posed by *The Eternal Road* are both practical and political. They are practical because of the fluid identity of the piece as reflected in the state of the sources, and political because of the work's ending, insofar as it is the conclusion of the fourth act that not only reflected philosophical differences among the collaborators but also, as a tool of propaganda, was rendered questionable, or at least in need of revision, by history.

Both of these challenges were tackled head on in the only full-length, fully staged revival to date, a production that received its premiere in the German city of Chemnitz on 13 June 1999 (from 1953 to 1990 the city was called Karl-Marx-Stadt). This was ostensibly a reconstruction not of *The Eternal Road* but of *Der Weg der Verheissung,* using Werfel's original German text and including the hitherto unperformed sections of act 4. Edward Harsh reassembled and edited the entire score and, together with composer Noam Sheriff, provided the missing orchestrations. The ending of act 4 was not so much a reconstruction as a dramatic "updating," with direct reference to the Nazi terror. Instead of the congregants being expelled from the synagogue to resume their "eternal road," they are marched off (presumably to their death) by the Gestapo, who shoot the Adversary when he heroically claims to be the Rabbi. Only the Estranged One's Son remains.

Revised or not, the ending could scarcely be anything but controversial. In Chemnitz—and the following year when the production moved to the Brooklyn Academy of Music, with the addition of English subtitles—it seemed to irritate almost everyone in one way or another. There were those who appreciated the revision but found the music inappropriate. Others found the revision itself patronizing. Rodney Milnes perhaps captured both sides best when he wrote, "*Weg* was conceived before the Holocaust, before *Kristallnach*t even. It doesn't quite rise to an occasion that hadn't yet happened. The short jaunty march to which the community marches away at the end is one of those moments that won't quite do."[121]

That Weill undertook subsequent pageants, utilizing material from *The Eternal Road,* attests to the fact that the project begun in 1934 remained a work in progress, mainly for reasons beyond the composer's control. Revival necessarily entails taking into account the various ephemeral aspects of this crucially time-bound work. A transitional "stage of exile," it was literally Weill's passport to his U.S. career, and for that and other reasons a key work. Its religious theme offers a striking contrast with his first "stage of exile," *Die sieben Todsünden,* a work whose religious theme, as discussed above, is utterly ironic. Any room for irony in *The Eternal Road,* at least potentially, occurs through Weill's allusive musical style. Yet here, too, despite the rich mix of styles and stylistic references, Weill largely abandons the more obvious disjunctions between text and music, often entailing the juxtaposition of incongruous cultural markers, that characterize many of his other works, especially those that utilize the so-called song style.

Although his incorporation of traditional Jewish formulae is an unequivocally serious matter, devoid of textual ironies, it remains one style among many, more indicative of Weill's overall approach to composition than of personal identification with the religious content. His background as the son of a cantor no doubt influenced his approach, and his Jewish upbringing in general determined his involvement in the project in a fateful way. Yet the temptation should be resisted to see *The Eternal Road* as either cause or effect of a reconversion to Judaism, as is often suggested (with better reason) in the case of Schoenberg and the composition of his unfinished opera *Moses und Aron*. "There can be no doubt," Alexander Ringer has persuasively argued, that Weill "remained at all times true to himself and his precious heritage." For him, that meant thinking of his "Jewish historical experience" primarily as "a universal lesson, 'never to forget' the enormity of humankind's mindless capacity for cruelty."[122] For Weill, this was as much a socialist as it was a Jewish lesson.

With all of the pageants that dealt with the plight of fellow Jews, not just *The Eternal Road,* Weill's involvement had as much to do with his response, both moral and professional, to the historical moment as it did with his own identity as a Jew. It is worth recalling here what he said in response to the question "What makes Weill Weill?" posed by host Boris Goldowsky during the intermission feature of a radio broadcast from the Metropolitan Opera in 1949: "Looking back on many of my own compositions, I find that I seem to react very strongly to the suffering of underprivileged people, of the oppressed, the persecuted. When my music involves human suffering, it is, for better or worse, pure Weill." This, too, was the spirit in which he became involved in *The Eternal Road* and the other pageants.

Consider, too, in this context his 1946 setting of "Kiddush," dedicated to his father. The text, set in a blues idiom, is the Jewish ceremonial blessing that marks the beginning of the Sabbath or any other Hebrew festival. Why the blues idiom? Perhaps because by invoking a musical "intonation" itself traditionally identified with "the suffering of underprivileged people," Weill could make an ecumenical gesture, beyond any single ethnic identity. That, at least, would be the positive resolution of juxtaposing otherwise incongruous cultural markers. Of personal significance here, too, is the import of inclusive mutual tolerance enshrined in Ruth's words "thy God is my God and thy folk is my folk," set so beautifully as a tango in her duet with Naomi in act 3 of *The Eternal Road.*

Matters of religious and ethnic identity aside, let us return to another of the questions posed at the outset: In what sense were Weill's theatrical aims realized, in what sense not? In spite of the issues it raises as a "stage of exile," but also partly because of them, *The Eternal Road*'s experimental qualities are undeniable. True, it exacted all manner of personal sacrifices from the composer and his collaborators, and hardly produced the balance Weill sought between "inner freedom" and "outer compulsion." Yet it also deserves recognition, to quote the verdict of David

Farneth, as "a novel experiment in [Weill's] search for the integration of drama, music, spoken word, and movement."[123] It made possible Weill's introduction to the world of American theater and his continuation of that search on Broadway. Yet even before his biblical show opened, Weill was busy completing a quite different project, his first "musical play."

9

Musical Plays

If the demands of musical theater are to be at all fulfilled, a play must be conceived from the very beginning as a musical play; the form of the play must be created from the musical point of view.

WEILL, "THE ALCHEMY OF MUSIC"[1]

In the United States, as in Europe, Weill's reforms of musical theater tended to blur rather than affirm generic boundaries. It is no coincidence that the rise in the currency of the umbrella term *musical*—incorporating and thereby rendering redundant the qualification of subgenres such as comedy, play, romance, and farce—occurred during the period of his activity on Broadway. "Musical play" nonetheless retains its significance for his work in its broader as well as in its more specific connotation, as both catch-all and delimiting term.

Because of this inherent ambiguity, "musical play" can be seen to function as the English-language counterpart to the German designation *Stück mit Musik* ("play with music"). By applying English terms to works formerly billed as *Stücke mit Musik,* Weill himself made a conceptual link between the European and American parts of his oeuvre. For example, he came to see *Die Dreigroschenoper* as "a musical play written by Bert Brecht and myself" and *Der Silbersee* as a "serious musical."[2] (Conversely, the sheet music of individual numbers from *Johnny Johnson* described the piece as "A Play with Music.") And in the 1941 interview "I'm an American," he offered a definition of musical play broad enough to encompass his work from both continents:

> It is a form of theatre which combines the elements of drama, musical comedy, ballet and opera. In collaboration with the German dramatists Georg Kaiser and Bert Brecht I had developed this form in the years between 1926 and 1933. Then suddenly all that we had done was wiped out by an iron hand. You can imagine what it meant to me when I arrived in this country and found a theatre full of creative impulse, freedom, technical possibilities—everything I needed to continue where I had left off. Leading playwrights like Paul Green, later Maxwell Anderson and

> recently Moss Hart were interested and willing to try out new forms of the theatre, great actors were looking for new opportunities and the audiences were completely open-minded.[3]

Restrictions to this definition reside in the historical specificity of the term *musical play* as determined by the traditions of Broadway theater, and in the significance of the "musical point of view," as Weill described it. Each piece mixes the ingredients of the musical play differently; there's no fixed formula.

Weill himself did occasionally refer to some of his American works as "musicals," albeit only informally, among them *One Touch of Venus* and *Love Life*. And *Firebrand of Florence*, best described as a Broadway operetta, was actually billed as "a new musical," leaving it unclear whether the modifier *new* referred to the work's substance or merely to its chronology. In the present context of his adapting to the customs of American musical theater, however, the term *musical* seems too broad, if not anachronistic. *Musical play* is surely more fitting as a general descriptor where both the music and the play are the thing. The historical reasons for the preference are also key.

If the term *musical play* is primarily associated with post-*Oklahoma!* shows (from 1943 onward), as *The New Grove Dictionary* has stated—with shows, that is, "in which music, drama and dance aspired to an integrated dramatic whole"—then Weill was surely one of the pioneers of that trend.[4] Alan Jay Lerner, Weill's collaborative dramatist for *Love Life* in 1948, similarly defined the genre with reference to the premiere of *Oklahoma!*, which he described as "a shining tower whose shadow fell on the musical theater from that day forth."

> The book was not a vehicle. The book was a play. The characters were not cartoons; the characters were characters. The music and lyrics, besides being memorable, seemed to flow more from the characters than from the composer and lyricist. And the now celebrated Agnes de Mille [who would soon work on *One Touch of Venus*] created choreography that was not only a brilliant ornament but an even more brilliant dramatic essential. For this was not an operetta, nor a musical comedy. This was a musical play, in which play, music, lyrics and dancing were fused into one living experience. In short, it was a milestone.[5]

Yet Lerner's article also acknowledges the contribution of Weill's early musical plays prior to *Oklahoma!*; these, it says, were "built with sound dramatic bricks" and "making strong advances in the field."

At the same time, if Weill's attitude toward tradition is reflected in the labels he used, that is only because there is a productive tension between implication and realization or, seen from the audience's as opposed to the author's perspective, between expectation and fulfillment. Genre, comprehensively defined, is a form of social contract. Mixed genres, in creating such tension, potentially destabilize or undermine the contract. Transcending generic conventions has social and sociological, even politically subversive, implications. Novelty may be liberating in more than just an aesthetic sense.

With generic labels going only so far, appearances are inevitably deceptive. *Love Life,* whose billing as a "vaudeville" seemingly (but only seemingly) belies both the coherence and originality of its conception, is perhaps the most striking but by no means the sole example. *A Kingdom for a Cow* is anomalous for different reasons. Really a satirical operetta, it was billed as a "musical play," chiefly for publicity reasons. Such issues also obtained on Broadway, of course, where producers as well as audiences harbored skepticism toward any label that included the word *opera* or even *operetta.*

Soon after his arrival in the United States, Weill described his creative task as a reformer of musical theater in the following terms: "The musical theater as it exists today consists on the one hand of the opera completely isolated from drama and on the other hand of musical comedy, which is to say a handful of topical events surrounding a group of hit songs. Without contesting the right to existence of both of these veins, since both have their audiences, it can be said that a reestablishment of the true musical theater is scheduled to take place inside of the enormous territory between the two genres."[6] The appeal to an ideal, a "true" form yet to be realized—or rather, realized again, after a hiatus—is characteristic. Weill says "reestablished," thereby suggesting the ideal had once existed. It is a notion familiar from Busoni's ideas about musical theater, as is the awareness expressed of a historical moment to be seized.

More than a decade devoted to American theater did little to change that view. In 1947, at the time of *Street Scene,* Weill wrote: "Through this show [*Johnny Johnson*] I learned a great deal about Broadway and its audience. I discovered that a vast, unexploited field lay between grand opera and musical comedy."[7] This was the territory not just of his musical plays but of all his principal American works. As he put it in 1950, "Ever since I started in Germany, my main interest has been somewhere between musical comedy and the opera."[8] Of those works written expressly for Broadway theaters, however, only one was actually labeled "musical play"—*Lady in the Dark. Knickerbocker Holiday,* which began as a "play with music," ended up as "a new musical comedy." *One Touch of Venus,* later referred to as a "musical comedy," initially had no designation. According to Weill's own definition, none of his theater pieces was ever merely "a handful of topical events surrounding a group of hit songs," although they could contain those elements, too. The "American opera" *Street Scene,* which includes its share of topical events and hit songs, is no less anomalous. (Here, too, several labels were considered, before the final one stuck.) Although it is the closest of the Broadway works to the operatic end of the spectrum, *Street Scene* is nonetheless far from being "completely isolated from drama." *Lost in the Stars* could also count as a "musical play" in the more general sense; yet Weill and Anderson chose to call it a "musical tragedy."

Despite his sometimes promiscuous use of them in private, the labels were as much a challenge for the composer and his collaborators as they were for his critics—that much is clear from the works' genesis and reception. In order to be useful as a general description, then, "musical play" has to be as capacious as "play with music" was. Using it more narrowly would imply a generic uniformity that Weill's works resist.

Contrary to the tradition to which Weill was keen to adapt, and as the quotation that heads this chapter suggests, "musical play" need not exclude its usual complement, "musical comedy." Given as he was throughout his career to satire and irony, and hence to juxtaposing or mixing the comic and the serious, he felt that "one of the most difficult form problems of contemporary playwrights is the balancing of the opposed values of humor and tragedy without having one destroy the other. . . . I have seen numerous plays," he wrote, "where I was unable to rise sympathetically to the dramatic climaxes of the story because the previous humorous scenes had not prepared me for them at all." The musical play, he thought, afforded special opportunities for mixing theatrical genres: "The author can mingle these elements with far greater freedom; his comic scenes can be more comic, his tragic more tragic, since music creates the balance." The presence of music informed both content and form: "The action of the musical play must be more pliable than that of sheer drama, so that lyrics can be planted; the suspense is created not so much through the progress of the action as through the dynamics of the epic tale; and psychology, which has been such an intrinsic feature of drama during recent decades, is replaced by simple, human, universal events."[9]

Nor did he limit the term *musical play* to the institution of the theater. The work that eventually became his "folk opera" *Down in the Valley* was initially conceived as one of "a series of musical plays around folk tunes for radio programs."[10] Distinctions between genres are significant, as reflected in the labels. Nonetheless, as a "theatrical composer," as opposed to a "symphonic composer," Weill found outlets for his ideas in a variety of forms and media.[11] "Musical play" connotes a play that has been "musicalized" in accordance with his aesthetic precepts.[12] The same can be said for his conceptions of film, also informed by those precepts. Conversely, the film adaptations of his musical plays largely entail a process that can be described as "demusicalization." Although there's no fixed formula, even within a single genre, the underlying precepts remain fairly consistent, regardless of the medium.

Taken together, Weill's four main contributions to the genre of the American "musical play"—*Johnny Johnson, Knickerbocker Holiday, Lady in the Dark* and *One Touch of Venus*—illustrate the striking variety of his conceptions and document the steady rise to prominence of a composer determined to succeed in his adopted country. In view of that variety, *Love Life* and *Lost in the Stars* more or less belong in this context, too, differing in degree rather than kind from their predecessors. Chiefly for reasons of chronology, however (both are from Weill's last years), they are discussed separately in the final chapter.

JOHNNY JOHNSON

The first piece Weill conceived expressly for the American theater owes its creation to long delays in the production of *The Eternal Road.* During this time he came into contact with members of the Group Theatre, a collective dedicated to presenting contemporary plays that dealt with social issues. Founded in 1931 by Harold Clurman, Cheryl Crawford, and Lee Strasberg, the Group remained in existence for ten years, staging some two dozen new plays, including *The House of Connelly* (1931, by Paul Green), *Men in White* (1933, by Sidney Kingsley), and *Waiting for Lefty* (1935, by Clifford Odets). As the fifteenth production, a collaboration between Weill and the American playwright Paul Green, *Johnny Johnson* came in the middle of that history, receiving its premiere at the 44th Street Theater on 19 November 1936, just under two months before the premiere of *The Eternal Road.*

Weill worked closely with Green and with other members of the Group, and contributed a substantial amount of vocal and instrumental music, not all of which found its way either into the premiere production or into the productions that followed soon thereafter (although the Los Angeles production mounted by the Federal Theater Project in May–July 1937 came close to including all the music). For some of the music he contributed to *Johnny Johnson* he drew on earlier compositions, thereby continuing a practice quite prevalent in the immediately preceding works.

The encounter with the Group Theatre amounted to a meeting of sympathetic, if not entirely compatible, minds. Despite perhaps inevitable obstacles, the collaboration proved successful enough to convince Weill of a future in the American theater. Activities with the Group can be reconstructed from a number of sources, including biographical accounts either by or about the Group's founders. Especially rich in information are two studies: W. David Sievers's 1944 master's dissertation, "The Group Theatre of New York City, 1931–1941," which provides potted accounts of each of the Group's productions based chiefly on contemporaneous published sources; and Wendy Smith's *Real Life Drama: The Group Theatre and America, 1931–1940,* which draws on an array of sources, including autobiographies and oral histories.[13]

In his prologue, Sievers describes how Clurman's dreams for the revitalization of American dramatic art crystallized while he was studying in France in the mid-1920s. It is there that Clurman developed his interest in European men of the theater, an interest shared by actor and fellow countryman Strasberg, with whom Clurman came into contact at the time. Together Clurman and Strasberg developed their vision of American theater in terms of a synthesis of their European idols' ideas: the ideas of Jacques Copeau, Gordon Craig, and Stanislavsky.

Meanwhile, both men continued their professional work as actors, performing in plays staged by the Theatre Guild. Through this work they came into contact with Crawford, an actress turned director and producer. (In the mid-1940s Crawford would found the American Repertory Theatre and create the Actor's Studio, which trained Marlon Brando, James Dean, and Bea Arthur, among others; she would also work again with Weill as producer of *One Touch of Venus* and *Love Life*.) After initial get-togethers on their own, the three of them began to hold public meetings at Steinway Hall in New York, where they discussed their reform ideas with hundreds of actors. Maxwell Anderson, with whom Weill would soon become close friends and also collaborate, came to one of those events, approving of "the idea of a permanent, integrated theater-group that would have the time and the solidity to make consecutive progress, to train actors and playwrights."[14]

Because training was considered as important as actual performing, membership of the collective involved participation in workshops, not just productions. After he was introduced by Crawford and Clurman to Paul Green, and several months before the premiere of *Johnny Johnson,* Weill took part in one of the regular summer workshops in Connecticut. Evidence of his contribution to the proceedings has survived in two important documents: the composer's own notes, prepared for the lecture he gave on 27 July 1936, and a typed transcription of notes taken at the lecture itself by one of the Group's members, Tony Kraber (stage name: Gerrit Kraber).[15] Because the two sets of notes are quite similar, in places identical, Weill must have followed his own set fairly closely.

Weill's lecture deserves scrutiny as a document of his thinking about musical theater at a crucial point in his career, as he reflects on his European achievements and, pending the realization of *The Eternal Road,* seeks to establish himself in the new context of American theater. Dealing with what his notes call "principal questions" (probably a literal, unidiomatic translation of *Grundsatzfragen;* Kraber renders this as "principles"), the composer reflects on his own experiences in musical theater and, in so doing, echoes much that he had formulated in earlier writings. Hardly surprising, perhaps, the lecture can be seen to relate most closely to the essay "The Alchemy of Music," written in the same year. Yet it also deals with performance matters scarcely touched on in the published essay.

The first paragraph of Weill's notes, where he states his own understanding of the Group's significance, is crossed out. Nor does that paragraph seem to have been used, as Kraber's notes corroborate, making only a brief reference to *Johnny Johnson* as the Group's "1st musical production" and the need to cover the theory and practice of "music in the theatre." Here's what Weill at least planned to say:

> The idea of the Group Theatre is the only way to create and cultivate a theatre art which will exist by itself and which cannot be touched by the success of movies, radio, television etc. Since the German theatre culture has been destroyed, there are, with the exception of the Russian theatre, not many Group theatres left in the world. That's why I am happy to be with you. I feel that I can here at least continue what I have built up in Europe, that I can bring to you my experiences and be certain that you will use them in the right way, and that your experiences will be helpful to me in my efforts towards the goal which I have set for me since the beginning of my career: the creation of a musical theatre for our time.

Among his "principal questions" Weill lists his opposition to "l'art pour l'art" and to "art which is a luxury for a few chosen people." That's hardly new. His solution—and here he begins a brief synopsis of his career thus far—is "popular art, which has a real appeal to the masses and which at the same time gives the masses something to think about, to learn, to comprehend." Conceived in terms of his own experience, he describes his ideal as contrary to the "idealism" of the nineteenth century, when artists believed they should "create eternal works, which could not be understood by their contemporaries" because "the artists wanted to be original." He later asserts, not without a little self-contradiction, that his *Dreigroschenoper* made musicians realize that "one can write simple music without giving up originality." Originality, then, is not the real problem, so much as a challenge. How to remain original without isolating oneself?

He rejects opera's status, as he did at the time of *Dreigroschenoper,* as "an aristocratic art." His rejection leads him "to leave the opera house" and "to go to the theatre." Without strict adherence to chronology, he outlines his own development as turning away from opera and then gradually returning to it. Defining the first tendency are: *Die Dreigroschenoper* ("the first opera for actors"), *Happy End, Mahagonny* (presumably the full-length version rather than the "Songspiel"), and *Silbersee.* "The way back to opera" is defined by the following group: *Der Jasager* ("model-opera"), *Bürgschaft* ("epic opera with social idea, sentence of Marx, proved by 3 stories of the life of two men"), *Die sieben Todsünden* ("ballet-opera"; Weill uses the title of the British premiere: *Anna-Anna*), *A Kingdom for a Cow* ("operetta"), and *Eternal Road* ("mysterium-opera"). This last work he describes as the "most consequent [i.e., consistent, as in the German word *konsequent*] amalgamation of singing and talking, of actor and singer." Another division defining the dynamic of his development is the difference, noted in the margin of the notes, between two kinds of works: those that use "actors who sing" and those that use "singers who act."

Dividing Weill's works according to these criteria—moving away from opera and back again; using either actors who can sing or singers who can act—is complicated by factors other than purely chronological ones. He continues to produce plays with music alongside works that signal a "return to opera." The latter group is not wholly the preserve of "singers who act" but also includes "actors who sing," such as Lenya in *Die sieben Todsünden.* By the same token, although the *Mahagonny-Songspiel* was conceived exclusively for singers, that changed with Lenya's last-minute inclusion. According to these criteria, *Eternal Road* was also mixed, an "amalgamation," as Weill says. Lenya was Weill's middle point in this regard, if not his blind spot. For him, she was both actor and singer, the center from which his works could go in either direction, toward and away from opera. (The part she would take as the Duchess in *The Firebrand of Florence* was considered by many, though not by Weill, to be miscast.) If he was referring not to the "Songspiel" as a member of the group to "leave opera," but rather to the full-length version of *Mahagonny,* this complicates the scheme to the point of making it irrelevant. The work was at once a departure and a return to opera, an ambiguity that no doubt contributes to its appeal.

Weill's distinctions are idealistic conceptions rather than clear-cut definitions, an attempt to capture tendencies and goals rather than pinpoint realities. The operas he lists are all qualified ("model," "epic," "ballet," "operetta," "mysterium"). *Dreigroschenoper* subverts the norm; it's an "opera for actors." Nothing is clear-cut. He draws his extreme, negative boundaries, in American terms: as "Metropolitan: worst example of old fashioned opera (museum)," on the one hand, and as "musical comedy, which tried to be sophisticated and low brow at the same time" with "nothing in between," on the other. His purpose, however, is clear: to stake out in positive terms the "enormous field," as he describes it, that he wants his work to occupy. The central point here is that musical theater of the kind he wishes to cultivate is "poetic theatre," which he sees as an antithesis to "realistic theatre."

Music, Weill says, "makes it possible to introduce the romantic element in modern theater as a new expression of modern life." Music "brings together the elements of theater: the idea, the humor, the sentiment." As in "The Alchemy of Music," he emphasizes music's role in creating "fantasy" and "unreality." He mentions, in an almost Schopenhauerian moment, "the powers behind man speaking through music," citing as examples "Goddess of liberty, canons." This is an explicit reference to two moments in *Johnny Johnson.* Music "is not descriptive," he concludes (Schopenhauer would have said "not representational"). He also reasserts another basic tenet of his musical theater, the primacy of song: "The action of the play comes to a point where a song can express the philosophie *[sic],* the general aspect of the scene."

With his insistence on "the romantic element" it might be suspected that

Weill is signaling a shift away from the anti-Romantic stance he had forcefully adopted in the late 1920s. Christian Kuhnt has made this very point, comparing a statement made by Weill in his 1928 essay "Der Musiker Weill" with one made in 1936 in "The Alchemy of Music." Kuhnt cites from the earlier essay the rejection of "extramusical content" as well as Weill's refusal to "convey philosophies," "depict external events" and "create atmospheres."[16] By way of contrast, he cites two passages from the 1936 essay: "Music can aid, for example, in restoring the romantic element, which the modern theater has had to do without for so long," a passage echoed in the lecture; and "Music can do what the greatest performer does at the height of his playing: it can win over the spectator with passion, it can create an exalted mood, which makes the poet's fantasy so much simpler to follow and accept."

Yet it would be wrong to construe the later text as amounting to an apostasy. Weill nowhere states that music should depict external events. On the contrary, he reasserts its nondescriptive nature. And a statement such as the following could be seen as perfectly consonant with his earlier, Busonian position: "In the musical theater the author is much better able to remain within the bounds of reality because the music assumes the task of widening and deepening the range of effects, of illuminating the action from within, of making the implications and the universality of the events clear to the spectator. Thus the musical theater creates a basic extension of the material of drama."[17] Weill had always held to the Busonian precept of where music had a place in the theater, where singing had a part to play, as opposed to speaking. Apropos *Die Dreigroschenoper* he stated: "With every musical work for the stage the question arises: how is music, particularly song, at all possible in the theater? I had a realistic plot, so I had to set the music against it, since I do not consider music capable of realistic effects."[18] In this he was echoing Busoni's conviction about the moments at which music is indispensable on the stage: "During dances, marches and songs—and when the supernatural enters the plot."

Nor should Weill's 1936 views have to be seen as revoking his basic commitment to an ideal of absolute music, conceived in Busonian (not Hanslickian) terms. What seems to have shifted is his anti-Wagnerian stance. Rather than define the ideal of his own theater negatively, in terms of what it is not, he is offering a largely positive definition. Anti-Wagnerian rhetoric would have been quite superfluous in the new American context. In Germany, that rhetoric informed not just the programmatic statements, but the music itself, especially during the period 1928–30. *Dreigroschenoper* was "the most thorough-going reaction to Wagner . . . the complete destruction of the concept of music drama."[19]

The 1928 essay "Der Musiker Weill" needs to be seen in terms of both its relationship to the other writings and its purpose; it is perhaps the closest Weill came to echoing Brecht's polemical position, a position he adopted in that particular essay in a somewhat ironic spirit, as the outpourings of an authoritarian schoolteacher. Weill's anti-Romantic views concerned principally his attitude toward musical form and toward the audience. In neither respect had he changed, although his views about audience reaction appear to have softened. Nor would it be hard to demonstrate that his actual practice, even in 1928, undermined the affected austerity of his theoretical position.

Kuhnt presses his case as part of his discussion of Weill's Second Symphony, a work that received its premiere in Amsterdam under Bruno Walter on 11 October 1934 as "Symphonische Fantasie" and its second performance in New York as "Three Night Scenes: A Symphonic Fantasy." He sees a contradiction between Weill's two descriptions of the work in the program note for the premiere—between, that is, "a piece of 'absolute' Music" and "the opposite of 'Pastoral.'" He finds it "surprising" that Weill would offer "an example for reading his work."[20] The example is one Weill hesitatingly quotes from "a Parisian female friend." Here is the passage in full: "It is not possible for me to say anything about the 'content' of the work, since it was conceived as a purely musical form. Perhaps the words of a Parisian female friend are right, who said that if a word existed that expressed the opposite of 'Pastoral,' that would be the title of this music. I don't know.[21]

There is much to unpack here. Weill is hardly embracing the idea of program music. Not only does he qualify the idea of his "female friend" (if she ever existed) with "I don't know," but he is also making a reference to Beethoven's Sixth, in which regard Beethoven's famous statement about "more feeling than painting" should be recalled (Kuhnt himself recalls it). Be that as it may, there are musical conventions for expressing the pastoral mode, and Weill makes copious use of them in his works, including in *Johnny Johnson*. By the same token, there are means to express the "opposite of 'Pastoral,'" without concrete programmatic implications.

Kuhnt's formalistic conception of the "purely musical" is not the same as Weill's, as can be seen from Weill's program note: "I believe that the most consummate theater musician from time to time feels the urge to create a piece of 'absolute' music. Since real theater music also needs to hold up as 'music per se,' it is very enticing to control the musical forms and style elements discovered in connection with verbal and scenic representation through the kind of work whose realization pursues a purely musical purpose, that is, in a concert."

For Weill, schooled in Busoni's "unity of music," there is no fundamental difference between theater and concert music. Transferring musical styles and idioms from the theater to the concert hall does not in itself bespeak any programmatic intention, at least in a representational sense. For Weill, as the quotation from the program note makes clear, "purely musical" refers merely to the use of the music as "absolute" music, a music free from any scenic or vocal context.

That Weill should hint at the expressive character of the music in no way detracts from that view. Nor, therefore, should it be "surprising," as Kuhnt asserts, that an understanding of the work demand "an analysis that goes beyond purely musical questions." "Purely musical" is not, for Weill, synonymous with a formalistic aesthetics. The music of the symphony may remind listeners such as Kuhnt of some of the theater works, almost to the point of quotation. But that is because of Weill's approach to composition in general, an approach grounded in the use of conventional musical rhetoric. True, he does include a melody in the first movement of the symphony whose march gestures and melodic contours may recall the "Ballad of Caesar's Death" from *Der Silbersee.* Partly no doubt because its composition overlapped with *Die sieben Todsünden,* there are a number of similarities between passages in these two works. And there are various other allusions, including from *Aufstieg und Fall der Stadt Mahagonny,* some of which Kuhnt catalogues, arguing that these references to "themes and motives" are "concretely occupied *[besetzt]* in terms of content." In this way, Kuhnt contends that Weill derives "extramusical material" from experiences. These experiences, he suggests, are processed in musical terms and create associations that can be understood as an "anti-idyll" or "the opposite of 'Pastoral.'"[22]

The question remains: how concretely is the material marked or "occupied," even the material that is quoted almost verbatim? Several qualifications are in order. The first, quite obvious one is that the interpretation will not be shared by those unaware of the associations; that includes above all those not familiar with the works alluded to, and even some who are. In such cases, any concrete program, if conceived as such by the composer, remains secret. David Drew has argued that Weill himself was not aware of what he was doing, referring to the symphony as a form of "unconscious leave-taking."[23]

One also needs to consider the topic of Weill's self-borrowings more generally. The symphony is hardly an isolated example of his reusing material from earlier works. He did so frequently. The works quoted verbatim tend to be those that received little exposure in his lifetime. *Happy End* is one such work; *Die Bürgschaft* another; *Der Silbersee* yet another. There is doubtless more than one reason why he should do this. Apart from pressures of time, and not wanting a perfectly good tune to go to waste, by drawing on little-known works he may have been hoping to avoid precisely the associations to which Kuhnt alludes. One could argue, rather, that the musical language is already marked, not because of the works in which it is employed, but in terms of its expressive content. Such "markedness" is certainly one reason, if not the sole reason, it was employed in the first place. The new works provide an opportunity for redeployment.

No less important is the abiding irony of Weill's inventions: music and text are rarely congruous. Idyllic music often underscores far from idyllic situations. In order to express "the opposite of 'Pastoral'" in a texted work, he may use pastoral music. Robbed of its text and presented in an "absolute" way, music may thus function quite differently from its original context.

Lastly, nearly all of his works, if not all of his music, treat the topic of cities, not the countryside. In that, too, they are "the opposite" of pastoral.

Johnny Johnson, Weill's most strident antiwar piece, is replete with musical material that echoes earlier works—sometimes extensive borrowings, at other times brief musical gestures previously employed in other contexts. The first and most literal borrowing is the instrumental Introduction, which reuses the melody of "Das Lied vom Branntweinhändler" from *Happy End.* (In similar fashion, *Marie Galante* had drawn on three songs from *Happy End,* including "Das Lied vom Branntweinhändler." The other two are the brief chorus "In der Jugend gold'nem Schimmer," borrowed for the main melody of the Introduction, and "Das Lied von der harten Nuss.") As the opening of Weill's first American work, the borrowing makes for a striking connection with his German oeuvre, the "Stück mit Musik" feeding into the "musical play." As with parts of Weill's Symphony, it is music that originally served a vocal context and is reused in an instrumental one. But unlike the Symphony, the new context here is not "absolute"; it is scenic and dramatic, as indicated in the version of the play that Green published in 1937.[24]

Although it does not always reflect what was actually done in the theater, Green's text preserves a large amount of stage business from the first production. After the initial fanfare, which Green describes as "the slightly mock-heroic overture," the new version of the melody from *Happy End* evidently accompanied an expository pantomime; and the same music, differently orchestrated, recurs during the first scene. Green's description of the stage setting and the action fills two full pages of text, beginning with a motto that quotes the opening line of the "Asylum Chorus": "How sweetly friendship binds." The reference is surely sardonic.

As in the chorus, whose melody invokes the classic pastoral topic of the siciliano, thereby reflecting the peace and happiness enjoyed by the inmates of the asylum to which Johnny Johnson has been admitted because of his antiwar views, Green begins with a pastoral scene: "A hill-top outside a small American town—April 1917."[25]

> The curtain rises on the level and clean-swept top of a little hill. The ground is covered with a carpet of green grass, and at the right front a quaint young arbor-vitae tree is growing. In the middle background is a funeral obelisk monument about ten feet high and draped in a dark low-hanging cloth. At the left is a naïve and homemade example of the Star-Spangled Banner hanging down from a hoe-handle staff which stands stuck in the ground. It is a beautiful day in spring, and far beyond the obelisk and far beyond the scene stretches the blue and light-filled sky with here and there a tiny billowy cloud hanging motionless in it.

EXAMPLE 38. *Johnny Johnson,* Introduction

EXAMPLE 39. *Happy End,* "Das Lied vom Branntweinhändler"

Weill's "Branntweinhändler" melody, presented initially as a mellifluous trombone solo accompanied by lilting woodwind and string accompaniment, expresses this idyllic mood (ex. 38, m. 9). But what about the preceding "mock-heroic" fanfare alluded to by Green? Comparison with the *Happy End* original reveals that it, too, is taken from the same song. The rhythm (not the melody) is identical to the chanting passage of the song's brief middle section: "An die Gewehre, Seele in Not" ("Take to arms, soul in distress") (ex. 39). In other words, Weill's self-borrowing nicely captures the pastoral gesture of the opening, and counterpoints this with an apt intertextual reference that is related to a principal theme of *Johnny Johnson,* the antagonism between war and spiritual well-being.

Green achieves an analogous juxtaposition by first painting a pastoral scene that accompanies celebrations of the southern American town's two hundredth anniversary and the consecration of a new peace monument fabricated by Johnny Johnson ("our gentle-hearted friend and artisan and tombstone carver of the skillful hand"), before moving to the announcement of President Wilson's declaration of war with Germany. (The town's inhabitants will just as soon sing a chorus to war as they will to peace, and to the same patriotic march tune.) Weill provides the ensuing contrast at the outset through antithetical gestures, one deriving from a belligerent march, the other peacefully lyrical. The reference to the earlier work must remain a relatively arcane matter, of course. That Weill seems to have found inspiration for the initial measures of *Johnny Johnson* in his earlier setting of Brecht's lines from *Happy End* is relevant more to the Introduction's genesis than to what the music might signify. The salient point is rather that the juxtaposed gestures and the musical language informing them are common to both works. Later in the piece, Weill similarly reemploys musical gestures from other works, among them *A Kingdom for a Cow, Der Silbersee,* and *Marie Galante.* In addition to dance types such as waltz and fox-trot, he also makes quite extensive use of familiar pieces of vernacular music, such as the "La Marseillaise" and "You're in the Army Now" and the bugle calls "Reveille" and "First Call," as part of the dramatic context.

Combined with newly appropriated American elements, notably the cowboy idiom of "Captain Valentine's Song" and the popular American song form of "Johnny's Song," the mix of musical styles is remarkably varied, even by Weill's eclectic standards. Besides enhancing the international character of the antiwar theme, which involves German, French, and British as well as American elements, such extreme diversity lends parts of the drama the feel of a revue with vaudevillian moments.

The work's subtitle, which changed several times, conveys nothing about what kind of "musical play" *Johnny Johnson* is. At its premiere, it was called "a Legend." Green's 1937 published text changes that to "The Biography of a Common Man"; other variants included the adjective "Kindly" instead of "Common," as well as "Good-Natured" and "Friendly." In each case the subtitle describes the content, not the form, which is hard to pin down. In his review of the premiere, the first of two notices he wrote for the *New York Times,* Brooks Atkinson provided multiple descriptions that effectively conveyed the confusion of the generic mix. The play, he wrote, is "part fantasy, part musical satire, part symbolic poetry, in the common interests of peace . . . part good and part bad, since new forms cannot be created overnight . . . a marriage of musical comedy and picaresque story-telling."[26]

Johnny Johnson is an everyman figure, so called because his was the most common name among American conscripts during the First World War. (Several commentators have talked in terms of an "American Schweik," which seems to have been Weill's initial idea for the piece, as he later claimed.) From his southern home Johnny embarks on an odyssey that begins with his enlistment in Woodrow Wilson's "war to end wars," justified at the time as a crusade "to make the world safe for democracy." As a soldier on the front in France facing the appalling realities of war, he attempts to put an end to armed combat with the help of laughing gas, whereupon he is committed to an asylum. After his release he becomes a maker of children's toys, selling his wares on the street.

For Johnny, the personal is political. Framing the drama is the sad fate of his love for Minny Belle Tompkins, who is presented during the pantomime that accompanies the Introduction as "a vision of loveliness with her golden hair, baby limpid eyes, and doll-like face." Johnny has to deal with a rival, Anguish Howington, Minny Belle's other suitor, who is described at the beginning as "a gangling young man resembling the stage undertaker type." Minny Belle and Anguish, who feature as prominent characters in Johnny's private life, symbolically represent all those citizens of American democracy who uncritically and opportunistically go along with the status quo. Johnny, by contrast, is the kind-hearted idealist who doesn't fit in—humanity as it should be rather than is.

At the very end, many years later, when he happens to encounter Minny Belle again, it turns out she has married Anguish, who has become mayor. She is accompanying her son, Anguish Howington, Jr., who wants to buy a toy soldier from Johnny. "No—no—I don't make soldiers," Johnny says sternly. Following this pathetic scene, and to quote one of the few pieces of stage business included in the piano-vocal score: "At the end of the play the American Legion band plays 'Democracy Advancing,' No. 3. [The actual title of the number in the piano-vocal score is "Democracy's Call."] They march off. Johnny is alone, there is a moment of silence, then the orchestra starts playing softly the introductory bars to 'Johnny's Song,' and Johnny sings." As a reminder of the opening scene's pomp and circumstance, this brief musical reminiscence creates a stark and ironic contrast to the title song, with which the show concludes.

Although the nature and extent of the musical contribution to the play fluctuated during the work's multifaceted history—a history that comprises the fraught production process, the initial run, and subsequent productions, including one by the Federal Theater Project in Los Angeles and another by the same organization in Boston, as well as the various published and unpublished sources—music was always an essential part of the conception. Weill himself stressed its antirealistic contribution in his comments on that conception by drawing particular attention to the "Song of the Goddess" and the "Song of the Guns." The former comes after Johnny's speech to the Statue of Liberty, in which he addresses her as "Mother of Liberty" and pledges that "neither by a look, a thought, or word will

I fail either you or Minny Belle." Liberty responds in her two-part song by first intoning her regret at having been "used to send men forth to die" and then, to the strains of Weill's "Youkali," longing for the day when "men and all their hates are done and deep in the earth I sleep again."

Ronald Sanders has likened the primal quality of the Statue's appearance to the moment when Erda rises up and addresses Wotan in Wagner's *Siegfried*. The quotation of the melody of "Youkali," a sensuous tango about a land of dreams and desires that doesn't exist, adds a bitter note of irony. "The melody is so beautiful," Sanders remarks, "that for a moment one thinks one is in that better world all the same."[27]

The "Song of the Guns," sung by (male-voice) cannons to the sleeping soldiers, was intended to have a similar effect, as Weill himself explained. "My idea was this: instead of doing what most composers would do—make the music grim and stark, with timpani and such devices—I wanted it to be seducing, almost sweet, as if sung perhaps by prostitutes. For cannons are like prostitutes; their metal would have been used to better purposes, and moreover they do anybody's bidding, right or wrong. They say to the soldiers: 'you sleep, we do the work for you.' The music should [be] almost a lullaby."[28]

Above all, the idea of having "Johnny's Song" recur at various places in the show implicates music as integral to the work's large-scale organization. That the complete sung version does not emerge until the very end reflects the protagonist's evolution as well as his essential humanity. (This is a dramaturgical idea that Weill would employ again to great effect in *Lady in the Dark*.) Here the song also serves to summarize the play's idealistically pacifist message.

When man was first created
I'm sure his maker meant
Him for some good intent,
Kind heart and love, forgiving wrong.

And though through ages fated
To climb our wandering way,
At last we'll find the day
When joy shall be our song.

One of Weill's first essays in the genre of American popular song, "Johnny's Song" has a form that is hardly standard, at least in the culminating complete version that concludes the play.[29] There is no introductory verse, a conventional feature that Weill will include in some (though by no means all) of the songs composed for later Broadway works. Although this absence is hardly unorthodox, the disposition of the "chorus" section certainly is. The standard chorus form is AABA, with B constituting the contrasting "bridge" or "release" and the repeats of A somewhat varied. Here, however, the form can be summarized as

AABACAD, with the formal function of C and D ambiguous, in that these two sections serve both as additional releases and as concluding gestures. The first "release" (B) provides both textual and musical contrast:

I hear them say it's all baloney
The world's a mighty cruel place
With tooth and claw and promise phoney,
An old hard guy he wins the race.

The return of A is addressed, as indicated in the published piano-vocal score, "*To the Audience*":

But you and I don't think so,
We know there's something still
Of good beyond such ill
Within our heart and mind.

The first additional release (C), which reinforces the collective sentiment, is written in the style of a homophonic anthem with steadily plodding bass:

And we'll never lose our faith and hope
And trust in all mankind.
We'll work and strive
While we're alive
That better way to find.

The second return of the main melody makes reference again to Johnny's song (earlier "our song"):

As up and down I wander
My weary way and long,
I meet all kinds of folks
Who listen to my song.

Following this is a dancelike instrumental section (D), part extra release, part coda, over which Johnny, resorting to speech, wistfully describes his new trade: "Toys, toys, for nice little girls and boys. Toys, toys . . ."

In an interview conducted with his longtime assistant, Rhoda Wynn, Green recalled Weill's telling him, "If we can send the audience out humming a melody . . . it will be like a leitmotif, you know, that Wagner thing." More important than "that Wagner thing" from the Broadway standpoint is the fact that the number is supposed to function as the work's "title song." Unusual in this case, however, is the placement within the play of the complete version. (In its sheet-music form, as discussed below, "Johnny's Song" acquires new lyrics as well as a new title.) In the play the song evolves from an instrumental interlude for solo banjo later in act 1, to brief reminiscence in act 2, to the most complex version at the end. How this actually played out varied in performance (in 1971 Green included a sung version in act 1 as well). Nor are the published sources consistent in placing the song within the whole. The principle of the song reappearing at different points in the play, however, remains. "The thing to do," Green said, is "sum up the whole philosophy of this play into the musical statement at the end."[30] In that sense, the "song" that Johnny refers to is not so much the musical number he happens to be singing as it is what his character and his story (the "legend") stand for—"the whole philosophy," as Green says, that the music is supposed to encapsulate.

In the same interview, Green also said: "Kurt Weill told me earlier that he had written a melody in Europe . . . and he wanted to use it . . . it was a beautiful melody, but complicated." Weill may well have may been alluding to an earlier version of "Johnny's Song" (to a quite different text) that J. Bradford Robinson has identified and described as a "dramatized theater song" *(dramatisiertes Theaterlied),* as opposed to a mere "hit song" *(Schlagerlied).* The reference seems plausible, except that the draft was likely composed in America, not in Europe.[31] The "earlier melody" could also have referred to "J'attends un navire," a song originally written for the "play with music" *Marie Galante* (and which would later become known on its own as an anthem of the French resistance). Certainly, the initial melody of "Johnny's Song" is similar to "J'attends," as several commentators have noted. But that is only one of the borrowings. The instrumental coda of "Johnny's Song," although rhythmically a fox-trot, recalls the tango that originated as incidental music for *Marie Galante,* later known with its own lyrics as "Youkali/Tango-Habañera"; it is also quoted, as mentioned, in the "Song of the Goddess." The material of "Johnny's Song" is, in sum, truly syncretic, drawn from a variety of sources, including earlier compositions, and at once lyrical, hymn-like, and inflected by the rhythms of contemporary dance music.

Weill wanted to send the people out of the theater humming "Johnny's Song," and in a letter to Max Dreyfus of the music publishing firm Chappell dated 20 December 1936 he claimed not only that the members of the audience were humming the music but that their doing so "is, I think, internationally the best test for the success of a music."[32] He admitted, however, that "we had difficulties in the beginning because we did not have the right material."

Before it could be issued as sheet music in a popular adaptation, the title song of *Johnny Johnson* had to be given new lyrics (by Edward Heyman); it even received a new title in the process. The dramatized theater song that preaches "faith and hope and trust in all mankind" was transformed into a more conventional love ballad, "To Love You and to Lose You." Curiously enough, in the 1937 published text, Paul Green also expunged the words of "Johnny's Song" at the end of the play and instead has Johnny "whistling his song again—a little more clearly now, a little more bravely." Also missing from his text is the "Song of the

Goddess," following Johnny's speech to the Statue of Liberty; it had been cut from the premiere, along with other parts of the score, despite Weill's repeatedly emphasizing its importance for his conception of the work.

Several reasons can be cited for the various cuts made during the production process and initial run. One reason is running time: the Group had too much material for a show of standard length. Another is the perhaps inevitable tension between composer, playwright, and director. Deriving from notions of epic theater and the gestic character of music, as evinced in his comments about the "Song of the Guns," Weill's antirealistic musicalizing conception of the play stood in stark contrast to the approach of Lee Strasberg, whose Stanislavskian training in spoken theater predisposed him toward naturalism. (Recall Weill's replacement of "psychology," "an intrinsic feature of drama during recent decades," by "simple, human, universal events.") Elia Kazan, who would direct Weill's *One Touch of Venus* and *Love Life,* remarked in his memoirs that Strasberg was not "suited for . . . material" that was "supposed to be funny" and that he "directed wearing a psychological straightjacket."[33] And in his second review of the premiere production, generally more enthusiastic than the first, Brooks Atkinson felt obliged to comment that "the Group Theatre actors are lacking in the comic spirit."[34]

By all accounts, the production process was fraught, bringing to the fore rifts in the leadership of the Group that would lead to its temporary dissolution after the show. Yet another reason for the cuts was the size of the 44th Street Theater, which proved too large for the untrained voices of the Group's cast. As Clurman recalled: "Many of the musical numbers were cut—in a smaller theatre they need not have been."[35] The initial previews were a disaster. Clurman remembered them as "the most distressing experiences I have ever gone through in the theatre . . . After the first five minutes of the first preview half the audience left."[36]

Yet despite these obstacles and setbacks, the show ultimately fared quite well. With a relatively modest run of sixty-eight performances, which failed to recoup the initial investment and can hardly be called a success by Broadway standards, *Johnny Johnson* nonetheless attracted favorable press notices and garnered several accolades. In his second notice, Atkinson concluded that the play was, "at its best, a deeply moving piece of work," despite its "theatre frailties." The panel responsible for deciding the New York Drama Critics' Award, of which Atkinson was a member, voted *Johnny Johnson* runner-up to Maxwell Anderson's *High Tor* in the category "Best American Play" in 1936–37. Among the subsequent productions organized under the auspices of the Federal Theater Project (FTP) was the well-received production in Los Angeles, which opened on 28 May 1937 for a six-week run (closing 4 July). According to the FTP reports, which Tim Carter cites in the exhaustive introduction to his edition of the score for the Kurt Weill Edition, "around 22,000 people attended the thirty-three performances of this production."[37] Weill can be forgiven, therefore, for perhaps exaggerating only a bit when he reported to Dr. Kalmus of Universal Edition in Vienna in July 1937 that his first American piece, which he calls a "musical comedy," had been a "sensational success."[38] But a success—critical if not popular or commercial—it certainly was.

Maxwell Anderson had been present at those early meetings in New York that led to the Group's formation (though he did not become a member himself), and it was to him that Weill would turn for his next musical play.

KNICKERBOCKER HOLIDAY

A measure of the early impact of Weill's second musical play, billed as "a new musical comedy," may be gleaned from two obliquely related events. On 15 October 1938, President Franklin D. Roosevelt attended a performance of *Knickerbocker Holiday,* the last of the five-day try-out run at the National Theater in Washington, before the production moved to New York for its premiere. According to a report in the *New York Times* the following day, the president "laughed heartily at the sallies poking fun at the government. . . . Many allusions in the play applicable to the present day," the report continued, "were not lost upon Mr. Roosevelt or the audience, who joined the president in a hearty response to Stuyvesant's definition of democracy. 'Democracy,' he said, 'is government by amateurs,' which sent the President's head back rolling in laughter."

A correction is in order here: the reviewer attributed the line to the wrong character. Stuyvesant does not answer the question "What's a democracy?" He asks it. And although he might already sense what the answer will be, he certainly doesn't like it. In the play's script it is Brom, the quintessential American protagonist and opponent of Stuyvesant's tyrannical ways, who supplies the definition. "It's—it's where you're governed by amateurs," Brom says. "It's a—a free country." To which Stuyvesant remarks, "Ridiculous." Be that as it may, was the audience laughing at the definition itself (implying perhaps that those in power are mere amateurs, not that they were living under a system of government by the people, for the people) or more at the fact that the president himself was laughing?[39] The point of the scene, and of much of the rest of the play—and surely a reason to make Roosevelt's laughter nervous—is the parallel drawn here and elsewhere between him and the play's overbearing tyrant, Governor Stuyvesant.

The *Times* report calls to mind the celebrated occasion, some two hundred years earlier, when the British prime minister, Sir Robert Walpole, attended a performance of John Gay's *Beggar's Opera.* In that work, the basis of Weill's *Dreigroschenoper,* Gay alluded to an affinity between Peachum and Walpole, something not lost on the audiences of the time—or on the lambasted politicians. Walpole is said to have saved face by rising and calling for an encore of the most damaging song, "When You Censure the Age." And as Jonathan Swift wrote to Gay shortly after the 1728 premiere, "We hear a million of stories about the Opera, of the encore at the song, 'That was levell'd at me,' when two great ministers were in a box together, and all the world staring at them."[40] In that respect at least, *Knickerbocker Holiday* is more like the *Beggar's Opera* than *Die Dreigroschenoper* is! Although Brecht and Weill evidently did not plant any such specific satirical barbs in their 1928 version of Gay's piece, in *Knickerbocker Holiday,* his first collaboration with Weill, Maxwell Anderson most certainly did.

But the topicality was problematic, such that Anderson sought to explain his intentions in an article that appeared, again in the *New York Times,* just a month after the premiere. Entitled "On Government: Being a Preface to the Politics of 'Knickerbocker Holiday,'" the piece attempted to defuse some of the criticism that had been leveled at Anderson, principally for political reasons—criticism that had begun before he finished the book, and then continued during the rehearsal period and into the premiere production's run.[41]

Knickerbocker Holiday, like *Johnny Johnson,* was presented under the auspices of a theatrical collective, in this case the Playwrights' Company, formed in 1938 by Elmer Rice, Maxwell Anderson, Robert E. Sherwood, S. N. Behrman, and Sidney Howard (all except Behrman recipients of the Pulitzer Prize for drama). Just days before *Knickerbocker Holiday* opened, the Company had staged its first production, Sherwood's *Abe Lincoln in Illinois,* directed by Rice and starring Raymond Massey. And they would continue their work until 1961, including among their sponsored productions *Street Scene* (1947) and *Lost in the Stars* (1949). Weill himself would become the only nonplaywright member of the Company in July 1946 and proudly use its letterhead, which included his name.[42]

Changes to Anderson's original script were suggested by other members of the collective, but they were also prompted by casting difficulties. Rice, who along with other members of the Company read drafts of the script and suggested cuts and changes, put the issue succinctly in his autobiography: "*Knickerbocker Holiday* was a not too subtle attack upon Roosevelt and what Anderson regarded as his highhanded measures of social reform. The rest of us were strongly pro-Roosevelt, and though, of course, we had no control over Anderson's script, we did succeed, mainly by cajolery, in getting him to delete some of the more pointed references to the New Deal."[43] Lines such as "My citizens, there is to be a complete reshuffling of the cards" (i.e., a new "deal"!), spoken by Stuyvesant before he promulgates his demagogic political program, are among the more obvious cases in point.[44]

In his letter to the *Times,* Anderson concedes that "there has been a good deal of critical bewilderment over the political opinions expressed in the play, and not a little resentment at my definitions of government and democracy." Based both on certain passages in the play and on the amplification of his opinions in the

Times article, one can see why. Anderson, in sum, adopts a belligerently libertarian stance. Not only does he read the American Constitution as "our forefathers' distrust of state," but he finds that laws enacted to "increase the power of the government over men's destinies" amount to "fighting a lesser tyranny [namely, the accumulation of wealth in the hands of a few] by accepting a greater and more deadly one." Social Security, he says, without mentioning President Roosevelt as its champion, "is a step toward the abrogation of the individual and his absorption into that robot which he has invented to serve him—the paternal state."

But he goes further (as, by inference, does the play), not stopping at issuing a blanket criticism of the birth of an American welfare state: "When a government takes over people's economic life it becomes absolute, and when it has become absolute it destroys the arts, the minds, the liberties and the meaning of the people it governs." He chooses to cite, of all countries, contemporary Germany and Russia as cautionary tales: "It is not an accident that Germany, the first paternalistic state in Europe, should be governed now by an uncontrollable dictator; not an accident that Russia, adopting a centrally administered economy for humanitarian reasons, should arrive at a tyranny bloodier and more absolute than that of the Czars." The warning is all too clear: "Men who are fed by their government will soon be driven down to the status of slaves or cattle."

The difficulty the piece presented for the other members of the Playwrights' Company, and for the audience as well, wasn't that Anderson wanted to present the early Dutch settlers grappling with the issue of government power, or that he wanted to do so in a comic vein (although the transliterated Dutch accents admittedly may seem silly, if not outright offensive, nowadays). Nor was it, on the face of it, objectionable that Anderson should want to write a satirical play with local political references, à la *Beggar's Opera;* nor, indeed, that he should want to issue a warning about the dangers of tyranny, again alluding to contemporaneous politics. The difficulty was that he wanted to do all of these things at once, thereby proposing an appalling affinity between the New Deal and European totalitarianism, and more specifically between F.D.R. and Hitler. Many thought the allegory reckless, even dangerous.

Not surprisingly, *Knickerbocker Holiday* received perhaps the most emphatic harangue from *New Masses,* the left-wing journal that published a mix of reportage, fiction, poetry, and art by figures such as Max Eastman and his sister, Crystal, Richard Wright, Ralph Ellison, Langston Hughes, John Dos Passos, Josephine Herbst, and satirists Art Young and William Gropper. "I didn't laugh," the *New Masses* critic Ruth McKenney wrote. "For I think calling the New Deal fascist is a poor sort of joke, and I consider labeling Roosevelt the American Hitler is a vicious perversion. . . . Mr. Anderson makes his points by indirection. His lyrics are suave. His jokes are disarming up to the stinger on the end." McKenney also thought it "a shame to have to add to this review of Mr. Anderson's attack on democracy in America, the words 'With Music by Kurt Weill.' And Mr. Weill's score for *Knickerbocker Holiday* is delightful. Many of the songs are hauntingly beautiful, and one at least, 'September Song,' will surely become a classic."[45] And so it did.

McKenney's strong reservations were echoed in other reviews, if less stridently. The 20 October 1938 critique by Richard Watts of the *Herald Tribune* was twofold. Not only is Anderson's view of democracy "cynical," says Watts, comparing *Knickerbocker Holiday* to *Abe Lincoln;* "the trouble is that the author fails to do his debating with the necessary light touch." In the piece's defense, one might say that it didn't meet conventional expectations for a production billed as a "new musical comedy." In that sense, the label was deceptive. But the charge of heavy-handedness, even dullness, was nonetheless widespread. Brooks Atkinson, for example, though also enthusiastic about Weill's score, described the book as "unwieldy" and, in his second review, as "considerably on the pedantic side."[46]

"September Song" found its way into the play as an afterthought. Accurately predicted by several critics to become an enduring gem, it initially formed part of a broader effort by the production team to humanize the role of Governor Stuyvesant, a particularly poignant means of strengthening the "love interest" part of the plot as a way of counterbalancing the tyrannical part.

The "holiday" of the work's title is supposed to be one celebrated by the Dutchmen—the "Knickerbockers"—with a hanging. And the victim is Brom, "the fellow who resents being ordered around." He describes himself as "the beginning of a national type . . . with an aversion to taking orders, coupled with a complete abhorrence for governmental corruption, and an utter incapacity for doing anything about it." Complicating the situation, and thereby bringing the two parts of the plot together, is Stuyvesant's attraction to Brom's fiancée, Tina, who resists the Governor's advances with an appeal to her youth. "I'm very young," she pleads, "not ready at all." Whereupon Stuyvesant grows wistful and ardent: "You are young, my sweet, you have the world and a lifetime before you, but the hair is graying at the temples—slightly—but graying—and the days begin to slip rapidly through my fingers. For my sake try to overcome your girlish modesty and let me lead you to the altar while the fire burns brightly."

Anderson's original text as set by Weill represents that future in the tentatively conditional: "These precious days I'd spend with you." But that would soon change. Innumerable renderings of the song's chorus—notably those by Bing Crosby and Frank Sinatra, but also by many others—alter the lyrics by turning the conditional into an indicative, in keeping with the sentiments of a crooner's sentimental ballad: "These precious days *I'll* spend with you" (emphasis added). The crooners also tend to omit the introductory verse section of the song, beginning instead with the chorus. "September Song" as sung in the show is more than a mellow reflection on the ephemerality of life, if not love. The original commercial recording of "September Song," made in 1938 by Walter Huston, who played Stuyvesant in the premiere production, conveys a nervous element of insecurity, even of midlife crisis—the reversed, more humanistic face of Stuyvesant's tyrannical nature. How and when the shift in syntax first occurred may be impossible to reconstruct, but by 1944 it was legitimized by Chapell's sheet music of the song, with the *I'd* replaced by *I'll.* Also included in Huston's original recording, but subsequently omitted in sheet music and Huston's later versions (in 1944 and 1950), is the self-deprecating line from Anderson's libretto: "And I have lost one tooth and I walk a little lame"—the latter due to the aging governor's silver peg-leg.

The year of Weill's death, 1950, marked an important milestone in the career of "September Song," thanks to the release of Paramount's *September Affair,* a film about a fateful romantic encounter starring Joseph Cotton and Joan Fontaine, for which Walter Huston made his third recording of the song, needless to say without the missing tooth, the lame gait, or the conditional tense. Some of the lyrics are also changed, with the painfully punning sentiment (already present in Huston's 1944 recording, albeit in the conditional tense) about "the wine [dwindling] down to a precious brew," followed by "these vintage years I'll spend with you." Just who was responsible for this vinous variant is unclear. In the movie soundtrack, the melody of the song's chorus features prominently as part of Victor Young's opulent underscoring. And the song itself is presented in a key scene between the two lovers, who listen to it being played on a gramophone (performed in the new version by Huston; that is, it is neither the classic 1938 recording nor the one from 1944). Not only does the plot echo David Lean's *Brief Encounter* (1941), but so does the use of Rachmaninov's second piano concerto as both background and source music (the Joan Fontaine character is a concert pianist). Young is especially artful in combining Weill's and Rachmaninov's music, revealing telling affinities between the expressive qualities of the two pieces. At one point, they are literally played together, as if Weill had cowritten the concerto's melodic material.

Although the song itself was an afterthought in the musical play, the melody was not new; it derived—rather than being merely borrowed—from an earlier score by Weill, *A Kingdom for a Cow* (originally conceived in German as *Der Kuhhandel*). In its original form the melody begins the first part of an aria in which the principal tenor, Juan, sings a catalogue of the sacrifices exacted from him, tolerable only thanks to his love for Juanita. It is a heartfelt, almost heroic love song, quite different from Stuyvesant's unseemly pleadings.

After the transformation from an extended rounded-binary song form into a Broadway ballad, what remains of the original aria, transposed from E to C, are the principal contours of one of Weill's most memorable melodic inventions. The first half of each phrase, in a gesture of lyrical expansiveness, outlines a seventh

EXAMPLE 40. *Der Kuhhandel,* "Juans Lied"

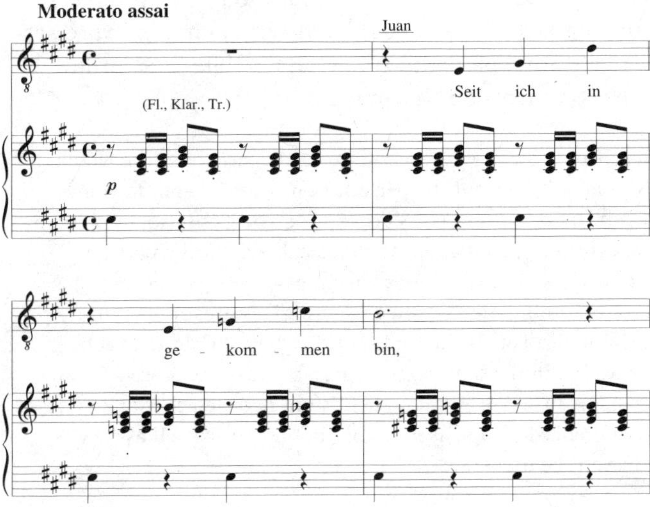

EXAMPLE 41. *Knickerbocker Holiday,* "September Song"

(major and minor respectively), whereas each of the second halves is more constricted. (One could argue that this gesture of expansion and constriction defines, in a very general way, the affinity between the Weill and the Rachmaninov in *September Affair.*) But the melody in the operetta aria goes on to form a sixteen-measure sentence that continues, as the list does, into the meandering expanded second section. The melody of "September Song" is organized in a formally simpler, more concise manner, articulating the first part of a conventional AABA chorus. The verse, on the other hand, sounds almost improvised, the accompaniment little more than a "vamp" to the soloist's recounting of earlier times ("When I was a young man courting the girls," etc.) (exx. 40 and 41).

Form and material tend to be discrete categories for Weill, as suggested by the remarkable note he sent Anderson during the inception of *Knickerbocker Holiday*. In describing an approach to the task at hand, the composer expresses ideas that apply to many of his other pieces, too. The call for "bite" and "irony" is noteworthy here, as are the comments on "the musical style of the play."

> The more I think about our play the more I get enthousiastic *[sic]* about the whole idea, the characters, the background and the period. I am sure we can do something very original, and in using music, you can express your philosophy with great bite and irony. I am thinking a lot about the musical style of the play and I have started to work out a style which would give a feeling of the period and yet be very up-to-date music. This combination of old and new gives great opportunity for humor in music, and my idea is that the music in this play should take active part in the humorous as well as in the sentimental parts, because the more we can say in fun the better it is. For instance if we have the fight between the flute and the trumpet, I want our audience to laugh as much about the music itself as they'll laugh about the situation and the dialogue.[47]

As befits a historical play with topical relevance, Weill's "combination of old and new" manifests itself on a number of levels. "How do you tell an American?"—that is the central question of *Knickerbocker Holiday*, addressed by Anderson as a didactically theatrical and by Weill as a musical theme. The song bearing this title occupies a prominent place in the piece, toward the end of the first act and as one of two reprises at the end. It is the culmination of Brom's heated exchanges with Stuyvesant highlighting the distinction between Old World and New. There is no doubt how Weill makes the point musically: by saturating the song's melody with syncopations, emblems of the New. In contrast to his German works, then, American jazz is invested here with wholly positive connotations, the expression of modern individualism as opposed to "the instinct of the masses," as Weill had defined it in the mid-1920s, or the symbol of urban decadence that it represents, among other things, in *Aufstieg und Fall der Stadt Mahagonny*.

Much more traditional, but no less contemporary in its sentiment, is the anthem "All Hail the Political Honeymoon," with its marchlike rhythms and verbal allusions to Nazi Germany: "Sing the news to hoi polloi / Of each individual man his boon in an age of strength through joy" (a chilling allusion to the Nazis' slogan *Kraft durch Freude*). The "American" theme contrasts, above all, rhythmically with "the regimented life" that is hailed in Stuyvesant's song "One Touch of Alchemy," at the end of which the "political honeymoon" is first introduced (to be reprised later). Multilayered, too, is the contrast between the "humorous" and the "sentimental parts." In the former, the tone comes closest to resembling Gilbertian operetta; in the latter, Weill draws rather on his vast experience with Viennese operetta, as reflected in, for example, *A Kingdom for a Cow*.

In addition to the unwelcome political allegory, "lines that have too much of a Gilbertian lilt" are something to which Elmer Rice drew attention after his second reading of the draft libretto. "Your script is fresh and original," he wrote to Anderson, "and doesn't need to lean upon Gilbert at all. . . . It isn't anything specific, just here and there a rhythm and a turn of phrase. I think I felt it particularly in some of Brom's lines. The notion of a timorous man who becomes fighting mad when anyone gives him orders is faintly Gilbertian and I think his autobiographical speeches will bear watching."[48]

Anderson seems not to have heeded Rice's advice. Nor, given Weill's own creative inclinations in this regard, should there have been any particularly compelling reason to do so. Thanks to both the tone and substance of the music as well as the mix of Offenbachian and Gilbertian satire, *Knickerbocker Holiday* is as much operetta as it is musical comedy. And the generic crossover is a product of a stylistic eclecticism that prefers to wear its sources on its sleeve rather than blend (still less suppress) them. "Faintly Gilbertian"—and in places more than just "faintly"—are not just turns of phrase, especially in the many "patter" elements, but also plot parallels with *The Mikado*. For example, the councillors' eagerness to organize a hanging for the Governor's holiday echoes the Mikado's own concern about the lack of executions in Gilbert and Sullivan's Savoy opera.[49] The old and the new are combined, then, without being homogenized beyond recognition. Certainly more problematic than the variety of artistic models invoked, at least as far as the critical reception of the piece is concerned, is the multiplicity of the satire's targets.

For Rice, "lumping F.D.R. with European dictators" was a "serious—but entirely personal—point," the "Gilbertian lilt" a "minor" one. In the latter category was his reservation about the opening. "I think Irving should clearly and unmistakably state . . . just who and what he is. He is never clearly identified and anyhow a lot of the customers will have only a vague idea who he is." Rice is referring to Washington Irving, the author who introduces himself with an opening monologue and song and provides a narrative frame for the entire piece, appearing intermittently to comment on the creation and outcome of the story. To judge by the published script, Anderson appears to have responded to this critique, such that Irving tells the audience of his history project and the tale he wants to tell with it:

> There's that history of Old Dutch New York I thought of writing;
> My Knickerbocker History.
> If it's funny enough it will be read;
> If it's good enough it will endure –
> And in all the history of the world
> There's never been such a gathering
> Of Pantalunatics
> As among those first fat Dutch settlers.

The title of the musical comedy is thereby partly explained, but only partly: Irving doesn't mention his pen name, Diedrich Knickerbocker, used for his satirical book *A History of New York*. In that work, published in 1809, Knickerbocker, an imaginary Dutch historian, presents himself as an eccentric twenty-five-year-old scholar who pokes fun at pedantic methods of scholarship and the Dutch colonization of New York. It was only after Irving's book that the name Knickerbocker came to be used to identify descendants of the early Dutch settlers and, more widely, any New Yorker. Anderson's "Pantalunatics" has sartorial connotations, of course, referring to the garment worn by the Dutchmen in early illustrations of Irving's book and later called "knickerbockers."

Anderson's libertarian sympathies no doubt warmed to Irving's portraits of the Dutch settlers, as satirically apposite in their lambasting of contemporary politicians in 1809 as they were in 1938. Take the description of the warring factions of Short Pipes and Long Pipes, which also serves as a representative sample of Irving's style:

> Thus did dame Wisdom (whom the wags of antiquity have humorously personified as a woman) seem to take a mischievous pleasure in jilting the venerable councilors of New Amsterdam. To add to the confusion, the old factions of Short Pipes and Long Pipes, which had been almost strangled by the Herculean grasp of Peter Stuyvesant, now sprang up with tenfold vigor. Whatever was proposed by Short Pipe was opposed by the whole tribe of Long Pipes, who, like true partisans, deemed it their first duty to effect the downfall of their rivals, their second, to elevate themselves, and their third, to consult the public good; though many left the consideration out of question altogether.[50]

Something of this humorous prolixity seems to have transferred itself to *Knickerbocker Holiday* in those passages where the actor playing Irving appears as narrator, self-consciously describing the import of the story, analyzing the creative process, and entertaining alternative plot twists by interacting with characters in the play, notably Brom and Stuyvesant. Whether this elaborate "epic" device was Weill's or Anderson's idea is hard to determine. It seems to have been inspired more by the fictional nature of Irving's *History* and that work's mode of presentation than by any Brechtian precedents. In any event, the narrator's interventions serve to cast a tone of qualifying humor over the whole satirical enterprise, contributing further to its bite and irony. Irving's voice also acts, at the end, as the tempering conscience of posterity that inspires Stuyvesant's clemency. Brom is reprieved. All ends happily, as everyone joins in a final rendition of "How Can You Tell an American?" Gilbertian patter lends itself here to lilting rhymes such as the last: "Without the supervision of a governmental plan— / And that's an American!"

Posterity has not been kind to *Knickerbocker Holiday*. Its topicality—whether to do with domestic or international politics, or with the rebarbative combination of the two—has not fared well. Some of its music has more than just survived, however: not just the perennial "September Song," but also the exquisite ballad "It Never Was You." Both of these songs, each an impressive document of Weill's rapidly advancing Broadway education, reveal a composer poised to make a significant impact on the American musical theater.

Critics at the time already recognized that he would do so. Several felt that Anderson's book was a hindrance rather than a help, and indeed, it would require a different project for him to realize the full extent of his abundant creative talents. Moss Hart and Ira Gershwin would eventually fit that bill very nicely. And Anderson's theatrical gifts would prove, with *Lost in the Stars,* to be better suited to a serious "musical tragedy" than to musical comedy, however much the oddly rich mixture that is *Knickerbocker Holiday* might appeal in its own unique, awkwardly problematic way.

Weill recognized Anderson's limitations in this regard and managed to work with them. In 1945, reporting to Lenya that Anderson had read *The Beggar's Opera,* Weill conceded that the playwright's mind-set differed significantly from his own: "He just doesn't understand this kind of negative humor," Weill explained; he "is always afraid of anything that is not on the line of straight idealism."[51] Although Weill made this observation some seven years after *Knickerbocker Holiday,* he is implying that he himself was after something a little different from Anderson's idealism. With respect to *Knickerbocker Holiday,* one might even infer that its tendency toward two-dimensional preachiness was not entirely to his liking. What Weill liked about Gay's theater, he wrote to Lenya, was this: "By showing with biting humor what the world would be like if it were inhabited by crooks and hypocrites, the 'Beggar's Opera' does more good than all the drama of 'noble souls.'"

The first Anderson-Weill collaboration remains a fascinating curiosity nonetheless, a period piece, admittedly, with more enduring musical than dramatic substance. Nor was the film version from 1944, a loose adaptation with reduced musical content, ever likely to do much to promote interest in the original stage work. Of all Weill's musical plays, posterity has, at least to date, deemed *Knickerbocker Holiday* the least revivable.

LADY IN THE DARK

After its opening at New York's Alvin Theatre on 23 January 1941, following a tryout run in Boston, the premiere production of *Lady in the Dark,* a collaboration with playwright Moss Hart and lyricist Ira Gershwin, ran for an impressive total of 545 performances. Yet the question of "revivability" has dogged Weill's third American musical play, too. The scholarly authority on the work, bruce mcclung, concluded his encyclopedic dissertation on *Lady in the Dark* by stating that "in its present condition, it is probably not revivable."[52] That was in 1994, and the reasons he gave were several. One was the length of the script, another the demands made by the title role—both important but not insurmountable challenges. A greater obstacle was the work's datedness, the fact that "the send-up of the fashion industry" can seem both "labored" and "tied too tightly to the times." According to mcclung, "Every aspect of this work reflects the moment of its composition."[53] Chief among these aspects, and hence the biggest challenge by far, was the blatant sexism of the book.

The titular "lady" is publishing executive Liza Elliott, whose recurring bouts of neurosis and depression lead her to seek help from psychoanalyst Dr. Brooks. The play's underlying misogyny manifests itself above all in the doctor's diagnosis, which is based on a quasi-Freudian interpretation of Liza's dreams and her current interpersonal troubles. Brooks views Liza's pursuit of success as a career women as compensation for experiences that traumatized her during childhood. According to this analysis, her female identity has remained effectively repressed—hence "in the dark"—as a consequence of those formative experiences; only the talking-cure allows her to discover her "true" nature.

By the time his monograph *Lady in the Dark: Biography of a Musical* appeared some twelve years later, in 2007, mcclung could report on a number of more recent productions, albeit without substantially altering his earlier assessment. At the top of the list was the major revival staged at the Royal National Theater in London in 1997, which yielded a new commercial recording. Another of this recent clutch of productions, at Philadelphia's Hal Prince Theater in 2001, attempted a radical revision by casting the role of the psychiatrist, Dr. Brooks, as a woman. Even though mcclung believes this intervention by the director "[makes] the subtext of *Lady in the Dark* more palatable," his reservations about the viability of a major Broadway production remain.[54] None of the revivals, he concludes, "has topped the original" (167).

"Completely updating *Lady in the Dark* is impossible," mcclung claims, "because its plot, dialogue and lyrics all reflect the year 1940" (197–98). He saves his strongest reservation, however, for the film version starring Ginger Rogers, which was released in 1944. "What had been literate in *Lady in the Dark*," he writes, "was dumbed down for the film" (174). Moreover, the cultural context that informed the book just four years earlier had already shifted quite perceptibly. No less problematic is the fact that the show's dramaturgical premise—the process, that is, whereby Liza's growing consciousness of a song from her childhood becomes a metaphor for an effective talking cure—is all but obliterated in the film version. Integral to an informed understanding of the work, including the nature of its sexist message, Weill's "musical point of view" effectively disappears in the translation from stage to screen.

Lady in the Dark's contemporaneous topicality—the datedness of the topics that the book treats and, above all, how it treats them—is not in doubt. Yet even if one is prepared to accept as valid the various reasons mcclung offers against the viability of revival, does that make *Lady in the Dark* the American musical equivalent of a *Zeitoper,* whose built-in obsolescence Weill had so vehemently chided in the closing years of the Weimar Republic? Or does it still contain aspects that can be seen to be doing more than reflect the moment of composition and instead contribute to a more enduring appeal, even to a kind of universality?

The piece's subject matter and tone are not so very different from, say, Hindemith's *Neues vom Tage* and *Hin und zurück,* both from the late 1920s. Yet insofar as Weill's musical play takes "the news of the day" as its theme, in the spirit of Weimar *Zeittheater,* it is a theme drawn not from historical news items so much as from the stuff of fashion pages and gossip columns. The twenty-first century calls this "soft news" and "infotainment," something quite different from the kind of topicality that dates the books of *Johnny Johnson* and *Knickerbocker Holiday,* both of which have overtly political content. Liza Elliott, with all of her personal problems placed in the spotlight, is portrayed as newsworthy in the same way that media personalities or celebrities are nowadays. Celebrity comes at a high price.

Moss Hart's book brings his own autobiography into play. Nor are those elements mere background information, though they are assuredly that as well. Hart wrote *Lady in the Dark* with several years of intense psychoanalysis behind him, going back to his consultations in the early 1930s with Russian émigré Gregory Zilboorg, whose celebrity patients included George Gershwin and Lillian Hellman. Hart himself suffered from neurosis and depression, and he had learned to talk about them using the technical language of the profession, at first from frequent sessions with Dr. Zilboorg and then with Lawrence Kubie, whose patient he became in 1937.

A neurologist, psychiatrist, and psychoanalyst, Kubie was drawn to the arts, particularly to celebrities in the arts, and counted among his patients Vladimir Horowitz and Tennessee Williams. His extensive list of publications includes titles such as "The Literature of Horror: An Analysis of *Sanctuary* by William Faulkner," an article from 1934, and *Neurotic Distortion of the Creative Process,* a book published in 1958. Of particular interest here is "Psychiatry and the Films," an article from 1947, in which he voiced criticism of recent attempts to "portray the technical process of psychiatric diagnosis and treatment." He directed his criticism first and foremost at the film industry, from whom he demanded greater responsibility in dealing with the topic of psychiatry, and second at all professional psychiatrists asked to serve as consultants. "It is not too much," he wrote, "to demand that, when the films deal with universal human suffering and the struggle to alleviate it, they should not distort it."[55]

When the first edition of the text of *Lady in the Dark* was published in 1941, with a dedication "*To* / L.S.K. / M.H.," Kubie wrote the preface for Hart using the pseudonym "Dr. Brooks" (playful quotation marks included). In offering qualified endorsement, Kubie's text served a double purpose. Not only did it underscore the connection between the plot of the musical play and the actual practice of Freudian analysis (and for those in the know, between playwright and analyst) by offering the analyst's own potted analysis; it also voiced qualifications about artistic uses of psychiatry and psychoanalysis that anticipate the criticisms contained in "Psychiatry and the Films."

In the book's preface, Kubie, using language with which Hart was doubtless familiar, describes the fulfillment of Liza Elliott's career ambition to become the editor of the fashion magazine *Allure* as a "Pyrrhic victory": every success in her life has "merely added to her accumulating burden of frustration"; she feels "empty-handed." He then elaborates on how Liza "plays out this aspect of her problem against the relatively inert images of three men and what they represent to her."[56] Each of these men plays a part in a Freudian family drama. Liza's long-time partner Kendall Nesbitt, an older man, assumes a role "not unlike that of a mother or father; or, under more usual circumstances, of a wife toward a busy husband—or perhaps all of them combined." Only when Kendall becomes free to marry her does she realize that their union is impossible. The true nature of their relationship becomes clear, "that he represented a fantasy of father and mother rolled into one." Randy Curtis, in contrast, is a "childlike juvenile glamour-boy, the movie-hero of adolescent fantasy literally come to life." Kubie sees Randy's "pseudo-virilism" as being "stripped from him to reveal the anxious and dependent child." Of the three principal men in her life, it is only her advertising manager, Charley Johnson, who "refuses to play the role either of the subservient parent or of the submissive child" and who "challenges her right to live in her no-man's land between the sexes" (x).

In Kubie's analysis, Liza's men are "dummies out of a window display, on whom she drapes the compelling fantasies of her childhood and the fear and hate of these fantasies which had formed in her in those nursery years" (ix). While her struggle would appear to be with the men themselves, in reality "it is wholly within herself, a struggle between the conflicting yearnings, fear and angers of her own nature" (x). Following Freudian orthodoxy, Kubie describes how Liza's nature is formed primarily through the disturbing and hence repressed experiences of childhood: "The illness of a woman of forty begins under our eyes in the exquisite forgotten agony of a little girl of four." The repressive mechanisms also apply to her memory of the song that she had happily performed during her childhood—until, that is, "her father's heedless phrases shame her" (xi). The shame results from his cruel, because unfavorable, comparison of Liza with her beautiful mother, as well as from his fury at his daughter's trying on one of her mother's dresses after the mother's untimely death. "Beauty becomes something," Kubie writes, "only to be offered up in sacrificial expiation. . . . Love becomes possible to her only when it can bring to her aid the protective love of a parent" (xii).

The "Dr. Brooks" of the preface and the Dr. Brooks of the play explain Liza's career in similar terms but with an important difference. The former describes it as "masking her jealousy of other women by devoting herself to making them beautiful and herself plain" (xiii). The latter states the premise rhetorically, in a blunt, confrontational manner, asking Liza: "Doesn't it strike you as curious, too, that you, who have rejected beauty for yourself, in reality, at least, should spend all your days, in fact, dedicate your life to the task of telling *other* women how to be beautiful? That is the function of your magazine, isn't it?"

In other words, although Kubie endorses Liza's story as a "case history" that is "wholly accurate," he voices professional reservations about "technical flaws to which the analyst might object." He writes that the procedure, as portrayed, is "more directly challenging, more provocative, than would be characteristic of the ordinary analytical situation." The above dialogue is an obvious case in point. For the sake of "scientific accuracy," he also suggests that the author "could easily have introduced an interval of weeks or months between the acts" in order to "give the impression of a longer period of treatment" (xiii). Yet he excuses "the condensation in time" as a "license due a poet." More fundamentally, he questions the portrayal of the dreams, "a series of rococo fantasies built around a core of valid dream ideas," which he describes as being closer to the "fantasies of children" (xiv).

Kubie also attempts to account for the work's success. At the end of his preface he suggests that the "ordinary playgoer" derives "deepening pleasure and understanding" by seeing *Lady in the Dark* repeatedly. "It is because," Kubie concludes, "he [the playgoer] has been awakened to a realization that subtle and powerful psychological forces play beneath the surface of his own life and of the lives of those around him. This awakening cannot fail ultimately to have profound social and cultural significance" (xiv). Earlier Kubie had referred to Liza's story of illness and recovery as "the saga of what can happen to any woman—and, with some transposition of forces, to any man" (viii). But he leaves it to the reader's own judgment what that transposition might entail. The masculine pronoun referring to "the ordinary playgoer" is intended to represent everyone, male and female. Yet it is also quite clear that the nature of Liza's illness as presented and diagnosed in the play is emphatically gender-specific. Therein lies the crux of the book's social and cultural significance as well as its datedness.

Analyzing *Lady in the Dark* from a contemporary perspective invites a dual focus. Apart from the social values reflected in the plot, there is the psychological theory itself to consider. In her study *Feminism and Its Discontents,* Mari Jo Buhle draws on Hart's book to describe the adoption and adaptation of psychoanalytic theory in midcentury America, calling the chapter in question "Ladies in the Dark." It was a period, Buhle argues, that witnessed the reinforcement of Freud's patriarchal family as the "natural" order, a reinforcement in which psychologists were largely complicit. The "censure of career women" in *Lady in the Dark,* Buhle writes, "makes it almost too perfect an example of psychoanalytic misogyny."[57] Such misogyny forms the play's premise or "subtext," as mcclung calls it.[58] In Buhle's words, by "opting for careers, women risked jeopardizing their femininity."[59]

Hart and Kubie accept without question the premise of mutually exclusive options, the one "natural," the other not. That Liza rejects her feminine role as "temptress" in pursuit of a career as "executive" they construe as the symptom of an illness. Accordingly, it is the job of Dr. Brooks to diagnose and treat this condition in therapy sessions whose putative success allows Liza to rediscover her "true" feminine identity. In a similar way, Kubie treated Hart and others with the aim of "curing" them of their homosexuality.[60]

There is no escaping the fact that Dr. Brooks's analysis comes across nowadays as at best irrelevant, at worst wholly offensive. The "either/or" ideology of gender roles and sexual orientation that informed psychoanalytic theory at the time and that, via Kubie, inspired Hart to write *Lady in the Dark* reflects more than anything the historical moment of the play's composition. Casting a woman as Dr. Brooks in the 2001 Philadelphia production may have been intended to make the subtext "more palatable," as mcclung suggests, but if the psychological theory remains intact, the gender switch could leave the audience thinking more than ever that the analyst really should know better.

No less "of the time" than the psychoanalyst's misogynistic mind-set, however, is the topic of psychoanalysis itself. By the late 1930s and early 1940s, Kubie's "subtle and powerful psychological forces" were achieving a measure of social and cultural significance as psychoanalysis entered the cultural mainstream. Evidence for this trend abounds on various levels. By the 1920s and 1930s in America, as Joel Pfister has shown, "we find a full-fledged pop psychological essence-and-identity culture." Not only did psychology play a crucial part in "glamorizing the lifestyles of the rich," but magazines such as *The Masses* promoted psychoanalytic language as a "script for new everyday rituals of middle- and upper-class social interaction and identification." As early as 1915, Pfister notes, the magazine *Vanity Fair*—a real-life precursor of Liza Elliott's *Allure*—published a piece called "Speaking of Psycho-Analysis: The New Boon for Dinner Table Conversationalists." Delving into psychological depths with the aid of recondite technical vocabulary acquired "an aura . . . associated with wealth, glamour and hidden mystery. . . . Women who styled themselves as neurotic and in need of therapy were regarded as charming and sexy." Connected to this trend were smash-hit plays such as Eugene O'Neill's *Strange Interlude* (1928) with its "neurotic heroine," as she was billed, played by the Theatre Guild's celebrated Lynn Fontaine.[61]

Against this cultural backdrop, Liza's staged dreams—especially the first one, the "Glamour Dream"—reflect the glitzy, show-biz aura with which psychoanalysis had become associated in the 1920s and 1930s. Although it would therefore have been hard for audiences in 1941 not to be familiar with Freudian concepts such as the "unconscious" (or "subconscious," as it was often called) that had infiltrated both high art and popular culture, they would have had little opportunity to encounter these concepts in a musical play. Insofar as *Lady in the Dark* had an immediate predecessor, it was not in the musical theater, but in the movies. A frequently cited example of a film involving psychoanalysis is *Carefree,* directed by Mark Sandrich and released in 1938, which expressly juxtaposes glamorous lifestyles and psychiatric treatment. The film "may well have been inspired," Andrew Velez wrote in his introduction to the screenplay's publication in 1965, "by the fact that half of Hollywood seemed to be undergoing psychoanalysis at the time."[62]

Carefree tells the story of a psychiatrist, played by Fred Astaire, who is asked by his friend for help in his relationship. The friend wants to understand why his fiancée, played by Ginger Rogers, keeps breaking off their engagement. (Rogers, as mentioned, would also star as Liza in the movie version of *Lady in the Dark.*) With music composed by Irving Berlin, *Carefree* incorporates extended dream sequences presented as lavish production numbers, which seem like sources of inspiration for the three production numbers in *Lady in the Dark* that Kubie described as "a series of rococo fantasies." The Astaire character even describes his patient as a woman "who can't make up her mind," a phrase echoed exactly in the musical play. The professional analyst in *Carefree* further qualifies his description of his patient by referring to her as "one of those dizzy, silly, maladjusted females" and says of her mind that "I'll probably find out she hasn't got one"; moreover, when he realizes in the process of administering hypnosis, with a view to stabilizing her relationship, that he has fallen in love with her, he selfishly reverses the treatment—all of which reflects a distinct difference between the film and the musical play. Apart from supplying a splendid pretext for Fred and Ginger to fall in love and dance, *Carefree* amounts to little more than a screwball comedy to which the description "dizzy and silly affair" readily applies. By comparison, *Lady in the Dark* is a much more serious, even authentic treatment of psychoanalysis. Not that *Lady in the Dark* doesn't have its fair share of "dizzy and silly" elements, but *Carefree* would have been unlikely to receive imprimatur from someone such as Kubie. "Clearly," as Krin and Glen Gabbard wryly observed in their book *Psychiatry and the Cinema,* "there was no psychiatric adviser on the set."[63]

Lady in the Dark, in contrast, is rightly celebrated as "the first musical drama based upon psychoanalytic therapy itself," according to W. David Sievers in his comprehensive study *Freud on Broadway,* "a milestone in American musical comedy as well as in the story of the influence of psychoanalysis upon the drama."[64] Those who had seen *Johnny Johnson* may have recalled Dr. Mahodan's "Psychiatry Song," a satirical number whose concluding message is that those who practice psychiatry are themselves healed lunatics. And audiences for Weill's next musical play, *One Touch of Venus,* would encounter Dr. Rook, also a figure of satire, who makes mention of various psychological theories to explain the curious behavior of the hapless barber, Rodney, and to whom Rodney says, "I'm not the loony one—you are!" Both of these examples, however, especially the last one, are more in the *Carefree* vein.

Hart's autobiographically significant book for *Lady in the Dark* was both of its time, reflecting the wider currency that psychoanalytic thought was acquiring, and artistically on the cutting edge. Orson Welles's film *Citizen Kane,* for example, which appeared in 1941, concerns itself in a similar way with the protagonist's repressed childhood memories. And movies such as Alfred Hitchcock's *Spellbound* (1945), for which Ben Hecht wrote the screenplay, would soon follow suit with references to guilt complexes and dream interpretation.[65]

Lady in the Dark is of *our* time, too, as suggested: the invasion of personal space, including the psychological probing of repressive family dramas, has continued to be one of the indispensable ingredients of celebrity culture. Such popularization of analytic psychology and the kind of public exposure that haunts Liza's worst dreams are nowadays even more commonplace than half a century ago. What was new back then survives into the present as a hackneyed part of popular culture. That *Lady in the Dark* might still seem topical, refunctioned more as a commentary *on* than as a reflection *of* the culture of its time, owes much to the way in which it explores the spheres of "reality" and "fantasy." The psychoanalytic theory that informs its book is itself an object of scrutiny.

Mixing psychoanalytic depth and Hollywood glitz, seriousness and humor, *Lady in the Dark* can seem both a celebration and a send-up of contemporaneous trends. Without question, Hart's book reinforces the ideology of the psychologically informed and gender-specific self that was prevalent in American culture by the late 1930s, while managing to adopt a certain ironic distance from that culture, thanks chiefly to the comic elements that infuse the work. Ira Gershwin's lyrics and Weill's music both have a substantial part to play here. Weill's self-contained "one-act operas," as he described the discrete musical portions of the piece, are an integral part of the psychoanalytic process.

No less critical, the tone of the individual musical numbers is frequently tongue-in-cheek, in a manner even more redolent of Gilbert and Sullivan than in *Knickerbocker Holiday.* Indeed, the creators of Savoy Opera are explicitly invoked in one of the piece's amusingly self-reflexive moments, where the performers question the appropriate style in which to conduct their dramatic business. The moment comes in the third musical sequence, the "Circus Dream," in which Liza finds herself in court standing trial for not making up her mind. In addition to the general confusion wrought by the logic of dreams, which locates her not in a courtroom but in a circus, the members of the jury before which she is forced to appear parody words and music from *The Mikado*.

The scene begins with the appearance of the Ringmaster, played in Liza's dream by staff photographer Russell Paxton. Described earlier as "Old World in manner and mildly effeminate in a rather charming fashion," Russell acts throughout the play in a decidedly camp manner. As Ringmaster, he itemizes Liza's professional and personal "offenses," doing so in formal legal language, with phrases such as "And inasmuch as" and "Moreover," but in a style of delivery familiar from the radio commercial in *Carefree,* articulating the charges on a repeated monotone, with each new sentence rising by a tension-tightening scale degree. Liza is charged with "not making up her mind" about three things: about "the Easter cover or the circus cover," about whether she is "marrying Kendall Nesbitt or not," and about the kind of woman she wants to be, "the executive or enchantress." Charley acts as attorney for the prosecution and Randy as lawyer for the defense. When the Jury enters, it is to the melody sung in *The Mikado* to the words:

My object all sublime
I shall achieve in time—
To let the punishment fit the crime—
The punishment fit the crime;
And make each prisoner pent
Unwillingly represent
A source of innocent merriment!
Of innocent merriment!

Ira Gershwin has the Jury sing a variant of this:

Our object all sublime
We shall achieve in time—
To let the melody fit the rhyme,
The melody fit the rhyme!

And then to a different melody:

This is all immaterial and irrelevant!
What do you think this is—
Gilbert and Sellivant *[sic]?*

The melody does fit the rhyme, if only briefly, but long enough to add a further, quite distinct layer of bizarrerie.

This is not the only instance of music taken from another composer. The borrowing continues in "Tschaikowsky" (Weill retains the German spelling), a Gilbertian patter-song sung by the Ringmaster, whose introduction quotes the theme from the third movement of Tchaikovsky's Sixth Symphony. Between Russell's "Tschaikowsky" and Liza's concluding "My Ship" comes "Saga of Jenny," a raunchy ballad with boogie-woogie accompaniment that Liza performs in her own defense before finding reconciliation with Charley.

Complementing these allusions to familiar music are numerous references throughout the work to all kinds of art and artists. Like "Tschaikowsky," a catalogue of Russian composers to be recited at tongue-twisting speed, the "Glamour Dream" is particularly full of glib name-dropping. Following Dr. Brooks's invitation to "hum what you remember of the song," which elicits from her the first four measures of "My Ship" (without the words), Liza fantasizes about being serenaded by members of the "New York Chapter—LIZA ELLIOTT Admirers," as a sign reads carried by one of "twelve men in faultless evening clothes, carrying lyres." They compare their love for her to a collection of famous couples, historical as well as fictional, beginning with Mélisande and Pelléas. Others that make it onto this motley list are Juliet and Romeo; Beatrice and Dante; Guinevere and Lancelot; Brunhilde *[sic]* and Siegfried; Pocahontas and Captain Smith; Martha and George Washington; Butterfly and Pinkerton; Calamity Jane and Buffalo Bill; Carmen and Don José.

Living artists also get a mention: Liza plans to visit Toscanini, who is on her calendar. "Huxley wants to dedicate his book to you / And Stravinsky his latest sonata . . . Shostakovich his latest cantata." "Epstein says I simply have to pose for him." The President requests that Liza's portrait be painted and her "likeness used on the new two-cent stamp." In breathless anticipation of the finished painting, Liza wonders aloud:

> Is it impressionistic?
> Or is it American Primitive?
> . . .
> Is it Pointillistic?
> Is it surrealistic?
> Or is it a W.P.A.-ish one?[66]

Given the kaleidoscopic assortment of elements in the work, Liza might as well be wondering how best to describe the style of the entire "Glamour Dream" and the other sequences as well, not just the portrait. No doubt intended to reflect Liza's disturbed state of mind, this manically eclectic quality makes the musicalized dreams, also in an aesthetic sense, "jokes in dubious taste," to use W. H. Auden's memorable phrase.[67] (Perhaps this is also why Kubie made light of the dreams from a psychoanalytic viewpoint as "a series of rococo fantasies.")

When finally unveiled, the painting elicits only derision from Liza's admirers, bringing the fantasy to an abrupt and bitter halt as she sees herself portrayed in an unflattering, realistic style and is thus forced to confront herself as "a woman who cares very little for any of the feminine adornments most women use to enhance their attractiveness." That, at least, is how Dr. Brooks interprets the symbolism of the dream-turned-nightmare. The glamorous woman about whom Liza fantasizes prior to the painting episode is, he sternly advises her, "the complete opposite of your realistic self."

Enriching further the surrealistic mix is the "Mapleton High School Song" in the "Wedding Dream," a fine example of Weill's ability to create anthemlike pastiches (other notable ones being the concluding chorale of *Die Dreigroschenoper* and the national anthem of *A Kingdom for a Cow,* which he recycled in *The Firebrand of Florence*). French nursery music is also invoked. And although the song "It's Never Too Late to Mendelssohn" was eventually cut, Charley murmurs some of its playful, punning text that references the musical bookends of the standard wedding ceremony as part of the sequence's dense counterpoint of interconnecting musical and verbal lines:

> It's never too late to Mendelssohn
> Two hearts are at Journey's Endelssohn
> Whate'er their future they must share it.
> I trust they Lohengrin and bear it.

Charley's witty recitation accompanies the melody of "This Is New," the love song that Liza's fantasies have screen idol Randy Curtis singing to her and that is being reprised here instrumentally to a bolero accompaniment. The musical texture, full of driving rhythms and rich in melodic descants, nicely represents the unresolved confusion of Liza's relations to the men in her life—psychoanalytic counterpoint, as it were.

The tableau of the "Circus Dream" is no less frenetic. A waltz borrowed from *A Kingdom for a Cow,* for example, now serves as the melody for "He gave her the best years of her life," sung in turns by the Ringmaster and Randy ("Mr. Bareback Rider") with choral support, and culminating in Liza's added descant ("When a maid gives her heart but does not give her word / How on earth can that maid have betrayed him?") that preempts her defense in the "Saga of Jenny."

Reviews of the premiere production stressed the impact made here and elsewhere by the visually arresting and lavishly expensive set pieces. Brooks Atkinson, for example, wrote that "Harry Horner's whirling scenery gives the narrative a transcendent loveliness"—a reference to the four revolving turntables created by set designer Horner, which accommodated the large amount of stage property and allowed for frequent and seamless changes of scene as the action shifted back and forth between reality and fantasy.[68]

Like Polly's "Seeräuberjenny" in *Die Dreigroschenoper,* a ballad whose out-of-character play-acting irritates Macheath, Liza's "Saga of Jenny" provocatively resolves the issue of her indecision by turning it on its head. Applying the logic of the person who claims that giving up smoking is easy, Jenny has no problem whatsoever making up her mind: she has done it many times. Each verse describes the kind of havoc that her decisiveness has wrought. Committing arson when she was three, learning languages when she was twelve (except for the word *no*), stealing other women's men, publishing her memoirs and thereby provoking wives to "[shoot] their husbands in some thirty-three states"—Jenny's story leads "anyone with vision," as the song's chorus concludes, to "[come] to this decision: don't make up your mind!"

True resolution comes only when Liza is able in her final session with Dr. Brooks to recall the situation from her adolescence when she was able to sing the song complete. Up to that point she had still been resisting, until, toward the end of the "Circus Dream," Charley confronts her without resorting to his usual sarcasm. When the Jury hums the song's opening measures, eliciting Liza's "Don't sing that," Charley exclaims: "You're hiding something! You're afraid of that music, aren't you? Just as you're afraid to compete as a woman."

Concerning the division of the piece into musical dream sequences that devote themselves to the world of unconscious fantasy, on the one hand, and spoken portions that present the real world of Liza's everyday dealings, on the other, Moss Hart wrote in the souvenir playbill: "Why not show someone in the process of being psychoanalyzed and dramatize the dreams? And what more natural than that the dreams be conveyed by music and lyrics so that the plane of reality and that of the dreams would be distinct?"[69] The link between the two "planes"—a device as inspired as it is simple—is the "lost song," Liza's *verlorenes Lied,* to use the title of the first of several German translations of the piece. The key to her emotional world and to her identity as woman, the song is literally an "inner song" (to use a favorite expression of Weill's that describes the function of music in the theater), one that remains partially repressed until the analysis is complete.

There is a precedent for such a musical evolution in *Johnny Johnson,* as discussed above. But there is also a critical difference in that "Johnny's Song" appears essentially as a complete song, first without words, before it is presented in its most complex and sophisticated variant at the end. In *Lady in the Dark,* the process is somewhat the reverse: "My Ship" emerges as a complete AABA form after partial exposure during the dream sequences, adumbrated as incomplete fragments that are incorporated into an array of musical styles and allusions.[70] Hearing the complete song creates a sense of clarification resulting from simplification.

With reference to the terminology of film studies, mcclung labels this aspect of Weill's score "metadiegetical": the two parts of the work's structure—the spoken and the sung—are brought together in a moment of symbolic reconciliation. The song itself is source music, but music that at the same time functions as a metaphor for Liza's restored personal harmony. The surreal world of dreams gives way to relived memory. The dreams themselves, as in Freudian theory, are not pictures of reality so much as an internalized narrative, "dream work" (or *Traumarbeit,* as Freud would say), a compression of conscious narrative with defamiliarized or "displaced" elements.

Concepts such as surreal "dream work" and inverted logic relate to the large-scale musical dramaturgy of *Lady in the Dark* as well as to other compositional choices made by Weill. The final song, heard as a collection of motivic or even leitmotivic fragments and ultimately as a complete composition, functions metaphorically as a musical analog of such work and logic. Liza's song, fully revealed, signifies an overcoming of the surreal displacement represented in the dream sequences. As a musical process it can be likened to Sibelius's approach to writing symphonies, an inversion of traditional symphonic logic. There is a gradual unfolding of the main theme, whose complete exposition is withheld until near the end.

Although the practice of psychoanalysis on the musical stage was novel, the formal idea behind the piece was not—at least not for Weill. For this reason, *Lady in the Dark* can be seen less as an abrogation or even suppression of his European roots and identity, as critics of the piece have sometimes claimed, than as the realization of a long-cherished musico-dramatic ideal. mcclung is surely right, in his entry on the work for the *Enzyklopädie des Musiktheaters,* to invoke the example of Ferruccio Busoni, the central influence on Weill's conception of musical theater, and also to point to earlier works, in particular *Royal Palace,* in which music serves a similar purpose.[71]

The separation of "realistic" scenes and "fantastic" musical numbers is arguably the most consistent application in Weill's oeuvre of the aesthetics of opera promulgated by his teacher. "The sung word on stage," Busoni had maintained, "will always remain a convention and an obstacle to any genuine impact: in order to emerge from this conflict with any degree of propriety a plot in which people act while singing has to be based on the unbelievable, the untrue, the improbable, so that one impossibility may support the other and both become possible and acceptable." The stage, he said, should be viewed as a "clear and unabashed distortion"; its essence resides "in the idea of the joke and unreality as opposed to the seriousness and verity of life." It is "fitting that people . . . behave differently from how they would in real life instead of unintentionally doing it the other way round (as in our theaters and especially opera houses)."[72]

One might even say that *Lady in the Dark* rises to the Busonian challenge and emerges from the generic conflict utterly unscathed. If that dramaturgy permits as complete a realization of Busonian precepts as any of Weill's works, then

EXAMPLE 42. *Lady in the Dark,* "Glamour Dream" (incipit of "My Ship")

EXAMPLE 43. *Lady in the Dark,* "This Is New" (beginning)

each of the individual dream sequences correspondingly invites the composer to deploy an unprecedentedly diverse range of musical idioms, some drawn from his earlier works, others more recent acquisitions, some even from the more distant past, especially (again, as in *Knickerbocker Holiday*) from Gilbert and Sullivan. Yet for all the topsy-turvy atmosphere created by the surreal jumble of musical styles and textual associations, a jumble reflective of the turbulent, overwrought state of Liza's unconscious, there are distinctive musical elements that appear at various points in the work and contribute to the overall sense of musico-dramatic coherence. They function in a number of different ways. Principal among these elements, as discussed below, is the frequently heard incipit of "My Ship" (ex. 42). Another is the melodic shape, a stepwise descending and rising figure, that occurs in the chorus of "This Is New" as a whole-tone collection outlining a tritone to the words "I was merely existing" and then, transformed into a diatonic collection, to the words "And I'm living at last" (ex. 43).

First, a few words are in order about the form and function of "This Is New," one of Weill's most exquisite and also most unusual love ballads. Although the overall division into verse and chorus is standard, the form of the chorus is quite unconventional. Rather than adhering to the Broadway form (AABA) or a creative variant thereof, as had become his usual practice, Weill casts this song in a form that on closer inspection turns out to have its origin in classical traditions.

EXAMPLE 44. *Lady in the Dark*, "This Is New" (end)

The thirty-one measures of the chorus possess a seamless unity that can be analyzed in terms of a single period. Comprising a sixteen-bar antecedent clause and fifteen-bar consequent, the two halves mirror each other melodically, the antecedent ending with a half-close cadence on the dominant, the consequent with an authentic cadence in the tonic. Particularly striking are the consequent's final six measures, which artfully disrupt the formal symmetry. The phrase begins at the words "I am hurled," as if mirroring the second phrase of the antecedent ("Head to toe you've got me so I'm spellbound"), but then at the words "up to another world where life is bliss" the melody eschews the expected sequence with an ascending figure that leads to a momentum-suspending doubling of note values before the concluding words "And this is new" (ex. 44). The expressive novelty of the chorus's cadence is the composer's inspired response to Gershwin's text, just as the formal syntax manages to invoke "another world," the effect of whose classical unity "is bliss."

To say that Randy sings this song in the middle of Liza's wedding to Kendall Nesbitt is not strictly true. The song is pure fantasy; its sensuous passion and romantic yearning are Liza's, not Randy's. (His unsuccessful proposal to her proves to be no less a projection, however, "in real life.") Liza is confronting in her dream the contradiction of her personal life writ large: making a marital commitment to one man while lusting after another. The choreography of the ensuing dance highlights her confusion: "Liza leaves Randy's arms, finds herself in Johnson's. They dance. Six girls in red wigs, with dresses like Liza's, come on. Johnson disappears. Randy is again discovered. He sings to the six. As they dance Liza merely watches. Finally Liza is alone on the stage. Slowly she hums the beginning of that phrase of song ['My Ship']."

The whole-note motif derived from the chorus of "This Is New" undergoes several transformations. One occurs in the song itself, as mentioned, where the unfolded tritone becomes a diatonic collection. Another is in the transitional music that precedes the song, where two whole-tone versions of the motif flank a chromatic one. The motif returns later in the dream, juxtaposed with the incipit of "My Ship," before the opening of "This Is New" is played by the orchestra *fortissimo* with church organ accompaniment. The chromatic variant of the motif also recurs during the ensuing bolero, mentioned above, where its appearance (like Randy's reprise of the song itself) is surely intended as an ironic interjection as the guests exclaim, "What a lovely day for a wedding," and Charley recites "It's Never Too Late to Mendelssohn." In his *Interpretation of Dreams,* Freud used the term *condensation (Verdichtung)* to describe various elements with diverse, incongruous origins combined into a composite figure. The same concept seems wholly appropriate here, in particular to capture the counterpoint of the "Wedding Dream's" tumultuous conclusion, where the ensemble simultaneously delivers five quite different texts and vocal lines to the bolero accompaniment. Condensation, indeed.

The incipit of "My Ship" is perhaps best labeled an "idée fixe" insofar as it recurs as a more or less unchanging musical object. (A parallel may be drawn here to Berlioz's *Symphonie fantastique* and to the musical reminder of the young artist's romantic obsession, the "idée fixe," as Berlioz himself describes it, that "reappears constantly" in all of the work's movements.) It is also the literal gateway to Liza's interior life, appearing at the beginning and end of her analysis sessions to signal the transition from reality to fantasy, from the conscious to the unconscious world, as "dark" thoughts are brought into the spotlight. So long as Liza is unable to overcome her deep-seated emotional fears, her "inner song" remains equivocal as a source of attraction as well as anxiety. Her profound sense of failure, as Dr. Brooks reminds her, occurred not once but twice: as a child in competition with her beautiful and adored mother and as an adolescent in competition with the student voted "the Most Beautiful Girl" in Mapleton High School. In providing access to the present, past, and future dimensions of her psychological state, the fragment also fulfills the essential functions of Wagnerian leitmotif: emotional identification, recollection, and presentiment.

There are a number of places where only the three initial pitches of the melody are heard, without the rest of the incipit. Inviting recognition as a snippet of Liza's song, this three-note tag or motif can also appear as part of the melodic fabric of other musical numbers. One such place is the opening of "One Life to Live." Another is the beginning of the verse to "This Is New." And there are several other instances in the "Wedding Dream": "There's a girl," "And now a Mapleton High girl," "Randy Curtis."[73] As these various instances suggest, the motif is linked primarily to Liza's unconscious, but also, by extension, to Randy's romantic projections. And in the final scene, when Charley suddenly starts singing along to Liza's humming, the song belongs to him almost as much as it does to her. "Why—do you know that song?" she asks. "Yeah," he replies, "haven't heard it since I was a kid, though." In the final rendition of "My Ship" just before the curtain, the two of them sing together. Having represented the first person singular, the music now says "we." The emotional condition associated with the song becomes shared.

It is a commonplace of opera studies to admit significant divergences between music and libretto. Even in the most tragic or oppressive circumstances, the act of singing tends to have a transformative, liberating effect. This tendency belongs to what the philosopher Bernard Williams in his reflections on the nature of the genre called opera's "special resources," evident above all in music's capacity to "[carry] layers of meaning of a kind inexpressible in the text."[74] Relevant in this connection is the way in which the melodramatic immediacy of Weill's vocal music can be perceived as running counter to the sociological theories of epic theater. A particular case in point is Jimmy Mahoney's defiant singing in *Aufstieg und Fall der Stadt Mahagonny;* a more general one is the constitutive tension in *Die Bürgschaft* between, on the one hand, the individual freedom demonstrated by the singing protagonists and, on the other, the constraining influence of social relations.

How are such "special resources" at work in the "three little one-act operas" of *Lady in the Dark?* On one level, the divergence between music and libretto is preprogrammed in the musical play's dramaturgy. The composer who stated in 1936 that psychology would be "replaced by simple, human, universal events" ends up creating a work not only *with* psychology but *about* psychology. *Lady in the Dark* is about Freudian analysis, or to be precise: it is about the American adaptation of Freud's theories as reflected in Kubie's work. Through the absurd and comic elements, especially in the musicalized dream sequences, it also satirizes that adaptation in the lives of the rich and famous. (Originally there was to be a "Hollywood Dream," but it did not make it into the performed version of the work.)

Strictly speaking, the psychological theory that informs the plot of the book departs significantly from the Freudian paradigm. In an orthodox account, libido problems associated with Liza's childhood would have a role to play. Instead, as Buhle noted, "her anxiety traces back to her parents, to fathers who fail to encourage a budding femininity and to mothers who prove insufficiently maternal."[75] As diagnosed by Dr. Brooks, the factors principally affecting Liza's emotional life are "interpersonal" rather than "intrapsychic." Taking the "special resources" of the dreams into account, however, shifts that perspective quite considerably.

It is the music of the dream sequences that is chiefly responsible for taking gender out of the equation and putting sex back into the mix. Liza's fantasy of screen idol Randy Curtis making love to her in the middle of her wedding to staid Kendall Nesbitt is one of several surreal examples. Another is Liza's penultimate number, "Saga of Jenny." In the original production, Gertrude Lawrence, the star for whom the role was created and this additional song composed, managed to turn the number into "a burlesque hall routine" in which, in the words of mcclung, she "bumps and grinds." Her performance is "all the more titillating," mcclung observes, "because the repressed Liza Elliott is now firmly in touch with her sexuality" (23). The censors were not amused. When Lawrence took the number on tour and wanted to include it in concerts given to members of the armed services, her performance was banned. Responding to protests at the song's exclusion, the Pentagon relented with the following directive: "Miss Lawrence may do the bumps, *provided she does them sideways*" (158).

As the most overtly sexual number in the show, particularly in Lawrence's rendition of it, the "Saga of Jenny" offers a libidinous corrective to the sanitized Freudian theory of Dr. Brooks's analysis. The more sedate and sentimental "My Ship" has its subversive side, too, potentially serving to undercut the theory's misogynist premise in a different way. In the broader scheme of the show, one could make the case that the resolution embodied in Charley and Liza's coming together in song does not represent her unilateral capitulation to the sexist environment so much as a rapprochement on the part of both of the sexes. Each of them, not just Liza, undergoes a transformation. There are even hints of this in the dialogue.

After behaving boorishly, for example by calling Liza "boss lady" throughout, Charley begins to see that he has "been rotten" to her; he even confesses that "I've kicked myself for it afterward." Although her offer to him that there be "two bosses" and that they share executive control seems to meet with his acceptance, her qualifying remark that she "might even step aside after a while" provided he "didn't get too drunk with power" leaves open how their personal as well as their business partnership will develop.

The deeper evidence for change is in the music. While Liza's coming to terms with her identity is represented on stage by the dramatization of early 1940s culture, in particular of that era's dated psychoanalytic practices, the "musical point of view" arguably transcends the values reflected in the book. The dramaturgy that serves as a metaphor for Liza's story finds expression in terms of an unfolding "inner song" that is "simple, human, universal."

ONE TOUCH OF VENUS

One of the songs in *Lady in the Dark* provides a brief but immediate link to Weill's next musical play. When publishing executive Liza Elliott fantasizes in her "Wedding Dream" about a sexy screen idol, his love song to her contains the following line: "This is new. Is it Venus insisting that I'm through with the shadowy past?" The eponymous ancient goddess in Weill's musical comedy *One Touch of Venus* is insistent that an unsuspecting barber try something new and disturb his shadowy *present* in wartime New York. She appears in two forms, animate and inanimate. Before being brought back to life by the barber, whose name is Rodney Hatch, she arrives as a priceless statue, the Venus of Anatolia, which wealthy art collector Whitelaw Savory, one of the Hatch's clients, has acquired after being tipped off by "a shady importer in Istanbul." (Demonstrating that he gives a damn about posterity, Savory provides these background details for "the Memoirs" that he is dictating to his long-suffering assistant.) The art collector's loss is the barber's gain. Rodney and Venus connect romantically, until she balks at the vision of married life in the suburban idyll of Ozone Heights and flees back to Olympus. Rodney, however, contents himself with someone who only *resembles* Venus.

One Touch of Venus, on which the composer collaborated with book author S. J. Perelman and lyricist Ogden Nash, works as a metaphor on several levels, musically as well as textually. The goddess of love is pitted against mere mortals, the rich and famous against the average citizen, city against suburb, new art against traditional art. The work has also been interpreted allegorically. Michael Baumgartner, for example, states that "Venus is, of course, an allegory for the emancipated, American, urbane female of the 1940s who is not prepared to subjugate herself to male dictates."[76]

This makes it sound as though *One Touch of Venus,* which received its premiere at New York's Imperial Theatre on 7 October 1943, were making amends for the blatant sexism of its predecessor. Certainly, sexual politics are in play, and there are a number of specific references to the role of women in the wartime context, such as the scene in the bus terminal (act 1, scene 5), which begins with a soldier "giving [a] girl a last kiss" and saying, "Good-by, darling—look up my wife, won't you?" In the same scene a Woman Welder appears, "dressed in rough work clothes, heavy gloves and a welder's helmet" (a colleague perhaps of "Rosie the Riveter," the wartime icon popularized the previous year by a song of the same name), "opens a locker, takes out a baby, and dandles it in her arms."[77] The first ballet, "Forty Minutes for Lunch" (act 1, scene 4), has Venus cavorting with a sailor. In the final ballet, the "Bacchanale" (act 2, scene 3), she is carried back to Olympus by an aviator.[78] And the pas de deux after Venus's torch song, "Foolish

Heart," concludes with an accelerating and crescendoing rendition of the sea shanty "What Shall We Do with the Drunken Sailor?" Venus's interest in the barber is, as much as anything, raunchily carnal: she describes her "condition" as "available," and Rodney's jealous girlfriend disparagingly apostrophizes her as "you libido."

But is the work as a whole—and Venus herself, for that matter—preaching emancipation? Does she reject the regimented married life in suburbia because Rodney and other men subscribe to it or simply because it is suburban? What about the story as a whole? Venus is different things to different people. Her image varies according to the eye of the beholder. The musical comedy's original title, *One Man's Venus,* tacitly invited completion (*is another man's . . . poison,* perhaps?). For the arrogant and snobbish collector Savory, and in apparent contradiction of his professed taste for the more expressionist forms of avant-garde art, Venus epitomizes classical beauty; above all, she triggers his nostalgia for an irretrievably lost love.

For Savory's assistant Molly, "a touch of Venus" is something that may be used in a male-dominated world to "equalize the odds." As someone whom the published script describes as "knowing, uninhibited, attractive in a cynical and disillusioned way," she sees the goddess's power as the influence women have over men by virtue of their physical beauty; they either have and use it—or they don't. For her, Venus is not the emancipated female so much as the woman who gets ahead by exploiting her looks. Even Venus, who could "dance with a new lover nightly," recognizes limitations because of her infatuation with "an obscure little barber." On earth, she succumbs to all-too human feelings ("Foolish Heart") and to celebrating Rodney's ordinariness ("That's Him").

And what are we to make of the ending? Originally the piece was to end after the "Bacchanale" that immediately follows "Venus in Ozone Heights." According to the scenario of these two ballets in the script, Rodney is "dividing his attention between the lawnmower and the comics" in front of "three identical suburban doorways." Venus, "in housewifely garments," tries to resist "the creatures of her magic world . . . but they will not be resisted." Now, as the stage directions indicate, "Ancient Greece is real, and Ozone Heights the myth, only the vast open sky remains. Venus, once again the goddess, returns to her people." This ending certainly supports an emancipatory reading of the goddess's significance, leaving open the question of whether she is critical of the loveless world as such, of the role she is expected to play in it as a woman, or of the limited options available to her in suburbia.

Be that as it may, it was decided during the Boston tryout in September 1943 that a short final scene should be tacked on. If the preceding ballet had forcefully conveyed the feminist allegory of Venus's rejection of the mortal world, this addition serves to soften, if not entirely eviscerate, that message while shifting the focus from Venus's displeasure to Rodney's romantic fantasy. Savory is reunited with his statue. "A masterpiece," he remarks, "but it doesn't do her justice." Molly *"(with genuine sympathy)"* consoles Rodney: "She was the nicest goddess I ever met." Rodney, still reeling from Venus's return to Olympus, reprises their beautiful duet about the ephemeral nature of love, "Speak Low." At the line "I wait, darling, I wait," a girl enters. "Her clothes are simple, and she has an attractive, awkward grace; she might be Venus' country cousin." The girl asks Rodney where she can register for the Art Course. (As we know from the opening scene, Savory chides all of the students at his foundation for not having "the faintest inkling of what I was saying," an observation with which they uniformly and unthinkingly agree.) Looking at the statue and then at the girl, Rodney asks her where she's from.

GIRL: Ozone Heights

RODNEY: Do you like it there?

GIRL: I wouldn't think of living any place else.

RODNEY: My name is Rodney Hatch

GIRL: Mine is—

RODNEY: *(Going quickly to her)* You don't have to tell me. I know.

(He takes the suitcase from her and offers her his arm. She takes his arm, their eyes never leaving each other, and as they start off . . .)

Preceding the final curtain, this brief exchange over the closing measures of "Speak Low" restores the spirit of musical comedy that informs the work but that the "Bacchanale" (as well as the earlier lunch ballet) had left behind. With five months still to go before the tryout and a number of major production decisions ahead, including the replacement of Marlene Dietrich by Mary Martin in the title role, Weill wrote to Ira Gershwin that the show was "witty and romantic at the same time, with good comedy situations."[79] The new ending nicely captures that combination. It suggests that the "touch of Venus," however defined and however ephemeral, is indeed in the eye of the beholder. It may be "one man's," but not another's. With this question of taste, the additional scene brings back the related theme of art with which the play began. And it also leaves intact the gentle note of satire targeted at contemporary America, and from which none of the characters is entirely spared.

In his study of Weill's stage works, Foster Hirsch suggests an allegorizing interpretation along biographical lines. "Did Weill perhaps see in the misadventures of Venus on earth an allegory of his own experience as an 'alien' in America? Was her odyssey somehow a submerged autobiography, a reflection of the way he and perhaps Lenya too had felt on their arrival in America in 1935 and perhaps still felt eight years later?"[80] Although he doesn't press the biographical case for Weill being a stranger here himself any further, Hirsch also mentions the attraction in "strictly professional terms," noting the wartime appeal of a goddess defying mortal limits as well as the specifically musical opportunities afforded by the story's fantastic elements.

Comparison of *Venus* with other works reveals a predilection for similarly treated topics that goes back to *Royal Palace* and *Der neue Orpheus* and that thus transcends Weill's American experience. Both of those collaborations with Iwan Goll deliver a provocative mix of classical myth and contemporary setting. Transplanted from their origins in antiquity, neither Dejanira nor Euridice fits comfortably into the modern world. Like Venus, both women in the earlier works are the object of male fantasies and projections—"the beloved of longing," as Goll describes Euridice. And the fantastic elements of the ballet scenarios, not just in *Venus* but also in *Lady in the Dark,* can be compared to the kind of surrealist pretext for musical invention that Weill seized on before.

Insofar as a biographical connection can be invoked, it is one that reflects the composer's lifelong sympathy for female characters who view themselves as outsiders. Among the characters who could join those just mentioned are both of the women called Jenny, from *Die Dreigroschenoper* and *Aufstieg und Fall der Stadt Mahagonny,* respectively; Angèle in *Der Zar lässt sich photographieren;* Anna in *Die sieben Todsünden;* Luise in *Die Bürgschaft;* Liza in *Lady in the Dark;* Anna and Rose in *Street Scene;* Susan in *Love Life;* Linda in *Lost in the Stars.* Women who feel in some way estranged tend to be the rule rather than the exception.

It was, in fact, the costume designer of *Lady in the Dark,* Irene Sharaff, who drew Weill's attention to the story of an ancient statue of Aphrodite being brought to life when, in 1941, she recommended that he read F. Anstey's *The Tinted Venus,* a "farcical romance" first published in 1885.[81] (A silent movie version, adapted by Blanche McIntosh and directed by Cecil M. Hepworth, was released in 1921.) Not surprisingly, perhaps, given his earlier interest in similar material, Weill responded enthusiastically, seeing in the story "a first-rate idea for a very entertaining and yet original kind of opera comique along the Offenbach-line," as he described the work to Ira Gershwin in November 1941 in an unsuccessful attempt to interest his recent collaborator in a new project.[82]

Unable to bring Gershwin onboard, Weill at first began working with the husband-and-wife writing team of Sam and Bella Spewack on an adaptation of Anstey's story (the couple would later work on *Kiss Me, Kate*), but he quit after the collaboration appeared to be going nowhere. Producer Cheryl Crawford, who had worked with Weill on *Johnny Johnson,* kept lyric writer Ogden Nash, but replaced the Spewacks with Nash's friend S. J. Perelman as book author (previously known for his scripts for the Marx Brothers)—a somewhat risky decision, perhaps, given that neither Nash nor Perelman had prior experience writing for the musical theater. Writing again to Gershwin on 5 April 1943, Weill reported on the difficulties he'd encountered trying to turn the idea into something viable: "I had terrible troubles with the Venus show. As expected from the beginning, Bella became more and more difficult . . . So we threw her out, and Sid Perelman, Ogden and I sat down and worked out an entirely new story line, in complete disregard of Bella's script, with entirely new characters and no Olympus." It was at this point that Anstey's setting of Victorian London was updated to wartime New York. In addition, the star playing the title figure would eventually be switched, as mentioned, from the sultry and temperamental Marlene Dietrich to the more upbeat and wholesome Mary Martin.

Countless cuts and changes would be made during the production process, which director Elia Kazan recalled as being a deflating experience. "We cut the dialogue scenes down," Kazan writes in his autobiography, "to little more than 'bridges,' introductions to the songs and dances, so we could move as quickly as possible from one musical number to the next." Moreover, Weill insisted that his songs "had to be sung down center, facing straight out front." The director consequently felt "reduced in rank. . . . I found out who was boss. Not me. I'd become a sort of overpaid stage manager, subservient to everyone else. I decided that this kind of theatre was another species, one for which I had no talent."[83] Kazan was trained in method acting, like fellow Group Theatre member Lee Strasberg before him. And as with *Johnny Johnson,* Weill's new musical comedy demanded an approach that ran counter to the director's theatrical doctrines. Thanks to the production's commercial and critical success, Kazan would nonetheless win an award as best director of a musical for that year.

In putting his own expectations and contribution in perspective, Kazan singled out the factors he considered primarily responsible for the show's appeal. Apart from Weill and his music, he drew particular attention to three women he describes as "marvelous" and "extraordinary": Mary Martin, Agnes de Mille, and the dancer Sono Osato. "I was deeply impressed," Kazan writes of *Oklahoma!* choreographer de Mille, "by the devotion and discipline of Agnes's dancers. They were devoted to Agnes as to a cult messiah—which is what she was. I used to sneak away from my silly 'book' rehearsals to watch Agnes's girls and boys work by the hour—hours I should have been trying to please Sid Perelman. . . . Her first dancer, Sono Osato, was a poem in movement."[84] Weill, too, found the collaboration with de Mille both intense and productive, as manifested by the substantial, well-received dance sequences that afforded him the opportunity for extended instrumental compositions based on the show's main songs. According to de Mille, he even confided that he considered the concluding ballet the best thing he had written since leaving Germany.[85]

De Mille and Weill contributed a total of seven dance sequences to the version of *Venus* performed at the premiere. The three extended ballets—"Forty Minutes for Lunch," "Venus in Ozone Heights," and the "Bacchanale"—narrate in dream-like sequences the protagonist's experiences of strangeness in the modern world. The others sequences include a "Boogie-Woogie" after "Way Out West in Jersey," the pas de deux that is danced after Venus's torch song "Foolish Heart," and the "Artists' Ball."

Although based mostly on the preceding song, the pas de deux ends, as mentioned, with the traditional sea shanty "What Shall We Do with the Drunken Sailor?" This concluding portion of the ballet, whose dynamics swell from *pianissimo* to triple *forte,* with a corresponding increase in tempo that culminates in a raucous, tonally destabilized presto section, abruptly shifting from D minor to C major, is the only moment in the work of literally quoted vernacular music. The contrast with the melancholy nostalgia of the waltz melody could scarcely be starker: Mars versus Venus. Apart from offering such stark oppositions, the ballets tend to rework previously heard material in ways that have a similarly ironic effect. Moreover, most of the dance sequences involving Venus or her songs deform her lyrical melodies by subjecting them to an array of variation techniques, often quite mechanical in effect, that reinforce her sense of alienation in wartime America.

If *One Touch of Venus* works as an extended metaphor for the state of heterosexual love in the modern world, a world of forty-minute lunches and cookie-cutter suburbia, then the love invoked is a love that is lost. Where amorous passion is concerned, Weill tends to look to the past. As the romantic emblem of a bygone era, Venus's backward-looking, operetta-inspired waltz is a musical facet of that extended metaphor. With her "Foolish Heart," the love goddess is forced to wonder: "Have I somehow lost my touch?" (The song is related to "Oh Heart of Love" from *Johnny Johnson,* whose waltz rhythm it shares and whose introduction it borrows wholesale.) In "Westwind," Savory reveals that he is anxious to rekindle the emotions he associates with a former "true love," to "recapture the past."

Nostalgia for that past may well seem justified in such an inhospitable world. Venus begins her song "I'm a Stranger Here Myself" by posing a rhetorical question whose answer is already implied by the play's satirical tone: "Tell me," she demands, "is love still a popular suggestion or merely an obsolete art?" Asking to be forgiven for posing "this simple question," she proceeds to add several more as the song unfolds. Her critique of the loveless present becomes more explicit and quite specific, as the questions pile up: "Does love embarrass him or does it bore him? . . . Have I missed the path, have I gone astray? . . . Is there really any danger that love is now outmoded? . . . With what have you replaced it? . . . What is your latest foible? . . . Is gin rummy more exquisite? . . . Is skiing more enjoyable? . . . For heaven's sake, what is it?"

The emphasis with which Venus gives vent to her frustration breaks the bounds of the Broadway song form. Her "stranger's" approach is "strange" in several ways; the overall form of the song resists conventional categorization. Whereas the opening strophe more or less adheres to the thirty-two-measure model with an eight-measure bridge/release passage, the following sections effectively elide the beginning and end of the chorus while expanding the bridge component. In other words, each of the three choruses in Venus's verseless song has its own unique release, each more artful than the last.

Most of Rodney's musical numbers are far less transgressive. They also tend toward the witty end of Weill's romantic-witty spectrum. In his first number, "How Much I Love You," Rodney tries to persuade himself of his continuing affection for his fiancée, Gloria (who doesn't warrant a solo song of her own). The four-square rhythms, plain melodic contours, and prosaic text conspire to suggest that he is either deluding himself or has a rather limited notion of love. How much does Rodney love Gloria? "More than a catbird hates a cat or a criminal hates a clue, / Or the Axis hates the United States." All the images of intensity, which include hangnails that hurt and grapefruits that squirt, are negative. He will later reprise the song invoking similar images but changing the title words to "that's how I'm sick of love." The catalogue of activities of his projected life with Venus that he later enumerates in "Wooden Wedding" is no less mundane in its portrayal of married existence.

Rodney also sings with Gloria and her mother in a trio that pays ironic tribute to the neighboring state, "Way Out West in Jersey." Containing as it does lines such as "Yippi-Yi I heard the natives talkin'," New York audiences at the time would no doubt have recognized this number as a patronizing, city-centric parody of the country-bumpkin world of Rodgers and Hammerstein's smash hit of the previous season, *Oklahoma!* By way of providing a musical contrast similarly stark to that after Venus's waltz, the number concludes with a boogie-woogie dance variant. As befits his profession, Rodney also gets to sing in the barbershop quartet "The Trouble with Women," whose self-pitying witticisms are trumped by the final realization that "the trouble with women is men." The exception in Rodney's music to all this comedy is his duet with Venus, "Speak Low," a sensuous rumba, that has proved to be one of the show's enduring hits. Like "September Song" and "My Ship," it has been adopted by a whole range of artists as a standard.

"Speak Low" also receives extensive exposure in the show itself. After being sung as a duet by Venus and Rodney, with the latter exclaiming, "I never felt like this before," the song is played as background music in the ensuing ball scene, juxtaposed with the music of the interlude's middle section, which anticipates music from the production number that follows, "Dr. Crippen." In this latter scene, Savory sings the ballad of a man executed for murdering his wife out of love for his secretary. The dramatically ironic reference to the situation in the play is quite overt: Rodney is suspected of murdering his wife-to-be, whom Venus

EXAMPLE 45. *One Touch of Venus,* "Venus Awakening"

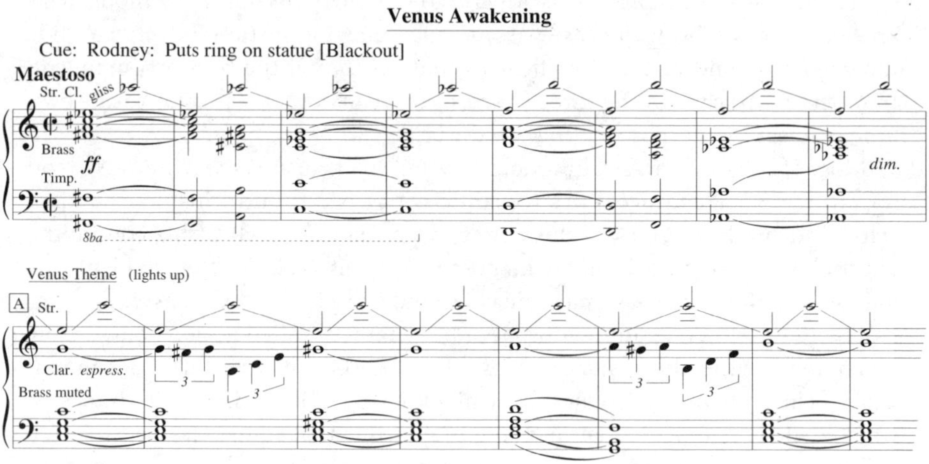

has temporarily pacified with her magic powers. When Venus visits Rodney in jail, they sing their duet, while she facilitates his escape, again using her magic. The melody features prominently in the final two ballets as well; in the last one, the "Bacchanale," the rumba rhythm accompanies Venus as she waltzes off with her aviator, "leaving the forlorn Rodney alone on the stage."[86] In the "Finaletto," Rodney sings "Speak Low" for a third time. No sooner has he rued yet again that love is "a spark lost in the dark too soon" than his next "Venus" appears. The curtain descends (literally).

The songs' melodies are not the only recurring elements. The musical means used to invoke the "true love" in "Westwind" is the so-called Venus theme, as it is referred to in the score when employed as incidental music. It first appears in the score at "Venus Awakening," the point in the drama where Rodney playfully places on the statue's finger the ring intended for Gloria (ex. 45). A melodic contour rising by sequence articulated with triplet quarter-notes coupled with the augmented-triad harmony in the third measure and unresolved major seventh in the seventh measure combine to express a sense of intense yearning. Preceding this theme however, is another, quite different one: a descending figure, also sequential, harmonized in floating minor tonality over a bass that rises by minor thirds, thereby creating "false relations" (c♯–c; a–a♭), and outlines two tritones (f♯–c; d–a♭).

Pointing out that these two musical devices were associated rhetorically with pain and suffering in baroque music, Michael Baumgartner has noted an affinity between this initial music that accompanies Venus's awakening (preceding the

EXAMPLE 46. *One Touch of Venus,* "Speak Low" (end)

"Venus theme" proper) and the recurring motif associated with Anna in *Die sieben Todsünden.*[87] Both of these musical elements associated with Venus—metaphors for the pain and passion of love—recur throughout the score. They are quoted quite specifically as an invocation of the goddess's powers, both in "Westwind" and in the instrumental dance sequences. More in "operetta" than in "Wagnerian" fashion, the "Venus theme" is played as an orchestral leitmotif at Venus's various entrances in both acts. The entr'acte music—an instrumental medley of Rodney's "Wooden Wedding," Savory's "Westwind," Venus's "Foolish Heart," the "Jersey Plunk," and "Speak Low"—commences with the above-mentioned "pain" motif. And the chorus intones it off stage (amplified in the premiere production by loudspeakers) as connecting material between the numbers that appear in different stylistic guises in "Venus in Ozone Heights" and the "Bacchanale."

As expressive-cum-rhetorical devices with their own natural history in eighteenth- and nineteenth-century composition, and adopted as such by Weill as facets of his musical language, these same motivic elements find their way into other parts of the score, too. Theme and motif are derived from that history and that language. Therein lies their metaphorical potential. Consider, for example, the melodic snatches from the end of the songs "Speak Low" and "Foolish Heart," all sung by Venus (exx. 46–48). Or the frequently occurring triplet rhythms in "Speak Low" and "A Stranger Here Myself" that have the effect of releasing the singer from the metrical constraints of the accompaniment (exx. 49 and 50). Or even Rodney's line "I love you more" (ex. 51). Either the pitch content or the

EXAMPLE 47. *One Touch of Venus,* "Foolish Heart"

EXAMPLE 48. *One Touch of Venus,* "Foolish Heart"

EXAMPLE 49. *One Touch of Venus,* "Speak Low"

EXAMPLE 50. *One Touch of Venus,* "A Stranger Here Myself"

EXAMPLE 51. *One Touch of Venus,* "How Much I Love You"

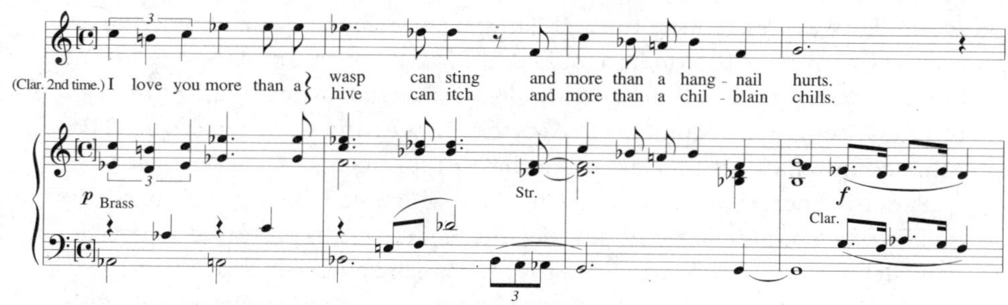

rhythm of these examples is related to the "Venus theme," and hence to its quotation in "Westwind."[88] In the last example, it's both.

Direct quotation of preexisting music in *One Touch of Venus* is rare, as mentioned. While the concluding "Bacchanale" no doubt suggested to Weill a connection to Wagner's opera *Tannhäuser,* with its Venusberg, and while one might have expected him, master of the furtive musical allusion, to invoke a work he knew well from his youth, he seems to have resisted the temptation here. Instead, in somewhat more chaste fashion, he turned to another of Wagner's works—specifically, to a particular motif from that work—to mark Venus's rude departure from the mortal world. The motif in question is a trochaically articulated ascending figure. Because it appears throughout *Der Ring des Nibelungen* in transformed guises, it becomes variously associated with nature (major mode); with the earth goddess Erda (minor mode); and with the twilight of the gods (descending form), the fundamental idea of the four-part cycle. In the symphonic treatment of the motif in the Prelude to act 3 of *Siegfried,* for example, all three connotations are in play. Appropriately enough, perhaps, the variant that comes closest to Weill's—in the minor mode and effectively double-dotted—appears near the opening of *Götterdämmerung,* after the initial nature theme switches from the major key (ex. 52).

A similar ascending figure appears twice in *One Touch of Venus* linked with the melody of "Speak Low," first toward the end of the instrumental entr'acte and again in the "Finaletto," as the barber Rodney mourns the loss of his goddess (a "Götterdämmerung" of sorts) by reprising the earlier duet, only then to recognize more than a touch of Venus in his fellow resident of suburban Ozone Heights (ex. 53).

Venus's departure and return in another guise (still a goddess in Rodney's romantic projection) piles on the irony in several deliciously thick layers. While it is the regular barber Rodney, not the pretentious art-lover Whitelaw Savory, who temporarily brings the statue to life, Venus flees not only from the petty-bourgeois routines of suburbia but also from a city of fast-paced, inhumane mechanization. Love expresses itself through familiar means; the mode of individuality is lyrical, even atavistic. Modern music, in contrast, the music of the city, belongs to the alienated masses. The rhythmically mechanical, ostinato-laden treatment of Venus's song "I'm a Stranger Here Myself" in the ballets, particularly in "Forty Minutes for Lunch," is a metaphor for that estrangement.

Parallels emerge with other works by Weill with urban themes, such as *Aufstieg und Fall der Stadt Mahagonny,* in which the modern city is portrayed as an essentially dehumanizing force. The music of the lunch ballet, which accompanies "a series of formalized dance patterns parodying the tension of metropolitan life" (to quote the stage directions), sounds familiar from the "New Objectivity" style that composers cultivated after the First World War, beginning with works such as Erik Satie's *Parade,* an important precursor of Weill's own motoric music of the late 1920s.

The mix of romantically lyrical melodies, on the one hand, and the various dance rhythms, on the other, and the way in which this mix is mapped onto a dichotomy that plays itself out on various levels between traditional and modern, the individual and the masses, love and estrangement—this, too, is common territory in Weill's theatrical imagination. It is a dichotomy that informs works as different as the surreal one-act opera *Royal Palace* and the penultimate work for the musical stage, *Love Life.*

EXAMPLE 52. Richard Wagner, *Götterdämmerung,* Prelude

EXAMPLE 53. *One Touch of Venus,* Finaletto

For all of this musical diversity, it has often been noted that in *One Touch of Venus* Weill sticks closer to the theatrical conventions of Broadway than in any of his other musical plays. Foster Hirsch, for example, has written that "of all Weill's Broadway shows *One Touch of Venus* would seem the most conventional and impersonal."[89] In his review of the premiere, which comes close to damning Weill's achievement with faint praise, Elliott Carter wrote: "Compared to his other American shows, the music is neither as ingenious and as striking as *Johnny Johnson* nor as forced as his made-to-order jobs for *The Eternal Road* and the railroad show at the World's Fair. But in the atmosphere of Broadway, where so much music is unconvincing and dead, Weill's workmanlike care and his refined sense of style make up for whatever spontaneity and freshness his music lacks."[90] Leaving behind the political idealism and satire of *Johnny Johnson* and *Knickerbocker Holiday,* and the precedent-setting dramaturgy of *Lady in the Dark, One Touch of Venus* is without question "the most completely 'Broadway' of Kurt Weill's scores," as Ronald Sanders puts it, "a first-rate Broadway musical."[91] It also enjoyed the longest initial run of any of Weill's works for the American stage (the premiere production at the Imperial Theatre ran for a total of 567 performances before going on tour, eclipsing the 462 achieved by *Lady in the Dark* in its initial run at the Alvin). Yet judging it merely by its shimmering comic surface and savvy adherence to conventions hardly does it justice.

As a whole, *One Touch of Venus* is so much more than the sum of its witty book, memorable individual songs, and arresting ballet sequences. On closer hearing it proves to be a richly nuanced response to Anstey's "farcical romance," whose subject matter seemed ideally suited to Weill's "musicalizing" treatment. In this respect, his approach is quite similar to that in many of his other works for the musical theater. Whether the topic is love and the human condition or the more self-reflexive one of art itself, the music's response to the thematic threads of the book is imbued throughout with metaphorical significance. Weill's musical ambitions no doubt shaped the book, too—and in many ways.

As the show evolved from Weill's enthusiastic response to Anstey's novel to theatrical performance, the book accommodated itself to the conception of the music rather than vice versa. Seen from this "musical point of view," the cultural dichotomy of past versus present that is embodied by Venus's revivified presence has an aesthetic dimension that correlates to the sociological one. The resulting combination of nostalgic romanticism and contemporary wit, both required to represent the complementary sides of Venus's appearance in wartime New York, may be familiar from many of Weill's other works for the musical theater. Each work mixes these essential ingredients differently, however. Here they form an especially balanced and harmonious partnership in which neither predominates.

10

Stage vs. Screen

Weill's involvement with the medium of film is a story of high hopes, countless frustrations, some major disappointments, and a handful of notable achievements. In several respects it can be likened to his experience with radio. Like many of his generation in the incipient era of mechanical reproduction, he welcomed technological innovation, inspired as he was by ideals that were artistic as well as political. And as music critic for *Der deutsche Rundfunk,* an activity that he began in November 1924, under his own by-line starting in January 1925, he had ample opportunity to contribute to the lively and productive discourse about the new media.

Yet when it came to his own creative projects, reality often fell short of the perceived potential. His last column for the radio journal, which appeared in May 1929, sounded a note of disillusionment over what he saw as censorship of one of his own compositions. It is a pattern that would repeat itself on a number of occasions: motivated to a greater or lesser degree by the prospect of a supplementary or alternative source of income as well as by the opportunity to explore novel artistic outlets, Weill was keen to explore the opportunities offered by new technology, but his initial enthusiasm often gave way to an increasing sense of frustration, as he found the means of mass production hindering rather than helping the realization of his musical conception.

He remained hopeful to the last, however, ready to entertain new projects that would enable him to translate his ambitions as a composer for the theater to the cinema, from stage to screen. As with the theater, he also left a body of theoretical writing that reflected those ambitions with a characteristic mix of pragmatism and idealism.

THE NEW MEDIA

In one of his earliest pieces as radio critic, published in 1925 and entitled "Possibilities of an Absolute Radio Art," Weill discussed cinema and radio together: both of these media, beyond the opportunities created by new modes of distribution, invited exploration in terms of their inherent artistic laws. In this respect, his approach was analogous to his work in musical theater, where creativity evolved from reflection about the possibilities and constraints imposed by the medium itself.

For Weill, committed as he was to theatrical reform, film held a greater appeal than radio as an alternative to live musical theater.[1] Apart from working with mixed success on all manner of movie projects, large and small, he continued throughout his career to harbor the ideal of creating a new genre, "film-opera." The abiding ambition was to transfer his aspirations from stage to screen with the aim of producing a hybrid form, something cinematic yet resting on musico-dramatic principles. It was an ambition left largely unfulfilled, however. Accordingly, the following discussion of Weill's cinematic ambitions has two aims, related but somewhat separate: first, to present the composer's ideas about music in the new media, in particular the unrealized dream of "film-opera"; second, to document the various film-related projects in which he was involved. Relevant here, too, is the fact not only that Weill sought to transfer his ideas about musical theater to the movies, but that the traffic also went the other way. Cinematic elements mark a number of the stage works, especially the later ones.

The 1925 essay on "radio art" is notable for the optimism and idealism that Weill conveys about the new media of the time. He focuses above all on "the innovations of film," drawing up a list of achievements that radio, he believed, should match in its own way: "The continuous change of location, the simultaneity of two separate events, the pace of real life and the larger-than-life pace of persiflage, the puppetlike fidelity of animated cartoons and the possibility of following a line from its inception to its transition into other forms—all this, translated into acoustic terms, must be created by the microphone." Although he sees film as the more advanced of the two media thanks to its longer history, he seems hopeful that radio, still in its infancy, will follow. "Just as the film has enriched the optical means of expression, so the acoustic ones must be multiplied in unforeseen ways by radio telephony. 'Acoustic slow-motion' *[Die akustische Zeitlupe]* must be invented—and much else besides. And all that could then lead to an absolute radio art."

The constraints are as much as anything technological. Even though film leads the way, there are important musical issues to consider. Weill goes on to draw parallels between his Busonian aesthetic of absolute music, on the one hand, and the idea of "absolute film," on the other. (The title "Possibilities of an

Absolute Radio Art" echoes Busoni's short treatise "The Possibilities of Opera" that appeared in several of his later published writings.) "The difficulty encountered by absolute film," Weill maintains, "has to do with our visual perception being tied too closely to translation into images from nature and life to apprehend a purely 'melodic' art."

Both the viewer and the artist may be at fault. And although it is rare for Weill to single out expressionism in the arts, he does so here: "Even the expressionism of the fine arts, which pursued similar goals, ultimately failed because the viewer and often even the painter himself conceived of these abstract domains too much as symbols of actual events. This danger is obviated for music and the verbal arts. Musical practice repeatedly refutes the dilettantish view that with every piece of music one has to 'think of something,' that in order to enjoy music we have to connect it with dramatic or idyllic images of one kind or another." The aim—presented here in high-flown language redolent more of his teacher than of Weill himself—is to avoid program music: aim "not [for] a nature symphony . . . but [for] an absolute, soulful work of art that hovers above the earth with no other aim than that of every true work of art: to provide beauty, and through beauty to make mankind good as well as indifferent to life's trivialities."

He is fascinated by the possibility of purely abstract film. Reporting on experiments by Walther Ruttmann and others, he senses "purely musical laws" at work. Yet the comparison with music goes only so far: "The shifting juxtaposition of purely optical forces, this contrapuntal intertwining—of lines and circles, to which color is added as the most expressive ingredient at the climax—all this may create the superficial impression of a piece of music, but it offers only the outlines, only the contours of music; it can channel expression, but what is supposed to be being expressed is missing: the soulfulness, the inner song."

That "inner song" is the domain of music, not of the abstract image. The following year Weill would use the very same expression in an article titled "Commitment to Opera": "If our music possesses typically operatic elements—strict accentuation, concise dynamics, eloquently moving melodic lines—opera can once again become the most precious vessel for capturing streams of inner song."[2]

For the next four years, Weill continued his regular commentaries on radio music, mixing general discussions of the psychology and sociology of the medium with previews and reviews of specific broadcasts (mainly concerts and opera performances but also some radio plays), while often holding out hope that technological advances would help bring about artistic ones. Because of the primitive state of technology, however—as Weill suggested on numerous occasions—some of the limitations of the medium were likely to be temporary rather than inherent.

But then, in 1929, his activity as a radio critic came to an abrupt end. The immediate cause was the broadcast of his own *Berliner Requiem*, a debacle on which he reports in his last column for *Der deutsche Rundfunk*, published in May 1929. There he groups the secular *Requiem* together with *Der Lindberghflug* as being "expressly intended for use by radio stations." "It went without saying," he adds, "that I should be acquainted with the acoustic conditions of the studio, with the orchestral and instrumental possibilities of the microphone, with the distribution of vocal registers and the harmonic boundaries imposed on a composition for radio." He was, he writes, drawing on "observations made over several years of listening to radio music."

Technological questions aside, his aims were in many respects congruent with those of his pieces for the musical theater. And in certain respects radio represented, at least potentially, an even better forum than the theater for realizing them.

> The primary consideration is that the radio audience consists of people from all social strata. It is therefore impossible to proceed from the same premises that apply to the concert hall. Concert music was always intended at the time of its genesis for a particular and limited group of listeners from the educated and well-to-do classes. Radio presents the serious musician of our time with the novel challenge of creating works that can be comprehended by as large a group of listeners as possible. The content and form of these radio compositions must be capable of reaching a large number of people from all groups, and the musical means of expression should not present the primitive listener with any difficulties.[3]

Weill's complaint stemmed from the fact that apart from the "Frankfurter Sender," which broadcast the *Berliner Requiem* on 22 May 1929, no other radio stations carried the piece on that or any subsequent date. The reasons for the suppression were evidently political. Weill writes of "strange goings-on behind the scenes" and "a few especially strict radio censors" whose views, he says, "reflect a shocking ignorance of the artistic needs of those groups that in the context of radio audiences occupy the largest space." That Weill ceased to write for *Der deutsche Rundfunk* no doubt reflects his disenchantment, not with the medium per se, but with its institutional and political dimensions. (That said, it should be noted that the enormous commercial success of *Die Dreigroschenoper*, which was reaching large groups of listeners, meant that he could now easily forgo the additional income from his journalistic by-line and focus exclusively on composition.)

Weill's collected statements on the medium of film similarly mix programmatic optimism and disillusioned critique: optimism about the artistic and sociological possibilities, especially early on; disillusionment about the negative costs of mass distribution, above all about industrialization. His first extensive statement appeared as an interview that he gave with film critic Lotte Eisner in 1927.[4] As far as his own creative work is concerned, his relationship with film had begun shortly before the interview, with his second opera, *Royal Palace,* into which he inserted a short cinematic sequence. Otherwise he had no practical experience with film. His views are, for the most part, necessarily prescriptive and programmatic, based on intimate knowledge of recent cinematic history, to be sure, but written in anticipation of eventual further involvement and of better and greater things to come.

Eisner quotes Weill as saying, "I view film as an art work . . . naturally only good ones," among which he includes Chaplin's *The Kid* and *The Gold Rush* and D.W. Griffith's *That Royle Girl.* He expressly does not include Walther Ruttmann's film *Berlin: Sinfonie der Grosstadt* (1927), whose music, by Edmund Meisel, he criticizes as failing to "solve the problem of 'film music.'" Meisel's score uses, as he puts it, "the expressive means of a superannuated age. . . . This music works with purely melodramatic means in a veristic style utterly opposed to the epic attitude of modern film." Instead, he argues, "we need film music that is objective, so to speak 'concertistic,' music fashioned under the influence of the film, not literary 'illustration.'"

The Eisner interview makes clear that Weill's thinking about film music differs little in its basic thrust from his thinking about musical theater. "There is only one art," he says, echoing a Busonian idea. "Basic laws are the same everywhere. That is why the forms of a good film correspond to those of a good work of music." But that is also why music in the cinema will be quite different from musical theater. "Film music needs only to act on the inner formal laws of film; like all art nowadays it must turn away from naturalism and symbolism and proceed to absolute construction *[absolute Gestaltung].*"

At this point, his experience was based largely on live music in movie theaters. "It may seem antisocial toward the musicians of the orchestra," he remarks, "but the mechanical film needs mechanical instrumentation—the mechanical organ or the mechanical piano. The film companies could record the film along with the music, they could send film roll and music roll together. Thereby an absolute filmic and musical unity would be achieved. Until that time is reached, one should at least try to reduce the all-too-intensified expressive means of film music." In this regard he welcomes experiments such as those conducted at the Baden-Baden chamber music festival, and concludes in an optimistic vein: "It is to be expected that there will soon be a truly decisive example of proper film music."

Perhaps the most remarkable and intriguing passage in the interview is the one where Weill comments in general terms on music's role in the movies. What is the alternative to the mere "illustration" that he rejects? How can music be both "absolute construction" and "fashioned under the influence of the film"? His answer touches on a core issue to do with musical representation and expression, referred to earlier as "inner song": "I see the most valuable support of the film by music in the blind force *[blinde Kraft]* of its interpreting the filmic events in a way formed by musical laws. The film itself brings scene after scene with changing moods. If music clings merely superficially to these scenes and moods—as is the case with illustration—instead of presenting the basic tempo in large musical forms, then it allows the film to fall apart."

The key phrase here is "blind force," an expression indicating the gulf separating Weill's notion of absolute music and a purely formalist view. Music may be conceived in absolute terms by virtue of its being fashioned and presented in large-scale forms; yet such formal concerns do not render it powerless or irrelevant with regard to the film's content. As with so many of Weill's statements, his choice of words seems to contain an element of irony. The expression "blind force" is literal (as "inner song," music doesn't see; it is not bound by the visual) and also allusive.

In religious and philosophical contexts, "blinde Kraft" possesses both positive and pejorative connotations—hence the ironic effect of Weill's choice of expression. In Kant's positive terms, it is the force behind synthesis, a kind of meta-rationality. It is we who are blind rather than the thing itself; as something akin to a force of nature, it eludes our rational grasp. In Freudian psychology, it is linked to the elemental power of sexuality, also the origin of neurosis. Aestheticians of music would most readily associate the idea of a "blinde Kraft," again both positively and negatively, with Schopenhauer, as a way of circumscribing the "Will," that which is essential, as opposed to the world of mere appearances. (The word *blind* occurs frequently in Schopenhauer's work, in both a literal and a metaphorical sense.) With reference to Wagner's music, Schopenhauer's ideas apply more to the later work than to the ideas promulgated in Wagner's principal theoretical tract, *Oper und Drama.* And it would be legitimate to go yet further back to E. T. A. Hoffmann, whose writings about music's role in the theater directly influenced Busoni.[5]

Music's "blindness" is ultimately more a virtue than a limitation: its power is located at a level more profound than the surface world of representations; it expresses a "rarer truth," as Weill would later say. Here again, he could be seen to be applying his teacher's theories about music in the theater to the world of the cinema. In this sense, Weill's later testimony was hardly hyperbolic when he acknowledged that his teacher provided an important stimulus. Busoni "foresaw," Weill said in 1937, "the enormous musical possibilities of the film as the vehicle of a new form of tone-drama."[6]

By 1930, when he published an even more extensive piece on film music,[7] his own experience had grown significantly, more or less in step with a rapidly evolving culture of filmmaking. Film and sound were things he could now talk about together, no longer simply as an aesthetic ideal of absolute construction or as a proposed corrective to the current practice of performing live music as accompaniment to silent movies, but as they might apply to realizable projects. And he was soon to become involved in a project of his own.

The title of the 1930 essay, "Tonfilm, Opernfilm, Filmoper," draws a critical distinction between the medium of sound film generally *(Tonfilm)* and two subgenres in which Weill declares a special interest. He uses the term *opera-film* to describe a film version of a preexisting opera. The term *film-opera* he reserves for original sound films conceived from the outset in terms of musical principles. Although his own involvement in film would largely occur in the former category, his creative ambitions tended more toward the latter. The essay, published in the *Frankfurter Zeitung* just as he was signing a contract for the film version of his own *Dreigroschenoper*, provides him with the opportunity to take stock of the medium and to make public his own position.

Before turning to sound, Weill pays tribute to silent film, describing it with the language of his own epic theater. "What used to lure us into the film was the silent acting, which made possible a heightening of gestic expression beyond a naturalistic attitude"—in other words, the attraction was not immediately musical, nor of course verbal. Only with the advent of sound film were the musician and the writer properly brought into the picture. But Weill's reservations about their role are several. One is a strong sense that sound movies "are way behind the possibilities that our imagination discovered when this new technology emerged." It's not simply a matter of "capturing theater on film *[Theater abfotografieren]* . . . sound film must find its own, independent forms of expression if it is to have a right to exist." At the same time, Weill feared, its mass appeal might mean that film would simply "replace theatrical production that is content to satisfy needs for entertainment." That would not be his aim, just as it was not the aim of "the productive forces" of the theater, among whom he no doubt includes himself.

"The question concerning the role of music in sound film," he asserts, "can only be resolved by musicians." This clearly stated principle leads Weill to raise an issue that he would continue to address for the rest of his career: "The musician can resolve this question only when he collaborates in the film from the very beginning." Future projects would be likely to succeed or fail, he presciently anticipates, depending on the level of the musician's active involvement. This may seem an obvious, even trite point, but it will continue to be a crucial one for a composer for whom control of the "sonic image" remained an essential aesthetic tenet.

Just as Weill repeatedly addressed the Busonian question of "how music, particularly song, is at all possible" in the musical theater, so he poses it here, too, with respect to the medium of film. "To begin with, we need to examine what possibilities there are to show a singing person in sound film." In this regard, he sees film as quite different from theater. "It seems almost out of the question that a person would stand there and sing in a sound film as on the operatic stage." But he does not rule out duets, "especially if they contain elements of the plot or of movement." He also entertains "new possibilities of presenting song in motion." The example he cites is the "singing chauffeur" in *Liebeswalzer* (Wilhelm Thiele, 1929). Another option is "disconnecting a song from the camera by showing its effect on the listener"; here he refers to Marlene Dietrich's song in *The Blue Angel.* Both examples belong to what film theorists would nowadays call "source" or "diegetic" music—music that is an integral part of the narrative as opposed to being merely a means of narration or representation; represented music, in other words, as opposed to the music of representation.

So much for singing. As with the human voice, Weill sees an opportunity in film for the musical instrument to "contribute to the plot *[Handlungsmoment].*" He takes his example from Mickey Mouse films, "rhythmically fixed animated films that establish a thoroughly new and original form of 'film ballet.'" These films point, he argues, to the possibility of an art "that shows people in relation to their living and inanimate environment," demonstrating "the relativity of all phenomena. Everything dissolves itself in movement but finds itself again in rhythm. A skeleton plays xylophone with its lower leg on the ribs of a neighboring skeleton, a locomotive strenuously drags itself up a mountain, and the jaw of a predator suddenly becomes the gentlest of all glockenspiels."

The problems addressed here, evidently with Weill's approval, are quite different from those posed by what he calls "Opern-Tonfilme." Although he concedes that filming repertory operas "seems from the outside alluring," he also says that "its execution will encounter difficulties that cannot be ignored." "Canned music" *(Musik in der Konserve),* as Weill calls it, may be significant "for pedagogical uses and the internal work of the musician," but the possibility of it providing "an adequate substitute" for live performances is "very doubtful. . . . Opera in particular, whose impact depends on the unmediated contact of the singer with the audience, seems the least suited of all forms of theater simply to be captured on film *[abfotografiert].*" The solution, as he sees it, would be "to produce a sound film so removed from the original that it amounted to a new creation." But that is not the main issue. "More important than such experiments is the creation of original sound films," namely "film-operas." That is Weill's priority: "Only when one has clearly established the basic formal tenets concerning the musical possibilities of sound film can one begin to think about transforming a classic opera into an 'opera-film.'"

PABST'S *3-GROSCHEN-OPER*

Given the specific ambitions that Weill's early writings on the medium of film circumscribe—concerning music's role, the composer's input to the film's conception, and the vision of creating a "film-opera"—it is not surprising that his first large-scale film project should end up in court or that the work in question would be *Die Dreigroschenoper,* an instant classic of the musical theater that G. W. Pabst transformed into a film in 1930. (Pabst's film was released with the title *Die 3-Groschen-Oper,* distinguishing it orthographically from the stage work.)

To begin the story at the end, on 13 February 1931, six days before the film's premiere in Berlin, Weill made the following public statement: "I went to court over the author's rights of participation in the production, and I reached a settlement because Tobis [acronym for *Ton-Bild-Syndikat,* the sound-picture company] made a commitment to include me in future productions."[8] The concerns voiced in his previous writings about participation in the production process had been justified. Both Brecht and Weill sued the Nero film company (an affiliate of Tobis-Klangfilm) over their contractual right of codetermination *(Mitbestimmungsrecht).* There were two separate suits, in fact, with different outcomes. Weill's claims, as he reports, were upheld; he reached an out-of-court settlement that included a payment of 50,000 marks and the option for the film company to acquire the film rights of future musical works. Brecht lost his suit, chiefly because he was deemed not to have met the terms of his contract, although he too managed to reach an out-of-court settlement that likely covered the considerable legal costs.

The lawsuit is hard to reconstruct in detail, as Steve Giles has shown in a lucid, well-researched and entertaining study, partly because there is no transcript of the court proceedings and partly because the surviving accounts do not always agree with one another.[9] Accounts vary depending on which side was taken, of course, whether in favor of the artist or the industry. Widely reported by the press at the time, the litigation was seen as an important test case of intellectual property rights as they pertain to creative artists working in the new film industry.

A crucial part of the contract on which the outcome of the lawsuit hinged concerns the extent of Weill and Brecht's right of codetermination. The right applied not to the "form and content of the film," but only to the screenplay adaptation (the "kurbelfertige Bearbeitung des Stoffes," as the contract stated). The distinction proved critical. Thus Nero engaged Brecht as a scriptwriter and was also required to consult Weill about the music. To quote the contract: "The composition of additional music and the arrangement of existing music may only be carried out by the composer Kurt Weill." The same applied to new lyrics, "only to be written by Brecht." Each of them would be remunerated separately for these activities. Yet because Brecht missed the deadline for submitting his manuscript, Nero was legally justified in making the film without him.

Hence the different outcomes. Brecht lost his suit because, by failing to deliver his version of the screenplay on time, he had invalidated the original contract. As Giles concludes, "Brecht had not acknowledged his legal obligation to Nero"; he had "refused to exercise his right of co-determination in a manner consistent with the terms of his contract and from a contractual point of view he had not acted in good faith."[10] Weill won his suit because he could claim, with some justification, that he had not been properly consulted during the preparation of the music used in the film.

The outcome of Brecht's suit was inevitable on more than one level. Brecht turned his withdrawal from the contractually arranged production into an "experiment," whose findings appeared in published form in 1931 as "Der Dreigroschenprozess: Ein soziologisches Experiment" (The Threepenny Lawsuit: A Sociological Experiment). The loss thereby served as a practical demonstration of his developing theory of the new media, a "media theory *avant la lettre,*" to use Kümmel and Löffler's term that describes the discourse surrounding the emerging media in the late nineteenth and early twentieth century.[11] Although Weill, for his part, had already raised some of the main issues in his previous writings, "Der Dreigroschenprozess" presents them more comprehensively and, above all, more systematically as part of the *Versuche.* As far as the evolution of his political ideology was concerned, Brecht had tended increasingly toward Marxist orthodoxy; the trial's outcome, as he writes at the very beginning of his report, was merely symptomatic of a broader malaise: "This winter the filming of the theater piece *Die Dreigroschenoper* provided us with the opportunity to encounter a number of ideas *[Vorstellungen]* characteristic of the current state of bourgeois ideology."[12]

Brecht's theoretical text is significant, as Giles has indicated, not least because of its influence on the perhaps most frequently cited text of media theory, Walter Benjamin's essay "The Work of Art in the Age of Mechanical Reproduction." (Benjamin's previous publications, for their part, had no doubt influenced Brecht in turn.) Both authors reflect the common concepts of media discourse at the time, such as "masses" vs. "individual"; "reproduction" vs. "uniqueness"; "entertainment" vs. "instruction"; "art" vs. "politics." Yet each of them delivers his unique constellation of these concepts in their respective views of contemporary culture; each grapples in his own way with the new roles that the artist and the spectator perform in the technological age. Relevant here is how Brecht's experience with film production and its legal underpinnings added a new dimension to his Marxist analysis of commodification. Weill may have shared that experience and given expression to it in relation to the prevalent dichotomies of the time, though he never articulated it in the clearly delineated socioeconomic terms preferred by his celebrated collaborator.

Although by failing to deliver his screenplay adaptation on time Brecht did not fulfill the terms of his contract, Pabst's film adheres nonetheless fairly closely to Brecht's original outline. To suggest that the lawsuit had little, if anything, to do with the substance of the film as produced, and almost everything to do with the process of production—as it evidently did for Weill, too—would be strictly correct, leaving aside any judgment as to whether either Brecht or Weill actually approved of the final product. In "Der Dreigroschenprozess," Brecht dismisses the film as "a botched job and shameless disfigurement of *Dreigroschenoper.*"[13] And Weill would later criticize it as "old-fashioned," as discussed below.

In his revision of *Die Dreigroschenoper,* also published in the 1931 *Versuche* volume, Brecht inserted portions of a speech from *Happy End* that compares the interests of petty criminals with those of the corporate world: "The days when you minor artisans, working with a conventional jemmy in your callused palms, broke into metal safes containing nothing more than shares and credit notes—these days are gone. You are being swallowed up by big corporations with the banks behind them. What's a jemmy compared with a share certificate? What's breaking into a bank compared with founding a bank?" (These concluding rhetorical questions paraphrase a passage from the introduction to Karl Marx's *A Contribution to the Critique of Political Economy* that compares the gods of ancient mythology with those of modern technology.) Following Brecht's draft scenario, Pabst makes the transition from "petty crime" to "big business" quite explicit. Brecht, in the published version of his scenario, added a new song to make the point, "Gründungssong [founding song] der National Deposit Bank"; it is not in the film, of course, which uses only music from the original *Dreigroschenoper.* The opening stanza of the new song begins: "Nicht wahr, eine Bank zu gründen / Muss doch jeder richtig finden / Kann man schon sein Geld nicht erben / Muss man's irgendwie erwerben. / Dazu sind doch Aktien besser / Als Revolver oder Messer / Nur das eine ist fatal—Man braucht Anfangskapital" (Everyone must find founding a bank okay. If you can't inherit your money, you somehow have to acquire it. Shares are better than a revolver or a knife. One thing, however, is fatal—one needs startup capital).[14] In the final scene, Pabst shows the founding of the bank, but has Macheath and the police chief celebrate their complicity as banking partners with a rendition of the relocated "Kanonensong."

What, to borrow Weill's expression, are the film's "formal tenets"? Musically speaking, apart from the drastic reduction in musical content to a mere thirty minutes (performed by the same musicians as in the stage premiere under the direction of Theo Mackeben), there are two principal differences between the stage and screen versions: (1) Pabst's repositioning of the sung finales; (2) the almost wholesale refunctioning of the musical numbers. The second finale replaces the Overture and is sung by an invisible chorus at the beginning; and the first finale is performed only instrumentally as an entr'acte, as is later "Die Ballade von der Unzulänglichkeit menschlichen Strebens." What's more, only a few of the musical numbers remain as separate formal units. Where possible, and in accordance with Weill's general theoretical leanings discussed above, the songs are treated as source or diegetic music. For example, Ernst Busch is literally a street singer at the beginning, relating the "Moritat" of Mack the Knife to a gathering at the London docks (or rather, the artificially painted backdrop thereof).

And at the end, he sings again, with the new verses taken from Brecht's scenario, concluding with the line "die im Dunkel sieht man nicht" (one doesn't see those [who are] in darkness). In the early scene in the "Tintenfischhotel," "Die Ballade vom angenehmen Leben" is played by the bar pianist as source music. Apart from the "Kanonensong," there are only two remaining pieces of diegetic vocal music: "Melodram" and "Seeräuberjenny," the latter appropriated by Jenny herself (played in the film by Lenya). "Hochzeitslied" and "Barbarasong" were already diegetic (the latter song replaces "Seeräuberjenny" in the wedding scene), and the "Tangoballade" becomes background music in one of the brothel scenes. The closing chorale, like the repositioned second finale, serves as a musical framing device and as background for the credits. Macheath, played in the movie by the Austrian actor Rudolf Forster, in a radical departure from the original doesn't sing at all.[15]

Clearly, Pabst's movie is anything but "theater captured on film," to use Weill's expression. His solution, to use Weill's words again, was "to produce a sound film so removed from the original that it amounted to a new creation." Nor, however, does Pabst's adaptation amount to the kind of film-opera that Weill envisaged. There is too little music for that. Although he used "considerable portions" of Brecht's scenario, as the court found in its verdict, and although he never fully comprehended why Brecht objected, he produced a film quite at odds with the aesthetic informing Brecht's ideas.[16]

Some segments of the film betray Pabst's own background in the presound era, especially the early sequences showing Macheath pursuing Polly on the streets of London, which are almost entirely silent, with no dialogue or music whatsoever. Suppressing the reception of the piece as a "Berlin operetta," the striking camera work—slow-paced, with starkly dramatic contrasts of light, shadow, and reflection—harks back to the medium's expressionist roots. Brecht's scenario, however, makes much of the punctuating titles—described in terms of "panoramas of the intellectual locations of entire segments," "dividing the film into chapters," and "guaranteeing the epic flow"—which Pabst ignores in favor of a more seamless montage. "To leave them out," Brecht remarked, would be "idiotic."[17] At the same time, the ending injects a political message in keeping with Brecht's latest revisions of the *Dreigroschen* material. The overall effect vis-à-vis the original stage version is to seem both dated and updated. In May 1937, when he saw the film again in Los Angeles, Weill inclined toward the "dated" assessment. It "feels quite old-fashioned," he wrote dismissively to Lenya, "which proves that it never was any good in the first place."[18]

UNFULFILLED HOPES

It would be another seven years before Weill became actively involved in another completed film project, though the long delay was not for want of interest. With the National Socialists' takeover of state-subsidized theater after their seizure of power in January 1933, Weill began to see the independent film industry as the only place to turn for work, however temporarily. In February of that year he wrote to Hans Heinsheimer of Universal Edition with a frank assessment of the situation: "I consider what is happening here to be so abnormal that I cannot imagine that it will last longer than a few months. But one can be quite mistaken, and it can't do any harm to begin securing all work opportunities outside the official German theater system. I'm thinking mainly of film, beyond that all non-German theater and concert opportunities, and finally a primitive form of theater that can be done by private theaters."[19]

The response that Heinsheimer sent two days later is remarkably prescient on both counts. Of possible film projects, he warns: "The struggle between business and art will be tougher to decide in favor of the latter in this sphere than in every other." He reports about the latest film hit in Vienna, the romantic comedy *Paprika* (directed by Carl Boese), and wonders whether Weill would really want to have been involved. "I see quite clearly the film problem confronting you," he continues; namely, "to make concessions as far as possible, right up to the limit, intellectually, socially, polemically, while preserving the highest artistic and musical standards. Otherwise no marriage will ever come about." On the matter of Germany's future, Heinsheimer emphatically contradicted Weill: "I cannot share your view that the new course in Germany could be a nightmare lasting only a few months. I am filled with deepest pessimism because I believe that underestimating the opposition will bring reprisals, that it will become evident that they [i.e., the Nazis] will maintain everything better, more securely and ruthlessly than the republicans ever dared for 15 years."[20] He was right, of course.

At the end of January 1933 it looked as though Weill would become part of a collective working on a film version of Hans Fallada's 1932 novel *Kleiner Mann, was nun?* Heinsheimer's remarks were partly a response to the shaky foundations on which the negotiations for that project seemed to have been based. As so often, Weill was initially full of optimism. "Things look very favorable and I believe it will work out this time," he wrote on 19 January. Referring to the collective, he hoped that "in this form" he could "organize a work that would depart from the usual routine and make possible the realization of at least some of the form of the musical film I have in mind."[21] Above all he saw "great possibilities" for his publisher, since he wanted to write music that was "as popular as possible, and place at the center a song with the refrain 'Kleiner Mann, was nun?'"

By late February, however, the whole matter had foundered, principally because the film company did not want to risk the political fallout (or the investment of 300,000 marks) on a film with music supplied by a Jewish composer, especially one as well known and as anathema to the Nazis as Weill. As Weill's correspondence with Heinsheimer reveals, further possible projects came briefly into focus, with René Clair and Jean Renoir and, perhaps most exciting of all, with Josef von Sternberg and Marlene Dietrich. Writing from France in 1934 while working on *Marie Galante,* he could report that "very favorable negotiations with Hollywood are under way, since Sternberg wants to have me for the next Marlene Dietrich film. . . . They were almost concluded a few weeks ago, but they then suddenly stalled, as per usual nowadays, because Marlene is having difficulties with Paramount."[22]

It wasn't until early 1937, after the New York premieres of *Johnny Johnson* (19 November 1936) and *The Eternal Road* (7 January 1937), that Weill started composing for the films. He moved to Los Angeles in late January, staying there until early July, to work on a film about the Spanish Civil War called *The River Is Blue,* which had begun as something of a Group Theatre project, based on a screenplay by author Clifford Odets, and with members of the Group as part of the cast. This time, the project progressed quite far before it, too, was abandoned—or rather, before Weill's music was abandoned. The film was eventually released under the title *Blockade* and with a score by Werner Janssen.

Because Lenya had remained in New York for performances of *Eternal Road,* Weill wrote to her regularly about his Hollywood experiences. On 1 February, for example, he confessed to her his sense of being an utter novice: "Work on the movie is slow, but it's quite interesting to learn the techniques of screenwriting. So far I haven't had any inspiration; it's really an entirely new medium for me, and I feel quite insecure."[23] On 3 March he reported that "[Walter] Wanger decided not to produce the movie for the time being but to wait until he finds the right all-star cast."[24] The indefinite postponement provided the context for Weill's telling comment to Group Theatre director Cheryl Crawford two days later, on 5 March (perhaps with Heinsheimer's words of advice still in his mind): "Don't worry, Hollywood will not get to me. A whore never loves the man who pays her, she wants to get rid of him as soon as she has rendered her services. That is my relation to Hollywood. (I am the whore.) Most people try to mix the whore-business with 'love'—that's why they don't get away."[25]

Having arrived in the United States without any money, with his considerable royalty income from *Dreigroschenoper* frozen, and having earned little from *Johnny Johnson* and *The Eternal Road,* Weill was desperate to find work. He knew his music for *The River Is Blue* might never be used (and it wasn't), yet he completed the score anyway so that he could receive payment—10,000 dollars, no less—in fulfillment of the contract. The idea of composing entirely for money, and not for a movie that was going to be shot, still less for one that was actually *being* shot, may help to explain the kind of music he composed. Writing as a self-declared "novice," he drew heavily on his stock of previous compositions for melodic and thematic material.[26] The burial music from *Der Silbersee* is there, as is the tango from *Marie Galante* that became the song "Youkali," and quite a few other materials that the composer "borrowed" from himself. If he was gaining experience with this trial run, testing his music in a new context, he was also hoping that the completed score might function as a kind of "business card," something he could use to demonstrate his aptitude as a composer of film music.[27]

He was pleased, it seems, with one idea in particular, the kind of musical pun he had appreciated in early cartoons, where music emerges from inanimate objects and vice versa. And so was Charlie Chaplin, as Weill reported in one of his letters to Lenya. The unabashed, almost schoolboyish pride Weill displayed on receiving approbation from the great man, whose silent movies he had so admired in the 1920s, is poignant in the extreme:

> In the afternoon I was with Wanger; I played some recordings for him and was just starting to play some of the music for Cliff's film (which belongs to Wanger anyway), when the door opened and—in came Charlie Chaplin. He is truly the most enchanting person I've ever seen; you can sense his genius ten miles away. We hit it off right away. You can't imagine how enthusiastic he was about the music, jumping up all the time and saying, "play that again," and everything he said showed extraordinary understanding. He was beside himself about the opening of the film, where I start with some wild Spanish music with a lot of castanets which suddenly give way to the clatter of machine guns, while the wild music continues. "*That's one of the greatest ideas I've ever heard,*" he said. We were together for an hour an a half, saw color tests for the new Wanger film *(Vogues of 1938),* and he talked only to me. You can imagine how that impressed Wanger.[28]

Weill would use a similar kind of musical pun in his next movie, *You and Me,* which includes a "Knocking Song."

YOU AND ME

The kind of "marriage" Heinsheimer had desired for Weill finally seemed to be in the offing when, shortly after the *Blue River/Blockade* debacle, the composer was engaged to work on *You and Me* with the German émigré director Fritz Lang. Yet when the movie was released, and despite its including a fair amount of the music he had composed, Weill was left doubting whether the project had been the kind of consummation he really wished for. The gap between ideal and reality can be measured quite closely by comparing his notes on the project to the film proper. Even more than the final product, the notes, which he wrote in English, afford an intriguing glimpse into his thinking about music in the movies in his early American years.

"At the end of the main title," the notes begin, "we hear the voice of a man singing a song which gives in very simple terms and with a popular tune a kind of philosophy of the whole picture."[29] In fact, Weill conceived of the whole opening scene as being informed by music. "The man is singing the song for a lady to whom he tries to sell the song. Now we discover that we are in a music shop and a little while later we see that the music shop is on the . . . th *[sic]* floor of a department store. . . . While the camera moves away from him, the song continues and we hear the song (instead of an underscoring) through all the first shots which make the audience acquainted with the locality of the department store."

The key principle of Weill's ideas is encapsulated in the negative definition "instead of an underscoring." Although the ideas are not totally abandoned in the film, music's role is certainly altered and diminished. The song remains, for example, but it is not integrated as the central part of the action in the way Weill hoped. Instead it is performed as part of the soundtrack by an off-camera tenor, declaiming the text by turns *parlando* and in rich sung tones, while the camera surveys a variety of images that illustrate individual words of the song, "You cannot get something for nothing." Punctuated by the recurring close-up of a cash register (in his correspondence Weill refers to the number as the "cash register song"), the stream of images includes cars, bottles of wine, food, scenic vacations, diplomas, and beauty parlors, thereby presenting "a kind of philosophy of the whole picture." Yet, all the more because of the *parlando* passages, the manner is less that of the musical film Weill had in mind than of didactic theater. (Apparently, it was Weill's *Jasager* that drew Fritz Lang to him.) Critical irony creeps in, too, as the singer embellishes on the song's title by proclaiming hyperbolically and with overdone rhyme: "You cannot rearrange a plan by man since the world began." So although the film at this point doesn't exactly resort to underscoring, and although the song's moral is illustrated by the ensuing action, the song itself was kept musically and visually separate from the primary action, in contrast to Weill's initial plan, which strives for maximum integration. Also, instead of slowly revealing the location in the course of the song, as Weill had wanted, the film begins with a shot of the storefront ("Morris Department Store") before going inside.

We soon learn that some of the store's employees are ex-convicts whom the manager, a kindhearted social reformer, hopes to help back onto the straight and narrow. The plot revolves around the relationship of two of these "jailbirds," Joe and Helen (played by Sylvia Sidney and George Raft). No longer on parole, Joe is about to leave town, but instead, on impulse, he and Helen get married. Little does Joe know that Helen also has a criminal past; not only that, but unlike him, she is still bound by parole regulations, which forbid marriage. It is just a matter of time before her efforts to keep the truth from him fail, whereupon he rejoins his group of fellow ex-cons, who are planning to rob the department store. Meanwhile Helen, who has informed the store manager of the break-in plans, assists in the interception of the crime before it is fully committed. After the manager gives the members of the gang yet another chance to go straight, she provides a mathematical demonstration, aided by a chalkboard, that crime literally doesn't pay. They are just "little crooks," she tells them in a gesture of social critique; the "big shots" are the politicians. That's not the end of it, of course. Helen is pregnant, another fact she has been withholding from her husband, who rejects her (because she lied to him) but then has second thoughts. Finding her involves a visit to the parole officer, who breaks the news of the impending birth, whereupon the whole group of reformed gang members goes in search of her. The final scene in the hospital has the members of the gang nervously awaiting the arrival of the baby boy, who has the final nonverbal word.

In his notes, Weill envisaged a "scene in the elevator" at the end of the scene in the department store: "we hear for the first time the rhythm of the knocking song," a rhythm that should be "typical [so] that the audience recognizes it immediately when it comes back." He explains the musico-dramatic significance of the scene as follows: "The rhythm and the tune of this knocking song (which is built on the knocking of the walls in prison, used as a mean[s] of communication between the prisoners) is one of the two 'Leitmotive' of our picture and is carried through the whole picture. It indicates the former life of these people and the danger which results out of their past for their present life." Fascinating, of course, if not entirely unexpected that Weill should use Wagnerian terminology, in German, and also invest the motive, as described, with such richly symbolic significance, even if his actual approach is thoroughly un-Wagnerian. He goes on to outline a later scene as a "knocking symphony," out of which the song grows. The principal characters have previously used the rhythm as part of a love song ("Do you love me?" "I do." etc.), but here "it really shows the dangerous background . . . a kind of revolt, a rebellion in prison." Moreover, "it builds up to a wild, savage, rude song, changing these people who had tried to go straight back into criminals."

In the movie proper, the planned "elevator scene" is reduced to a brief encounter (without music) between the two protagonists, who briefly touch hands as they pass on an escalator. After the store has closed, the two repair to a bar; in this scene, according to his notes, Weill's intention was to include a "torch song." Although the notes identify the title as "You and Me" and specify that the song be "carried through the picture as a sort of Leitmotive *[sic]*," in the movie proper it is replaced by another song, called "The Right Guy for Me." For this reason, the leitmotivic integration of the song isn't as extensive as hoped for. However, the immediate dramatic point is as the composer wished it to be: "Sung by a torch singer," as the notes describe, the song "tells everything that Raft would like to tell the girl, and in showing Raft's and Sylvia's reaction to the song, we show what is going on between them." He wanted to "see Sylvia taking Raft's hand in hers, under the table . . . we know it's she who says it, through the mouth of the torch singer."

An ingenious and effective use of source music similar to that planned (but not executed) for the first scene and also reflective of Weill's theoretical writings from the early 1930s, the song functions on two levels at once. As source music, it is utterly realistic; but it is also "inner song," reflecting the protagonists' own emotions. With its blues-inflected idiom and its flashback illustrations of scenes from harbor-town low life, the song expresses a sentiment reminiscent of "Seeräuberjenny" and "Surabaya-Johnny": the right guy may be a "good-for-nothing," but he's still right.

Particularly affecting is the opening incipit of the song's refrain, "they call him 'Good for Nothing'" (ex. 54). The melodic inflection D–F♮ suggests a blues lament—5th degree to flattened 7th degree. It should be noted, too, that the opening music also invokes the topic of lament with its chromatically descending bass, in both the telescoped introduction and the accompaniment to the sung verse. But the harmonization of the F♮ on "nothing" moves away from the tonic to E♭, the flattened 6th degree of G major, thereby producing a whole-tone cluster (thanks to the added seventh and ninth over the E♭ root). It is a magical lament, a lament of love! Weill will use the cluster again for moments of bewitching disorientation, such as in "This Is New," in *Lady in the Dark,* at the words "Am I really existing?" The flattened sixth degree also relates back to the harmonic sphere of the verse, which is not in G, but in the key of A♭, more clearly defined by the key signature than by the music itself, which evades that particular tonic in favor of the "interrupted" area of F minor.

The incipit's oscillation between the tonic and the whole-tone cluster also fits the phrase "Just a bit of driftwood," given the "funny feeling" the singer has about the guy, a feeling announced by a rising figure that begins with a semitone appoggiatura in finest operetta mode. It is vintage Weill, singing the love song of society's underclass, mixing heterogeneous "love" elements, from Léhar and Wagner to modern tango; it also reveals a quickly acquired mastery in a new context, not only of Gershwinesque harmonies but also of the American song form, which Weill first experimented with in *Johnny Johnson.*

If the refrain's melody counts as the most affecting moment, then the preceding verse surely contains the most dramatic one, with the melodic line at the end reduced almost to recitative, the urgent, quoted pleas of an operatic scena, spoken in slang: "'Doggone you, snap out of it! This is love!' There wasn't a doubt of it." Weill may even have smuggled in here a reference to Wagner's *Tristan und Isolde* with an allusion to that work's so-called motif of longing (see ex. 54, mm. 5–6).

Here, as with the earlier examples, the song tells a double story. Beyond that, Weill intended it to function more broadly as a device perhaps best known in cinema from a later movie, *Casablanca* (1942), with its principal "leitmotivic" popular song "As Time Goes By" (written not by the film's composer, Max Steiner, but by Herman Hupfeld in 1931). Although "The Right Guy for Me" as a replacement

EXAMPLE 54. *You and Me,* "The Right Guy for Me" (conclusion of verse, opening of refrain)

for the envisaged title song "You and Me" doesn't receive the same pervasive treatment as "As Time Goes By," one can see that Weill was at least thinking creatively along the same lines five years before *Casablanca*.

Other of Weill's unrealized ideas include a second elevator scene ("Song of the Lie") as the couple are on their way to get married. Weill again wants an animated inanimate object to make music: "The camera turns down to [the] wheels of the elevated [*recte:* elevator] and they begin to sing: Don't lie, don't lie, and then the rattling voice of the wheels is the voice of Sylvia's conscience, it follows her when they leave the elevated *[sic]*, it stops for a moment, but it starts again when they get the information where to get married, and maybe it follows them and is still warning, whispering when the big door of the marriage bureau has already closed behind them."

In addition, he imagined a scene with "The Song of the Baby," blurring the distinction between diegetic and nondiegetic music. This is the moment where Helen has decided to tell Joe that she's pregnant: "She is working in the kitchen, perhaps she is preparing whipped cream, the underscoring music follows the rhythm of her hands which beat the cream, and out of the rhythm she begins to hum a simple little folksong which expresses her deep happiness that she can give him a baby—and her fear that their happiness could be destroyed. Here also the song expresses the idea of the scene instead of a dialogue."

What does remain are fragments of another idea, connected to the "Knocking Song." "The preparations for the burglary which is an almost silent sequence is underscored with a kind of fugue on the theme of the knocking song." The scene in the movie itself is certainly not silent, and it is more extended than Weill's description. Before preparing the break-in, the men recall a break-out, with their chants emerging as translations of the messages encoded in the rhythms. As the scene intensifies, their call-and-response unison chants become polyphonic, almost in the manner of Ernst Toch's "Geographical Fugue." Fugue as flight, perhaps?

Weill's notes "About the music for 'You and me'" are dated 24 May 1937—written, that is, during his first stay in Hollywood and long before his return for final dubbing the following year. They describe in a fair amount of detail the role he envisaged for music in the movies, even if in this instance he was not charged to realize the ideal of a "film-opera." As the quoted excerpts demonstrate, his express aim was to avoid traditional underscoring and, where possible, to replace dialogue with song. They also show that his conception allowed for "leitmotivic" connections, especially where they were constitutive for the plot and where they complicated the film's symbolic content through "inner song."

After final dubbing, *You and Me* represented only a partial realization of Weill's ideas, as various comments made to Lenya in their correspondence indicate. The opening music, which recurs throughout the movie, must have derived from the song "You and Me," as described in the notes. Nowhere in the film, however, do we hear it with any words (although it's easy to imagine how those words might fit the incipit). The melody supplies the thematic material for a set of instrumental character variations during the "honeymoon" visit to four restaurants—Swedish, Italian, Chinese, and Austrian. And the latter variation, a waltz (needless to say), is used as underscoring during the brief visit to the registry office (which we don't see).

Otherwise, underscoring is used only sparingly, though perhaps more than Weill cared for. On 21 April 1938, during his second stay in Hollywood, he told Lenya that "doing the *underscoring* [is] rather boring work."[30] Apart from the examples already cited, there is brief underscoring at the following moments: as atonal build-up to the break-in; when Joe decides after all to pay for the "Ecstasy" perfume rather than steal it (theme from "Cash Register Song" followed by "You and Me"); music of steady momentum during the search for Helen before she is found in the hospital; and as the closing music (same as beginning, but now as upbeat waltz).

Visually and in terms of plot, especially with its exploration of the darker side of the human psyche and the tension between love and the law, *You and Me* belongs to the genre of film noir. But it is hardly pure noir. It also contains some elements of heavy-handed comedy mixed with moments of law-abiding rectitude, and even a dash of social critique. With Lang at the helm, and with Weill supplying the music, one might be forgiven for thinking that George Raft had assumed the persona of a reformed Macheath from *Die Dreigroschenoper* who had relocated with his gang from Soho in London to somewhere in New York. It is an odd mixture, a psychological gangster movie lightened by satirical humor and tempered by somewhat sanctimonious moralizing—nicely captured by the self-admonishing comment of one of the gang members, who, on seeing a newspaper headline about a gangster slaying, exclaims, "That could happen to us, couldn't it?" A cautionary tale!

The film's hybrid nature was recognized at the time by the critic of the *New York Times* who respected Lang's credentials and aims but found the result disappointing, despite Weill's "impressive score": "[Lang] has been trying to break with the Hollywood formula, to bring into closer unity the still-disjointed sound and picture tracks of the talking screen. It is a good cause he is fighting, but it is one which cannot be fought with compromises. No director can serve two styles at once. 'You and Me' is torn both ways and emerges, in consequence, as a ragged drama with comic overtones." The "net effect," he concluded, "is remarkably bad."[31]

Weill's own reports on the production process are similarly mixed, registering the occasional triumph, but also giving vent to enormous frustration with the director and his assistants. His own verdict on the film itself, which he voiced privately about a partial screening before editing reduced the final product to ninety minutes of screen time, is contained in the letter to Lenya dated 19 April 1938:

> This morning at 8:30 Fritz showed me about two thirds of the movie. It's very beautiful, at times excitingly so, but *zu lang* (i.e. too long and too Lang), often very draggy and very German, but of a much higher standard than anything they're doing here. The songs are definitely the highlights, and one could just cry (or laugh) to think that in this movie all my ideas have again proved to be right and new and exciting—and nobody will ever know they were my ideas. "The Right Guy" is terribly effective; "Song of the Lie" [ultimately dropped] comes through much better than I had thought. The best thing is the *cash register* in the beginning, but of course they won't understand it (except for Lang), and I'm more convinced than ever that it isn't worth it getting irritated, because you're dealing with the lowest human scum.[32]

On balance, it seems, Weill's motion-picture glass was both half full and half empty. Just eighteen months after the film's release, a critic for the *New York Times,* discussing the state of "composing for the films," singled out Weill for special mention. "Hollywood in exceptional instances," he wrote, "has allowed the composer a hand in a plot. Kurt Weill was called in from the start by Producer-Director Fritz Lang on 'You and Me.' Here music was psychologically of first importance, being heard on occasions as 'the voice of conscience.'"[33] Whom the critic was quoting in his assessment, he doesn't say. Yet the quoted words succinctly capture the role Weill's notes assign to music in a number of ways, not only in the torch song, but above all in the novel (albeit unrealized) second elevator scene, and also through underscoring in the scene where Joe resolves to pay for the perfume. As Weill himself said in 1946, looking back at his work of nine years earlier, "I tried out a new technique by using songs as a part of the background music, expressing the 'inner voice' of the characters."[34] Had Weill had his way, the musical "voice of conscience" or "inner voice" would likely have been even stronger.

STAGE TO SCREEN

None of the three Hollywood movies derived from Weill's American stage shows was ever likely to meet with the composer's full-blown approval. To a greater or lesser degree, they are all notable for being adaptations that ran counter to the composer's precepts and expectations. In the case of *Knickerbocker Holiday,* there exist several pages of notes, similar to those Weill drafted for *You and Me,* that provide a telling point of comparison. In the other two cases—*Lady in the Dark* and *One Touch of Venus*—Weill's reactions document countless frustrations with a production process whose tendency was to exclude the composer while reducing the role of his music.

There was no reason for Weill to feel as though he was being singled out for unusually negligent treatment, however. In his study *Through the Screen Door: What Happened to the Broadway Musical When It Went to Hollywood,* Thomas S. Hischak presents case after case of disaffected composers, from Richard Rodgers to Stephen Sondheim. "Hollywood was wary of songs," he writes. "It didn't know at first exactly what to do with them. Film tends to be realistic, and the narrative is primary. Songs are not realistic and, until the fully integrated musicals of the 1940s, did not advance the story. The studios knew the songs were the heart of the musical, yet they were suspicious of them."[35]

Weill's own early diagnosis of the medium is echoed in Hischak's summary description: "An actor bursting out in music because an emotion had overcome him was what made the theater songs soar. But would audiences as easily accept screen characters in realistic settings breaking into music? How does one move from dialogue into a song lyric? And where was the music coming from?" Moreover, "the studios never came up with new songs in filming Broadway shows that matched the quality of those eliminated. . . . What puzzles is how good songs were so often replaced by mediocre ones."[36] Weill would experience all of this, the cuts as well as the mediocre replacements.

Because of his own insights into the differences between the media and their respective institutions, Weill was less interested in attempts to turn his musicals into the equivalent of "opera-films" than he was in starting afresh and creating the Hollywood equivalent of "film-opera." Yet he wasn't entirely uninterested either, not least for financial reasons. With his typescript "Notes for Movie *Knickerbocker Holiday*" (dated in Weill's hand "Suffern, N.Y Dec. 5 1939," just over a year after the work's stage premiere), he again revealed the yawning gap between ideal and reality.[37] The ideas sketched in the notes evidently had little bearing on the film that was eventually released in 1944, some four years later. Werner R. Heymann, not Weill, was responsible for arranging the music. Apart from providing insight into Weill's own and largely neglected conception of the cinematic adaptation, the notes can also be read as an expression of his own thinking, as opposed to Anderson's, about the original musical play.

At the beginning he replaces the original epic frame, which had author Washington Irving reflecting on himself and the story he is writing. Instead he stresses the contrast between now and then:

> Suggested opening for picture: we show a modern street in the downtown part of New York which was "New Amsterdam" 300 years ago (Wall Street and Battery), with skyscrapers, automobiles, people rushing to their business with a modern New York music. Then the people disappear from the street, ducks, chickens and pigs appear, the skyscrapers shrink down to little old dutch houses and the music dies down to the idyllic harmonies of the beginning of "Knickerbocker Holiday," the dutch maidens appear and begin the opening chorus ("Clickety Clack") while they are washing the steps of the market place on old "New Amsterdam."

Neither the Irving frame nor the musical or visual connection to contemporary New York remains in the movie (directed by Harry Joe Brown), which presents itself rather in the manner of a historical costume drama, however anachronistically. The "basic idea" for the picture *does* remain, as described in Weill's notes: "the story of the 'First American,' the boy who cannot take orders and gets into trouble because he does not agree with the laws of the city council." But several of the numbers disappear, including "How Can You Tell an American?" and "It Never Was You." The latter survives only as underscoring, a recurring leitmotif of the bond between Tina (Constance Dowling) and Brom (Nelson Eddy). Stuyvesant (Charles Coburn) keeps his "September Song," performed in an upbeat, jaunty manner with a dance sequence in which he hobbles around on his silver peg-leg. The opening notes of the melody also serve as leitmotivic material for Stuyvesant, often with a dotted rhythm that suggests a curious affinity with a very different Dutchman, Wagner's eponymous *fliegender Holländer.* And there is quite a bit of new musical material not by Weill, attributed in the credits to Jule Styne and a quartet of lyricists. Given the importance Weill attached to the "sonic image" of his stage works, it is not without more than a tinge of irony that Heymann shared the 1944 Oscar nomination with Weill for best "Scoring of a Musical Picture." (The winners that year were Carmen Dragon and Morris Stoloff for *Cover Girl.*)

Weill's notes prescribe that "the comic situations of the play should be retained." And they are. But he also asks for satire, whose "main source" he sees in "the parallel between Stuyvesant and the modern dictator of the Mussolini type, the regimentation of everybody and everything, the parody of militarism (with General Poffenburgh as a take-off of Goering)." None of this finds its way into the film, any more than the prescribed contemporary frame did (although the caricature of sadistic German militarism would find its way into *Where Do We Go from Here?* as discussed below). Missing, too, is any overtly allegorical link to contemporaneous politics (thereby serendipitously precluding the fatal connection between European dictators and FDR).

Weill concludes his notes by stating that the "picture should not be conceived as an old production musical. . . . The music and the songs should be worked into the plot very naturally and should become really an essential part of the picture as it was in the stage production of 'Knickerbocker Holiday.'" Despite the sheer amount of sonic material, much of it admittedly underscoring but also a fair number of set pieces, albeit not all of them drawn from Weill's score, the music in the film cannot be said to form "an essential part." Still less does it approximate the model Weill proposes in the final sentence of his notes: "the kind of musical film as it had been started by Lubitsch some 10 years ago and which, strangely enough, never has been continued." Knowing with hindsight how badly other musical plays of Weill's would fare as screen adaptations, one can at least pay

Knickerbocker Holiday the backhanded compliment that, from a musical point of view, things could have been worse.

Lady in the Dark and *One Touch of Venus*—Weill's two biggest Broadway successes—were likely candidates to attract attention from Hollywood, just as other smash-hit shows such as *Show Boat* had done before them. Both of these musical plays received lavish treatment by major studios, each of them cast with top-tier screen actors. *Lady in the Dark,* which went on general release on 10 February 1944, starred Ginger Rogers as the neurotic publishing executive Liza Elliott. *One Touch of Venus,* which had to wait until August 1948 before finding its way into theaters, boasted Ava Gardner in the sexy title role.

The resources expended on the movie version of *Lady in the Dark* were particularly extravagant. Quite apart from the almost unprecedented $2.6 million spent on production costs, Paramount Pictures had paid the then record sum of $285,000 to secure the film rights ($115,000 to producer Sam Harris, $85,000 to librettist Moss Hart, and $42,500 each to composer Kurt Weill and lyricist Ira Gershwin). *Lady in the Dark* thus acquired, as bruce mcclung notes, "the dubious distinction of being the most expensive picture ever made since *Gone With the Wind.*" Although filming ended on 20 March 1943, the studio delayed the film's release for well over a year, in part because it was embarrassed by the size of the budget. "Concerned with the exorbitant price tag," says mcclung, "Paramount was quick to publicize that the rights had been purchased and the production planned prior to America's involvement in WWII." Even so, *Lady in the Dark* easily covered the investment with receipts of $4.3 million, making it "the fourth-largest grossing film of 1944."[38]

One Touch of Venus encountered quite different sorts of obstacles in reaching the movie theaters. Having acquired the screen rights in 1945, while the memory of the theatrical premiere was still fresh, United Artists intended to cast Mary Martin from the stage show as Venus, with Mary Pickford producing. Agnes de Mille, also from the Broadway production, was announced as the choreographer. But Pickford, who had paid $150,000 for the rights, finally sold them to Lester Cowan at Universal after Martin became pregnant. After initially considering Deanna Durbin, Universal cast Ava Gardner in the title role, securing for her a one-time contractual release from MGM.

Easily discounted as mere "movie trivia," these facts illustrate the complex negotiations and considerable investments involved in transferring a musical play from Broadway to Hollywood. Given that Weill had felt impelled to file a lawsuit against the company that produced the film version of his *Dreigroschenoper,* he surely had even more reason to complain about how these two American works were treated. As with *Knickerbocker Holiday,* he was obliged to accept wholesale removal of instrumental and vocal numbers to a degree even more radical than with Pabst's *3-Groschen-Oper.* As long as Martin and de Mille were involved in

One Touch of Venus, and even allowing for industry pressures, it might have been possible to approximate "theater captured on film," to use Weill's expression, for that production at least. Yet neither of these screen adaptations ended up anywhere close to that, being notable more for what is missing from the original score than for what is left. Nor, because of the removal of so much of the music, do they qualify as "film-opera." In each case, the final product fell far short of the composer's expectations.

Amounting to a radical "demusicalization," the adaptation from stage to screen severely diminished in length whole sections of the stage work that rely on music, while reducing others from sung foreground to mere instrumental background. Arranging and orchestrating this material was not the composer's responsibility; it was done by specially hired arrangers and orchestrators. Granted, *Lady in the Dark* reflects at least a rudimentary attempt to retain the original's form-defining principle separating spoken reality from musicalized dreams. And thanks in large part to fabulous costume designs by the legendary Edith Head, Mitchell Leisen's technicolor movie is visually quite arresting, especially so in the four dream sequences. Yet both here and in *One Touch of Venus,* the suppression of Weill's score substantially alters the work's dramaturgy.

Liza's music is the principal victim of this suppression, with just a single number left for her to sing. Ginger Rogers's performance of "The Saga of Jenny" in the "Circus Dream" (omitting the fourth of the song's five stanzas) seems oddly demure compared to the raunchier rendition of the stage production's Gertrude Lawrence. The song "This Is New," originally written for the character of Randy Curtis (played in the movie by Jon Hall), is relegated to underscoring in the preceding "Wedding Dream." (In the stage production Liza had performed the number, and then only the chorus, because of the limited vocal talents of the actor playing Randy, Victor Mature.) The show-stopping "Tschaikowsky," brilliantly performed in the stage version by Danny Kaye as the Ringmaster (a.k.a. the photographer Russell Paxton in the "real" scenes of the play), is cut from the movie altogether. (In the movie the dual role of Russell/Ringmaster is played by Misha Auer.) And a fair amount of Weill's circus music is cut and replaced by more generic, clichéd fare, such as Julius Fučík's "Entrance of the Gladiators" and the theme to *The Lone Ranger* (taken from Rossini's overture to his opera *William Tell*), the latter being fleetingly used to identify screen idol Randy with the title character of the film series.

Perhaps the most puzzling omission of all, however, and something that especially irked lyricist Ira Gershwin, is Liza's song "My Ship" following the "Childhood Dream." As in the stage version, the incipit of the song appears throughout, either hummed by Liza or played instrumentally. To cite a couple of examples: as recollected in one of the therapy sessions with Dr. Brooks, Liza's childhood persona haltingly and perfunctorily attempts the opening measures of the song at one of her parents' dinner parties (the only time any of the words are heard), only to abandon the effort in a state of acute embarrassment and shame. Liza's absent-mindedly humming the song's melody as an adult prompts the query: "Didn't you know you did that?" Thus, as in the stage show, "My Ship" works as a metaphor of her unconscious, and its dissonantly harmonized underscoring (played in the film soundtrack on the theremin, an electronic instrument whose eerie sonorities conventionally conjure up otherworldly phenomena) is especially effective in expressing inner anxiety and estrangement. Not just the plot but also the soundtrack can be called "psychological." Yet by omitting "My Ship" in the final scene, the film deprives the song of the central role that it plays in the stage show.

Whereas the play celebrates in music the success of Liza's talking cure, as she recalls the song in its entirety, with her newly acquired partner, Charley Johnson, joining in, the movie concludes in a less sentimental, almost flippant manner. As discussed in the preceding chapter, the music of the dream sequences takes gender out of the equation and puts sex back into the mix. By the same token, the film's relegating music to the background or removing much of it entirely mirrors an evident (and in 1940s America perhaps inevitable) discomfort with the theme of psychoanalysis in general and female sexuality in particular. In this connection, it is pertinent to note that in *The Great Hollywood Musical Pictures,* James Robert Parish and Michael R. Pitts, who dismiss the film adaptation as "a gaudy abortion," claim that the final song "was excised from the movie because Paramount executive producer Buddy G. DeSylva, himself a songwriter, did not like Weill's style and was upset that the movie (and this song) referred to the leading lady's mental aberrations."[39]

Maggie, Liza's assistant, seems to have similar qualms about her boss's psychoanalysis. When Liza gains insight into her unequal relationships with Kendall and Randy (the former providing a father substitute, the latter wanting her to dominate him), she rejects them both, making up her mind instead in favor of a grown-up relationship with Charley (played in the movie by Ray Milland). Maggie reacts to the commotion by joking that "I want a big picture of Freud in my office." Russell expresses disapproval in his own characteristic style, with camp outrage. Walking in on Liza and Charley, who are sealing their new business and romantic partnership with a kiss, he vents: "This is the end, the absolute end."[40] Indeed, it is "The End," as these two concluding words appear on the screen and the soundtrack intones the song's unsung as well as previously unheard final phrase.

With Paramount's treatment of *Lady in the Dark* quite fresh in his mind and the movie still running in the theaters, Weill made an attempt to gain tighter artistic control over *One Touch of Venus* by proposing to his agent, Leah Salisbury, several conditions for the production of a screen version. In a memo to

Salisbury dated 4 September 1944, he delivered what he calls "the content of the non-interpretation clause as I want it in the contract for 'Venus.'" Specifically, and by way of corrective to his experience with *Lady in the Dark,* he made two stipulations regarding the music. First, he required that "all the songs in the picture have to be taken from the score of the original show and the underscoring of the picture has to be based on themes from the original score." Second, he stated that the studio should "call on me . . . to write any new songs or musical material as might be necessary for the moving picture treatment of the original show . . . to select and place the original songs for the requirements of the movie script and make any necessary changes . . . [and] to select themes and material from the original score for underscoring purposes." The remaining details of the document concern the terms of his work "according to my Hollywood salary of 2500.- a week for my last job at 20th Century" and also the matter of credits.

The movie would indeed have, as requested, "a special frame with the following text":

> Based on the musical play "One Touch of Venus"
> Music by Kurt Weill
> Book by S. J. Perelman and Ogden Nash[41]

Although the contract stipulated that Weill would be "responsible for the entire music in the picture," things did not quite turn out that way. For a while, with Mary Pickford and Sam Coslow still involved, it looked as though Weill would indeed continue to work on the score as he had envisaged. In May 1945 he mentioned to Lenya that they were "keeping 'Speak low,' 'That's him' and 'Foolish Heart'" and that he was "trying also to get the Barbershopquartett [*sic;* i.e., 'The Trouble with Women'] in," adding that "I have to write about four new numbers," which he promptly set about doing.[42] By the end of the month he could report to her that he had "now finished 3 songs for Venus (2 good ones) and have one more to write."[43] And on 1 June he was "[working] with Coslow to wind up my business on the picture."[44] With the shift to a different studio, however, the supervision of the music fell to Ann Ronell, a versatile songwriter, lyricist, and musical director for films, who was married to Universal's producer Lester Cowan. Weill had made her acquaintance on the set of *The River Is Blue* and seems to have trusted her with representing his best interests. Weill and Ronell both appear in the credits: there is a separate frame with the words "Music by Kurt Weill" (as per contract), whereas Ronell receives mention for contributing the "musical score and new lyrics."

Yet Ronell had even less control than Weill over which numbers remained and which were to be eliminated. As with *Lady in the Dark,* much of the music was either cut or radically altered, despite Ronell's apparent protestations. "I know you are putting up a very brave fight to keep my material, as far as it is being used, intact," Weill wrote to Ronell in February 1948, "and I appreciate very much the fine integrity which characterizes your fight in defense of the work of a fellow artist and a friend. I realize full well what that means, and I want you to know that I realize it."[45] The previous month, he had described Ronell's "battle with the mighty music department" as "comparable only to the fight of little David against Goliath." Ronell had reported that "regarding adapting your orchestrations for the film score, I have found a general indisposition on the part of Hollywood men to join me in my enthusiasm."[46] To which Weill sarcastically responded, "What would become of [Milton] Schwarzwald [head of Universal's music department] and his arranger friends if they would allow the spirit of my orchestration to enter the sacred Wagnerian halls of Hollywood motion picture scoring."[47]

Not only did Ronell have to fight a losing battle with the studio in defense of Weill's music, but the Motion Picture Association of America (MPAA) took exception to the lyrics of two of the songs, "The Trouble with Women" and "Wooden Wedding," as well. As it turned out, neither of the songs was included in the film, even with expurgated lyrics (although the melody of "The Trouble with Women" can still be heard as background music, during the opening credits). The MPAA censors also rejected some of the lyrics in "Foolish Heart," so Ronell rewrote them with a new title, "(Don't Look Now but) My Heart Is Showing." She also rewrote the text of "West Wind" as "My Week." Both retexted songs were eventually published as sheet music, even though "My Week" did not make it into the movie (the melody can be heard as underscoring during Savory's failed seduction of Venus). When all was said and done, only the numbers that Weill originally mentioned remained more or less intact—"Speak Low," "My Heart Is Showing," and "That's Him"—without any new ones added.

Apart from omitting all but three of the songs, William A. Seiter's black-and-white picture introduces numerous other departures from the original play, some of them quite extensive. Hatch, whose first name is changed from Rodney to Eddie, is no longer a barber but a "window trimmer." Mr. Savory, formerly associated with a foundation, is now the owner of the department store where Eddie is employed. Perhaps the main difference between the stage and screen versions, however, has to do with the disappearance of Agnes de Mille's ballet sequences, and along with them the original's socially critical themes of urban alienation and the one-dimensional boredom of domestic life in suburbia (not to mention Weill's critically acclaimed dance music). Nor does the film make much of the musical comedy's self-reflexive quips about the value of modern art. The element of satire is substantially toned down. True, the various scenes in the home furnishings section of the department store could be seen to be poking fun at shallow materialism. But with all of her low-key eroticism, Ava Gardner's Venus visits earth not to indict New Yorkers for a state of affairs in which "passion [is] passé" or love "merely an obsolete art" (how can she possibly do that, having lost her torch song "I'm a Stranger Here Myself"?); her mission is rather to inspire the population to "speak love." The result of her divine intervention, expressed through music literally filling the sky (and lip-synched in her case), is a sudden spike in marriage licenses. Even Savory and his cynical, wise-cracking assistant, Molly, get hitched. And Venus's mortal likeness appears at the end not bound for the art class, but looking instead for the department store's model home.

WHERE DO WE GO FROM HERE?

The screen versions of *Lady in the Dark* and *One Touch of Venus* fell either side of another Hollywood project, *Where Do We Go from Here?*, with which Weill declared himself to be "on the whole very pleased."[48] "A sort of humorous fantasy," as Weill described it, the movie concerns a man called Bill Morgan (played by Fred MacMurray) who is eager to serve his country by enlisting in the armed forces.[49] He also wants to impress the uniform-obsessed Lucilla at the local USO (United Service Organizations) headquarters, thinking he loves her—not realizing that it is the more sympathetic Sally who craves his attention. But he fails his medical examination and is classified 4-F.

Assigned to help on the home front with the scrap drive, the hapless Bill stumbles across an old lamp donated by an elderly woman with a German accent. Rubbing the lamp to remove a thick layer of dust, he inadvertently brings to life a bibulous genie called Ali who, as Weill describes the story, "gets mixed up in his time sense."[50] Hence the title: the plot is structured around defining moments in American history, beginning and ending in the present with excursions—courtesy of Ali's undependable magic watch—to the eighteenth, fifteenth, and seventeenth centuries, in that order. (In this regard, the film prefigures the time travel in Weill's later musical play *Love Life*.) An advertisement in the July issue of the monthly magazine *Movie Show* touted *Where Do We Go from Here?* as "a century-hopping lyrical miracle!"

Yet the title acquired an unanticipated historical relevance insofar as, when the movie opened on 23 May 1945, less than a month after the end of WWII in Europe, the present looked very different from when the film was made in 1944. Had Bill been transported by the genie to the future of the film's reception rather than back to its inception, the aspiring soldier might well have revoked his wish for military service (and looked for other ways to impress the opposite sex). As Miles Kreuger puts it, "The story of a man desperate to join the armed forces had become ludicrously anachronistic at a time when everyone was thinking about getting out of the armed forces."[51] At the end of the movie, thanks to Ali's sly intervention, Bill is finally declared fit to serve. Yet the premiere audience may well have wondered about his enthusiasm at being drafted: where do we go from *here?*

In addition to reflecting the uncertainty of the historical destinations for the movie's protagonist and the suddenly altered vantage point of the cinema-going public at the time of the film's release (the dawning of a new "here"), the title also fits on a generic level in nicely capturing the personal sense of expectation that Weill himself attached to the movie in the context of his composing career. He had lofty ambitions for the creative direction in which his first original screen musical might take him. "It is a pretty safe bet," he predicted a year after the film's release, "that eventually something like a 'film-opera' will grow out of all this." He even went so far as to envisage a convergence of his aspirations as a composer for the musical theater on the one hand and for the cinema on the other. "It is quite possible," he ventured, "that the much-talked-about 'American opera' will come out of the most popular American form of entertainment—the motion picture."[52] Granted, as discussed below and in the following chapter, there is indeed a sense in which Weill's "American opera" was indebted to the motion picture, albeit not the one he had in mind here.

"The picture is excellent," Weill remarked to Lenya, "and comes over as something very fresh and completely original and utterly different from any musical they've made so far."[53] He was proud of one sequence in particular that he saw as a sign of things to come, "a regular little comic opera for the scene on Columbus' ship" written with lyricist Ira Gershwin.[54] At the same time, he conceded that "there are weak spots in the picture, especially in the end."[55] By the time he wrote these remarks, he was doubtless aware of the conclusion's sudden datedness. Despite almost uniformly favorable press reviews, box office receipts were modest. The composer remained upbeat about his achievement, for example in a letter to his agent, Irving Lazar: "The great acclaim which the score for *Where do we go from here* got is an indication of the vast new possibilities for music in pictures and there is nobody like me when it comes to discovering new grounds." He was "convinced," he wrote, "that someday somebody will write a 'film-opera' which will start a new trend in musical pictures—and I hope it will be me."[56] If the Columbus scene was only a foretaste of the possibilities he envisaged, it was a substantial, precedent-setting one nonetheless: a musically continuous dramatic unit in the form of an opera travesty à la Gilbert and Sullivan lasting a full nine minutes (fig. 4).

In its basic outline, the film's plot structure resembles a fairy tale, with the Columbus scene resulting from the second of Bill's three wishes with Ali. In response to the first wish—"to get in the army"—Ali's defective timepiece transports Bill back to the outpost "USO Valley Forge" at the time of the American Revolutionary War, where he is a soldier in the Continental Army under General George Washington. As in many time-travel movies—notable examples of which include *Back to the Future* (1985) and its two sequels—hindsight coupled with intentional anachronism provides the principal source of wit. Thus Bill's rudi-

FIGURE 4. Fortunio Bonanova as Christopher Columbus in the movie *Where Do We Go from Here?* (1945). Weill described this musically continuous scene, which lasts a full nine minutes, as "a regular little comic opera." Courtesy of 20th Century–Fox.

mentary grasp of American history allows him to demonstrate his superior knowledge to his commanding officer by predicting with certainty the outcome of the forthcoming battle against the Hessians and even to warn of duplicity in the ranks (by Benedict Arnold). Impressed, Washington presses him into service as a spy behind enemy lines in Trenton. But his cover is blown by a troop of partying Germans, who sentence him to death by firing squad. Facing the unique fate of being "born in 1910 and dying in 1776," he is rescued by Ali posing as a soldier on the other side, who "wishes" him into the navy. The musically rich scene affords ample opportunity to send up German culture, with Weill and Gershwin's delightfully over-the-top beer-drinking ditty ("Song of the Rhineland") and the playful caricature of Nazi military figures.

Next, it is 1492, and Bill finds himself in the midst of an attempted mutiny aboard the ships of Christopher Columbus. Bill feels bound to intervene as a member of the crew, thus allowing Ira Gershwin to rise to the occasion of supplying him with some wonderfully parochial words of warning to sing to his fellow sailors in the crowning song of the nine-minute sequence, and to have those words rhyme at all costs. In a triple-time allegro *("a la Tarantella"),* with accompanying castanets, Bill invites the disaffected sailors to "imagine what happens to posterity without Columbus." Published posthumously under the title "The Nina, the Pinta, the Santa Maria," the number incorporates four stanzas, the first two preceded by an introduction and the second by a "Recitativo *(Free).*" Here, by way of illustrating the Gilbertian flavor of the opera travesty, are the third and the fourth:

No automat nickels
No Heinz and his pickles
No land of the brave and the freeah,
Just think what you're losing
If you don't keep cruising
the Nina, the Pinta, the Santa Maria.

No Radio City
And who'll feed the kitty
At Belmont Park and Hialeah!
But you'll be unveiling
A new world by sailing
the Nina, the Pinta, the Santa Maria.

The music of this through-composed dramatic unit effectively served as a stylistic study for *The Firebrand of Florence,* the Broadway operetta that Weill and Gershwin were working on with Edwin Justus Mayer around the same time.[57] In terms of its underlying aesthetic principle, the composer described the film as "frankly an experiment with an opera form in that the music and lyrics are integrated with the story, advancing it rather than retarding it, as is the case with most musical films."[58]

This approach, which recalls his concern with the integration of music in the *Tonfilm* essay of 1930, can be said to apply almost as much to the other musical numbers of *Where Do We Go from Here?* as it does to the Columbus sequence, with one crucial difference. Whereas the "little comic opera" is self-contained, the musical numbers in the other parts of the film flow more or less seamlessly in and out of the dramatic dialogue. Take, for example, the movie's most prominent song, "All at Once," a fox-trot whose suave melody is a Weillian self-borrowing from a song written to a text by Oscar Hammerstein in 1942, "The Good Earth."[59] In the opening sequence, the melody drifts from diegetic background (as dance music), to foreground (as song), and back again to background. In the eighteenth-century episode it forms the basis of a minuet presented in period style, prior to the transformation of another central song, "If Love Remains," into a thoroughly anachronistic "1776 Boogie." As such, the recurring musical objects are analogous to Lucilla and Sally's appearing in different guises, and even with different names, as the narrative unfolds from epoch to epoch.

Consistent with the "experiment," to use Weill's own description of his innovative approach, the origin of each historical episode in the making of the movie was supposed to be a musical one. True, some of the songs that Weill and Gershwin wrote and recorded for demonstration purposes in January 1944 would end up on the cutting-room floor during the production process. One such victim is "It Could Have Happened to Anyone."[60] Another is "Woo, Woo, Woo, Manhattan," the production number originally planned for the scene in Manhattan following the Columbus episode, in which Bill enters into a shady real-estate deal with a Native American and buys the island for $24. In the preceding 1776 scene, the other key song, "If Love Remains," had marked the turning point in the story at which Bill begins to transfer his affections from Lucilla (June Haver—ironically, Fred MacMurray's bride-to-be) to Sally (Joan Leslie). And in the succeeding episode in Dutch-colonial "Nieuw Amsterdam" set in the mid-1600s (shades here of *Knickerbocker Holiday*), which is triggered by Bill's hubristic wish to "see the faces of those Dutchmen when they get a load of this," this key number appears prominently as underscoring, without any vocal numbers as such. Again, with Ali's help, Bill manages to escape, this time fulfilling his wish to take Sally (alias Katrina) with him back to the twentieth century and to become a marine.

Such was Weill's contribution as the "composer." Standard studio practice dictated that after delivering the songs conceived as the screen musical's dramaturgical basis he was obliged to cede final creative decisions to a large production team, this one headed by director Gregory Ratoff and producer William Perlberg. David Raksin and David Buttolph supplied additional and incidental music; Maurice DePackh and his associates from the Music Department were responsible for arrangements and orchestrations.[61]

UNREALIZED PROJECTS

Electing to cooperate with the film industry's division of labor while remaining critical of it, and yet at the same time hopeful of somehow transforming it, Weill continued to nurture ambitions for further film projects. None of them progressed beyond the outline or "treatment" stage, however. In 1948, hoping to sell the film rights to their musical play *Love Life,* he and Alan Jay Lerner worked on a plan for a movie tentatively titled *Miss Memory.* "It turned out to be an enchanting yarn," Weill wrote to Irving Lazar on 24 October 1948, "full of charm, humor, warmth, and building up to a very good climax. It was much more work than we had anticipated, because we wanted to present it as a complete story. We worked on a first draft all week, and yesterday we dictated all day until the synopsis was finished." Lazar, he hoped, would promote the idea as his agent, such that "when you discuss the picture, I want you to point out that all the scenes with Miss Memory will be treated musically, in song and dance and the kind of underscored dialogue which I am using so successfully in the theatre." He left the extent of his own involvement flexible, however: "We can either sell the idea in connection with a deal for the score (lyrics and music), or we can make a deal to write the entire picture (book, lyrics and music)."[62]

Around the same time he created by himself yet another "story idea for a motion picture," as he described the three-page typed manuscript titled "I Married a King."[63] Weill's narrative outline tells the story of King Peter of Sylvania, "a small kingdom in Southern Europe." Threatened by a revolutionary mob in front of his palace, Peter flees the country for New York, leaving behind his security double called Pedro. Looking for the quiet life, he becomes an expert adviser for a Hollywood picture about a royal romance after falling in love with the movie's female star, Lorna Stevens. Threats to his life by Sylvanian revolutionaries continue, however, so he requests that Pedro join him again to take over all of his public appearances, while he himself settles down on a ranch in the valley. Lorna consequently becomes confused by the two quite different sides of the king's personality. Leading the life of a normal person, Peter is "simple, a little shy and very lovable," whereas his double is "somewhat arrogant and slightly snobbish and behaves as people think an ex-king would behave." In suggestions for further development, Weill writes that in the making of the picture about royal romance, "Pedro's ideas about royalty could be quite contrary to the real king's ideas." The story ends happily, however, after Pedro has been chased away by the assassins. Lorna returns to the ranch thinking she has been forsaken, only to find "Peter waiting for her, and it is the real Peter, the one she always loved."

Noblesse oblige? An allegory of the authentic European émigré? Presumably Weill intended his motion picture to become a musical, although the outline makes no mention of music. What is perhaps most striking is the reappearance of key plot threads from the one-act opera *Der Zar lässt sich photographieren:* the man of noble birth who hankers after a "normal" existence in the midst of threats to his life by revolutionary assassins.

Weill's attitude toward the movies remained equivocal to the end. "I keep coming back to the theatre," he said in an interview given in 1950, just months before he died. "It's more fascinating. . . . It's not an industry. The rest are industries, and the creative artist has to adapt himself to the requirement of that industry. There's no use fighting it. There are enormous amounts of money involved and the industries want certain rules followed to protect those investments . . . Since the theatre is smaller, the investments are smaller so one is much freer."[64] At the same time, he was aware of the theater's limitations, where movies could offer advantages. "One of the difficulties in casting a stage musical," he said, was "to find actors who can sing or singers who can act. It's very hard to get a combination of the two. But in pictures you can take actors who don't need to know anything more than how to carry a tune and the mike will do the rest.

Like these aviators, our movie actors can sing by instrument."[65] In fact, although MacMurray managed to sing his own songs in *Where Do We Go from Here?*, Joan Leslie (playing the role of Sally) was dubbed by Sally Sweetland.

Despite the numerous frustrations and setbacks of his experiences as a composer for the cinema, it is fair to say that he never sank to the cynical disdain of fellow émigré and near-contemporary Hanns Eisler, who had to rely more heavily on movie work than Weill ever did. "The truth is," Eisler declared in the book *Composing for the Films* that he co-authored with Theodor W. Adorno, "no serious composer writes for the motion pictures for any other than money reasons; and in the studios he does not feel that he is a beneficiary of utopian technical potentialities, but a regimented employee who can be discharged on any pretext."[66] Certainly more utopian than Eisler's, Weill's attitude can be perhaps best described as one of abiding ambivalence—idealism tempered by realism.

It is therefore perhaps fitting that his engagement with the film industry after *Where Do We Go from Here?* found two principal and quite different outlets. One was the adaptation of *One Touch of Venus*, as described above, a sobering reminder of the limitations imposed by the Hollywood studio system on transferring a stage musical to the screen. The other was his "big article," as he described it, "Music in the Movies," which *Harper's Bazaar* published in September 1946.[67]

Apart from seizing the opportunity of this public forum to articulate his aspirations as a composer, Weill took pains to display his in-depth knowledge of cinema from its beginnings to the present and to invoke a broad historical context for his contributions. "It would not be the first time in the history of music," he stated,

> that a powerful institution became a sponsor for musical creation. The great polyphonic masters of the sixteenth century worked in the service of the Catholic Church; Bach had to write a cantata for the Sunday service in his church every week—and the early symphonic and operatic works of the eighteenth century were commissioned by European princes and aristocratic landowners for the entertainment of their guests. Today, in a more democratic world, music has become a powerful medium in the hands of those who provide entertainment for the masses. The men who make our movies are well aware of this. In their projection rooms they have seen many pictures without music, and they know how much the score helps to "warm up" the action of the picture, to heighten the emotional impact, to cover up weaknesses in the plot development or in the acting of certain scenes, and to hold together episodes which would seem quite disconnected without a musical bridge. They know that a scene which is slow and dragging can be made exciting with the proper musical treatment. They know that a good melody will move an audience when the words or the acting don't succeed. (257)

The article goes on to outline the workings of the "very efficient musical departments" and praise "the amount of work, the craftsmanship, which goes into the recording of a score" (257). It is no wonder," Weill continues, bemoaning the limited opportunities to find outlets for new music, "that many composers look to the movies as a possible solution of their problems." His account outlines an evolutionary, future-oriented trajectory: "There is hardly any doubt that some day the motion picture will take its place beside the musical theatre as a free, unrestricted outlet for a composer's imagination. . . . The position of music in general and of the contemporary composer in particular is rather encouraging if we consider the fact that the whole development of music in the movies is only about forty years old and that the whole field of 'musical pictures' has been hardly scratched" (398).

He writes as an eyewitness, as someone to whom "the sound of the piano in the nickelodeons is a cherished childhood memory, and many times when we see one of those standard situations in a movie—the villain triumphing over his innocent victim; the daughter being expelled from her father's house; the mother being separated from her child—we are longing to hear again that tinny old worn-out piano, playing 'The March of the Gladiators,' 'The Virgin's Prayer,' or the William Tell overture" (398). Weill's choice of examples is hardly random. The second of the pieces (normally titled in English "The Maiden's Prayer"; Weill was no doubt translating from the German title, "Gebet einer Jungfrau") found its way into *Aufstieg und Fall der Stadt Mahagonny* as "eternal art," ironically apostrophized as such and presumably with the intended allusion to its cinematic associations. The other two were both added to the film version of *Lady in the Dark,* alongside the portions of Weill's score retained from the original musical play.

In passing, "Music in the Movies" mentions a veritable "who's who" of other musicians associated with the medium, from Erich Korngold to Victor Young.[68] Among "outstanding contemporary composers" Weill further lists Milhaud, Honegger, Auric, Copland, Antheil, Janssen, Herrmann, Tansman, and Toch. Yet as someone writing "from the standpoint of the creative musician," he cannot "help feeling that all the enthusiasm, all the hard work, all the ingenuity that goes into the making of these film scores, is . . . more or less wasted, as long as the composer's task is not more than to provide a musical background for a picture which is completely finished at the time when he starts working." His dream for the future remained: "The motion picture is a perfect medium for an original musico-dramatic creation on the same level as the different forms of the musical theatre: musical comedy, operetta, musical play and opera. If we want to develop an art form (or a form of entertainment) in which music has an integral part, we have to allow the composer to collaborate with the writer and director to the same extent as he collaborates in the musical theatre" (400).

To date he saw the main opportunities for such collaboration having been afforded by documentaries and cartoons as well as by "a sort of glorified amplification of the musical-comedy format," citing Lubitsch's early musicals and

Rouben Mamoulian's *Love Me Tonight*, "a really intelligent, uncompromising musical picture which has become a kind of classic of its genre" (400). He concludes by citing several of his own works that "develop certain elements of this genre": his *Dreigroschenoper* film, *You and Me*, and *Where Do We Go from Here?*

On the face of it, "film-opera" seems an odd choice of label to describe Weill's aspirations in the world of motion pictures. His imagining that "the much-talked-about 'American opera' will come out of the most popular American form of entertainment" was no doubt a tall order. Yet it should be recalled that when he published this prognostication, in 1946, he was hard at work on *Street Scene*, an American opera that, at least for a while, he considered a possible candidate for cinematic treatment.[69] How much that treatment would have yielded a "film-opera" in the sense later applied by the director Franco Zeffirelli to describe a genre of adaptation that leaves the structural integrity of the composer's score more or less intact, or whether a more extensive transformation of the stage version would have occurred, is hard to say. (It would have been unimaginable in the mid-1940s that opera houses would one day broadcast live performances of their productions to sold-out movie theaters.)

And on 23 March 1949, Weill wrote to Alan Jay Lerner entertaining "picture possibilities" for *Down in the Valley*, while insisting that "it should only be sold to movies if we have a guaranty *[sic]* that it is being made as a *film-opera*." He had quite specific restrictions in mind, however: "The story cannot be changed into a Hollywood musical, but has to be the technique of our piece translated into the medium of film. I doubt very much if anyone *[sic]* of the big studios will do that, or even know what t'hell I am talking about, and we all feel we might be better off to wait until we can make the picture ourselves."[70] Had Weill lived a bit longer, it seems more likely that opportunities would have arisen for the creation of another original screen musical, following in the footsteps of *Where Do We Go from Here?*, rather than a fully executed American opera.

So much for speculation about how Weill's career in the movies might have continued to evolve along the lines adumbrated by his article "Music in the Movies." There is the other side of the story to consider as well: the impact of the screen on the musical stage. Several specific elements have been cited already, such as the use of film in *Royal Palace* and the ironic quotation of quintessential silent-movie music in *Aufstieg und Fall der Stadt Mahagonny*. The allusion to Chaplin's *The Gold Rush* in *Der Silbersee* is another case in point. (The double scene of Anna's abandonment in *Die Bürgschaft* anticipates the technique of the "split screen" employed in later cinema.) Then there is the broader question of narrative structure in Weill's musical theater and the debt it owes to the medium of cinema. The "underscored dialogue" mentioned earlier, which can be found in Weill's last three works for the musical stage, *Street Scene*, *Down in the Valley*, and *Lost in the Stars*, surely follows the example of the "talkies," just as the placards in epic theater suggest an affinity to the plot-summarizing title cards of the silent era. Flashback technique in *Down in the Valley* and the stretching of "narrative time" in *Love Life* are yet other ways in which Weill's intimate familiarity with cinematic art informed his stage works. "Of course, it is safer to work in the movies," he wrote to Lenya prior to the release of *Where Do We Go from Here?* "But how dull, how uninspiring!"[71] Insofar as his ambitions as a movie composer remained largely unfulfilled, it seems fitting to conclude that the impact of film on Weill's reforms of musical theater was greater than the other way round.

11

American Opera

"You can imagine what this means to me," Weill wrote to his parents in 1949, gratified by the success of the first professional performance of his college opera *Down in the Valley.* "This recognition of my efforts," he continued, "allows me to work again in the world of opera, which has been my real field of activity *[eigentliches Betätigungsfeld]* all along."[1] Writing in German, he paraphrases a review from the *New York World-Telegram* in which the critic suggested that Weill might become known as "the founder of American opera."[2] Weill's other principal "effort" in this field was *Street Scene,* first performed in 1947 and subtitled in the piano-vocal score "An American Opera." In describing the connection between the two works, Olin Downes, the composer's foremost champion at the *New York Times,* wrote that the "little folk-opera is in a sense a pendant to *Street Scene.*" *Street Scene,* he said, "is a lyric drama of the city, couched partly in the musical patois of its streets. *Down in the Valley,* in its structure, method, and point of poetical and musical approach, deserves the closest scrutiny by those interested in the evolution of a native operatic form. It is a folk form, masterly fabricated."[3]

The critics believed *Street Scene* and *Down in the Valley* had something significant to contribute to a specifically American form of opera. Downes went further, encapsulating with his description some of the central questions reflected in the works' reception. How is *Street Scene* a "lyric drama of the city," something that could also be said, albeit in an utterly different way, of *Aufstieg und Fall der Stadt Mahagonny?* What is "the musical patois" of the city's streets, and what is its role in the piece? What, with respect to *Down in the Valley,* does Downes mean by the "structure, method, and point of poetical and musical approach" that he deems deserving of "the closest scrutiny"? How is it a "folk form"; how "masterly fabricated"? And lastly, in what ways do the two works complement each other? How is the one a "pendant" to the other?

That Weill should consider opera his "real field of activity" may seem surprising; it certainly invites qualification. In the same letter to his parents, he explained that the performance of *Down in the Valley* was done "in a small theater, where a group of young singers have been performing opera with great success for a number of years. They call themselves 'Lemonade Opera' because they sell lemonade in the intermission in order to emphasize the difference from the formality of grand opera (as we did with *Die Dreigroschenoper* all those years ago)." He was pleased, moreover, that "the critic of the 'Times' compared [my opera] to the original *Beggar's Opera,* which was the origin of English opera, and said *Down in the Valley* will go down in history as the 'fountain head' of American opera."[4]

Although excluding opera that has associations with social formality and ceremony (the German word he uses is *pomphaft,* as in pomp and circumstance), Weill was willing to include in his endeavors *Die Dreigroschenoper,* strictly speaking a "play with music," and its model, *The Beggar's Opera,* a "ballad opera." In other words, his conception of opera was both broad and limited: broad enough to accommodate experiments in mixed genres that function as operatic prototypes, yet limited to more popular, vernacular endeavors. At this point in his creative career, "opera" for him was effectively synonymous with "American opera." And for this reason he made no secret of the fact that he considered *Street Scene* his *chef d'oeuvre.* It represented, as he put it, "two dreams come true." The first dream had to do with "a special brand of musical theater that would completely integrate drama and music, spoken word, song and movement"; the second was "the dream of an American opera on Broadway."[5]

As always with Weill, the boundaries remained fluid. In a 1947 essay titled "Broadway and the Musical Theatre," he left the distinction between "musical theatre" more generally and opera specifically as something to be challenged:

> It has been my opinion for a long time that the Broadway stage can become an important outlet for the American composer and might even become the birthplace of a genuine American "musical theatre" or, if you wish, an American opera. That this theory has been widely accepted lately, is to me one of the most gratifying results of the success of *Street Scene.* I never could see any reason why the "educated" (not to say "serious") composer should not be able to reach all available markets with his music, and I have always believed that opera should be a part of the living theatre of our time.[6]

As mixed genres, the majority of Weill's works for Broadway belong more or less in the tradition of the musical play. The "more or less" has to do with the extent of their conformity with generic traditions. The reasons why *Street Scene* and *Down in the Valley* qualify as opera, setting themselves apart from the musical plays, are at once structural and aesthetic: structural, because of the preponderance of music as opposed to spoken dialogue and because of the large-scale musical organization; aesthetic, because of the various ways in which the two works invoke the conventions of mainstream opera. The various forms of musical play that Weill created do not qualify on either count, though they may have more to do with opera aesthetically than structurally. *Lady in the Dark* is a true hybrid insofar as it juxtaposes uninterrupted stretches of spoken dialogue and self-contained musical units, which Weill conceived as "three little one-act operas." The institutional question hardly obtains at all: for all their ambitions as far as operatic conventions are concerned, the "American operas" were not performed in or intended for traditional opera houses, at least at the time of their conception.

The other work that comes closest to being an "American opera" in the sense outlined above is *The Firebrand of Florence,* a project no doubt inspired by Weill's "two dreams." Inspired, yes, but even the composer would never have said in full confidence that *Firebrand* had made those dreams "come true." It had been a flop, as he conceded in a single parenthetical word when reacting to *Life* magazine's description of him as "a German composer": "I am an American citizen," he insisted in his letter to the editor, "and during my dozen years in this country have composed exclusively for the American stage, writing the scores for *Johnny Johnson, Knickerbocker Holiday, Lady in the Dark, One Touch of Venus, The Firebrand of Florence* (ouch) and *Street Scene.*"[7]

In 1941, still enjoying the successful Broadway premiere of *Lady in the Dark,* which would eventually run for 462 performances, Weill wrote to Ira Gershwin that he would like to write "a very entertaining opera comique on the Offenbach line."[8] As with other American works, the way in which *Firebrand*'s label changed during its inception vividly illustrates the challenges connected with Weill's attempts to establish himself in the musical theater in America. Early on he decided "to treat great parts of the score in real opera style, without any attempt to write American popular songs.... The whole thing," he confided to Lenya during the work's genesis, "might very well become an Opera for Broadway."[9] Other letters to Lenya conveyed similar, if diminishing, ambitions: "*Firebrand* might become what you and I have been waiting for: my first Broadway Opera."[10] "It probably will become almost an opera because I hear music almost all the way through, except for the comedy scenes."[11] "The score will have the size of an opera."[12] And two days after the show had closed, he would proudly write to his parents that "musically it was the best thing I've written in years, a real opera with choruses and ensemble numbers, full of melodic invention, using all the technical craft that I've acquired over the years."[13] On opening night, *Firebrand* was billed as "a New Musical." Yet as Joel Galand remarks, "Nearly all the opening night reviews of *Firebrand* noted that the new offering was an operetta."[14]

That was the path from conception to reception: "opera comique," to "Opera for Broadway" to "almost opera" to "size of an opera" to "New Musical" to "operetta." *Firebrand* is all of these things—that is to say, a large-scale work conceived with operatic ambitions for the Broadway theater, drawing throughout on the conventions of European operetta and with a European theme. (The libretto by Edwin Justus Mayer is based on his 1924 play *The Firebrand,* a theatrical treatment of the memoirs of the sixteenth-century sculptor and goldsmith Benvenuto Cellini.) In that sense, the epithet *American* applies less than the descriptor *opera* does. The work's "Americanness" is chiefly an institutional matter, more to do with its conception for Broadway than with either its form or its content. *Street Scene* and *Down in the Valley* are quite different in this regard.

As Weill's published "ouch" poignantly indicates, *Firebrand*'s lack of success was a source of pain. Written in Hollywood and New York in the latter part of 1944, its three-week tryout with the title *Much Ado about Love* at Boston's Colonial Theater began in late February 1945. The New York premiere, with the new title *The Firebrand of Florence,* opened at the Alvin Theater on 22 March and closed, after just forty-three performances, on 28 April. The reasons for the flop were complex, according to Galand, "stemming partly from weaknesses specific to Max Gordon's production, such as casting and direction, partly from structural flaws in the work itself, and partly from critical consternation over what appeared to be nothing more than an old-fashioned costume operetta. . . . The verdicts on *Firebrand* were also verdicts on a genre widely perceived as epigonic."[15]

Whether the circumstances surrounding the ill-fated production were more at fault than the work itself must remain a matter of conjecture. Galand is surely right to identify a constellation of factors. More European than American in theme and tone, *Firebrand* is nonetheless a substantial score, impressive in its large-scale formal design and lyrical invention. Its nearest relative in Weill's oeuvre is to be found not in any of the preceding musical plays but in *A Kingdom for a Cow.* By way of emphasizing that link to the European past, beyond reliance on the formal and expressive conventions of operetta, Weill reused the earlier work's anthem at the beginning of *Firebrand's* orchestral Prelude, where the melody anticipates the later choral panegyric to "Alessandro the Wise."

Except for the four isolated numbers published as sheet music—"Sing Me Not a Ballad," "There'll Be Life, Love, and Laughter," "You're Far Too Near Me," and "A Rhyme for Angela"—*Firebrand* had to wait more than half a century for its musical qualities, of which Weill was rightly proud, to be fully rediscovered. In 2002 a critical edition, prepared by Galand, was published as part of the Kurt Weill Edition. In conjunction with that publication, Ohio Light Opera staged a revival in 1999. Two concert performances followed in 2000, one by the BBC in London that was given during the Weill centenary celebrations (and subsequently issued commercially on compact disc) and another by the Radio Symphony Orchestra Vienna; further performances followed at the Kurt-Weill-Fest in Dessau in 2005 and by the Collegiate Chorale in New York in 2009. Acknowledging its place in the history of American musical theater as a large-scale work with continuous music that is neither emphatically operatic nor emphatically American, the critical edition applies a new, more appropriate descriptor to *The Firebrand of Florence:* "Broadway Operetta."

STREET SCENE

Billed as a "dramatic musical," Weill's *Street Scene* received its premiere at New York's Adelphi Theatre on 9 January 1947 and would run for a total of 148 performances, a fairly modest number by Broadway standards but uncommonly high for an opera. Reporting on the critically well-received production in a letter to his friend Caspar Neher, co-librettist of *Die Bürgschaft,* the composer described his latest work as "a type of number opera. . . . But," he continued, "I composed right through the spoken dialogues between the musical numbers, like a recitative, so that the dialogue melts into the musical numbers and creates a unity of drama and music that I had never achieved before." He was evidently proud of his new work, which he had referred to elsewhere as a "real Broadway opera" and whose label he would eventually change to "An American Opera" for the publication of the piano-vocal score; he frequently promoted it, in public as well as in private communications, as the culmination of his career in the musical theater. And not just for reasons of tact and courtesy toward Neher, he was no doubt justified in adding (parenthetically) that "among all of my former works, only the first act of *Bürgschaft* had this same kind of unity of drama and music."[16]

Claiming greater unity than in other works for the whole of *Street Scene* and also for the first act of *Bürgschaft* (otherwise "never before") suggests that Weill was not merely describing his approach to composition in those two works but also, with pride, passing a favorable judgment on them. His description of the way in which he attempted to create continuity points to an essential difference between the genre of opera, in which music is pervasive, and musical plays, in which the clear distinction between musical numbers and a substantial amount of dialogue are a defining, characteristic feature. At the same time, however, by singling out just one act of his earlier opera for comparison, he is also stating his view that the approach in *Street Scene* had been particularly successful, overall even more so than before.

"Unity" is both a descriptive and a normative term. Saying that *Street Scene* achieves a "unity of drama and music" is valid as a statement about the fact that its ingredients are designed to cohere. Yet it also amounts to an invitation to consider the critical judgment, voiced by the composer himself and shared by a number of critics, that the work's ingredients actually do cohere as a unified whole. How, then, does Weill's recipe for composing *Street Scene* as an opera, rather than as a musical play, allow its unification of text and music to become dramatically effective? And is the classicizing aesthetic that Weill invokes not only appropriate but also justified?

Applying the concept of unity in *Street Scene* certainly seems appropriate on a number of levels. Weill himself referred to the unities of classical drama when describing the time and place of the action. In his attempt, ultimately unsuccessful, to interest Rouben Mamoulian as director of the premiere production, he mentioned "some important decisions for this show" that he and playwright Elmer Rice had "agreed on immediately." One that he singled out was the decision "to do it in one set like the original play."[17] The segment of time presented to the audience spans a twenty-four-hour period: an evening in June (act one); the following morning and the afternoon of the same day (act two). In an interview for *P.M.* magazine given a month after the premiere, Weill not only stressed the unity of time and place but drew an analogy also with the dramatic content of classical models, as he had similarly done in the letter to Mamoulian. *Street Scene* was constructed, he said, "very much like Greek tragedy, with tight unity of time and space and the inescapability of fate."[18] But is the motivation for this approach solely "classical"? One could well argue that the frame for the action derives as much from naturalistic as it does from classical models.

By way of emphasizing the unity of the action, which takes place for the most part in front of a New York apartment house (and also partly *in* the house) during that twenty-four-hour period, Weill's score introduces elements of formal symmetry through the cyclical repetition of previously heard material. This occurs both in the large and in the small. The opening blues-inflected ensemble number "Ain't It Awful the Heat" frames the entire opera, repeated as it is at the very end as a reminder of the sweltering weather conditions. Like the storm in Verdi's *Otello,* the conditions relate symbolically to the tragic action. Unlike in *Otello,* however, the conditions remain the same at the end as they were at the beginning. The formal symmetry not only reflects the unity of action but suggests an analogue to cyclical time: the "awful heat," a force of nature, is bound to persist during the days ahead and summers to come.

Similarly, at a more local level, following a snatch of Henry the janitor's earlier blues number "I Got a Marble and a Star," the first-act finaletto ultimately concludes with a brief reminiscence of Sam's signature aria, "Lonely House," whose swooping melody to those titular words appears at the very beginning of the opera as the work's motto, dissonantly harmonized (ex. 55). (The melodic tag will

EXAMPLE 55. *Street Scene,* opening ("Lonely House" motto)

recur in the same jarring, *fortissimo* variant prior to the off-stage murder scene.) Each of these large-scale formal symmetries creates a sense of unity and closure while also contributing to the overall scene painting.

Many of the opera's recurring elements, in contrast, recalling Verdian as well as Wagnerian techniques, seem less formally than dramatically motivated. The most obvious case in point is the short motif that appears throughout the opera and whose foreboding quality is initially and principally associated with the perpetrator of the murder, Frank Maurrant. But thanks to its frequent recurrence, the motif ends up standing for much more than either Frank or the crime of passion he commits in the heat of the moment. When it puts in its last, arguably incongruous, appearance in the lower instrumental voices of the opera's penultimate measure, as a summarizing epic aside to the "Heat" ensemble and, indeed, to the entire work, the motif seems to have transcended Frank's actions and the misfortune they have wrought to represent symbolically the all-too-human element that inescapably injects itself into the lives of the community (ex. 56).

If this briefly recurring "fate" motif, which has been likened to a similar figure in Bizet's *Carmen,* creates unity, it is surely of a quite different kind either from the invocation of the formal traditions of classical theater or from the repeated ensemble that underscores the unity of time and place. Comparison of the comments Weill made to Neher and Mamoulian about the unity of *Street Scene* thus reveals inherent tensions in the work's conception: between classical and naturalistic form, on the one hand, and two competing types of musical coherence, on the other, namely large-scale, number-based formal correspondence and the through-composed fluidity of a dramatically motivated web of recurring motifs. The tensions no doubt reflect the creative challenges that Weill set himself in translating Rice's play into music and, rather than being resolved in the process of composition, serve to define the relationship among the diverse elements constitutive of the opera's distinct style. Beyond that, they also play a critical role, as discussed below, in informing the work's reception.

The genesis of the "American opera" that Weill promoted as the culmination

EXAMPLE 56. *Street Scene,* conclusion ("fate motif")

of his career in the musical theater is quite well documented, from initial inspiration through opening night. Before being introduced to Elmer Rice "during a rehearsal of *Johnny Johnson,*" as he recalled, the composer had seen the play *Street Scene* while still in Europe. He must have attended Heinz Hilpert's 1930 production in Berlin, the year after the Pulitzer Prize–winning play had received its highly successful premiere in New York.[19]

Looking back in 1947, Weill claimed to have "thought of [Rice's work] many times as a perfect vehicle for a musical play." He was not alone. "Elmer told me that he had been approached by several composers with the same idea."[20] Already on 7 March 1929, two months after the play's New York premiere, the *New York Times* published an unsigned article with the headline "Deems Taylor Writing 'Street Scene' Opera: Bases Piece for Metropolitan on Current Play by Elmer Rice." But this project went unfulfilled. By December of that year, Taylor, who had been searching for the appropriate vehicle for a commission from New York's Metropolitan Opera—initially, before toying with *Street Scene,* he had considered Heywood Broun's 1926 novel *Gandle Follows His Nose*—had changed his mind again, this time in favor of George du Maurier's novel *Peter Ibbetson,* an opera completed and given its successful Met premiere in 1931. In his autobiography, *Minority Report,* Rice identifies William Schuman as another composer, along with Taylor, who had approached him about turning his play into a piece of musical theater.[21]

The transformation of Rice's play occurred in several stages. The impulse to start the project began when Weill approached Rice in the mid-1940s. They knew each other already, from their original encounter in 1936 and soon thereafter through the Playwrights' Company, of which Rice was one of five founding members—Sidney Howard, Robert E. Sherwood, S. N. Behrman, and Maxwell Anderson being the others. *Knickerbocker Holiday* had been one of the first plays produced after the company formed, their express aim being to preserve the integrity of their scripts as well as to retain the profits that otherwise went to producers.[22] Anderson took part in initial discussions, in 1945, with his close friend

Weill about adapting Rice's play before Rice himself and Langston Hughes took over.[23] And, no less important, Weill joined the Playwrights' Company in 1946 as the first composer and first new member since its inception eight years earlier.

As far as musical influences go, Weill mentioned in the interview with *P.M.* magazine that he had studied Verdi's treatment of Shakespeare plays, namely *Othello, Falstaff,* and *Macbeth,* while working on *Street Scene.*[24] But there are other influences, too, among them Bizet, Wagner, Puccini, and Gershwin.

That Deems Taylor was widely reported to be working with the playwright on an operatic version of *Street Scene* in 1929 could appear to be at odds with Weill's account, according to which Rice told him not only that other composers had approached him with the idea, but also that "he thought it too early for a show of that type." At the very least, the apparent discrepancy raises several questions. What type of show would Weill and Rice have had in mind when they first met in 1936? Were they both thinking along the lines of a musical play like *Johnny Johnson,* or was Rice imagining a full-length opera of the "Met" kind envisaged by Taylor and others? Or did Weill, already then, imagine following the example of Gershwin's *Porgy and Bess,* which he mentions having heard in rehearsal at the composer's invitation "a few weeks after my arrival in this country" and cites as evidence "that the American theatre was already on the way to the more integrated form of musical that we had begun to attempt in Europe?"[25]

Certainly, when Rice agreed to the collaboration with Weill in 1945, things were quite different from in the 1930s. "The Broadway musical scene," as Weill remarks, "had changed quite a bit in the ten years since we first discussed the plan. Broadway composers had become more 'book conscious.' Opera was now a popular entertainment: the public had become interested in singing."[26] Weill was speaking in part for himself, of course; his work since *Johnny Johnson* had contributed in large measure to that development. And with *Street Scene* he intended to take it to a new level in a career-defining way. Apart from being quite obviously "book conscious," *Street Scene* achieved a form more integrated than any of the works since *Die Bürgschaft*—a piece that Weill continued to invoke, at least in private, as a benchmark.

Two months before the premiere of *Street Scene,* he wrote to his brother Hans that "it is without doubt the most important piece I've written since *Die Bürgschaft,* and it might turn out to be the best of all my works."[27] And in his letter to the co-librettist of *Die Bürgschaft,* his friend Caspar Neher, he drew a direct parallel with the first act of that work: "It was a tough nut to crack this time around," he wrote. "I had made up my mind to really write an opera for Broadway, something I had been planning and preparing for years. If you knew Broadway a little better, you would have some idea of what a daring enterprise this was. . . . The great challenge for me was to find a form that translated the realism of the plot into music. The result is something entirely new and probably the most 'modern' form of musical theater, since it applies the technique of opera without ever falling into the artificiality of opera."[28]

While repeating some of his other remarks made at the time in essays and interviews about the challenge of setting Rice's "realistic" play, and about seeing the achievement as the culmination of earlier efforts, the letter to Neher is notable because of the distinction Weill draws between technique and artificiality in opera. By "technique" he is referring specifically to the way in which he divides the work into musical numbers while integrating dialogue and song through musical links that are created between the discrete numbers. What he means by "artificiality" *(Unnatürlichkeit)*—something he claims to avoid—is less apparent but can be inferred from other remarks made at the time and from his earlier writings on opera. The musical links, which can be likened to the underscoring that accompanies dialogue in film, allow the characters, drawn from everyday life as opposed to myth or history, to have everyday conversation without relying on opera's "artificial" conventions, such as arioso or recitative. Elsewhere, in cast notes, he spoke of *Street Scene* as "a show that flows naturally [i.e., *not* artificially] from dialogue into music and back." This is what he describes as a "musicalized STREET SCENE."[29] The connecting elements, he hoped, would serve to unify music and drama: on a structural level, by sustaining the musical flow, and on a dramatic one, by functioning as musical motifs that relate to the enacted drama in various ways. The degree of integration is all the more remarkable in view of the heterogeneity of the materials the composer was working with. This goes both for the choice of the play itself—the source material—and for the actual means of its "musicalization."

In describing with hindsight the type of show he had in mind, and why, as he claimed, *Street Scene* was "the perfect vehicle," Weill repeatedly drew attention to the play's "realism" as something complementary to, even at odds with, his music: "It was a simple story of every-day life in a big city, a story of love and passion and greed and death. I saw great musical possibilities in its theatrical device—life in a tenement house between one evening and the next afternoon. And it seemed like a great challenge to me to find the inherent poetry in these people and to blend my music with the stark realism of the play." At the same time, he "discovered that the play lent itself to a great variety of music, just as the streets of New York themselves embrace the music of many lands and many people."[30] The urban space, which *Street Scene* represents, thus finds an analogue for its *ethnic* diversity in its *musical* diversity. The music gives voice to the disparate identities of the citizens who go about their business in America's urban melting pot, while providing a foil to the "stark reality" of city life.

Street Scene's realism, as discussed above, could be seen to derive from naturalistic models as much as from classical ones. Indeed, the play's "stark realism," which Weill saw as an obstacle to its musicalization, is also naturalistic in the sense applied to the nineteenth-century movement of Zola, Gerhard Hauptmann et al. Naturalist plays can be seen, in the words of theater historian Edwin Wilson, as an "attempt to achieve verisimilitude of a documentary film, to convey the impression that everything about the play—the setting, the way the characters dress, speak, and act—is exactly like everyday life."[31] The description fits Rice's play perfectly, and also suggests why *Street Scene* lent itself so well to King Vidor's successful film version of 1931.

Street Scene is naturalistic not just in terms of technique, however, but also in terms of its underlying philosophy. Rice, a socialist, portrays his characters more or less objectively as products and victims of their environment. He does not appear to stand in judgment of their actions, even the actions of Frank Maurrant, the theater stagehand who, in a crime of passion, kills his wife Anna because of her affair with the collector for the milk money. Rice presents scenes of intertwined existences, played out in front of the "exterior of a 'walk-up' apartment-house, in a mean quarter of New York. . . . It is an ugly brownstone," the play's published script continues in its description of the monolithic set, "and was built in the '90's." The slice of metropolitan life that the audience witnesses in all its melodramatic richness has its correspondingly "ugly" and "mean" sides. "Rusted" and "rotting" are other adjectives used to describe the state of the brownstone, whose house number is "half-obliterated."[32]

The music works both with and against this naturalism. It can be quite mundane, with mixed elements of contemporary, multicultural local color; and it can be poetic. The "lyric drama," as Downes observed, is "couched . . . in the patois of the streets," but only "partly." Complementing the music's naturalistic dimension is the predominant transcendental tendency toward the idealistic. But it is only a tendency: the two roles that the music is required to perform do not demarcate easily classifiable types so much as they mark the end points of a varied spectrum of forms and idioms that Weill uses in *Street Scene,* from the cheerful strains of the literally quoted school song at one end to the evocative intonations of tragic music-drama at the other.

Insofar as Weill creates unity in *Street Scene,* he does so out of abundant diversity. And the degree to which he is considered to succeed or fail in this endeavor, and the various means he employs in doing so, are persistent themes of the work's critical history. The composer's own frequently quoted remarks made at the time of the premiere established the terms of a discourse that has continued to the present with numerous commentaries, some of them quite substantial. Representative of the negatively inclined camp is Elise K. Kirk's unfavorable comparison of Weill with Gershwin in her 2001 history of American opera: "*Street Scene*'s integration of jazz and popular styles within a large symphonic score," she writes in a chapter called "The New American Verismo," "is less successful than *Porgy and Bess*'s."[33]

FIGURE 5. Opera baritone Randolph Symonette as Frank Maurrant in the premiere of the American opera *Street Scene* (1947). Weill and Elmer Rice, author of the Pulitzer Prize–winning play of 1929 on which *Street Scene* was based, decided "to do it in one set like the original play . . . very much like Greek tragedy, with tight unity of time and space and the inescapability of fate." Courtesy of the Weill-Lenya Research Center, Kurt Weill Foundation for Music, New York.

Kirk's assessment echoes the conclusion reached by Larry Stempel in his landmark essay on the opera from 1986. Stempel diagnoses an unresolved tension between opera and musical theater in *Street Scene.* The presence of musical comedy numbers "in form and function," Stempel observes, "may well have resulted from compromises demanded by the collaborative process that shapes the Broadway musical to a degree few opera-house operatic composers would tolerate."[34] Stempel is referring here primarily to three numbers: "Moon-Faced, Starry-Eyed," "Wouldn't You Like to Be on Broadway?," and "Wrapped in a Ribbon and Tied in a Bow." Stempel's remark may seem odd, given Weill's collaborative ways, yet it is one frequently encountered in the literature on Weill.[35] Suggesting that the composer would have done something different without the constraints of the Broadway theater, as if hankering after greater artistic autonomy, really misses the point of what he was trying to do and how he went about it. Stempel concludes, citing the "give-and-take" of the production process, that Weill "may not have been solely responsible (as an operatic composer would have been) for the gallimaufry of musical styles that *Street Scene* ultimately became" (330).

Although true as a statement of fact, Stempel's observation is questionable as criticism, based as it is on the assumption of unrealized and unrealizable intentions. It is hard, in many cases impossible, to distinguish between Weill's creative decisions and those of his collaborators. Arguably, it is also futile to try. "But Weill cannot be let off the hook so easily," Stempel insists, "for he felt and acted as if he *were* the operatic composer and thus ultimately responsible for the fact that in his 'Broadway Opera' the Broadway elements and the operatic elements were working at cross-purposes" (330).

Where Kirk claims that Weill fails to integrate the diversity of styles in *Street Scene* as an aesthetic unity, Stempel accounts for that putative failure with reference to the creative process, which, he claims, compromised the composer's intentions. But he goes further, suggesting that Weill's commentaries rationalized the creative compromises by presenting them as intentions. "Indeed," he writes, "Weill even went so far as to embrace the contradictions at the heart of his 'Broadway opera' concept as if it were something purposeful. . . . Weill's appeal to the musical variety . . . is an attempt to justify the conflict of styles as if there *were* some point to be made by it. . . . But its appearance," he concludes, "remains unmotivated" (332–33).

Stempel's aesthetic criticism of the musical comedy numbers in *Street Scene* is really twofold. First, he claims, they lack the kind of overt irony that he sees as having justified banality in the European works. The song "Wrapped in a Ribbon and Tied in a Bow," he says, "even goes so far as to [imitate] Richard Rodgers outright." Second, the Broadway "forms of expression" are not "the structural principle behind the show," (332) which Stempel equates with the story of the four central characters: Frank and Anna Maurrant, their daughter, Rose, and her friend Sam Kaplan. "That opera," Stempel writes, referring to the overtly operatic parts of the score, "almost a self-contained piece, has virtually nothing to do with the Broadway-style view of 'the streets of New York themselves.'" The "melting-pot episodes," he feels, "interrupt the operatic momentum to provide the slice-of-life background that might otherwise have brought the *opera* into relief" (333). Though "perhaps," he suggests, "the dilemma was built into the very structure of Weill's endeavor from the start" (334). It should be noted here that Weill did not orchestrate all the Broadway numbers himself. Ted Royal's orchestrations of "Moon-Faced, Starry-Eyed" and "Wrapped in a Ribbon" have their own discrete "sound" quite different from Weill's. Insofar as there's a dilemma, outsourcing the orchestrations only accentuated it.

How to account for the disparate elements in *Street Scene,* either the Broadway parts of the "Broadway Opera" or, conversely, the operatic parts of the "Dramatic Musical"? On what basis do the elements cohere, if they do? Stempel's remarks suggest an operatic structure with superimposed musical episodes, a conflation of two incompatible genres rather than a unified whole. Referring to the production numbers, including Henry's blues number, Stempel states that "all these Broadwayisms could be cut from *Street Scene* without disturbing the heart of the work in the least. Clearly 'Broadway' is not the street where *Street Scene* lives" (333).

Stempel quotes from two documents to bolster his argument. One of them is the fascinating set of notes that Weill sent to the creative team on 21 December 1946 during rehearsals for the tryout performances in Philadelphia, which began the following month. Weill himself was certainly aware of the challenge that the juxtaposition of the elements presented in performance. He explained that "the most important job to be done on STREET SCENE is to decide on a definite *form* for the show and then to be consistent in carrying through this form." By this he meant the "natural flow" mentioned earlier, having "the numbers grow out of action, to have the dialogue underscored, to avoid the break between spoken and sung word. . . . We always were aware," he writes, "of falling into the conventional musical-comedy pattern of dialogue—number—dialogue—number." His aim, rather, was "a complete blending of music and words and action. . . . But in some parts," he continues, and this is the passage cited by Stempel, "specially in the first act, we have not succeeded yet in blending the elements of the show. In some places we try to be too legitimate, in other places, too musical comedy. We are definitely using too much the number technique of musical comedy instead of the flowing technique we had in mind." Weill proceeded to list in detail the ways in which he thought the production could achieve a more successful result, including tightening the pace of the performance and adopting quite a few specific cuts and revisions.[36]

The other item cited by Stempel in support of his analysis concerns Anna Maurrant's big aria in the first act. This extended number—six and a half minutes on the cast recording, more than seven on recent recordings—lies at the very heart of the opera, according to Stempel's reading. He cites Weill's insisting that the number be left intact, not trimmed, as director Charles Friedman had requested. In Lenya's telling of the story, Weill responded to the request by remarking, "If this aria goes over, it will prove to me that I have written the opera I wanted to write."[37] Foster Hirsch cites the anecdote as evidence of Weill's having resisted the temptation to comply with the "American way." In Hirsch's estimate, "Anna's act I aria became the reason he did the show, and a preview of the kind of American opera he hoped to continue to write."[38] Stempel's essay, published before Hirsch's book, offers a similar perspective. Quoting Weill's own various definitions of *Street Scene,* and with reference to "European-style . . . assumptions of opera" that he believes "determine the stylistic as well as structural underpinnings of the 'American opera,'" Stempel uses the anecdote to support his contention that what "Weill wanted to write" was "a real opera . . . on Broadway," not "a real Broadway opera" (327).

The emotional depth of Anna's aria, in part a function of its formal complexity and motivic richness, certainly provides a striking contrast with the numbers performed by the subsidiary characters. Formally, the aria resembles in miniature the large-scale design of the opera as a whole, with repetition of entire syntactical units creating formal symmetries and with a richly allusive web of motivic reference to other parts of the opera. The life story that is contained in Anna's text and its musical presentation suggest a debt to the narrative form of the big first-act duet in Verdi's *Otello,* where Otello and Desdemona recall episodes from the past. Here, as in the Verdi, each episode corresponds to a new section, defined by a change of musical character, texture, key, etc. This is Anna's cavatina, the introductory aria in which the principal female character tells us (1) about her "dull and grey" existence; (2) about the unfulfilled longings of her childhood (for a "party dress"); (3) about her move to New York in search of "a fairy prince to love me"; (4) how her "dream of love" found only temporary fulfillment in her marriage to Frank; (5) about the joy derived from the birth of children before (6) domestic drudgery set in ("the greasy soap-suds drown our wishes"); (7) about her faith that "there must be two smiling eyes somewhere that will smile back into mine"; and hence (8) about her resolute belief in "a brighter day."

But if the formal precedent for Anna's touching narrative is Verdian, the first of the eight sections, in ABA form and marked "with great feeling and warmth," is indebted to the expressive world of Puccini's *Madama Butterfly,* evoked above all by the stepwise descending parallel triads that produce the trademark consecutive perfect fifths. The connection to that world becomes more explicit with the varied repeat of the opening section, where Anna sentimentally recalls her marriage to Frank. The flower imagery could also be taken from *Butterfly.* Anna sings, "Oh, on the day that we were married I took a flower from my bouquet. And I pressed it in a book and put the book away" (ex. 57). For Anna, like the principal female in the Puccini opera, only the petrified memory remains: "the flower's dry, the perfume's gone, the petals all turned grey." (Earlier, to the same melodic material, she quoted "the fairy tales I read" about "a fairy prince to love me.") But the pentatonic tranquillity of her wistful recollection gives way to an impassioned exclamation, preceded by a rising sequence of heart-tugging appoggiaturas in the orchestra. To the words "Oh dream of love!" Anna's melody abruptly shifts from the world of Butterfly's muted longing to more highly charged Wagnerian intensity, with an allusion to the "motif of longing" from *Tristan und Isolde,* followed by the question "Should love turn out that way?" (ex. 58).

The musical and textual parallels of the first and fourth sections are substantial, generating formal correspondences with wholesale repetition of melodic phrases and other syntactic units. Connections between the third and fifth sections are of a somewhat different kind. The textual theme of New York, symbol of enterprise and optimism, brings to the fore a motif first heard in the bustling

EXAMPLE 57. *Street Scene,* "Somehow I never could believe"

orchestral Introduction at the very beginning of the opera (ex. 59). In the fifth section, where Anna mentions the arrival of babies, the motif reappears, retaining the note of optimism but transformed into something much gentler. The same motif is then subjected to developing variation to produce a lilting figure that depicts "their little arms [that] made a ring-around-a-rosy about me" (ex. 60, mm. 3–4). But the episode is brief, as befits Anna's narrative. Her lament resurfaces, with the falling bass-line echoing the opening, and another exclamation, like before, to the words "There's got to be a little happiness somewhere." After the opening music reappears, Anna expresses her hope for a "brighter day," which is followed by a concluding snatch of the "New York" motif in the orchestra. As

EXAMPLE 58. *Street Scene,* "Somehow I never could believe"

a musical symbol, the motif transcends any direct association with a specific place, signifying through transformation a universal hope of anticipated and real personal fulfillment.

As Weill describes in his commentaries, the singing emerges in an unforced way out of the spoken dialogue, which is accompanied by underscoring. Anna's aria grows out of the preceding scene, in which she and Frank bicker about their daughter under the all too watchful eye of the neighbors. Especially prevalent in the underscoring is the "fate" motif associated with Frank's aggressively saturnine temperament.

EXAMPLE 59. *Street Scene,* Introduction ("bustle motif")

EXAMPLE 60. *Street Scene,* "Somehow I never could believe"

The aria is both self-contained and integrated; the orchestral introduction acts as a prolonged, composed-out anacrusis. As far as the structure of the aria proper is concerned, this is less clearly articulated than the following diagram might suggest.

[1]	[2]	[3]	[4]	[5]	[6]	[7] [8]
F min.	C maj.	B♭ maj.	F min.	C maj.	F min.	F min./F maj.

It is a design based on large-scale harmonic organization, but also on the kind of syntactic repetitions discussed above. The blurring of foreground formal articulation owes to both of these factors: to floating tonality, especially in the harmonically meandering second and third sections, and to artful dovetailing and elisions. The third section, for example, seems cut short syntactically, ending on the dominant of F minor. Rather than completing the melody as expected, however, the following section, which develops the textual theme of the flower "pressed . . . in a book," reiterates thematic material drawn from the very opening of the aria. Just as Anna's life quickly turned "grey," so the music finds abrupt resolution in her earlier, quite contrary expression of discontent: "somehow [she] never could believe."

Before resolving in the major key on a note of optimism and hope, one that the tragic denouement of the opera ultimately belies, Anna's involved, formally sophisticated narrative has covered a lot of emotional ground. Conversely, as Kim Kowalke states in his wide-ranging, finely observed comments on the work, "the most 'conventional' and seductive music in *Street Scene* is reserved for its shallowest, least mature characters." These are the "Broadway" numbers, which use the standard forms of American popular songs that include the 32-bar refrain (or chorus) of four 8-bar phrases in AABA or ABAB patterns. Kowalke posits, moreover, a correlation between "the extent to which each of these numbers departs from or distorts the 32-bar conventional form" and "the degree of independence and spontaneity of thought expressed by the character who is singing."[39] By that measure, Anna's aria, exhibiting a high degree of independence and spontaneity, is anything but "shallow."

Although this emotional depth derives from the aria's individuality and studied spontaneity, its musical means also integrate it into the work as a whole. Apprehension of this integration, acquired in the ways described, including the richly motivic orchestral texture, lends support to Stempel's point about the difference between the "operatic" numbers composed for the principal roles and the "Broadway" numbers for the more minor ones. The extent of the aria's integration militates against its being detached from the original dramatic context and performed as an individual number. Such integration and hence lack of "detachability" are less evident for the "Broadway numbers." Yet the difference—both a structural matter and a fact of the work's reception—is hardly absolute.

The concept of a "Broadway opera" informs the composition of the work less in terms of discrete elements that can be readily separated from one other than as competing ideas that coexist in tension on a number of levels. Thinking of *Street Scene* as essentially a European opera in Broadway clothing misses two critical points about Weill's approach. One is the extent to which the Broadway elements are themselves integrated into the work's overall structure. The other is the way in which the American vernacular and the European classical elements complement one another.

Of all Weill's American shows, *Street Scene* may well be the one, apart from *The Firebrand of Florence,* with the commercially least exploited songs. A handful of songs sheets were published, but none of them caught on in the way individual numbers from other shows had done. Nor did the composer himself consider them especially exploitable. "It is no use fooling ourselves," he wrote to Langston Hughes on 19 April 1947, "that the songs we have written are hit-parade material."[40] Of those published as song sheets, one belongs to Anna ("A Boy Like You"), one each to Rose ("What Good Would the Moon Be") and Sam ("Lonely House"), plus their duet ("We'll Go Away Together"). Of the songs sung by the subsidiary characters, only the jitterbug "Moon-faced, Starry-eyed" was published separately. Insofar as the songs were considered worthy of commercial exploitation, even as potential "hit-parade material," they belonged more to the principal characters than not.

Whatever the potential of the jitterbug to become a hit on its own independent of the show, it is certainly required to be one *in* it. The orchestral Introduction before the opening ensemble comprises three segments. The first, as mentioned, is the *fortissimo* "Lonely House" motto, which precedes the motoric portrait of the hustle and bustle of the city, including the motif referred to earlier as "New York," which is later transformed into a motif associated with children and hope. The third section, as the curtain rises, introduces a dance-band version of "Moon-Faced, Starry-Eyed" coming from a "radio off stage" (ex. 61). Weill had already set a precedent for mechanically reproduced music with the Tango Angèle in *Der Zar lässt sich photographieren.* In this case, the piece is in effect referring to itself, one of several such moments in *Street Scene.* Another one comes in the scene between Rose and her office colleague Harry Easter. Harry, who is vying for her affections and whom she addresses as "Mr. Easter," says to Rose: "A girl like you has got no business to be working all day in a real estate office. . . . Why, you ought to be on the stage." Rose responds: "Don't be silly, how could I ever get a job on the stage?" It is a nicely self-referential moment that calls to mind Macheath's witty line from *Die Dreigroschenoper:* "I'm not exactly asking for an opera." Just as the actor playing Macheath is "not exactly" getting an opera with the piece he is starring in, so the actress playing Rose obviously has "a job on the stage." Harry's ensuing song, "Wouldn't You Like to Be On Broadway?," could be taken

EXAMPLE 61. *Street Scene,* Introduction ("Moon Faced, Starry Eyed")

the same way, as an ironic reference to itself and to its place in the institutional home of Weill's American opera.

The jitterbug's brief presence on the radio as part of the Introduction precedes its being performed by Dick and Mae in the extended dance sequence. Which of the two incarnations is the primary one, the broadcast excerpt or the longer danced version with jazz breaks that incorporate the janitor's blues? On one level, the radio version forms part of the traditional medley that functions as a preview or overture to the ensuing work, whether it be an opera, an operetta, or a musical. But its appearance here in a different medium delivers a defamiliarizing jolt. On another level, then, the number that Dick and Mae perform could be based on a preexisting, well-disseminated piece that is no more a discrete, unique part of the American opera than, say, the quoted school song from Julia Richmond High. That, at least, is the conceit. Not only does the switch of medium to radio at once broach and breach the boundaries between art and life, but *Street Scene* seems also to be posing a question about its own popularity.

Such reflexiveness, an aesthetic self-consciousness for which David Kilroy uses the theoretical term *metadramatic,* is both cause and effect of the hybrid genre.[41] Nor is it limited to the obviously popular elements. The "opera" side of the equation has its part to play as one of the work's themes alongside the "Broadway" ingredients. The two mutually dependent sides complement each other as the musical cultures that Weill brings to bear in a variety of ways. It's the interplay between the two that makes *Street Scene* what it is.

The culture of opera manifests itself in *Street Scene* both as a technical-cum-formal approach, as Weill described in his letter to Neher, and as a pervasive metadramatic topic. Stylistically, however, that culture is hardly monolithic but appears in various guises. Among the Italian ingredients, the over-the-top Ice Cream Sextet is the most "bel canto" moment of the work. An extended ensemble that recalls the Columbus sequence in Weill's 1944 movie *Where Do We Go from Here?,* a composition similarly indebted to the spirit of Gilbert and Sullivan, the sextet is obviously parodic. The divergence between the extravagant operatic form and the banal content lends the whole thing a deliciously camp tone. There is a humorous congruence, of course, in that both bel canto opera and the ice cream cone being celebrated are Italian imports. The "American" opera assimilates them both.

Of the various operatic influences that make themselves felt in *Street Scene,* that of Puccini is the most profound and extensive, as both idiom and source of specific allusions. Several critics of the premiere established the debt, some pejoratively with expressions such as "secondhand Puccini." In addition to Anna's aria, which invokes the tone and imagery of *Madama Butterfly,* as mentioned, Rose's duet with Sam contains quite specific allusions to Puccini's opera at the point where Sam begins to recite Walt Whitman's poem "When Lilacs Last in the Dooryard Bloom'd." In his detailed analysis, Kowalke describes how the music of Rose's cavatina, an "intratextual reference" in the duet, gives way to an "intertextual allusion" to Butterfly's "Dammi sul viso un tocco di carmino" ("Put on a touch of rouge") from act 2 of Puccini's opera. Kowalke notes that although Puccini's and Weill's melodies

> are nearly identical for three measures . . . there seem to be no directly congruent textual parallels that might account for the musical reference. However, the moment in Puccini follows immediately upon Butterfly's and Suzuki's famous "flower duet," where images of fragrant cherry blossoms, lilies, jasmine, and violets from the spring garden give Butterfly new hope as she decorates the house in anticipation of Pinkerton's arrival: "diedi pianto alla zolla, essa i suoi fior mi da" (I have given tears to the earth and she gives her flowers to me). Suspicions, voiced by numerous critics ever since *Street Scene*'s premiere, that the allusion might be fortuitous or the musical idiom merely "secondhand Puccini" in a more general sense may be dispelled if one recalls that the corresponding pastoral moment in *Madama Butterfly* is prompted by the appearance of an American warship in port: "Hold my trembling hand so that I may read the name: ABRAHAM LINCOLN!"[42]

What amounts to a sophisticated, multilayered musical pun, Kowalke argues, potentially both "distances" and "affects." Butterfly's "pastoral respite is now recognized to have been false hope"; the allusion "tells us that Sam and Rose's relationship is doomed, before it has a chance to blossom."[43]

Incorporating not only a variety of styles but also allusions to specific composers and their works is a common feature of both Weill's European and American periods. In *Street Scene,* Puccini joins Bizet, Verdi, and Wagner among the opera composers. From the canon of popular American composers, it is above all Richard Rodgers who makes his influence felt with "Wrapped in a Ribbon." In that sense, the operatic style is no more Weill's "personal style" than the Broadway idiom is. Both are essential to the work's dramaturgy.

The operatic and popular sources serve a variety of dramatic purposes, including specific allusions such as the near-quotation from *Madama Butterfly* and Wagner's *Tristan.* Yet irrespective of whether such allusions are immediately evident or not (and there may be some of which even the composer himself was not entirely conscious), the chosen style always has to work expressively and in terms of the overall "Gestus." Weill invokes Puccini's opera, not simply because of the parallels it may or may not suggest between the fates of the two quite different lead females, Butterfly and Anna Maurrant, but because of its cultural currency as a certain kind of mainstream opera. The same goes for Wagner, whose musical language, like Puccini's, both draws on and establishes rhetorical conventions. Throughout his career, Weill was a master of those conventions. He had a keen sense not only of *when* it was appropriate for characters to sing but also of *how* they should sing. Even those who don't know *Tristan und Isolde,* for example, will still grasp the emotional significance of the "motif of longing" in terms of its expressive content. Even those who don't apprehend the intertextual details of the *Butterfly* allusion will appreciate the operatic conventions that Puccini's music brings to bear. Weill is able to draw liberally on those conventions, whatever their provenance. The juxtaposition is key.

The ability to hit upon the appropriate theatrical register, whether vernacular or operatic, is no doubt based as much on Weill's control of a vast repertory of tonal music as it is on an intuitive grasp of musical vocabulary. Yet it is hard, if not impossible, to determine the extent to which that vocabulary is historically and culturally mediated or whether it can be extrapolated and defined in terms of expressive universals, as Deryck Cooke attempted to do in his 1959 book *The Language of Music.* What one can say is that Weill's own music often relies on identifiable models, in part on the very same canonic repertory on which Cooke's own generalizations are based, in part on the vernacular music of the time. And even where the models are not immediately apparent, Weill's urge to communicate in a shared musical language is undeniable. In this respect, his command of musical topics and other expressive devices can be compared to that of eighteenth-century composers such as Mozart and Handel and also to that of two particularly formative influences from the nineteenth century that he shares with Cooke, Wagner and Mahler.

Although it is hard to say for certain how specific any of them are, Sam's arioso "Lonely House" appears to combine several sources of inspiration. We briefly hear the theme for the first time at the very beginning of the opera, as noted earlier, in a version quite different from its presentation in the arioso. The blues-infused lyricism of Sam's swooping melody, with which he expresses his sense of spiritual isolation, initially appears in a jarringly dissonant harmonization. The tone is suggestive of the city's hubbub, even cacophony, conveyed by the Introduction's motoric second section. Life in the collective urban dwelling only heightens the sense of individual alienation: self-pitying reflection is transformed into a scream of despair. Hence Weill's own description of the house as "a prison for the human spirit."[44]

In sharp contrast to the earlier daytime sounds of the city, the arioso invokes the sounds of the night, with the orchestral accompaniment to the verse providing an evocative sonic tableau. "At night everything is quiet," Sam sings, accompanied by a recurring jazzlike lick that appears in the preceding mood-setting measures on the solo violin, sonic emblem of romantic subjectivity. The accompaniment is evocative of the nocturnal atmosphere to which Sam's text refers, without there being any word-painting as such. The sustained creeping bass line, played here on the cello—which could have been lifted wholesale from the introduction to Pablo de Sarasate's *Introduction et Tarentelle* for violin and piano—is punctuated, if not to say punctured, by percussive semitonal clashes provided by the harp, celesta, and clarinet (exx. 62 and 63). "Sometimes I hear a neighbor snoring. Sometimes I hear a baby cry. Sometimes I hear a staircase creaking. Sometimes a distant telephone." The sonic layers of the verse may suggest all these things. We don't hear any of them, however, at any rate not literally, but are invited to do so imaginatively, to enter Sam's world, in which, as he sings in the chorus, "you can be so lonely with all these folks around." The same layers reappear at the end of the verse to restore the mood of the opening, cadencing in E♭ with the two-note appoggiatura (B♭, C), added by the trumpet, to which Sam had already intoned the word *quiet* (ex. 64).

"Lonely House"—the show's "theme song," as Weill called it—is at once song and aria, a soulful blues that crosses over into the sound world of late-nineteenth-century opera. The climax of the refrain occurs where one would normally expect a concluding return to its opening after the bridge. Instead Sam sings an impassioned variant marked "free" that packs an ironic punch: "The night for me is not romantic;" he sings on his way up to an eventual high B♭. "Unhook the stars and

EXAMPLE 62. Pablo de Sarasate, *Introduction et Tarentelle,* op. 43 (opening)

EXAMPLE 63. *Street Scene,* "Lonely House" (opening)

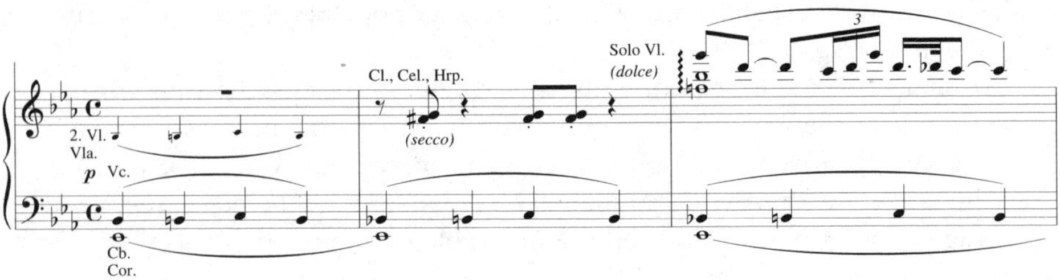

EXAMPLE 64. *Street Scene,* "Lonely House" (ending)

take them down. I'm lonely in this lonely house in this lonely town." The topic of the isolated, self-pitying hero and the Mahlerian, harp-tinged orchestral color make it one of the most romantic moments in the entire opera.

Another such moment is the pastoral dimension of Sam and Rose's interaction. Both of them long to escape from their life in the city, experienced as the tragic dramas of family and race, in contrast to the promise of harmony contained in the Whitman poem that unites them emotionally. "We'll Go Away Together," Sam and Rose's other duet, conveys that sentiment in both the text and the music. It can be read as another of the metadramatic moments derived from Weill's melting pot of musical styles, as if Sam and Rose were also longing, however vainly, for a return to the earlier, simpler world of operetta. Several commentators have remarked that the piece, with its "Pollyanna sentimentality," sounds like music from the earlier generation of American operetta à la Romberg and Kern.[45]

This is the strong sense in which the concept of "pastoral" applies to *Street Scene,* a critique as much as a celebration of urban existence in contemporary America. "Pastoral" traditionally depends on a philosophical opposition, whether "between art and nature or between country and city," as Geoffrey Chew has defined it. Musically, Chew observes, referring chiefly to eighteenth-century artistic practices, the opposition is "usually reinforced by the use of distinctive styles, with the 'natural' style falling appreciably short of the complexity of the conventional style of the day."[46] A pastoral reading of Weill's "American opera" along these lines would account for the atavism of the operetta style as projecting an alternative sphere to life in the modern city. Sam and Rose's desire to flee New York, stated verbally and already fulfilled by a shift of musical register, brings them closer to nature, allowing them to share their personal feelings and emotions in unbridled song. Not that the musical register is any more "natural" than the idioms of the street. The artistic convention, traditionally associated with romantic communion, is merely marked as such; the immediacy is necessarily mediated.

Other allusions suggest themselves, in addition to those mentioned already. Apart from spotting the connection to the language of *Tristan,* as several others have, Andreas Hauff identifies parallels to Eugen d'Albert's *Tiefland,* a relatively obscure opera nowadays, that Weill knew well from his youth. Of particular interest to Hauff is the motif outlining a falling fifth (5–4–5–1) common to *Tiefland* and *Street Scene,* in the former where Pedro sings, "I now have a woman, . . . Heaven gave her to me," and later, "all around there is peace"; in the latter where Sam sings, "remember that I care." For Hauff, however, the significance extends beyond construable parallels between the works' plots to matters of biography. He suggests "a special affinity" on Weill's part for the figure of Sam, "perhaps even identification" with him, and hence a biographical significance attaching to the *Tiefland* quotation at the end of the "Lilacs" duet. "Perhaps," Hauff writes, "the composer has encoded here a personal commitment to his wife as well as the hope for a happier common future."[47]

The *Tiefland* allusion, which is employed both as motif and cipher in *Street Scene,* supports Hauff's argument in favor of the unity of Weill's work. By this he means not only the unity of the "individual work," but, thanks to the specific reference to Weill's European roots, also "the unity of the entire oeuvre" as well as "the unity of the biography"—a bold claim to make on behalf of a single motif that will likely elude most listeners.[48]

Establishing the unity underlying the American opera's eclectic diversity represents a critical challenge that has been addressed in various ways. Biographical decoding, bolstered by leitmotivic analysis and suggesting thereby a subjective, inner program on the composer's part, seems ultimately as untenable as peeling away the accretions of popular music in an attempt to reveal an essential, inner opera. Both approaches tend to minimize what David Kilroy identifies as the quality "that makes [Weill's] late works so fundamentally dramatic"—namely conflict, a "pastoral type of conflict," he suggests, "that resolves only in the hearts and minds of its beholders."[49] Conflict in *Street Scene* takes place on several levels, in terms of dramatic idea and musical style: the city versus its pastoral counterpart; the individual versus the community; traditional versus modern; character versus fate. The one side both determines and qualifies and hence gives enriched meaning to the other.

It is this notion of constitutive conflict that left its mark on the work's conception from the outset and for which Weill himself used an inherently musical term: *counterpoint*. There can be little doubt that conflict manifests itself musically in *Street Scene* via all manner of contrapuntal juxtapositions—tonal, timbral, idiomatic, historical. With respect to "so many diverse idioms," for example, Kowalke writes of a "centripetal force," which "might threaten musical coherence." Yet "despite] its collage-like surface," he concludes, "there is no score of Weill more tightly interwoven motivically and thematically than *Street Scene*." He is referring here to "all manner and scale of musical repetition, development, and transformation to unify seemingly un-unifiable elements: reprise of large sections of numbers; refrains within musical scenes; motivic generation and thematic reminiscence, transformation, and development." Such integration of these musical aspects "within a single distinctive voice and coherent musical structure," he concludes, is "virtually unique in the Broadway musical theater of Weill's time."[50]

There is no question that quasi-symphonic coherence is an indispensable factor contributing to *Street Scene*'s unity. Yet that is not all that is at stake. How to combine the musical with other factors? Annotations made by the composer in his copy of Rice's play, doubtless at an early stage of the work's genesis, make a connection between music and drama in a way that allows unity to be considered from a comprehensive, dramaturgical perspective. Toward the end of Rice's second act, where the children are daring one another to perform somersaults, Weill inserted three marginal notes in the text. The first is "children's song." The second and third belong together, just before Rose appears again at the window: "*children games*" and immediately following, in parentheses, "Sam counterpoint."[51]

Counterpoint in Weill's note relates not merely to the musical design but to the more encompassing level of dramaturgy, which subsumes music. In the play, as indicated in the stage directions, the note refers specifically to the children playing games "undisturbed by Sam's presence." In the more extensive "musicalized" version, it refers to musical factors as well. Sam's physical presence may be initially ignored, as Rice wanted it to be in the play, but his *musical* presence makes itself felt through the rhythm of the "Lonely House" motif. Along with a whole array of recurring elements, the motif provides a foil to the pentatonic chanting of the children and, in juxtaposition with the games, contributes to the musical basis of the scene's elaborate musico-dramatic tableau.

Defined in terms of the "musicalized" realization, then, Weill's annotation signals how as a composer for the musical theater he intended to exploit contrast and conflict on a dramatic as well as a musical level—in short, to create dramaturgical counterpoint. It is a poietic principle, at work not just in this portion of the work but throughout *Street Scene*. As I will argue in the following chapter, dramaturgically motivated counterpoint informs Weill's conception of musical theater throughout his career. Even though this American opera may be considered a paradigmatic case (if not *the* paradigmatic case in his oeuvre, as the composer's own testimony suggested), other examples are not hard to find.

DOWN IN THE VALLEY

The American subject matter of their librettos, the connection to American vernacular music, the conception for American performers and audiences—these are the common elements that define *Street Scene* and *Down in the Valley* as "American operas." Yet there are more specific features, to do with formal design and content, that link them in other quite substantial ways, such that they can be considered companion pieces. The latter, smaller-scale work thereby becomes (to use Olin Downes's expression) a "pendant" to the former.

The origins and purpose of the two American operas could suggest alternative companions in Weill's oeuvre. Thoroughly urban in conception, *Street Scene* can readily be compared, as suggested above, to *Aufstieg und Fall der Stadt Mahagonny* as well as to other of Weill's musical explorations of the metropolis. Moreover, *Street Scene* is not only an opera *about* the city; like *Mahagonny*, it was conceived *for* the city, as a work to be presented by professional performing forces. *Down in the Valley* is quite different in both origin and purpose, as Weill was keen to stress in his own quite detailed account of the work's genesis, which appeared in the *New York Times* on 5 June 1949. Responding to an article by H. W. Heinsheimer published the previous week, Weill wished to make what he calls "correcting remarks." (Heinsheimer, it should be recalled, was Weill's editor at Universal Edition in Vienna. After emigrating to the United States to escape the

Nazi annexation of Austria in 1938, he worked for the music publishers Boosey & Hawkes before moving to G. Schirmer in 1947.)

In his version, Heinsheimer effectively took credit for having inspired the work's inception. Motivated by resistance he had encountered toward opera in America, he writes that in 1947 he had gone to visit "my old friend, the composer, Kurt Weill." Weill's works, he explains, "were not conceived, as were most operas of the past, with the lavish public subsidies in mind that had made opera possible in Europe and did not exist in America. . . . We had a long talk," Heinsheimer relates. "The result is the opera 'Down in the Valley.'"[52]

Weill's riposte effectively disputes the account of the inception in Heinsheimer's *Times* article, an account often repeated in the secondary literature. As editor at Schirmer, Heinsheimer was responsible for publishing the score of *Down in the Valley.* And even if he may have provided encouragement and support to Weill, he omitted mentioning that the opera already existed, albeit in a different form, before being turned into a stage work. Hence Weill's need to provide a correction, which he does by rehearsing "facts connected with the early origin of the piece." As he makes clear, the inception predated Heinsheimer's version by a couple of years. If credit should go to anyone, he suggests, it is to Olin Downes: "In 1945 Olin Downes acquainted me with his concept of finding a new artistic form through which American composers might evolve a native art by the utilization for dramatic purposes of American folksong. He had been approached by Charles McArthur, a business man of exceptionally thoughtful and idealistic aims, who had asked him whether he thought he could build a series of musical plays around folk tunes for radio programs."[53]

Weill goes on to describe how he "suggested as a basic form for this radio program a weekly dramatization of a specific folksong" and that "this formula was accepted." The search for a collaborator, which lasted several weeks, ended with Arnold Sundgaard, "a fine, young playwright and expert in American folklore." Weill explains that Sundgaard "created a story idea which he had found in the verses of *Down in the Valley.*" He then mentions how they "cast the opera" and "made what in radio circles is known as an audition, a recording of which, in turn, was submitted to prospective sponsors." But it all came to naught because of lack of support from the sponsors: "We found these sponsors frightened by the idea that they might be accused of submitting an opera to the public. It seemed that our project for radio advertisers was somewhat ahead of its time."

As Weill reports, the radio project languished until "about a year later a friend of mine who is dean of a Midwestern university asked me if I knew of a dramatic work to be performed in his school." It is not clear to whom Weill is referring here, most likely to Hans Busch, director of the premiere production at Indiana University, where Busch joined the School of Music faculty in 1948, though not as dean. (Fritz Busch, Hans's father, had conducted the 1926 premiere of Weill's first opera, *Der Protagonist,* in Dresden.) In conceiving of the revision, Weill could certainly refer to his earlier work, as Heinsheimer had done. Weill writes:

> I remembered a wonderful experience I had had with a school opera which I wrote in Europe years ago, and it occurred to me that the piece we had written for Mr. Downes' radio program would be readily adaptable for an American school opera.
>
> So Sundgaard and I went to work again. We changed the original radio piece into a musico-dramatic form, about twice as long as the original, with new scenes, new lyrics and new music, and a brand-new orchestration for the special requirements of school orchestras. This is the folk-opera, "Down in the Valley," as it was first performed at Indiana University last summer.

In both of its incarnations, for broadcast on radio and for college performance, *Down in the Valley* has roots that go back to Weill's attempts in Europe to create artistically valuable *Gebrauchsmusik.* Where he mentions "a school opera which I wrote in Europe years ago," he is no doubt thinking of *Der Jasager,* while the earlier commission for radio suggests a connection to his experimental piece for radio, *Der Lindberghflug.* Not least because of the basis in American folk culture, however, *Down in the Valley* also has antecedents in more recent work that he doesn't mention.

Down in the Valley was not Weill's first American work conceived for radio. Nor was it the first to be based on particular folk songs. In 1938–39 he had composed for the New York World's Fair *Railroads on Parade,* a "Pageant-Drama of Transport," which paid tribute to the American railroad system from the mid–nineteenth century to the present. Presented in two separate versions, in 1939 and 1940, the pageant draws on a number of well-known songs, most of them added to the 1940 version, which are interwoven with accompanied narration and orchestral interludes. The interludes are written for the most part in a style familiar from Weill's motoric music of the late 1920s; intermittently, the building momentum of these interludes could be interpreted as imitating the sound of an accelerating steam locomotive, in a manner redolent of Honegger's "Pacific 231." The songs include such evergreens as "This Train Is Bound for Glory" and "I've Been Working on the Railroad" (this last arranged as a canon).

Between the 1939 production of *Railroads on Parade* and the revised version the following year, Weill composed with Maxwell Anderson *The Ballad of Magna Carta* in fulfillment of a commission from the Columbia Broadcasting System. Concerning the title of this radio piece, Weill explained: "It's a ballad like the old Scottish ones, set to music, but between the stanzas there are prose passages, sometimes spoken, sometimes in recitative. Even the spoken parts, though, are in rhythm, so that the whole thing has a definite pattern."[54]

Radio attracted Weill as an artistic alternative to live theater, an alternative he was keen to explore, even though, as with film, he often found his interest and idealism dampened by the obstacles and challenges posed by the industry. *The Ballad of Magna Carta* is at once an exception to and confirmation of the rule of his frustrated ambitions in the medium.[55] Broadcast live on 4 February 1940, with Burgess Meredith as the singing narrator, it was originally intended as the first part of a trilogy of contributions to a series of radio programs called *Pursuit of Happiness*. The remaining parts of the trilogy never materialized for reasons that are not entirely clear.

One of the reasons must have been the advent of the Second World War. *Pursuit of Happiness* was, in the words of an announcement heralding the series, "dedicated to the brighter side of the American scene." The broadcasts expressly did not "deal with war or issues growing out of the war which divide our minds. . . . Instead," the program information stated in lofty vein, "these new programs each Sunday for a little while will turn aside from the stream of grave events and bring us reminders that today, with thankfulness and humility, we Americans still enjoy our constitutional rights to life, liberty, and the pursuit of happiness." It was, as Meredith made clear in his introductory words, "a show about the United States—of American things and American places and American people."[56]

The program information suggests that a dramatized narrative of the signing of the Magna Carta in 1215 justified itself as a contribution to the series, since that document laid the foundation stone of freedoms enshrined in the Constitution of the United States. Yet the connection between the Constitution and the title of the series is, strictly speaking, misleading. The "pursuit of happiness" (along with "life" and "liberty") is one of the "unalienable rights" enumerated in the Declaration of Independence, not in the U.S. Constitution. Be that as it may, the contemporary relevance of the broadcast was really twofold. Not only did the work construe this defining moment in British history as having paved the way for political values in America; the "resistance unto tyrants" being celebrated also suggested an unmistakable parallel to the current situation in Europe, immediately prior to U.S. entry into the war. To that extent, although the "grave events" were not being addressed directly, they did provide at least an implied backdrop to the upbeat American theme.

The two remaining parts of the trilogy were no doubt intended to bridge the considerable historical and cultural gap between King John's England and Roosevelt's America. One of them was to deal with the Boston Tea Party, the other with the Declaration of Independence. History, however, intervened. Reasserting U.S. political independence from its chief ally likely seemed insensitive, even entirely inappropriate, as the United States became increasingly involved in the war.

Instead of continuing with the other two parts of the trilogy, Weill was invited by Norman Corwin, the director of *Pursuit of Happiness*, to contribute, again with Maxwell Anderson, to *This Is War!,* a series of broadcasts intended to raise the consciousness of the American public in the wake of the Japanese attack on Pearl Harbor. Entitled *Your Navy,* Anderson and Weill's contribution, broadcast on 28 February 1942, drew on sea shanties and war songs that the composer had researched in the New York Public Library.[57]

This, then, is the cultural and musical background to the folk opera *Down in the Valley,* a period during which Weill worked on a variety of projects that incorporated folk songs at the service of markedly American themes. The projects mixed idealism and opportunism in equal measure. As Weill assimilated himself into American culture quite consciously and with a distinct sense of patriotic purpose, he looked beyond the regular theater as a way of establishing himself as an American artist, whether through immediate involvement in the war effort or more generally by creating distinctly American forms of art.

The list of war-related projects between 1941 and 1945 is substantial. It includes incidental music for *Fun to Be Free,* a 1941 pageant staged at New York's Madison Square Garden and sponsored by Fight for Freedom, Inc., a group that supported U.S. involvement in the European war. The next year, in 1942, Weill arranged four patriotic melodramas—the "Battle Hymn of the Republic," "The Star Spangled Banner," "America," and his setting of Walt Whitman's "Beat! Beat! Drums!"—which the actress Helen Hayes narrated on an RCA Victor recording issued with the title *Mine Eyes Have Seen the Glory.* He wrote numerous propaganda songs for the war effort that were performed as part of the *Lunch Hour Follies,* a series of variety shows staged by the American Theatre Wing for workers in munitions factories. (Of these, "Schickelgruber" [words by Howard Dietz] and "Buddy on the Nightshift" [Oscar Hammerstein] have become quite well known in our own era.) In 1943 he provided incidental music for the pageant *We Will Never Die,* a memorial to the Jewish victims of Nazi persecution, which received its premiere at Madison Square Garden on 9 March and was subsequently performed in Washington, D.C., Philadelphia, Chicago, Boston, and Hollywood, and also broadcast widely on radio. In 1944 he was involved in two projects for the Office of War Information: in one, Lenya recorded Weill's setting of "Wie lange noch?" (words by Walter Mehring) for broadcast in Germany behind enemy lines; and in the other, he wrote the score for a film called *Salute to France,* starring Burgess Meredith, which was released in English and French versions.

Down in the Valley comes at the end of this period of *Gebrauchsmusik* composed for patriotic and consciousness-raising purposes. Nor should this work, which was initially conceived as a "ballad opera" for radio and then refunctioned as a "folk opera" for nonprofessional performing forces, be entirely divorced from those preceding endeavors. Certainly, in a 1946 letter to businessman Charles McArthur, who along with Downes was one of the instigators of the radio version, Weill expresses an idealism similar to that which informed the wartime projects.[58] And he obviously still has on his mind the practical question of finding a sponsor. But in explaining his decision to base the work on folk song, he also voices deeply held convictions about what it means to him to be an American artist. Even though the American aspect of his art features prominently in his statement, two principal themes he introduces are familiar from his European days. One of them has to do with the democratic aspirations of his art; the other with the notion of service to institutions that he sees in a broad historical perspective, invoking Bach and Mozart as composers whose music was at once useful and great. Thus he frames his own ambition—to create "great American art": "I have been convinced for a long time that in a deeply democratic country like ours, art should belong to the people. It should come out of their thinking and their emotions, and it should become part of their lives. It should become 'popular' in the highest sense of the word. Only by making this our aim can we create an American art, as opposed to the art of the old countries which belongs to a selected class of aristocrats or 'connoisseurs.'"[59]

Weill's letter continues in unabashedly patriotic vein, describing folk song as "the natural basis for the creation of an American music. . . . American folk song," he writes, "overshadows the folk songs of all other countries . . . not only in quantity but also in the quality of its texture, in the depth of its emotion, in the exuberance of its humor, in the beauty of its melody, and in the strength of its rhythm." He then describes how "for our new radio program we have found a new way of making the folk song the basic element of an American art-form." In this he seeks "to dramatize the folk song itself," producing what he calls a "modern 'ballad opera.'" "There is," he explains, "a great variety of songs which have enough 'story' in themselves to build a folk play around. Sometimes, like in the case of 'Down in the Valley' there is only a line in the song which indicates a story, but there are always good dramatic situations and rich characterizations in these songs."

Among the numerous transmitted versions of the folk song "Down in the Valley," there are really two lines, not just one, that indicate the story of the opera. One tells of enduring love, the other of imprisonment. Here is a version published in 1917:

Down in the valley, valley so low,
Late in the evening, hear the train blow;
The train, love, hear the train blow;
Late in the evening, hear the train blow.

Go build me a mansion, build it so high,
So I can see my true love go by,
See her go by, love, see her go by,
So I can see my true love go by.

Go write me a letter, send it by mail;
Bake it and stamp it to the Birmingham jail,
Birmingham jail, love, to the Birmingham jail,
Bake it and stamp it to the Birmingham jail.

Roses are red, love, violets are blue;
God and his angels know I love you,
Know I love you, know I love you,
God and his angels know I love you.[60]

Text and music vary considerably, however, depending on the version. Just among the published versions contained in Weill's personal library alone, for instance, there is "a surprising degree of variation," as John Graziano remarked in his essay on the opera.[61] Nor does the opera follow any one version faithfully.

Apart from the titular song, Weill and Sundgaard also drew on four other folk songs, as the published piano-vocal score acknowledges beneath the *dramatis personae*: "Parts of this score are based on American folk songs. Besides 'Down in the Valley' the following songs have been used: 'The Lonesome Dove,'* 'The Little Black Train,' 'Hop Up, My Ladies,' and 'Sourwood Mountain.'"[62] The footnote indicated by the asterisk supplies details of a single source, the 1939 collection *The Singin' Gatherin'*.[63] Although they relied on other folk song collections as well, the authors must have been obliged to cite this one for copyright reasons.

Transforming the folk song's opposing motifs of imprisonment and enduring love into an opera required the invention of two elements missing in the original source. The first is the dramatic narrative that serves as the basis of the operatic plot: the story of a killing (a crime of passion) and the subsequent execution of the perpetrator. The second element is the *dramatis personae* themselves: Brack Weaver (tenor or high baritone), Jennie Parsons (lyric soprano), Thomas Bouché (bass), the Leader and the Preacher (baritone), a handful of speaking roles, including Jennie's father, and the Chorus. So artful is Weill's manipulation of the folk idiom, however, that one could be forgiven for mistaking details of the resulting scenario as having been lifted directly from a traditional American ballad. The simple strophic songs "Brack Weaver, My True Love, They've Taken Away," which lends expression to Jennie's grief and undying love, and Brack's "Where Is the One Who Will Mourn Me When I'm Gone?" sound as authentic in their lilting modality as any of the borrowed material.

The work's structure is quasi-cinematic, comprising interpolated dramatic scenes that emerge seamlessly from the epic narration. The titular song, presented through varied repetition, forms the principal musical element of the narrative frame, while the content of that narrative is dramatically enacted in a series of flashbacks. Some of the spoken dialogue is also cinematic in that it is accompanied by underscoring—a technique similar to that employed in *Street Scene.* Again, as in *Street Scene,* dialogue is also incorporated into the main songs. And, more sparingly, there is some traditional recitative.

Highlighting the work's use-value, the composer begins his foreword to the piano-vocal score by stating that *Down in the Valley* "was mainly conceived for production by non-professional groups. It can be performed," he writes, "wherever a chorus, a few singers, and a few actors are available. . . . The physical production can be as simple as a 'dramatic' concert performance where the principals act their scenes in front of the chorus, without any help of scenery." The simple style of *Down in the Valley* is a function not just of the work's origin in folk song and the radio series for which it was conceived, but also of its ultimate purpose as a college opera. Weill further emphasizes this latter aspect when he writes in the foreword that the "leading parts should provide good training for the specific type of singing actor who has become such an important asset of the musical theater in America."

Although markedly different in both form and content from its austere predecessor *Der Jasager, Down in the Valley* similarly pursues the aim of schooling the participants in the rudiments of the genre. Both are operas about opera. Yet the impulse toward metadramatic distance is not so much ironic (as in, say, *Die Dreigroschenoper*) as it is educational. *Down in the Valley* nonetheless thrives, like *Street Scene,* on the interplay between two distinct levels of musical expression, in this case folk music and operatic music. The following critical assessment will attempt to maintain these distinctions.

Within a year of its premiere at Indiana, Weill's college opera had received eighty productions. Citing this figure in a 23 July 1949 article titled "Home-Grown Opera" published in connection with the Madison Square Garden production, *Time* magazine described the work as "the biggest hit in the three-year history of Manhattan's zestful Lemonade Opera company" and "a sensational hit on the campus theater circuit all over the U.S." NBC, whose radio division had broadcast a performance by the University of Michigan on 7 August 1948, just three weeks after the premiere production at Indiana, launched its inaugural series of televised operas in 1950 with a studio production of *Down in the Valley.* Within nine years, more than 1,500 productions with some 6,000 performances, most of them at American colleges, universities, and conservatories, had been staged.

Both in spite and because of the success reflected in these remarkable performance statistics, *Down in the Valley* has had perhaps the most mixed reception of all Weill's works, dividing its critics from the very beginning. The constellation of topics addressed has remained consistent throughout: the sentimental nature of the libretto, the heterogeneous mix of musical idioms, and the marked contrast between the European artifice of Weill's compositional technique, on the one hand, and the naïveté of the American folk song material, on the other. Even though the composer receives copious credit for having forged a path toward the establishment of a new genre of American opera, the means for doing so have frequently been called into question.

In support of his own critique, for example, Foster Hirsch draws on a number of earlier writers, such as Harold Schonberg and Cecil Smith, both of whom reviewed the Lemonade Opera production in 1949.[64] Schonberg identified a basic dichotomy: "The theme is American, Weill's setting is based on European concepts. The story, whatever its lack of literary merit, is basically simple, whereas Weill's treatment is slick and sophisticated. As such, *Down in the Valley* impresses as a synthetic, and a pretty obvious one at that."[65] Smith, writing in *Musical America*, described the work along similar lines but was more conspicuously negative in his critique: "The innocent folk melodies are subjected to chromatic harmonizations that artificialize and cheapen them. . . . If *Down in the Valley* represents the ultimate Americanization of Mr. Weill, the news is bad, for he has thrown away his fine-grained sandpaper and reached for a trowel."[66]

The *Time* article quoted above struck more of a balance between criticism of the libretto and admiration for Weill's technique: "The story is pathetic enough to sluice any church basement with tears. . . . Some customers feel that the libretto should have been poured over a waffle instead of an audience, but most of them like Weill's witty, musicianly development of the folk themes." Among the wholly positive notices was Wilfred Bain's review of the piano-vocal score, which hailed the work as "a departure in the field of American opera selected from American folk songs, which are expressive of American events, ideas and experiences." Bain also praised the "full learned and skillful orchestral treatment . . . a series of small musical forms or pieces."[67]

If the constellation of critical topics remains more or less the same, their weighting and appraisal clearly differ depending on the sensibilities of the critic. When the score was reissued in the 1960s, David Drew acknowledged the work's success as both "immediate" and "enduring," but he otherwise echoed the negative verdict offered by a number of earlier writers such as Schonberg and Smith: "The fact remains that *Down in the Valley* is not the kind of work likely to find favour in the higher reaches of the musical world. It is too obviously subservient to the commercial circumstances of its composition. At best it has a certain folksy charm. . . . At worst it is the merest tear-jerker. If one can stomach the sentimentality of the libretto, it is possible to find something to admire in the musico-dramatic form."[68]

Drew singled out a few aspects as "effective" and "well done," but "as a whole," he opined, "the music, apart from the still masterly instrumentation, lacks conviction and coherence." He disapproved, for example, of the way in which "gobbets of undigested Wagner or Puccini are lumped together with stock Tin Pan

Alley formulae," and how "empty ostinati do service for real invention." Hirsch would later refer to "aesthetic misjudgments" for similar reasons. Drawing on psychological criteria, Drew interpreted *Down in the Valley* as a symptom of a personal crisis in Weill's biography that began in the late 1930s, specifically as an unconscious reaction to "the crushing reception of *The Firebrand of Florence*, his last work in any kind of European tradition"—in short, as a manifestation of "the ultimate Americanization of Mr. Weill," as Smith had put it. Whatever this transformation held for Weill, Drew suggests, "he concealed it . . . from his friends and not least from himself."

Such a psychological interpretation, positing repressive mechanisms at work, necessarily undermines Weill's public opinion of his work's significance, which positively embraces its Americanization. According to him, as with *Street Scene*, "Everything I have done so far has been working toward this."[69] Critic John Rockwell, writing about *Down in the Valley* in 1984, drew attention to the challenge of finding appropriate criteria for judging the work while qualifying his comment that "the deliberate naïvete" was "too extreme." "Weill's sentimentality," he ventured, "needed the balance of a sharper, wittier, more ironic mind; Bertolt Brecht, for instance." He also felt that "the innocent purity of the folk songs is more subverted than exalted by Weill's European-symphonic gussying up." Calling *Down in the Valley* "a historical curiosity," he nonetheless conceded that it "may well appeal to many *on its own terms*."[70] But how might those terms be construed?

Weill's American folk opera may be simple because of the melodic material it presents (and in two instance fabricates) and because of its catering to college performers, but it is hardly unsophisticated. Even the work's critics have conceded this point, whether or not they end up finding that sophistication ill-conceived or inappropriate. The composition is technically artful in the way Weill treats the basic material through varied repetition to create a cyclically seamless structure. (It should be recalled that in a much-quoted letter to Chicago music critic Irving Sablosky, he remarked that "its very limitations as musical material seemed attractive to me for the piece.")[71] And it is dramatically effective—a "red-hot piece of theatre," as Weill himself put it—thanks to the range of expression that he achieves with relatively limited means.[72] Again, in both of these respects, formal and expressive, *Down in the Valley* invites comparison with *Street Scene* and hence poses a similar critical challenge.

In his study of the piece, John Graziano states that the Introduction "has no thematic relationship to the remainder of *Down in the Valley*."[73] While this is true with respect to the folk song material, the passage does in fact recur twice: first as almost literal repetition, the second time at the very end, somewhat varied. The first time is a crucial moment of flashback, creating a transition between Jennie's encounter with Brack after his jailbreak to their meeting in church a year earlier.

It's as though the opera were starting over, albeit at a happier juncture in their relationship. This time the fanfare quality of the opening (again analogous to *Street Scene*'s opening "Lonely House" motto) is followed by an ascent to a high ethereal passage in the strings that reverses the motion of the beginning of the opera, where a similarly contoured figure descends as part of the prolonged upbeat to the Leader's presentation of the titular song. There is a further parallel between the earlier and later sections in that the same baritone performs the role of Leader and Preacher, with the latter singing the spiritual "The Little Black Train" as atmospheric local color for the church setting of Brack and Jennie's tryst.

A similar string figure, again descending, supplies the transition to the next flashback, which presents the preparation for the Shadow Creek dance at which, in the succeeding scene, Jennie goes against the financially motivated wishes of her father by spurning the advances of Thomas Bouché, and at which Brack kills Bouché, after Bouché has pulled a knife from his pocket. All this occurs against the mounting frenzy of the folk dance, which is based on material drawn from "Sourwood Mountain."

Following the fatal fight, two women (like the nursemaids and other gossips in the closing scene of *Street Scene*) offer laconic spoken commentary:

1ST WOMAN: Trouble at Shadow Creek again. Tom Bouché's got killed.

2ND WOMAN: Might've known Jennie would be gettin' somebody in trouble.

1ST WOMAN: Have they caught him yet?

2ND WOMAN: Caught him in the hills before sunrise . . . Took him to Birmingham jail . . .

This time the Leader sings an "artificial" variant of the titular song in the minor key, followed by the rising transition similar to that heard before the church scene. Now, however, it is early morning as the lovers await Brack's capture following his nocturnal jailbreak. Their rendition of "The Lonesome Dove" intermingles with a musical reminiscence of the ostinato figure and wind fanfare that illustrated the drama of that incident (ex. 65). (The fanfare itself, alternating triplets and dotted rhythms, recalls the motoric style of *Mahagonny*.) This transition in turn brings the action back—or rather, forward. The love story is about to conclude, with the poignant stage direction "Brack is back in jail, as in the beginning, leaning against the wall, but now with a quiet expression of fulfillment." He is united with his beloved, in death. The operatic topic par excellence dramatically recasts the sentiments of the folk songs, lending individual expressive nuance to the culture of the community.

This dovetailing of simple folk song melodies and the melodrama of grand opera is an essential ingredient of *Down in the Valley*. The one element plays off the other in dramaturgical counterpoint, just as popular song and opera do in

EXAMPLE 65. *Down in the Valley,* "The Lonesome Dove"

Street Scene. The music of the people and the idiom of passionate individualism feed off each other. The expressive nuance is already present in the first presentation of the folk song, where the tenors' flattened sixth injects an alteration of the song's mode from major to minor (ex. 66). As noted, the folk melody itself appears in various guises, with the shift between major and minor being one of the principal means of variation.

The moment of starkest contrast between the folk and operatic elements comes after Brack's escape. Brack identifies himself by whistling the "Down in the Valley" melody—the work's leitmotif, as it were—accompanied only by tremolando strings. Between the two clauses of the opening melodic period, Jenny responds: "Brack, I can hear you." What we hear while she "hurries out the gate" and "they embrace," however, is the musical language of longing and emotional communion supplied by the orchestra (ex. 67). As in *Street Scene,* one could speak of an allusion to Wagner's *Tristan und Isolde,* if not of actual quotation. ("Gobbets of undigested Wagner," according to Drew's assessment, quoted above.) Common expressive devices are the chromaticized contours of appoggiaturas and the heightened tension achieved via sequential repetition.

EXAMPLE 66. *Down in the Valley,* "Down in the Valley"

EXAMPLE 67. *Down in the Valley,* Jennie and Brack embrace

Yet there is another element of repetition here, a counterpart to sequence, that provides dramatic tension as well as continuity—namely, ostinato. This, too, manifests itself in a variety of ways. In its initial use, it serves to imitate the sound of the train, the means of Brack's flight, recalling a similar effect at the beginning of *Street Scene,* where it functions as a marker of urban bustle. (A common source here is Weill's own *Railroads on Parade.*) Ostinato is also evident in other motoric figures, some of them reduced in their later appearances to brief snippets with motivic significance. For instance, the repeated four-note figure that accompanies the conversation of the women immediately following the fatal dance scene derives from the earlier "train" music. Here the motif associates that

EXAMPLE 68. *Down in the Valley,* underscored spoken dialogue ("flight motif")

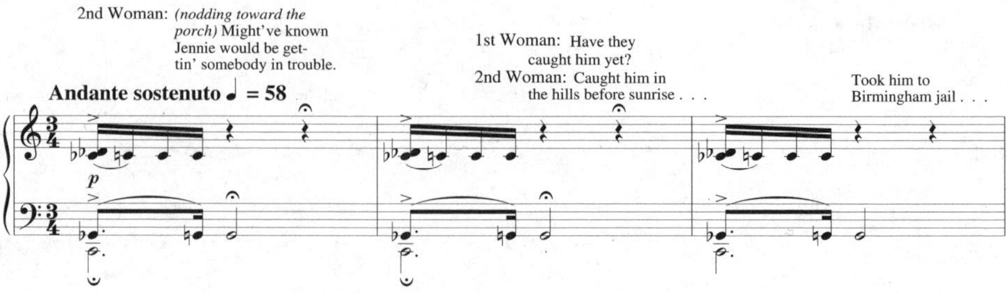

first moment of flight from the jail with the second moment, Brack's flight from the scene of accidental manslaughter (ex. 68).

Both of these devices central to the art of varied repetition—ostinato and sequence—alternate throughout the scene of Brack's escape and his reunion with Jennie. Each performs its traditional task of musical signification throughout the opera: ostinato representative of action, sequence of emotion. The extended action sequence of the dance, which forms the dramatic high point of the opera, relies heavily on driving repeated figures whose material is derived, as mentioned, from the song "Sourwood Mountain." At the moment of climax, which continues the process of repeating melodic modules lifted from the song, the rhythmic units undergo metrical variation, with alternating triple and duple meter, culminating in the irregular dissonant strikes of Brack's fight with Bouché. It is Weill at his most Stravinskian, conjuring up the ritual violence of *Le sacre du printemps.* Nor is it surprising that in his 1950 obituary of the composer, Theodor W. Adorno paid particular tribute to "the garish and confused fiddling at the start of the village dance," which for him "stuck out" from the otherwise (at least to him) "dreary surroundings" of the folk opera.[74]

As with *Street Scene,* the integration of heterogeneous materials into a tightly controlled large-scale structure raises questions about coherence. Both works evince a symmetrical design that links individual numbers with various techniques of through-composition. The alternation of folk song refrains and operatic episodes in *Down in the Valley* is rondo-like. Yet as with *Street Scene,* any formalistic considerations need to take into account the overarching perspective of dramaturgy. Both works contextualize a crime of passion. *Street Scene*'s cyclical structure, defined by the repeated blues number, brackets the awfully hot day on which Frank's murder of Anna occurs. *Down in the Valley* is more literally symmetrical. Apart from the reiterated main song, the opera's opening fanfare recurs at the very end, broken down into its constituent parts. As a motif common to the fanfare and the incipit of the song, the basic rhythm (short-short-short-long)

EXAMPLE 69. *Down in the Valley,* "opening fanfare"

EXAMPLE 70. *Down in the Valley,* "concluding fanfare"

occurs twice during the final curtain before the additional iambic element (short-long) concludes the work, this time inverted as an affirmatively rising element (exx. 69 and 70).

In each of Weill's American operas, the protagonists' destinies play themselves out operatically against the backdrop of community. Although both *Street Scene* and *Down in the Valley* are tragedies, the latter conveys a sense of transcendence that is missing from its urban counterpart. Rose and Sam espy pastoral escape only in daydreaming and lyrical fantasy. Unlike Frank Maurrant, whose life and fate symbolize the dysfunction of existence in the modern city, Brack overcomes his incarceration in a conclusion that reconciles the preceding counterpoint of folk song and opera. In this, he is supported first by the choral rendition of the folk song with its closing line "Angels in heaven know I love you" and then by the grand fanfare.

Rather than implying the eternal recurrence of earthly suffering, as the recapitulated blues does in *Street Scene,* the concluding measures of *Down in the Valley* supply the musical gesture of religious affirmation that corresponds to Brack's "expression of fulfillment." That, too, is a way in which Weill's college opera demonstrates the lessons of the genre: tragedy transcended. The fanfare makes an emphatically affirmative point. "Almost too effective" was the verdict of Cecil Smith, one of the work's early critics. "It sounds like a choral-orchestral montage at the end of a Hollywood epic—a sumptuous noise, but overwritten and spurious."[75] There is no denying that the tone of the conclusion is somewhat hackneyed—even corny, to quote Sablosky. But if Weill's response to Sablosky's charge is worth anything, then that's precisely the point. Like *Street Scene, Down in the Valley* relies on a variety of expressive conventions and techniques, including film. Instead of censuring the ending for its proximity to Hollywood or dismissing it for being "subservient to the commercial circumstances of its composition," one could legitimately say that these are the very terms on which the piece should be judged to succeed.

Companion pieces on account of their common musical aesthetic and complementary purpose, *Street Scene* and *Down in the Valley* can lay claim to a substantial measure of success, each on its own terms. Inspired by George Gershwin's example, Weill's "quest for American opera," as Kowalke has shown, either succeeded where others had made little impact or inspired further experiments.[76] That Weill planned to continue working "in the world of opera"—his "real field of activity," as he called it—is clear from the numerous ideas he was considering until the very end of his life. These included operas based on literary sources such as *The Grapes of Wrath* and *Moby Dick;* composing for the Metropolitan Opera was even a possibility. In the end, however, although the two completed American operas did much to realize an abiding artistic ambition, it was an ambition sadly cut short.

12

Concept and Commitment

Weill's last two works for the musical theater, which had their premieres on Broadway within a year of each other, in 1948 and 1949, offer an intriguing study in contrasts. Subtitled "A Vaudeville," *Love Life* looks in a critical, yet entertaining way at the institution of marriage in a broad historical context. *Lost in the Stars,* billed as a "musical tragedy," represents a serious, humanistically committed attempt to examine race relations in a society oppressed by bigotry.

By looking back to earlier forms of American theatrical entertainment, Weill's "vaudeville" also looks forward. Its subversion of conventional linear plot-construction foreshadows a genre that would not become commonplace until a couple of decades later, the "concept musical." In this, Weill was building on recent trends in musicals, such as Rodgers and Hammerstein's *Allegro* and his own *Lady in the Dark,* as well as on innovations in dramaturgy evinced in plays such as Thornton Wilder's *Our Town,* all of which have demonstrable connections to Weill's own earliest German stage works.

The "musical tragedy," by contrast, challenges conventions in quite different ways. As Weill told the music critic Olin Downes, he considered his last completed work for the musical theater an "experiment" conceived for "the typical American audience," but with "a lot of very serious, tragic, quite un-Broadwayish music of operatic dimensions, together with some songs written in a more familiar style."[1] Whether or not the experiment succeeded, and on what terms, became a matter of some controversy. Downes, among others, had his doubts. Nor was the controversy resolved in the composer's lifetime. The reactions that *Lost in the Stars* elicited can be seen as having prepared the ground for Weill reception more generally.

Forty-Sixth Street Theatre

Operated by City Playhouses Inc. — Louis A. Lotito, President

FIRE NOTICE: The exit indicated by a red light and sign nearest to the seat you occupy is the shortest route to the street. In the event of fire please do not run—WALK TO THAT EXIT.

Frank J. Quayle,
FIRE COMMISSIONER

Thoughtless persons annoy patrons and distract actors and endanger the safety of others by lighting matches during the performance and intermissions. This violates a city ordinance and renders the offender liable to a summons from the fireman on duty. It is urged that all patrons refrain from lighting matches in the auditorium of this theatre.

THE · PLAYBILL · A · WEEKLY · PUBLICATION · OF · PLAYBILL · INCORPORATED

Week beginning Monday, December 13, 1948 • Matinees Wednesday and Saturday

CHERYL CRAWFORD

presents

LOVE LIFE

A Vaudeville

Book and Lyrics by
ALAN JAY LERNER

Music by
KURT WEILL

Directed by ELIA KAZAN

Choreography by MICHAEL KIDD

with

NANETTE FABRAY **RAY MIDDLETON**

Settings designed by
BORIS ARONSON

Costumes designed by
LUCINDA BALLARD

Musical Director: Joseph Littau

Lighting by Peggy Clark

Musical Arrangements and Orchestrations by MR. WEILL

"Love Life" is presented in two parts, each consisting of a series of acts. The sketches, which start in 1791 and come up to the present day, are presented in the physical style of the various periods. The four main characters, Susan and Sam Cooper, and their children, Johnny and Elizabeth, who present the story, do not change in appearance as time moves on. The vaudeville acts which come between each sketch are presented in a set vaudeville pattern.

PART I — Act 1

THE MAGICIAN

Cast

(In order of appearance)

The Magician .... Jay Marshall
Susan .... Nanette Fabray
Sam .... Ray Middleton

FIGURE 6. Playbill for the premiere production of *Love Life* (1948), with a significant gap between the two title words.

The culmination of the composer's career, as they turned out to be, the last two works represent complementary sides of a creative personality whose oeuvre, to quote Weill himself, "[approached] the form-problems of the musical theatre . . . from all different angles."[2] *Love Life* and *Lost in the Stars* are indeed quite different in their respective approaches; and their complementary nature, insofar as it can be seen as characteristically Weillian, lends both unity and nuance to the composer's posthumous image.

LOVE LIFE

Weill described *Love Life* as "a study of marriage in the last 100 years."[3] His description raises a question about the subtitle "A Vaudeville," which sits uneasily with the notion of "a study," as it was no doubt intended to. What are the precedents for this contradiction? Or are Weill and his collaborator Alan Jay Lerner establishing one? Take, for example, Kander and Ebb's line "Life is a cabaret," which they have Sally Bowles sing in the 1966 musical *Cabaret*. Weill and Lerner's pre-*Cabaret* musical does something similar: "Love Life" is a "vaudeville." The musical "studies" life, that goes without saying. Yet the influence cuts both ways. Life imitates art, the art of vaudeville. The title is thus multilayered. Not only does it link "Love Life" with "vaudeville," but by inviting the spectator to appreciate the art in life, it also accommodates an exhortation, akin to "Come to the cabaret!" Seen in this way, the "love" of *Love Life* could suggest an imperative.

Irony is never far from the surface, however, for example when the male lead, Sam, celebrates his divorce in the soliloquy (more *scena* than song) "This Is the Life!" Here, "love" and "life" have little to do with each other. They have become incompatible substantives, not a harmonious compound. That is the story of Sam and Susan's marriage: a story of growing incompatibility, told in terms of an ineluctable social and historical process during the era of industrialization. By way of emphasizing the rift, the program booklet for the premiere production printed the title both on the cover and in the credits with a graphically, and presumably intentionally, large gap between its two constituent words, *Love* and *Life* (fig. 6). The work is about the two—visually quite separate—concepts, if anything more about their estrangement than about their interaction as a compound. Appearing in varying constellations, separately and in combination, the two words function as verbal motifs in a way analogous to music. Sam's soliloquy is a case in point.

An analogous connection between the work's musical title and its conceptual theme is similarly evident in Rodgers and Hammerstein's *Allegro*, from the year before *Love Life*. The self-defining title song, "Allegro," contains numerous musical allusions that serve to gloss a socially critical concept, as in lines such as these from the first verse:

We know no other way
Of living out a day.
Our music must be galloping and gay!
We muffle all the undertones,
The minor blood-and-thunder tones,
The overtones are all we care to play!

And the chorus:

Brisk, lively,
Merry and bright!
Allegro!
Same tempo
Morning and night!
Allegro!
Don't stop whatever you do,
Do something dizzy and new,
Keep up the hullabaloo!
Allegro! Allegro!
Allegro! Allegro!
Allegro! Allegro!

The title of Weill's "vaudeville" constituted a play on words even before it became *Love Life.* The original title, "Dish for the Gods," works on several levels, as David Kilroy makes clear in his wide-ranging study of the work's genesis and reception.[4] Both substantives are ambiguous. *Dish* signifies a literal and figurative comestible and, in vernacular usage, an attractive woman. *Gods* refers both literally to deities and figuratively, as theatrical jargon, to the audience, especially those in the gallery. Yet the phrase as a whole doubtless owes something to Shakespeare, who uses it in two of his historical plays. In *Julius Caesar,* Brutus says of Caesar: "Let's kill him boldly, but not wrathfully; Let's carve him as a dish fit for the gods." In *Anthony and Cleopatra,* Anthony comments: "I know that a woman is a dish for the gods, if the devil dress her not." As such, the original title works not only as a literary reference but also as a bitterly ironic one, especially if one ties the Caesar allusion to one of *Love Life's* vaudeville acts, the one at the very beginning where the female lead, Susan, is cut in half as part of the magician's show. A dish fit for the gods, indeed!

What's more, the scene itself creates an internal reference. Susan's bifurcation in the world of theatrical entertainment mirrors in wry fashion her increasingly divided roles in "real" life.

SUSAN: Well, this is what I really am, isn't it? Split in two and severed in the middle? I'm half homemaker, half breadwinner, half mother, half provider; I'm over there a woman and up here a man.

Compared with the theatrical variety, then, her own personal vaudeville is hardly an entertaining matter. That is the point. The audience—"the gods"—are served two dishes: the vaudeville entertainment and the story of Sam and Susan. And it is the counterpoint between the two—the thematic resonances tossed back and forth between the show interludes and the cautionary tale of marital decay in the modern world—that generates the dramaturgical sophistication of *Love Life*. *Cabaret* would follow this precedent by juxtaposing the story of the Nazis' rise to power with satirical cabaret numbers.[5]

Frames such as these, playing two discrete levels off against each other, are hardly novel in Weill's works. They are the rule rather than the exception, a modus operandi established by his very first work for the musical theater, *Der Protagonist,* and employed in a variety of ways in most of the other works as well. The dramatic levels in the one-act *Protagonist* are in fact remarkably similar to those in *Love Life.* Both works adopt the Shakespearean precedent of the play-within-a-play—in the earlier work, the tragicomic pantomimes; in the later one, the vaudeville acts. And both exploit the opposition not so much to uphold the distinction between illusion and reality as to complicate it. In both cases, the play-within-a-play functions as commentary on the play proper, casting in a critical light the enacted parallels and disjunctions between art and life. It's as if Weill's "form problems" habitually pose themselves in terms of such oppositions, with the various frames—how the contrasting levels relate to each other and interact—representing the "different angles."

The oppositions are first and foremost structural and hence dramaturgical. Striking examples include the surreal ballet and film sequences in *Royal Palace;* the fashionable gramophone tango in *Der Zar lässt sich photographieren;* the lowlife boxing ring in the *Mahagonny-Songspiel;* the epic narration that articulates the neoclassicist frame in *Die Dreigroschenoper;* the choral commentary in *Die Bürgschaft;* pastoral milieu versus military state in *A Kingdom for a Cow;* the alternation (on separate stages) of scenes drawn from biblical tales and the story of a "timeless community" in exile in *The Eternal Road;* the spoken plot "proper" and the interspersed musicalized dreams in *Lady in the Dark;* traditional operatic arias and ensembles juxtaposed with Broadway production numbers in *Street Scene;* folk song versus filmlike melodrama in *Down in the Valley.* In each case, however, the frame has significant stylistic and, more broadly speaking, conceptual consequences.[6]

Of the works listed above, *Der Protagonist, The Eternal Road,* and *Lady in the Dark* stand out as radical implementations of dramaturgical counterpoint insofar as the opposition informing the structural levels seems at its starkest in these works. In each case, the second level presents an additional narrative layer that complements the first: the transition from "artificial" comedy to "real" tragedy in *Der Protagonist;* the parallels between ancient scripture and modern history in

The Eternal Road; the dramatically formalized contrast between the outer world of Liza's career and the inner world of her repressed emotions (her conscious versus her unconscious life) in *Lady in the Dark*. In terms of its conceptual implications, however, *Love Life* is not only comparable to its predecessors but arguably surpasses them.

The means whereby Weill's "vaudeville" becomes "a study," as Weill described it, and hence a prototype of the concept musical, are twofold. The dramaturgical counterpoint, as described, is one factor: Sam and Susan's marriage becomes an object of ironic commentary through juxtaposition with the vaudeville acts. The other factor is the expansion of the narrative structure, which Weill's earlier-quoted definition somewhat imprecisely describes as "the last 100 years." Time marches on for more than a century (157 years, to be precise) without Sam and Susan appearing to age in the least. In this way, they, too, become "objectified." Yet as time passes, not only does their marriage deteriorate, but society "progresses." Or does it? That's the human question that *Love Life* doesn't so much answer as pose, through its formal dialectic and historical plot structure. The "vaudeville" invites us to conduct the conceptual study ourselves.

The program booklet for the premiere production prefaced the detailed description of the piece's two "parts," which are divided into acts, scenes, and songs, with the following matter-of-fact note: "*Love Life* is presented in two parts, each consisting of a series of acts. The sketches, which start in 1791 and come up to the present day, are presented in the physical style of the various periods. The four main characters, Susan and Sam Cooper, and their children, Johnny and Elizabeth, who present the story, do not change in appearance as time moves on. The vaudeville acts which come between each sketch are presented in a set vaudeville pattern." Part 1 comprises ten separate acts, Part 2 just six. The dovetailing of "sketch" and "vaudeville acts," described here in dry, formalistic terms, suggests a plan that is at once carefully worked out and quite flexible. In fact, to quote Foster Hirsch's succinct account of *Love Life*'s genesis, "the musical went through more drafts, revisions, and out-of-town surgery than any other Kurt Weill project. . . . The road from original concept to opening night on Broadway was bumpy," with a "sizable discard section."[7]

One of Weill's most experimental pieces, *Love Life* was also the one most experimented with, from conception to realization. Its prolonged "tryout" process was no doubt a function of the casting process, also prolonged because of several failed attempts to fill the two principal roles and find a suitable director. Yet to talk here of "the production process" is really a misnomer. Elements such as casting and finding a director belong to a greater or lesser degree to the process of composition. And in *Love Life* that degree was, if anything, at the "greater" end of the spectrum. In other words, the traditional distinction between composition and realization, a distinction that became solidified in the nineteenth century, hardly applies here. Instead, as in the discussion of stylistic matters, it seems more apt to apply earlier, eighteenth-century categories derived from theories of classical rhetoric. These are based not on a binary model (opposing "creation" and "reproduction"), but on a more nuanced division of the creative process into three stages: invention *(inventio),* disposition *(dispositio),* and elocution *(elocutio),* with two further stages for actual presentation or performance.

The first term, invention, applies to the choice of material, the general plan of the composition worked out by the collaborators before its initial execution in a sketch; disposition refers to a preliminary draft that gives a clear indication of the outlines of the final form, reflecting the relation of parts to the whole; elocution is the final rendering, in this case an actual theatrical production. The distinction between composition and realization thereby collapses; production and creation go hand in hand. Continuing the parallel with rhetorical categories, "production" would also embrace the memorization of the work during the final stages of rehearsal *(memoria)* and actual performance *(pronunciato).* Applying this model to Weill's musical theater allows the initial invention, the *Einfall* (or *Idee,* as the Busoni pupil might have said), to remain intact as an idea that informs the work, in a process of transformation, throughout its creation. Translated into Weillian terms, the invention, as an underlying theatrical concept, could be seen to correspond to the constantly reconceived *Urform,* a new solution to the "form-problems of the musical theatre."

The tripartite "invention-disposition-elocution" model fits particularly well Weill's conception of film at the time. A few weeks after *Love Life*'s premiere, Weill wrote to his agent, Irving Lazar, to report on the idea that he and Lerner were meanwhile developing for a movie called "Miss Memory."

> It was much more work than we had anticipated, because we wanted to present it as a complete story. We worked on a first draft all week, and yesterday we dictated all day until the synopsis was finished. By the way, when you discuss the picture, I want you to point out that all the scenes with Miss Memory will be treated musically, in song and dance and the kind of underscored dialogue which I am using so successfully in the theatre.
>
> To avoid any misunderstanding I want to make it clear, that "Miss Memory" is entirely the result of a collaboration and can only be negotiated as a joint effort of Alan and me, with no strings attached. We can either sell the idea in connection with a deal for the score (lyrics and music), or we can make a deal to write the entire picture (book, lyrics and music).[8]

The "idea" represents the initial invention, available in the form of a finished synopsis with general indications for the assorted uses of music. Not yet available is the actual score, the initial stage of a disposition, in whose elaboration Weill would necessarily have to be involved. That being the case, he would presumably work hand in hand with the author of the book, likely to be Lerner, who would anyway be contracted to write the lyrics for Weill's music. The "elocution" would then rest with the film studio, the part of the process that Weill felt more often than not detracted from his conception. The theater, by contrast, tended to offer him more control in this vital third stage of the collaborative process.

Even though the stages were not so neatly delineated with *Love Life,* the model still serves a useful heuristic purpose. The genesis began with what Weill described as "an interesting idea which Lerner brought to me . . . and which we are investigating now."[9] From the start, it seems, the form was intended to be both "loose" and "American," as described by Lerner shortly after the premiere:

> Kurt Weill and I discussed the basic story idea first. We knew what we wanted to say. And then we talked and talked—for about two months before we figured out the form our story would take. That, from the writing standpoint, was the most important problem we had with *Love Life*—finding a way to tell our story. Finally, after discussing hundreds of notions, the idea of doing the show as a vaudeville found its way into our misty heads. We decided on it for a host of reasons. To begin with, we were telling a basically American story and we feel that vaudeville is a basically American form. Secondly, the form was loose enough to allow for any kind of invention.[10]

Lerner's "invention," as he called it, more or less accords with the "disposition" of the classical model, the process of creating the initial text of the work before it was ready to go into production. In this case, as Lerner recounted, "we spent almost a year on the actual writing of the show." This is where the distinction between the "disposition" and "elocution" becomes somewhat blurred. At this point, the authors had "assembled [the show] into what we fondly thought was its final form." But of course the "tryouts" in New Haven and Boston were just that, further stages of revision, which in this case would turn out to be uncommonly extensive, even by Broadway standards. Between the opening in New Haven and "the day—three and a half weeks later—when we opened in New York," Lerner recalled, "practically every scene in the play was rewritten and three completely new scenes were added."

The protracted period of casting had influenced the work's shape quite significantly, particularly as far as the principal parts of Sam and Susan Cooper were concerned. The producer, Cheryl Crawford, had approached two leading ladies from other Weill shows—Gertrude Lawrence, from *Lady in the Dark,* and Mary Martin, from *One Touch of Venus*—and Weill and Lerner had asked Ginger Rogers, star of the screen version of *Lady in the Dark,* before Nanette Fabray joined the show. As Kilroy notes, the casting of Fabray as Susan and Ray Middleton, a Julliard-trained baritone, as Sam occasioned the insertion of "two new solo numbers in both parts of the show for each of the two protagonists . . . specifically tailored to suit Fabray and Middleton."[11]

The tryouts in New Haven and Boston, in turn, revealed the necessity of cuts: the show was far too long. Two of the main sources for reconstructing the genesis of *Love Life,* the theater programs and the orchestra parts, both reflect frequent changes, whether cuts, additions, or reorderings.[12] Once the show opened in New York, however, the form of the show, its "elocution," appears quite settled; the order of numbers listed in a sample of programs from October, November, and December remains the same. The copy of the holograph piano-vocal score that Weill gave to Lerner "as a token of my affection" closely reflects this version, too.[13] Three of the cut songs are included at the end of the holograph score: "Susan's Dream," "There's Nothing Left for Daddy," and "Locker Room"—just some of the copious material left, so to speak, on the cutting-room floor, as the work developed from abundant disposition to actual performance.

If Weill's own works provide ample examples of contrapuntal musical frames, as detailed above, *Love Life*'s particular narrative structure has more immediate and obvious antecedents in American spoken theater of the time, notably Thornton Wilder's *Our Town.* Wilder's Pulitzer Prize–winning play from 1938 offered a much-invoked example, one that other writers seemed to follow and critics admired. In his review of the premiere of *Allegro,* for example, *New York Times* critic Brooks Atkinson compared *Allegro* with *Our Town.* Rodgers and Hammerstein, Atkinson wrote, "have composed a musical play without any of the conventions of form. . . . For at least half its length it is a work of great beauty and purity, as if 'Our Town' could be written in music."[14]

Atkinson's reservations had to do with the second act, which begins with the economic crash of 1929 and deals, as Atkinson observed, "with materials that cannot be recollected through the golden haze of sentiment, for the period after 1929 belongs all too graphically with recorded time." These aspects, he felt, "do not belong in the old legend." Above all, he thought they possessed "a hackneyed moral overtone." (Similar objections would, in turn, be raised regarding the socially critical aspects of *Love Life.*)

Weill, for his part, had met Wilder in 1938, the year of *Our Town*'s publication, in the hope of a possible collaboration, and he continued to think that the celebrated playwright was, as he wrote in 1945, one of "the guys to work with."[15] After studying the completed draft of *Love Life,* the show's producer, Cheryl Crawford, wrote to Weill: "I feel you are prepared now to do something which has long been in my mind—an opera on 'Our Town.'"[16] Wilder was just the kind of leading playwright, like Brecht, Kaiser, Anderson et al., whom Weill liked to seek out as an equal partner.

Of special relevance here is what the theorist of modern drama Peter Szondi identified in *Our Town* as "the epic *I*" of the narrator and the dramatic "play of time."[17] The two are closely linked. Central to the play's unconventional structure, the way in which it creates a window onto the events of thirty-five years, is the presence of the pipe-smoking Stage Manager. He is the omniscient guide, providing continuity between the three acts, which he refers to, in act 2, as "Daily Life," "Love and Marriage," and, with reference to act 3, "I reckon you can guess what that's about." He not only sets the scene in his avuncular way, framing the theatrical space and time, but, like a *conférencier,* he also acts as an intermediary between audience and action, providing perspective as well as inviting personal introspection; he even joins the cast to play two of the characters, the minister in the wedding scene and Mrs. Morgan. Weill and Anderson's *Knickerbocker Holiday,* from the same year as *Our Town,* has a similar figure in the guise of "the author" Washington Irving. Here, however, Weill and Anderson more likely drew on earlier European models for such a device, whether on Weill's own work with Brecht or his earliest musical influence in this regard, Stravinsky, whose *L'histoire du soldat* and *Oedipus rex* use narrators.

Wilder, who attended German school in Hong Kong when he was nine and studied in Kiel as a young man, was no doubt indebted to European models of epic theater, and to a few German playwrights in particular, including Brecht and Piscator. He visited Berlin twice before the Second World War, in 1928 and 1931, and dedicated his first collection of plays to Max Reinhardt. German writers have been especially inclined to note the parallels between Brecht and Wilder. For example, while extolling Brecht as a classic, Max Frisch, an admirer of Wilder, described Wilder's techniques as a "glorious imitation" of Brecht.[18] In particular, there are "a great number of similarities" between Brecht's *Mother Courage* and Wilder's *The Skin of Our Teeth,* as Charles H. Helmetag has observed.[19] Yet one also needs to take into account the very different purposes that each of these celebrated playwrights pursued in his work. As Helmetag puts it, "Brecht and Wilder of the thirties and forties were kindred spirits in choice of form and theme, though not, obviously, in ideology."[20] Brecht himself was equivocal about the matter: he may have had, as Eric Bentley wrote, "paranoid suspicions" about Wilder having copied his epic techniques, but he also admired Wilder; he considered him "the ideal translator" for his *Der gute Mensch von Sezuan,* for example, and he added *The Skin of Our Teeth* to his own repertory at the Berliner Ensemble.[21] Balancing these various factors, one might say that anything Weill took from Wilder could be seen as a debt repaid for Weill's own influence (principally via his collaborations with Brecht) on the American playwright.

The fact remains that, in the late 1930s and 1940s, *Our Town* was the successful, Pulitzer Prize–winning example of innovative, unconventional theater in the United States, the American version of Epic Theater. For all their differences, musical theater works such as *Love Life* and *Allegro* reflected commonalities, sharing not only Wilder's interest in "epic" narrative techniques but also some of his thematic concerns.

One of the principal thematic similarities is what the Narrator in *Our Town* calls "citification," variously captured in the generational divides of that play, in *Allegro*'s title song, and in the breakdown of family communication in *Love Life*. The Cooper family, for example, is disunited by radio in the contemporaneous era of mass media: each of its members wants to be alone to listen to his or her favorite show. This is clearly a facet of *Love Life*'s central theme, the human cost of technological progress. In *Our Town* that kind of alienation is really only a side issue. More central here is the making strange via epic commentary—and hence the making special—of the commonplace. Wilder put it succinctly in the preface to *Three Plays* (1957): "It is an attempt to find a value above all price for the smallest events in our daily life. I have made the claim as preposterous as possible, for I have set the village against the largest dimensions of time and place."[22]

Both *Our Town* and *Love Life* give the audience ample occasion to view the fate of the principal characters dispassionately, as generalized cases, and hence to compare these cases to their own lives. Yet although both create dramatic frames to this end, the perspectives adopted are utterly different. In *Our Town,* the connection between the "epic *I*" and the "play of time" is of the essence, leading from the portrayal of act 1's single day, via act 2's marriage and its enacted prehistory, to the simultaneity of multiple temporal planes in act 3, as the dead revisit themselves as the living. All this—existentially quite mind-boggling—complexity is negotiated by the Stage Manager, whose all-knowing perspective leads Emily to precipitate the gloomy conclusion with her question "Do any human beings ever realize life while they live it?—every, every minute?" The Stage Manager provides the blunt answer: "No."

The audience at once enjoys the Stage Manager's perspective and is given pause to reflect, having witnessed the suggestive tale of small-town life. However cautionary the tale may seem, it is nonetheless anything but preachy. (The Stage Manager, after all, only *plays* the minister.) Wilder's epic theater, an antidramatic play of temporal levels, is more sentimentally metaphysical than it is critically didactic. A play of time, certainly; but "Wilder's philosophy lacks the historic dimension," to quote Francis Ferguson's penetrating comparison of Wilder and Brecht as allegorists.[23]

Brecht's plays, by radical contrast, not only tend to be historical in nature but are informed through and through by a philosophy of history, something also true of *Love Life,* albeit not by a Brechtian one. Like Brecht, Lerner and Weill explore the contradictions between industrial capitalism and human relations, between the political and the personal. But unlike Brecht, they do not imply, still less offer, any concrete political solutions. The question that *Love Life* poses—will Sam and Susan find reconciliation? ("Can we make it?" asks Susan at the end)—requires facing personal reality ("We've got to!" answers Sam) beyond the world of illusion, beyond the world of the minstrels. Social relations have plainly affected their extensive past. How those relations will affect their future remains, of course, unclear. The tightrope on which they nervously approach each other at the end could be read metaphorically as an allusion to Nietzsche's *Also sprach Zarathustra,* in particular to the passage in the Prologue where Zarathustra helps the fallen tightrope-walker overcome his superstitions. Will Susan and Sam, by implication, remain in their current stage of consciousness or achieve a more advanced stage?[24]

Insofar as there is a narrator in *Love Life,* it is not so much the entertainment figures like the Magician at the beginning or the Minstrels at the end, but Sam and Susan themselves, taken out of their immediate lives into the two vaudeville acts that frame the show. After complaining about being "split in two and severed in the middle," Susan lays the blame squarely in Sam's court: "Every single thing that's happened to us and the children for the last hundred and thirty odd years has been your fault." Their argument elicits the flashback, all the way back from 1948 to 1791. "A hundred years ago," Susan says, "it was beginning to slip." "A hundred and fifty years ago?" Sam asks and then supplies the answer: "We had it then, Susan." And Susan agrees. This is the "decent existence" that Susan says "wasn't perfect but at least it made sense." Each succeeding sketch involving the protagonists documents the "slip"; everything enacted takes place in the knowledge of this inevitable decline. All talk of the "industrial age" in terms of "real progress"—a "chance for every man to improve his lot," as one of the inhabitants of Mayville, Connecticut, remarks in the 1791 scene—necessarily has ironic connotations for Sam and Susan's century-and-a-half-long marriage. We know in advance that it will founder. If it's Sam's fault, that's not because he "set out to change" things, as Susan claims at the retrospective outset, but because of the circumstances, which Sam is forced to go along with.

This is quite different from the Stage Manager's recital of details of small-town life at the beginning of *Our Town* and his forecasting of Dr. Gibbs's death in 1930, or indeed from Wilder's one-act play *The Long Christmas Dinner* (1931), "which represents," as the stage directions tell us, "in accelerated motion ninety Christmas dinners in the Bayard household."[25] Whereas Wilder opens a window onto existential issues raised by the play of time, creating through the montage of episodes in *The Long Christmas Dinner* what Szondi calls "a secular mystery play about time,"[26] Lerner and Weill repeatedly raise the question of both historical and personal agency, urging us to consider the connection between technological progress and the institution of marriage. There is an intimate connection, they suggest, which they conceive in terms of a historical dialectic. In both *Our Town* and *Love Life,* the play of time occurs through an "epic" laying-bare of dramatic mechanisms and conventions: in Wilder's play, through the interventions—the "epic posture," as Szondi calls it[27]—of the Stage Manager, who literally sets the stage for the dramatic action, splicing together a series of scenes that document the themes of life, love, and death; and in *Love Life,* whose contrast between "narrative time" and "narrated time" outstrips *The Long Christmas Dinner* by some sixty years, through the mixing of historical vignettes that document a dialectic of technological progress and personal estrangement with vaudevillian entertainment. Whereas Wilder's anachronisms and use of the same characters in various historical periods reveal human experience to be more or less the same irrespective of time or place, *Love Life* seems to be suggesting that historical circumstances play a decisive role. It is a perspective that recalls the theme of *Die Bürgschaft*.

The concept of a "love life" is tainted in advance. Our foreknowledge, gained from the opening vaudeville, colors the meaning of the ensuing sketches to the point of subversion—a dramatic irony that applies in particular to the musical numbers. Consider, for example, Sam and Susan's duet "Here I'll Stay." On the face of it, read as a self-contained number, this touching ballad expresses romantic commitment. Sam sings in the first verse:

> Susan, this is all I'm searching for
> A place to live with you forever more
> A sign that says it's Samuel Cooper's store
> There is no other world awaiting me
> That meadow is as far as I can see.
> My heaven is no higher than that tree.

In the first part of the forty-measure refrain, the contentment seems qualified, tinged with a certain melancholy resignation:

> There's a far land I'm told
> Where I'll find a field of gold,
> But here I'll stay with you.

The eight-measure bridge passage, however, rejects the lure of the "field of gold":

> For that land is a sandy illusion!
> It's a theme of a dream gone astray.

The point of the conclusion of the refrain is to reconcile the apparent opposition between illusion and reality:

> And the world others woo
> I can find loving you,
> And so here I'll stay.

But in the context of the scene, following their vaudevillian prologue, the lyrical moment is contaminated by the epic sweep of the whole; we know as Sam and Susan sing that they won't stay "there"; the gradual process of estrangement will lead them to grasp at all manner of "sandy illusions," symbolized in the bridge by the chromatically downward-shifting bass line and the attendant lack of tonal stability, including the ambiguously "floating" augmented chord under *illusion* (ex. 71). Melodically, against this shifting bass, the bridge comprises two short identical phrases that reproduce the internal rhymes (*land/sand-y* and *theme/dream*) on the same note (d") before falling down an octave (to *illusion* and *astray* respectively). Its division into two melodically identical four-bar phrases makes the bridge even more perfunctory than a single eight-bar section. Following this, by way of extreme contrast, the melody then climbs a tenth by step, diatonically, before resolving as part of the perfect cadence on "Here I'll Stay." The cadence itself is prepared by a minor secondary dominant on *Here,* sustained for a full six beats—a signature Weillian sonority that echoes as a pitch collection Wagner's so-called Tristan chord. "Here," the music seems to be indicating, is less a place than it is a romantic feeling (ex. 72).

Hearing the duet in the context of the show complicates the opposition of reality and illusion: reality will threaten feeling, life will impinge on love. Sam and Susan's pledge to stay "here" proves to be a vain wish whose fulfillment remains in question, even at the end: "it's the theme of a dream gone astray." *Love Life*'s central, ultimately unanswered question—concerning the compatibility of life and love—recurs throughout the piece as a kind of leitmotif that is both verbal and musical.

This dramatically ironic context prompts consideration of significant differences among three notated versions of the song: Weill's manuscript piano-vocal score, the full score, and the separately published piano-vocal sheet music. Although the sheet music furnishes sufficient information for the kind of formal and harmonic analysis presented above, it conveys nothing of the song's deployment as a duet and as instrumental reprise—nothing, that is, of the discrete setting of Sam's and Susan's respective stanzas or of the instrumental introduction contained in the other sources, and nothing (needless to say) of the instrumentation, including a transformed "sonic image" (to use Weill's expression) for Susan's strophe.

The introduction in the sheet music, marked "Moderato," is utterly different from the version in the show. A four-measure piano vamp, it could be pressed into service for any number of popular-song arrangements (ex. 73). The melodic contours, seemingly unrelated either to the succeeding verse or to the chorus, outline an octave descent to the tonic B♭ that commences after the pickup with an expressive appoggiatura on the downbeat (the appoggiatura figure is repeated in the second half of the second measure). The accompanying broken chords outline a simple approach of the tonic harmony via secondary dominants and a dominant minor-ninth, and the arrival itself lingers with chromatic oscillations. In Weill's piano-vocal score, in contrast, there are just two measures, which do no more—and no less—than arpeggiate what appears to be the tonic harmony

EXAMPLE 71. *Love Life,* "Here I'll Stay" (bridge)

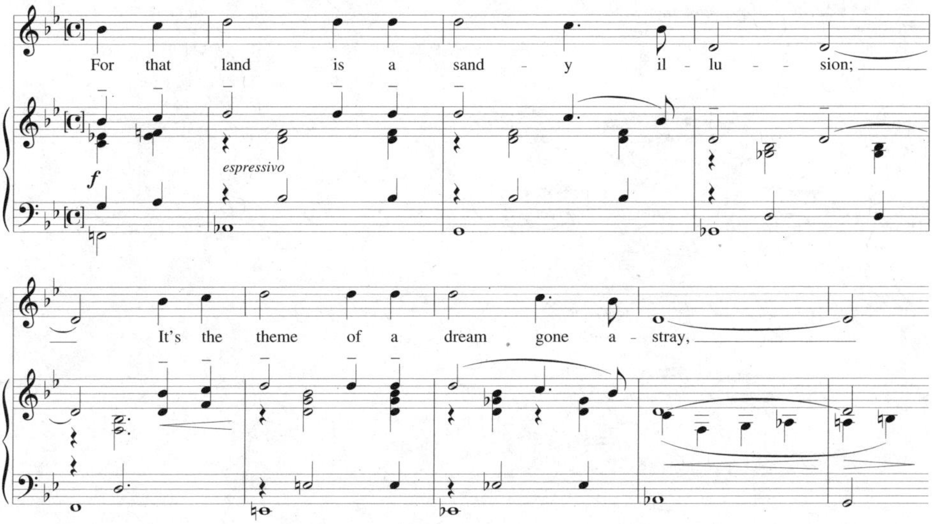

EXAMPLE 72. *Love Life,* "Here I'll Stay" (conclusion)

EXAMPLE 73. *Love Life,* "Here I'll Stay" (opening, sheet music)

EXAMPLE 74. *Love Life,* "Here I'll Stay" (opening, autograph piano-vocal score)

of E♭ with the all-important added sixth and ninth, but in fact turns out to be a pentatonically inflected subdominant (ex. 74).

It is the same collection of pitches with which the music of *Love Life* commences in the second scene, the same swelling sonority from which the opening ensemble piece emerges. It carries over into the duet as a musical motif that identifies Sam while recalling the opening question: "Who is Samuel Cooper?" The full score orchestrates this version of the introduction to "Here I'll Stay" with strings and clarinet, continuing into the chorus with rich-toned lower-register saxophone writing and many extra brass and string embellishments, most of which are not reproduced in either the piano-vocal score or the sheet music. Just as the latter's introduction turns out to be the link in the duet between Sam's chorus and Susan's verse, so Susan sings the music reproduced in the sheet music, albeit with different words. Sam's verse exclaims *(Andante rubato, con passione):* "Susan, this is all I'm searching for" (continuing the theme of *his* identity). Susan's is more reflectively lyrical: "Since I was old enough to long and harken to a tender song," as reflected in her contrasting melody and in the lighter instrumentation of her chorus.[28]

The difference between the sheet-music arrangement and the theater duet is, in short, significant, not only in itself but also with regard to the overall musical design of Weill's vaudeville. Both text and music of the duet are colored by their role within the whole. Both have "motivic" connections to other parts of the show.

The dramatic context of the sung words renders the "sandy illusion" that Sam and Susan resist doubly ironic. The basis of their own arrangement, the "here" where their feelings are committed to stay, is hardly stable. While expressing commitment to the reality of their situation, their romantic duet is subtly tinged with the epistemology of the "Liebeslied" from *Die Dreigroschenoper:* "love lasts—or it doesn't." Although in this case love ends up inevitably diminished by life, the traditional reminiscence of the duet during the reprise sequence of the finale adds a further, untraditionally ironic note. It's the same song, but the people and their feelings are different. For their love to survive, Sam and Susan will need to move on—not stay "here." Their life, along with the circumstances of society at large, will have to change accordingly.

Even though long-range connections outlined above serve as unifying devices, their prevalence and importance should not be overstated. *Love Life* is a work of stark juxtapositions, more hetero- than homogeneous. It thrives on the kind of musico-dramatic coherence that emphasizes the dichotomies indicated by the title rather than its apparent harmony. Sam and Susan are challenged to make sense of their marriage against the expansive historical panorama of 150 years of American history. And the music reflects that panorama, not just the contemporaneous setting of 1948. Weill himself stressed this stylistic heterogeneity in a newspaper piece he and Lerner published in the *New York Times* on 4 October 1948, three days before the premiere. Published under the title "Two on the Street," with the heading "Collaborators Stage a Scene Aimed at Explaining Their Musical Play," the article takes the form of a conversation among Lerner, Weill, and "a man" who "comes by and stares at the theatre marquee" outside the Shubert Theatre, Boston, where the show's tryout took place. On being told by Weill that the show "tells the saga of 150 years of American home life but also the love life of two people and the gradual changing of their personalities as life becomes more complex," the man wonders how that is possible. "With vaudeville," Lerner answers. "Isn't that simple?" Weill asks rhetorically. The man then remarks, "(Wiping his forehead) I don't know. Is it like a lot of little plays strung together?" Weill explains: "Not exactly. One sketch is a musical play, one is an American ballad, one is a straight comedy, one is a satire, one is danced, one is a musical comedy, one is dramatic. All different styles." (Weill's "American ballad" presumably refers to the "Love Song" sung by the Hobo in the penultimate scene of part 1; "satire" to the Punch and Judy episode; "danced" to "Green Up Time"; "straight comedy" to the cruise scene; "musical play" to the suffragettes; and "dramatic" to Sam's scena.) These "styles"—the theatrical genres of the sketches—vary just as the "physical style of the various periods" does. And both of these shifting "styles" are complemented by the various musical idioms brought to bear.

Because Susan and Sam's story takes the form of a historical "study of marriage," to use Weill's description, it is not merely a lesson to be learned by the couple alone, but one with seemingly broader, more didactic implications. The question mark hanging over the chronicle's conclusion leaves the audience with something to think about: the present is their own, Sam and Susan's unknowable future something in which they are all implicated.

How did the lesson go down? Already at the tryout, Elliot Norton of the *Boston Post* (14 September 1948), while praising *Love Life* as "perhaps the most mature musical play the American stage has yet produced," predicted that it "will create controversy and perhaps indignation." He proved to be correct. He likened the work to *Allegro,* "which delighted some of us and infuriated others. . . . It's a dream of a show," he went on, "about the American dream: sentimental, hopeful, satirical, ironic, and even bitter." On the same day, Norton's counterpart at the *Boston Daily Globe* echoed this prescient evaluation almost exactly: "This is a show bound to arouse diverse opinion, for it is at once sentiment and acid satire, serious and gay, reality and fantasy, and touched over with something of the moralistic preachment of *Christopher Blake* and *Allegro.*" It's as if the two Boston critics had compared notes before going to press.

The critical reception of the premiere, even more than the tryout, was decidedly mixed. Brooks Atkinson of the *New York Times,* generally sympathetic to Weill, dismissed the book while praising the music. *Love Life,* he wrote in a review of 8 October 1948, "is an intellectual idea about showmanship gone wrong. Vaudeville has nothing to do with the bitter ideas Mr. Lerner has to express about marriage." The show "gets lost in some strange cerebral labyrinth, and the pretense that is vaudeville is a pose." But he thought that Weill "has never composed a more versatile score with agreeable music in so many moods—hot, comic, blue, satiric and romantic." Group Theatre cofounder Harold Clurman, writing for the *New Republic* (8 October 1948), described *Love Life* as "an educated musical" but felt that "its multiple ingenuity is overstrenuous."

Critical assessments hinged largely on whether the lack of conventional plot structure was seen as a virtue or a vice. William Hawkins, critic of the *New York World-Telegram,* wrote on 8 October 1948 that the show "tries too hard for comfort to be different," even though he considered it "wicked to discourage novelty in the theater." His ultimately conservative verdict: *Love Life* "suggests that theatrical conventions like unities of time, place and subject were developed over the years for pretty good reasons." George Freedley of the *New York Telegraph,* by radical contrast, saw virtue in the work's sophistication, while recognizing that it "may keep it from the wide popularity of simpler musicals. . . . For many of us," he continued in his review of 9 October, "it is sheer delight. [Producer] Cheryl Crawford, always an innovator despite a canny knowledge of where her feet are, has given us a show which is iconoclastic in every direction."

In the end, *Love Life*'s innovations may have limited its acceptance among theatergoers expecting more traditional, less challenging fare. Weill and Lerner were no doubt aware of that, as their "Two on the Street" interview suggests. Yet both of them would surely have been gratified to know that later composers, such as Sondheim, would happily enter that "cerebral labyrinth" and draw on the same unconventional aspects for their own reforms of the musical theater.

In his biography of Weill, Ronald Taylor remarks that "the story-line that Lerner laid out almost precluded a convincing coherence in a musical score, Weill's or anyone else's, and would rather have lent itself to the medium of film—time-splits, flash-backs, techniques part realistic, part surrealistic."[29] Taylor has a point. The historical panorama that *Love Life* presents does indeed recall the even larger time frame of Weill's movie *Where Do We Go from Here?*, which takes the viewer from the wartime present of 1944, via the era of George Washington (roughly contemporaneous with the historical starting-point of *Love Life*), all the way back to the discovery of America by Christopher Columbus. Work on film in general, a potent aesthetic influence on Weill's work throughout his career, and on *Where Do We Go from Here?* in particular, left its mark on Weill's conception of the "vaudeville." Yet in suggesting an affinity between stage and screen, Taylor does not consider two crucial factors. The first is the composer's own involvement as committed collaborator in laying out the "story-line" of *Love Life*. The second is the question begged about "convincing coherence"—a question often raised in the early reception of the piece. Seen in the broader context of Weill's ideas about the reform of musical theater, *Love Life* represents the birth of the concept musical out of the spirit of cinema.

LOST IN THE STARS

Weill's last completed work for the musical theater was long in the making. In search of suitable theatrical material for a musical play to succeed *Knickerbocker Holiday*, Weill and Anderson eventually settled on Alan Paton's novel *Cry, the Beloved Country*, published in 1948, which they transformed into a "musical tragedy" called *Lost in the Stars*. (The reasons for the name change are explained below.) The search had occupied them for close to a decade, producing a couple of false starts, a few "keeper" songs, and an abiding sense of their common commitment to the themes of liberty and democracy. For each of them, these themes constituted two sides of the same ideological coin, even if their close personal friendship could not disguise certain differences in their respective outlooks, as *Knickerbocker Holiday* had already revealed. Their cantata *The Ballad of Magna Carta* belongs in this thematic context as well, as does Weill's "American opera" *Street Scene* with its urban "melting-pot" theme.

That Anderson was initially involved in the adaptation of Elmer Rice's play *Street Scene* before Rice and Langston Hughes replaced him on Weill's creative team no doubt reflects the keen interest he and his good friend and neighbor shared in working together in the musical theater and tackling socially committed topics. For their next project after *Lost in the Stars* they began adapting Mark Twain's picaresque novel *Adventures of Huckleberry Finn,* a work whose treatment of racism and social hypocrisy has continued to generate controversy. Envisaged by Weill as "essentially a light musical comedy" (at one point provisionally titled *River Chanty* and at another *Raft on the River*), the adaptation remained unfinished because of Weill's sudden death from a coronary attack in 1950.[30]

The process of transformation from which *Lost in the Stars* emerged as Weill's last work was certainly more protracted than was the case with *Love Life,* and also more circuitous. Moreover, as with *Love Life,* it was a process decisively influenced by production contingencies. A decade before Anderson hit on the idea of adapting Paton's then–recently published novel, he and Weill began working on a musical play with a scenario suggested by *Eneas Africanus,* the popular epistolary novella by Harry Stillwell Edwards that describes the quest of a slave during the post–Civil War ("Reconstruction") era to find his former master and return a family heirloom to him. That Anderson and Weill should be drawn to such an unabashedly racist tale, first published in 1920, may seem particularly odd given the anti-apartheid message at the core of *Lost in the Stars.*[31] The choice certainly seemed odd to Paul Robeson, whom Anderson had in mind as he began the new work, hoping to create a suitable musico-dramatic vehicle for the celebrated black singer. Indeed, envisaging Robeson in the lead role was no doubt a key factor in the work's conception at this stage. "Without you, frankly," Anderson wrote to Robeson, "I shouldn't think much of the project. With you I would think it would make an excellent and most unusual play. . . . I don't know of anybody who could both act and sing it and the script might be wasted completely if you were not available."[32] Although the script wasn't entirely wasted, Robeson's unwillingness to take on the role of Eneas did cause Anderson and Weill to thoroughly reconceive their project.

The reason for Robeson's reluctance had little to do with the work itself, which existed only in outline form at that point. More decisive was his negative reaction to the source material and, above all, his own iconic role in American culture, as Eslanda Robeson explained to Anderson in a lengthy and incisively thoughtful letter written on behalf of her husband. The fact that Anderson sent along with his query to Robeson a copy of Edwards's novella no doubt gave a disconcertingly negative impression of how the adaptation might eventually come across. Whether Anderson and Weill's reworking would have done enough to transform the questionably anachronistic premise of the novella, in which a freed slave demonstrates his sense of social responsibility by remaining faithful to his former master, remains an open question. In any event, the letter to Anderson emphasized the outdated views on race that the story embodies:

> Mr. Robeson feels that one of the reasons for the almost universal prejudice against our race is the fact that very few people know anything about us (as a race). The ignorance is largely deliberate, we feel. The general public's idea of a Negro is an Uncle Tom, an Aunt Jemima, Mammy, and Jack Johnson. These types have always been sold to the public deliberately. Well, now that they dont *[sic]* exist any more except in the sentimental minds of credulous people, and we feel we certainly must not do anything in any way, to prolong their non-existent lives!!! We feel Mr. Robeson must play a negro who does exist, who has something to do with reality. That's all he asks.

With respect to Robeson's public image as a performer, the letter explained: "Mr. Robeson REPRESENTS, to some exten[t], the Negro race, the Negro thought, and the Negro behaviour. This is extremely inconvenient for us, as it limits our scope a great deal. . . . If we play the Negro slave, everyone immediately decides that the slave is the complete picture of the Negro."[33] With that, Robeson was also making it clear that Anderson and Weill would need to consider carefully the topical relevance of their project, with or without him.

After receiving Robeson's polite but firm rejection, which Robeson biographer Martin Duberman characterizes as "an attempt to blend diplomacy and self-respect," Weill and Anderson decided to approach the revue-artist, actor, and legendary tap dancer Bill "Bojangles" Robinson, a casting change that would call for a quite different kind of show.[34] Anderson and Weill sought to accommodate Robinson by substantially altering the plot of what Anderson had described to Robeson as "essentially . . . the story of a man in a chaotic world in search of his own manhood and his rules of conduct."[35] Instead of managing a stable of horses, as originally envisaged, following Edwards's story, the principal character, now named Ulysses rather than Eneas, takes over a minstrel show for which he directs and performs in a musicalized version of Homer's *Odyssey.*

It is likely that the differences between the two characters and their exploits were in part influenced by Robeson's initial reaction to the project. Whereas Edwards had borrowed little from Virgil, apart from the name of the protagonist and the idea of a journey of self-discovery, Anderson's adaptation of the story contains numerous intertextual references to Homer. Principal among them is the journey (or *katabasis*) to the Underworld that symbolizes a rebirth of the individual: abetted by another freed slave, called Nicodemus (again with historical allusion), the leading character is forced to confront the bigoted culture in which he has lived up to that point and in the process call into question his own (and his race's) belief system.[36] The idea of casting Robinson in this role also prompted Weill to begin studying the tradition of the minstrel show and acquaint himself with songs as well as films related to it. By July, he and Anderson had finished their new script, now called *Ulysses Africanus,* and a month later much of the music had been composed. Discussions were already under way for a production with director Joshua Logan (who had directed *Knickerbocker Holiday*) and the Playwrights' Company.

But a number of factors conspired to hinder and ultimately halt further progress. Anderson had other obligations (notably, his play *Key Largo*). Robinson was performing in the smash hit *Hot Mikado* and was therefore uncertain when he would be available for other engagements. There was also the question of acquiring the underlying literary rights for a musical adaptation of Edwards's story. Elmar Juchem cites the difficulty and prohibitive cost of this acquisition as having been ultimately responsible for the demise of the project.[37] An additional factor was the cultural shift that took place as the United States joined the international fight against fascism with active involvement in the Second World War.

Both race and religion played a role as well: the Underworld scene of *Ulysses Africanus* involves Ulysses and Nicodemus being pursued by the Ku Klux Klan, and the theme of religious doubt—later transferred more or less directly into *Lost in the Stars*—pervades the work. In his pivotal song "Lost in the Stars," Nicodemus challenges Ulysses to consider the possibility that "sometimes it seems maybe God's gone away" and that "the Lawd God" might not be "watching over them." Nicodemus's song is, in the words of Robert J. Rabel, "highly appropriate and absolutely crucial for the development of the plot of *Ulysses Africanus.*"[38] Whereas Nicodemus feels quite helpless—"lost out here in the stars"—without direction in a literally god-forsaken universe, Ulysses is set on a path to his own freedom and autonomy as an artist, but also to a growing sense of responsibility toward others. As David Kilroy suggests, wartime was surely not the moment for Broadway audiences to be confronted with the unresolved racial tensions of their own culture, inherited from an ignominious past, or be invited to question the tenets of Judeo-Christian faith.[39]

Choosing Paton's novel about the current situation in South Africa would effect a twofold shift of focus, into the present and away from the United States. Accordingly, parallels to contemporary experience would be both more and less evident. The challenge for Anderson and Weill was to find the appropriate form and, above all, the appropriate tone for a theme of such urgency and relevance. It is perhaps only to be expected, therefore, that the means with which they attempted to meet that challenge would continue to divide critical opinion, even among those positively disposed toward Weill's American works.

After they had abandoned *Ulysses Africanus,* and before deciding to adapt Paton's novel, Anderson and Weill briefly contemplated writing what Weill referred to as "our spaceship-musical." On 22 June 1947 he wrote to Anderson summarizing a recent discussion with John Wharton, fellow member and legal counsel of the Playwrights' Company.

> [John] thinks if we mention the spaceship at all, it would be too overpowering an idea to use it just as a sort of background. So his idea includes a real trip on a spaceship, and I think he has a nice idea to have the people arrive, after hundred *[sic]* years of travelling, at a place which is really earth again, but a different kind of earth, different not in appearance or in more technical perfection, but in spirit and emotion. He thinks that would give you a good opportunity to say, in an amusing, light way, a lot of things you want to say about the state of the world we live in. I know you have the same apprehension about a play that takes place in the future that I have. But if this future world would look very much like our world, only the human race has developped *[sic]* into a higher form of spiritual and emotional life, and if these new members of the human race would be confronted with some people who still have our way of thinking and acting, it might make for a very nice high comedy situation. (My idea would be that the man, before he goes on the spaceship, would find himself in a difficult emotional situation with his girl, or wife, that for some reason she goes along, and that they both have to adjust their way of thinking when they are faced with the new humanity.) I don't know if this is any good, but I thought it worthwhile mentioning to you—and anyhow, I promised John to do so.[40]

Anderson responded testily: "I resent a little [John's] attempts to guide the erring playwrights—or set tasks for them." He also pointed out that the envisaged work "begins to seem to me like a plain play." The play was to be called *Lost in the Stars* and the titular song, salvaged from the discarded *Ulysses Africanus,* was to be used to convey one of the work's central themes: "Please don't discuss this with John, but my present notion is that [of] a scene in the kitchen of 220 C.P.S. [220 Central Park South, the address of Anderson's son in Manhattan], with a negro singing *Lost in the Stars* at the opening as he's washing the dishes—and a group of youngsters living there who don't know what to do with their lives."[41]

If collaborative works all involve accommodation and compromise, then the genesis of *Lost in the Stars* evidently demanded more than most. This is only partly a function of the extensive process of transformation—the collapsing of creation and production—customary in Broadway musical theater. *Love Life* had emerged out of that process, too, yet still with a firm sense that the members of the creative team were pursuing common goals. To apply the rhetorical model invoked earlier, Weill and Lerner's initial "invention" remained essentially intact during the phases of the work's "disposition" and "elocution," through production in the theater, the "pronunciation." The same can hardly be said of *Lost in the Stars,* whose genesis followed a quite different course.

The protracted and circuitous creative process that produced Weill's last work certainly contradicts the notion that his oeuvre developed in a clearly linear or sequential fashion. It reveals, rather, the recurrence of a range of artistic interests that the American works brought to the fore in various ways. Although the idea of time travel had to be dropped here, it had already been used in the film *Where Do We Go from Here?* and would inform the narrative structure of *Love Life,* as discussed above. Similarly, although the self-reflexive play-within-a-play idea of *Ulysses Africanus* could not be transferred to *Lost in the Stars,* it became the principal structural device in *Love Life.* Nor was Weill's research into minstrelsy in vain. That, too, came in handy in the latter work's vaudeville scenes.

Emblematic of the salvaging process is the song "Lost in the Stars," the most conspicuous link between the various theatrical projects from which the show of the same name grew. Before it eventually made its way onto the musical stage, the song (devoid of the offensively patronizing dialect of the original version) was recorded three times: by Lenya in 1943, by Walter Huston in 1944, and by Frank Sinatra in 1946. It was also published in sheet-music form in 1946. Lenya's recording was issued as part of a disc of six songs prepared under Weill's supervision for Bost Records; the other songs were "Lover Man" (which would become "Trouble Man" in *Lost in the Stars*), "Surabaya-Johnny" (from *Happy End*), "Denn wie man sich bettet" (from *Aufstieg und Fall der Stadt Mahagonny*), "J'attends un navire" (from *Marie Galante*), and the chanson "Complainte de la Seine." Huston included "Lost in the Stars" as the flip-side to his second recording of "September Song." Sinatra's recording, whose release was supposed to coincide with the publication of the sheet music, did not appear until the time of the premiere production of *Lost in the Stars,* in 1949.

Insofar as there is an idea common to the work's various incarnations, from the initial plan to adapt Edwards's story to the staged version of Paton's novel, Anderson's statement to the hoped-for principal Robeson still holds true, albeit in a general and therefore limited sense: "essentially . . . the story of a man in a chaotic world in search of his own manhood and his rules of conduct." The switch of book to Paton's novel called for a whole new musico-dramatic conception. This in turn became significantly altered as a result of the numerous interventions by director Rouben Mamoulian, whose imperious directing style caused well-documented tensions among the members of the production team. Because of the influence Mamoulian exerted on the work's final form, Foster Hirsch has gone so far as to describe the director of *Lost in the Stars* as "the show's third author."[42] True, the director's input decisively affected the final version, requiring Anderson and Weill to accept a number of critical adjustments. Yet it was they who were ultimately responsible for transforming the novel. And their departures from Paton's original, as discussed below, incurred the novelist's displeasure.

Not only did the song "Lost in the Stars" play a constant and pivotal role connecting the disparate materials discussed so far; it would be no exaggeration to say that the sentiments the song expresses were leitmotifs of Anderson's entire oeuvre. The poetic figure of stars recurs throughout his plays and poems, as does the theme of a God-forsaken world whose inhabitants are "lost out here in the stars." Figure and theme, as here in the song, often go together. Small wonder, then, that Anderson would want to salvage this song in particular from the various aborted projects he worked on with Weill, electing twice to use it as the title song, in the last and enduring instance even as the title song for the adaptation of a novel. He had even considered incorporating it in *Street Scene* during his involvement in the American Opera's initial conception, along with "The Little Gray House," which would likewise make its way from *Ulysses Africanus* to *Lost in the Stars*.[43] (The ending of that song is one of Weill's self-borrowings, having been lifted from his setting of Brecht's "Nannas Lied," where the poet asks, partly borrowing from François Villon, "Where are the tears of last evening, where is the snow of yesteryear?")

Probably the two best-known instances of the "star" figure in Anderson's writing occur in the play *Star-Wagon* and the poem "Epilogue." The titular star-wagon of the play, which received its premiere in 1937, is a time machine built by the protagonist, an unhappy inventor named Stephen. Space becomes time, and vice versa. The star-wagon enables Stephen to return to his youth at the beginning of the twentieth century and relive his life in an alternate version, which he ends up finding inferior to the original.

"Epilogue," first published in 1925, was selected as the inscription for Anderson's gravestone. Written in the prosodic form known as "rime royal" (ababacc), the original version of the poem comprises three stanzas. Here are the first of them and the beginning of the second:

> Children of dust, astray among the suns,
> Children of earth, adrift upon the night,
> Who have shaken the pageants of old gods and thrones,
> And know them crushed and dead and lost to sight,
> What is there in our darkness or our light
> To linger in prose or claim a singing breath
> Save the curt history of life isled in death?—
>
> Life climbing blind through sunlight desolate
> Upon this saddest satellite of stars,
> Fearless and steadfast, holding toward the fate
> Of men and their little earth and sorrow-scars . . . [44]

Anderson's vision, which became immortalized in the words his family chose and amended for his gravestone, was an essentially tragic one. Replacing the "suns" of the first line (and thereby disturbing the rhyme scheme) with his beloved "stars" of the ninth, the inscription on the gravestone also suppresses the poem's revolutionary overcoming of gods and kings by removing the third and fourth lines:

> Children of dust astray among the stars
> Children of earth adrift upon the night
> What is there in our darkness or our light
> To linger in prose or claim a singing breath
> Save the curt history of life isled in death

The version of the poem preserved in the inscription nicely captures the worldview underpinning Anderson's later works. Not that his democratic libertarianism, already sharply in evidence in *Knickerbocker Holiday,* was incompatible with the essentially secular, antiroyalist message of the omitted lines. Rather, the ideology of the later work no longer embraced the left-wing political leanings of his youth; instead, it is imbued with a sense of almost resigned idealism, as his theoretical statements about playwriting make abundantly clear.

One such statement, and among the most widely cited, is "The Essence of Tragedy." In this brief essay, first delivered to the Modern Language Association in New York in January 1938 and subsequently published in a collection of the same name, Anderson offers a potted digest of his theatrical poetics. Privileging tragedy over comedy, he describes the basic lessons he learned from Ancient Greek drama and how they might offer guidance for modern playwrights. In particular, he prides himself on having formulated a rule for his *own* guidance, describing it as "more concise than any other." According to Anderson, a play "should lead up to and away from a central crisis, and this crisis should consist in a discovery by the leading character which has an indelible effect on his thought and emotion and completely alters his course of action. The leading character, let me say it again, must make the discovery; it must affect him emotionally; and it must alter his direction in the play."[45]

Anderson builds on this idea by stipulating that the leading character should have a tragic fault and that the purpose of the discovery is therefore to trigger "a change for the better." The tragic hero, he writes, "must pass through an experience which opens his eyes to an error of his own." Anderson's definition further stipulates, following classical precedents, that even though the leading character must die, his character will first be transformed: "In a tragedy [the hero] suffers death itself as a consequence of his fault or his attempt to correct it, but before he dies he has become a nobler person because of his recognition of his fault and the consequent alteration of his course of action" (9). The reason Anderson offers is quite basic: "[The] audience will always insist that the alteration in the hero be for the better. . . . [It] will go along with it only when the leading character responds in the end to what it considers a higher moral impulse" (11). This, then, is what should guide the playwright in his writing: "He must arrange his story that it will prove to the audience that men pass through suffering purified, that, animal though we are, despicable though we are in many ways, there is in us all some divine, incalculable fire that urges us to be better than we are" (13).

Anderson's theoretical understanding of the genre of tragedy is narrowly circumscribed by the express requirement that the hero must die. If he doesn't die, yet the play still contains the other requisite ingredients and thereby succeeds in appealing to a "higher moral impulse," Anderson refrains from applying the label "tragedy" and talks instead of "a serious play." Based on this definition, few, if any, modern plays can strictly be classified as tragedies. Either they are "serious plays," according to Anderson's definition, or they are comedies, or they may draw on the example of the tragicomedy practiced by Euripides and amount to some form of hybrid. Anderson defines the latter, quite common approach as "Greek New Comedy," by which he means a form of theater that "[celebrates] man's virtue and his regeneration in hours of crisis." This form of theater is accepted, now as in the past, as "having the more important function" relative to the purely ribald "Old Comedy," which he calls "a celebration of the animal in us" (12). In conclusion, he calls theater "at its best . . . a religious affirmation," not in any theological or denominational sense, but as the expression of "faith in evolution," the "groping of men toward an excellence dimly apprehended, seldom possible of definition" (14).

Against the background of the theoretical precepts that Anderson put forth in his 1938 lecture, and given the generic label that he and Weill attached to *Lost in the Stars,* the following question arises: how do these precepts or "rules" apply, if they do, to the "musical tragedy"? Or conversely, how does Anderson's concept of tragedy affect the significance of that label? Of course, it is to the final, the performed, version of *Lost in the Stars* that such questions must ultimately be addressed, particularly in view of the vagaries of the work's genesis. However, the many changes of conception introduced during that protracted process—changes both great and small—are also instructive in explaining what it took to realize the experiment of a tragedy conceived for Broadway.

After reading *Cry, the Beloved Country,* Anderson wrote to Alan Paton expressing his admiration for the novel. "For years I've wanted to write something which would state the position and perhaps illuminate the tragedy of our own negroes. Now that I've read your story I think you have said as much as can be said both for your country and ours." In proposing to "arrange it for the stage," as he put it to Paton, Anderson evidently conceived of the question of race relations in South Africa that the novel depicts as pertinent to the situation in his own country, too. Yet the fuller explanation of his artistic motivation downplays that aspect as well as the specifically political dimensions of the conflict, instead pursuing a more universal message: "It would be our task—as we see it—to translate into stage form without dulling its edge or losing its poetry, this extraordinarily moving tale of lost men clinging to odds and ends of faith in the darkness of our modern earth. For the breaking of the tribe is only a symbol of all tribes and all the old ways and beliefs."[46]

Anderson's reading of the novel emphasized the questioning of faith that is experienced by the protagonist of *Ulysses Africanus* and which receives direct expression in the text of the song "Lost in the Stars." There's also a hint of the original version of "Epilogue," with the "shaken . . . pageants of old gods and thrones." In other words, Anderson viewed the "tragedy of our negroes" in terms that ultimately transcend race. At the same time, if he was going to turn the tragedy of black people, whether South African or American, into a stage work and, in so doing, follow his own rule for the composition of a theatrical tragedy, he would have to find a way for the collective tragedy to be conveyed by the actions of the individual protagonists, foremost by those of "the hero."

One passage in the novel in particular seems likely to have struck a chord in Anderson's mind; it obviously suggests a thematic link to the earlier unfinished work written with Weill and, above all, to the salvaged song.

> I shall devote myself, my time, my energy, my talents, to the service of South Africa. I shall no longer ask myself if this or that is expedient, but only if it is right. I shall do this, not because I am noble or unselfish, but because life slips away, and because I need for the rest of my journey a star that will not play false to me, a compass that will not lie. I shall do this not because I am a negrophile and a hater of my own, not because I cannot find it in me to do anything else. I am lost when I balance this against that. I am lost when I ask if this is safe, I am lost when I ask if men, white men or black men, Englishmen or Afrikaners, Gentiles or Jews, will approve. Therefore I shall try to do what is right, and to speak what is true.[47]

The images and sentiments conveyed by these words, which appear in the novel as quoted text, are familiar from the lyrics of the song "Lost in the Stars." They also capture the essence of "a man in a chaotic world in search of his own manhood and his rules of conduct" that Anderson was aiming for a decade or so earlier. In the narrative of the novel, however, the words are not directly associated with the Reverend Stephen Kumalo, who becomes the principal singing character in *Lost in the Stars* and who performs the titular song; they appear, rather, in the form of written text from the pen of another character, who has only a brief speaking role in the musical tragedy. That character is Arthur Jarvis, author and liberal activist, whose murder constitutes the dramatic crux both of the novel and of the musical. In the novel, the quoted material is one of several such passages from Arthur Jarvis's essays about apartheid in South Africa that his white supremacist father, James Jarvis, discovers following his son's murder.

In the musical, in the second scene of the first act, the content of the extended quotations from Arthur's writings becomes telescoped into a dialogue between father and son immediately preceding a chance encounter between Arthur and Stephen and well before the murder takes place (in the eighth scene of the same act). In the brief exchange (a snippet of which is preserved in the cast recording), James voices his habitual support for the customs of apartheid ("in our village one does not go out of his way to speak to a black"), while Arthur makes it clear with his curt retort that he is "not bound by these customs."

Taken as a whole, the musicalized scene realizes the main idea behind the adaptation that Anderson proposed when he initially approached Paton: "My first concern would be to keep as much as possible of the dialogue and the story structure, just as they stand. Your effects are both powerful and delicate—and both the power and the delicacy could be lost in an ordinary dramatization. And to keep the plot and the dialogue form you gave them would only be possible if a chorus—a sort of Greek chorus—were used to tie together the great number of scenes, and to comment on the action as you comment in the philosophic and descriptive passages."[48]

Partly in the interests of compression, and also as their work evolved during the production process, Anderson and Weill would make numerous adjustments to the original. The above example from the second scene of act 1 illustrates the kind of transformation that occurred. And, as projected, they would employ the chorus as a framing device. For instance, both before and after the father-son confrontation, which takes place at a railway station, we hear a group of Zulus "singing [as the stage direction puts it] a farewell to one of their number who has been called to work in the mines." The song is "Train to Johannesburg," with motoric rhythms imitative of a locomotive and with contrasting lines of verbal commentary: "White man go to Johannesburg—He come back, he come back. Black man go to Johannesburg—Never come back, never come back!" The words harbor a note of dramatic irony, however: in search of his lost son Absalom, Stephen does come back. But neither Arthur, a white man, nor Absalom, Arthur's black assailant in a failed burglary, returns from Johannesburg. Absalom is tried and executed for Arthur's murder committed during a botched break-in.

The personal and the political are intertwined. Each of them having lost a son, Stephen and James face the daunting challenge of coming to terms with the emotions that threaten to undermine the possibility of friendship and that, seen in a broader context, reflect the human tragedy of South African society at large—or, by extension, of any society—struggling to overcome entrenched racial divisions. For Anderson, as he made clear in his letter to the author, the tragedy of the novel possessed broad symbolic significance, allowing its narrative to function as an allegory for contemporary American society. He also wanted it to capture the nature of social change and the supplanting of ruling ideologies more generally.

Commonalities between the conception of *Lost in the Stars* and Weill's earlier works are not only thematic. Similarities of style and expression are in evidence, too, some of them going back as far as his German period. Employing a chorus as a central structural component calls to mind the choral writing in *Die Bürgschaft* and *Der Jasager*, both didactically conceived works that foreground the relationship of the individual to the community (and vice versa). Unlike the two earlier operas, however, which are sung throughout, *Lost in the Stars* is a singspiel-like hybrid with an unusually asymmetrical constellation—or counterpoint—of dramaturgical elements.

The fact that only the black characters are "musicalized" no doubt adds particular emphasis to Stephen's personal crisis as well as to the experience of his fellow black South Africans. From the perspective of Anderson's conventional understanding of the genre, this asymmetry makes for an especially unorthodox tragedy. The character with whom readers of the novel, Anderson included, might be inclined to sympathize the most—Arthur Jarvis—is assigned to a small speaking role, as mentioned. And it is his father, James, also a purely speaking part, who arguably displays the most significant change of heart toward the end of the dramatization. The death prescribed by Anderson's concept of tragedy, along with the most far-reaching transformation elicited by that death—both of these elements are associated with characters who don't sing. The essential ingredients of tragic drama in this "musical tragedy" are not musical. (The transformation that Stephen Kumalo undergoes in the musical belongs to the adaptation rather than being derived from the original.)

Several, not necessarily congruent factors account for these departures from the model. One of them has to do with genre: Weill and Anderson were adapting a novel, not a play (which would anyway have been written quite differently). In the dramatization, Arthur's quoted writings, which convey the central political and ethical message of *Cry, the Beloved Country,* all but disappear. Another factor is largely pragmatic: from the beginning, Anderson and Weill wanted to provide a vehicle for a star performer. The role of Stephen, eventually taken by Todd Duncan, dominates the stage proceedings. In the novel, Stephen is one of two main protagonists. And although James Jarvis joins him in the second half, he is one among a host of characters, all of them described, in part, by the third-person narrative voice that intersperses reports of human interactions with lyrical portraits of the South African settings in which those interactions occur. Yet another factor has to do with the conception of the piece as a variant of epic theater: the tragedy is personal, certainly, but it is also social and historical. The dramaturgical counterpoint of *Lost in the Stars* may seem oddly asymmetrical when judged in conventional terms. In terms of the piece's social commitment, however, the formal experiment is an essential part of the work's message. Yet another factor is philosophical. By focusing on Stephen's personal crisis in the aftermath of Arthur Jarvis's murder, Anderson and Weill manage to introduce an ideological dimension wholly at odds with the novelist's own beliefs.

In his memoirs, Paton pointedly disagreed with one review of *Lost in the Stars* in particular, an unequivocal rave from the critic Howard Barnes: "I did my best to join in the rejoicing, but my heart wasn't in it. I am sure that *Cry, the Beloved Country* had moved [Anderson] deeply, and that his musical play was 'based on' the book. But his view of life and the world was very different from mine. Barnes was wrong; Anderson did not capture 'the full essence of the original.'"[49] Barnes, in his 6 November 1949 review for the *New York Herald Tribune,* had in fact written: "Out of Alan Paton's fine book of racial tension in South Africa, *Cry the Beloved Country,* Maxwell Anderson has designed a story line and lyrics which capture the full burden of a great tragedy." That does not alter the point of the novelist, who took issue with the content of the titular song "Lost in the Stars" in particular and with the musicalized characterization of Stephen Kumalo in general.

> The song "Lost in the Stars," sung by Todd Duncan playing the part of the humble and unsophisticated black priest Stephen Kumalo, was highly sophisticated, and it was extremely painful to me to hear my humble hero in a role that he could never have taken. It was made still more painful for me by the fact that the song belonged to the death-of-God genre, or to put it more accurately, to the desertion-of-God genre. God had created the universe, and more especially He had created the earth, but now He had gone away, "forgetting the promise that we heard him say." So "we are lost out here in the stars."[50]

Lost in the Stars ends quite differently from *Cry, the Beloved Country.* Paton concludes his novel with an interior monologue for Stephen in which the black preacher poses a long, somewhat desultory list of existential questions, about knowledge of God, about the conditions in his village, about Jarvis's role in restoring order, all of which leads to the comment: "But his mind would contain it no longer. It was not for man's knowing. He put it from his mind, for it was a secret." Stephen's stream of consciousness elicits an appeal to God's mercy coupled with a note of resignation: "And now for all the people of Africa, the beloved country, *Nkosi Sikel' iAfrika,* God save Africa. But he would not see that salvation. It lay far off, because men were afraid of it" (275). Blending Stephen's voice with his own, and echoing the preceding remark, the author suggests that the end of apartheid, as inevitable in its way as the cycles of nature, is also beyond comprehension: "For it is the dawn that has come, as it has come for a thousand centuries, never failing. But when that dawn will come, of our emancipation, from the fear of bondage and the bondage of fear, why, that is a secret" (276).

The musical tragedy, by contrast, presages the achievement of social liberation with a final scene of reconciliation between Stephen and James. In their closing dialogue, Stephen repeats the underlying theme of the work's title ("We are all lost here, black and white, rich and poor, the fools and the wise! Lost and hopeless and condemned on this rock that goes 'round the sun without meaning!"), whereupon Jarvis counters: "Not hopeless, Stephen, and not without meaning. For even out of this horror of this crime some things have come that are gain and not loss. . . . Let us forgive each other," he proposes. "Let us be neighbors. Let us be friends."[51] As mentioned above, it is up to Jarvis to introduce the constructive, transformative element and overcome old prejudices. In celebratory affirmation of this change of heart, the chorus reprises the conclusion of the song Stephen had sung earlier as he embarked on the journey in search of his son, the words serving to express his own personal faith in human nature:

> Each lives alone in a world of dark,
> Crossing the skies in a lonely arc,
> Save when love leaps out like a leaping spark
> Over thousands, thousands of miles!

Now the same words are meant to give voice to a common faith that transcends all differences of race or creed.

The human tragedy experienced by two men, each of whom loses a son, forms the basis of a didactically conceived play with a broad appeal to universal brotherhood. The immediate source for that conception was the kind of secular humanism enshrined in the writings of historian Arnold Toynbee, as Anderson himself made explicit. In February 1950, in an acceptance speech at the National Conference of Christians and Jews, which had selected *Lost in the Stars* to receive its "Brotherhood Award," Anderson explained how shortly before reading Paton's novel he and other members of the Playwrights' Company had been inspired by a meeting with the famous historian in New York. (The previous year Toynbee's picture had appeared on the cover of *Time* magazine.) Anderson credited Toynbee's own commitment to "brotherhood, amity, tolerance, understanding—understanding that crosses all boundaries" as having galvanized his own resolve to write a play on the topic. And it was with this goal in mind that he then read *Cry, the Beloved Country* and went about adapting it for the theater in the hope of promoting "mutual tolerance and understanding that refuses to recognize any barriers between neighbor and neighbor."[52]

If the conclusion of the musical tragedy represents a significant and telling departure from that of the novel, the opening is quick to establish specific connections. One of them is contained already in the opening musical theme of the instrumental introduction, even though its actual nature becomes evident only later in the show. By setting the tone for the ensuing work and presenting musical material that appears later in a vocal context, the instrumental introduction to the opening number performs the conventional function of an overture (ex. 75).

In its foreshadowing of the later sung version, the opening theme calls to mind musical gestures that function in an analogous way in earlier works. For example,

EXAMPLE 75. *Lost in the Stars,* "The Hills of Ixopo" (opening)

the introduction to *Street Scene* starts with the melody of "Lonely House," dissonantly harmonized; the "Glamour Dream" of *Lady in the Dark* begins with the incipit of "My Ship," which appears throughout the musical play in the manner of a leitmotif, until the song appears in its entirety at the very end. In *Der Zar lässt sich photographieren,* the initial measures perform a slightly different function: the terse musical gesture is vocal, delivered by the chorus, which announces the title of the work itself. Here, in *Lost in the Stars,* the melody is both enunciative and anticipatory: prefiguring the song of the same name, it is associated note-for-note with the novel's title, "Cry, the beloved country."

Following the wordless allusion to the musical tragedy's source, the opening sung text of this number ("The Hills of Ixopo") comes well-nigh verbatim from the novel, from chapter 1. (Snippets of the same text appear again, like repeated motifs, at the beginning of chapter 18.) Here are the words of Anderson and Weill's tripartite sung version (A-B-A'), with ellipses indicating where portions of Paton's prose were not set:

> There is a lovely road that runs from Ixopo into the hills. These hills are grass-covered and rolling, and they are lovely beyond any singing of it. . . . About you is grass and bracken and you may hear the forlorn crying of the titihoya bird. . . . The grass is rich and matted, you cannot see the soil. The grass holds the rain and mist, they seep into the ground, feeding the streams in every clove. The clove is cool and green, and lovely beyond any singing of it. . . . Where you stand the grass is rich and matted . . . but the rich green hills break down. They fall to the valley below, and falling change. . . .

> For they grow red and bare; they cannot hold the rain and mist; the streams run dry in the cloves. Too many cattle feed on the grass . . . ; it is not kept or guarded or cared for. It no longer keeps men, guards men, cares for men. The titihoya cries here no more.
>
> The great red hills stand desolate. And the earth has torn away like flesh. . . . These are the valleys of old men and old women, of mothers and children. The men are away, the young men and the girls are away. The soil cannot keep them any more.

The melody's pentatonically inflected character carries over into the musical material of the entire number, which plaintively paints the environmental setting. In fact, the melody to the words of Paton's text is a variation of the opening pentatonic collection, as is the accompanying ostinato. Moreover, that Weill was able to abridge this number for the cast album by simply removing selected measures owes to the music's essentially static, repetitive character.

In dramatic contrast with the directionless feel of pastoral pentatonicism, the chromatically descending bass line that accompanies the wordless allusion lends expression to the work's underlying affect of lament. Weill had utilized this centuries-old expressive convention in earlier works, notably at the beginning and end of *Die sieben Todsünden,* where it serves to convey the work's aura of uprootedness, and in his score of *Lost in the Stars,* too, it becomes a prominent motivic element. (The bass line of the opening varies the convention by beginning its descent on the flattened supertonic B♭, thereby extending the figure while also creating a jarring tritone with the initial melodic tone of E. In its second iteration, the chromatic line is extended even further to cover a full octave and a half.) Apart from the very opening, where it underpins the literal lament of the "Cry" theme, the chromatically descending bass line appears in a number of other places throughout the score, usually spanning the conventional tetrachord: as ostinato accompaniment to the number "Murder in Parkwold"; at the beginning of Stephen's soliloquy "O Tixo, Tixo, Help Me!"; and in the choral number "Four o'Clock." A variant marks the double chorus "Fear!," and yet another accompanies "The Wild Justice."

To call chromatically descending and ascending motifs unifying devices would go too far, however. They constitute prominent affective figures, nothing more, but also nothing less. More obviously and immediately constitutive of musical continuity is Weill's use of recurring themes from the musical numbers, both in the instrumental interludes and in quasi-filmic underscoring. Immediate precedents for such underscoring are the two American operas, portions of which are couched in an overtly operatic style.

In *Lost in the Stars,* the "very serious, tragic, quite un-Broadway-ish music of operatic dimensions," to use Weill's own description, reaches its apogee in Stephen's extended soliloquy, a number comparable in scale and emotional depth to Anna Maurrant's big aria in *Street Scene*. Like Anna's "Somehow I Never Could Believe," Stephen's "O Tixo, Tixo, Help Me!" is a personal narrative comprising several sections that build to a climax toward the end. If the style and language of the two numbers are comparable—including close correspondences between some of the musical gestures—Stephen appears to give vent to even greater desperation than Anna. "I shall lose Absalom," he exclaims in the climactic fifth section, resigning himself in the muted and partly spoken conclusion to finding "some other hope" and wondering, "Where can I turn now?" In the preceding sections he recounts his son's failure to heed his advice ("Speak truly, evade nothing, what you have done, let it be on your head") and how this failure caused a lapse into crime: Absalom "ran far into evil." Stephen appreciates, however, the bitter irony of the confession uttered by his son when charged with murder: "I shall do no more evil, tell no more untruth. I shall keep my father's ways and remember them." By belatedly heeding his father's advice and speaking the truth, Absalom places himself at the mercy of the court—a court that condemns him to death. (His accomplices are acquitted on lack of evidence.)

The ambiguity of the aria's conclusion is encapsulated in the final chord, which switches from the prevailing key of D minor to a D-major harmony that incorporates a major sixth and ninth. Not only does this harmony (on the final word *me*) arise contrapuntally from the voice-leading of the preceding chromatic descent, but the nontriadic "added" notes are themselves related to the repeated accompaniment figure in the second and fourth sections, which recall in relative tranquillity the father's advice to be truthful unto oneself. Even in the depths of his despair, Stephen does not lose sight of his personal integrity (ex. 76).

Such "serious" features of the score have to be balanced against the more obviously popular elements, which include the numbers imported from *Ulysses Africanus*. (The chorus "Bird of Passage," discussed in the Coda below, is at once serious and popular thanks to its hymnlike tone and texture.) The amalgam of serious and popular traditions, which Weill would defend as an "experiment," became even more pronounced during the production process, largely as a result of Mamoulian's involvement. The nature and extent of the director's intervention can be gauged from the memorandum he wrote to the authors and, even more, from how they responded to it. That may not elevate his role to that of coauthor, as Hirsch suggested, but he certainly left a decisive mark on the final mix of stylistic elements as well as on a whole host of details.

With his memorandum, dated 27 August 1949, Mamoulian pursued two complementary goals. On the one hand, he aimed to inject as much humor as possible into the dramatic proceedings. "Every chuckle or smile that can be honestly brought into our play," he forthrightly advised, "will be like a drink of water in the desert." On the other hand, he sought to ensure that Todd Duncan be allowed to shine in the role of Stephen. (Mamoulian had already directed Duncan as

EXAMPLE 76. *Lost in the Stars,* "O Tixo, Tixo, Help Me!" (conclusion)

Porgy in the premiere production of Gershwin's *Porgy and Bess.*) Rather than being sung by the leader of the chorus, in keeping with the original concept of a "choral play," the soliloquy would now be sung by Stephen—offering "a chance for Kurt's score to rise to a high operatic level"—as would the titular song "Lost in the Stars." "With Todd Duncan playing the part," Mamoulian wrote, "let's have a sweeping, powerful aria, deeply emotional and of tragic dimensions."[53] As Elmar Juchem observes, "a comparison of Mamoulian's suggestions with the actual revisions reveals a large amount of agreement."[54] Prominent among those suggestions is the insertion of a new song, "Thousands of Miles," whose melody Weill derived at Mamoulian's suggestion from an instrumental interlude. With this added song the director intended to "show [Stephen] as he was before all the tragic events. . . . He should be a man of clear and happy convictions . . . All of his wife's skeptical forebodings cannot affect his bright faith in life and in ABSALOM." For a similar reason, it was decided that the chorus should reprise this new number at the end of the final scene, instead of the inherently skeptical "Lost in the Stars."

Nor was Mamoulian the first to suggest making such adjustments with the aim of producing a viable work for the Broadway theater. After being approached by Anderson and Weill as a possible director for the show, and then having read the script and heard the music, Agnes de Mille (choreographer for *One Touch of Venus* and director of *Allegro*) responded that "The play is static . . . too much of the action is carried by the chorus." In addition, she was bothered by an "aura of unrelieved tragedy."[55] Mamoulian's revisions sought to address these very issues. Yet further changes would occur as a matter of course during rehearsal. For example, according to Anderson's daughter, Hesper, it was decided that "a respite was needed between the heartbreak of the choral 'Cry, the Beloved Country' and the quiet sadness of the ending."[56] The satirical song about diamond drilling, "Big Mole," sung by Stephen's nephew Alex, provides such relief.

Not everyone found the solutions to their taste, however, as can be seen from critical reactions to the premiere production, which opened at the Music Box Theatre on 30 October 1949 and ran for a respectable 281 performances. Among the wholly favorable reviews were those by Brooks Atkinson and Howard Barnes. Atkinson, writing on 31 October for the *New York Times,* praised book and music alike: "When he comes to the overwhelming climax of this terrible tragedy [Mr. Anderson] takes the time and has the words to write a grand and enlightening scene with unadorned beauty. . . . In the past Mr. Weill has given the theatre some fine scores. But at the moment, which is forty minutes after the final curtain, it is difficult to remember anything out of his portfolio as eloquent as this richly orchestrated singing music. Some of it is as artless as a Broadway song. But most of it is flowing with the same compassion that Mr. Paton brought to his novel." Although Atkinson articulated a fairly common reaction at the time—"Probably, *Cry the Beloved Country* should not be translated into a drama"—he followed that caveat with the concluding line: "But it has been [translated], and into a drama that is illuminating and memorable."

In his review for the *New York Herald Tribune* that appeared on 6 November (it was his second notice, the first having appeared a week earlier, on 31 October), Barnes posited and then responded to similar charges, thereby incurring Paton's principled objection, as mentioned above. He observed, for example: "There are those who relished the book who feel that the surging conflict between black man and white man has not been fully realized in the stern musical tragedy which has emerged at the Music Box." But he then immediately countered: "They are mistaken. For the theater employs its own terms in its particular fashion and needs no antecedent references for its magic." In addition, he stated that "Kurt Weill's score is no counterpart of George Gershwin's music for the classic musical tragedy *Porgy and Bess,*" only to continue that "it always carries the melodrama to its inexorable and moving conclusion." Finally, after praising the novel as "superior in its own right," he concluded that "it is somewhat astounding to find its transmutation into musical terms so tremendously effective," including in his glowing assessment the various facets of Weill's musicalization. "The Messrs. Anderson, Weill, Mamoulian and their colleagues have composed an engrossing stage threnody which enriches the theatrical season immeasurably. Even in such bits as the number 'Who'll Buy?' [the bawdy song of the nightclub entertainer Linda] in which Sheila Guyse is torridly attractive, *Lost in the Stars* is a completely satisfying entertainment."

Among the less favorably disposed were two critics who succeeded with their comments in eliciting immediate and detailed responses from the composer: the *New York Times* music critic Olin Downes and theater critic Harold Clurman. Each of them knew Weill well—Downes as a longtime supporter and advocate, Clurman from the Group Theatre days. Whereas Downes's reservations, which he communicated in private, were admittedly qualified and well intended, Clurman used the occasion of the release of the cast recording to publish a blanket dismissal of Weill's American career.

Because music critics were not expected to write about musicals, Downes did not review the premiere of *Lost in the Stars.* Instead he offered his candid opinion of the musical tragedy in a personal letter to the composer. (The task of covering a musical theater piece for the *New York Times,* even such an overtly operatic one as this, typically fell to the theater critic, not the opera critic. Hence Brooks Atkinson's opening-night review. Even *Street Scene,* billed a "dramatic musical" before being called an "American opera" for the publication of the piano-vocal score, received its initial notice from Atkinson. Downes's assessment of the piece, in an article titled "Opera on Broadway," appeared in the *Times*'s Sunday edition some two weeks after the premiere.)[57] In his letter to Weill dated 9 December 1949, Downes explains that he was going to write about Weill's new work as well as "Blitzstein's mishandling of *The Little Foxes*" (that is, *Regina,* which Downes dismisses as "awfully bad and dramatically false"), but he had learned that another of the newspaper's music critics, Howard Taubman, would be touching on these works in an omnibus piece on New York's musical theater. (Taubman's article, which appeared on 11 December, dealt only briefly with *Lost in the Stars,* describing it as "a disappointment" compared with the original, and the music as "too commonplace to evoke the atmosphere of South Africa." He reserved his harshest criticism for the titular song, describing it as "embarrassing." It seemed, he said, "to be the maudlin, torchy kind of thing that Tin Pan Alley grinds out by the yard. I thought it demeaned the old preacher, not revealed him." Meanwhile, unlike Downes, Taubman liked *Regina,* praising it as "exciting musical theater.")

In his letter to Weill, Downes sticks close to his brief as an opera critic: he tempers his appreciation of Weill's operatic achievement with doubts (similar to Taubman's) about the work's more popular aspects. "In many respects I think it is the best thing you've done yet for the theater," he writes. "It has a remarkable technique, too. I have reservations that evidently the audience has not, concerning the Broadway touches of the show."[58] He specifically identifies "numbers in the form of song hits" as a "kind of formalism that disturbs me a little bit."

The letter's conclusion is similarly ambivalent. He first places *Lost in the Stars* alongside *Street Scene* as "the most significant steps which have so far been taken both to modernize and popularize the operatic principle, and say something worthwhile in the artistic sense." Yet there follows a substantial *but:* "But I am still waiting for the day when you get exactly the subject which you can treat without the faintest consideration of public taste or expediency of any sort, while in the meantime you are constantly developing a reputation for making it more and more possible for you to do exactly what you want to do ultimately in the music field."

This well-meaning and hopeful expectation of future developments amounted to an appeal to embrace the very autonomy that had been anathema to Weill for much of his career. Small wonder that he felt impelled to defend his "experiment" in the very terms that informed Downes's reservations: "It must be somewhat surprising indeed," he wrote in response, "to find a serious subject treated in a form which (in this country at least) has been used so far only for a light form of entertainment. But that was exactly the nature of my experiment—to do a 'musical tragedy' for the American theater so that the typical American audience (not a specialized audience) can accept it; and the real success of the piece is the fact that the audience did accept it without hesitation, that they accepted a lot of very serious, tragic, quite un-Broadway-ish music of operatic dimensions, together with some songs written in a more familiar style."[59]

Collaboration involves compromise, as the genesis of *Lost in the Stars* amply documents. Yet here Weill explicitly rejects any such notion with regard either to the audience he was trying to reach or to his use of vernacular musical forms. For him, "the American popular song" forms the basis of the American musical theater, "growing out of the American folk-music." (In parentheses he remarks that *Regina* suffered precisely from Blitzstein's lack of success in writing songs.) He does, however, concede that this genre of theater is still "in this early state of development."

Clurman's essay, which appeared in the *Saturday Review of Literature* on 31 December, ostensibly as a review of the recently released cast album, is not only more exacting in its negative criticisms than Downes's letter; it is also more sweeping and comprehensive.[60] Weill evidently took it seriously enough to draft a lengthy response, albeit one he did not complete, much less submit for publication. Rather than prescriptively envisioning an operatic future toward which *Lost in the Stars* and other recent pieces might serve as significant stepping stones, as Downes had done, Clurman inserts the latest work into a narrative of artistic decline, a process that he associates with Weill's attempts to adapt himself to a new environment after emigration from Germany. "Weill is so much the adaptable artist," he writes, "that if he were forced to live among the Hottentots he would in the shortest possible span of time become the leading Hottentot composer." (The hypothesis of Clurman's rhetorical flourish calls to mind the comment about Weill quoted earlier that Elia Kazan would include in his memoirs: "If he'd been dumped on an African savannah, he'd quickly have mastered the tribal drum!")

For Clurman, *The Threepenny Opera* serves as his benchmark—"a masterpiece of its time"—even though he claims it is not his intention "to indulge in that other form of critical sadism, which consists of hanging an artist on the hook of his most notable work." In effect, though, this is precisely what he does. Not only is he delighted by *Threepenny*'s wit, but "one is captivated" as well, he suggests, "by its sweet raffishness, its poisonously warm abandon, its drugged back-alley romanticism, its occasional burst of buoyant populism and street-corner bravery." He then provides a list of Weill's major American works that do not meet this standard. They include *Street Scene,* which he disparages as "a smooth amalgam of Puccini, jazz, and Viennese operetta for the purpose of putting over the opera form among those prejudiced against it," and *Lost in the Stars,* which he dismisses as "slickly impressive and as basically void as the architecture of our giant movie emporia." Among the American works, he is prepared to name *Johnny Johnson* as the sole exception, describing its music as "a strange but affecting mixture, superior, in my opinion, to most of what Weill has subsequently written" (but without mentioning his own involvement in that work's production as a founding member of the Group Theatre).

"There is nothing wrong in adapting oneself to a new environment," Clurman is quick to point out, "but one must adapt oneself upward rather than downward, that is, to the more challenging and difficult as well as to the simpler and safer." He thus sees Weill's protean gifts of adaptability as both symptom and cause of a putative diminishment of artistic authenticity and originality, and hence of quality, as he defines it. This criticism betrays a strong ideological dimension, evident above all in the remarks on *Lost in the Stars,* in which Clurman insinuates willing complicity on the composer's part in the superficiality and emptiness of mass culture and its institutions. Insofar as it anticipates a prevalent tradition of postwar Weill reception, in which these three themes often appear (sometimes only singly, frequently in combination), Clurman's review of *Lost in the Stars* has a valid claim to being that tradition's agenda-defining origin and source.

Clurman's criticisms resonate, for example, in Carl Dahlhaus's review of the Stuttgart production from 1962 (Dahlhaus was music critic at the time for the *Stuttgarter Zeitung*)—though Adorno's later writings on Weill, such as the 1950 obituary in the *Frankfurter Rundschau,* were no doubt a more obvious and immediate influence. Even so, the parallels to Clurman's views are striking. Dahlhaus refers to Weill as "the composer of *Mahagonny,*" who "in *Lost in the Stars* has degenerated into a technician of the music industry," and to Weill's music as "hewing to a carefully calculated median between aria and hit tune." The use of popular song comes in for particularly harsh criticism: not even a performance of "Stay Well" (the song of Absalom's fiancée, Irina), sung in Stuttgart by Lucretia West "as if Schubert had composed it," could entirely erase awareness of "fox-trot schemata and glazed harmonies" and thereby "transform musical jargon back into language." With the expectation that the sober reality of apartheid would make itself felt, Dahlhaus registered barely any opportunity for "a suggestion of the real horror" to penetrate "the smooth, even surface *[glatt gefügte Oberfläche]* of the musical tragedy." He was disturbed, rather, by what he calls "Weill's tendency toward partly coy, partly aggrandizing kitsch."[61]

Weill drafted a response in which he set out to counter Clurman's charges of change and concomitant decline by claiming continuity and progress in his new work: "This musical drama represents to me the furthest advance in a direction which I laid down for myself in the early years of my life as a composer." Nonetheless, he stressed its American origins, stating that his "new musical theater [grows] . . . partly out of the Broadway theater, partly from the steadily expanding theatrical life in schools and universities." (In mentioning "schools and universities, he was no doubt thinking of his college opera *Down in the Valley*.) "Confusion originates mostly in certain musical circles," he maintained, "which . . . are so far removed from the living theater that they have little understanding for a movement which has its roots more in theatrical than in musical developments." (Although valid, this seems an odd point to make to Clurman, a theater critic.) In justifying his approach he invoked the examples of Bizet and, above all, Verdi. "We began to study Verdi's scores and discovered behind those popular melodies the emotional depth and the textural brilliance of a great composer." Presumably he expected similar shifts in perception to occur in his own case. Ultimately, though, by not submitting his response for publication, he ended up honoring what he calls "one of the more commendable customs of our time," namely, "that a man should not talk back to his critic."[62]

Talking back to critics on behalf of the composer and his works, however, is one of the historian's legitimate jobs. Connections between the early and late work to which Weill was alluding in his unpublished response to Clurman were typically downplayed or went entirely unappreciated during the so-called Cold War period, whose reception of the composer largely rested on the aesthetic precepts and prejudices—"superstitions," as Nietzsche would have called them—that were analyzed in chapter 1, ostensibly modernist conceptions of artistic biography as well as musical style. Weill's commitment to working creatively within the institution of the Broadway theater fundamentally contradicted such conceptions, either because of a general suspicion harbored against cultural adaptability (a suspicion with an anti-Semitic antecedent in Wagner's diatribe against Mendelssohn) or because such an "adaptive" musical development was considered a failure on the composer's part to cultivate a personal style or "language." But to invoke such aesthetic prejudices against "other-directedness" and the practices of popular culture—prejudices that undoubtedly inform Clurmanesque critiques of *Lost in the Stars*—is not necessarily to discount any and all negative criticisms of the work (including well-meaning ones such as that privately volunteered by Downes), any more than it is to condone unconditionally the wholly positive reviews by critics such as Atkinson and Barnes. (In that sense, the interpretive challenges are closely related to those discussed with regard to *Street Scene* and *Down in the Valley*.) Interrogating the terms on which a musico-dramatic work is deemed to succeed or fail may point, rather, to the contingent nature of the critical act itself.

The same goes for the testimony of Weill and Anderson, all the more so in view of the work's uncommonly protracted genesis. Although exploring that genesis should shed light on how the creators at least hoped it would succeed, the various production contingencies described above had an uncommonly significant part to play in influencing the final outcome and thereby in causing conceptions to shift. Consideration of that genesis, along with the early reception history, reveals the description of the work that appeared on the original playbill—*Lost in the Stars: A Musical Tragedy (based on Alan Paton's novel "Cry, the Beloved Country")*—and, above all, the nature of the relationship among its title, genre, and source, to have been nothing if not problematic.

As far as the song "Lost in the Stars" is concerned, and hence the title of the "musical tragedy" itself, it proved a less propitious fit than Anderson had hoped for. Having served well the demythologizing purposes of the abandoned *Ulysses Africanus,* the song continued to transmit an abiding idea in search of a work. But its eventual integration into the adaptation of Paton's novel would meet with principled resistance on several fronts. The novelist thought it too sophisticated for his "humble hero," objecting that it conveyed a worldview at odds with his novel. For similar reasons, in order to conclude the show on a more uplifting note, the director urged that "Lost in the Stars" be replaced at the end by the song he had asked to be inserted at the beginning so as to convey the principal character's "clear and happy convictions." The *Times* music critic Taubman found the titular song "embarrassing," not only because it "demeaned the old preacher," but because of its "Tin Pan Alley" quality. His sympathetically inclined colleague, Downes, thought that Weill's score should have relied much less on popular song forms—a view that would be shared by his much less sympathetically inclined German counterpart, Dahlhaus.

When, after reading the novel, Anderson wrote to Paton that he had "for years . . . wanted to write something which would state the position and perhaps illuminate the tragedy of our own negroes," not only was he alluding to the origin of *Lost in the Stars* in the quite different *Ulysses Africanus;* he was also presaging a crux of the work's reception. Should *Lost in the Stars* be judged in relation to its

South African topic or on account of its relevance to the situation in the United States? Conversely, is the theme of apartheid to be understood, as Anderson also claimed, merely as "a symbol of all tribes and all the old ways and beliefs"? Or are the personal relations between two fathers and their respective sons supposed, as Weill put it, to "give a picture of the whole world today?"[63]

There can be little question that *Lost in the Stars* distances itself from the original South African setting. As Weill put it, "I wasn't trying to reproduce the native music of Africa any more than Maxwell Anderson was trying to provide with words a local-color picture of life there. I'm attempting to get to the heart of the public, and my public wouldn't feel anything if I gave them African chimes."[64] And yet, enough of the original milieu remains as to be at least somewhat relevant in assessments of the work. Eleanor Roosevelt went so far as to suggest that an appreciation of the novel and the conditions it describes could actually detract from the theatrical experience. After seeing the show in New York, she wrote in her syndicated newspaper column "My Day": "Perhaps reading the book, which gives a more complete picture of the whole problem, will make it difficult for some people to enjoy the play."[65]

Against the stark background of historical realities, whether South African or indeed American, is the work's "message of hope," as Weill called it, likely to come across as politically naïve and inadequate? "The really fine thing about this story," he volunteered, "is that it carries a message of hope that people through a personal approach will solve whatever racial problems exist."[66] In other words, does the theme of "brotherhood, amity, tolerance, understanding—understanding that crosses all boundaries" (the message that Anderson expressly associated with Toynbee's philosophy of history) serve less to illuminate than to gloss over, even to sugarcoat, the real tragedy of racism in the twentieth century? Dahlhaus's review of the 1962 Stuttgart production certainly suggested as much, underpinned as his views seemed to be by an aesthetics of critical realism. Howard Barnes, in contrast, came away from the premiere with the impression that "the story line and lyrics" had managed to "capture the full burden of a great tragedy" and that the work as a whole offered "a completely satisfying entertainment."

The critical question revolves around the nature of the tragedy and the theatrical means employed to represent it. In both respects, *Lost in the Stars* steers something of a middle course: in terms of its subject matter, between the social reality of a specific culture divided by apartheid and a universalized human experience; in terms of its genre, between musical play and opera. The significance of the label *musical tragedy* is therefore hard to pin down. Is the tragedy being presented specifically social or is it universally personal? Even though the work evolved away from the former and more toward the latter, as Stephen's dramatic role expanded and the part played by the epic chorus and its Leader correspondingly contracted, it would be difficult to make the case that *Lost in the Stars* achieved the condition of a musicalized tragedy in the emphatic sense that applies to, say, *Down in the Valley.*

Weill's "college opera" meets Anderson's definition with nothing left over, whereas *Lost in the Stars* complicates the model in various ways, as discussed above. The principal singing character (the black priest Stephen Kumalo) and the supporting spoken role (the white landowner James Jarvis) each must deal with the death of his son, and with how those inextricably connected tragic events affect their personal relations. This is already a major departure from Anderson's classical model. More unusual still, it is the spoken supporting role, not the principal singing role, who undergoes the all-important change of heart and who initiates the symbolic transformation of race relations. (Quite apart from the structural asymmetry here, it seems patronizingly, even offensively one-sided, not to mention historically problematic, that seizing the initiative for change should fall solely to the white man.) The tragedy does not reside merely in Stephen's lyrically expressed personal crisis, in *his* being "lost out here in the stars." As a story of individual human relations, specifically one that is acted out in the context of a racist society in which the two protagonists are presented as representatives of their respective races, *Lost in the Stars* is a hybrid on several levels, each of which defines as well as qualifies the label "musical tragedy." That is the idiosyncratic challenge of Weill's Broadway experiment: it is epic *and* dramatic, spoken *and* sung, musical *and* opera, didactic *and* entertaining. Mode, medium, genre, aesthetic purpose—all are mixed.

Coda

MIXED GENRES AND THE POSSIBILITIES OF OPERA

In an article titled "Music Written for the Theater: A Summary of the Early Season," which appeared in the *New York Herald Tribune* on 13 November 1949, the composer and music critic Virgil Thomson eschewed the label *musical tragedy.* Instead he described *Lost in the Stars* as "a play with musical numbers, a *singspiel.*" His reason for doing so: "It is not . . . either purely or chiefly a musical narrative." Even though one might take issue with Thomson's assertion that this and Blitzstein's *Regina* are plays in which "music is employed copiously but incidentally," his judgment seems fair enough. He does, after all, concede that "the composer's contribution" is "not quite so incidental" in Weill's case (nor is it in Blitzstein's either). As in his other plays with music, whether "Stücke mit Musik" or "musical plays," Weill's music resists conventional critical distinctions. For this reason, Thomson's alternate German description seems quite apt, given its connotation of works for the theater in which music's role is both substantial and indispensable, not merely "copious."

Yet the fact that the music alternates with spoken dialogue and is not entirely incidental to the drama is not the only reason Thomson's label seems well chosen. Granted, *singspiel* is a term generally applied to operatic works from the German-speaking lands of the late eighteenth century written in the vernacular. Applying this foreign term to a mid-twentieth-century musical performed on Broadway may seem culturally odd as well as anachronistic—a shock effect Thomson presumably intended his remark to have in some measure but one that, on closer inspection, proves to be hardly gratuitous or meaningless. The associations that emerge are several.

Thomson had touched on something that he would soon have occasion to discuss more extensively. Just five months after the above-quoted article, he published an obituary of Kurt Weill (one of the most incisive and insightful of any that appeared), praising not only the composer as "a master of musico-dramatic design" but also *Lost in the Stars* as "a masterpiece of musical application to dramatic narrative" and its score for twelve players as "Weill's finest work of orchestral craft." Again he brought up the connection to the eighteenth century: the "lighter wing [of American musical theater] has lost in Kurt Weill a workman who might have bridged for us the gap, as he did in Germany, between grand opera and the *singspiel.*"[1]

Following Thomson's cue, it can indeed be argued that thinking of *Lost in the Stars* as a latter-day singspiel rather than as a "musical tragedy" is an especially fruitful premise for appreciating Weill's last "play with music" and thereby understanding how it represented for him "the furthest advance in a direction which I laid down for myself in the early years of my life as a composer."

Balancing continuity and change in assessments of Weill's career poses a peculiar challenge. His own self-assessments stressed both of these aspects, drawing attention to his Busonian roots while at the same time "defining a new direction for musical comedy" (an expression he used to describe a rivalry with Richard Rodgers).[2] Whereas the critical literature on Weill, following the lead of critics such as S. L. M. Barlow and Harold Clurman, has been inclined to evaluate Weill's career in terms of a decline in originality and authenticity, Thomson's obituary furnishes a wholly positive example. A much-quoted sentence toward the end conveys how each of Weill's works for the musical theater was sui generis, the product of unceasing innovation: "But his output of new models—every new work was a new model, a new shape, a new solution of dramatic problems—will not continue." And so Thomson concluded: "Music has lost a creative mind and a master's hand."[3] (Compare this eulogistic assessment with the negatively critical verdicts of Barlow and Clurman. In Barlow's judgment [quoted in chapter 1], Weill's earlier music came from "a man almost inflexibly remote from any other style but his own," whereas the American works wholly lacked the European works' "curious individuality." Clurman, in his review of *Lost in the Stars,* went so far as to equate Weill's later music with the "void" manifestations of mass culture.)[4]

According to Thomson's criteria, Weill's innovation and creativity, along with his mastery, are principally reflected in the sheer range of the "solutions" he explored: from one-act operas in German to full-scale dramatic musicals in English; from "epic opera" to prototypes of the so-called concept musical; from plays with music to musical plays; various works with dance, including a "ballet chanté"; several pageants, including a "circus opera"; a number of compositions that draw in different ways on the traditions of operetta; others that expressly serve the needs of amateur musicians; and on and on. Yet throughout his career, and behind all of this remarkable diversity, the singspiel idea offers a crucial point of origin on a number of levels.

In a quite basic way, it manifests itself as an ongoing commitment to the creation of mixed genres between spoken theater and opera written in the vernacular—the conventional understanding of the term. Furthermore, it is the singspiel tradition that serves as the exemplar of a popular, bourgeois form of musical theater born out of a spirit of artistic reform. (It should be noted here that in the late eighteenth century the term *singspiel* could also connote what we would normally classify as opera: Mozart's *Le nozze di Figaro,* for example, a "commedia per musica," as the first published libretto described it, was billed in German at its premiere in 1786 as "ein italienisches Singspiel in 4 Aufzügen." This broader usage is consistent with the word's origin as a literal translation of the Italian *melodramma.*) Yet the principal point of orientation for Weill is not the mixed genre as such or the association of that genre with Enlightenment culture so much as one German-language singspiel in particular, and the best known of them all: Mozart's *Die Zauberflöte.* It is arguably to this work that Weill owed a lifelong debt more extensive and profound than to any other work of the entire operatic repertory.

The Mozart paradigm formed the core of Busoni's teachings, into which Weill immersed himself as a member of Busoni's master class in Berlin in the early 1920s, with particular focus on an aesthetics of opera that his mentor defined negatively in terms of an aversion toward Wagner and positively as boundless, unconditional admiration for Mozart. Although we cannot know exactly what Busoni said about *Die Zauberflöte* to his students, we do know that he used it as a preferred model in his classes. In addition, he had his pupil Weill copy out his two-piano arrangement of the overture, which was performed by two former pupils, Egon Petri and Michael von Zadora, at Berlin's Volksbühne on 10 December 1923; and Busoni's two-hand piano transcription and arrangement of the scene from *Die Zauberflöte* with the "Armed Men" forms the last of his *Fünf kurze Stücke zur Pflege des polyphonen Spiels* (also from 1923).[5]

In his essay "The Possibilities of Opera," a short treatise on the genre that appeared in several of his published writings, Busoni extols *Die Zauberflöte* as "opera *par excellence" (die Oper "schlechtweg")* and expresses his amazement that "in Germany at least it hasn't been established as a signpost for opera." For him it was "the only example" of an opera he could name that "comes closest to the ideal"—an ideal that his manifestolike essay attempts to circumscribe—"uniting instruction and spectacle, solemnity and entertainment, to which a captivating music is added, or rather above which the music hovers and which it holds together." He quotes with approval Goethe's characterization of the libretto as being "full of improbabilities and jest that not everyone knows how to reconcile and appreciate" as well as his exhortation "to concede that its author knew to a high degree the art of using contrast and of creating big theatrical effects." Invoking "the miracle" that the music "draws near," he singles out the "trial of fire and water" and the "two armed guards before the gates of the trial [who] issue their warning in the rhythms of an ancient chorale tune" (the same passage that he transcribed for the last of his *Fünf Stücke*).[6]

Busoni does not mention that the chorale in its entirety (not just the rhythm) dates back to Luther, an omission that seems quite surprising, given that another of Busoni's idols, J. S. Bach, quoted it in two of his cantatas. One of the cantatas is "Ach Gott, vom Himmel sieh' darein" (the words of the Lutheran incipit); the other is "Schau, lieber Gott, wie meine Feind." (In the *Fünf Stücke,* Busoni marks the "Corale," as he calls it in Italian, with an asterisk, merely noting in both German and Italian that it is sung by "The Two Armed Men" in Mozart's opera.) Not only is the chorale tune "ancient"; this whole section of the work is composed in the strict contrapuntal style—the "learned style" or *stile antico,* as it is sometimes called—that becomes quite common in Mozart's later music alongside the more modern "gallant style." In this scene of the opera, even if the Lutheran source as such is not explicit, the "old style" in general and the chorale quotation in particular serve as musical markers. Such markers, as Stephen Rumph has demonstrated with reference to Mozart's music, cannot simply be reduced to topics with fixed meanings; rather, "a topic assumes meaning only within an oppositional context."[7] Here, the strict contrapuntal style combined with the Lutheran tune creates a suggestive mix of order and solemnity, rationality and communal religiosity.

Weill would soon have occasion to write about Mozart's work himself. Of the many operas covered in the previews and reviews he produced as music critic for the weekly journal *Der deutsche Rundfunk,* none received a more enthusiastic and reverential treatment than *Die Zauberflöte.* Echoing his mentor's panegyric, he defends the libretto against the charge that it was "badly chosen," quoting Goethe's defense verbatim: "One needs to be more cultured to recognize the value of this libretto than to deny it." For him, "the enchanting play of princes, gods and mysterious powers" deserves to be interpreted as "an allegory of a deeply religious idea . . . a statement of faith." As he puts it, "The goal of all overcome dangers" is "not money, fame and honor, but admission into a brotherhood of believers, a temple of purity and altruism." Furthermore, he recognizes the "unaffected symbolism" of "the fairytale opera" as "providing the suitable garb for the musical forms," whether the music is "depicting the amusing joys and hardships of love experienced by Papageno" or "conveying with dramatic vigor Pamina's trials."[8]

Mozart's singspiel had an enduring impact on Weill's conception of musical theater, first and foremost as the cornerstone of a philosophy of opera that his teacher promulgated in the master class and that Weill then preached and practiced in his own way. Just as it more closely approximated his teacher's ideal than any other single work, so it can be said to have similarly informed the pupil's conception of the genre, which he described theoretically in terms of an *Urform*. Moreover, in order to elucidate the concept of *Gestus* that he introduced in his essay "On the Gestic Character of Music"—and that would become one of the central tenets of Brecht's theory of epic theater as well—he drew on just two music examples: his own "Alabama Song" from the *Mahagonny-Songspiel* and Tamino's opening aria ("Dies Bildnis ist bezaubernd schön") from *Die Zauberflöte*. And just as he would repeatedly acknowledge his teacher's influence throughout his career, so he continued to cite the example of Mozart generally and *Die Zauberflöte* particularly as prefiguring the kind of popular contemporary theater toward which his own work aspired.

A return to eighteenth-century principles forms a common theme in Weill's programmatic statements. "Opera found in the masterpieces of Mozart," he wrote in 1936, "a new blend of speech and music where the drama justifies its right to existence in spite of the clear predominance of the music. It was the nineteenth century which brought the definite break."[9] In 1937, as he was beginning his career on Broadway, he went even further in defining his model: "Paralleling the subsidized product was a different kind of opera, reared on a far healthier basis as part of the amusement business by entrepreneurs who recognized and tried to satisfy the need of the masses for a music theatre. The artistic value of such operatic works is often underestimated, because they are popular, completely comprehensible, and have a direct effect on the public. Mozart's *Zauberflöte* was written on commission and in collaboration with a commercial theatre impresario; it is an ideal example of the union of popular music and the highest degree of artistic power."[10] And seven years after that, around the time he was working on *One Touch of Venus*, he was even quoted as having said in an interview, "*The Magic Flute*, you know, was the first Broadway musical comedy."[11] In his scribbled notes in response to Clurman he remarked that "Mozart wrote Magic Flute for the 'Broadway' of Vienna of his time."[12]

Insofar as Mozart's work—or rather, Mozart's work mediated through Busoni's tutelage—inspired Weill to invent a whole series of new mixed genres, the debt remained one of creative appropriation. The "signpost for opera," as Busoni called it, pointed in several directions. Far from representing a fixed formula for emulation, the prototype influenced the new genres in different ways and to differing degrees, from the earliest through the last works. Some aspects of that influence are more concrete and hence more obvious than others, of course. The spectrum ranges from almost literal quotation, via veiled allusion and parallels in dramaturgical design, to more general questions of aesthetic purpose and function.

To return to *Lost in the Stars* as an example, the parallels certainly go well beyond the hybrid of opera and spoken theater inferred by the mention of *singspiel* in Thomson's review. One of the key similarities is the mix of high and low, serious and light, a chief cause of consternation for a number of the work's critics. Even at the end of his career, the guiding compositional precedent remained *Die Zauberflöte,* the model par excellence of an opera whose plot as well as its music incorporates the dimensions of serious and light by integrating *seria* and *buffa* elements along with other stylistic markers, such as Baroque counterpoint and Lutheran chorales. Weill's review of 1925 had specifically acknowledged such contrasting elements in Mozart's opera by describing the "dramatic" music of Pamina on the one hand and the "amusing" music of Papageno on the other.

Another, related aspect that invites comparison is the religious one, highlighted by Weill both in his 1925 review of *Die Zauberflöte* and in his 1949 interview with Harry Gilroy about *Lost in the Stars.* For the twenty-five-year-old Weill, Mozart's opera possessed validity as "an allegory of a deeply religious idea . . . a statement of faith." "In general," the 49-year-old Weill is reported to have said in rehearsals for *Lost in the Stars,* "the whole play has a Biblical tone that we hope the public will like." Musically, the common denominator is the chorale. Although the chorale in *Lost in the Stars* is not a literal quotation from Bach, as it is in the Mozart, the chorus "A Bird of Passage" is couched in the style of a four-part hymn. The number's concluding lines were even considered appropriate in their tone and sentiment to serve as the epitaph for Weill's gravestone (fig. 7):

> This is the life of men on earth:
> Out of darkness we come at birth
> Into a lamplit room and then
> Go forward into dark again.[13]

"Thousands of Miles," which concludes *Lost in the Stars* following the chorale, is similarly hymnlike. Overall, Weill's last work is one that aimed as much as any of his, and perhaps more than most, at "uniting instruction and spectacle, solemnity and entertainment," to use Busoni's characterization of the Mozartian ideal. *Love Life* does so, too, in its way. It may be less solemn than its successor, but its combination of "vaudeville" and conceptual "study" arguably derives from a common notion of mutually inclusive opposites. On a thematic level, an analogy to Tamino and Pamina's rite of passage suggests itself at the end of the show when Sam and Susan face their own trial, symbolized by their tightrope walk.

These are just two works that can be cited from an entire oeuvre that reveals Mozartian traits in comparable ways. Other instances of chorales used as cultural markers are not hard to find. Probably best known is the one that concludes *Die Dreigroschenoper,* a work that "gave us the opportunity to make opera the subject matter for an evening in the theater," as Weill claimed.[14] The finale, with

FIGURE 7. Weill's tombstone in the nondenominational Mount Repose Cemetery in Rockland County, New York. The inscription quotes the chorale "Bird of Passage" from his last stage work, *Lost in the Stars* (1949), albeit with an engraving error. The note over *earth* should be a tied A♭, not a G. Photo: Irma Commanday. Courtesy of the Weill-Lenya Research Center, Kurt Weill Foundation for Music, New York.

its artificial happy end, is one such moment, drawing on the conventions of operatic recitative and religious chorale while pursuing an unconventional objective. Earlier in the same scene, the musical gesture of the three chords that punctuate the recitative in which Brown announces the Queen's pardoning of Macheath could be construed as a direct allusion to the ceremonial music with which the overture to *Die Zauberflöte* begins and which recurs with symbolic significance during the rituals in the temple (exx. 77 and 78).

Chorales appear in earlier works, too, for example those in the First Symphony and the String Quartet, opus. 8, which, as Antony Beaumont points out, are not only related to each other but are quite similar to the chorale in *Die Zauberflöte*.[15] Immediately following *Die Dreigroschenoper*, there are, in *Aufstieg und Fall der Stadt Mahagonny* and in *Die Bürgschaft*, male choruses with their own "rhythms of an ancient chorale tune."

The list of such allusions goes on: the quotation of Papageno's aria "Ein Mädchen oder Weibchen" in the song "Zu Potsdam unter den Eichen" that Weill originally included in *Das Berliner Requiem* (a provocatively secular requiem); the near-literal quotations from *Die Zauberflöte* in *Der Silbersee* and that work's bitterly allegorical "Wintermärchen," announced already in its subtitle (i.e., not

EXAMPLE 77. Wolfgang Amadeus Mozart, *Die Zauberflöte,* Overture (opening)

EXAMPLE 78. *Die Dreigroschenoper,* Drittes Dreigroschenfinale (Brown's recitative)

a "Märchenoper").[16] There is also the subversively ironic punning on the word *singspiel* in the title *Mahagonny-Songspiel,* which plays on connotations of the genre that Weill characterized in relation to Mozart's work as "the foundation stone of 'German' opera."[17]

On a more fundamental level, Mozart represents the paradigm of an opera composer whose use of a variety of idioms and registers juxtaposed with one another to meaningful dramatic ends challenges the notion of a unity of style.[18] For all the historical distance between them, a close affinity exists between Mozart's predilection for the "learned style" in his mature works and Weill's shift to what he called "a perfectly strict, thoroughly responsible style" in *Aufstieg und Fall der Stadt Mahagonny, Der Jasager,* and *Die Bürgschaft.* For the composer of musical theater, cultivating such a style is not to be explained merely as an exhibition of handicraft and technical prowess, although it is that, too. Topical appropriateness and significance are decisive.

Style, according to this Mozartian paradigm, is a function of dramaturgy. It plays a pivotal role in the composer's "art of using contrast and of creating big theatrical effects," as Busoni described Mozart's approach to opera in *Die Zauberflöte.* While specific features of Weill's works for the musical theater either derive directly from or can be linked to this particular work in the ways described, its example as a model of "dramaturgical counterpoint" is among its most profound and enduring lessons. Citing Goethe, the same authority on which his teacher drew, Weill made an emphatic point of defending the libretto, whose alleged inconsistencies and rifts have often been declared weaknesses that needed to be explained away in terms of the text's origins in disparate sources. The result is a contamination of genre—in this case, the provocative mix of elements from fairy tale and ritual, comedy and tragedy, *buffa* and *seria*—that lends a remarkable, much-discussed, and variously interpreted richness to the layers of symbolic meaning in Mozart's work.

Weill's own theatrical imagination positively thrives on the possibilities afforded by Mozart's example. Comparable contaminations, which are the rule rather than the exception in his musical theater, begin already with *Der Protagonist,* the precedent-setting first opera (which otherwise has little in common with the singspiel), and continue through *Lost in the Stars.* (The connections between Weill's first stage work proper, the children's ballet *Zaubernacht,* and *Die Zauberflöte* certainly go beyond the "magic" of the titles, the appeal to children being only one of them.) Weill's inclination as an artist to savor the tensions between two distinct cultures or practices has its biographical basis in a defining experience of his whole life: "People like us," he confided to his brother at the age of nineteen, referring to their dual identity as German *and* Jewish, "are caught between two worlds."[19]

The application of "dramaturgical counterpoint" finds its most radical incarnation in *Love Life,* as suggested already. In *Lost in the Stars* the principle still obtains, however, both in how Weill conceives the "musical tragedy" as a singspiel along Mozartian lines and in how he confuses epic and dramatic moments. This latter aspect of the "experiment" creates unusual asymmetries, as discussed, that arose in part from Weill and Anderson's attempt to adapt Paton's novel to preexisting musico-dramatic material, in part from the need to accommodate specific production contingencies.

Yet the most controversial feature of *Lost in the Stars* that finds a precedent in Mozart is its ending. In their revision of the novel, Weill and Anderson turned Paton's note of muted, theologically grounded faith in the future into a symbolic overcoming of social differences. Like *Die Zauberflöte, Lost in the Stars* represents a commitment to a sense of "common humanity" which, as Weill stated, "everyone should learn."[20] No less than all the musical influences, this idealistic trait comprises another essential link between Weill's musical theater and the Mozartian model, at least as Weill conceived of it.

In his appreciation of Mozart's work as the embodiment of an operatic ideal, Weill may have appeared to concur for once with Theodor W. Adorno, his erstwhile friend who had lent qualified support to earlier works of his, notably *Die Dreigroschenoper* and *Aufstieg und Fall der Stadt Mahagonny,* but who would eventually become one of his sternest critics. In the article "On the Fetish Character of Music and the Regression of Listening," written in 1938, when Weill was busy working on *Knickerbocker Holiday*, Adorno singled out *Die Zauberflöte* as an opera "in which the utopia of human emancipation and the enjoyment afforded by a *singspiel* couplet exactly coincide." But how differently the two of them viewed the contemporary relevance of that ideal! Unlike Weill, Adorno saw that coincidence as a unique occurrence or "a moment by itself," for "after *Die Zauberflöte* serious and light music did not allow themselves to be forced together again."[21] Therein lies the fundamental difference in their respective aesthetic positions.

For the critical theorist Adorno, who subscribed to a negative dialectics of cultural history straddling the disciplines of philosophy and sociology, and for whom popular music functioned in modern society as a capitalist commodity and hence primarily as a tool at the service of the cultural industry, the world of *Die Zauberflöte* represented an almost Edenic condition, a state of affairs never to return on this earth. His utopia was backward-, not forward-looking. According to this gloomy and pessimistic worldview, subsequent history delineated a process of decline, an ineluctable fall from grace that brought with it an increasing and irreparable schism between "high" and "low."

Weill may have paid homage to the same historical prototype as Adorno—after all, they shared common roots as middle-class German Jews from the same era with similar educational backgrounds—but his outlook was generally more optimistic, and also more cosmopolitan. For him, "high" and "low" or "serious" and "light" were not mutually exclusive. Nor did he consider art that attempted to embrace a utopia of human emancipation as something that was incompatible with entertainment. Nor, indeed, did that entertainment preclude popular strophic songs. If Weill's works teach us about "the common property of all music theater," as Daniel Albright remarked, it is because they draw freely on the example of many composers, not just one, as the foregoing chapters have shown.[22]

Mozart's work was not his sole source of inspiration. It was demonstrably the principal source, however. A product of Enlightenment culture, the singspiel still contained valid lessons to be absorbed by composer and audience alike. For the émigré musician who remained committed to the reform of musical theater in his adopted homeland, it represented neither an impasse nor an aporia, but a viable set of possibilities.

STAGES OF RECEPTION

After the premiere production's respectable run of 252 performances, *Love Life* effectively disappeared from the theater for almost four decades until its revival at the University of Michigan in 1987. Three further productions have been mounted during the past two decades, none of them at major professional venues.[23] Among the factors that impeded the work's transmission and kept *Love Life* out of public view for so long were two industrial strikes at the time of the premiere. The first was a nearly yearlong strike known as the second "Petrillo Ban," named after James Caesar Petrillo, president of the American Federation of Musicians, which prevented a cast album from being recorded; meanwhile, an ASCAP embargo precluded any of the songs, eight of which had been published as sheet music, from being performed on the radio during much of the work's run. Neither the book nor the score was published or even available as rental material. Yet another obstacle was Lerner's opposition to the show's being revived because of the well-publicized vicissitudes of his own love life (he married eight times). He allegedly quipped to his associate and friend Miles Kreuger that he had "turned into everything he satirized in that show."[24] Not that the work was without influence on subsequent developments—quite the contrary; but the vagaries of reception history would not allow the connection to be appreciated for quite some time.

Lost in the Stars did not encounter the same immediate obstacles as *Love Life.* Its titular song was already well known from earlier recordings; a cast album appeared under the composer's supervision; and both the book and piano-vocal score were published. As for the premiere production itself, its run of performances in New York, twenty-nine more than *Love Life,* was extended by a road tour that took the show to California and the Midwest. Negative notices in Chicago brought the premiere's extension to a premature end, however, and the performances planned for several cities on the East Coast had to be canceled. The work waited until 1958 for its first major revival, at New York's City Opera, and until 1972 for the second Broadway production, this time closing after only thirty-nine performances of the radically altered score.[25] In addition, there were a handful of performances in Germany in the early 1960s, as indicated above. These came after the production of another of Weill's stage works from his American years, *Street Scene,* which had taken place in Düsseldorf in 1955 to a mixed reception. While most of the professional music critics voiced reservations about Weill's American opera, many of them nonetheless reported that the audience response had been favorable, even enthusiastic.

Critics in Germany, perhaps more than anywhere, were inclined to discredit Weill's American works as historically and aesthetically negligible, at the same time as they were rediscovering and rehabilitating the earlier music in the wake of its vilification and suppression during the Nazi period. The larger context for the German revival was the process known as "overcoming the past" *(Vergangenheitsbewältigung),* a coming-to-terms with a political and cultural history that had forced German artists such as Weill into exile. Similarly motivated was the somewhat later flourishing of scholarship known as "exile studies" *(Exilforschung),* leading to publications such as the book *Musik im Exil,* which placed questions concerning the cultural identity of German émigré artists at the forefront of an interdisciplinary discourse.

Two works above all acquired a central role in the early stages of this posthumous reception history of Weill's music. The undisputed centerpiece of the Weill renaissance, *Die Dreigroschenoper,* attracted recordings on both sides of the Atlantic, in Marc Blitzstein's translation in 1954 and the original German in 1958. Lotte Lenya, who starred in the 1928 premiere and the off-Broadway revival, sang the role of Jenny for both recordings. In 1956, the Philips and Columbia record labels issued the first complete recording of *Aufstieg und Fall der Stadt Mahagonny,* again featuring Lenya.

When Dahlhaus wrote in reaction to the Stuttgart performance of *Lost in the Stars* that "the composer of Mahagonny" had "degenerated into a technician of the music industry," he was doubtless prompted to make the comparison because of recent exposure to the earlier opera. He was also transmitting an image of the composer that had become de rigueur in European intellectual circles. Adorno's obituary along with other writings of his played a significant role in shaping that image, of course, as did the cultural politics of postwar Germany more broadly.

For the production of *Street Scene* in Düsseldorf, Adorno contributed an essay to the program booklet that omitted any mention of the work whatsoever and instead used the occasion to rehearse the blanket criticisms contained in the obituary written five years earlier. As before, he described the composer as a *Musikregisseur* and defined the creative type negatively as one that "defied the concept of composer." Weill, he opined, would "rather sacrifice musical standards than the immediate context for which his artistic response was tailored like that of Offenbach."[26] His discussion dwelled for the most part on the 1920s, especially on the feelings of nostalgia for that era that Weill's music readily conjured up.

The essay clearly left its mark on how the production was received, to judge from the notices that appeared in various newspapers. After reading the opinion of such a prominent voice in German cultural life, the critics, to quote Wolfgang Jansen's analysis of the reviews, "could no longer express an unbiased positive view without the risk of appearing to their colleagues as philistines and clueless bunglers."[27] One of the rare exceptions was Horst Koegler, a dance critic quite familiar with Broadway repertory in general and Weill's American works in particular. In a spirited diatribe against Adorno's critique, which in turn elicited a published reply from Adorno in defense of the musical avant-garde, Koegler portrayed the critical reaction to *Street Scene* as a "first-class opera burial."[28]

Both halves of the politically divided nation were confronting questions about their own musical heritage, often providing quite different answers based on diverging political interests. In what respect could the work of émigré artists be construed as German culture? In what ways could it be distinguished from the German culture promoted under the name of National Socialism? If Adorno served as the *spiritus rector* of Weill reception in the West, in the East it was Brecht and his disciples. Both sides tended to disparage the Broadway music, if they did not ignore it entirely, owing to its putative subservience to American commercial values. Where the one side found it wanting by applying the criteria of high German modernism, the other did so more in terms of politics and ideological engagement.

Fritz Hennenberg, a Brecht specialist from the German Democratic Republic, conveyed a persistent and commonly held view when he described Weill's career pejoratively in terms of a trajectory of "turning away" from association with and sympathy for "communist activities" and "seizing the commercial opportunities of Broadway": "This went hand in hand with his music giving up its critical aggressiveness. His view of political connections became obstructed, and (unlike Brecht, who knew how to draw distinctions) he developed a hatred of all things German *[das Deutsche an sich]*. He became intent on assimilating himself as quickly and seamlessly as possible, avoided writing and speaking German, and protested vociferously when *Life* magazine called him a 'German composer.'"[29]

Summaries such as this one—Hennenberg included it in a study of the Brecht-Weill partnership that he submitted as part of his second doctorate *(Habilitationsschrift)* to Humboldt University just two years before the fall of the Berlin Wall—represent a polarizing caricature. Despite his association with Brecht, Weill was never a communist, much less affiliated with the Communist Party. Although his works produced on Broadway relied on financial support from individual backers, they often lost money rather than amounting to sound business investments. Circumstances required him to conduct business affairs in English, it is true, and he and Lenya eventually corresponded mainly in English, but he continued to write and speak German whenever he needed to. And although he surely felt an antipathy toward the German culture that had driven him into exile, as he made clear in his letter to *Life* magazine, and although his assimilation as a composer in the United States was as rapid as it was successful, it is also a willful distortion to suggest that his embrace of American culture entailed hating "all things German."[30]

Shaping such points of view was not only a superficial grasp of Weill's non-German works, in part stemming from a politicized reading of the German ones, but also an anti-Americanism that was part and parcel of Cold War propaganda. The separation of East and West Germany was impossible to ignore, not least because of the existence of the Wall from 1961 through 1989. Yet in matters of aesthetic ideology the divide would prove less clear-cut. Positing two quite separate reception histories, one in each half of the two Germanys, is complicated by the fact that a number of musicologists and critics, especially those who came out of the West German student movement in the late 1960s and early 1970s, several of them pupils of Dahlhaus, disavowed Adorno's negative dialectics in favor of a position somewhat closer to the more orthodox Marxist one of Brecht and his disciples.[31]

Against this general background of postwar Weill reception, the most immediate sources influencing the terms of Dahlhaus's comparison were two related events in the West German city of Darmstadt: the performance of the *Mahagonny* opera given as part of the Darmstadt International Summer Course for New Music in 1959 (a production that received its premiere at the city's Landestheater in 1957) and, eight months later and with the active participation of the composer's widow, the "Kurt-Weill-Memorial" organized by the Kranichstein Institute for Music on the occasion of the sixtieth anniversary of Weill's birth and the tenth anniversary of his death. The memorial featured a recital by "Lotte Lenya-Weill," as the program lists her, with a preceding lecture by the composer Hans Ulrich Engelmann, who also provided piano accompaniment for the songs. Selected from Weill's German period, the songs were all to texts by Brecht: "Bilbao-Song," "Ballade vom ertrunkenen Mädchen," "Havanna-Lied," and "Seeräuber-Jenny."

The memorial became itself memorialized when Engelmann's lecture appeared in print later that year as "Kurt Weill—Today" in the third volume of the *Darmstädter Beiträge zur neuen Musik* (1960), coming after articles by Stockhausen ("Music and Graphics"), Ligeti ("On Harmony in Webern's First Cantata"), Edgard Varèse ("Memories and Thoughts"), and Werner Meyer-Eppler ("On Systems of Electronic Sound Transformation"). The juxtaposition is revealing: Weill is very clearly the odd man out. The published text itself, moreover, warrants scrutiny as a key document of West German Weill reception in the early postwar period. None reflects more clearly and succinctly what might be called the "cultural imperatives" of the moment.

Engelmann, who counted Adorno and Horkheimer among his former teachers, was a composition pupil of Wolfgang Fortner. Fortner and Adorno regularly taught at the Darmstadt Summer School. Both would have read the *Darmstädter Beiträge,* if not attended Engelmann's actual lecture. Dahlhaus attended those summer courses, too. In addition, as a musicologist and critic with an active interest in West Germany's musical avant-garde, he not only followed the journal but, like Adorno, also contributed to it.

With the sensibilities of his potential audience evidently in mind, Engelmann begins his text on a note of apprehension by pointing out "the attraction and difficulty of talking about Weill's musical work for a young composer nowadays." The attraction, he says, is for those "peculiarly drawn to the colorful world of musical theater"; the difficulty presents itself to those "to whom music appears hallowed only in its autonomous purity." Invoking the language of his philosophy teachers, he describes such purity as music's "truth"—a truth that "in the final analysis nonetheless pays tribute to the essence of aesthetic appearances *[Schein].*" Hence Engelmann's (and his generation's) dilemma. While acknowledging the Weimar

Republic as "uncommonly stimulating and fruitful for new art," he admits a difficulty in interpreting Weill's legacy, namely "the situation of the development of today's modern music, whose method of composition is developing in exactly the opposite direction from that of the 1920s." Thus while recognizing the historical achievements of the earlier era, Engelmann is invoking a spirit of the age that has rendered those achievements "antiquated and superseded."[32]

In both cases, however, Engelmann draws on the music of Schoenberg and the Second Viennese School for historiographical orientation. Whereas the 1920s considered this music "an endpoint . . . a superseded extension of romanticism," in Engelmann's apt phrase, the postwar period reengaged with it. "Precisely in 1945," he writes, "it occurred to history to reconnect [with that era], and the evolution of new music took a diametrically opposed path to the aesthetic *Zeitgeist* of the 1920s, to whom the New Objectivity had been the egg of Columbus" (88).

Note the agency to which Engelmann ascribes this sudden aesthetic shift. He is appealing to "history," in the impersonal, Hegelian singular. Only toward the end of the piece, in a brief remark and quite euphemistically, does he allude to any actual historical reason for his periodization. After quoting the opening words of the "Berlin im Licht-Song," he states that "the breezy, popular Berlin song tells us more about a genuine *[echte]* bond with a German city than all disingenuously mawkish sentiment about the homeland. In 1933 these lights of Berlin went out one by one, until it had become truly dark there and in the whole of Germany. Weill had escaped to America" (94).

Engelmann thus reclaims Weill's "song style" as authentically German, albeit as the product of an age whose time has come and gone. According to this interpretation, Weill's music is at once relevant and irrelevant, an ambiguity nicely captured by Engelmann's describing it as "a living document," at the same time as he voices deep concern that his interpretation may not—indeed, cannot—be shared by all. He reports that the recent production of *Mahagonny* was an "ostentatious success" with the Darmstadt audience, yet he also claims that most people were unable to grasp the work's parodic qualities, instead taking it in merely as "an entertaining undertaking, leaving all ideology behind" (89). The thrust of his argument is familiar from the interpretation proposed in 1928, when Adorno asserted that audiences who flocked to see *Die Dreigroschenoper* for the most part failed to grasp the piece's subversive import. "It's not the socially critical relevance," Engelmann writes, "that still generates its immense success, but its theatrical vigor and the popularity of its hit tunes and songs" (92). In drawing a direct comparison with Offenbach as a popular composer whose music similarly risked being enjoyed uncritically and hence "misunderstood," Engelmann is recalling an affinity that Adorno had suggested both in the obituary and the Düsseldorf essay.[33] It should be remembered that Adorno believed the model of Offenbach "wasn't repeatable." As he put it in the obituary, "The grimness of reality" had become "too overwhelming for a parody to measure up to it."[34] Engelmann appears to be making an analogous point about the place of Weill's prewar music in postwar Germany.

Engelmann's analysis of Weill reception thus relies on a sharp distinction being drawn between the general audience and the "radical-critical circle," to use his own label. The former group, according to him, failed to grasp the point of the opera's musical language or *Gestus,* as he calls it with explicit reference to Weill's writings. Only the exclusive group of initiates was capable of appreciating the work's cultural significance as a "living document," one that documents a piece of socially critical art. (As an aside, and by way of illustrating how differently Weill's prewar music was remembered across the channel in postwar England, it is worth recalling a passage from Nancy Mitford's 1945 novel *The Pursuit of Love.* There the aesthete and modernist Lord Merlin—Mitford's affectionate literary portrait of the real Lord Berners—invites his neighbors "to attend such puzzlers as Cocteau plays, the opera 'Mahagonny,' or the latest Dada extravagances from Paris.")[35]

The remainder of Engelmann's talk supplies an outline of Weill's career, focusing on the music prior to 1933 and quoting further excerpts from various of Weill's own writings. (Lenya may well have shared some of this information with Engelmann, especially the more obscure sources.) Only at the end, in the final paragraph, does the author touch on the second half of Weill's career, seemingly as an afterthought, which permits little more than a recital of "a series of American stage works" resulting from what he prosaically describes as "diligent work" (94).

The conclusion is as guarded and equivocal as the opening. Although he acknowledges Weill's role as having "shown the legitimate and qualitative way" as a composer of musical plays for Broadway, he feels obliged to assert without further analysis that "not all these works possess the musical substance of *Dreigroschenoper* or *Mahagonny*" (94–5). What he means by "musical substance" is left unclear; it needs to be considered in light of the initial comments about "the colorful world of musical theater" and the lack of autonomous purity. Besides, even if he does allow that at least *some* of the American works possess such substance, it is not germane to the principal point of his talk, which is to redeem the Weimar works by insisting on their significance at the time of their composition in terms of political ideology. This more than anything is the yardstick that lends works such as *Die Dreigroschenoper* and *Mahagonny* their value and significance as Engelmann's historical documents, though it also renders them incommensurable with any of the American works.

Hellmut Kotschenreuther emphasizes this very point at the end of his book *Kurt Weill,* the first monograph on the composer in any language, which was published in West Berlin in 1962. (Kotschenreuther worked for years as a music critic of the Berlin daily newspaper *Der Tagesspiegel.*) The relative amount of space accorded the different stages of Weill's career by Kotschenreuther's 103-page study corresponds almost exactly to that of Engelmann's eight-page essay. After stating at the outset that *Die Dreigroschenoper* "stands at the center of Weill's work" and represents "as it were the key to understanding Weill's work,"[36] Kotschenreuther focuses the majority of his attention in a central chapter of some fifty-four pages on Weill as "composer of epic theater." The chapter titled "The Creator of Modern Musical Theater," which deals with the fifteen years of the American period, contains a mere fourteen pages, followed by a brief epilogue in which the author arrives at the following conclusion: "The criticism directed at some of the works from Weill's American period is justified insofar as Weill may lay claim to being judged by the criteria that he himself established in his central works. Sweeping commendation would do him an injustice by reducing *Die Dreigroschenoper* to the level of *Johnny Johnson.* In other words, whoever accepts *Johnny Johnson* also forfeits the right to accept *Die Dreigroschenoper, Aufstieg und Fall der Stadt Mahagonny,* and *Die sieben Todsünden*" (92).

Like Engelmann, Kotschenreuther feels drawn to the Weill-Brecht works principally because of what he sees as their social criticism. But is that a criterion inherent in the works themselves or an interpretive perspective brought to them by the critic or theater director? "Properly staged," Kotschenreuther concludes in a paragraph addressing performance practice, "the socially critical works of Brecht and Weill still reveal their provocative power wherever oppressors oppress, exploiters exploit, and terrorists terrorize. What Brecht and Weill said will no longer need to be said only when a social order exists without injustice. Until that time the works of Brecht and Weill remain what they were and are: an admonition, a warning, and an artistically shaped negative example" (94).

The interpretation of *Die Dreigroschenoper* as conveying an unheeded warning of impending political "darkness," to borrow Engelmann's metaphor for National Socialism, became commonplace after 1945, decisively shaping postwar reception on either side of the Iron Curtain. To recall the obituary written in 1950 by author and theater director Karl Lustig-Prean quoted earlier: "Weill had recognized these brown portents well in advance and alerted us to them."[37] It might be tempting to discount this consummation of the work's symbolic content as merely a form of nostalgic projection—though it is doubtless that too, as Adorno's Düsseldorf essay suggested. The socially critical interpretation can also be understood, however, as belonging to the vexed process of atonement for the atrocities of the immediate past, a broader effort to reclaim the work of exiled German-Jewish composers whose reputations had been ignominiously defamed. Several German critics heralded the production of *Street Scene* in 1955 as Weill's "Come-back," using the original English word (i.e., the *Fremdwort*).[38] The irony is that their reviews betrayed their predilection for Weill to return not as a composer of American operas but as the German Weill of old as they now remembered him.

It is in the cultural and intellectual milieu that nurtured accounts such as Engelmann's and Kotschenreuther's that in 1957 the Englishman David Drew, just twenty-seven at the time, received a commission from the Academy of Arts in West Berlin to prepare a catalogue of Weill's *Nachlass.* The catalogue was to appear in the same series as that of the Schoenberg manuscripts in Los Angeles, which was being prepared by Josef Rufer. The time taken by each of the two scholars to publish their respective catalogues is indicative of the very different states in which the oeuvres of the two composers were preserved at the time of the commission. Rufer was able to prepare his catalogue in short order and have it published in 1959. Drew, however, faced a far more daunting task, and it was not until 1987, a full three decades after receiving the commission, that he published *Kurt Weill: A Handbook.*

In the handbook's Introduction, subtitled "Report to the Academy of Arts, West Berlin," Drew accounts for the delay by pointing out how "profoundly different" Weill was not only from Schoenberg, but also from Brecht. Both Schoenberg and Brecht, he writes, "in the course of their circuitous emigrations, had clung tenaciously to whatever manuscripts they could save, as if every line bore witness to the integrity of their work" (DDH, 9). Both, in other words, projected an inner-directed image. Schoenberg, above all, had taken meticulous care archiving his legacy in its entirety as well as providing interpretive commentary on the organic evolution and historical importance of his work. Brecht had overseen the publication of his collected works, beginning with the *Versuche* in the early 1930s, which had the effect of unifying his oeuvre. (The *Versuche* series, as with all subsequent Brecht editions, contained revised "literary" versions of the stage works, not originals.) Not so Weill, the traces of whose career had first to be painstakingly uncovered and reconstructed before the catalogue could be compiled and submitted. "To design his own monuments and pave the way for future processions of researchers and biographers," Drew observes, "was wholly foreign to his nature" (9). In that sense, at least, Weill did indeed care very little about posterity.

Darmstadt definitely played a role for Drew in his formation as a scholar and critic, but its significance became equivocal. While attending Cambridge University as a student in the early 1950s, he had deepened his burgeoning interest in contemporary music by attending the International Summer Courses. But by 1954, as he explains in the introduction, he "found it harder than ever to reconcile the school's dogmatic objections to much that Schoenberg and all that Stravinsky had achieved after the early 1920s with what I heard and was moved by in both composers, throughout their work, irrespective of date, style, or method" (5). It was two years later, after a trip to the festival of contemporary music in

Venice, that he decided to write a book about Weill, "a composer at the furthest conceivable remove from the ethos and preoccupations of Darmstadt" (6). One of the consequences of his decision was that he contacted and eventually met Lotte Lenya, who, together with her husband, George Davis, would lend him encouragement and support as an ally in the Weill renaissance, which she and Davis were doing so much to define and promote.

Drew's letter of introduction, dated 3 November 1956, nicely captures the historiographical and aesthetic framework within which he wished to cast the proposed project: "What I would like to try to do is to demonstrate, on purely musical grounds, the reasons why I feel Kurt Weill to be one of the very few genuinely original composers of our day, and a composer who should, moreover, take a place in the general hierarchy of music that is at least equal to the position occupied by, say, Hugo Wolf." At the same time, he wanted to set his "purely musical" analysis "against a detailed consideration of the musical, artistic, social and political life of Germany in the inter-war-years." He did not intend to "cover 'The Broadway Years' in quite the same way," but he still planned to "devote quite a lot of space to it."[39]

Writing as someone who had still been at school during the war—as "a member of the younger generation," as he describes himself—Drew confesses to Lenya that he still "feels extraordinarily close . . . to it all." He shares with her the foreboding he had sensed as a schoolboy "that Europe was about to be involved in a major catastrophe" and how this, in turn, created in him a feeling of "complete, and at times frightening, sympathy with Kurt Weill's music." As a result, he finds it "so easy to involve myself in the hopes and doubts underlying the music that I can hardly persuade myself that I did not grow up with it."

As for the commission for the catalogue, which he received the following year, Drew describes in the *Handbook* (8) being approached by the academy's vice president, Boris Blacher, a composer who had survived the war in "inner emigration," as Drew refers to it, using a term from exile studies that describes the disposition of those who, although they did not leave Germany, remained ideologically and spiritually detached from Nazi culture. Blacher expressed "gratitude" toward Weill and appreciated what the latter's "path had signified to him and to some of his fellow composers amid the darkness of the Third Reich"; there was, Drew notes, an "intensity" and "urgency" to how Blacher remembered "the subversive liberties and illegal escapes" of inner emigration that Weill's example had made possible.

The fond recollection of Weill's banned music lending countercultural inspiration during Nazi rule played a role in Blacher's commissioning of the catalogue, as Drew recalls. It also resonated with Drew's own identification with Weill's music and its connection to the European "catastrophe"; in this way, it was one of several defining factors for the Englishman to consider, not all of them "purely musical," as he sought to determine the composer's "place in the general hierarchy of music." Comparisons to Schoenberg and other masters, great and not so great, would continue to absorb his interest (his Weill entry for *The New Grove Dictionary* replaced Hugo Wolf with Carl Maria von Weber), as did weighing the competing aesthetic dogmas of Adorno, Brecht, and others. These were all vital issues confronting him in the European context as he began his own multifaceted championing of the composer's music, something that would preoccupy him for the next half century. In light of Blacher's commission and in view of Drew's own testimony to Lenya, it is quite easy to appreciate how preserving an image of the music written *during* the Weimar years was a more immediate concern than coming to terms with the music composed *after* Weill left Germany.

The catalogue and the life and works were just two of the many projects that Drew undertook in conjunction with diverse professional activities in the world of twentieth-century music, including criticism, editing, publishing, and record producing. The catalogue, which contains individual entries on Weill's entire oeuvre, did not materialize for thirty years, as mentioned, and the life and works, which went through countless revisions, remained unpublished at his death in 2009. The first major scholarly projects to appear in print were two paperback volumes published together in West Germany by Suhrkamp Verlag in 1975. One of them is a selection of Weill's writings, the *Ausgewählte Schriften*. The companion volume, a collection of writings about Weill entitled *Über Kurt Weill*, is of particular relevance here in that it constitutes the first substantial conspectus of reception history.

Über Kurt Weill divides the bulk of its contents into four sections delineating stylistic-cum-biographical periods: 1920–27, 1928–33, 1933–39, and 1940–50. Yet almost half of the collection's 179 pages are dedicated to the second period, twenty-five to the first, seventeen to the third, and a mere ten to the fourth (and longest) period—approximately the same proportions are found in Engelmann's and Kotschenreuther's texts. The emphasis on the second period no doubt reflects Drew's own priorities and values at the time, as reinforced by his substantial foreword, the English original of which appeared in the *Times Literary Supplement* under the title "Kurt Weill and His Critics."[40] Moreover, and perhaps not surprisingly, five of the fifty-one items included in the anthology are by Adorno, the most prominent and also the most influential critical voice in Drew's essay. "It would be folly," Drew states, "to conclude that Adorno's contributions to the pre-war Weill literature are of anything less than commanding importance."[41] (By extension, one might say the same about Adorno's writings in the immediate postwar period as well.) Of the other authors represented by more than one piece, all are German. The critic Oskar Bie has three, while philosopher Ernst Bloch and the German critics Heinrich Strobel and Paul Bekker each have two.

Drew's choice of opening and closing pieces further supports the centrality of middle-period Weill. In his obituary, included as the anthology's first item, the French pianist and composer Jean Wiener claims well-nigh total ignorance of the American works, relying chiefly on the songs of *Die Dreigroschenoper* for his rhapsodic assessment. "I do not know enough of Kurt Weill's work since he settled in the United States," Wiener writes. "I have heard from Milhaud [a former fellow student of Wiener's and close friend of Weill's] that he has written much and achieved terrific success. Hence I cannot say anything about it" (2). Similarly, Ian Kemp's essay on Weill's harmony, translated from the original English and included as an appendix, focuses its analytic gaze exclusively on Weill's music from the second period. There, Kemp concludes, "we may find a logic and a sense of growth which at once proclaims his kinship with the main German tradition, and his special role of reasserting the primacy of the closed musical form in the wake of the Wagnerian and the Schoenbergian revolutions."[42]

Based on judgments such as these that define Weill's second-period style in terms of an organic evolution out of mainstream German traditions but also with specific reference to Schoenberg's more "revolutionary" achievements, Drew makes his case for a "central style" in Weill's music, a style "defined . . . by the very bone structure . . . voice-leading and the interrelation of timbre and tempo, and so on," and for seeing his subsequent development not only as an aberration but as something "unique in the history of significant composition," as discussed in the opening chapter. "This has nothing to do with normal evolutionary processes," Drew explained to Hans Curjel in a letter from 1969; "it is . . . a psychological and indeed historical phenomenon for which there is no parallel in music. It means that in Weill we have not one, but two composers. The first and important one can and should be evaluated without reference to the second."[43] Drew concludes his foreword by recasting Adorno's dialectical opposition between Schoenberg and Stravinsky in the *Philosophie der neuen Musik* as one between Schoenberg and Weill: "Linked by their irreconcilable differences no less than by their secret affinities, they are the two hostile consciences of modern music: the anguished father and the disinherited son" (1200).

Drew's restatement of the "two Weills" construct in *The New Grove Dictionary of Music and Musicians* (1980) marked the culmination of the first thirty years of posthumous reception history. Not only did the dictionary entry reaffirm Weill's unique status as "perhaps the only [notable artist] to have done away with his old creative self in order to make way for a new one," but its positioning of Weill as "one of music's great 'might-have-beens'" claimed his place in the hierarchy of composers in terms of unrealized potential as much as actual achievement.

One might counter that calling Weill's case "unique" derives more from perceptions of the "divided world" that Weill inhabited than from "purely musical" considerations. It is a judgment call informed by an unparalleled set of cultural and historical circumstances. Reception, after all, is always a matter of selection. In making sense of a composer's work, critics, audiences, and the composers themselves are necessarily partial in their focus. It follows that reception history—the process whereby artists influence other artists and acquire a reputation among audiences, critics, and scholars, and how that influence and reputation change over time—challenges us to account for such selective views. One era's preferences become another's myths, topics that are subject to critical interrogation.

Partial views are therefore partial in two respects: first, they tend to be predicated on just a part of a composer's oeuvre. In that sense, Weill is not entirely unusual, though he is certainly an extreme case. And second, such views invariably reflect values whose significance shifts over time. Reception generates a gallery of mutable images, and the documents of its history invite interpretation in terms of a sequence of synecdoches: rhetorical figures that take a part for the whole. The "two Weills" theory is not only partial in its construal of Weill's identity as a composer; it also quite consciously rejects the part that doesn't fit, as Drew's letter to Curjel makes quite clear, "evaluating" the one Weill "without reference to the second." And if the image of a "might-have-been" composer similarly qualifies as such a rhetorical figure, it stands for a part of the composer's legacy that never existed. It is pure construction, based on an imagined creative response to a quite different set of historical circumstances.

The values informing earlier interpretations such as these might easily be discounted or qualified as aesthetic prejudices. Yet the resulting judgments cannot, or at least should not, be dismissed as merely arbitrary or avoidable. Rather, they are the grounds upon which a particular generation of critics and scholars came to terms with Weill's music in the ways described. The interpretive act is necessarily interactive. Different groups and generations of listeners and critics bring into play their own terms of reception, or "horizon of expectations" ("Erwartungshorizont") as this variable is called in the reception aesthetics pioneered by Hans Robert Jauss.[44]

The "German" Weill as he was understood during this postwar stage of reception is no more an inherently false image than, say, the "heroic" Beethoven. Each is the result of a particular kind of exclusivity that precludes taking account of other parts of their respective oeuvres—the "non-German" in Weill's case, the "non-heroic" in Beethoven's. The image of Beethoven as the "heroic" composer along with musical values that attach to it privileges the middle-period works over the late, the instrumental music over the vocal, the odd-numbered symphonies over the even, and so on.

Yet the image has also been called into question, especially in the latter part of the twentieth century, with increased attention paid to the private, more introspective, and more "modern" qualities of Beethoven's late music. Something analogous occurred with Weill, although for diametrically different reasons. For the first few decades after his death, the "German" Weill held sway in the critical reception of his music as a whole to the detriment of the later works, which were neglected not because of their difficulty and complexity, as with late Beethoven, but because of their avowed accessibility. Only relatively recently have the later works begun to receive their critical due as part of an overall shift from an exclusive to a more inclusive reception.

Increasing historical distance no doubt promotes "understanding life backwards," in Kierkegaard's trenchant phrase. Threads of tradition and continuity may emerge where previously the impression of change and discontinuity predominated. If the sixtieth-anniversary celebrations in Darmstadt epitomized the first, exclusive stage of posthumous reception—reflective of a Cold War culture that, for better and for worse, sought to define Weill's place in music history in relation to German modernism—numerous events and publications, perhaps not surprisingly, could be singled out as doing something analogous for the remainder of the century until the present. Likely candidates for this second, inclusive stage would be any of the centenary celebrations that occurred around the world in 2000, offering wide-ranging retrospectives of Weill's career. Audiences in London, for example, were able to hear the first European performance of *The Firebrand of Florence* alongside the first British performance of *Royal Palace* and a new English version of *Der Kuhhandel* (translated as *Arms and the Cow),* in addition to many other works in a variety of genres.

Heading the list of scholarly publications that epitomize this shift is Kim Kowalke's seminal essay "Kurt Weill, Modernism, and Popular Culture," published in 1995, which discusses the composer's cultivation of popular forms of musical theater against the backdrop of modernist resistance to it. With its German subtitle, "Öffentlichkeit als Stil" (Public Accessibility as Style), the essay at once references and inverts the title Adorno gave to one of the sections dealing with Schoenberg in his *Philosophie der neuen Musik,* namely "Einsamkeit als Stil" (Loneliness as Style).

Belonging on that same list is bruce mcclung's "From Myth to Monograph," a comprehensive review of scholarship that subjects to scrutiny "Weill's disputed reception history."[45] The "myths" that mcclung identifies concern four principal areas: the significance attached to Brecht in understanding Weill's development as a composer; the role played by singing actors (Lenya in particular) in the music's conception; the connection, or lack thereof, between Weill's European and American works; and the extent to which Weill adopted the forms and idioms of American popular music. mcclung's review, published in the centenary year, amounts to a plea for the qualities it so amply exemplifies itself: a more informed and nuanced understanding in all of these areas.

Reception is not just critical or scholarly evaluation, of course, but also creative appropriation—a fact demonstrated with both poignancy and wit at the celebration that took place at Tanglewood to mark Leonard Bernstein's seventieth birthday in 1988. As a birthday offering and tribute to his friend and former collaborator, Stephen Sondheim refunctioned "The Saga of Jenny" from *Lady in the Dark*, changing just a single letter in the title and substituting a mischievously entertaining new text in order to present "The Saga of Lenny." The singer was Lauren Bacall.

Sondheim could not claim to be the first author of a contrafactum based on a famous Weill tune. That distinction is more likely to go to Erich Kästner, who in 1930 created a biting parody of "Surabaya-Johnny" from *Happy End* (titled "Surabaya-Johnny II, freely after Kipling and Brecht"), in which he mocked Brecht's notorious "fundamental laxity in matters of intellectual property," as Brecht himself had called it. To quote part of the first refrain:

Das war gemein, Johnny.
Ich fiel drauf rein, Johnny.
Du hast gelogen, Johnny, du bist nicht echt.
Du bist nicht gereist, Johnny.
Du bist nicht von Kipling, Johnny.
Nimm die Pfeife raus. Du bist von Brecht.[46]

(That was mean, Johnny.
I was taken in, Johnny.
You lied, Johnny, you're not *echt*.
You didn't travel, Johnny.
You're not by Kipling, Johnny.
Take the pipe out. You're by Brecht.)

For all the similarities between the two parodies, Sondheim's barbs are quite different from Kästner's. Here's the relevant refrain from "The Saga of Lenny":

Poor Lenny,
Ten gifts too many,
The curse of being versatile,
To show how bad the curse is
Will need a lot of verses
And take a little Weill.[47]

In relating the poetic subject of the poems to Brecht and Bernstein respectively, both texts allow the performer to poke fun at the artists' creative habits. Sondheim's tone is as affectionate as Kästner's is bitter. Where Kästner rhymes "von Brecht" with "nicht echt" to ridicule the poet's well-publicized practice of frequent and sometimes unacknowledged borrowings, Sondheim's multilayered pun on "a little Weill" could be heard as connoting (1) the composer of the song; (2) his small physical stature; (3) his musical influence on Bernstein; (4) the

German aspect of Bernstein's artistic apprenticeship; (5) an analogy between Weill's protean nature and Bernstein's inability to "make up his mind" about the kind of musician he wanted to be; or (6) the amount of time required to capture Bernstein's versatility.

What "little Weill" did Bernstein take? As far as the conducting part of his multitasking career is concerned, the connection began with the revival of *The Threepenny Opera* at Brandeis University in 1952, where he was on the faculty as a visiting professor. Starring Lenya as Jenny, this was the first performance of Blitzstein's translation, paving the way for the record-breaking "off-Broadway" production at the Theatre de Lys two years later.[48] In this regard, Bernstein played a pioneering part in the transatlantic Weill renaissance, in which the revived German works temporarily suppressed general awareness of the recent American ones.

As another aside, it should be pointed out that awareness of *The Threepenny Opera* has never dwindled since Blitzstein's adaptation and its spinoffs took American culture by storm in the 1950s. In his *Chronicles,* Bob Dylan recounts "the raw intensity" that the songs from the Theatre de Lys production conveyed, "a combination of both opera and jazz. . . . They were like folksongs in nature, but unlike folksongs, too, because they were sophisticated." He singles out "Pirate Jenny" as a "show-stopping ballad [that] made the strongest impression."[49]

A very different, "cutting-edge" instance of awareness in the current century can be found in the work of cocreators Alan Moore (writer) and Kevin O'Neill (artist), who draw heavily on *The Threepenny Opera* in *Century,* a graphic novel planned for publication in three parts as the third volume of their series *The League of Extraordinary Gentlemen.* The first part of *Century,* subtitled *1910,* whose opening chapter is called "What Keeps Mankind Alive?" and replaces Blitzstein's translation of that number with new lyrics, appeared in 2009.[50]

Back to Bernstein: his career as a composer tells a somewhat different story from his career as a conductor. He knew the recent American works firsthand, of course, and Weill's creative path no doubt seemed paradigmatic for a composer with a background in high culture and deep aspirations to reach a broader public, especially on Broadway. Of the musical-theater works, *1600 Pennsylvania Avenue,* which received its premiere in 1976, evinces the largest debt, specifically to the dramaturgy of *Love Life*—perhaps not surprising, since the musical's book author was again Alan Jay Lerner. In this last connection, at least, Sondheim's birthday tribute applied as much to himself as it did to the honoree. It is a connection that has increasingly come to light during the second stage of Weill reception history: his "vaudeville" served as a prototype, as mentioned already, not only for Kander and Ebb's concept musicals, such as *Cabaret, Chicago,* and the recent *Scottsboro Boys,* but also for many of Sondheim's own, such as *Company* and *Assassins.*[51] It should also be noted that Boris Aronson, the scenic designer for *Love Life,* worked with Kander and Ebb on *Cabaret* and with Sondheim on *Company, Follies,* and *Pacific Overtures.*

A topic-based study of reception tracing connections like these between *Love Life* and the work of other composers provides a necessary complement to the chronological approach that narrates how Weill's image changed over time. A related topic would be the kind of epic music theater developed by Weill and Neher in *Die Bürgschaft,* which Neher continued to pursue in his collaborations with the composer Rudolf Wagner-Régeny during the years of the Third Reich. (Would Weill himself have continued along a similar path had he remained in Germany? The impossibility of supplying an answer to that question should only sharpen appreciation of what he did in fact accomplish after circumstances compelled him to leave.) In addition to dramaturgical matters, other topics might include Alban Berg's admission in 1928 that "the likes of us cannot make up our minds in favor of a 'Threepenny Opera' or a 'Ten-Thousand-Dollar Symphony,'" an aesthetic quandary that certainly left its mark on Berg's own opera *Lulu* and found frequent echoes in reactions to Weill's musical theater ever since.[52] As Sondheim's seventieth-birthday tribute illustrates, Bernstein's career as a whole offers a celebrated example.

Another topic to consider in more detail, touched on only briefly here, would be the vast and seemingly inexhaustible array of literary responses to the composer's works, as varied in the aggregate as Mitford's fictional portrayal of Lord Berners, Sondheim's "Saga of Lenny," and a twenty-first-century graphic novel. Yet another would be the inspiration Weill has provided to rock musicians such as Dylan or the Doors, whose recording of the "Alabama Song" appeared on their debut album in 1967, or Tom Waits, who learned that his music was like Weill's before he had even heard any.[53] Having thus discovered Weill by being alerted to similarities to his own "sound," Waits contributed to the "tribute album" called *Lost in the Stars*—not to be confused with the stage work, although it does feature the title number of that show in an instrumental arrangement by Carla Bley. Produced by Hal Willner and Paul M. Young and released by A&M Records in 1985, *Lost in the Stars* presents new renditions of Weill's music done in a variety of idioms; the project can thus be seen as having a distant precedent in earlier arrangements, such as those for dance band from the 1920s and 1940s.[54] Other "stars" performing in this eclectic collection, which draws its material from all the stages of Weill's career, include Charlie Haden, Dagmar Krause, Marianne Faithfull, John Zorn, Van Dyke Parks, Lou Reed, and Sting. Each of them, in his or her own way, contributes to a vital strand of reception history that has allowed many of Weill's songs to have an enduring impact outside the musical theater for which they were originally but not exclusively conceived.

Those who have taken "a little Weill" are legion.

APPENDIX

Weill's Works for Stage or Screen

The works are listed chronologically; dates indicate the stage premiere or motion picture release.

Zaubernacht (ballet with song, Wladimir Boritsch), Berlin, Theater am Kurfürstendamm, 18 November 1922; arranged by Weill as orchestral suite *Quodlibet (Eine Unterhaltungsmusik)*, op. 9, 1923.

Der Protagonist, op. 15 (one-act opera, Georg Kaiser), Dresden, Staatsoper, 27 March 1926.

Royal Palace, op. 17 (one-act opera, Iwan Goll), Berlin, Staatsoper, 2 March 1927 [full score lost]; reorchestrated version, Nederlands Congresgebouw, The Hague, 25 June 1971.

Na und? (two-act operetta, Friedrich Joachimson), 1926–27 [unperformed, lost].

Mahagonny (*Songspiel*, after texts by Bertolt Brecht), Baden-Baden, Kurhaus, Grosser Bühnensaal, 17 July 1927.

Der Zar lässt sich photographieren, op. 21 (one-act opera, Georg Kaiser), Leipzig, Neues Theater, 18 February 1928.

Die Dreigroschenoper (play with music, Bertolt Brecht and Elisabeth Hauptmann; after John Gay: *The Beggar's Opera*), Berlin, Theater am Schiffbauerdamm, 31 August 1928. Film adaptation by Georg Pabst, *Die 3-Groschen-Oper*, 19 February 1931.

Happy End (play with music, Dorothy Lane [Elisabeth Hauptmann] and Bertolt Brecht), Berlin, Theater am Schiffbauerdamm, 2 September 1929.

Aufstieg und Fall der Stadt Mahagonny (epic opera, Bertolt Brecht), Leipzig, Neues Theater, 9 March 1930.

Der Jasager (school opera, Bertolt Brecht; after the Japanese Noh play *Taniko*), live broadcast on Berliner Rundfunk, 23 June 1930; Berlin, Zentralinstitut für Erziehung und Unterricht, 24 June 1930.

Die Bürgschaft (epic opera, Caspar Neher; after Herder: *Der afrikanische Rechtspruch*), Berlin, Städtische Oper, 10 March 1932.

Der Silbersee: Ein Wintermärchen (play with music, Georg Kaiser), simultaneous premieres at Leipzig, Altes Theater; Erfurt, Stadttheater; and Magdeburg, Städtisches Theater, 18 February 1933.

Die sieben Todsünden (ballet chanté, Bertolt Brecht and Edward James), Paris, Théâtre des Champs-Elysées, 7 June 1933.

Der Kuhhandel (operetta, Robert Vambery), 1934 [incomplete]; revised as *A Kingdom for a Cow* (musical play, Reginald Arkell; lyrics Desmond Carter), London, Savoy, 28 June 1935.

Der Weg der Verheissung (biblical drama, Franz Werfel), 1934–35 [incomplete]; revised by Weill and Ludwig Lewisohn as *The Eternal Road,* New York, Manhattan Opera House, 7 January 1937.

Johnny Johnson (musical play, Paul Green), New York, 44th Street Theatre, 19 November 1936.

The River Is Blue (screenplay by Clifford Odets, directed by Lewis Milestone), 1937; released with new score by Werner Janssen and directed by William Dieterle under the title *Blockade,* 17 June 1938.

Knickerbocker Holiday (musical comedy, Maxwell Anderson), New York, Ethel Barrymore Theatre, 19 October 1938; film adaptation directed by Harry Joe Brown, released 17 March 1944.

You and Me (film, Norman Krasna, Virginia Van Upp; lyrics Sam Coslow), directed by Fritz Lang, released 3 June 1938.

Railroads on Parade (Pageant-Drama of Transport, text by Edward Hungerford), New York World's Fair, 30 April 1939; revised version performed at the Fair in 1940.

Lady in the Dark (musical play, Moss Hart; lyrics Ira Gershwin), New York, Alvin Theatre, 23 January 1941; film adaptation directed by Mitchell Leisen, released 10 February 1944.

Fun to be Free (pageant, Ben Hecht, Charles MacArthur, Moss Hart), New York, Madison Square Garden, 5 October 1941; sponsored by Fight for Freedom, Inc.

We Will Never Die ("A memorial dedicated to the Two Million Jewish Dead of Europe," Ben Hecht, Moss Hart), New York, Madison Square Garden, 9 March 1943; the production traveled to Washington, D.C., Philadelphia, Chicago, Boston, and Hollywood; it was also widely broadcast.

One Touch of Venus (musical comedy, S. J. Perelman and Ogden Nash), New York, Imperial Theatre, 7 October 1943; film adaptation directed by William A. Seiter, released 28 October 1948.

Salute to France (propaganda movie, screenplay by Maxwell Anderson, directed by Jean Renoir and Garson Kanin), released 13 October 1944; produced by the U.S. Office of War Information.

Where Do We Go from Here? (film, Sig Herzig, Morrie Ryskind, Ira Gershwin), directed by Gregory Ratoff, released 23 May 1945.

The Firebrand of Florence (Broadway operetta, Edwin Justus Mayer; lyrics Ira Gershwin), New York, Alvin Theatre, 22 March 1945.

Street Scene (American opera, Elmer Rice; lyrics Langston Hughes), New York, Adelphi Theater, 9 January 1947.

Down in the Valley (folk opera, Arnold Sundgaard), Bloomington, Indiana, School of Music, 15 July 1948.

Love Life (vaudeville, Alan Jay Lerner), New York, Forty-sixth Street Theatre, 7 October 1948.

Lost in the Stars (musical tragedy, Maxwell Anderson; after Alan Paton: *Cry, the Beloved Country*), New York, Music Box, 30 October 1949.

ABBREVIATIONS

BBA	Bertolt Brecht, *Grosse kommentierte Berliner und Frankfurter Ausgabe,* 30 vols. plus index (Berlin: Aufbau-Verlag, 1988–)
BF	Kurt Weill, *Briefe an die Familie,* ed. Lys Symonette and Elmar Juchem (Stuttgart: Metzler, 2000)
DDH	David Drew, *Kurt Weill: A Handbook* (London: Faber, 1987)
GS	Kurt Weill, *Musik und musikalisches Theater: Gesammelte Schriften,* ed. Stephen Hinton and Jürgen Schebera, with Elmar Juchem (Mainz: Schott, 2000)
GS1	Kurt Weill, *Musik und Theater: Gesammelte Schriften,* ed. Stephen Hinton and Jürgen Schebera (Berlin: Henschelverlag, 1990)
KWE	The Kurt Weill Edition (New York : Kurt Weill Foundation for Music/ European American Music Corp., 1996–). The edition comprises four series: I—Stage; II—Concert; III—Screen; IV—Miscellanea.
KWNL	*Kurt Weill Newsletter* (1983–)
PDE	David Farneth, with Elmar Juchem and Dave Stein, *Kurt Weill: Pictures and Documents* (Woodstock, N.Y.: Overlook Press, 2000)
PDG	David Farneth, with Elmar Juchem and Dave Stein, *Kurt Weill: Ein Leben in Bildern und Dokumenten* (Berlin: Ullstein, 2000)
ÜKW	*Über Kurt Weill,* ed. David Drew (Frankfurt am Main: Suhrkamp, 1975)
WLE	Lys Symonette and Kim H. Kowalke, ed. and trans., *Speak Low (When You Speak Love): The Letters of Kurt Weill and Lotte Lenya* (Berkeley: University of California Press, 1996)
WLG	Lys Symonette and Kim H. Kowalke, ed. and trans., *Sprich leise, wenn du Liebe sagst: Der Briefwechsel Kurt Weill–Lotte Lenya* (Cologne: Kiepenheuer & Witsch, 1998)
WLRC	Weill-Lenya Research Center, New York, N.Y.
WUE	Kurt Weill, *Briefwechsel mit der Universal Edition,* ed. Nils Grosch (Stuttgart: Metzler, 2002)

NOTES

PREFACE

1. "Two Dreams Come True," undated typescript (copy in WLRC); used without title as liner notes to the cast recording of *Street Scene* (Columbia OL 4139).

2. Kurt Weill, "Bekenntnis zur Oper," originally published in the program booklet for the premiere production of his one-act opera *Der Protagonist* on 27 March 1926 and in *Blätter der Staatsoper Dresden,* no. 131 (April 1926): 97–99; reprinted in GS, 45–47. A second, somewhat amended version of the essay appeared in *25 Jahre Neue Musik: Jahrbuch 1926 der Universal-Edition* (Vienna: Universal Edition, 1926), 226–28; reprinted in GS, 47–49.

3. "Fidelio—die schönste Oper!" Weill's contribution to a collection of opinions published as "Bekenntnisse zu Beethoven," *Magdeburgische Zeitung,* 27 March 1927; reprinted in GS, 52–54, here 54.

4. "Der Komponist der *Dreigroschenoper* über sein neues Werk," *Berlin am Morgen,* 6 September 1929; reprinted in GS, 446. Also quoted in "'Nichts Höheres': Auch Kurt Weill blamiert sich," *Chemnitzer Tageblatt,* 28 September 1929.

5. The original manuscript of Weill's schoolboy lecture "Richard Wagner / 'Meistersinger von Nürnberg' / Ein Vortrag von Kurt Weill.Ib" is housed in WLRC (ser. 30, box 5, folder 9). The letter to his brother, Hans Weill, reporting on the performance of the *Liebestod* is dated 23 March 1917; it is reprinted in BF, 21–23, here 22. The endorsement of *Tristan und Isolde* is contained in a letter to Hans Weill dated 25 April 1917; reprinted in BF, 47–49, here 49. For a detailed discussion of Weill's shifting attitudes toward Wagner, see my article "Weill contra Wagner: Aspects of Ambivalence," in "*. . . dass alles auch hätte anders kommen können*": *Beiträge zur Musikgeschichte des 20. Jahrhunderts,* ed. Susanne Schaal-Gotthardt, Luitgard Schader, and Heinz-Jürgen Winkler (Frankfurt am Main: Schott, 2009), 155–74.

6. Kurt Weill, "The Alchemy of Music," *Stage* 14, no. 2 (November 1936): 63–64.

7. Letter dated 11 December 1948, in WUE, 499.

8. Somewhat tongue-in-cheek, and forcing the polarization, the critic Edward Rothstein distinguished between Weill who "wrote 'authentic' works with a claim on the art music world" and Weill who "'sold out' for popular success." See his "On Music: Kurt Weill's Deadly Sin," *New Republic*, 23 November 1987, 25–26.

CHAPTER 1

1. S. L. M. Barlow, "In the Theatre," *Modern Music* 22, no. 4 (1945): 275–77, here 276. Barlow's column includes a brief review of Weill's operetta *The Firebrand of Florence*, which had just received its Broadway premiere.

2. Daniel Albright, "Kurt Weill as Modernist," *Modernism/Modernity* 7, no. 2 (2000): 273–84, here 283. Albright reuses the same passage almost verbatim (substituting "legible music-figures" with "hieroglyphs") in his book *Untwisting the Serpent: Modernism in Music, Literature, and Other Arts* (Chicago: University of Chicago Press, 2000), 180.

3. Ronald Taylor, *Kurt Weill: Composer in a Divided World* (London: Simon & Schuster, 1991), vii.

4. See KWE, ser. 4, vol. 2: *Popular Adaptations, 1927–1950*, ed. Charles Hamm, Elmar Juchem, and Kim H. Kowalke (New York: Kurt Weill Foundation for Music / European American Music Corporation, 2009).

5. Elia Kazan, *Elia Kazan: A Life* (New York: Knopf, 1988), 72.

6. David Drew, "Kurt Weill and His Critics," *Times Literary Supplement*, 3 and 10 October 1975, 1142–44 and 1198–1200, here 1199.

7. Robin Holloway, review of Lys Symonette and Kim H. Kowalke, ed. and trans., *Speak Low (When You Speak Love): The Letters of Kurt Weill and Lotte Lenya* (Berkeley: University of California Press, 1996), in *Tempo*, n.s., no. 201 (July 1997): 43. Holloway's comment closely echoes the opinion of Philipp Jarnach, Weill's fellow Busoni pupil and counterpoint teacher, who wrote in 1958 that Weill's "later production [i.e., in America] signifies a complete abandonment of the earlier serious goals of this composer" (letter from Jarnach to Heinz Tiessen, 24 March 1958, Heinz-Tiessen-Archiv, Akademie der Künste, Berlin; quoted in Kim H. Kowalke, "Hin und zurück: Kurt Weill heute," in *Vom Kurfürstendamm zum Broadway: Kurt Weill [1900–1950]*, ed. Bernd Kortländer et al. [Düsseldorf: Droste Verlag, 1990], 16–27, here 16). For a radical recasting of the "two Weills" theory, see Claire Taylor-Jay, "The Composer's Voice? Compositional Style and Criteria of Value in Weill, Krenek, and Stravinsky," *Journal of the Royal Musical Association* 134, no. 1 (2009): 85–111. "There are two Weills," Taylor-Jay writes, "who sound fundamentally different, and the American works are just as good as the European ones; reclaiming the worth of the American Weill does not require the composer to be seen through the lens of lifelong compositional or aesthetic consistency" (97).

8. Letter from 27 June 1919 to Hans Weill, in BF, 234.

9. Theodor W. Adorno, "Kurt Weill: Musiker des epischen Theaters," *Frankfurter Rundschau*, 15 April 1950; reprinted in *Gesammelte Schriften*, vol. 18 (Frankfurt am Main: Suhrkamp Verlag, 1984), 544–47, here 544.

10. William G. King, "Composer for the Theater: Kurt Weill Talks about 'Practical Music,'" *New York Sun,* 3 February 1940. Reception history would have it that this very excerpt appeared, in German and without commentary, on the inside cover of the program booklet for the Weill centenary celebrations in Berlin (in 2000), in connection with which a preliminary version of part of this chapter was first presented. The same passage serves as the opening motto for Pascal Huynh's monograph *Kurt Weill, ou la conquête des masses* (Arles: Actes Sud, 2000). For additional commentary on the passage, especially on Weill's attitudes toward Schoenberg, see the "editor's preface" to Alan Chapman's essay "Crossing the Cusp: The Schoenberg Connection," in *A New Orpheus: Essays on Kurt Weill,* ed. Kim H. Kowalke (New Haven: Yale University Press, 1986), 103–29, esp. 103–6.

11. Oscar Thomson, "New Rides for Music at Fair," quoted in PDE, 193.

12. David Drew concluded his entry "Kurt Weill" for *The New Grove Dictionary of Music and Musicians,* ed. Stanley Sadie (London: Macmillan, 1980), by apostrophizing the composer as "one of music's great 'might-have-beens'" (20:309). In 1919, Weill briefly considered studying with Schoenberg but then dropped the idea, ostensibly for financial reasons. See David Drew, "Weill and Schoenberg," *KWNL* 12, no. 1 (1994): 10–13; and Jürgen Schebera, ". . . jedenfalls schreibe ich heute noch an Schönberg . . . ," *Neue Zeitschrift für Musik* 25, no. 2 (2000): 25–27.

13. "Music in the Movies," *Harper's Bazaar* 80, no. 9 (September 1946): 257, 398, 400.

14. Kurt Weill, "Die Oper wohin? 'Gebrauchsmusik' und ihre Grenzen," *Berliner Tageblatt,* 31 October 1929; reprinted in GS, 92–96.

15. As Tobias Fasshauer has remarked, "Where boundaries are to be transcended *[aufgehoben],* it is hard to speak of a dualistic aesthetics"; see Fasshauer's study *Ein Aparter im Unaparten: Untersuchungen zum Songstil von Kurt Weill* (Saarbrücken: Pfau, 2007), 7. Heinz Geuen (*Von der Zeitoper zur Broadway Opera: Kurt Weill und die Idee des musikalischen Theaters* [Schliengen: Edition Argus, 1997], 332) also challenges the notion of a dualistic aesthetics, but for different reasons. "The question of aesthetic value," he writes, "can be discussed only as a variable depending on function."

16. Kurt Weill, "Broadway and the Musical Theatre," *Composer's News-Record,* no. 2 (May 1947): 1.

17. Kurt Weill, "The Alchemy of Music," *Stage* 14, no. 2 (November 1936): 63–64.

18. Kurt Weill, letter to Irving Sablosky, 24 July 1948; copy in WLRC.

19. Drew, "Kurt Weill and His Critics"; David Drew, "Kurt Weill," in *The New Grove Dictionary of Music and Musicians,* ed. Stanley Sadie (London: Macmillan, 1980), 20:300–310; David Drew and J. Bradford Robinson, "Kurt Weill," in *The New Grove Dictionary of Music and Musicians,* 2nd ed. (London: Macmillan, 2001), 27:220–32; Taylor, *Weill: Composer in a Divided World;* Jürgen Schebera, *Kurt Weill: Eine Biographie in Texten, Bildern und Dokumenten* (Mainz: Schott, 1900)—translated by Caroline Murphy as *Kurt Weill: An Illustrated Life* (New Haven: Yale University Press, 1995); Foster Hirsch, *Kurt Weill on Stage: From Berlin to Broadway* (New York: Knopf, 2002).

20. Ronald Sanders, *The Days Grow Short: The Life and Music of Kurt Weill* (London: Weidenfeld & Nicolson, 1980).

21. Douglas Jarman, *Kurt Weill: An Illustrated Biography* (Bloomington: Indiana University Press, 1982).

22. These issues have been discussed in a broad historical context (and with particular reference to Smetana) by Hermann Danuser; see his "Biographik und musikalische Hermeneutik: Zum Verhältnis zweier Disziplinen der Musikwissenschaft," in *Neue Musik und Tradition: Festschrift Rudolf Stephan zum 65. Geburtstag,* ed. Josef Kuckertz et al. (Laaber: Laaber Verlag, 1990), 571–601.

23. Wolfgang Hildesheimer, *Mozart* (Frankfurt am Main: Suhrkamp Verlag, 1977).

24. "Die Biographen der siebziger Jahre versuchen die Klippe der Heroisierung und Mythisierung zu umschiffen." See Helmut Scheuer, "Biographische Modelle in der modernen deutschen Literatur," *Österreichische Zeitschrift für Geschichtswissenschaft* 5, no. 4 (1994): 457–87, here 478. See also Scheuer's article "Biographie" in *Historisches Wörterbuch der Rhetorik,* ed. Gerd Ueding (Tübingen: Max Niemeyer Verlag, 1994).

25. See Taylor, *Weill: Composer in a Divided World;* also Jarman, *Kurt Weill: An Illustrated Biography.* The impact of Adorno's writings is explored further in the Coda following chapter 12, in the section "Stages of Reception."

26. "Die Figur des Komponisten, der in Amerika starb, wird vom Begriff des Komponisten kaum recht getroffen." Theodor W. Adorno, "Kurt Weill: Musiker des epischen Theaters," in *Gesammelte Schriften* 18:544.

27. Adorno made essentially the same judgment about Weill's teacher Busoni: "There are extraordinary intentions and perhaps even significant things that he realized, and yet I repeatedly have the reaction: he was actually not a composer. If I'm not mistaken, a curious "as if" quality is responsible, an element of playacting, as it were, that gets in the way of the thing itself, the composition [*das Komponierte*]" (letter from Theodor W. Adorno to the music critic Hans Heinz Stuckenschmidt, 13 December 1968; in: *Hans Heinz Stuckenschmidt: Der Deutsche im Konzertsaal,* Archive zur Musik des 20. Jahrhunderts, vol. 10, ed. Werner Grünzweig and Christiane Niklew [Hofheim: Wolke Verlag, 2010], 168).

28. Eduard Hanslick, *Die moderne Oper,* vol. 3: *Aus dem Opernleben der Gegenwart* (Berlin, 1885), 324; quoted in David J. Levin, "Reading a Staging/Staging a Reading," *Cambridge Opera Journal* 9, no. 1 (1997): 47–71, here 52.

29. Having introduced his "new type" in the obituary, Adorno would have occasion to invoke it in two subsequent pieces from the 1950s, each time with specific reference to Weill. In a follow-up article to the obituary, written in connection with the German premiere of *Street Scene* in Düsseldorf in 1955, he described Weill's whole "attitude" *(Haltung)* as "that of the *Musikregisseur,*" noting that "it is not the musical composition as such that struck people, but the change in dramaturgical function"; see "Nach einem Vierteljahrhundert," *Gesammelte Schriften* 18:550. The term also appears in the radio lectures that Adorno published in 1962 as *Einleitung in die Musiksoziologie,* where he rejects the apparent reconciliation of "the separate spheres of production, performance, and reception" represented by the figure of the "music director" as a "false rationalization"; in *Gesammelte Schriften* 14:393. With specific reference to Weill he coins the synonym *Manager-Komponist* (manager-composer) (392).

30. "Fragen des gegenwärtigen Operntheaters," in program booklet to *Tannhäuser,* Bayreuther Festspiele 1966, 1–15; reprinted in *Gesammelte Schriften* 19 (Frankfurt am Main: Suhrkamp Verlag, 1984), 481–93, here 486. An earlier version appeared in *Neue Deutsche Hefte* 31 (January 1957): 526–35. Sarah Whitfield's study "Kurt Weill: The 'Com-

poser as Dramatist' in American Musical Theatre Production" (Ph.D. diss., University of London, 2010) represents an attempt to neutralize the negative connotations attaching to Adorno's criticism of Weill's American works. As Whitfield explains, her thesis "establishes how Weill can be seen through his own model of the 'composer as dramatist' and through Adorno's depiction of the composer as a *Musikregisseur*" (2).

31. None of the quotations here from Drew's *New Grove* article have found their way into the revised edition, written in collaboration with J. Bradford Robinson and published in 2001. In that sense they reflect an earlier image of Weill, now superseded. The biographical decoding of *Lady in the Dark* has gone. It is replaced by the following assessment: "Exemplary yet inimitable, the score resembles a surreal montage of *Royal Palace* and *Die Dreigroschenoper,* and was fiercely rejected by admirers of the latter (Stravinsky excepted)." Weill is also credited with "[retaining] from his discarded background two notable advantages over his popular competitors." One is "an aural imagination that . . . compelled him to make his own orchestral scores"; the other a "highly cultivated sense of musical character and theatrical form." In a section on "posthumous reputation," Robinson states that the difference between the European and American works was "long thought to be unbridgeable and to stand in need of special biographical or even psychological pleading." Now, however, it is acknowledged that the works "spoke to quite different audiences and require different sets of categories for their appraisal."

32. Drew, "Kurt Weill and His Critics," 1200.

33. See Herbert Fleischer, "Kurt Weill: Versuch einer einheitlichen Stilbetrachtung," *Anbruch* 14 (1932); reprinted in ÜKW, 102–7.

34. Drew, "Kurt Weill and His Critics," 1198–99.

35. For an excellent "unitary" account of Weill's career that specifically takes issue with modernist prejudices toward Weill's populism in the writings of Adorno and others, see Kim Kowalke, "Kurt Weill, Modernism, and Popular Culture: *Öffentlichkeit als Stil,*" *Modernism/Modernity* 2, no. 1 (1995): 27–69. See also the section "Stages of Reception" in the Coda for further discussion of Kowalke's essay.

36. Kurt Weill, "Two Dreams Come True," undated manuscript, published without title on the cover of the cast recording of *Street Scene* (Columbia OL 4139).

37. In the 1929 essay "Die Oper—wohin?" (GS, 93): "Fear of banality has finally been overcome (something demanded by Busoni ten years ago)."

38. David Drew, "Musical Theatre in the Weimar Republic," *Proceedings of the Royal Musical Association* 88 (1961–62): 89–108. See also Giselher Schubert, "Hindemith und Weill: Zu einer Musikgeschichte der zwanziger Jahre," *Hindemith-Jahrbuch* 25 (1996): 158–78.

39. Apart from the work itself, one of the few documents pertaining directly to the process of collaboration is an interview by Weill, published as "Keine Differenz Weill-Hindemith" in the Berlin journal *Filmkurier,* 8 August 1929. An unsubstantiated rumor had been circulating that Hindemith had forbidden any further performances after the successful 1929 premiere in Baden-Baden. Weill responded as follows:

> There is no conflict whatsoever between Hindemith and me. Together Brecht and I wrote *Der Lindberghflug* in the autumn of last year, with my having already sketched the music when the work was first published in a journal

[in *Uhu* 5 (1929)] . . . Hindemith took over the composition of the elements and the words about America, and I the part in which Germany speaks. We both viewed this Baden-Baden version merely as an interesting, one-off experiment created for a particular purpose. We were quite aware that no artistic unity could emerge, given our different natures. The work indeed revealed a great divergence, which—and that was part of the purpose—was interesting to observe. (Reprinted in GS, 444–45.)

40. Beeke Sell Tower, *Envisioning America: Prints, Drawings, and Photographs by George Grosz and His Contemporaries, 1915–1933* (Cambridge, Mass.: Busch-Reisinger Museum, Harvard University, 1990).

41. Two studies by J. Bradford Robinson shed considerable light on the German conception of jazz peculiar to the Weimar Republic: "Jazz Reception in Weimar Germany: In Search of a Shimmy Figure," in *Music and Performance in the Weimar Republic,* ed. Bryan Gilliam (Cambridge: Cambridge University Press, 1994), 107–34; and "The Jazz Essays of Theodor Adorno: Some Thoughts on Jazz Reception in Weimar Germany," *Popular Music* 13, no. 1 (1994): 1–25.

42. "Vorwort zum Regiebuch der Oper *Aufstieg und Fall der Stadt Mahagonny,*" GS, 103–6.

43. Hindemith's publisher, Schott, wrote to him proposing a new version of *The Beggar's Opera* on 28 January 1925: "The way you drew the foxtrot of your Kammermusik No. 1 into the sphere of serious music would be the right thing in this case: refined popular music or a caricature thereof, at the same time a satire of the sort of modern opera music composed by d'Albert." Hindemith, it would appear, never responded. See Stephen Hinton, ed., *Kurt Weill: The Threepenny Opera* (Cambridge: Cambridge University Press, 1990), 16.

44. Weill, "Notiz zum *Berliner Requiem,*" *Der deutsche Rundfunk* 7 (1929); reprinted in GS, 409.

45. Writing in 1927, Weill singled out Hindemith (along with Ludwig Weber) as one of a number of musicians within the youth movement *(Jugendbewegung)* who were attempting "directly to attract a public for understanding and cultivating new music." Approving in principle, Weill nonetheless wondered "whether this youth movement is not too restricted to certain circles of the population really to create the basis of a rejuvenation of musical culture or even of forming a people's art *[Volkskunst].*" See "Verschiebungen in der musikalischen Produktion," *Berliner Tageblatt,* 1 October 1927; reprinted in GS, 61–64.

46. In the introduction to his edition of the opera, Christoph Wolff described *Cardillac* as Hindemith's "first really large-scale *[grossformatige]* composition"; the reception, in Wolff's informed description, was a *succès d'estime* ("Achtungserfolg"). See Paul Hindemith, *Cardillac* (= Sämtliche Werke 1/4, Mainz: Schott, 1979), ix–xxiii.

47. Letter from Kurt Weill to G. F. Stegmann, 14 February 1949; copy in WLRC.

48. See my article "Hindemith: Pedagogy and Personal Style," *Hindemith-Jahrbuch* 17 (1988): 54–67.

49. Giselher Schubert, "Vorgeschichte und Entstehung der *Unterweisung im Tonsatz,*" *Hindemith-Jahrbuch* 9 (1980): 16–64.

50. Reinhold Brinkmann has expounded on the late Hindemith's "sense of isolation and artistic uncertainty," even "melancholy"; see Brinkmann's article "Über Paul Hindemiths Rede *Sterbende Gewässer,*" *Hindemith-Jahrbuch* 13 (1984): 71–90.

51. See my article "Großbritannien als Exilland: Der Fall Weill," in *Musik in der Emigration, 1933–1945: Verfolgung—Vertreibung—Rückwirkung,* ed. H. Weber (Stuttgart: Metzler, 1994), 213–27.

52. For an account of the "Fall Hindemith," with particular reference to the Symphony *Mathis der Maler,* see my introduction to Paul Hindemith, *Orchesterwerke 1932–34: Philharmonisches Konzert—Symphonie "Mathis der Maler"* (= Sämtliche Werke, ser. 2, vol. 2, Mainz: Schott, 1991).

53. Paul Hindemith, *Unterweisung im Tonsatz: Theoretischer Teil* (Mainz: Schott, 1937), 251.

54. Other revised works are *Cardillac* (1926; 2/1952), *Frau Musica* (1928; 2/1943), and *Neues vom Tage* (1929; 2/1953; 3/1960).

55. David Neumeyer, *The Music of Paul Hindemith* (New Haven: Yale University Press, 1986), esp. 137–67.

56. Paul Hindemith, *Das Marienleben* (London: Schott, 1948), iv.

57. Ibid., x.

58. Ibid., iv.

59. Ibid., x.

60. See Kim Kowalke, "*The Threepenny Opera* in America," in Hinton (ed.), *Kurt Weill: The Threepenny Opera,* 78–119. In June 1939, Weill wrote to Brecht: "It wouldn't be impossible to mount *Die Dreigroschenoper* again in America at some point. . . . One could risk it, of course, only with a completely new adaptation . . . and with one of the best Broadway producers" (90).

61. A comprehensive study of Weill's self-borrowings remains a desideratum of Weill scholarship. The borrowings, linking works otherwise quite dissimilar in style and type, are too numerous to list here. In DDH, Drew has detailed thirteen borrowings from A *Kingdom for a Cow* alone. *Der Silbersee* (1933) borrows from *Die Bürgschaft* (1932), and *Die sieben Todsünden* (1933) from *Der Silbersee.* But early and late works also share common material: the orchestral introduction to act 2 of *Street Scene* (1946) borrows from Weill's own theater music to Erwin Piscator's 1928 production of *Konjunktur.*

62. See my "Hindemith: Pedagogy and Personal Style" for a discussion of this issue.

63. David Riesman (in collaboration with Reuel Denney and Nathan Glazer), *The Lonely Crowd: A Study of the Changing American Character* (New Haven: Yale University Press, 1950).

64. The final two quotations here are from Riesman, *Lonely Crowd,* preface to abridged edition of 1961 (New Haven; Yale University Press, 1969), xxxii.

65. Riesman in fact posits a third type: "tradition-directed." It is redundant here, however, in that he restricts its applicability to less developed countries: "in India, Egypt, and China . . . for most preliterate peoples in Central Africa, parts of Central and South America, in fact most of the world relatively untouched by industrialization" (*Lonely Crowd* [1950 ed.], 10). But it also applies to earlier historical periods in the West: "In western history the Middle Ages can be considered a period in which the majority were

tradition-directed" (13). In any event, certain aspects of "tradition direction," as defined by Riesman, are clearly pertinent to Hindemith's case, especially the emphasis he placed on *Gemeinschaft* (community) as against *Gesellschaft* (society), a distinction also drawn by Riesman (13).

66. See especially Elisabeth Young-Bruehl, *Creative Characters* (New York: Routledge, 1991); and *Culture and Social Character: The Work of David Riesman Reviewed*, ed. Seymour Martin Lipset and Leo Lowenthal (New York: Free Press of Glencoe, 1961).

67. See his "Conformity and Nonconformity in the Fine Arts," in Lipset and Lowenthal (eds.), *Culture and Social Character*, 389–403.

68. Ibid., 399.

69. "Das 'So kann es nicht weiter gehen' [ist] gleichsam mitkomponiert." Quoted from the "Postludium" to "Ad vocem Hindemith: Eine Dokumentation," in Theodor W. Adorno, *Impromptus* (Frankfurt am Main, 1968); reprinted in *Gesammelte Schriften*, vol. 17 (Frankfurt am Main: Suhrkamp Verlag, 1982), 210–46, here 242.

70. There may be, as Hindemith experienced, particularly in the 1930s, a clash between tradition and character. In defining the "inner-directed type," Riesman writes of a "psychological gyroscope." "This instrument, once it is set by the parents and other authorities, keeps the inner-directed person . . . 'on course' even when tradition, as responded to by his character, no longer dictates his moves" (*Lonely Crowd*, 16). Riesman's contrasting metaphor for the "other-directed" type is that of radar: "As against guilt-and-shame controls, though of course these survive, one prime psychological lever of the other-directed person is diffuse *anxiety*. This control equipment, instead of being like a gyroscope, is like radar" (26).

Another attempt to apply Riesman's model of "other direction" to the arts can be found in Helmut Lethen's book *Verhaltenslehren der Kälte: Lebensversuche zwischen den Kriegen* (Frankfurt am Main: Suhrkamp Verlag, 1994), a study of interbellum cultural shifts in Germany as reflected in literature. Lethen quotes from Helmut Schelsky's introduction to the German edition of *The Lonely Crowd* (*Die einsame Masse: eine Untersuchung der Wandlungen des amerikanischen Charakters* [Reinbek bei Hamburg: Rowohlt, 1965]), in which the author shows how difficult it is for German sociologists to detach the "other-directed" type from associations with Nazi collectivism on the one hand and bourgeois ideals on the other (297). Especially relevant to the cases of Weill and Hindemith against the background of recent *Exilforschung* is the following remark: "Thus [because of the Nazi regime] possibilities once accorded the *Neue Sachlichkeit* were obscured" (243).

71. Young-Bruehl, *Creative Characters*, 251

72. Adorno's views on the problems of intellectuals exiled from Germany and on his status as an emigrant are summarized in the lecture entitled "Fragen an die intellektuelle Emigration," which he gave to the Jewish Club of Los Angeles on 27 May 1945; published in *Gesammelte Schriften*, vol. 20.1 (Frankfurt am Main: Suhrkamp Verlag, 1986), 352–59. The lecture concludes with four theses:

1. The thinking person in emigration should not pretend to begin a new life, but should proceed from the past life, from his entire experience, including the European catastrophe and the difficulties in his new country . . .

2. The power of the immeasurable industrial apparatus over the individual should not seduce us into idolizing the world in which we live and which controls us . . .
3. We should remain unswerving in our objective work. That is to say, we should seek to express things for their own sake, without regard to ends and communication . . .
4. We should not succumb to stupidity. We should not assume for ourselves a suspension of thought because of the pressure to translate everything into facts and figures. While we should learn here everything that can cure us of the manic aspect of German thought, we should not rob ourselves of imagination, speculation, unrestrained insight . . .

The theses both characterize his attitude to his own work during his American period and serve as a reminder of why he failed to appreciate Weill's position.

73. Helmut Lethen has pertinently suggested that the "inner-directed" prototype may ultimately serve a compensatory purpose: "Inner direction, which shines forth in such an exemplary fashion in cultural criticism, is empirically difficult to prove. That is why the nineteenth-century public devoured it so readily in novels so as to assimilate it as a compensatory yardstick. The numerous documents of the bourgeoisie stylizing itself as inner-directed subjects in bourgeois novels do not permit the automatic conclusion that inner direction ever existed. . . . We should probably assume the norm of other direction, which appears in epoch-specific variations *as if* human beings were guided 'from within'" (*Verhaltenslehren der Kälte,* 267).

74. The issue of terminology is a sensitive one, as discussed in chapter 8.

75. Edward W. Said, *Culture and Imperialism* (New York: Knopf, 1993), 336.

76. Ibid., 335.

77. Lipset and Lowenthal (eds.), *Culture and Social Character,* 171; see also the preface to the 1961 edition of *The Lonely Crowd,* where Riesman comments on "the tendency among readers . . . to equate inner-direction with autonomy" (xxiv).

78. Taylor, *Weill: Composer in a Divided World,* 306.

79. http://classicalcdreview.com/weillnax.html.

80. Herbert Fleischer, *Philosophische Grundanschauungen in der gegenwärtigen Musikaesthetik* (Berlin-Charlottenburg: Buch- und Kunstdruckerei "Sonne," 1928). Weill, it should be noted, was also a fan of Dessoir's work, having attended his lectures as a student. Dessoir was a friend of Weill's teacher, Busoni, and gave the oration at Busoni's funeral.

81. Herbert Fleischer, *Strawinsky* (Berlin and New York: Russischer Musik Verlag, 1931).

82. Letter from Weill to Universal Edition, 20 August 1932, in WUE, 410.

83. Herbert Fleischer, *La musica contemporanea,* translated from the German by A. Hermet in collaboration with the author (Milan: Hoepli, 1938).

84. Fleischer, "Versuch," in ÜKW, 102.

85. Ibid., 105.

86. Ibid., 103.

87. WUE, 194.

88. Ibid., 195.

89. Letter from Weill to Lenya, [6? September 1934], in WLG, 147: "Mit dem Bibelstück komme ich jetzt, unberufen, ganz gut weiter, da ich mich allmählich in den Stil hineinarbeite."

90. Letter from Weill to Lenya, 13 March 1934, in WLE, 120.

91. Letter from Weill to Irving Sablosky, 24 July 1948; copy in WLRC.

92. Kurt Weill, "Score for a Play," *New York Times,* 5 January 1947. Elsewhere Weill compared "attempts in the United States and Palestine to create original music," saying that "Jewish music had made further progress toward a style of its own than American music and that he thought that, in style, Palestinian music had a labour spirit" (Weill, "Palestine Music Has 'Labour Spirit,'" *Palestine Post,* 2 June 1947). He also suggested: "It takes time to develop a creative style. I find it so in myself" (R.C.B., "Kurt Weill Has Secured Niche of His Own at 35," *New York World Telegram,* 21 December 1935). He is talking here, in 1935, less about work style or national style than about personal style.

Apropos his Second Symphony he said that he composed "absolute music in order to—how can I say it?—control my own style. You must turn away from your own habitual way occasionally. So then I write symphonic works. Last year Bruno Walter played my latest symphonic composition, 'Nocturne Symphonique.' He plays it everywhere." Even if it isn't habitual, but controlled, it remains recognizable: "My style is melodious. People say they can recognize my music when they hear only three measures of it. I believe in the simplification of music. If someone has something to say, it is not important what means he uses so long as he knows how to use them." Again, there is an inferred tension between a plurality of means and a singularity of approach. "Musicians too often become musical historians. They think too much about what has been written before. Personally they are afraid not to be original" (ibid.).

For Weill, style is as much means as end: "I'd never write a single measure for purely aesthetic reasons in an effort to create a new style. I write only to express human emotions. If music is really human, it doesn't make much difference how it is conveyed. And as long as it is able to reach its audience emotionally, its creator should not worry about its possible sentimentality or banality" (William G. King, "Composer for the Theater Kurt Weill Talks about 'Practical Music,'" *New York Sun,* 3 February 1940). This echoes almost exactly the statement "Nor would I ever compose a single bar for esthetic reasons in order to try to create a new style. I write to express human emotions, solely. If music is really human, it doesn't matter to me how it is conveyed" (N.S., "Kurt Weill's New Score," *New York Times,* 27 October 1935). In the same interview, he reflected again on his Mahagonny project: "This first *Mahagonny* was merely an attempt to invent a new style for use in the larger work, in which the atrocities referred to were eliminated. Bert Brecht, the librettist of *Mahagonny,* and I had a moral idea as the background of that opera, namely, that a city given over to pleasure must perish, which is hardly sardonic." As the interviewer summarized, "All he knows about composition he feels that he learned from his principal teacher, Ferruccio Busoni, from whom he imbibed the fundamental principle of simplicity. Yet Mr. Weill claims that he did not find his own style until he began to write for the theatre. Then his method changed fundamentally, due to the demands of the stage. It has become, he feels, altogether a style for, and of, that realm" (ibid.). Again, if one of Fleischer's concepts applies here, it is the syncretic "stage style."

93. W.B. Gallie, "Essentially Contested Concepts," *Proceedings of the Aristotelian Society* 66 (1956): 167–98, here 168.

94. Wilhelm Seidel, "Stil," in *Die Musik in Geschichte und Gegenwart,* ed. Ludwig Finscher, Sachteil 8 (Kassel: Bärenreiter, 1998), cols. 1740–59.

95. Ibid., cols. 1741, 1743.

96. Guido Adler, *Der Stil in der Musik. I. Buch: Prinzipien und Arten des musikalischen Stils,* 2nd ed. (Leipzig: Breitkopf & Härtel, 1929), 6. The first edition of Adler's book appeared in 1911.

97. Ibid., 27.

98. Richard L. Crocker, *A History of Musical Style* (New York: McGraw-Hill, 1966), vi. Another such narrative, reflected in its title, is Robert P. Morgan's *Twentieth-Century Music: A History of Musical Style in Modern Europe and America* (New York: Norton, 1991).

99. Charles Rosen, *The Classical Style: Haydn, Mozart, Beethoven* (London: Faber, 1971), 22.

100. Ibid., 460.

101. Leonard B. Meyer, *Style and Music: Theory, History, and Ideology* (Philadelphia: University of Pennsylvania Press, 1989), 13.

102. E.H. Gombrich, "Style," in *International Encyclopaedia of the Social Sciences* (New York: Macmillan, 1968), 15:352–61, here 360.

103. Meyer, *Style and Music,* 352.

104. Immanuel Kant, *Critique of Judgment,* trans. Werner S. Pluhar (Indianapolis: Hackett, 1987), §§ 57, 215.

105. See also Fasshauer, *Ein Aparter im Unaparten.* Fasshauer, as the subtitle of his study, *Untersuchungen zum Songstil von Kurt Weill,* indicates, is interested in Weill's song style in particular, which he describes in terms of "an individual structural characteristic . . . that has been found wanting, whether rightly or not, in the 'American Weill'" (50). For a critical discussion of Fasshauer's attempt to construe the song style as "personal style," see my review in *KWNL* 25, no. 2 (2007): 14–15. Nils Grosch, in contrast, has drawn attention to "the problem of a concept of style well-nigh inseparable from a hermetically sealed language of the work of art" as something "that the *New Objectivity* expressly rejects." See Grosch's *Die Musik der Neuen Sachlichkeit* (Stuttgart: Metzler, 1999), 18–19.

106. Marc Silberman, "Gestus," in *Wörterbuch der Theaterpädagogik,* ed. Gerd Koch and Marianne Streisand (Berlin: Schibri-Verlag, 2003), 127–29.

107. Gotthold Ephraim Lessing, *Hamburgische Dramaturgie* (Stuttgart: Reclam, 1981), 30. The quoted passage comes from the "4. Stück," dated 12 May 1767.

108. It is hard to disagree with the following observation from Matthias Tischer: "Neither from the relatively few passages in Brecht's theoretical oeuvre where there is mention of 'Gestus' nor from word's use in the secondary literature is it possible to form a clearly delineated concept." See his article "Musik im Zeichen Bertolt Brechts: Versuch über das Gestische in der Musik," *Communications from the International Brecht Society* 34 (2005): 94–105, here 96.

109. Kurt Weill, "Über den gestischen Charakter der Musik," *Die Musik* 21 (1928–29): 419–23; reprinted in GS, 83–88.

110. Letter to Universal Edition dated 24 November 1932, in WUE, 422.

111. Adorno, "Kurt Weill," 545.

112. For a discussion of the distinction between "text" and "script," see "Foreword to the New Kurt Weill Edition," *Music Library Association Notes* 56, no. 2 (December 1999): 315–18.

113. In 1979, two years before she died, Lenya wrote: "Nobody really knew Kurt Weill. I wonder sometimes whether I knew him. I was married to him twenty-four years and we lived together two years without being married, so it was twenty-six years together. When he died, I looked at him, and I wasn't sure I really knew him." Quoted in the prefatory matter to WLE.

114. Søren Kierkegaard, *Journals and Papers,* ed. and trans. Howard V. Hong and Edna H. Hong (Bloomington: Indiana University Press, 1967–), 4A:164.

115. The opposite (not necessarily formalist) position has been nicely summarized by the novelist Martin Amis: "But the fit reader, the ideal reader, regards a writer's life as just an interesting extra. On good days, when you have the sense that you are a mere instrument of the work you were sent here to do, this is what a writer's life actually feels like: an interesting extra. And there is no value correlation between the life and the work" (*Experience: A Memoir* [New York: Hyperion, 2000], 117).

CHAPTER 2

1. Journal entry of 16 October 1940, in Bertolt Brecht, *Journale I,* BBA vol. 26, ed. Marianne Conrad and Werner Hecht (Berlin: Aufbau-Verlag, 1994), 436.

2. Letter to Hans Weill, 21 February 1919, in BF, 207–9, here 208.

3. "[Franz Schreker dirigiert im Funk]," *Der deutsche Rundfunk;* reprinted in GS, 344–46, here 345.

4. "Über den gestischen Charakter der Musik," *Die Musik* 21 (1928–29): 419–23; reprinted in GS, 83–88; here 86–87.

5. Joachim Lucchesi,"Versuch eines Vergleichs: Kurt Weill als Mittler zwischen Brecht und Busoni," *Musik und Gesellschaft* 40, no. 3 (1990): 132–34; Vera Stegman, "La nuova commedia dell'arte: Ferruccio Busoni als Vorläufer von Brecht und Weill," *Brecht Yearbook* 21 (1996): 141–57.

6. Transcript held in WLRC. At the beginning of the broadcast the announcer states: "The Department of Justice of the United States in cooperation with the National Broadcasting Company presents a program for all Americans—from Plymouth Rock to Ellis Island! We have invited a number of distinguished naturalized citizens to talk about the American citizenship which they have recently acquired—a possession which we ourselves take for granted—but which is still new and thrilling to them!"

7. Weill describes Busoni as having "made Berlin his *Wahlheimat*" in a discussion of the chamber music of fellow Busoni pupil Jarnach in the journal *Der deutsche Rundfunk* 3, no. 41 (1925): 2615–16; reprinted in GS, 288.

8. Ralph Winett, "Composer of the Hour: An Interview With Kurt Weill," *Brooklyn Daily Eagle,* 20 December 1936.

9. Kurt Weill, "Busoni: Zu seinem einjährigen Todestage," *Berliner Börsen-Courier,* 26 July 1925; reprinted in GS, 31–34, here 32–33. The phrase "last renaissance man" also

appears in "Todestage Bachs und Busonis," *Der deutsche Rundfunk* 3, no. 30 (1925): 1883–84; reprinted in GS, 272–74, here 274.

10. "Busoni und die neue Musik," *Der neue Weg* 54, no. 21 (1925): 282–83; reprinted in GS, 39–42, here 39–40.

11. Weill, "Busoni: Zu seinem einjährigen Todestage," in GS, 34.

12. Paul Bekker, *Neue Musik* (Stuttgart: Deutsche Verlagsanstalt, 1923), xi.

13. Hugo Leichtentritt, *Music, History, and Ideas* (Cambridge, Mass.: Harvard University Press, 1939), 254–55. Leichtentritt published his Busoni biography in 1916.

14. "Ferruccio Busoni: Zu seinem 60. Geburtstage am 1. April," *Der deutsche Rundfunk* 4, no. 13 (1926): 872; reprinted in GS, 302–3, here 303.

15. BF, 314.

16. Letter from Weill to Irving Sablosky, 24 July 1948; copy in WLRC. Sablosky served as music critic of *Chicago Daily News.*

17. "National Music, Opera, and the Movies: An Interview with Kurt Weill," *Pacific Coast Musician,* 3 July 1937, 12–13. According to Tamara Levitz (*Teaching New Classicality: Ferruccio Busoni's Master Class in Composition* [Frankfurt am Main: Peter Lang, 1996], 276), Busoni's attitude toward the new technology was ambivalent at best. Even so, films were screened in his own home, with the encouragement and assistance of his pupils.

18. Letter from Weill to Lotte Lenya, 8 May 1947, in WLG, 472.

19. Ferruccio Busoni, *Selected Letters,* ed. and trans. Antony Beaumont (New York: Columbia University Press, 1987), 373.

20. On Wolpe's relation to Busoni, see Tamara Levitz, "The Would-Be Master Student," in *On the Music of Stefan Wolpe: Essays and Recollections,* ed. Austin Clarkson (New York: Pendragon Press, 2003), 31–39.

21. In his review of Weill's one-act opera *Der Protagonist,* the critic O. Schmidt associated Weill with the "Busoni school" and implied, moreover, that the school was responsible for "literary" tendencies evinced by the opera itself: "The whole thing is a stage play written from a completely literary standpoint, without taking account of the fact that music is not an art form of the mind. That Kurt Weill, coming from the Busoni school, chose this product of a frankly perverse mind-set demonstrates that he, too, is more a musician of the mind than of the heart" (*Chemnitzer Zeitung,* 3 April 1926).

Adorno, in contrast, detected an element of "playfulness," which he likewise associated with the Busoni school:

> If, especially in *Der Protagonist,* everything doesn't quite come off, one is inclined from the start to place the blame on the school: for all of Busoni's inspirational power, his mistrust of musical construction and his resistance to any kind of vivid profile has spread confusion among a generation that is no longer satisfied with the aestheticizing rehearsal of a lost *serenitas.* There is the danger, above all, that the Busonian doctrine of resolute technical introspection stands in the way, just as Busoni's compositional technique has never quite consolidated itself. Hence a number of solutions in *Der Protagonist* are technically not the most sophisticated; there is an occasional lack of contrasting characters construed in opposition to one another, and

> for all the clarity and precision of the voice-leading, Weill's instrumental imagination seems a little insecure when it comes to writing for orchestra. (Theodor W. Adorno, "Frankfurt a. M.," *Die Musik* 20, no. 12 [September 1928]: 923)

22. John Waterhouse has discussed the specific issue of "semitonal instability" in his article "Weill's Debt to Busoni," *Musical Times* 105 (1964): 897–99. He also discusses this issue in "Busoni: Visionary or Pasticheur?" *Proceedings of the Royal Music Association* 92 (1965–66): 79–93.

23. Weill, "Busoni: Zu seinem einjährigen Todestage," in GS, 33.

24. Levitz, *Teaching New Classicality*, 5. Petri's essay "How Busoni Taught" was published in *The Etude* 58, no. 10 (1940): 657, 710.

25. Weill's letters to Busoni are housed in the Staatsbibliothek zu Berlin; they have been edited by Jutta Theurich and published as "'. . . wenn Sie doch auch hier wären!' Briefe von Kurt Weill an Ferruccio Busoni," *Musik und Gesellschaft* 40 (1990): 114–26.

26. On Weill's studies with Jarnach, see Levitz, *Teaching New Classicality*, 256–60.

27. "Impotenz—oder Potenz?" *Frankfurter Zeitung*, 15–16 January 1920. The newspaper published Busoni's response on 2 February 1920; it was reprinted that same year in a special Busoni issue of *Der Aufbruch* and, in 1922, in Busoni's collection of writings *Von der Einheit der Musik* (Berlin, Max Hesses Verlag, 1922). An English translation is in Ferruccio Busoni, *The Essence of Music, and Other Papers*, trans. Rosamond Ley (London: Rockliff, 1957), 19–22. See also Robert P. Morgan, "'A New Musical Reality': Futurism, Modernism, and 'The Art of Noises,'" *Modernism/Modernity* 1, no. 3 (1994): 129–51

28. Levitz, *Teaching New Classicality*, 293.

29. Ibid., 140.

30. Ibid., 142.

31. Weill, "Korrespondenz über *Dreigroschenoper*," *Anbruch* 11, no. 1 (1929): 24–25; reprinted in GS, 72–74, here 73.

32. Letter to Hans Heinsheimer, 14 October 1929, in WUE, 196.

33. "Tonfilm, Opernfilm, Filmoper," *Frankfurter Zeitung*, 24 May 1930; reprinted in GS, 109–14; here 113.

34. Ferruccio Busoni, *Sketch of a New Esthetic of Music*, trans. Theodore Baker (New York: G. Schirmer, 1911), 34: "Let us take thought, how music may be restored to its primitive, natural essence; let us free it from architectonic, acoustic and esthetic dogmas; let it be pure invention and sentiment, in harmonies, in forms, in tone-colors (for invention and sentiment are not the prerogative of melody alone)." Busoni's *Sketch* was originally published as *Entwurf einer neuen Ästhetik der Tonkunst* (Trieste: C. Schmidl, 1907) and later issued in an expanded edition under the same title (Leipzig: Insel Verlag, 1916).

35. Busoni, *Sketch*, 18.

36. Busoni, *Entwurf einer neuen Ästhetik der Tonkunst* (*ergänzte und kommentierte Neuausgabe*), ed. Martina Weindel (Wilhelmshaven: Florian Noetzel, 2001), 26. The English translation is quoted here from Busoni, "The Future of Opera," in *The Essence of Music*, 39–41, here 41.

37. Busoni, *Entwurf einer neuen Ästhetik der Tonkunst*, ed. Weindel, 62.

38. *Sketch,* 9.

39. Busoni, "The Essence of Music: A Paving the Way to an Understanding of the Everlasting Calendar," in *The Essence of Music,* 193.

40. Ibid., 199–200.

41. "Korrespondenz über *Dreigroschenoper,*" *Anbruch* 11 (1929): 24–25; reprinted in GS, 72–75, here 72.

42. "Die Oper—Wohin?" *Berliner Tageblatt,* 31 October 1929, reprinted in GS, 92–96, here 95.

43. "Two Dreams Come True," undated typescript; used without title as liner notes to the cast album of *Street Scene* (Columbia OL 4139).

44. Weill, "The Alchemy of Music," *Stage Magazine* (November 1936): 63–64.

45. Ibid.

46. Francesco Algarotti, "Saggio sopra l'opera in musica" (1755). The anonymous English translation "An Essay on the Opera" was first published in 1767; it is quoted here from the reprinted excerpt in *Strunk's Source Readings in Music History,* rev. ed., gen ed. Leo Treitler (New York: W. W. Norton, 1998), 909–22, here 921.

47. "Der Irrthum in dem Kunstgenre der Oper bestand darin, daß ein Mittel des Ausdruckes (die Musik) zum Zwecke, der Zweck des Ausdruckes (das Drama) aber zum Mittel gemacht war" (Richard Wagner, *Oper und Drama, erster Theil: Die Oper und das Wesen der Musik* [Leipzig: Verlagsbuchhandlung von J. J. Weber, 1852], 21).

48. For an account of the *Entwurf*'s genesis, see Weindel's *Neuausgabe,* esp. 67–78.

49. Busoni, *Entwurf,* 23–24.

50. Weill, "Über den gestischen Charakter der Musik," *Die Musik,* 21, no. 6 (March 29): 419–23; reprinted in GS, 83–88, here 83.

51. Busoni, *Entwurf,* 24.

52. Weill, "Korrespondenz über *Dreigroschenoper,*" GS, 73–74.

53. Busoni, *Entwurf,* 24.

54. Weill, "Die neue Oper," *Der neue Weg* 60, no. 2 (1926): 24–25; reprinted in GS, 42–45, here 42.

55. Busoni, *Entwurf,* 18.

56. Weill, "Bekenntnis zur Oper," *Blätter der Staatsoper Dresden* (April 1926): 97–99; reprinted in GS, 45–47, here 46.

57. Theodor W. Adorno, *Philosophie der neuen Musik* (Frankfurt am Main: Europäische Verlagsanstalt, 1958), 36.

58. Ernst Robert Curtius, *Europäische Literatur und lateinisches Mittelalter* (Bern: A. Francke, 1948), 275. An English translation was published as *European Literature and the Latin Middle Ages* (Princeton: Princeton University Press, 1952). Curtius describes the systematic use of his terminology as follows:

> This is not the place to discuss whether the word "Mannerism" is a good choice as the designation of a period in art history and to what extent it is justified. We may borrow it because it is well adapted to fill a gap in the terminology of literary science. For that purpose, to be sure, we must free the word from all art-historical connotations and broaden its meaning until it represents simply the common denominator for all literary tenden-

> cies which are opposed to Classicism, whether they be pre-classical, post-classical, or contemporary with any Classicism. Understood in this sense, Mannerism is a constant in European literature. (273)

59. For an interpretation of Stravinsky's music as "mannerist," see Carl Dahlhaus, "Igor Strawinskijs episches Theater," in *Vom Musikdrama zur Literaturoper* (Munich: Piper 1989), 186–227, esp. 225–27.

60. Rudolf Stephan, "Zur Deutung von Strawinskys Neoklassizismus," in *Vom musikalischen Denken: Gesammelte Vorträge*, ed. Rainer Damm and Andreas Traub (Mainz: Schott, 1985), 243–48; see also Rudolf Stephan, "Der Neoklassizismus als Formalismus," in *Funk-Kolleg Musik*, vol. 1, ed. Carl Dahlhaus (Frankfurt am Main: Fischer, 1981), 307–31. Stephan takes the central concepts of Russian formalism—"automatism," "defamiliarization," "parody," and "mechanization"—and applies them to the music of Stravinsky's so-called neoclassical period. Of mechanization, "preventing automatic, i.e. effectively unconscious, habitual perception," he writes: "That exactly corresponds with Stravinsky's approach in his neoclassical works, whose precursor may be seen as his ballet music *Pulcinella*. The automatism of the underlying music, whose language is assumed to be familiar, is purposely defamiliarized, that is, mechanized by various devices available in the twentieth century but not available two centuries earlier, when the compositional technique was not yet recognized as merely a technique" (315).

61. Jack O'Brien (Jakob Schmidt) utters the phrase in act 1, scene 9, at the point where the onstage piano plays that timeless piece of nineteenth-century kitsch, "The Maiden's Prayer" by Tekla Badarzewska-Baranowska. Weill would later recount the "cherished childhood memory" of hearing the "tinny old worn-out piano" play this piece as quintessential silent-film music. See "Music in the Movies," *Harper's Bazaar* 80, no. 9 (September 1946): 257, 398, 400. See also chapter 10 for a detailed discussion of Weill's essay.

62. Kurt Weill, letter to the editor in "Trybuna artystów," from *Muzyka* 6 (20 January 1929): 27; translated by Geoffrey Chew. I am grateful to Karol Berger for his help with this translation.

63. The context of Adorno's quoting Goebbels by way of polemicizing against "Neoklassik" is his review of choral music by Herbert Müntzel. Quoting Adorno here is neither to condemn nor to exonerate him for his baffling action. The volume of the *Gesammelte Schriften* in which the review is reprinted (vol. 19, Frankfurt am Main 1984, pp. 331–32) also contains, in an appendix, Adorno's open letter from 1963 in which he explained his action and voiced his regret. In the central portion of the letter, he writes: "The true error lay in my wrongly assessing the situation; if you like, in the foolishness of one who found making the decision to emigrate infinitely difficult. I believed that the Third Reich could not last long, that one had to remain in order to salvage whatever was possible. Nothing else prompted these words and the stupid tactics that went with them" (638).

64. Ferruccio Busoni, letter to Paul Bekker ["Junge Klassizität"], dated January 1920, published in *Frankfurter Zeitung*, 7 February 1920; reprinted in *Von der Macht der Töne: Ausgewählte Schriften*, ed. Siegfried Bimberg (Leipzig: Reclam, 1983), 115–18.

65. Busoni, *Entwurf*, 26.

66. Bertolt Brecht and Peter Suhrkamp, "Anmerkungen zur Oper *Aufstieg und Fall*

der Stadt Mahagonny," *Versuche* 2 (Berlin: Kiepenheuer, 1930), 107–15; reprinted in BBA 2:74–86, here 79. An earlier version of the "Notes" appeared as "Zur Soziologie der Oper—Anmerkungen zu 'Mahagonny'" in the journal *Musik und Gesellschaft* 1, no. 4 (1930): 105–12.

67. Weill, "Über den gestischen Charakter der Musik," in GS, 84.

68. Weill, "Der Rundfunk und die Umschichtung des Musiklebens," *Der deutsche Rundfunk* 4, no. 24 (June 1926): 1649–50; reprinted in GS, 311–14, here 313.

69. A facsimile of the original playbill of Weill's *Mahagonny: Ein Songspiel nach Texten von Bert Brecht,* which included the short text quoted here, is reproduced in the published score, *Mahagonny-Songspiel,* ed. David Drew (Vienna: Universal Edition, 1963), n.p.

70. "Korrespondenz über *Dreigroschenoper.*" See also "Gesellschaftsbildende Oper," in GS, 76–77; originally published in *Berliner Börsen-Courier,* 19 February 1929.

71. BF, 209.

72. BF, 265.

73. Paul Bekker, *Das deutsche Musikleben* (Berlin: Schuster & Loeffler, 1916), 11. See also Matthias Schmidt: "Ernst Krenek, Paul Bekker und die 'gesellschaftsbildende Macht' der Oper," *Musiktheorie* 16, no. 1 (2001): 59–72.

74. Bekker, *Das deutsche Musikleben,* 129.

75. Paul Bekker, *Die Sinfonie von Beethoven bis Mahler* (Berlin: Schuster & Loeffler, 1918), 17.

76. As Bekker writes in *Das deutsche Musikleben* (120): "In Mahler's symphonies, especially in the Eighth, we find the ideal conception of the new form of our instrumental and vocal concert, our new society."

77. Heinrich Besseler, "Grundfragen des musikalischen Hörens," in *Jahrbuch der Musikbibliothek Peters für 1925* (Leipzig: Peters, 1926), 35–52.

78. See Weill's article "Zeitoper," *Melos* 7 (1928): 106–8; reprinted in GS, 64–67.

79. These and other writings are published in Philipp Jarnach, *Schriften zur Musik,* ed. Norbert Jers (Kassel: Merseburger Verlag, 1994).

80. Ibid., 113. Jarnach spoke these words as part of a homage to Schoenberg broadcast on Northwest German Radio just days after the composer's death on 13 July 1951. In Jarnach's *Schriften,* the text of the broadcast appears without a title, serving as a postlude to the script of a longer encomium to Schoenberg originally delivered on the same radio station the previous month. The essay "Das Romanische in der Musik," also included in the *Schriften* (170–73), was first published in *Melos* 4 (1924–25): 191–95.

81. Letter from Philipp Jarnach to Heinz Tiessen, 24 March 1958, Heinz-Tiessen-Archiv, Akademie der Künste, Berlin; quoted in Kim H. Kowalke, "Hin und zurück: Kurt Weill heute," in *Vom Kurfürstendamm zum Broadway: Kurt Weill (1900–1950),* ed. Bernd Kortländer et al. (Düsseldorf: Droste Verlag, 1990), 16–27, here 16.

82. Busoni, *Sketch,* 15.

83. John Williamson, "The Musical Artwork and Its Materials in the Music and Aesthetics of Busoni," in *The Musical Work: Reality or Invention?* ed. Michael Talbot (Liverpool: Liverpool University Press, 2000), 187–204, here 187.

84. Albrecht Riethmüller, *Busonis Poetik* (Mainz: Schott, 1988).

85. Busoni, *Sketch,* 17.

86. Busoni, *Sketch,* 18.

87. Williamson, "Musical Artwork and Its Materials," 192.

88. Busoni, "Essence of Music," 200.

89. Ibid., 194

90. Cited in Williamson, "Musical Artwork and Its Materials," 203.

91. Notes on orchestration, taken from lessons given to Philipp Jarnach in Zurich during 1917–18, Staatsbibliothek zu Berlin, Busoni-Nachlass CI, 135: "Die Wahl der Mittel: Präzisierung des Gedankens, Gewand der Form, Form selbst." I am grateful to Larry Yeaw for drawing my attention to this document in connection with his work on the genesis of Busoni's *Entwurf.*

92. Winett, "Composer of the Hour: An Interview With Kurt Weill."

93. "Even in The Threepenny Opera (where we're dealing with only 7 instruments) the conductor's score has not proven its worth, since no one can form an impression of the sonic-image, which is always especially important with me" (letter to Universal Edition, 24 November 1932).

94. Busoni, "Liszt," in *Essence,* 150 and 139.

95. N.S., "Kurt Weill's New Score: Music for 'Road of Promise' Written in Modern Contemporary Style," *New York Times,* October 27, 1935.

96. Weill, "Music in the Movies."

97. "Bekenntnis zur Oper," *Blätter der Staatsoper Dresden: 1925/26,* no. 13 (1 April 1926): 97–99; reprinted in GS, 45–47. In the version of Weill's "Bekenntnis" published the following year by Universal Edition *(25 Jahre Neue Musik),* the phrase "streams of inner song" was changed to "all forms and genres of this music"; see GS, 49.

98. Weill, "Score for a Play," *New York Times,* 5 January 1947.

99. See Martina Weindel, *Ferruccio Busonis Ästhetik in seinen Briefen und Schriften* (Wilhelmshaven: Florian Noetzel, 1996), esp. 26–30.

100. Busoni, *Entwurf einer neuen Ästhetik der Tonkunst,* ed. Weindel, 136.

101. "Fort vom Durchschnitt! Zur Krise der musikalischen Interpretation,"*Berliner Börsen-Courier,* 20 August 1925; reprinted in GS, 35–39, here 38.

102. Weill, "Alchemy of Music," 63–64.

103. Levitz, *Teaching New Classicality,* 143.

104. Levitz writes: "In terms of musical aesthetics, compositional practice, and means of operatic production, *Arlecchino* had a far greater influence on Busoni's students than his esoteric project, *Doktor Faust*" (ibid.).

105. "Busonis *Faust*-Oper," *Der deutsche Rundfunk* 5 (1927): 3028–29; reprinted in GS, 367–68, here 368.

106. "Über meine Schuloper *Der Jasager,*" *Die Scene* 20, no. 8 (1930): 232–33; reprinted in GS, 119–20, here 119.

107. Winett, "Composer of the Hour: An Interview With Kurt Weill."

108. Weill, "The Future of Opera in America," *Modern Music* 14 (May–June 1937): 183–88.

109. Antony Beaumont, "Arlecchino," in *The New Grove Dictionary of Opera,* ed. Stanley Sadie, *Grove Music Online, Oxford Music Online,* www.oxfordmusiconline.com/subscriber/article/grove/music/O004034 (accessed 20 July 2011).

110. Waterhouse, "Weill's Debt to Busoni."

111. For a discussion of Fleischer's writings on Weill, see chapter 1; further aspects of Busoni's influence on *Der Protagonist,* such as the mock quartet of the first pantomime and its model in *Arlecchino,* are discussed in Levitz, *Teaching New Classicality,* 294–98.

CHAPTER 3

1. "WCBS Presents Margaret Arlen," a radio program hosted by Margaret Arlen and Harry Marble and broadcast on 7 January 1950; transcription in the Maxwell Anderson Papers, Harry Ransom Humanities Research Center, University of Texas, Austin (first two pages missing); published in *KWNL* 10, no. 1 (1992): 11–13, here 13.

2. On the phenomenon of *Literaturoper,* see *Für und wider die Literaturoper: Zur Situation nach 1945,* ed. Sigrid Wiesmann (Laaber: Laaber Verlag, 1982); and Carl Dahlhaus, *Vom Musikdrama zur Literaturoper: Aufsätze zur neueren Operngeschichte* (rev. ed. Munich: Piper, 1989).

3. In his review of the premiere, quoted at greater length below, Oskar Bie (*Berliner Börsen-Courier,* 29 March 1926) suggested that Kaiser made the "small changes." It is much more likely, however, that Weill at least collaborated with him on this process, or even made all the changes himself as he composed. Gunther Diehl's published Ph.D. dissertation, *Der junge Kurt Weill und seine Oper "Der Protagonist": Exemplarische Untersuchungen zur Deutung des frühen kompositorischen Werkes* (Kassel: Bärenreiter, 1994), contains important source material, including a detailed comparison of the text of Kaiser's play and the text of the libretto. For additional documents, including an extensive set of early reviews of the work, see the introduction by Gunther Diehl and Giselher Schubert to the relevant volume of the Kurt Weill Edition (KWE), ser. 1, vol. 1: *Der Protagonist,* ed. Gunther Diehl and Jürgen Selk (New York: Kurt Weill Foundation/European American Music Corporation, 2006), 13–32.

4. Perhaps not normally thought of as a ballet composer, Weill in fact created a large amount of dance music for his works, not just through his pervasive use of dance rhythms, but by writing music that is actually danced to onstage. This latter kind occurs in *Zaubernacht,* of course, in the "sung-ballet" *Die sieben Todsünden,* as well as in the extended dance sequences in works such as *Royal Palace, Lady in the Dark, One Touch of Venus,* and *Street Scene.* Even *Die Dreigroschenoper* was turned into a ballet and performed in London in 1938.

5. "Bekenntnis zur Oper," published in the program booklet for the premiere of *Der Protagonist,* 27 March 1926, and the *Blätter der Staatsoper Dresden,* no. 13 (1 April 1926): 97–99; reprinted in GS, 45–47, here 46–47.

6. DDH, 155.

7. KWE, ser. 1, vol. 0: *Zaubernacht,* ed. Elmar Juchem and Andrew Kuster (New York: Kurt Weill Foundation for Music/European American Music Corporation, 2008).

8. DDH, 137.

9. Review signed by "E.N.," *Berliner Börsen-Zeitung* (morning edition), 21 November 1922.

10. WUE, 2.

11. BF, 295.

12. GS, 47.

13. Oskar Bie, "Der Protagonist," *Berliner Börsen-Courier,* 29 March 1926.

14. Theorists of film and musical theater would talk of an intentional inversion of the distinction between diegetic and nondiegetic music: music that normally underscores the action becomes part of the action.

15. Weill stated in 1926 that "what Stravinsky attempts in *L'histoire du soldat* can count as the mixed genre *[Zwischengattung]* most assured of a future . . . perhaps it can form the basis of a certain type of new opera." See Kurt Weill, "Die neue Oper," *Der neue Weg* 55 (1926): 24; reprinted in GS, 42–45, here 44.

16. Maurice de Abravanel, "Allemagne," *La Revue musicale* 7, no. 9 (July 1926): 77: "The music does not illustrate the plot; it is itself the plot. The text expresses the superficial, visible action. It is at a deeper level that music expresses the psychological plot, which is inaccessible to language." In a letter to Abravanel dated 9 June 1926 (held in WLRC), Weill wrote: "I was especially pleased by your assertion that I do not wish to promote any sympathy for my characters."

17. Theodor Wiesengrund-Adorno, "Frankfurt a. M.," *Die Musik* 20, no. 12 (September 1928): 923; reprinted in Theodor W. Adorno, *Gesammelte Schriften* (Frankfurt am Main: Suhrkamp Verlag, 1986), 19:134–36; here 134–35.

18. Georg Kaiser, *Werke,* ed. Walther Huder, vol. 5: *Stücke 1896–1922* (Frankfurt am Main: Propyläen, 1971–72), 821.

19. Kaiser's earlier brush with the law, which led to his brief imprisonment in 1921, elicited from him the notorious remark that "crime should be permissible for the creative person and the poet, if his work so requires, should be allowed to kill his own children." The Protagonist does not exactly kill his own children, just his own sister! See Wilhelm Steffens, *Georg Kaiser* (Velber: Friedrich Verlag, 1969), 26.

20. In his review of the premiere production in the *Breslauer Zeitung* (1 April 1926), the critic Alfred Dressler emphasized the "jostling array of moods" and Weill's skill in effecting the transitions between them:

> Kurt Weill's composition has several interesting characteristics. The two contrary style types—here drastic comedy, there dark tragedy—occasion Weill's use of two orchestras, the regular one in front of the stage, a second one on it. This last group, a wind octet, accompanies the more external events of the actors' rehearsal in the form of two pantomimes. The main orchestra serves to support the singing. For the most part, the two play separately. The frequent use of recitative is noticeable, demanded by Kaiser's modern notional dialogue. Among recent composers, Weill is a talent to be reckoned with. The way in which he expands and lays bare the psychological bond between Protagonist and Sister, something merely outlined in rudimentary fashion by Kaiser, demonstrates his born musical temperament. The disposition of the climaxes and transitions of the jostling array of moods in this hard-to-compose work betrays a remarkably secure dramatic instinct. The climax with the Protagonist's murder of the Sister is a splendid achievement. The orchestra is gripping in the captivating immediacy of its expression, ineluctably proceeding toward the catastrophe. The long fermata after the deed is especially impressive.

For a comprehensive account of the work's performance history and reception, see the introduction to Kurt Weill, *Der Protagonist*, KWE, ser. I, vol. 1.

21. Postcard from early June 1924, in BF, 295.

22. Of Berg's opera, Weill wrote in 1925: "This work is the first attempt to transfer to the stage Arnold Schoenberg's musical style, which breaks with everything conventional. The result is a work of art unique in its kind. Although not forward-looking, it may be seen as the grandiose conclusion of a development that leads from Wagner's *Tristan* via Debussy's *Pelléas et Mélisande* and Strauss's *Elektra* to this completely negative art. One may relate to this music as one will—the unbiased listener will receive the compelling impression of a strong musical personality in possession of a rare wealth of invention and a singular ability" (*Der deutsche Rundfunk* 3, no. 52 [1925]: 3422; in GS, 294).

23. WUE, 22.

24. BF, 306.

25. Ibid.

26. The story has been told in some detail by Robert Vilain and Geoffrey Chew, "Iwan Goll and Kurt Weill: *Der neue Orpheus and Royal Palace,*" in *Yvan Goll—Claire Goll: Texts and Contexts,* ed. Eric Robertson and Robert Vilain (Amsterdam and Atlanta, Ga.: Rodopi, 1997), 97–126.

27. See "Fort vom Durchschnitt!" *Berliner Börsen-Courier,* 20 August 1925, reprinted in GS, 35–39; English translation as "Say No to Mediocrity!" by Stephen Hinton, in *KWNL* 5, no. 2 (1987): 6–7.

28. "Kurt Weill i Exil," *Aften-Avisen* [evening edition of *Berlingske politiske og Avertissements-Tidende*], 21 June 1934.

29. Iwan Goll, "Flucht in die Oper," *Blätter der Staatsoper* [Berlin] 7, no. 8 (February 1927): 10–11; reprinted in ÜKW, 19–21, here 19.

30. Oskar Bie, "Royal Palace: Berliner Opernaufführung," *Breslauer Neueste Nachrichten,* 5 March 1927.

31. Karl Holl, *Frankfurter Zeitung,* 4 March 1927.

32. Rudolf Kastner, *Berliner Morgenpost,* 4 March 1927.

33. For a discussion of reviews of the premiere, including some not mentioned here, see David Drew, "*Royal Palace* and its Critics," in *Words on Music: Essays in Honor of Alexander Goehr on the Occasion of his 75th Birthday* (New York: Pendragon Press, 2003), 91–119. In seeking to account for the work's reception, Drew makes a case for Goll's libretto, defending it against an otherwise enduringly pervasive tradition of negative criticism.

34. Jonathan Eaton, "*Royal Palace:* A Translator's Note," *Theater* 30, no. 3 (2000): 23–25, here 24.

35. "Fragen an Nicolas Brieger," Program booklet of the Bregenzer Festspiele, *Oper im Festspielhaus 2004,* 44–59, here 54.

36. *Leipziger Bühnenblätter,* no. 14 (1927–28): 117–18; reprinted in GS, 67–68.

37. WUE, 53.

38. Alexander Rehding, "On the Record," *Cambridge Opera Journal* 18, no. 1 (2006): 59–82, here 64–65.

39. Letter from Heinsheimer to Weill, 29 March 1928, in WUE, 119.

40. For a critical discussion of the concept of surrealism as applied to *Royal Palace,* see Ricarda Wackers, *Dialog der Künste: Die Zusammenarbeit von Kurt Weill und Yvan Goll* (Münster: Waxman, 2004), esp. 280–91.

CHAPTER 4

1. The published libretto omitted the indefinite article in the title: *Mahagonny: Songspiel nach Texten von Bert Brecht. Musik von Kurt Weill. Gesangstexte entnommen aus Brechts "Hauspostille"* (Berlin and Vienna: Propyläen-Verlag/Universal-Edition, 1927).

2. Hans Curjel, "Die grossen Berliner Jahre," *Neue Zeitschrift für Musik* 133, no. 9 (1972): 503–6.

3. David Drew, "Kurt Weill and His Critics," *Times Literary Supplement,* 3 and 10 October 1975, 1142–44 and 1198–1200, here 1144.

4. Ernst Josef Aufricht, *Erzähle, damit du dein Recht erweist* (Berlin: Propyläen Verlag, 1966), 126. Aufricht recalls an episode when Weill and Brecht were photographed together during the strained rehearsals of the *Mahagonny* opera, at which "Brecht argued for the priority of the word, Weill for that of music." Brecht, according to Aufricht, "knocked the camera out of the photographer's hands [and] shouted after Weill, 'I will throw that phony Richard Strauss down the stairs with my war paint on.'"

5. Letter from Weill to Erika Neher, 18 April 1933, in WLRC.

6. "Kurt Weill i Exil," *Aften-Avisen* [the evening edition of *Berlingske politiske og Avertissements-Tidende*], 21 June 1934; German translation in GS 458–62.

7. See Felix Jackson, "Portrait of a Quiet Man: Kurt Weill, His Life and His Times," unpublished biography (photocopy in WLRC), 110; quoted in Kim H. Kowalke, "Singing Brecht versus Brecht Singing: Performance in Theory and Practice," in *Music and Performance in the Weimar Republic,* ed. Bryan Gilliam (Cambridge: Cambridge University Press, 1994), 80.

8. WLE, 52.

9. Letter dated 12 July 1950 from Lotte Lenya to Olin Downes, in WLRC.

10. Lotte Lenya, transcription of an interview by Robert Wennersten, 27 November 1971 (WLRC, ser. 30, box 11, folder 17, p. 4); partially quoted in *Lenya the Legend,* ed. David Farneth (New York: Overlook Press, 1998), 56–57.

11. The collection had been privately published the previous year in a very small print run as *Taschenpostille* (Pocket Breivary), but it is unlikely that Weill had acquired one of those copies.

12. "That was a Time!" *Theatre Arts* (May 1956), reprinted as "August 1928" in *The Threepenny Opera,* trans. Eric Bentley and Desmond Vesey (New York: Grove Press, 1964), v–xiv.

13. See Helga Kliemann, *Die Novembergruppe* (Berlin: Gebr. Mann, 1969); also Joachim Lucchesi, "Einsatz für die 'junge Kunst': Musik und Musiker in der Berliner Novembergruppe," *Musik und Gesellschaft* 37 (1987): 18–22.

14. Kurt Weill, *Der deutsche Rundfunk* 3, no. 21 (1925): 1323; reprinted as "[Abend der Novembergruppe]" in GS, 257–58. See also Albrecht Dümling, *Lasst euch nicht verführen: Brecht und die Musik* (Munich: Kindler, 1985), 141. In rehearsing much of the available

information, Fritz Hennenberg cites Nicolas Nabokov's recollection of having been in Berlin with both Weill and Brecht at Stanislawski's production of Chekhov's *Three Sisters* in 1923 (though that performance actually occurred two years earlier, in 1921). See Hennenberg, "Neue Funktionsweisen der Musik und des Musiktheaters in den zwanziger Jahren: Studien über die Zusammenarbeit Bertolt Brechts mit Franz S. Bruinier und Kurt Weill" (diss., Martin-Luther-Universität, Halle-Wittenberg, 1987), 56. Esbjörn Nyström's impressively exhaustive source-critical study *Libretto im Progress: Brechts und Weills "Aufstieg und Fall der Stadt Mahagonny" aus textgeschichtlicher Sicht* (Bern: Lang, 2005) deals only with the textual history of the full-length opera, not with biographical matters.

15. Joachim Lucchesi and Ronald K. Shull, *Musik bei Brecht* (Frankfurt am Main: Suhrkamp Verlag, 1988), 106.

16. Dümling, *Lasst euch nicht verführen,* 144.

17. Kurt Weill, "Anmerkungen zu meiner Oper *Mahagonny,*" *Die Musik* 22 (March 1930): 440–41; reprinted in GS, 102.

18. Kurt Weill, "Die Affäre Brecht," *Der Montag Morgen,* 10 June 1930, reprinted in GS, 114–15.

19. Fritz Voigt, "Um 'Mahagonny'—Eine kritische Auseinandersetzung," *Der Abend,* 16 June 1930; reprinted in *Brecht/Weill "Mahagonny,"* ed. Fritz Hennenberg and Jan Knopf (Frankfurt am Main: Suhrkamp Verlag, 2006), 285–89.

20. Curjel, "Die grossen Berliner Jahre," 503–4.

21. Drew (DDH, 189) has remarked that "Curjel's memory must have been at fault when he claimed . . . that the idea of the opera arose only from the experience, and the success, of the *Songspiel* at Baden-Baden in July 1927."

22. Facsimile of the original playbill of Weill's *Mahagonny: Ein Songspiel nach Texten von Bert Brecht,* reproduced in the published score, *Mahagonny-Songspiel,* ed. David Drew (Vienna: Universal Edition, 1963), n.p.

23. "Korrespondenz über *Dreigroschenoper,*" *Anbruch* 11, no. 1 (1929): 24–25; reprinted in GS, 73.

24. Heinrich Burkard, "Donaueschingen—Baden-Baden: Zum Program 1927," reprinted in *1927–1929: Badener Musiktage—Texte, Bilder, Programme,* selected by Klaus Schultz (Baden-Baden: Südwestfunk, 1977), 5–8, here 8.

25. Letter to UE, 4 June 1929, in WUE, 168.

26. WUE, 205.

27. In a letter to UE dated 26 December 1932 (in WUE, 431), he described "an old plan of mine . . . arranging the songs from *Happy end* into a kind of Songspiel with short spoken scenes etc." He thought that "Brecht could of course do it, but it is a dreadful thought, just because of a small and simple thing, to have to deal again with all the difficulties of working with Brecht."

28. Kurt Weill, "Opern-Rück- und Vorschau," *Der deutsche Rundfunk* 3, no. 2 (11 January 1925): 84–85; reprinted as "[Mozarts *Entführung aus dem Serail* als Sendespiel]" in GS, 217–18, here 218.

29. Kurt Weill, "Carl Maria von Weber: Zum 100. Todestag des Komponisten," *Der deutsche Rundfunk* 4, no. 22 (30 May 1926): 1517–18; reprinted in GS, 307–11, here 308.

30. Jürgen Schebera, *Kurt Weill: An Illustrated Life* (New Haven: Yale University Press,

1995), 93. Schebera's biography first appeared in German in 1990. See also Andreas Hauff, "Mahagonny . . . Only a Made-Up Word?" *KWNL* 9, no. 1 (1991): 7–9.

31. Olin Downes, "Savage Song-Spiel by a Bold and Bad Young Man," *New York Times*, 14 August 1927..

32. Ronald Sanders, *The Days Grow Short: The Life and Music of Kurt Weill* (London: Weidenfeld & Nicolson, 1980), 91.

33. Paul Bekker, *Briefe an zeitgenössische Musiker* (Berlin: Max Hesses Verlag, 1932), 104.

34. WUE, 194.

35. WUE, 78–79.

36. Letter dated 16 December 1927, in WUE, 96.

37. Letter dated 27 December 1927, in WUE, 98.

CHAPTER 5

1. In 1920s popular music, asparagus *(Spargel)* functioned as a lewd code word, as in the line from the popular song "Veronika" by Walter Jurmann: "Veronika, der Spargel wächst, / Die ganze Welt ist wie verhext!" (Veronika, the asparagus is growing, the whole world is bewitched!). The same innuendo was no doubt intended in *Der Zar lässt sich photographieren*, where the Zar in an amorous mood likens the Eiffel Tower to a "giant asparagus." In a letter to Weill written in May 1942, Lenya kept the tradition alive by saying that when she first met him he was a "thin turnip" *(dünne rübe)*, but in the meantime he had become "a very intelligent asparagus *[spargi]*," even providing her own graphic illustration (reproduced, along with the letter, in WLE, 345).

2. Weill, "Korrespondenz über *Dreigroschenoper*," *Anbruch* 11, no. 1 (1929): 24–25; reprinted in GS, 72–74, here 74.

3. Michael Morley hears an allusion to Bach's *Weihnachtsoratorium*; see Morley's review of the *Die Dreigroschenoper*, KWE, ser. 1, vol. 5; reprinted in *KWNL* 18, nos. 1–2 (2000): 35.

4. Aufricht related the early history of the piece, from his first meeting with Brecht through opening night, in his memoirs *Erzähle, damit du dein Recht erweist* (Berlin: Propyläen Verlag, 1966), 60–79.

5. Brecht's response to Kerr appeared in the *Berliner Börsen-Courier* on 6 May 1929. See *Kurt Weill: The Threepenny Opera*, ed. Stephen Hinton (Cambridge: Cambridge University Press, 1990), 10–11.

6. For a legal perspective on the contract that Brecht and Weill drew up with the literary agency Bloch Erben, see Ulrich Fischer, "Erfolgsstory im Paragrafendschungel: Fünfundsiebzig Jahre 'Dreigroschengesellschaft,'" *Neue Musikzeitung* 52, no. 5 (2003): 5–6.

7. On the origin of the "Kanonen-Song," see *Brecht-Liederbuch*, ed. Fritz Hennenberg (Frankfurt am Main: Suhrkamp Verlag, 1984), 391–93. Brecht knew Kipling's "Screw-Guns" in the German translation of the "Barrack-Room Ballads" (*Balladen aus dem Biwak*, trans. Marx Möller [Berlin: Vita Verlag, 1911]).

8. Oskar Bie, *Berliner Börsen-Courier*, 1 September 1928. The following day Bie published a second, more extensive notice for the same newspaper with the title "Die Musik zur Dreigroschenoper."

9. Theodor Wiesengrund-Adorno, "Zur Dreigroschenoper," *Die Musik* 22 (1929): 424–28; translated by Stephen Hinton in Hinton (ed.), *Weill: Threepenny Opera,* 129–33: "The success [of the piece] entices one into believing that here, with simple means, with utter comprehensibility, operetta has quite simply been exalted and made palatable for the requirements of the cognoscenti."

10. Elias Canetti, *Die Fackel im Ohr: Lebensgeschichte 1921–1931* (Munich: Carl Hanser Verlag, 1980), 286: "An opera it was not, nor a send-up of opera, as it had originally been; it was, and this was the one unadulterated thing about it, an operetta. What one had done was to take the saccharine form of Viennese operetta, in which people found their wishes undisturbed, and oppose it with a Berlin form, with its hardness, meanness, and banal justifications, which people wanted no less, probably even more, than all that sweetness."

11. Aufricht, *Erzähle,* 65.

12. Letter to UE, 10 September 1928, in WUE, 135.

13. Weill talked initially in terms of a "farce": "During work on *The Beggar's Opera* I have rapidly developed the impression that the piece is out of the question as 'opera,' and that one can best choose the form of a farce *[Posse]* with music, which cannot be considered for opera houses because of the preponderance of dialogue" (letter to Schott-Verlag, 14 March 1928; quoted in Hinton [ed.], *Weill: Threepenny Opera,* 18). The critic Heinrich Strobel confirmed this impression by drawing attention in his review of the premiere to "an unbuttoned performance with Nestroyesque traits" ("Melosberichte," *Melos* 7 [1928]: 498).

14. See my "Misunderstanding *The Threepenny Opera,*" in Hinton (ed.), *Weill: Threepenny Opera,* 181–92.

15. Bertolt Brecht, *Journale 1,* BBA, vol. 26 (Frankfurt am Main: Suhrkamp Verlag, 1994), 299.

16. John Willett put it this way: "The work as Brecht and Weill conceived it is still something of a bomb planted not so much beneath our society (because I don't really believe it blew all that much of a hole even in the flimsy Weimar structure) as beneath its more outmoded art forms and the snobberies which these reflect" ("Brecht's *The Threepenny Opera* at the Adelaide Festival," *Theatre Quarterly* 7 [1977]: 100).

17. Erich Fried, "The Day Hitler Marched In," *Observer* [London], 8 March 1988.

18. Karl Lustig-Prean, "Der Tod des Avantgardisten," *Arbeiter-Zeitung* [Vienna], 9 April 1950.

19. Of all the works listed in the "play" category in the 2005–6 season, *Die Dreigroschenoper* was seen by more theatergoers than any other work—199,308 in total. However, it came in a distant second to *Die Zauberflöte,* which was listed in the "opera" category and attracted 320,474 audience members during the same period. These data are drawn from the web pages of the Deutscher Bühnenverein (www.buehnenverein.de).

20. See Kim H. Kowalke, "'The Threepenny Opera' in America," in Hinton (ed.), *Weill: Threepenny Opera,* 78–119.

21. Weill, "Korrespondenz," GS, 74. Somewhat baffling is Weill's preceding remark that "the last Threepenny Finale is by no means a parody." It is certainly one in both senses of the term: it self-consciously uses convention, and it functions as a kind of burlesque.

22. The first published full score of *Die Dreigroschenoper* omitted these instructions, but they were reinstated in the Kurt Weill Edition.

23. The verses were apparently never set to music. In this they parallel Brown's closing verse addressing the public at the end of *Dreigroschenoper.*

24. Fragment of an undated letter [1929] from Brecht to Hauptmann, quoted in Elisabeth Hauptmann, *Julia ohne Romeo: Geschichten, Stücke, Aufsätze, Erinnerungen,* ed. Rosemarie Eggert and Rosemarie Hill (Berlin: Aufbau-Verlag, 1977), 246.

25. Paula Hanssen has asserted that because of the central importance of the songs to the piece, some of them were probably Hauptmann's; see *Elisabeth Hauptmann: Brecht's Silent Collaborator* (Berlin: Peter Lang, 1994), 42. Not only did the original contract list Hauptmann as the author of *Happy End,* but the texts of the following songs were first published under her copyright in 1977: "Das Lied von der harten Nuss," "Der kleine Leutnant des lieben Gottes," "Geht hinein in die Schlacht," "Bruder gib dir einen Stoss," "Fürchte dich nicht," "In der Jugend goldnem Schimmer."

26. Kurt Weill, "Der Komponist der *Dreigroschenoper* über sein neues Werk," *Berlin am Morgen,* 6 September 1929; reprinted in GS, 446; also quoted in "'Nichts Höheres': Auch Kurt Weill blamiert sich," *Chemnitzer Tageblatt,* 28 September 1929.

27. I am grateful to Elmar Juchem for having established the length of *Happy End*'s run at the Theater am Schiffbauerdamm.

28. Letters to UE of 11 and 15 June 1932, respectively; in WUE, 392–93 and 395–98.

29. Kurt Weill, "Tanzmusik," *Der deutsche Rundfunk* 4, no. 11 (14 September 1926): 732; in GS, 299.

30. Karl Marx, *Preface and Introduction to a Contribution to the Critique of Political Economy* (Peking: Foreign Languages Press, 1976), 45. The introduction derives from the economic manuscripts *(Grundrisse)* of 1857–58.

31. Alfred Kerr, *Berliner Tageblatt,* 3 September 1929.

32. *Dresdner Neueste Nachrichten,* 4 September 1929; the same review appeared simultaneously in the *Breslauer Neueste Nachrichten.*

33. *Hannoverscher Courier,* 8 September 1929.

34. *Berliner Börsen-Courier,* 3 September 1929; the review also appeared in *Magdeburger Zeitung,* 6 September 1929, and *Thüringer Allgemeine Zeitung,* 7 September 1929.

35. *Die Weltbühne* 30, no. 37 (10 September 1929): 406–7.

36. Letter of 14 October 1929, in WUE, 194–95.

37. Letter of 3 June 1932, ibid., 388.

38. Letter of 11 June 1932, ibid., 392.

39. Letter of 15 June 1932, ibid., 395.

40. Letter of 26 December 1932, ibid., 431.

41. Such an arrangement was eventually prepared by David Drew and given its premiere in Berlin with the London Sinfonietta under David Atherton in 1975. The same forces subsequently recorded Drew's arrangement for Decca. See DDH, 221–22.

42. A version prepared by Hauptmann in the 1950s was published in Hauptmann, *Julia ohne Romeo,* 65–135. This version cuts "Hosiannah Rockefeller" but retains the Marxist speech.

43. Quoted in Andreas Hauff, "Nicht denkbar 'ohne die sozialen und ethischen Hin-

tergründe': Zum politischen Kontext des Weill'schen Musiktheaters," *Neue Zeitschrift für Musik* 25, no. 2 (2000): 36–41.

44. Ibid., 40–41.

45. Ulrike Zitzlsperger has noted how differing critical responses to the piece were conditioned, in part, "by the ways in which the different producers emphasized different aspects of the work." See her essay "Caught between Two Eras: Georg Kaiser's *The Silver Lake*," in *Georg Kaiser and Modernity*, ed. Frank Krause (Göttingen: V&R Unipress, 2005), 123–40, here 128. Additionally, she points out that in Leipzig, the role of Olim was played by Erhard Siedel, a comic actor, who "created a lightness of tone clearly absent from the Magdeburg production" (132).

46. Zitzlsperger has proposed a "further parallel" with George Grosz's collection of satirical montages from 1917–18, also entitled "Ein Wintermärchen." See ibid., 125.

47. Letter of 29 July 1932, in WUE, 406–7, here 407.

48. Letter of 2 August 1932, ibid., 407–8, here 407.

49. The minimum of twenty-five players can be inferred from a letter of 16 January 1933 (WUE, 443), where Weill mentions the objection to an orchestra of that size from Erich Ziegel, director of the Hamburger Kammerspiele. Although Ziegel was interested in staging the work at his theater, he was reluctant, Weill reports, to hire more than eighteen players.

50. Letter of 11 November 1932, in WUE, 417.

51. Letter of 14 November 1932, ibid., 418–19, here 418.

52. Letter of 24 November 1932, ibid., 421–23, here 422.

53. Cited in Peter K. Tyson, *The Reception of Georg Kaiser (1915–45)*, Canadian Studies in German Language and Literature, vol. 32 (New York: Peter Lang, 1984), 555. Tyson's study provides extensive documentation of the work's early production history and reception.

54. Kurt Weill, "Vorwort zum Regiebuch der Oper *Aufstieg und Fall der Stadt Mahagonny*," *Anbruch* 12 (January 1930): 5–7; in GS, 103–6, here 104.

55. Kurt Weill, "Zur Uraufführung der *Mahagonny*-Oper," *Leipziger Neueste Nachrichten*, 8 March 1930; in GS, 106–9, here 108.

56. Kurt Weill, "Zeitoper," *Melos* 7, no. 3 (March 1928): 106–8; in GS, 65.

57. See Hauff, "Nicht denkbar," 40.

58. There is a small difference between Kaiser's text and the one actually set by Weill: the former has the line "*Nothing* will be forgiven . . ." (my italics).

59. See Hauff, "Nicht denkbar," 38–39.

60. Ian Kemp, "Music as Metaphor: Aspects of *Der Silbersee*," in *A New Orpheus: Essays on Kurt Weill*, ed. Kim Kowalke (Yale University Press, 1990), 131–46.

61. Theodor W. Adorno, *Beethoven: Philosophie der Musik* (Frankfurt am Main: Suhrkamp Verlag, 1993), 22: "The difficulty of all musical analysis consists in the following: the more one resolves music into its smallest units, the nearer one gets to the single tone, and all music is comprised of single tones. That which is most specific becomes that which is most general and negatively abstract. Eschewing such close analysis, however, means missing all the connections."

62. Accounts of the National Socialist propaganda mobilized against the production

in Magdeburg can be found in both Tyson, *The Reception of Georg Kaiser (1915–45)*; and Ziztlsperger, "Caught between Two Eras."

CHAPTER 6

1. See Carl Dahlhaus, "Igor Strawinskijs episches Theater," in *Vom Musikdrama zur Literaturoper: Aufsätze zur neueren Operngeschichte*, rev. ed. (Munich: Piper, 1989), 186–227; and Vera Stegman, *Das epische Musiktheater bei Strawinsky und Brecht: Studien zur Geschichte und Theorie* (New York: Peter Lang, 1991).

2. Heinrich Strobel, "Erinnerung an Kurt Weill," *Melos* 17 (1950): 133–36; reprinted in ÜKW, 146–51, here 150.

3. Kurt Weill, "Protagonist of Music in the Theatre," unsigned article in *The American Hebrew* [New York], 8 January 1937, 756–57, 760.

4. Interview dated 7 December 1978 for Skyline (WNET/13 TV); transcript in WLRC: "I stopped in the middle [of 'Surabaya-Johnny'], I said 'Brecht, I want to ask you something. Now you have that theory of epic theater, maybe you want me to sing that different, you know.'" But the insecurity about her grasp of the playwright's celebrated theories was misplaced, and Brecht was quick to supply words of encouragement. "He got up . . . and he said, 'Anything you do, Lenya, is epic enough for me.'"

5. Bertolt Brecht and Peter Suhrkamp, "Anmerkungen zur Oper *Aufstieg und Fall der Stadt Mahagonny*," *Versuche* 2 (Berlin: Kiepenheuer, 1930), 107–15; reprinted in *Schriften*, vol. 4, BBA 24, ed. Marianne Conrad, Sigmar Gerund and Benno Slupianek (1991), 74–86. An earlier version of the "Notes" appeared as "Zur Soziologie der Oper—Anmerkungen zu 'Mahagonny,'" in the journal *Musik und Gesellschaft* 1, no. 4 (1930): 105–12.

6. A notable exception was Arnold Schoenberg, who polemicized vehemently against Brecht's theory as he found it summarized in an article by Hans Heinrich Stuckenschmidt. See Alexander Ringer, "Schoenberg, Weill, and Epic Theater," *Journal of the Arnold Schoenberg Institute* 9 (1980): 77–98.

7. John Locke, *An Essay Concerning Human Understanding* [1690] (Oxford: Oxford University Press, 1975), book 3, chap. 10, sec. 14, 497: "Another great *abuse of Words is, the taking them for Things* . . . To this Abuse, those Men are most subject, who confine their Thoughts to any one System, and give themselves up into a firm belief of the Perfection of any received Hypothesis: whereby they come to be persuaded, that the Terms of that Sect, are so suited to the Nature of Things, that they perfectly correspond with their real Existence."

8. Werner Hecht, *Brechts Weg zum epischen Theater* (Berlin: Henschel, 1962), 146.

9. Jürgen Schebera, *Kurt Weill: Leben und Werk* (Leipzig: Deutscher Verlag für Musik, 1983), 112. Fritz Hennenberg similarly interprets Weill's and Brecht's theories as essentially congruent, despite "contradictions in a few political and artistic views"; see his dissertation "Neue Funktionsweisen der Musik und des Musiktheaters in den zwanziger Jahren: Studien über die Zusammenarbeit Bertolt Brechts mit Franz S. Bruinier und Kurt Weill" (diss. [B.] [= Habilitationsschrift], Martin-Luther-Universität, Halle-Wittenberg, 1987), 137.

10. "Vorwort zum Regiebuch der Oper *Aufstieg und Fall der Stadt Mahagonny*,"

Anbruch 12, no. 1 (1930): 5–7 (reprinted in GS, 103–6); "Zur Uraufführung der Mahagonny-Oper," *Leipziger Neueste Nachrichten,* 8 March 1930 (reprinted in GS, 106–9); "Anmerkungen zu meiner Oper *Mahagonny,*" *Die Musik* 22 (March 1930): 440–41 (reprinted in GS, 102–3).

11. David Drew, "Kurt Weill and His Critics," *Times Literary Supplement,* 3 October 1975, 1143.

12. For a critique of Drew's view, see Hennenberg, "Neue Funktionsweisen der Musik," 108.

13. Weill, "Zur Uraufführung der Mahagonny-Oper," in GS, 107.

14. Considered for a while to be lost (see GS, 106), there have survived two typescript versions, both entitled "Vorschläge zur szenischen Ausführung der Oper AUFSTIEG UND FALL DER STADT MAHAGONNY," copies of which are held in the WLRC (ser. 33/[19308]). Consisting mainly of suggested stage directions, the text duplicates or paraphrases much that is already in the published piano-vocal score. The musical/scene numbers as well as the page numbers refer to those in the first edition of the published score. See Esbörn Nyström, *Libretto im Progress: Brechts und Weills "Aufstieg und Fall der Stadt Mahagonny" aus textgeschichtlicher Sicht* (Bern: Peter Lang, 2005), 286–93.

15. WUE, 92.

16. Quoted from "Protagonist of Music in the Theatre."

17. Brecht, "Anmerkungen," BBA 24:74–86, here 79.

18. Ibid.

19. Weill, "Anmerkungen zu meiner Oper *Mahagonny,*" in GS, 102.

20. Weill, "Das Formproblem der modernen Oper," *Der Scheinwerfer* 5, no. 2 (1931–32): 3–4; in GS, 134–36, here 136.

21. "Aktuelles Theater," *Melos* 8 (1929): 524, 527; in GS, 96–100, here 100.

22. Weill, "Über den gestischen Charakter der Musik," *Die Musik* 21 (1928–29): 419–23; in GS, 83–88, here 84.

23. Brecht, "Anmerkungen," in BBA 24:81.

24. Ibid., 83.

25. Ibid., 77.

26. Ibid., 81–82.

27. Ibid., 84.

28. Weill, "Zur Uraufführung der Mahagonny-Oper."

29. Emil Staiger, *Grundbegriffe der Poetik* (Zurich: Atlantis, 1961), 235.

30. Peter Szondi, *Theorie des modernen Dramas* (Frankfurt am Main: Suhrkamp Verlag, 1959), 115.

31. Ibid., 118.

32. Ibid., 13.

33. Peter Szondi, *Schriften* (Frankfurt am Main: Suhrkamp Verlag, 1978), 2:198–204.

34. Bertolt Brecht, "Die Strassenszene: Grundmodell einer Szene des epischen Theaters," *Schriften zum Theater* (Frankfurt am Main: Suhrkamp Verlag, 1957), 99.

35. For a general discussion of this issue, see Wolfgang Ruf, "Modernes Musiktheater: Studien zu seiner Geschichte und Typologie" (Habilitationsschrift, University of Freiburg, 1983).

36. Erik Fischer, *Zur Problematik der Opernstruktur: Das künstlerische System und seine Krisis im 20. Jahrhundert* (Wiesbaden: Franz Steiner, 1982).

37. Carl Dahlhaus, "Traditionelle Dramaturgie in der modernen Oper," *Musiktheater heute,* Veröffentlichungen des Instituts für Neue Musik und Musikerziehung Darmstadt, vol. 22 (Mainz: Schott, 1982), 25.

38. "Korrespondenz über *Dreigroschenoper,*" *Anbruch* 11, no. 1 (1929): 24–25; in GS, 73.

39. Weill, "Vorwort zum Regiebuch," in GS, 103.

40. Weill, "Zur Uraufführung der Mahagonny-Oper," 108.

41. Brecht, "Anmerkungen," in BBA 24:80.

42. Ibid., 79.

43. Carl Dahlhaus, "'Am Text entlang komponiert': Bermerkungen zu einem Schlagwort," in *Für und wider die Literaturoper,* ed. Sigrid Wiesman (Laaber: Laaber, 1982), 194.

44. For a discussion of parallels between Wagner's music dramas and Brecht's epic theater, see Hilda Meldrum Brown, *Leitmotiv and Drama: Wagner, Brecht, and the Limits of "Epic" Theatre* (Oxford: Clarendon Press, 1991).

45. W.H. Auden, "Notes on Music and Opera," in *The Dyer's Hand* (New York: Random House, 1962), 470.

46. Ibid, 474.

47. *New Statesman,* 30 November 1979, 870.

48. William Empson, *Seven Types of Ambiguity* (London: Chatto & Windus, 1953), 24: "We are concerned here with a sort of dramatic ambiguity of judgment which does not consider the character so much as the audience."

49. Weill, "Situation der Oper," *Melos* 10 (1930): 45; in GS, 457.

50. Letter from Weill to his publisher (Hans Heinsheimer of Universal Edition), 14 October 1929, in WUE, 194.

51. Letter from Heinsheimer to Weill, 10 October 1929, in WUE, 193. On the eve of the opera's premiere, which took place in Leipzig on 9 March 1930, Weill gave a radio broadcast (the text of which has not survived) in which he reportedly made a comparison between his new opera and Wagner's *Tristan und Isolde,* thereby adding a piquant twist to his anti-Wagnerian stance. "In his introductory talk," the arch-conservative critic Alfred Heuss reported, "Mr. Weill did not shy away from saying that the five Mahagonny songs that received their first performance in Baden-Baden three years ago were of no greater significance than—pay attention, dear reader!—than the *Wesendonck-Lieder* are to *Tristan und Isolde!* . . . Wagner of all people, with his greatest love poem, is supposed to furnish the stirrups upon which they can mount their nag!" See Alfred Heuss, "Wird es endlich dämmern? Zur Mahagonny-Theaterschlacht am 9. März im Neuen Theater Leipzig," *Zeitschrift für Musik* 97 (May 1930): 392–95, here 394; quoted in Jürgen Schebera, "*Mahagonny*—Songspiel und Oper: Aufführungs- und Rezeptionsgeschichte 1927–1933," *Communications* 33 (2004): 22–32, here 25. The verb of Heuss's title ("dämmern") is likely intended to have Wagnerian connotations, too. See also my article "Weill contra Wagner: Aspects of Ambivalence," in ". . . *dass alles auch hätte anders kommen können": Beiträge zur Musikgeschichte des 20. Jahrhunderts,* ed. Susanne Schaal-Gotthardt, Luitgard Schader, and Heinz-Jürgen Winkler (Frankfurt am Main: Schott, 2009), 155–74.

52. Kurt Weill, "Vorwort zum Regiebuch der Oper *Aufstieg und Fall der Stadt Mahagonny,*" *Anbruch* 12, no. 1 (1930): 5–7; reprinted in GS, 103–6.

53. Ralph Winett, "Composer of the Hour: An Interview with Kurt Weill," *Brooklyn Daily Eagle,* 20 December 1936.

54. Georg Simmel, some two decades prior to the Weimar Republic, had already drawn attention to the dehumanizing effects of the big city. For a discussion and contextualization of his classic essay of 1902, "The Metropolis and Mental Life," see Harry F. Mallgrave's introduction to Otto Wagner, *Modern Architecture* (Santa Monica: Getty Center for the History of Art and the Humanities, 1988), 1–51. In his summary of Simmel's ideas, Mallgrave notes how the "blasé attitude" engendered by the fast pace of city life "[led] to a cold and calculating behavior in which people were products to be bought, sold, and manipulated" (11). For a broad range of recent musicological papers dealing with the city in general and Weill's *Mahagonny* in particular, see *Mahagonny: Die Stadt als Sujet und Herausforderung des (Musik-)Theaters,* ed. Peter Csobádi et al. (Salzburg: Verlag Mueller-Speiser, 2000).

55. Kurt Weill, "Notiz zum *Berliner Requiem,*" *Der deutsche Rundfunk* 7, no. 20 (17 May 1929): 613; reprinted in GS, 409–11, here 410.

56. The "phony Richard Strauss" anecdote, discussed in chapter 2, originated in the memoirs of the impresario Ernst Josef Aufricht, who produced the 1928 premiere of *Die Dreigroschenoper* and the 1931 production of *Aufstieg und Fall der Stadt Mahagonny,* both in Berlin. See *Erzähle, damit du dein Recht erweist* (Berlin: Propyläen Verlag, 1966), 126.

57. See the Coda following chapter 12 for a discussion of Mozart's singspiel and its influence on Weill.

58. Letter from Emil Herztka (director of Universal Edition) to Weill, 16 December 1927, in WUE, 96.

59. DDH, 185.

60. Nyström, *Libretto im Progress,* 405.

61. Kurt Weill, *Aufstieg und Fall der Stadt Mahagonny,* piano-vocal score, ed. David Drew (Vienna: Universal Edition, 1969), n.p. [preface to 1969 ed.].

62. For a discussion of the origins of Brecht's text, see Jan Knopf, *Bertolt Brechts "Terzinen über die Liebe"* (Frankfurt am Main: Suhrkamp Verlag, 1998).

63. See *Brecht/Weill "Mahagonny,"* ed. Fritz Hennenberg and Jan Knopf (Frankfurt am Main: Suhrkamp Verlag, 2006), 21–39. The provenance of the manuscript, which came to light in Vienna in 1953, is murky. Less a reduction of the opera than an expansion of the *Songspiel* using additional material from the full-length work, it may, the editors claim, reflect the version of *Mahagonny* performed in Paris in 1932 or perhaps the revised version made for Paris, London, and Rome the following year, or, indeed, yet a further revision for a performance in Venice in 1949. They also note that it remains an open question whether the text is "an adaptation by a third party or an authentic version by Weill." Esbjörn Nyström (*Libretto im Progress,* 148) doubts its authenticity, not only because of the way Brecht's first name is spelled (as "Berthold"), which "does not make an especially reliable impression. . . . It seems," he writes, "to mix several works together—*Songspiel* (subtitle), opera (title), and the later versions of the *Songspiel,* the Parisian (idea of the expanded *Songspiel*) and Venetian (text)." Because the authenticity of this surviving version is at

best dubious and at worst entirely bogus, the so-called "Pariser" or "Kleines Mahagonny" is of little consequence for the opera's textual history.

64. The typescript of Weill's notes is held in WLRC. A German translation of the lecture, "Was ist musikalisches Theater?," is in GS, 144–48.

65. Karl Marx, "Vorwort," in *Zur Kritik der politischen Ökonomie,* Marx-Engels-Werke, vol. 13 (Berlin: Dietz, 1971), 9.

66. See Andreas Hauff, "Elemente romantischer Tradition im Musiktheater Kurt Weills: Überlegungen zur Nebelszene der Bürgschaft," in *A Stranger Here Myself: Kurt Weill-Studien,* ed. Kim H. Kowalke and Horst Edler (Hildesheim: Georg Olms Verlag, 1993), 185–206.

67. The story was originally published in the fourth installment of Johann Gottfried von Herder's *Blätter der Vorzeit: Dichtungen aus der morgenländischen Sage,* a collection whose first two installments bore the subtitle "Jüdische Dichtungen und Fabeln." Published in 1802, shortly before Herder's death, as "Jüdische Parabeln," the fourth installment contained stories related mainly to the Old Testament, as were many of the "fables" in the earlier collections. "Der afrikanische Rechtsspruch," demonstrably of Jewish origin, is "identical in content" to a parable in Moses Mendelssohn's *Proben rabbinischer Weisheit* from 1775, which itself drew on the Talmud, as David Drew has noted. See Drew's searching essay "The *Bürgschaft* Debate and the Timeliness of the Untimely," in Kowalke and Edler (eds.), *A Stranger Here Myself,* 161; and the "Afterword" by Fritz Bamberger to the 1936 edition of *Blätter der Vorzeit* (Berlin: Schocken Verlag, 1936), 87–91.

68. Ulrich Fischer, "Rechtliche, rechtshistorische und rechtssoziologische Anmerkungen zu Kurt Weills und Caspar Nehers Oper *Die Bürgschaft,*" *Neue Juristische Wochenschrift* 57, no. 9 (2004): 558–66.

69. Letter from Weill to UE, 19 November 1931, in WUE, 343–45, here 345.

70. Letter dated 14 December 1931, in WUE, 354–55.

71. David Drew, "Topicality and the Universal: The Strange Case of Weill's *Die Bürgschaft,*" *Music and Letters* 39 (1958): 242–55, here 255 n. 6: "The static, 'monumentalized' forms and the stylized characterization of *Die Bürgschaft* clearly owe something to Stravinsky's example."

72. Letter from Weill to UE, 1 August 1931, in WUE, 308–9.

73. Diana Stacie Diskin, "The Early History of Kurt Weill's *Die Bürgschaft,* 1930–33" (Ph.D. diss., University of Southern California, 2004), 525–27.

74. Ibid., 525.

75. Letter from Weill to UE, 13 August 1931, in WUE, 313–15, here 315.

76. Herbert Trantow, "Fragen an Kurt Weill, seine *Bürgschaft* betreffend," *Melos* 11 (September 1932): 276–77; reprinted in GS, 141.

77. Weill, letter to the editor, *Melos* 11 (October 1932): 336–37; reprinted in GS, 139–40.

78. A fuller context for Weill's and Trantow's differences, with discussion of other opinions, is provided by Drew's "*Bürgschaft* Debate."

79. Diskin, "Early History," 159.

80. Paul Bekker, *Briefe an zeitgenössische Musiker* (Berlin-Schöneberg: Max Hesses Verlag, 1932).

81. Drew, "*Bürgschaft* Debate," 175.

82. Diskin, "Early History," 467.

83. Herbert Trantow, "Weill: *Die Bürgschaft,*" *Sozialistische Monatshefte* 38 (October 1932): 877–79; quoted in Drew, "*Bürgschaft* Debate," 177.

84. Ernst Bloch, "Fragen in Weills *Bürgschaft,*" *Anbruch* 14 (1932): 207; reprinted in ÜKW, 82–84, here 84; Drew, "*Bürgschaft* Debate," 177.

85. David Drew, "Topicality and the Universal," 255.

86. "Darf die Musik politisieren?" *Deutsche Allgemeine Zeitung,* 14 December 1930; reprinted in GS, 122.

87. "Das Formproblem der modernen Oper," *Der Scheinwerfer* 5, no. 2 (February 1932): 3–4; reprinted in GS, 136. Weill specified the elements here as "forgoing the illustrative effect of music, eliminating false pathos, dividing the action into closed numbers and the dramaturgical exploitation of absolute musical form."

88. Brecht, "Anmerkungen," in BBA 24:79.

CHAPTER 7

1. Kurt Weill, "Aktuelles Zwiegepräch über die Schuloper," *Die Musikpflege* 1 (1930); reprinted in GS, 447–54, here 448.

2. "Kurt Weill Has Secured a Niche of His Own at 35" (interview), *New York World-Telegram,* 21 December 1935.

3. A list and description of the principal writings on the "Lehrstück" are contained in the following books: Reinhold Grimm, *Bertolt Brecht* (Stuttgart: J. B. Metzler, 1971); Jan Knopf, *Bertolt Brecht: Ein kritischer Forschungsbericht* (Frankfurt am Main: Suhrkamp Verlag, 1974); Juliane Eckhardt, *Das epische Theater* (Darmstadt: Wissenschaftliche Buchgesellschaft, 1983), esp. 78–104; Rekha Kamath, *Brechts Lehrstück-Modell als Bruch mit den bürgerlichen Theatertraditionen,* Europäische Hochschulschriften 605 (Frankfurt am Main: P. Lang, 1983); Matthias-Johannes Fischer, *Brechts Theatertheorie: Forschungsgeschichte—Forschungsstand—Perspektiven,* Europäische Hochschulschriften 1115 (Frankfurt am Main: P. Lang, 1989); Klaus-Dieter Krabiel, *Brechts Lehrstücke: Entstehung und Entwicklung eines Spieltyps* (Stuttgart: J. B. Metzler, 1993); and Joy H. Calico, *Brecht at the Opera* (Berkeley: University of California Press, 2008).

4. Jacob und Wilhelm Grimm, *Deutsches Wörterbuch,* vol. 12 (Leipzig: S. Hirzel, 1885), 578.

5. The *Lehrstück* entry in Wahrig's *Deutsches Wörterbuch* (Munich: Mosaik-Verlag, 1980) offers the following definition, which is specific about genre but not about authorship: "Theaterstück, das eine Lehre oder Erkenntnis vermitteln soll." The *Brockhaus Wahrig Deutsches Wörterbuch* (Wiesbaden: Brockhaus, 1982) also restricts itself to drama but gives Brecht as an example: "Drama, das belehren will, dramatische Lehrdichtung; die Lehrstücke Brechts." The *Wörterbuch der deutschen Gegenwartssprache* (Berlin: Akademie-Verlag, 1969), produced in the former German Democratic Republic, defines *Lehrstück* as "didactic theater" *(belehrendes Theater);* it does not mention Brecht, but it does list the term as a "neologism" *(Neuprägung).*

6. In his study *Brecht und das Fastnachtspiel* (Göttingen: Arbeitsstelle für Renaissanceforschung am Seminar für deutsche Philologie der Universtität Göttingen, 1978), which

draws parallels between Brecht's plays and sixteenth-century religious dramas, Thomas Habel remarks that Brecht often uses the terms *episch* and *lehrhaft* as synonyms (32).

7. See note 3 above.

8. Krabiel, *Brechts Lehrstücke,* 95.

9. Johann Balthasar Schupp, *Lehrreiche Schriften* (Frankfurt: Wust, 1677): "Lasse dir Gottes Exempel in dieser Sach ein Lehrstück sein" (755) and "sollen meine Schäden dein Lehrstück sein" (756); quoted in Grimm, *Deutsches Wörterbuch* 12:578.

10. For example, Yizhak Ahren, *Das Lehrstück "Holocaust": Zur Wirkungspsychologie eines Medienereignisses* (Opladen: Westdeutscher Verlag, 1982); and Fritz Schweighofer, *Das Privattheater der Anna O.: Ein psychoanalytisches Lehrstück—ein Emanzipationsdrama* (Munich: E. Reinhardt, n.d. [1987?]).

11. Ingrid Craemer-Ruegenberg, "Die Seele als Form in einer Hierarchie von Formen: Beobachtungen zu einem Lehrstück aus der De-Anima-Paraphrase Alberts des Großen," in *Albertus Magnus Doctor Universalis 1280/1980,* ed. G. Meyer et al. (Mainz: Matthias-Grünewald-Verlag, 1980), 64. This is also the earliest sense of the word cited in the Grimms' *Deutsches Wörterbuch:* "Unter des Plato alten Lehrstücken war auch dieses, das anders nichts von den Göttern solle gebeten werden, als: zu geben dasjenige, was dem Menschen am nützlichsten" (Samuel von Butschky, *Hochdeutsche Kanzeley* [Leipzig, 1659], 347).

12. See, for example, the entry *Lehrstück-Katechismus* in the *Lexikon für Theologie und Kirche,* 6 vols. (Freiburg: Herder, 1961).

13. This general sense is conveyed in E. Christian Achelis's absorbing historical study of the utilization of the decalogue in catechistic teaching: *Der Dekalog als katechetisches Lehrstück* (Giessen: Alfred Töppelmann, 1905). Achelis is concerned with the decalogue's didactic status as such rather than with its particular mode of presentation in the type of catechism known as "Lehrstück-Katechismus."

14. The first part of Carl Philip Emanuel Bach's *Versuch über die wahre Art das Clavier zu spielen* ([Berlin: C. F. Henning, 1753] Leipzig: Breitkopf & Härtel, 1981), for example, is divided into three "Hauptstücke" (fingering, ornamentation, and performance), which constitute the foundation of keyboard musicianship.

15. Quoted in the entry *Katechismus* in *Die Religion in Geschichte und Gegenwart,* vol. 3 (Tübingen: J. C. B. Mohr, 1959), 1180.

16. "The common people, especially those who live in the country, have no knowledge whatever of Christian teaching, and unfortunately many pastors are quite incompetent and unfitted for teaching" (Luther's preface to *The Small Catechism,* in *Three Reformation Catechisms: Catholic, Anabaptist, Lutheran,* ed. Denis Janz [New York and Toronto: E. Mellen Press, 1982], 182).

17. The so-called *Hessische Fragestücke,* first published in 1574 and intended expressly for such instruction, were later incorporated into the widely used *Darmstädter Katechismus.*

18. See "Katechismus," in *Religion in Geschichte und Gegenwart* 3:1184.

19. A cogent summary of these issues can be found in Bernhard Truffer, *Das materialkerygmatische Anliegen in der Katechetik der Gegenwart: Zur Geschichte der inneren Stoffgestaltung des Lehrstück-Katechismus* (Freiburg: Herder, 1963).

20. From an unpublished paper of 1860, quoted in Henry Tristram, "On Reading Newman," *John Henry Newman: Centenary Essays* (London: Burns, Oates & Washbourne, 1945), 226.

21. Franz Michel Willam, *Die Erkenntnis Lehre Kardinal Newmans: Systematische Darlegung und Dokumentation* (Bergen-Enkheim: Gerhard Kaffke, 1969).

22. See *Lehrstück-Katechismus* entry in the *Lexikon für Theologie und Kirche.*

23. See the foreword to the first edition of Mey's *Vollständige Katechesen für die untere Klasse der katholischen Volksschule* (Freiburg im Breisgau: Herdersche Verlagshandlung, 1871), v.

24. Achelis, *Der Dekalog als katechetisches Lehrstück*, 75.

25. Karl Laux, "Skandal in Baden-Baden," *Hindemith-Jahrbuch* 2 (1972): 166–80.

26. Cited in Monika Wyss (ed.), *Brecht in der Kritik* (Munich: Kindler, 1977), 97.

27. The text of the opening chorus of *Lehrstück* is identical to the closing chorus of *Der Lindberghflug.*

28. Reiner Steinweg, "*Das Badener Lehrstück vom Einverständnis:* Mystik, Religionsersatz oder Parodie?" in *Bertolt Brecht II,* Sonderband aus der Reihe Text und Kritik, ed. Heinz Ludwig Arnold (Munich: Edition Text + Kritik, 1973), 109–30. See also Andreas Lehmann, "Hindemiths Lehrstück," *Hindemith-Jahrbuch* 11 (1982): 36–76.

29. Ernst Schumacher, *Die dramatischen Versuche Bertolt Brechts 1918–1933* (Berlin: Verlag Rütter & Loening, 1954), 329.

30. Steinweg, "*Das Badener Lehrstück,*" 110.

31. Krabiel, *Brechts Lehrstücke*, 95.

32. Thomas O. Brandt, "Brecht und die Bibel," *Proceedings of the Modern Language Association* 79 (1964): 171–76; Hans Pabst, *Brecht und die Religion* (Graz: Verlag Styria, 1977); G. Ronald Murphy, *Brecht and the Bible: A Study of Religious Nihilism and Human Weakness in Brecht's Drama of Mortality and the City* (Chapel Hill: University of North Carolina Press, 1980); Eberhard Rohse, *Der frühe Brecht und die Bibel: Studien zum Augsburger Religionsunterricht und zu den literarischen Versuchen des Gymnasiasten* (Göttingen: Vandenhoeck & Ruprecht, 1983).

33. I am indebted to the painstaking research of Eberhard Rohse, whose study *Der frühe Brecht* reconstructs the entire curriculum of Brecht's religious education at grammar school in Augsburg. In the segment of religious instruction called "Catechism and Faith," each Hauptstück was treated in turn. The year 1908–9 was devoted to the first Hauptstück and the first and second articles of faith (the second Hauptstück). The following year concentrated on the second article, while introducing the third Hauptstück, and so on, until the fourth year, when all six Hauptstücke were reviewed.

34. Bertolt Brecht, *Versuche*, vol. 2 (Berlin: Gustav Kiepenheuer Verlag, 1930), 148.

35. Bertolt Brecht, "Aus der Musiklehre," in *Schriften*, vol. 1, ed. Werner Hecht, BBA, 21 (Berlin and Weimar: Aufbau-Verlag, 1992), 267–68.

36. Cited in Reiner Steinweg (ed.), *Brechts Modell der Lehrstücke: Zeugnisse, Diskussion, Erfahrungen* (Frankfurt am Main: Suhrkamp Verlag, 1976), 38.

37. The first edition of *Lehrstück* has been recently published in Paul Hindemith, *Szenische Versuche,* Sämtliche Werke, ser. 1, vol. 6, ed. Rudolf Stephan (Mainz: Schott, 1982). The latest edition of Brecht's works (BBA) curiously reprints *Das Badener Lehrstück*

vom Einverständnis, despite its declared policy of publishing "as a matter of principle the authorized and established *[wirksam gewordene]* first editions." The period 1929–33 has thirteen productions of the first version of *Lehrstück* on record and none of the revised version.

38. Heinrich Strobel, "Musikerziehung—die Forderung der Zeit," *Berliner Börsen-Courier,* 8 August 1929. See also Dorothea Kolland, *Die Jugendmusikbewegung: "Gemeinschaftsmusik"—Theorie und Praxis* (Stuttgart: J.B. Metzler, 1979); and Heide Hammel, *Die Schulmusik in der Weimarer Republik: Politische und gesellschaftliche Aspekte der Reformdiskussion in den 20er Jahren* (Stuttgart: J.B. Metzler, 1990).

39. On several occasions Besseler acknowledged an intellectual debt to Martin Heidegger, his philosophy teacher. In Heideggerian terms, *Gebrauchsmusik* belongs to the more immediate, primordial realm of *Zeug* ("equipment") as opposed to that of *Ding* ("thing"). *Zeug* is *zuhanden* ("ready-to-hand"), an object of manipulation (or *umgangsmässig,* as Besseler says), in contrast to objects of bare perceptual cognition or reflection, which Heidegger describes as *vorhanden* ("present-at-hand").

40. Originally published in the *Zeitschrift für Musik,* Laux's review has been reprinted as part of his article "Skandal in Baden-Baden," *Hindemith-Jahrbuch* 2 (1972): 166–80.

41. The article originated from the lecture that Besseler delivered as part of his "Habilitation" ritual at the University of Freiburg. See Stephen Hinton, *The Idea of Gebrauchsmusik* (New York: Garland, 1989), 6–23; and the terminological monograph "Gebrauchsmusik," *Handwörterbuch der musikalischen Terminologie,* vol. 15 (Wiesbaden: F. Steiner, 1988).

42. Hans Joachim Moser openly attacked Besseler's essay in *Archiv für Musikwissenschaft* 7 (1926): 380. Besseler responded in the same issue with a "critical remark," in which he commented that the *Jugendbewegung* had "been strongest and most decisive in preparing the ground."

43. Gerhart Scherler, "Lehrstück und Theater," *Musik und Gesellschaft* 1 (1930–31); reprinted in *100 Texte zu Brecht: Materialien aus der Weimarer Republik,* ed. Manfred Voigts (Munich: Fink Verlag, 1980), 276–78, here 277; and Hilmar Trede and Hans Boettcher, "Lehrstück," *Musik und Gesellschaft* 1 (1930–31); reprinted in *100 Texte zu Brecht,* 268–76, here 276.

44. Siegfried Günther, "Lehrstück und Schuloper," *Melos* 10 (1931): 410–13.

45. Ernst Schoen, "Die Rundfunkkompositionen für Baden-Baden," *Melos* 8, no. 6 (1929): 313–15.

46. See Hindemith, *Szenische Versuche,* especially the extensive documentation included in the editor's introduction. For a recent discussion of the cultural context in which *Der Lindberghflug* was conceived, see Alexander Rehding, "Magic Boxes and *Volksempfänger:* Music on the Radio in Weimar Germany," in *Music, Theatre, and Politics in Germany: 1848 to the Third Reich,* ed. Nikolaus Bacht (Aldershot, Eng.: Ashgate, 2006), 255–71.

47. Weill's statement was published in "Keine Differenz Weill-Hindemith," *Filmkurier,* 8 August 1929. The article was partially reprinted in the *Zeitschrift für Musik* 96, no. 10 (1929), and is reprinted in full in GS, 444–45.

48. Weill's letter to Curjel, dated 22 June 1929, is quoted in Giselher Schubert, "Hin-

demith und Weill: Zu einer Musikgeschichte der zwanziger Jahre," *Hindemith-Jahrbuch* 25 (1996): 158–78, here 173.

49. The letter to Curjel, dated 2 August 1929, is quoted ibid., 174.

50. Schubert, "Hindemith und Weill," 174.

51. "Notiz zum *Lindberghflug,*" program booklet of the third symphony concert of the Berlin Staatskapelle, 5 December 1929; reprinted in GS, 100–101.

52. Weill's statement on the matter, which examines among other things the relationship between "Gebrauchskunst" and state subvention, was published in his article "Musikfest oder Musikstudio," *Melos* 9 (1930), 230–32; it is reprinted in GS, 115–18. An abbreviated version of Eisler's open letter to the festival's committee was published as "Offener Brief an die künstlerische Leitung der neuen Musik Berlin 1930" in the *Berliner Börsen-Courier,* 13 May 1930; it is published in full in Hanns Eisler, *Musik und Politik: Schriften 1924–1948* (Leipzig: Deutscher Verlag für Musik, 1973), 102–5.

53. Weill, "Über meine Schuloper *Der Jasager,*" *Die Scene* 20 (1930): 232–33; reprinted in GS, 119–20.

54. See the "Nachwort" to Bertolt Brecht, *Der Jasager und Der Neinsager: Vorlagen, Fassungen, Materialien,* ed. Peter Szondi (Frankfurt am Main: Suhrkamp Verlag, 1978).

55. "Aktuelles Zwiegespräch," in GS, 451.

56. Paul W. Humphreys, "Expressions of *Einverständnis:* Musical Structure and Affective Content in Kurt Weill's Score for *Der Jasager*" (Ph.D. diss., University of California, Los Angeles, 1988), 21–23. Other recent studies that focus on the music lessons contained in Weill's school opera include Ian Kemp, "*Der Jasager:* Weill's Composition Lesson," in *A Stranger Here Myself: Kurt Weill Studien,* ed. Kim H. Kowalke and Horst Edler (Hildesheim: Olms Verlag, 1993), 143–57; and Daniel Albright, *Untwisting the Serpent: Modernism in Music, Literature, and Other Arts* (Chicago: University of Chicago Press, 2000), especially the section entitled "*Der Jasager:* Teaching Acquiescence," 170–81.

57. "Art Must Serve Society, Says Writer Bert Brecht," interview with Helge Bonnén, *Radiolytteren* 8, no. 31 (30 July 1933), 6; translated from the Danish by Niels Krabbe. I am grateful to Professor Krabbe for permission to quote from his translation.

58. "Der 'Jasager' in Arnstadt: Freunde und Gegner," *Melos* 10 (1931): 86.

59. Reprinted in Bertolt Brecht, *Der Jasager und Der Neinsager,* 73.

60. Hanns Gutman, "Eine Schuloper von H. J. Moser," *Melos* 10 (1931): 425–26.

61. Sergei Tretjakov, "Hanns Eisler," in *Die Arbeit des Schriftstellers,* ed. H. Boehncke (Reinbek bei Hamburg: Rowohlt, 1972), 182.

62. See Werner Fuhr, *Proletarische Musik in Deutschland 1928–1933,* Göppinger Akademische Beiträge (Göppingen: Verlag Alfred Kümmerle, 1977).

63. The fate of the German New Music festivals in the years immediately preceding and subsequent to the Nazi seizure of power is extensively documented in Werner Zintgraf's study *Neue Musik 1921–1950* (Horb am Neckar: Geiger, 1987).

64. The designation "Thingspiel" was suggested by the drama professor Carl Niessen, who had in mind the ancient concept of a judicial-cum-political meeting at which free men assembled in order to deliberate over matters of state. Especially significant for the Nazi tradition was the function of the "Thing" as the highest judicial authority at which the assembled company made a collective judgment. See Johannes M. Reichl, *Das Thing-*

spiel: Über den Versuch eines nationalsozialistischen Lehrstück-Theaters (Frankfurt am Main: Misslbeck, 1988).

65. An analogous kind of musical symbolism (jazz vs. neo-baroque) pervades the Lehrstücke of Eisler: while *Die Maßnahme* (1930) keeps the dualism in balance, *Die Mutter* (1931) tends more toward the austere neo-baroque.

66. Recounting the genesis of *Down in the Valley,* Weill wrote: "I remembered the wonderful experience I had had with a school opera in Europe years ago and it occurred to me that the [new] piece . . . would be readily adaptable for an American school opera" (*New York Times,* 5 June 1949).

67. For a fuller account of the points summarized here, see my article "Hindemith: Pedagogy and Personal style," *Hindemith-Jahrbuch* 17 (1988): 54–67.

68. Heinrich Strobel, *Paul Hindemith* (Mainz: B. Schott's Söhne, 1948), 54.

69. See Hinton, "Hindemith: Pedagogy and Personal style."

70. For a detailed discussion of Steinweg's theory, see Krabiel, *Brechts Lehrstücke,* esp. 295–312.

71. Quoted in Steinweg, *"Das Badener Lehrstück,"* 87.

72. Julius Bab, "Lehrstück in Gegenwart und Vergangenheit," *Die Literarische Welt,* 19 February 1932; reprinted in Bertolt Brecht, *Die Maßnahme: Kritische Ausgabe mit einer Spielanleitung von Reiner Steinweg* (Frankfurt am Main: Suhrkamp Verlag, 1972), 402–7, here 407.

CHAPTER 8

1. Hanns-Werner Heister et al., *Musik im Exil: Folgen des Nazismus fur die internationale Musikkultur* (Frankfurt am Main: Fischer Taschenbuch Verlag, 1993).

2. For a detailed interdisciplinary history of the exile concept *(Exilbegriff),* including a rejection of the term *emigration* as "eviscerating" *(verharmlosend),* see Claudia Maurer Zenck, *Ernst Krenek—ein Komponist im Exil* (Vienna: Lafite Verlag, 1980), esp. 11–42. Zenck applies the distinction with devastating effect to Hindemith, such as when she observes that it is "difficult to define Hindemith's emigration as exile." See also her article "Zwischen Boykott und Anpassung an den Charakter der Zeit: Über die Schwierigkeiten eines deutschen Komponisten mit dem Dritten Reich," *Hindemith-Jahrbuch* 9 (1980): 65–129. For another, more conciliatory perspective, see my own "Emigration and Self-Discovery," *Hindemith-Jahrbuch* 27 (1998): 12–24.

3. Radio program broadcast 9 March 1941 by NBC Blue Network on behalf of the U.S. Department of State, some two years before Weill received his certificate of naturalization in 1943. Transcribed from an audiocassette held by WLRC, ser. 122/3. See also Kim H. Kowalke, "Formerly German: Kurt Weill in America," in *A Stranger Here Myself,* ed. Kim H. Kowalke (Hildesheim: Olms Verlag, 1993), 35–57.

4. WLE, 427.

5. *Life* magazine, letter from Weill with the (probably editorial) heading "Gentle Beef," 17 March 1947.

6. Arnold Whittall, *Musical Composition in the Twentieth Century* (Oxford: Oxford University Press, 1999), 81. Comparing works from the German and the American peri-

ods, Whittall writes: "Whatever one's response to the theatrical works that Weill wrote during his enforced exile in America, like the 'musical play' *Lady in the Dark* (1940) or the 'American opera' *Street Scene* (1947), it is difficult to argue convincingly that they sustain, or aspire to sustain, such a 'less superficial' modern quality." In "'Bargain and Charity'? Aspekte der Aufnahme exilierter Musiker an der Ostküste der Vereinigten Staaten" (in *Musik im Exil,* 308), Werner Grünzweig offered a similar assessment underpinned by more overtly national distinctions: "Weill . . . thoroughly made America his new home, which had a decisive effect on his composing. Without wishing to belittle his American works, and despite all the connections with his earlier oeuvre, one has to conclude that he subjugated his creativity, with all the artistic consequences attending that goal, to his Americanization (and hence to his turning away from Germany). Weill placed himself in the front rank of 'adapted' *[hineinkomponiert]* American musical composers; at the same time, however, the characteristic aspect of his early music disappeared." In his biography *Kurt Weill: Composer in a Divided World* (London: Simon & Schuster, 1991), Ronald Taylor, despite the singular "composer" and "divided world" of his title, follows the critical orthodoxy, which he summarizes as follows: "People perceive a split in [Weill's] musical personality which fatally divides the European from the American, the former brilliant and sparklingly original, the latter a sad regression and capitulation to inferior values" (vii). Taylor thus observes that the "characteristic sound [of the European Weill] was becoming less characteristic, blander, almost more commonplace [in the American Weill]" (213). For further discussion of Taylor's and other biographies, see chapter 1.

7. *Musik im Exil,* 435.

8. Esbjörn Nyström, "Neuentdeckungen zur Arbeit Bertolt Brechts am Ballettprojekt *Die sieben Todsünden,*" in *Editio: Internationales Jahrbuch für Editionswissenschaft,* ed. Bodo Plachta and Winfried Woesler, vol. 20 (Tübingen: Niemeyer, 2006), 171–99, here 194.

9. See, in particular, John Fuegi, *Brecht and Company: Sex, Politics, and the Making of Modern Drama* (New York: Grove Press, 1994).

10. Barbara Münch, "Die Götterdämmerung der Kleinbürger: Sozialkritik und Tragik in Bertolt Brechts und Kurt Weills *Die sieben Todsünden*" (M.A. thesis, Ludwig-Maximilian-Universität, Munich, 1992).

11. Jan Knopf, *Brecht-Handbuch: Theater* (Stuttgart: Metzler, 1980), 139.

12. Münch, "Götterdämmerung der Kleinbürger," 97.

13. Ibid., 102.

14. Postcard to Helene Weigel, 10 June 1933, in BBA 28:361.

15. See Werner Hecht, *Brecht-Chronik 1898–1956* (Frankfurt am Main: Suhrkamp Verlag, 1997), 354. According to Hecht, Brecht's stay in Paris lasted from 7 through 20 April 1933. The most detailed account of the work's genesis to date is in Kim H. Kowalke, "Seven Degrees of Separation: Music, Text, Image, and Gesture in *The Seven Deadly Sins,*" in *Music, Image, Gesture,* ed. Bryan Gilliam, a special issue of the *South Atlantic Quarterly* 104, no. 1 (2005): 7–62. See also Nyström, "Neuentdeckungen"; and Joachim Lucchesi and Ronald K. Shull, eds., *Musik bei Brecht* (Frankfurt am Main: Suhrkamp Verlag, 1988).

16. The correspondence between Weill and Erika Neher is held in the WLRC. Excerpts are quoted in Kowalke, "Seven Degrees of Separation," and in Joanna Lee and Kim Ko-

walke, eds., *Die 7 Todsünden / The 7 Deadly Sins: A Sourcebook* (New York: Kurt Weill Foundation for Music, 1997).

17. The term *ballet-opera* occurs in the notes that Weill prepared for his lecture to the Group Theatre on 27 July 1936. The notes, partly typed and partly handwritten, are housed at Yale (MSS 30); there is a copy at WLRC; for facsimiles, see PDE, 165.

18. The description "more cantata than ballet" comes from the review in *Paris-soir* (12 June 1933), reprinted in PDE, 140; the term *Kurzoper* occurs in Walter Mehring, "Ein neuer Brecht-Weill," *Das neue Tagebuch,* no. 1 (July 1933); reprinted as "*Die sieben Todsünden* in Paris," in ÜKW, 116–18; the description "immorality play" occurs in a "Paris letter" published in the *New Yorker* on 8 July 1933, reprinted in PDE, 140.

19. Mehring, "*Die sieben Todsünden* in Paris."

20. Busoni included reflections on opera in the second edition of his *Entwurf einer neuen Ästhetik der Tonkunst* (1916), but without a significant passage that was added to the 1922 version: "it ought to be possible to consider the form of a scenario accompanied by music and illustrated by song, without words, producing a kind of 'sung pantomime'"; quoted in *Musik—zur Sprache gebracht: Ästhetische Texte aus drei Jahrhunderten,* ed. Carl Dahlhaus and Michael Zimmermann (Kassel: Bärenreiter, 1984), 345.

21. See Kowalke, "Seven Degrees of Separation," 59 n. 53: "There is no documentary evidence to suggest that Weill associated the bass role with the mother in the Family. This was probably a contribution of Kochno and/or Balanchine." This performing tradition eventually found its way into the published piano-vocal score, which specifies the bass part as "The Mother."

22. The untitled typescript belongs to the Weill-Lenya papers at Yale University Music Library. The WLRC has a copy of the typescript as part of its "Yale Collection."

23. Nyström corroborates this finding; see "Neuentdeckungen," 194.

24. Bertolt Brecht, *Die sieben Todsünden der Kleinbürger,* in BBA 4, ed. Johanna Rosenberg and Manfred Nössig (1988), 265–77, with critical notes on pp. 492–502; here, 499.

25. Based on scrutiny of various unpublished papers kept in the Bertolt-Brecht-Archiv and the Elisabeth-Hauptmann-Archiv, Nyström ("Neuentdeckungen," esp. 181–87) has shown that the playwright was working on a quite different scenario, which he may have wanted to use as the basis for the ballet until he was persuaded to go along with the project proposed by Weill, James, and Kochno.

26. DDH, 247.

27. It is possible that the journalist did not know the piece and misinterpreted Brecht's statement. Brecht surely meant plot rather than dialogue. See "Art Must Serve Society, Says Writer Bert Brecht," interview with Helge Bonnén, *Radiolytteren* 8, no. 31 (30 July 1933), 6; translated from the Danish by Niels Krabbe. I am grateful to Professor Krabbe for permission to quote from his translation.

28. Brecht, *Die sieben Todsünden der Kleinbürger,* BBA 4:267.

29. Ronald K. Shull makes the rift between Brecht and Weill the basis of his interpretation; see "The Genesis of *Die sieben Todsünden,*" in Kim H. Kowalke, ed., *A New Orpheus: Essays on Kurt Weill* (New Haven: Yale University Press, 1990), 203–16.

30. For a discussion of musical allusions in *Die sieben Todsünden,* including to the music of Bach, see Franz Willnauer, "'Bedenk, was geschieht, wenn du tätst, was dir läge!'

Dialektik und Parodie in Brecht/Weills Ballett von der pervertierten Moral," in *Ordnung und Freiheit: Almanach zum Internationalen Beethovenfest Bonn 2000* (Laaber: Laaber Verlag, 2000), 135–53.

31. *La revue musicale,* June 1933, quoted in Kowalke and Lee (eds.), *A Sourcebook,* 15.

32. 20 June 1933, in PDE, 140.

33. Ralph P. Locke, "What Are These Women Doing in Opera?" in *En travestie: Women, Gender Subversion, Opera,* ed. Corinne E. Blackmer and Patricia Juliana Smith (New York: Columbia University Press, 1995), 59–98.

34. Lambert continues: "For example, the churchy four-part chorus 'Here is a wire from Philadelphia' with the unctuous solo 'But our Anna really is quite sensible; she will know a contract is a contract' would lose its point without the visual accompaniment of the wretched Anna doing slimming exercises and being kept away from the dish of fruit at the point of a revolver." Parts of Lambert's review, which was initially published in the *Times* of London (and reprinted in PDE, 141), found their way into his book *Music Ho! A Study of Music in Decline* (London: Faber & Faber, 1934). Favorable comments on Weill's works occur at various places in the book; those on *Die sieben Todsünden* appear on 225–26 in the chapter called "Symphonic Jazz."

35. Eric Salzman reviewed the New York production in *KWNL* 26 (2009): 17–19. Salzman's review essay, which includes an account of the work's genesis, combines comments on the production itself with fine critical insight.

36. Weill's *Recordare* of 1923 is a setting of the Lamentations of Jeremiah in the Latin vulgate.

37. DDH, 271.

38. Letter from Weill to Lenya, 25 January 1934, in WLE, 112.

39. Letter from Weill to Lenya, [29 March 1934], ibid., 122.

40. Letter from Weill to Lenya, [6 April 1934], ibid., 123–24.

41. Letter from Weill to Abravanel, 21 January 1935, quoted in PDE, 156.

42. Pascal Huynh, *Kurt Weill, ou La conquête des masses* (Arles: Actes Sud, 2000), 263.

43. John Mucci and Richard Felnagle, "Marie: Still Waiting . . . ," *KWNL* 9, no. 1 (1991): 14–17.

44. Foster Hirsch, *Kurt Weill on Stage: From Berlin to Broadway* (New York: Knopf, 2002), 120.

45. Letter from Weill to Lenya, [17 July 1935], in WLE, 183.

46. The evidence of the reviews from the mainstream British newspapers and journals quoted here does not support David Drew's statement, often echoed in other secondary literature, that *A Kingdom for a Cow* "was well received by the press." See David Drew, "Reflections on the Last Years: *Der Kuhhandel* as a Key Work," in *A New Orpheus,* ed. Kowalke, 217–67, here 220.

47. Heine: "Denk ich an Deutschland in der Nacht, / Dann bin ich um den Schlaf gebracht. / Ich kann nicht mehr die Augen schließen, / Und meine heißen Tränen fließen."

48. For many musician émigrés, England was just a temporary refuge: these include Theodor W. Adorno, Hanns Eisler, Ernst Toch, Carl Flesch, Otto Erich Deutsch, Ernst Hermann Meyer, Walter Goehr, the architect Erich Mendelsohn, and the actors Fritz Kortner and Peter Lorre. Others succeeded in making Britain their permanent new home,

among them Egon Wellesz, Berthold Goldschmidt, Leopold Spinner, Mischa Spoliansky, Franz Reizenstein, Josef Zmigrod (Allan Gray), Bernhard Grün, Hans Gál, Mátyás Seiber, Hans Ferdinand Redlich, Mosco Carner, Peter Stadlen, Richard Tauber, Hans Keller, Max Rostal, Albi Rosenthal, Erwin Stein, Ernst Roth, and three-quarters of the Amadeus Quartet. Among the nonmusicians one could mention above all E. H. Gombrich and Nikolaus Pevsner, without whom British art history would hardly be what it is today. Others include the dancer Kurt Joos and Rudolf von Laban and, of course, Sigmund Freud. And they are just a few of the better-known names. See *Second Chance: Two Centuries of German-speaking Jews in the United Kingdom,* ed. Julius Carlebach et al. (Tübingen: Mohr, 1991).

49. Letter from Weill to Lenya, 17 May 1934, in WLE, 126–28.

50. Weill to Curjel, 19 April 1934; copy held in WLRC, original in Deutsches Literaturarchiv, Marbach.

51. A copy is held in WLRC (ser. 20/K9/1934a).

52. Letter to Hans Weill, 11 January 1920, in BF, 254.

53. Letter to Hans Weill, 26 April 1920, ibid., 269.

54. Letter to Hans Weill, ibid., 264–65.

55. "Alchemy of Music," *Stage* 14, no. 2 (November 1936): 63–64.

56. "Die fehlende Operette," *Der deutsche Rundfunk* 3, no. 40 (4 October 1925): 2547; reprinted in GS, 285–87.

57. "[Offenbachs *Großherzogin von Gerolstein*]," *Der deutsche Rundfunk* 4, no. 47 (21 November 1926): 3331; reprinted in GS, 335–36.

58. See Stephen Hinton, ed., *Kurt Weill: The Threepenny Opera* (Cambridge: Cambridge University Press, 1990), 36–37.

59. See PDE, 47, 52, 57. Composed in 1925–27, *Na und?* was sadly lost after it failed to attract the interest of a publisher. See also the entry on *Na und?* in David Drew's *Handbook* (DDH, 163–68), where he describes the little that is known about the work's composition and the circumstances surrounding its loss.

60. Letter from Weill to UE, 29 July 1932, in WUE, 406–7. He would later describe his conception of *The Firebrand of Florence* as "a very entertaining *opéra-comique* on the Offenbach line" (letter to Ira Gershwin, 13 November 1941, in WLRC).

61. Letter to UE, 29 July 1932, in WUE, 406–7.

62. Letter from Weill to UE, 13 January 1932, in WUE, 361.

63. Letter from Hans Heinsheimer to Weill, 26 January 1932, in WUE, 363.

64. See Susanne Rode-Breymann, "'Gegen die Operettenschande der Gegenwart': Anmerkungen zu den Offenbach-Vorlesungen von Karl Kraus," in *Jacques Offenbach und seine Zeit,* ed. Elisabeth Schmierer (Laaber: Laaber Verlag, 2009), 249–60.

65. See Stephan Stompor, "Die Offenbach-Renaissance um 1930 und die geschlossenen Vorstellungen für Juden nach 1933," in *Offenbach und die Schauplätze seines Musiktheaters,* ed. Rainer Franke (Laaber: Laaber Verlag, 1999), 257–66. For a discussion of the Offenbach renaissance with specific reference to Weill, see Joel Galand, "Weill, the *Operettenkrise,* and the Offenbach Renaissance," *KWNL* 22, no. 2 (2004): 9–15.

66. Karl Kraus, "Grimassen über Kultur und Bühne," *Die Fackel,* nos. 270–71 (19 January 1909): 1–18; reprinted in Karl Kraus, *Schriften,* ed. Christian Wagenknecht (Frankfurt am Main: Suhrkamp Verlag, 1987), 2:141–56.

67. Kraus's essay appeared in *Die literarische Welt,* 20 April 1928. Benjamin incorporated it into his big essay "Karl Kraus," which appeared in four installments of the *Frankfurter Zeitung* in 1931. See also Christian Schulte, *Ursprung ist das Ziel: Walter Benjamin über Karl Kraus* (Würzburg: Königshausen & Neumann, 2003); and Stefan Bub, "Jacques Offenbach bei Walter Benjamin und Siegfried Kracauer," *Euphorion* 100, no. 1 (2006): 117–28.

68. Theodor W. Adorno, "Einleitung zu Benjamins Schriften," in *Noten zur Literatur, Gesammelte Schriften* 11 (Frankfurt am Main: Suhrkamp Verlag, 1974), 574.

69. Walter Benjamin, "Karl Kraus," reprinted in *Gesammelte Schriften* vol. 2, pt. 1, ed. Rolf Tiedemann and Hermann Schweppenhäuser (Frankfurt am Main: Suhrkamp Verlag, 1977), 334–67, here 356.

70. Siegfried Kracauer, *Jacques Offenbach und das Paris seiner Zeit* (Amsterdam: Allert de Lange Verlag, 1937); reprinted in *Werke* 8, ed. Inka Mülder-Bach and Ingrid Belke (Frankfurt am Main: Suhrkamp Verlag, 2005), 265.

71. Letter from Kracauer to Julius Meier-Graefe, December 1934, quoted in *Werke* 8:531.

72. Harald Reil, *Siegfried Kracauers Jacques Offenbach: Biographie, Geschichte, Zeitgeschichte* (New York: Peter Lang, 2003), 82.

73. Alfred Döblin, "Der historische Roman und wir," *Das Wort* [Moscow] 1, no. 4 (1936): 56–71; reprinted in *Ausgewählte Werke in Einzelbänden,* ed. Walter Muschg (Freiburg im Breisgau: Olten, 1963), 12:163–86, here 184.

74. Drew, "Reflections on the Last Years," 221.

75. Quoted ibid., 219.

76. Josef Heinzelmann, "Kurt Weill im Exil: Pazifismus oder Defätismus? Drei verdrängte Werke 1933–1937," in *Das (Musik-)Theater im Exil und Diktatur: Vorträge und Gespräche des Salzburger Symposions 2003,* ed. Peter Csobádi et al. (Salzburg: Verlag Mueller-Speiser, 2005), 436–52, here 441. As Drew reports in DDH (260), the libretto revisions that Weill and Heinzelmann produced did not meet with approval of the original librettist, Robert Vambery, who would eventually prepare his own revised version. It is this latter version that forms the basis of the completed work edited by Lys Symonette in the late 1970s. The piano-vocal score of Vambery's revised version was published by Schott in 1988.

77. Letter from Weill to Lenya, [10 June 1934], in WLE, 132.

78. Letter from Weill to Lenya, [4 February 1935], ibid., 157.

79. Andreas Hauff, "Ein Komponist auf Abwegen? Kurt Weills Operette *Der Kuhhandel,*" in *Festschrift Christoph-Hellmut Mahling zum 65. Geburtstag,* ed. Axel Beer et al. (Tutzing: Hans Schneider, 1997), 1:501–16.

80. DDH, 259.

81. Letter from Weill to Lenya, [13 March 1934], in WLE, 120.

82. Letter from Weill to Lenya, [4 February 1935], ibid., 115.

83. David Drew, "Weill, Kurt," in *The New Grove Dictionary of Music and Musicians,* ed. Stanley Sadie (London: Macmillan, 1980), 20:309.

84. Drew has identified fourteen borrowings from *A Kingdom for a Cow* in subsequent compositions, notably *Johnny Johnson, Knickerbocker Holiday, Lady in the Dark, One Touch of Venus,* and *The Firebrand of Florence*—all works with ties to satirical operetta. See DDH, 274.

85. Letter to Meyer Weisgal, 12 August 1936; copy in WLRC.

86. The principal publications are Meyer Weisgal, . . . *So Far: An Autobiography* (New York: Random House, 1971); Guy Stern, "The Road to *The Eternal Road,*" in Kowalke (ed.), *A New Orpheus,* 269–84; Gottfried Reinhardt, *The Genius: A Memoir of Max Reinhardt* (New York: Knopf, 1979); Christian Kuhnt, *Kurt Weill und das Judentum* (Saarbrücken: Pfau, 2001); Jonathan C. Friedman, *The Literary, Cultural, and Historical Significance of the 1937 Biblical Stage Play "The Eternal Road"* (Lewiston, N.Y.: Edwin Mellen Press, 2004); Helmut Loos and Guy Stern, eds., *Kurt Weill: Auf dem Weg zum "Weg der Verheissung"* (Freiburg im Breisgau: Rombach, 2000); David Farneth, "Weill: *Der Weg der Verheissung:* Bibelspiel in vier Teilen," *Pipers Enzyklopädie des Musiktheaters,* ed. Carl Dahlhaus (Munich: Piper Verlag, 1997), 6:709–11; Stephen J. Whitfield, "The Politics of Pageantry, 1936–1946," *American Jewish History* 84, no. 3 (1996): 221–51; David Drew, "*Der Weg der Verheissung:* Weill at the Crossroads," *Tempo,* n.s., no. 208 (April 1999): 33–50; "*The Eternal Road* and Kurt Weill's German, Jewish, and American Identity: A Discussion with Kim H. Kowlake, Jürgen Schebera, Christian Kuhnt, and Alexander Ringer," in *Theater* (100 Years of Kurt Weill: A Special Centenary Issue, ed. Tom Sellar) 30, no. 3 (2000): 83–95; Alexander Ringer, "Strangers in a Strangers' Land: Werfel, Weill, and *The Eternal Road,*" in *Driven into Paradise: The Musical Migration from Nazi Germany to the United States,* ed. Reinhold Brinkmann and Christoph Wolff (Berkeley: University of California Press, 1999), 243–60; and Tamara Levitz, "Either a German or a Jew: The German Reception of Kurt Weill's *Der Weg der Verheissung,*" *Theater* 30, no. 3 (2000): 97–105.

87. "Wagner to Give Aid to Jewish Pageant," *New York Times,* 11 September 1933.

88. "125,000 See Drama of Jews at Fair," *New York Times,* 4 July 1933.

89. Ringer, "Werfel, Weill, and *The Eternal Road,*" 248–49. David Drew is perhaps even harsher in his criticism of the English title, associating it with a different aspect of Nazi propaganda: "It is hard to resist the conclusion that *The Eternal Road* was almost fatally flawed from the start," he contends. "The very title which had been wished upon the English-language version of *Der Weg der Verheissung* was a technicolor folly worse than any in Hollywood's *Song of Bernadette.* Was no one in Reinhardt's production team aware, or did no one care, that 'The eternal road' was an image favoured by Germany's new leadership, for whom 'Der ewige Weg des Nationalsozialismus' was not only a foregone conclusion but also part of the daily round of speech-making and leader-writing?" (Drew, "*Der Weg der Verheissung:* Weill at the Crossroads," 47).

90. See "Romance of a People: Jewish History in Chicago 1833–1933," www.wttw.com/main.taf?p=1,7,1,1,24 (accessed 19 August 2011).

91. Cited in Atay Citron, "Art and Propaganda in the Original Production of *The Eternal Road,*" in Loos and Stern (eds.), *Kurt Weill: Auf dem Weg zum "Weg der Verheissung,"* 205.

92. Meyer Weisgal, . . . *So Far,* 116–17. *The Eternal Road* ended up being one of the last major theatrical productions at the Manhattan Opera House before it became a meeting hall in 1940. Having built the venue in 1906 in direct competition with the Metropolitan Opera House, Oscar Hammerstein ended up selling it to the head of the Met, Otto Kahn, in 1911. The Shuberts leased it from 1911 to 1917, and Warner Bros. leased the space as a sound stage starting in 1927. The House's repertory over the years covered a broad spec-

trum of spoken and sung productions, from highbrow opera and Shakespeare to much lighter fare, including operettas and musicals.

93. Weisgal, . . . *So Far,* 120

94. Letter to Reinhardt, 6 October 1934: "Now that I know the whole book and the more I am involved with it, the more puzzling it appears to me that Werfel thinks of the work as a 'spoken drama.' Leaving aside the large spaces that swallow every spoken word, it would be unperformable even in smaller theaters given that it contains scarcely a page that doesn't cry out for music" (copy in WLRC).

95. WLE, 187.

96. Quoted in Kuhnt, *Weill und das Judentum,* 94.

97. Letter to Lenya, [26?] February 1934, in WLE, 113–14, here 114.

98. "Kurt Weill's New Score: Music for 'Road of Promise' Written in Modern Contemporary Style," *New York Times,* 27 October 1935.

99. Franz Werfel, *The Eternal Road: A Drama in Four Parts,* trans. Ludwig Lewisohn (New York: Viking Press, 1936), xi.

100. Ibid., ix.

101. A copy is located in WLRC.

102. Gottfried Reinhardt, "The Eternal Road," in *The Odyssey of an Optimist, Meyer W. Weisgal: An Anthology by His Contemporaries* (New York: Atheneum, 1967), 97–98.

103. The Eternal Road by Franz Werfel, 10 January 1937, Alexander Leftwich Jr., Typescript, carbon copy, 129 pp., Revised Script, [Box 17] Department of Special Collections, Charles E. Young Research Library, University of California, Los Angeles.

104. For a discussion of the word *Tendenz* and an alternative translation, see Drew, "*Der Weg der Verheissung:* Weill at the Crossroads," 37.

105. This is put quite poetically in the synopsis of the souvenir program (in WLRC), 18: "There is a continuous interchange of dramatic effect, of meaning and emotion, between the watchers and listeners in the synagogue, with doom hanging over their heads, and the mighty figures moving through the immense Biblical scenes." An abridged version of the same synopsis from the souvenir program is reprinted in the *KWNL* 17, nos. 1–2 (1999): 18–21. This version does not contain the passage in question.

106. Kuhnt, *Weill und das Judentum,* 114–18.

107. Souvenir program (WLRC), 22.

108. Kurt Weill, "The Future of Opera in America," *Modern Music* 14, no. 4 (May-June 1937): 183–188.

109. Writing in the *New York Herald Tribune* on 14 November 1940, the day after *Fantasia*'s premiere, Virgil Thomson commented that "Stokowski, whatever one might think of his musical taste, is unquestionably the man who has best watched over the upbringing of Hollywood's stepchild, musical reproduction and recording. Alone among successful symphonic conductors, he has given himself the trouble to find out something about musical reproduction techniques and to adapt these to the problems of orchestral execution."

110. Letter from Weill to Leopold Stokowski, 12 September 1935; copy in WLRC.

111. Telegram to Reinhardt, 19 October 1935; see Friedman, *Literary, Cultural, and Historical Significance of "The Eternal Road,"* 74.

112. G. L. Dimmick, "The Eternal Road," *Electronics* (April 1937): 28–29, 75–77, here 29. See also Andrew Halbran, "'The Eternal Road' Introduces a New Era in Theatre 'Sound,'" *Radio-Craft*, May 1937.

113. Dimmick, "Eternal Road," 76.

114. In her autobiography, published in 1960 with the Wagnerian title *Mein Leben* (Frankfurt am Main: Suhrkamp Verlag), Alma Mahler wrote: "The biblical story cannot end without Jesus Christ; and the Jews will not allow it with Christ. It would have to end with Zion—but Franz Werfel was not a Zionist and didn't believe in it" (255).

115. "Über 'The Eternal Road'," in *Max Reinhardt: Ich bin nichts als ein Theatermann*, ed. Hugo Fetting (Berlin: Henschelverlag, 1989), 296–97.

116. Norbert Abels, "Von den Mühen des Bibelspiels: Franz Werfel und Kurt Weill, *Der Weg der Verheissung*," in Loos and Stern (eds.), *Kurt Weill: Auf dem Weg zum "Weg der Verheissung,"* 134–56, here 154.

117. Citron, "Art and Propaganda," 203.

118. Whitfield, "Politics of Pageantry," 234.

119. Ibid., 250–51.

120. Friedman, *Literary, Cultural, and Historical Significance of "The Eternal Road,"* 126.

121. Rodney Milnes, review in *Opera* (September 1999), quoted in *KWNL* 17, nos. 1–2 (1999): 17. David Drew characterizes Weill's ending as "blithely triumphalist"; see "*Der Weg der Verheissung:* Weill at the Crossroads," 46.

122. See Alexander Ringer's contribution to the panel discussion "*The Eternal Road* and Kurt Weill's German, Jewish, and American Identity," 95; and Tamara Levitz, "Kurt Weills Identität als deutsch-jüdischer Komponist vor 1933," in *Amerikanismus, Americanism, Weill: Die Suche nach kultureller Identität in der Moderne*, ed. Hermann Danuser and Hermann Gottschewski (Schliengen: Edition Argus, 2003), 221–45.

123. Farneth, "Weill: *Der Weg der Verheissung* (1935)," 711.

CHAPTER 9

1. Kurt Weill, "The Alchemy of Music," *Stage* 14, no. 2 (November 1936): 63–64.

2. Letter to attorney Howard Reinheimer, 10 November 1942; copy in WLRC. The description "serious musical" risks seeming anomalous in light of Weill's frequent rejection of the distinction between "serious" and "light" music.

3. Radio program broadcast, 9 March 1941, by NBC Blue Network on behalf of the U.S. Department of State, some two years before Weill received his certificate of naturalization in 1943. Transcribed from audiocassette held by WLRC, ser. 122/3.

4. John Snelson and Andrew Lamb, "Musical," in *Grove Music Online. Oxford Music Online*, www.oxfordmusiconline.com/subscriber/article/grove/music/19420 (accessed 25 July 2011).

5. Alan Jay Lerner, "Oh, What a Beautiful Musical," *New York Times*, 12 May 1963.

6. Weill, "Alchemy of Music."

7. "Two Dreams Come True," undated typescript; used without title as liner notes to the cast recording of *Street Scene* (Columbia OL 4139).

8. "WCBS Presents Margaret Arlen," radio program hosted by Margaret Arlen and

Harry Marble, broadcast 7 January 1950; transcription in the Maxwell Anderson Papers, Harry Ransom Humanities Research Center, University of Texas, Austin; copy in WLRC.

9. Weill, "Alchemy of Music."

10. Letter from Weill to *New York Times,* published 5 June 1949.

11. Weill makes this distinction in "WCBS Presents Margaret Arlen."

12. Weill frequently used the verb *musicalize* during his later years in the United States, for example in a letter to Sir Alexander Korda dated 11 December 1948 in which he considers the possibility of doing a musical version of *The Ghost Goes West,* a British romantic comedy/fantasy film starring Robert Donat, Jean Parker, and Eugene Pallette, directed by René Clair as his first English-language film. Weill wanted to arrange with Korda multiple screenings of the picture, thereby "[making] it possible for me to make a more detailed study of how to musicalize it." Copy of letter in WLRC.

13. W. David Sievers, "The Group Theatre of New York City, 1931–1941" (M.A. thesis, Stanford University, 1944); Wendy Smith, *Real Life Drama: The Group Theatre and America, 1931–1940* (New York: Knopf, 1990).

14. John Paxton, "The Fabulous Fanatics," *Stage* 16 (December 1938): 22; quoted in Sievers, "Group Theatre of New York," 8.

15. Copies in WLRC.

16. Christian Kuhnt, "Das Gegenteil von 'Pastorale': Anmerkungen zu Kurt Weills 2. Sinfonie," in *Exilmusik: Komposition während der NS-Zeit,* ed. Friedrich Geiger and Thomas Schäfer (Hamburg: von Bockel, 1999), 315–32, here 321–22.

17. Weill, "Alchemy of Music."

18. Kurt Weill, "Korrespondenz über *Dreigroschenoper,*" *Anbruch* 11, no. 1 (1929): 24–25; reprinted in GS, 72–74, here 73–74.

19. "Kurt Weill, der Komponist der Dreigroschenoper, will den Begriff des Musikdramas zerstören," *Wiener Allgemeine Zeitung,* 8 March 1929; reprinted in GS, 442–44, here 443. For a detailed discussion of this statement, see my "Weill Contra Wagner: Aspects of Ambivalence," in "*. . . dass alles auch hätte anders kommen können*": *Beiträge zur Musikgeschichte des 20. Jahrhunderts,* ed. Susanne Schaal-Gotthardt, Luitgard Schader, and Heinz-Jürgen Winkler (Frankfurt am Main: Schott, 2009), 155–74.

20. Kuhnt, "Das Gegenteil von 'Pastorale,'" 317.

21. Weill's note appeared in German in the program booklet for the symphony's premiere at the Concertgebouw Amsterdam on 11 October 1934; it is reprinted in GS, 143.

22. Kuhnt, "Das Gegenteil von 'Pastorale,'" 329.

23. DDH, 44.

24. Paul Green, *Johnny Johnson: The Biography of a Common Man, in Three Acts* (New York: Samuel French, 1937).

25. The synopsis of the scenes in the playbill of the premiere production similarly combines scene descriptions and quoted lines. For scene 1, it listed "A hilltop in a small town. April 1937," with the same quoted line from the Asylum Chorus.

26. *New York Times,* 20 November 1936.

27. Ronald Sanders, *The Days Grow Short: The Life and Music of Kurt Weill* (London: Weidenfeld & Nicolson, 1980), 234.

28. Ralph Winett, "Composer of the Hour: An Interview with Kurt Weill," *Brooklyn Daily Eagle,* 20 December 1936.

29. For a discussion of the genesis of "Johnny's Song" and its various incarnations in the play, see J. Bradford Robinson, "Kurt Weills Aneignung des amerikanischen Theaterliedes: Zur Entstehungsgeschichte von *Johnny's Song,*" in *Kurt-Weill-Studien 1,* ed. Nils Grosch et al. (Stuttgart: Verlag für Wissenschaft und Forschung, 1996), 133–52. An abbreviated version of Robinson's essay was published as "Learning the New Ropes: Kurt Weill and the American Theater Song," *KWNL* 15, no. 2 (1997): 3–7. The form of the song is also discussed in Michael Morley, "'I cannot/will not sing the old songs now': Some Observations on Weill's Adaptation of Popular Song Forms," in *A Stranger Here Myself: Kurt Weill Studien,* ed. Kim H. Kowalke and Horst Edler (Hildesheim: Olms Verlag, 1993), 220–34.

30. Quoted in Joel Cohen, "Metamorphosis and Parody in Kurt Weill's 'Johnny Johnson,'" liner notes for *Music for Johnny Johnson,* Otaré Pit Band, Erato CD 0630-17870-2,14.

31. Robinson, "Kurt Weills Aneignung des amerikanischen Theaterliedes," 143.

32. Copy in WLRC.

33. Elia Kazan, *A Life* (New York: Knopf, 1988), 154–55.

34. *New York Times,* 29 November 1936.

35. Harold Clurman, *The Fervent Years: The Story of the Group Theatre and the Thirties* (New York: Knopf, 1945), 177.

36. Ibid.

37. Kurt Weill, *Johnny Johnson,* in KWE, ser. 1, vol. 13, ed. Tim Carter (forthcoming).

38. WUE, 491.

39. The director Joshua Logan later recalled that "the play went to hell that night. The entire audience turned compulsively to FDR's box at each funny line to see if he was laughing. Since he howled at each joke, they didn't have time to follow suit, so they turned silently back to the stage. To a blind man, it must have seemed like an empty auditorium for one crazy, laughing fool" (quoted in Elmar Juchem, *Kurt Weill und Maxwell Anderson: Neue Wege zu einem amerikanischen Musiktheater, 1938–1950* [Stuttgart: Metzler, 2000], 102).

40. Cited in Lewis Melville, *Life and Letters of John Gay, 1685–1732* (London: O'Connor, 1921), 90.

41. *New York Times,* 13 November 1938.

42. See John F. Wharton, *Life among the Playwrights* (New York: Quadrangle Books, 1974), 151.

43. Quoted in Juchem, *Weill and Anderson,* 89–90, fn. 48.

44. Rice's comments, sent in a letter dated 11 July 1938 to his colleagues in the Playwrights' Company, are quoted ibid., 81.

45. Ruth McKenney, "Abraham Lincoln Lives Again," *New Masses* 29, no. 6 (1 November 1938): 27–28. In response to Anderson's *Times* article, McKenney followed her review with a piece called "Notes on Maxwell Anderson" (*New Masses* 29, no. 10 [29 November 1938]: 27–28), in which she described his "philosophy of government" as "a remarkable combination of romantic anarchism and black Republicanism—Herbert Hoover wearing a Proudhon toga."

46. *New York Times,* 20 November and 29 November 1938.

47. Weill to Maxwell Anderson, Hollywood, 14 May 1938; copy in WLRC.

48. See Juchem, *Weill and Anderson,* 81.

49. For a discussion of *Mikado* references in *Knickerbocker Holiday,* see John Bush Jones, "Maxwell Anderson, Lyricist," in *Maxwell Anderson and the New York Stage,* ed. Nancy J. Doran Hazleton and Kenneth Krauss (New York: Library Research Associates, 1991), 97–111.

50. Diedrich Knickerbocker, *A History of New York* (New York: Putnam, 1868), 487.

51. Letter from Weill to Lenya, 11–12 May 1945, in WLE, 458.

52. bruce d. mcclung, "American Dreams: Analyzing *Lady in the Dark*" (Ph.D. diss., University of Rochester, 1994), 469.

53. Ibid., 470.

54. bruce d. mcclung, *Lady in the Dark: Biography of a Musical* (New York: Oxford University Press, 2007), 197.

55. Lawrence Kubie, "Psychiatry and the Films," *Hollywood Quarterly* 2, no. 2 (1947): 113–17, here 116.

56. *Lady in the Dark: A Musical Play by Moss Hart with Lyrics by Ira Gershwin and Music by Kurt Weill* (New York: Random House, 1941), ix.

57. Mari Jo Buhle, *Feminism and Its Discontents: A Century of Struggle with Psychoanalysis* (Cambridge, Mass.: Harvard University Press, 1998), 167.

58. mcclung, *Lady in the Dark,* 197.

59. Buhle, *Feminism and Its Discontents,* 173.

60. For detailed information on Hart's experiences with psychoanalysis, see Steven Bach, *Dazzler: The Life and Times of Moss Hart* (New York : Knopf, 2001); and Jared Brown, *Moss Hart: A Prince of the Theatre—A Biography in Three Acts* (New York: Back Stage Books, 2006).

61. Joel Pfister, "Glamorizing the Psychological: The Politics of the Performances of Modern Psychological Identities," in *Inventing the Psychological: Toward a Cultural History of Emotional Life in America,* ed. Joel Pfister and Nancy Schnog (New Haven: Yale University Press, 1997), 167–213, here 170–72.

62. *Carefree* (RKO Classic Screenplays) (New York: Frederick Ungar, 1965), [vi]. The screenplay's authors were Allan Scott and Ernest Pagano.

63. Krin and Glen O. Gabbard, *Psychiatry and the Cinema* (Chicago: University of Chicago Press, 1987), 56.

64. W. David Sievers, *Freud on Broadway: A History of Psychoanalysis and the American Drama* (New York: Cooper Square, 1955), 291–94.

65. Kubie, echoing his comments on *Lady in the Dark,* would also criticize the portrayal of diagnosis and treatment in *Spellbound* as "too quick and easy"; see his "Psychiatry and the Films," 116. Weill would get to know Hecht while working on the two pageants *Fun to Be Free* and *We Will Never Die.*

66. The Works Progress Administration (WPA) was established in 1935 as a relief measure during the Great Depression. Its special programs included the Federal Writers' Project and the Federal Arts Project, the latter giving unemployed artists the opportunity to decorate post offices, schools, and other public buildings with murals, canvases, and sculptures, while musicians organized symphony orchestras and community singing.

Weill embarked on several collaborations as part of the Federal Theatre Project, which was responsible for productions of his *Johnny Johnson* in Boston and Los Angeles in 1937.

67. From the poem "Lullaby" (1937):

> Should dreams haunt you, heed them not,
> for all, both sweet and horrid,
> are jokes in dubious taste,
> too jejune to have truck with.

68. Atkinson's review: *New York Times,* 24 January 1941; Harry Horner, "Of Those Four Revolving Stages," *New York Times,* 6 April 1941.

69. Moss Hart, "The How and Why of *Lady in the Dark,*" souvenir playbill; copy in WLRC.

70. See J. Bradford Robinson, "Learning the New Ropes: Kurt Weill and the American Theater Song," *KWNL* 15, no. 2 (1997): 3–7, here 7.

71. "Weill: *Lady in the Dark* (1941)," in *Pipers Enzyklopädie des Musiktheaters,* ed. Carl Dahlhaus (Munich: Piper, 1997), 6:712–15.

72. Ferruccio Busoni, "The Future of Opera," trans. Rosamond Ley, in *The Essence of Music* (London: Rockliff, 1957), 39–40.

73. Calling this "a motivically saturated score," mcclung (*Lady in the Dark,* 68) has drawn attention to the motif's presence in several of the cut songs as well.

74. See the article "Opera" in *The New Grove Dictionary of Music and Musicians,* ed. Stanley Sadie (London: Macmillan, 1980), in particular the initial section by Bernard Williams called "The Nature of Opera and Its Place in Society," 13:545–46.

75. Buhle, *Feminism and Its Discontents,* 172.

76. Michael Baumgartner, "Venus in Manhattan: Konträre Räume in *One Touch of Venus,*" in *Street Scene: Der urbane Raum im Musiktheater des 20. Jahrhunderts,* ed. Stefan Weiss and Jürgen Schebera (Münster: Waxmann, 2006), 69–89, here 79. Baumgartner's essay incorporates revised portions of his dissertation, "Exilierte Göttinnen: Die Darstellung der weiblichen Statue in Othmar Schoecks *Venus,* Kurt Weills *One Touch of Venus* und Thea Musgraves *The Voice of Ariadne*" (Ph.D. diss., University of Salzburg, 2005).

77. The script of the play is published as S. J. Perelman and Ogden Nash, *One Touch of Venus* (Boston: Little, Brown, 1944). See also Penny Colman, *Rosie the Riveter: Women Workers on the Home Front in World War II* (New York: Crown, 1995).

78. For details on the ballet sequences, related by the choreographer and cast members, see Carol Easton, *No Intermissions: The Life of Agnes de Mille* (Boston: Little, Brown and Company, 1996), esp. 216–24.

79. Letter to Ira Gershwin, 5 April 1943; copy in WLRC.

80. Foster Hirsch, *Kurt Weill on Stage: From Berlin to Broadway* (New York: Knopf, 2002), 219.

81. According to Michael Baumgartner ("Exilierte Göttinnen," 262–63), Sharaff felt she was never properly credited for her part in the work's inception.

82. Letter to Ira Gershwin, 13 November 1941; copy in WLRC.

83. Kazan, *A Life,* 234.

84. Ibid., 235.

85. Peggy Meyer Sherry, interview with Agnes de Mille, quoted in Baumgartner, "Venus in Manhattan," 81.

86. See the reminiscences of dancer Robert Pagent, who danced the part of the aviator in the premiere production, in Easton, *No Intermissions,* 219. In 1999, Pagent was invited by the University of Minnesota to reconstruct de Mille's dances for *One Touch of Venus* for a video recording.

87. Baumgartner, "Exilierte Göttinnen," 298.

88. For a discussion of the use of triplet rhythms in Broadway musicals generally, not just in *One Touch of Venus,* see Geoffrey Block, *Enchanted Evenings: The Broadway Musical from Show Boat to Sondheim* (Oxford: Oxford University Press, 2004), 151–52.

89. Hirsch, *Weill on Stage,* 219.

90. Elliott Carter, "Theatre and Films, 1943," *Modern Music* 21, no. 1 (1943): 50–53.

91. Sanders, *The Days Grow Short,* 329.

CHAPTER 10

1. Wll. [i.e., Kurt Weill], "Möglichkeiten absoluter Radiokunst," *Der deutsche Rundfunk* 3, no. 26 (28 June 1925): 1625–28; reprinted in GS, 264–70. In addition to the writings for the *Deutscher Rundfunk,* the list of radio-related projects is quite long, even though much of the music is now lost. The two best-known and most substantial are the collaborations with Brecht *Der Lindberghflug* (composed in 1929 jointly with Hindemith, but then withdrawn and revised as a concert work; see chapter 7) and *Das Berliner Requiem.* Others include music to radio broadcasts of Grabbe's *Herzog Theodor von Gothland* (1926, lost); Strindberg's *Gustav XII* (1927); *Konjunktur* (Leo Lania and Felix Gasbarra, 1927, partially lost); *Katalaunische Schlacht* (Arnolt Bronnen, 1928, lost); *Petroleuminseln* (Lion Feuchtwanger, 1928, partially lost); *Mann ist Mann* (Brecht, 1931, lost); *La grande complainte de Fantômas* (Desnos, 1933, lost); and *Your Navy* (Anderson, 1942, lost). *Down in the Valley* also began as a radio project before being turned into a college opera (see chapter 11). See also Elmar Juchem, "Kurt Weill und die Radiokunst in den USA," in *Emigrierte Komponisten in der Medienlandschaft des Exils 1933–1945,* ed. Nils Grosch et al. (Stuttgart: Metzler, 1998), 55–72.

2. Kurt Weill, "Bekenntnis zur Oper," originally published in the program booklet for the premiere production of *Der Protagonist* on 27 March 1926 and in *Blätter der Staatsoper Dresden,* no. 131 (April 1926): 97–99; reprinted in GS, 45–47. A second, somewhat amended version of the essay appeared in *25 Jahre Neue Musik: Jahrbuch 1926 der Universal-Edition* (Vienna: Universal Edition, 1926), 226–28; reprinted in GS, 47–49. Although the expression "streams of inner song" is replaced there by "all forms and genres of this music," Weill refers to "the crystal-clear quality and inner tension of musical diction" as being "based in the transparency of our emotions *[Gefühlsinhalte]*" (49). See also Viktor Rotthaler, "Der innere Gesang: Kurt Weill und seine Leidenschaft fürs Kino," *Filmdienst* 53, no. 7 (2000): 41–44.

3. "Notiz zum *Berliner Requiem,*" *Der deutsche Rundfunk* 7, no. 20 (17 May 1929): 613; reprinted in GS, 409–11.

4. "Musikalische Illustration oder Filmmusik? Gespräch mit Lotte H. Eisner," *Film-Kurier,* 13 October 1927; reprinted in GS, 437–40.

5. See Susanne Fontaine, *Busonis "Doktor Faust" und die Ästhetik des Wunderbaren* (Kassel: Bärenreiter, 1998).

6. "National Music, Opera, and the Movies: An Interview with Kurt Weill," *Pacific Coast Musician,* 3 July 1937, 12–13.

7. Kurt Weill, "Tonfilm, Opernfilm, Filmoper," *Frankfurter Zeitung,* 24 May 1930; reprinted in GS, 109–14.

8. "Die andere Seite: Kurt Weill zum 'Dreigroschenoper'-Vergleich," *LichtBildBühne,* 13 February 1931; reprinted in GS, 126–27.

9. For a detailed account of the lawsuit, see Steve Giles, *Bertolt Brecht and Critical Theory: Marxism, Modernity, and the "Threepenny" Lawsuit,* 2nd ed. (Bern: Peter Lang, 1998), 13–37.

10. Ibid., 23.

11. Albert Kümmel and Petra Löffler, eds., *Medientheorie 1888–1933* (Frankfurt am Main: Suhrkamp Verlag, 2002), 539.

12. Bertolt Brecht, "Der Dreigroschenprozess: Ein soziologisches Experiment," in *Versuche,* vol. 3 *[Versuche 8–10]* (Berlin: Kiepenheuer, 1931); quoted from BBA 21:448–514, here 448.

13. Ibid., in BBA 21:458.

14. Bertolt Brecht, "Die Beule: Ein Dreigroschenfilm," in *Versuche* 3:244–55; quoted from BBA 19:315.

15. The best source of information about the Pabst film, including extensive materials pertaining to the law lawsuits, is Hans-Michael Bock and Jürgen Berger, eds., *Photo: Casparius* (West Berlin: Stiftung Deutsche Kinemathek, 1978). Hans Casparius, a member of the film's production team, was responsible for still photography, and the volume contains a lot of Casparius's work. See also Anno Mungen, "Theatermusik als Filmmusik: Kurt Weills 'Dreigroschen'-Musik als Adaption für den Film von G. W. Pabst," *Filmexil,* no. 14 (2001): 9–22.

16. For a Brechtian analysis, see Wolfgang Gersch, *Film bei Brecht* (Munich: Hanser Verlag, 1975), 51–58.

17. Brecht, "Die Beule," 307.

18. Letter to Lenya, 29 May 1937, in WLE, 242–43. It should be noted that on this occasion Weill saw the French version, *L'opéra de quat'sous,* which Pabst had shot at the same time as the German version, using the same musicians (i.e., members of the Lewis Ruth Band), but with a different, French-speaking cast.

19. Letter to Heinsheimer, 6 February 1933, in WUE, 451.

20. Heinsheimer to Weill, 8 February 1933, in WUE, 452. Heinsheimer had taken an intense interest in the possibilities of opera on screen. His article "Film Opera—Screen vs. Stage," published in *Modern Music* 8, no. 3 (1931): 10–14, concludes with a summary of Weill's ideas about film-opera and describes the lawsuit in connection with Pabst's *3-Groschen-Oper* as having "an historical significance."

21. WUE, 446.

22. Letter from Weill (in Louveciennes) to UE, 5 May 1934, in WUE, 481.

23. WUE, 200.

24. Ibid., 212.

25. Copy in WLRC.

26. Both David Drew and Nils Grosch have discussed details of Weill's unused score. See DDH, 282–86; and Nils Grosch, "'Jahre warten auf einen Film': Kurt Weills Filmmusiken im US-Exil," *Filmexil,* no. 10 (1998): 37–49.

27. Grosch, "'Jahre warten auf einen Film,'" 40.

28. Weill [in Hollywood] to Lenya, [13 March 1937], in WLE, 216–17.

29. The notes "About the music for 'You and me'," which Weill wrote in English, bear the date 24 May 1937; a copy is held in WLRC. They were also published in German translation in GS1, 123–25.

30. WLE, 253.

31. Frank S. Nugent, "The Avant-Garde Retreats with 'You and Me' at the Paramount," *New York Times,* 2 June 1938.

32. WLE, 251.

33. Bruno David Ussher, "Composing for Films," *New York Times,* 28 January 1940.

34. Kurt Weill, "Music in the Movies," *Harper's Bazaar* 80, no. 9 (September 1946): 257, 398, 400.

35. Thomas S. Hischak, *Through the Screen Door: What Happened to the Broadway Musical When it Went to Hollywood* (Lanham, Md.: Scarecrow Press, 2004), 2.

36. Ibid., 2, 18.

37. Copy in WLRC.

38. bruce d. mcclung, *Lady in the Dark: Biography of a Musical* (New York: Oxford University Press, 2007), 172, 174.

39. James Robert Parish and Michael R. Pitts, *The Great Hollywood Musical Pictures* (Metuchen, N.J.: Scarecrow Press, 1992), 374.

40. In the film, even more than in the stage work, Liza capitulates to the sexist environment that created her problems in the first place. However, through Russell's verbal parting shot, as Edward Gallafent (*Astaire & Rogers* [Moffat, Scot.: Cameron & Hollis, 2000], 202–3) has proposed, "*Lady in the Dark* may perhaps register a sense of its own preposterousness."

41. Copy in WLRC.

42. Letter from Weill to Lenya, 11–12 May 1945, in WLE, 458.

43. Letter from Weill to Lenya, 26 May 1945, ibid., 462.

44. Letter from Weill to Lenya, 1 June 1945, ibid.

45. Letter from Weill to Ann Ronell, 5 February 1948, in WLRC. See also Tighe E. Zimmers, *Tin Pan Alley Girl: A Biography of Ann Ronell* (Jefferson, N.C.: McFarland, 2009), esp. 92–99.

46. Letter from Ronell to Weill, 18 December 1947; original in New York Public Library; quoted in Zimmers, *Tin Pan Alley Girl,* 93.

47. Letter from Weill to Ronell, 22 January 1948, in WLRC.

48. Letter from Weill to Lenya, 1 May 1945, in WLE, 455.

49. Thornton Delehanty, "Kurt Weill, a Commuter to Hollywood," *New York Herald Tribune,* 3 June 1945.

50. Ibid.

51. Miles Kreuger, "Some Words about *Where Do We Go from Here?*" *KWNL* 14, no. 2 (1996): 10–12, here 12.

52. Weill, "Music in the Movies," 400.

53. Letter from Weill to Lenya, 1 May 1945, in WLE, 455

54. Weill, "Music in the Movies," 400.

55. Letter from Weill to Lenya, 1 May 1945, in WLE, 455.

56. Letter dated 28 November 1946; copy in WLRC.

57. Joel Galand has observed that the Columbus sequence is "stylistically of a piece with *Firebrand.*" See Galand's "Introduction" to Kurt Weill, *The Firebrand of Florence,* in KWE, ser. 1, vol. 18 (Miami: European American Music, 2002), 19.

58. Quoted in Delehanty, "Kurt Weill, a Commuter to Hollywood."

59. "The Good Earth" is published in *Unsung Weill,* ed. Elmar Juchem ([Miami:] European American Music, 2002), 86–88. In a letter to Lenya dated 16 April 1942, Weill described the song as "definitely a hit. We'll try to sell it to the movies" (WLE, 328).

60. Published in Juchem (ed.), *Unsung Weill,* 59–61.

61. A complete list of "musical entries" in *Where Do We Go from Here?* along with attributions to the specific staff members of the music department at Twentieth Century–Fox can be found in DDH, 338–39.

62. Copy in WLRC.

63. WLRC, ser. 31, box 1.

64. "WCBS Presents Margaret Arlen," radio program hosted by Margaret Arlen and Harry Marble, broadcast 7 January 1950; transcription in the Maxwell Anderson Papers, Harry Ransom Humanities Research Center, University of Texas, Austin; copy in WLRC.

65. Delehanty, "Kurt Weill, a Commuter to Hollywood."

66. Hanns Eisler and Theodor W. Adorno, *Composing for the Films* (London: Athlone, 1994), 55. Although he served as coauthor, Adorno did not want to be acknowledged as such when the book was first published in 1947. As Graham McCann remarks in his introduction to the Athlone edition, "Adorno withdrew his name as co-author in order to avoid being implicated in the House Un-American Activities Committee's investigations into Eisler's political associations."

67. The description "big article" is quoted from Weill's letter dated 29 September 1946 to his film-production agent Arthur Lyons; copy in WLRC.

68. Others mentioned—"to name only a few"—include Hugo Riesenfeld, Erno Rapee, Edmund Meisel, Alfred Newman, Max Steiner, Miklós Rósza, Herbert Stothart, and Franz Waxmann.

69. Weill specifically mentioned "that he would like to make a picture after 'Street Scene'" in a letter to Arthur Lyons from 14 February 1947. The "new form of musical entertainment which 'Street Scene' has started," he suggested, "could easily be translated into the field of motion pictures and could probably make film history as it has already made theatre history. I have pretty definite ideas how this could be done, but I doubt if Hollywood would let me do it." Copy in WLRC.

70. Weill to Alan Jay Lerner, 28 March 1949; copy in WLRC.

71. Letter from Weill to Lenya, 18 April 1945, in WLE, 451. The context for Weill's remark is the early demise of *The Firebrand of Florence.*

CHAPTER 11

1. Letter dated 11 July 1949, in BF, 417–18.

2. The opening sentence of the original reads, "For all we know, Kurt Weill, a composer born in Dessau, Germany, and now here to stay, may yet become known as the man who founded American opera" (Robert C. Bagar, "Lemonade Opera Has Pioneer Flavor," *New York World-Telegram;* undated copy in WLRC).

3. Downes's article, "Folk-Song Opera," was published in the *New York Times* on 11 July 1948.

4. The critic was Noel Straus, whose review appeared on 7 July 1949 in the *New York Times.*

5. Weill, "Two Dreams Come True," published in 1947 as liner note for the original cast recording of Street Scene, CBS OL 4139.

6. Weill, "Broadway and the Musical Theatre," *Composer's News-Record* 2 (May 1947): 1

7. *Life* 22, no. 11 (17 March 1947): 17. The original letter bears the date 21 February 1947.

8. Letter dated 13 November 1941, held in WLRC.

9. Letter dated 14 July 1944, in WLE, 391.

10. Letter dated 12 July 1944, ibid., 388

11. Letter dated 3 July 1944, ibid., 378.

12. Letter dated 28 July 1944, ibid., 404.

13. Letter dated 30 April 1945, in BF, 397.

14. Joel Galand, "Introduction" to Kurt Weill, *The Firebrand of Florence,* KWE, ser. 1, vol. 18 (Miami: European American Music, 2002), 15.

15. Ibid., 13, 15.

16. Letter to Caspar Neher, 16 February 1947, in PDE, 250.

17. Letter to Rouben Mamoulian, 22 January 1946; reprinted in *Street Scene: A Sourcebook,* ed. Joanna Lee et al. (New York: Kurt Weill Foundation, 1994), 9.

18. Shana Ager, "Broadway's First Real Opera: Kurt Weill's Music Has Made Something New Out of *Street Scene,*" *P.M.,* 9 February 1947.

19. See "Street Scene," in *Handbuch des Musicals: Die wichtigsten Titel von A bis Z,* ed. Thomas Siedhoff (Mainz: Schott, 2007), 580.

20. Kurt Weill, "Score for a Play," *New York Times,* 5 January 1947; the essay was reprinted in the souvenir program of the original Broadway production of *Street Scene.*

21. Elmer Rice, *Minority Report: An Autobiography* (New York: Simon & Schuster, 1963), 411.

22. Oscar G. Brockett and Robert R. Findlay, *A History of European and American Theatre and Drama Since 1870* (Englewood Cliffs, N.J.: Prentice-Hall, 1973), 510.

23. For details of Anderson's involvement in the initial stages of the work's creation, see David Kilroy, "Kurt Weill on Broadway: The Postwar Years (1945–1950)" (Ph.D. diss., Harvard University, 1992), 75–77.

24. Ager, "Broadway's First Real Opera."

25. Weill, "Score for a Play."

26. Ibid.

27. Letter from Weill to his brother Hans, 26 November 1946, in BF, 404.

28. Letter to Caspar Neher, 16 February 1947, in PDE, 250.

29. "Kurt Weill's notes on STREET SCENE, DEC. 21st," published in *Street Scene: A Sourcebook,* 17–19.

30. Weill, "Score for a Play."

31. Edwin Wilson, *The Theater Experience,* 4th ed. (New York: McGraw-Hill, 1988), 447–48.

32. Elmer L. Rice, *Street Scene: A Play in Three Acts* (New York: Samuel French, Inc., 1956), 5.

33. Elise K. Kirk, *American Opera* (Urbana: University of Illinois Press, 2001), 262.

34. Larry Stempel, "*Street Scene* and the Enigma of Broadway Opera," in *A New Orpheus,* ed. Kim H. Kowalke (New Haven: Yale University Press, 1986), 321–41, here 329.

35. See, for example, William Thornhill, "Kurt Weill's *Street Scene*" (Ph.D. diss., University of North Carolina, Chapel Hill, 1990). According to Thornhill, the collaborative process "made *Street Scene* into a work at odds with the one [Weill] originally envisaged."

36. "Kurt Weill's notes on STREET SCENE, DEC. 21st." A copy of Weill's typescript notes is kept in WLRC; they are reprinted in *Street Scene: A Sourcebook,* 17–19.

37. Lenya's recollection of the incident, which occurred during the tryout period in Philadelphia, is cited in *Street Scene: A Sourcebook,* 16.

38. Foster Hirsch, *Kurt Weill on Stage: From Berlin to Broadway* (New York: Knopf, 2002), 272, 271.

39. Kowalke, "Kurt Weill, Modernism, and Popular Culture: *Öffentlichkeit als Stil,*" *Modernism/Modernity* 2, no. 1 (1995): 27–69, here 45.

40. Letter from Weill to Hughes, quoted in Kilroy, "Kurt Weill on Broadway," 117; the original Hughes letter belongs to the Langston Hughes Papers held at Yale University's Beinecke Library.

41. Kilroy, "Kurt Weill on Broadway," 43: "'Metadrama' is an umbrella term that theorists have adopted to describe a script's reflexive techniques and the function they can play within a theatrical event."

42. Kowalke, "Kurt Weill, Modernism, and Popular Culture," 49.

43. Ibid., 51.

44. Weill, "Score for a Play."

45. Kowalke, "Kurt Weill, Modernism, and Popular Culture," 44.

46. Geoffrey Chew, "Pastoral," in *The New Grove Dictionary of Opera,* ed. Stanley Sadie (London: Macmillan, 1992), 3:910–13.

47. Andreas Hauff, "Orientierungsversuche in der Großstadt: Verweise und Bekenntnisse in Kurt Weills *Street Scene,*" in *Street Scene: Der urbane Raum im Musiktheater des 20. Jahrhunderts,* ed. Stefan Weiss and Jürgen Schebera (Münster: Waxmann, 2006), 35–55, here 53–54.

48. Ibid., 55.

49. Kilroy, "Kurt Weill on Broadway," 201.

50. Kowalke, "Kurt Weill, Modernism, and Popular Culture," 42.

51. Weill's annotated copy of Rice's play is held in WLRC. The page in question is also reproduced in *Street Scene: A Sourcebook,* 8.

52. H.W. Heinsheimer, "Right Kind of Opera Has Market in America," *New York Times,* 29 May 1949.

53. "More Light on 'Valley': Kurt Weill Makes 'Correcting Remarks' about His Opera's Inception," *New York Times,* 5 June 1949. The next year, Heinsheimer published an amended account of the genesis in which he absorbs Weill's "correcting remarks" by acknowledging Downes's role; see H.W. Heinsheimer, "Opera for All the Valleys," *Educational Music Magazine* (March–April 1950): 25, 54–56.

54. Interview in the *New York Sun,* 3 February 1940.

55. See Elmar Juchem, "Kurt Weill und die Radiokunst in den USA," in *Emigrierte Komponisten in der Medienlandschaft des Exils 1933–1945,* ed. Nils Grosch et al. (Stuttgart: Metzler, 1999), 55–72.

56. Quoted in Elmar Juchem, *Kurt Weill und Maxwell Anderson: Neue Wege zu einem amerikanischen Musiktheater, 1938–1950* (Stuttgart: Metzler, 2000), 64.

57. See ibid., 68–70.

58. McArthur is not to be confused with Charles MacArthur, playwright and husband of Helen Hayes, with whom Weill had worked on *Fun to Be Free.*

59. Weill's letter to McArthur is held in the WLRC and published in PDE, 242–43.

60. G.L. Kittredge, "Ballads and Songs," *Journal of American Folklore,* 30 (July–September 1917): 283–369, here 346–47.

61. John Graziano, "Musical Dialects in *Down in the Valley,*" in Kowalke (ed.), *A New Orpheus,* 297–319, here 300 n. 12.

62. *Down in the Valley,* music by Kurt Weill, libretto by Arnold Sundgaard (New York: G. Schirmer, Inc., 1948), n.p.

63. Jean Thomas and Joseph A. Leeder, *The Singin' Gatherin': Tunes from the Southern Appalachians* (New York: Silver Burnett Company, 1939).

64. Hirsch, *Kurt Weill on Stage,* 292. Hirsch misidentifies Schonberg's review as having appeared in the *New York Times* on the day of the Indiana premiere, 15 July 1948.

65. Harold Schonberg, "Lemonade Opera gives 'Down in the Valley,'"probably from *New York Sun,* 7 July 1949; undated copy in WLRC, ser. 50A/D5. Schonberg's later verdict, issued in a review of the opera version of *Mahagonny* done at the Stratford Festival of Canada in 1965 ("Musical Parable of Sheer Despair," *New York Times,* 25 July 1965), pulled no punches: "It is not in his nature to be sentimental. 'Down in the Valley,' for example is embarrassing and even cheap, a cowboy opera for the old lady in Dubuque [Iowa, i.e., the Midwest]. It is to 'The Threepenny Opera' and 'Mahagonny' what the Little Orphan Annie is to a Rowlandson or a Hogarth drawing."

66. Cecil Smith, "Kurt Weill Folk Drama," *Musical America,* August 1949; copy in WLRC.

67. Wilfred C. Bain, review of *Down in the Valley* in *Notes* 5, no. 4 (1948): 521–22, here 522.

68. David Drew, "Two Weill Scores," *Musical Times* 107 (September 1966): 797–98. Concerning the "commercial circumstances" of *Down in the Valley,* it is worth noting that Weill and Sundgaard requested that the publisher Schirmer waive royalties and hence earned little from the circa 6,000 performances of the work.

69. Quoted in "Home-Grown Opera," *Time,* 25 July 1949.

70. "Weill's Opera 'Down in the Valley,'" *New York Times,* 16 April 1984; emphasis added.

71. Letter to Irving Sablosky, 24 July 1948; copy in WLRC.

72. Letter to Max Leavitt, director of the Lemonade Opera production, 29 June 1949; cited in Hirsch, *Kurt Weill on Stage,* 291.

73. Graziano, "Musical Dialects in *Down in the Valley,*" 217.

74. Theodor W. Adorno, "Kurt Weill: Musiker des epischen Theaters," *Frankfurter Rundschau,* 15 April 1950; reprinted in *Gesammelte Schriften* (Frankfurt am Main: Suhrkamp Verlag, 1984), 18:544–47, here 546.

75. Smith, "Kurt Weill Folk Drama."

76. Kim H. Kowalke, "Kurt Weill and the Quest for American Opera," in *Amerikanismus, Americanism, Weill: Die Suche nach kultureller Identität in der Moderne,"* ed. Hermann Danuser and Hermann Gottschewski (Schliengen: Edition Argus, 2003), 283–301.

CHAPTER 12

1. Letter to Olin Downes, 14 November 1949; copy in WLRC.

2. "Two Dreams Come True," undated typescript (copy in WLRC); used without title as liner notes to the cast recording of *Street Scene* (Columbia OL 4139).

3. Letter to Irving Sablosky, 24 July 1948; copy in WLRC.

4. David Kilroy, "Kurt Weill on Broadway: The Postwar Years (1945–1950)" (Ph.D. diss., Harvard University, 1992).

5. For a discussion of the parallels between *Love Life* and *Cabaret,* see Kim H. Kowalke, "Today's Invention, Tomorrow's Cliché: *Love Life* and the Concept Musical," "*. . . dass alles auch hätte anders kommen können": Beiträge zur Musikgeschichte des 20. Jahrhunderts,* ed. Susanne Schaal-Gotthardt, Luitgard Schader, and Heinz-Jürgen Winkler (Frankfurt am Main: Schott, 2009), 175–93.

6. In her typological study *Il musical di Kurt Weill (1940–1950): Prospettive, generi e tradizioni* (Rome: Edizioni Studio 12, 2006), Marida Rizzuti makes the case for a "third genre" between musical and opera in the works composed during the decade 1940–1950, positing a "hybrid form" that she presents not as a mere "contamination" of different genres, but as a "fusion" of them. (The original subtitle of Rizzuti's Master's thesis. was "Fusione di prospettive, generi e tradizioni," Università degli Studi di Pavia, 2005.) By contrast, the concept of dramaturgical counterpoint being proposed here embraces a wide range of mixed-genre solutions from all three decades of Weill's career and emphasizes the book-specific nature of the constitutive elements.

7. Foster Hirsch, *Kurt Weill on Stage: From Berlin to Broadway* (New York: Knopf, 2002), 279–80. A comparable case could be made for *Happy End,* whose book underwent a radical transformation from initial conception through opening night. Materials housed in the Elisabeth-Hauptmann-Archiv (Akademie der Künste Berlin) include multiple versions of the play's script that document this transformation.

8. Weill to Irving Lazar, 24 October 1948; copy in WLRC.

9. Weill to Maxwell Anderson, 25 July 1947; copy in WLRC.

10. Alan Jay Lerner, "Lerner's Life and Love Life," *PM,* 14 November 1948; quoted in Kilroy, "Kurt Weill on Broadway," 213.

11. Kilroy, "Kurt Weill on Broadway," 233. Middleton had played Irving in *Knickerbocker Holiday.*

12. The orchestral parts are preserved in the Irving S. Gilmore Music Library of Yale University as part of the Papers of Kurt Weill and Lotte Lenya, MSS 30.

13. The holograph is located at Harvard University: Weill, Kurt, 1900–1950. [Love life. Vocal Score]. [S.I. : s.n., 1948?]. Loeb Music: Mus 865.13.610.

14. Brooks Atkinson, "*Allegro:* A Fragment of the American Legend," *New York Times,* 2 November 1947.

15. Letter to Lenya, 18 May 1945, in WLE, 460.

16. Letter from Cheryl Crawford to Weill, n.d.; copy in WLRC.

17. Peter Szondi, *Theory of the Modern Drama,* ed. and trans. Michael Hays (Minneapolis: University of Minnesota Press: 1987), esp. 83–91. Szondi's two sections devoted to Wilder are called "The Epic *I* as Stage Manager" and "The Play of Time."

18. Max Frisch, "Brecht als Klassiker," *Weltwoche* (Zurich), 1 July 1955; quoted in Charles H. Helmetag, "Mother Courage and Her American Cousins in 'The Skin of Our Teeth,'" *Modern Language Studies* 8, no. 3 (1978): 65–69, here 65.

19. Helmetag, "Mother Courage and Her American Cousins," 68.

20. Ibid.

21. See Donald Haberman, "'Preparing the Way for Them': Wilder and the Next Generations," in *Critical Essays on Thornton Wilder,* ed. Martin Blank (New York: G. K. Hall, 1996), 129–37, esp. 130.

22. Thorton Wilder, *Three Plays: Our Town, The Skin of Our Teeth, The Matchmaker* (New York: Harper, 1957), xii.

23. Francis Fergusson, "Three Allegorists: Brecht, Wilder, and Eliot," in Blank, (ed.), *Critical Essays on Thornton Wilder,* 68; originally published in *Sewanee Review* 64 (1956): 544–73. Because it lacks a historical dimension, Fergusson goes on to say, the "intellectual freedom" of Wilder's philosophy "is therefore in danger of irrelevancy, pretentiousness and sentimentality."

24. The allusion is bitterly ironic in its implications. As Nietzsche (*Thus Spoke Zarathustra,* trans. Adrian Del Caro [Cambridge: Cambridge University Press, 2006], 11–12) writes,

> After a while the shattered man regained consciousness and saw Zarathustra kneeling beside him. "What are you doing here?" he said finally. "I've known for a long time that the devil would trip me up. Now he is going to drag me off to hell: are you going to stop him?"
>
> "By my honor, friend!" answered Zarathustra. "All that you are talking about does not exist. There is no devil and no hell. Your soul will be dead even sooner than your body—fear no more!"
>
> The man looked up mistrustfully. "If you speak the truth," he said, "then I lose nothing when I lose my life. I am not much more than an animal that has been taught to dance by blows and little treats."
>
> "Not at all," said Zarathustra. "You made your vocation out of danger,

and there is nothing contemptible about that. Now you perish of your vocation, and for that I will bury you with my own hands."

When Zarathustra said this the dying man answered no more, but he moved his hand as if seeking Zarathustra's hand in gratitude.

25. Thornton Wilder, *The Long Christmas Dinner and Other Plays in One Act* (London: Longmans, Green & Co., 1931), 3.

26. Szondi, *Theory of the Modern Drama,* 91.

27. Ibid., 85.

28. For an extensive, multiperspectived reading of "Here I'll Stay," see Kilroy, "Kurt Weill on Broadway," 284–316.

29. Ronald Taylor, *Kurt Weill: Composer in a Divided World* (New York: Simon & Schuster, 1991), 312.

30. Weill's own description of the adaptation is quoted in Lawrence Perry, "*Huckleberry Finn* Will Be a Musical," *New York Times,* 5 February 1950. Incidentally, Weill's former apologist and later detractor Theodor W. Adorno left musical sketches and two completed songs, written in 1932–33, for a projected *Singspiel* called *Der Schatz des Indianer-Joe.* Based on Twain's novel *The Adventures of Tom Sawyer,* Adorno's work was no doubt influenced by Weill and Brecht's *Aufstieg und Fall der Stadt Mahagonny.* See Rolf Tiedemann, "Adorno's *Tom Sawyer* Opera Singspiel," in *The Cambridge Companion to Adorno,* ed. Tom Huhn (Cambridge: Cambridge University Press, 2004), 376–94; and Karla Schultz, "Utopias from Hell: Brecht's *Mahagonny* and Adorno's *Treasure of Indian Joe,*" *Monatshefte* 90, no. 3 (1998): 307–16.

31. As George Hutchinson observes, "The book was 'plantation school' fiction of the deepest dye, extreme if unintended testimony to the racial delusions to which upper-class white Southerners were prone" (*In Search of Nella Larsen: A Biography of the Color Line* [Cambridge, Mass.: Belknap Press, 2006], 214).

32. Letter dated 3 March 1939; quoted in Laurence G. Avery, ed., *Dramatist in America: Letters of Maxwell Anderson, 1912–1958* (Chapel Hill: University of North Carolina Press, 1977), 84–86. Also in Elmar Juchem, *Kurt Weill und Maxwell Anderson: Neue Wege zu einem amerikanischen Musiktheater, 1938–1950* (Stuttgart: Metzler, 2000), 133.

33. Letter dated 29 March [1939], in Juchem, *Kurt Weill und Maxwell Anderson,* 134.

34. Martin Duberman, *Paul Robeson* (New York: Knopf, 1988), 230.

35. Letter from Anderson to Robeson, 3 March 1939; in Avery (ed.), *Dramatist in America,* 85.

36. For an illuminating reading of *Ulysses Africanus* in relation to Homer's *Odyssey,* see Robert J. Rabel, "Odysseus Almost Makes It to Broadway: The *Ulysses Africanus* of Kurt Weill and Maxwell Anderson," *International Journal of the Classical Tradition* 13, no. 4 (2007): 550–70.

37. Juchem, *Kurt Weill und Maxwell Anderson,* 144–45.

38. Rabel, "Odysseus Almost Makes It to Broadway," 559 n. 24.

39. Kilroy, "Kurt Weill on Broadway," 345–47.

40. Letter from Weill to Anderson, 22 June 1947; in the Maxwell Anderson Collection

of the Harry Ransom Humanities Research Center, University of Texas, Austin; quoted in Juchem, *Kurt Weill und Maxwell Anderson,* 161.

41. Letter from Anderson to Weill, undated except for "Sunday" (probably 13 July 1947), in WLRC; quoted in Juchem, *Kurt Weill und Maxwell Anderson,* 162.

42. Hirsch, *Kurt Weill on Stage,* 304.

43. See Elmar Juchem, "Lost in the Stars," *Kurt Weill Newsletter* 26, no. 1 (2008): 4–12. In this documentary essay Juchem also mentions that another song from *Ulysses Africanus,* "Forget," was being considered for insertion into *Street Scene.*

44. Maxwell Anderson, Epilogue to *You Who Have Dreams* (New York: Simon & Schuster, 1925), 58.

45. Maxwell Anderson, "The Essence of Tragedy," in *The Essence of Tragedy and Other Footnotes and Papers* (New York: Russell & Russell, 1939), 3–14, here 7.

46. Letter from Maxwell Anderson to Alan Paton, 15 March 1948; in Avery (ed.), *Dramatist in America,* 221–22.

47. Alan Paton, *Cry, the Beloved Country* (New York: C. Scribner's Sons, 1948), 175.

48. Avery (ed.), *Dramatist in America,* 221

49. Alan Paton, *Journey Continued: An Autobiography* (Oxford: Oxford University Press, 1988), 23.

50. Ibid., 20.

51. Maxwell Anderson, *Lost in the Stars* (New York: William Sloane Associates, Inc., 1950), 85.

52. The text of Anderson's speech is reproduced as an appendix to Avery (ed.), *Dramatist in America,* 298–301.

53. A copy of Mamoulian's twelve-page memorandum is held in WLRC. Excerpts are quoted in Juchem, *Kurt Weill und Maxwell Anderson,* 187–90.

54. Ibid., 190.

55. Letter from Agnes de Mille to Maxwell Anderson, 24 April 1949, quoted ibid., 177–78.

56. Hesper Anderson, *South Mountain Road: A Daughter's Journey of Discovery* (New York: Simon & Schuster, 2000), 17.

57. Olin Downes, "Opera on Broadway: Kurt Weill Takes Forward Step in Setting Idiomatic American to Music," *New York Times,* 26 January 1947.

58. Downes's letter, dated 9 December 1949, was published in *KWNL* 12, no. 2 (1994): 8; copy in WLRC.

59. A copy of Weill's letter of reply to Downes, dated 14 November [*recte:* December] 1949, is in WLRC. The letter was published in *KWNL* 12, no. 2 (1994): 10.

60. Clurman's review, entitled "Lost in the Stars of Broadway," is reprinted in *KWNL* 12, no. 2 (1994): 10–11.

61. Carl Dahlhaus, "Musical der Angst: Kurt Weills *Lost in the Stars* in der Stuttgarter Liederhalle," *Stuttgarter Zeitung,* 3 March 1962; reprinted in Carl Dahlhaus, *Gesammelte Schriften,* vol. 10, ed. Hermann Danuser (Laaber: Laaber Verlag, 2007), 417–19.

62. Notes for a response to Harold Clurman, published in *KWNL* 12, no. 2 (1994): 20. The manuscript belongs to the Weill-Lenya Papers, Yale University Music Library.

63. Quoted in Harry Gilroy, "Written in the Stars: Composer Kurt Weill and Playwright Maxwell Anderson Air Views on Racial Harmony in Latest Collaboration," *New York Times,* 30 October 1949.

64. Ibid.

65. Roosevelt's remarks on *Lost in the Stars* were published on 19 November 1949. The complete collection of her syndicated columns is available at www.gwu.edu/~erpapers/myday/.

66. Quoted in Gilroy, "Written in the Stars."

CODA

1. Virgil Thomson, "Kurt Weill," *New York Herald Tribune,* 9 April 1950; reprinted in *A Virgil Thomson Reader* (Boston: Houghton Mifflin, 1981), 342–44.

2. Letter to Lenya, 18 May 1945, in WLE, 460.

3. Thomson, "Kurt Weill," 344.

4. S. L. M. Barlow, "In the Theatre," *Modern Music* 22, no. 4 (1945): 275–77, here 276; Clurman's review, entitled "Lost in the Stars of Broadway" and originally published in the *Saturday Review of Literature* on 31 December 1949, is reprinted in *KWNL* 12, no. 2 (1994): 10–11. See chapter 12 for a discussion of Clurman's critique.

5. See Tamara Levitz, *Teaching New Classicality: Ferruccio Busoni's Master Class in Composition* (Frankfurt am Main: Peter Lang, 1996), 250.

6. Ferruccio Busoni, "Über die Möglichkeiten der Oper," written in Berlin in August 1921 and first published in *Die Revue "Faust,"* 1 (1921). A slightly longer version appeared in *Von der Einheit der Musik* (1922) as "Entwurf eines Vorworts zur Partitur des *Doktor Faust* enthaltend einige Betrachtungen über die Möglichkeiten der Oper" and later in *Wesen und Einheit der Musik* (1956) as "Die Einheit der Musik und die Möglichkeiten der Oper." It was also issued as a separate publication in 1926 as "Über die Möglichkeiten der Oper und über die Partitur des *Doktor Faust.*" See the editor's notes in Ferruccio Busoni, *Von der Macht der Töne: Ausgewählte Schriften,* ed. Siegfried Bimberg (Leipzig: Reclam, 1983), 135; the essay appears in this volume as "Über die Möglichkeiten der Oper," 121–35.

7. Stephen Rumph, "Mozart's Archaic Endings: A Linguistic Critique," *Journal of the Royal Musical Association* 130, no. 2 (2005): 159–96, here 191.

8. Kurt Weill, "Opern-Rück- und Vorschau," *Der deutsche Rundfunk* 3, no. 11 ([15 March] 1925): 681–82; 3, no. 13 ([29 March] 1925) : 809; reprinted as "Mozart's *Zauberflöte* als Sendespiel," GS, 230–35. It seems likely that in writing his article, Weill consulted Ernst Lert's book *Mozart auf dem Theater,* which was published in 1918 and issued in a third edition in 1921 by Schuster & Loeffler (Berlin). The Goethe quotation appears in Lert's text as a motto to the section on *Die Zauberflöte.* Moreover, several of Weill's formulations are near quotations or paraphrases from that section. Where Lert writes about "naive Symbolik" (385), Weill mentions "ungekünstelte [i.e., unaffected] Symbolik"; where Lert refers to "ewige Allegorie der Humanität" (385), Weill writes of an "Allegorie eines tief religiösen Gedankens." Similarities to Lert's text in matters of content, not just in the words used, are also apparent in Weill's review.

9. Kurt Weill, "The Alchemy of Music," *Stage* 14, no. 2 (November 1936): 63–64.

10. Kurt Weill, "The Future of Opera in America," *Modern Music* 14, no. 4 (May–June 1937): 183–88.

11. Julian Seaman, "Breath from Broadway," *Cue* 12, no. 46 (13 November 1943): 16.

12. Notes for a response to Harold Clurman, published in *KWNL* 12, no. 2 (1994): 20. The manuscript belongs to the Weill-Lenya Papers, Yale University Music Library.

13. Whether Anderson was familiar with an often-quoted passage from the Venerable Bede's *Ecclesiastical History of the English People* as an inspiration for "A Bird of Passage" is hard to establish with any certainty. There is little doubt that the Anglo-Saxon literature classes Anderson took at Stanford in 1914 could have exposed him to it. And even if the connection could be demonstrated, it's presumably a somewhat secular refunctioning. Be that as it may, that the text quoted on Weill's gravestone may have originated in a seventh-century story about King Edwin being converted to Christianity is not without a certain piquancy. The connection between Bede's and Anderson's texts has been pointed out by several authors, including Janet Duthie Collins in her article "The Reality of the Classification 'Poetry' for Old English," *Lacus Forum* 24 (1998): 389–97. The passage in question is the following:

> When compared with the stretch of time unknown to us, O king, the present life of men on earth is like the flight of a single sparrow through the hall where, in winter, you sit with your captains and ministers. Entering at one door and leaving by another, while it is inside it is untouched by the wintry storm; but this brief interval of calm is over in a moment, and it returns to the winter whence it came, vanishing from your sight. Man's life is similar; and of what follows it, or what went before, we are utterly ignorant.

14. Weill, "Korrespondenz über *Dreigroschenoper*," *Anbruch* 11, no. 1 (1929): 24–25; reprinted in GS, 72–74, here 74.

15. See Antony Beaumont, "Chamber Music: The Kurt Weill Edition, Series II, Volume 1" (a review), *KWNL* 23, no. 1 (2005): 13–15.

16. For an interpretation of Weill's quotation from Papageno's aria, see Anton Heuff, "Papageno in Potsdam: Kurt Weill's Parody of Prussian Militarism," *KWNL* 12, no. 2 (1994): 12–13. Following detective work done by the singer Gisela May, Heuff convincingly identifies the carillon of Berlin's Garnisonskirche as the likely source of the melody. The association is thereby equivocal: on the one hand with Mozart's operatic character, on the other with Prussian militarism. In military circles, the church's tune had become underlaid with the words "Üb immer Treu und Redlichkeit ("be always obedient and honorable").

17. Kurt Weill,"Opern-Rück- und Vorschau," *Der deutsche Rundfunk* 2, no. 49 (7 December 1924): 2967–68; reprinted as "Opern im Rundfunk" in GS, 218.

18. In "Mozart's Archaic Endings," Rumph presents a critique that, he says, "questions the unity of Mozart's style" (161).

19. Letter to Hans Weill, 27 June 1919, in BF, 234.

20. Harry Gilroy, "Written in the Stars: Composer Kurt Weill and Playwright Maxwell Anderson Air Views on Racial Harmony in Latest Collaboration," *New York Times*, 30 October 1949.

21. Theodor W. Adorno, "Über den Fetischcharakter in der Musik und die Regression des Hörens," *Zeitschrift für Sozialforschung* 7 (1938): 321–56; reprinted in *Dissonanzen: Einleitung in die Musiksoziologie* (Frankfurt am Main: Suhrkamp Verlag, 1973), 14–50; the essay was published in English as "On the Fetish Character of Music and the Regression of Listening" in *The Culture Industry: Selected Essays on Mass Culture,* ed. J. M. Bernstein (London: Routledge, 1991). The translation here, which attempts as far as possible to preserve Adorno's terminology, is my own. In an essay from the early 1960s on another singspiel, Weber's *Der Freischütz,* Adorno describes Mozart's singspiel in terms of "the heritage of the singspiel [creating] world theater, in which high and low, *opera seria,* couplet, lied, coloratura and enlightened mysticism come together for the last time in a unified cosmos, without any fissure between the sphere of Sarastro and that of Papageno." By way of comparison, he suggests that Weber's opera "draws from the singspiel the power of the unmediated and the disparate," suggesting that both its form and musical style are less unified than in Mozart. *Der Freischütz,* he declares, "is the first opera that modestly and involuntarily discharges style from itself" (quoted from "Bilderwelt des Freischütz," originally written for the *Programm der Hamburger Staatsoper,* no. 5 [1961–62] and anthologized in *Moments musicaux* [1964]; reprinted in *Gesammelte Schriften* [Frankfurt am Main: Suhrkamp Verlag, 1982], 17:36–41, here 39). Weber's music, which is parodied at the beginning of the *Mahagonny-Songspiel,* no doubt left its mark on Weill's work, too, albeit not as pervasively as Mozart's.

22. Daniel Albright, "Kurt Weill as Modernist," *Modernism/Modernity* 7, no. 2 (2000): 273–84, here 283.

23. The American Music Theater Festival in Philadelphia in 1990; Opera North in England in 1996; the workshop production by the Hochschule der Künste Berlin in 2000, with repeat performances at the Kurt-Weill-Fest in Bitterfeld in 2001.

24. Quoted in Foster Hirsch, *Kurt Weill on Stage: From Berlin to Broadway* (New York: Knopf, 2002), 297. Kreuger's anecdote comes from an interview he did with Hirsch in 1999. Almost identical wording can be found in Gene Lees's book *The Musical Worlds of Lerner and Loewe* (London: Ronson, 1991), 325; according to Kreuger, as Lees reports it, Lerner had said: "I can't ever allow *Love Life* to be revived [because] I have turned into everything I satirized in that show."

25. See Juchem, *Kurt Weill und Maxwell Anderson,* 215–22.

26. Theodor W. Adorno, "Nach einem Vierteljahrhundert," *Programmheft der Städtischen Bühnen Düsseldorf* (1955–56), 6:131–40; reprinted in *Gesammelte Schriften* (Frankfurt am Main: Suhrkamp Verlag, 1984), 18:548–51, here 550.

27. Wolfgang Jansen, "'. . . eine Räuberpistole aus New Yorker Hinterhöfen': Zur europäischen Erstaufführung von Kurt Weills *Street Scene* 1955 in Düsseldorf," *Musicals,* no. 121 (October–November 2006): 42–45, here 44.

28. Horst Koegler, "Der Vortrupp des Musicals," *Der Monat* 8 (January 1956): 68–71, here 69. The typescript of Adorno's reply, "Vortrupp und Avantgarde: Replik an Horst Koegler," is housed in the Weill/Lenya Archive at Yale (box 74, folder 1, 3); the text appeared in *Der Monat* 8 (March 1956): 76–78, and was reprinted in Adorno, *Gesammelte Schriften* 18:800–804.

29. Fritz Hennenberg, "Neue Funktionsweisen der Musik und des Musiktheaters in

den zwanziger Jahren: Studien über die Zusammenarbeit Bertolt Brechts mit Franz S. Bruinier und Kurt Weill" (diss., Martin-Luther-Universität, Halle-Wittenberg, 1987), 105–6.

30. "I do not consider myself a 'German composer,'" he wrote in a letter entitled "Gentle Beef," *Life,* 17 March 1947. "The Nazis obviously did not consider me such either."

31. See Jürgen Engelhardt, "Fragwürdiges in der Kurt-Weill-Rezeption: Zur Diskussion über einen wiederentdeckten Komponisten," in *Angewandte Musik 20er Jahre,* ed. Dietrich Stern (Berlin: Argument-Verlag, 1977), 118–37. The essay is ostensibly a critical review of the writings of Weill scholar David Drew, whom Engelhardt charges with wanting to make Weill "acceptable to the avant-garde" (135). Rejecting also "Adorno's brilliant one-sidedness" (121), the author concludes with a plea to take account of "the intentions of Brechtian music theater" (135).

32. Hans Ulrich Engelmann, "Kurt Weill—heute," *Darmstädter Beiträge zur neuen Musik* 3 (1960): 87–95, here 87.

33. See Stephen Hinton, "Misunderstanding 'The Threepenny Opera,'" in *Kurt Weill: The Threepenny Opera,* ed. Stephen Hinton (Cambridge: Cambridge University Press, 1990), 181–92.

34. Quoted in David Drew, "Reflections on the Last Years: *Der Kuhhandel* as a Key Work," in *A New Orpheus: Essays on Kurt Weill,* ed. Kim H. Kowalke (New Haven: Yale University Press, 1986), 219.

35. Nancy Mitford, *The Pursuit of Love and Love in a Cold Climate* (New York: Random House, 1994), 56.

36. Hellmut Kotschenreuther, *Kurt Weill* (Berlin: Max Hesses Verlag, 1962), 3.

37. Karl Lustig-Prean, "Der Tod des Avantgardisten," *Arbeiter-Zeitung* (Vienna), 9 April 1950. See also chapter 5.

38. See, for example, the review by Wolfgang Steinecke, "Kurt Weills Come-back: 'Street Scene' als europäische Erstaufführung in Düsseldorf," *Der Mittag,* 28 November 1955. In another review, which bore the title "Zwischen Ironie und Pathos" (*Der Tagesspiegel,* 30 November 1955), the famous critic and musicologist H. H. Stuckenschmidt wrote that prior to the Düsseldorf production Weill remained "the only famous émigré without a comeback *[Come back].*"

39. Published in *KWNL* 27, no. 2 (2009): 5.

40. David Drew, "Weill and His Critics," *Times Literary Supplement,* 3 and 10 October 1975, 1142–44 and 1198–1200. The same essay appears in German translation as the foreword to David Drew, ed., *Über Kurt Weill* (Frankfurt am Main: Suhrkamp Verlag, 1975), vii–xxxiii, here xi.

41. Drew, "Weill and His Critics," 1143.

42. Ian Kemp, "Weills Harmonik: Einige Beobachtungen," in Drew (ed.), *Über Kurt Weill,* 155–61; originally published as "Harmony in Weill: Some Observations," *Tempo,* n.s., no. 104 (1973): 11–15, here 15.

43. Letter from Drew to Hans Curjel, 26 November 1969; original in the Deutsches Literaturarchiv/Schiller-Nationalmuseum, Marbach am Neckar; quoted in Kim H. Kowalke, "Kurt Weill, Modernism, and Popular Culture: *Öffentlichkeit als Stil,*" *Modernism/Modernity* 2, no. 1 (1995): 27–69, here 28.

44. Hans Robert Jauss, "Der Leser als Instanz einer neuen Geschichte der Literatur," *Poetica* 7 (1975): 325–44.

45. bruce d. mcclung, "From Myth to Monograph: Weill Scholarship, Fifty Years After," *Theater* 30, no. 3 (2000): 107–17.

46. Kästner's "Surabaya-Johnny II" first appeared in print as "Surabaya-Johnny der Zweite" in *Simplicissimus* 52 (24 March 1930): 638. According to the collected edition of Kästner's works, the song had its first performance at the political-literary cabaret *Katakombe* in Berlin on 5 March 1930. See Erich Kästner, *Wir sind so frei: Chanson, Kabarett, kleine Prosa,* ed. Hermann Kurzke (Munich: Carl Hanser Verlag, 1998), 464. Kästner's parody appears in that edition on pp. 334–35. It is also included in *Brecht-Liederbuch,* ed. Fritz Hennenberg (Frankfurt am Main: Suhrkamp Verlag, 1984), 406.

47. The lyrics of "The Saga of Lenny" have been published as "Leonard Bernstein's 70th Birthday Song" in *Bernstein Remembered: A Life in Pictures,* ed. Jane Fluegel (New York: Carroll & Graf, 1991), 134. The Tanglewood celebration, including Bacall's rendition of the song, was broadcast as part of PBS's *Great Performances* on 19 March 1989.

48. See Kim H. Kowalke, "'The Threepenny Opera' in America," in Hinton (ed.), *Kurt Weill: The Threepenny Opera,* 78–122.

49. Bob Dylan, *Chronicles,* vol. 1 (New York: Simon & Schuster, 2004), 272–73.

50. Alan Moore and Kevin O'Neill, *The League of Extraordinary Gentlemen Volume 3: Century, part 1: 1910* (Marietta, Ga.: Top Shelf Productions, 2009). *Century, part 2: 1969* was published in 2001. The preceding two volumes, neither of which bears a subtitle, appeared in 2002 (vol. 1) and 2004 (vol. 2). Moore and O'Neill's graphic novel entitled *The League of Extraordinary Gentlemen: Black Dossier* was published as a stand-alone sourcebook in 2008; it has no volume number.

51. See Kim H. Kowalke, "Today's Invention, Tomorrow's Cliché," in "*. . . dass alles auch hätte anders kommen können*": *Beiträge zur Musik des 20. Jahrhunderts,* ed. Susanne Schaal-Gotthardt and Luitgard Schader (Mainz: Schott, 2009), 175–93; and Lara E. Housez, "Kurt Weill's *Love Life* in a Comparative Analysis with Stephen Sondheim's *Assassins*" (M.A. thesis, University of Western Ontario, 2004) and "Becoming Stephen Sondheim: From *Forum* to *Company*" (Ph.D. diss., Eastman School of Music, University of Rochester, N.Y., in progress).

52. Alban Berg, "Zu Franz Schuberts 100. Todestag" (1928), in Berg, *Schriften zur Musik,* ed. Frank Schneider (Leipzig: Reclam, 1981), 308.

53. "Well, the weird thing about Kurt Weill is that after I made a few records in the '80s, people started to tell me that I was sounding like this guy, or that I must be listening to this guy. So I figured I should probably go out and listen to him, because I'd never heard of him before. I did listen, and then I thought, 'Oh, I hear that.'" Quoted in Michael Barclay, "Tom Waits, In Dreams," *Exclaim!* (April–May 1999); also at www.tomwaitslibrary.com/interviews/99-apr-exclaim.html (accessed 17 February 2011).

54. The A&M catalogue number for the original vinyl release of *Lost in the* Stars is SP-95104. A newly recorded compilation of dance-band arrangements of Weill's songs called *Charming Weill* was issued in 2001, featuring the German singer Max Raabe and his Palast Orchester, conducted by H. K. Gruber (RCA Red Seal 09026 63513 2). The CD was released in the United States with the alternate title *Life, Love, and Laughter.*

CREDITS

The author is grateful to the publishers for permission to use portions of the following articles in revised form:

"The Concept of Epic Opera: Theoretical Anomalies in the Brecht-Weill Partnership," in *Festschrift Carl Dahlhaus,* ed. Hermann Danuser et al. (Laaber: Laaber Verlag, 1988), 283–94.

"Lehrstück: An Aesthetics of Performance," in *Music and Performance in the Weimar Republic,* ed. Bryan Gilliam (copyright © 1994 Cambridge University Press), 59–73.

"Grossbritannien als Exilland: Der Fall Weill," in *Musik in der Emigration 1933–1945: Verfolgung—Vertreibung—Rückwirkung,* ed. Horst Weber (copyright © 1994 by J. B. Metzler'sche Verlagsbuchhandlung und Carl Ernst Poeschel Verlag GmbH in Stuttgart), 213–27.

"Kurt Weill's Modern Classical Art," in *Die klassizistische Moderne in der Musik des 20. Jahrhunderts,* ed. Hermann Danuser (Winterthur: Amadeus Verlag, 1997), 115–22.

"Hindemith and Weill: Cases of Inner and Other Direction," in *Driven into Paradise,* ed. Christoph Wolff and Reinhold Brinkmann (Berkeley: University of California Press, 1999), 261–78.

"Kurt Weill: Life, Work, and Posterity," in *Amerikanismus, Americanism, Weill. Die Suche nach kultureller Identität in der Moderne,* ed. Hermann Danuser and Hermann Gottschewski (Schliengen: Edition Argus, 2003), 209–20.

Material from "1928, August 31: The Urform of Opera" reprinted here, in revised and expanded form, by permission of the publishers from *A New History of German Literature,* David Welberry, Editor-in-Chief, Judith Ryan, General Editor

(Cambridge, Mass.: The Belknap Press of Harvard University Press, copyright © 2004 by the President and Fellows of Harvard College), 758–64.

The quotation from *Allegro* by Richard Rodgers and Oscar Hammerstein II (copyright © 1947 by Richard Rodgers and Oscar Hammerstein II) is used by permission of Williamson Music, a Division of Rodgers & Hammerstein: An Imagem Company. Copyright renewed. International copyright secured. All rights reserved.

The quotation from "The Saga of Lenny" is reprinted by permission of Hal Leonard Corporation. Words by Stephen Sondheim. The lyrics are a parody of "The Saga of Jenny" by Ira Gerswhin and Kurt Weill. Copyright © 1989 Stephen Sondheim. All rights reserved. Used by permission.

The music example from "The Right Guy for Me" is reprinted by permission of Hal Leonard Corporation. Words by Sam Coslow. Music by Kurt Weill. Copyright © 1938 Sony/ATV Music Publishing LLC. Copyright renewed. This arrangement copyright © 2011 Sony/ATV Music Publishing LLC. All rights administered by Sony/ATV Music Publishing LLC, 8 Music Square West, Nashville, TN 37203. International copyright Secured. All rights reserved.

The following music examples are used by permission of Alfred Music Publishing Co., Inc.:

Die Dreigroschenoper. Words by Bert Brecht. Music by Kurt Weill. © 1928 (Renewed) WB Music Corp. & Kurt Weill Foundation for Music, Inc. All rights on behalf of Kurt Weill Foundation for Music, Inc. Administered by WB Music Corp.

Johnny Johnson. Lyrics by Paul Green. Music by Kurt Weill. © 1936 (Renewed) Chappell & Co., Inc. and Tro-Hampshire House Music, Inc. All rights reserved.

Knickerbocker Holiday. Lyrics by Maxwell Anderson. Music by Kurt Weill © 1938 (Renewed) Chappell & Co., Inc. and Tro-Hampshire House Music, Inc. All rights reserved.

Lady in the Dark. Lyrics by Ira Gershwin. Music by Kurt Weill. © 1941 (Renewed) Ira Gershwin Music and Tro-Hampshire House Publishing Corp. All rights for Ira Gershwin Music. Administered by WB Music Corp. All rights for the world outside of the U.S. controlled by Chappell & Co., Inc. All rights reserved.

One Touch of Venus. Words by Ogden Nash Music by Kurt Weill © 1944 (Renewed) Ogden Nash Music Publishing and Tro-Hampshire House Publishing Corp. All rights on behalf of Ogden Nash Music Publishing administered by WB Music Corp.

Street Scene. Lyrics by Langston Hughes. Music by Kurt Weill. © 1945 (Renewed) Chappell & Co., Inc. and Tro-Hampshire House Publishing Corp. All rights for the world outside of the U.S. administered by Chappell & Co., Inc. All rights reserved.

Love Life. Lyrics by Alan Jay Lerner. Music by Kurt Weill. © 1948 (Renewed) Chappell & Co., Inc. and Tro-Hampshire House Publishing Corp. All rights for the world outside of the U.S. administered by Chappell & Co., Inc.

Lost in the Stars. Words by Maxwell Anderson. Music by Kurt Weill. © 1946

(Renewed) Chappell & Co., Inc. and Tro-Hampshire House Publishing Corp. All rights for the world outside of the U.S. administered by Chappell & Co., Inc. All rights reserved.

The following music examples are used by permission of European American Music Corporation:

Kurt Weill, *Der Protagonist,* op. 15. Libretto by Georg Kaiser. Copyright © 1926 by European American Music Corporation (for the U.S.A., Canada, and other British reversionary territories) and Universal Edition (all other countries). Copyright renewed. All rights reserved.

Kurt Weill, *Royal Palace,* op. 17. Libretto by Iwan Goll. Copyright © 1926 by European American Music Corporation (for the U.S.A., Canada, and other British reversionary territories) and Universal Edition (all other countries). Copyright renewed. All rights reserved.

Kurt Weill, *Der Zar lässt sich photographieren,* op. 21. Libretto by Georg Kaiser. Copyright © 1927 by European American Music Corporation (for the U.S.A., Canada, and other British reversionary territories) and Universal Edition (all other countries). Copyright renewed. All rights reserved.

Kurt Weill, *Mahagonny Songspiel.* Text by Bertolt Brecht (and Elisabeth Hauptmann). Copyright © 1927 by European American Music Corporation (for the U.S.A., Canada, and other British reversionary territories) and Universal Edition (all other countries). Copyright renewed. All rights reserved.

Kurt Weill, *Happy End.* Book by Dorothy Lane (pseudonym for Elisabeth Hauptmann and Bertolt Brecht). Lyrics by Bertolt Brecht. Copyright © 1929 by European American Music Corporation (for the U.S.A., Canada, and other British reversionary territories) and Universal Edition (all other countries). Copyright renewed. All rights reserved.

Kurt Weill, *Der Silbersee.* Libretto by Georg Kaiser. Copyright © 1933 by European American Music Corporation (for the U.S.A., Canada, and other British reversionary territories) and Universal Edition (all other countries). Copyright renewed. All rights reserved.

Kurt Weill, *Aufstieg und Fall der Stadt Mahagonny.* Text by Bertolt Brecht and Kurt Weill. Copyright © 1930 by European American Music Corporation (for the U.S.A., Canada, and other British reversionary territories) and Universal Edition (all other countries). Copyright renewed. All rights reserved.

Kurt Weill, *Die Bürgschaft.* Libretto by Caspar Neher and Kurt Weill. Copyright © 1931 by European American Music Corporation (for the U.S.A., Canada, and other British reversionary territories) and Universal Edition (all other countries). Copyright renewed. All rights reserved.

Kurt Weill, *Der Lindberghflug.* Libretto by Bertolt Brecht. Copyright © 1930 by European American Music Corporation (for the U.S.A., Canada, and other British reversionary territories) and Universal Edition (all other countries). Copyright renewed. All rights reserved.

Kurt Weill, *Der Jasager.* Libretto by Bertolt Brecht, after the Japanese play *Taniko* (translated into German by Elisabeth Hauptmann from the English translation by Arthur Waley). Copyright © 1930 by European American Music Corporation (for the U.S.A., Canada, and other British reversionary territories) and Universal Edition (all other countries). Copyright renewed. All rights reserved.

Kurt Weill, *Die sieben Todsünden.* Lyrics by Bertolt Brecht. Copyright © 1956 by Schott Music GmbH & Co. KG. Copyright © renewed. All rights reserved.

Kurt Weill, *A Kingdom for a Cow (Der Kuhhandel).* Book and lyrics by Robert Vambery. Copyright © 1981 by Schott Music. All rights reserved.

Kurt Weill, *The Eternal Road.* Lyrics by Franz Werfel. Copyright © 1980 by European American Music Corporation. All rights reserved.

INDEX

TEXT
10/12.5 Minion Pro
DISPLAY
Minion Pro (Open Type)
COMPOSITOR
BookMatters, Berkeley
INDEXER
Andrew Joron
PRINTER/BINDER
Maple-Vail Book Manufacturing Group